THEY WERE ALL TOGETHER IN ONE PLACE?
TOWARD MINORITY BIBLICAL CRITICISM

Society of Biblical Literature

Semeia Studies

Gale A. Yee, General Editor

Number 57

THEY WERE ALL TOGETHER IN ONE PLACE?
TOWARD MINORITY BIBLICAL CRITICISM

THEY WERE ALL TOGETHER IN ONE PLACE?
TOWARD MINORITY BIBLICAL CRITICISM

Edited by

Randall C. Bailey,
Tat-siong Benny Liew,
and Fernando F. Segovia

Society of Biblical Literature
Atlanta

THEY WERE ALL TOGETHER IN ONE PLACE?
TOWARD MINORITY BIBLICAL CRITICISM

Library of Congress Cataloging-in-Publication Data

They were all together in one place : toward minority biblical criticism / edited by Randall C. Bailey, Tat-siong Benny Liew, and Fernando F. Segovia.
    p. cm. — (Society of Biblical Literature semeia studies ; no. 57)
    Includes bibliographical references.
    ISBN 978-1-58983-245-9 (paper binding : alk. paper)
    1. Bible—Social scientific criticism. 2. Marginality, Social—Biblical teaching. I. Bailey, Randall C., 1947– II. Liew, Tat-Siong Benny. III. Segovia, Fernando F.
    BS521.88.T44 2009b
    220.6'089—dc22   2009001212

17   16   15   14 13 12 11 10 09   5 4 3 2 1
Printed in the United States of America on acid-free, recycled paper conforming to ANSI/NISO Z39.48-1992 (R1997) and ISO 9706:1994 standards for paper permanence.

To all those who have preceded us,
to all those who stand alongside of us,
and to all those who will follow us
in this ongoing struggle to render our invisibility visible

Contents

PREFACE

We would like to say a few words about our choice of book cover, for the photograph and design of which we are indebted to Pamela K. Liew. The wood structure, which is not only artificially constructed but also slightly skewed, represents the model or edifice of traditional (read: white) scholarship. It appears inflamed and lit up—as well as partially burnt—by the color-full fire from within. Like a fire, minority biblical scholarship defies containment, whether attempted by whites or persons of color. Various sparks within the fire represent not only the multiple locations of minority biblical criticism but also the varied illuminations it may shed on the Bible. Like the book cover, biblical criticism—minority or not—is an art that, as Odette Lockwood-Stewart reminds us, requires creativity as well as courage and may function at times to disturb and destabilize.

In light of the preceding paragraph, we also need to be very clear about our usage of the word "minority," found throughout the volume as well and even in the subtitle. We employ the term with reference to "minoritization" or the process of unequal valorization of population groups, yielding dominant and minority formations and relations, within the context, and through the apparatus, of a nation or state as the result of migration, whether voluntary or coerced. We are, therefore, using "minority" simultaneously to signify (on) this demeaning practice and to challenge, contest, or change the term's meaning, even when we are no longer putting the term in quotation marks. By "minority," it should be understood, we always include "minoritized" or "being minoritized" as part of its meaning.

In this regard we should further like to point to a striking though fortuitous conjunction of developments. While in the process of writing this preface and putting the final touches on the manuscript for publication, a front-page article appeared in *The New York Times* ("In a Generation, Minorities May be the U.S. Majority," 14 August 2008) with the remarkable demographic news that, according to the latest projections of the U.S. Census Bureau, racial-ethnic minorities will displace "non-Hispanic whites" as the numerical majority in the U.S. by 2042—an acceleration of a full eight years from the previous projections of but a few years ago. This revision, according to the Bureau, is due to both higher birthrates among recent immigrants and an increasing influx of immigrants. We find the following comments imperative:

▶ We would question whether even this revision is accelerated enough in light of the following key factors: (1) the current definition of "whites" by the U.S. Office of Management and Budget as descendants of "the original peoples of Europe, *North Africa or the Middle East*" (emphasis added, given the tendency to write the latter two areas out of Africa and Asia, so that Christianity can be seen as basically European or Eurocentric); and (2) the inability of the Census Bureau to have an accurate count of racial-ethnic minorities who work and live in the country without legal documentation.

▶ We would underscore the likelihood—as evidenced by the repeated references in the article to "overpopulation," "foreign-born," and "immigration policies"—that the national abjection of minorities will only intensify even or especially as minorities increase in number.

▶ We would stress the unmistakable reality of change, whether with regard to the changing faces of the U.S. or the changing constructions of race.

▶ We would point out that these dynamic demographics are not yet reflected in the U.S. contingent of the Society of Biblical Literature.

Given such radical demographic developments, and such qualifications on our part (overdefinition of whiteness and undercounting of minorities; sharpening marginalization; unstoppable change; lagging responsiveness within the guild), we see this collection of essays as a response—courageous and creative, destabilizing and disturbing—to the challenge of change, as African American, Asian American, and Latino/a American scholars of the Bible come together to discuss, debate, develop, and demonstrate "minority biblical criticism." Although we recognize that this collection is but an initial and limited response, we hope that it will turn out to be only one of the ever-multiplying sparks within the color-full fire of such criticism.

Randall C. Bailey
Tat-siong Benny Liew
Fernando F. Segovia

Acknowledgments

This volume has been made possible due to the assistance and support of many individuals and institutions. To all we are deeply indebted and most thankful.

First and foremost, to our fellow participants in the project, for having graciously accepted our invitation to join us in this important undertaking.

Second, to the Wabash Center for Teaching and Learning in Religion and Theology and to its former Director, Dr. Lucinda Huffaker, for their generous grant in support of the project.

Third, to Mrs. Elizabeth Littlejohn, Vice-President for Administration and Finance at Interdenominational Theological Center in Atlanta, and to her staff, Mr. Damon Cosby and Ms. Sharon Morgan, for their impeccable management of all matters financial.

Fourth, to Dr. James Hudnut-Beumler, Dean of the Divinity School at Vanderbilt University, for his unreserved backing of the project and much-appreciated support toward editing expenses.

Fifth, to the Rev. Rohun Park, who, as a doctoral student in New Testament and Early Christianity within the Graduate Department of Religion at Vanderbilt University, served as editorial assistant for the project, for his superb editing of the manuscript.

Sixth, to Ms. Vanessa Lovelace and to Ms. Pamela Liew, for their exceptional attention to detail in organizing and facilitating our week-long consultations in Chicago in the summers of 2004 and 2005, respectively.

Finally, to the General Editor of Semeia Studies, Dr. Gale Yee, and to the entire staff of SBL Publications, especially its Editorial Director, Bob Buller, for their keen counsel in all matters editorial.

Abbreviations

AB	Anchor Bible
ABD	*The Anchor Bible Dictionary.* Edited by David Noel Freedman. 6 vols. New York: Doubleday, 1992.
AJT	*Asia Journal of Theology*
BA	*Biblical Archaeologist*
BibInt	*Biblical Interpretation*
CBQ	*Catholic Biblical Quarterly*
CSCO	Corpus scriptorum christianorum orientalium
FCB	Feminist Companion to the Bible
FCNTECW	Feminist Companion to the New Testament and Early Christian Writings
HSM	Harvard Semitic Monographs
HSS	Harvard Semitic Studies
HTR	*Harvard Theological Review*
IBC	Interpretation: A Bible Commentary for Teaching and Preaching
ICC	International Critical Commentary
JBL	*Journal of Biblical Literature*
JFSR	*Journal of Feminist Studies in Religion*
JITC	*Journal of the Interdenominational Theological Center*
JNES	*Journal of Near Eastern Studies*
JSJ	*Journal for the Study of Judaism in the Persian, Hellenistic, and Roman Periods*
JSNT	*Journal for the Study of the New Testament*
JSNTSup	Journal for the Study of the New Testament Supplement Series
JSOT	*Journal for the Study of the Old Testament*
JSOTSup	Journal for the Study of the Old Testament Supplement Series
JSS	*Journal of Semitic Studies*
LCBI	Literary Currents in Biblical Interpretation
LSJ	Liddell, H. G., R. Scott, H. S. Jones, *A Greek-English Lexicon.* 9th ed. with revised supplement. Oxford: Clarendon, 1996.
NAB	New American Bible
NCBC	New Cambridge Bible Commentary

NIB	*The New Interpreter's Bible*. 12 vols. Nashville: Abingdon.
NIBC	New International Biblical Commentary
NRSV	New Revised Standard Version
NTS	*New Testament Studies*
OBT	Overtures to Biblical Theology
OTE	*Old Testament Essays*
OTL	Old Testament Library
OtSt	*Oudtestamentische Studiën*
RSV	Revised Standard Version
SBLAcBib	Society of Biblical Literature Academia Biblica
SBLDS	Society of Biblical Literature Dissertation Series
SBLGPBS	Society of Biblical Literature Global Perspectives on Biblical Scholarship
SemeiaSt	Semeia Studies
SFSHJ	South Florida Studies in the History of Judaism
SNTSMS	Society for New Testament Studies Monograph Series
USQR	*Union Seminary Quarterly Review*
VT	*Vetus Testamentum*
WBC	Word Biblical Commentary
ZAW	*Zeitschrift für die alttestamentliche Wissenschaft*

INTRODUCTION

Toward Minority Biblical Criticism: Framework, Contours, Dynamics

Randall C. Bailey, Tat-siong Benny Liew, Fernando F. Segovia

In 2003 we received a generous grant from the Wabash Center for Teaching and Learning in Theology and Religion for a project entitled "Reading and Teaching the Bible as Black, Asian American and Latino/a Scholars in the U.S." That year, it should be recalled, also marked the centenary of W. E. B. Du Bois's great book, *The Souls of Black Folk* (1903). The two volumes are not unrelated.

In a way that is true to his idea of a "double consciousness," Du Bois's celebrated book may have been written and may be read with a double vision. On the one hand, Du Bois clearly had one eye on the black-versus-white "color line"; on the other hand, he also had a broader, more complicated—almost "universal"—vision involving people other than or alongside "black folk" (Mullen and Watson 2005). Du Bois would—for example, in his call for the First Universal Races Congress in London in 1910—mention not only "Chinese and Hindus" but also that we live in a world "where most men [*sic*] are colored" (cited in Gilroy 2005, 38).[1] As Paul Gilroy suggests in his reading of Du Bois, "'Negro blood' had a message for the wider world beyond the narrow American space" (2005, 35). Du Bois's vision or double vision is about transforming the world, and he is clear that much of that transformation is dependent on or indebted to the marginalized people of color. Our volume on "minority biblical criticism" has a similar but more modest

---

1. A similar gathering of not only Buddhists, Muslims, and Hindus but also peoples of India, Africa, and the Americas is found in Du Bois's *Dark Princess* (1995, 297–98), which Du Bois once proclaimed to be his favorite among his own books (1940, 270). We have no interest to join in the debate over the "real identity" of Du Bois's Princess Kautilya (see Bhabha 2007, 186–87), but a couple of things about this novel are particularly relevant to our project: (1) Du Bois's clear affection and admiration for this novel's female protagonist even though or especially because she is from India; and (2) this novel's theme centers on "the betrayal of common purpose amongst minorities who share a common historic condition of racial oppression" (Bhabha 2007, 188). While we are highlighting the positive *potentials* of Du Bois's novel for our project, we are not romancing it, as we are well aware of other readings of the novel that point to its Orientalist tendencies or its parodic dimensions (see, e.g., Edwards 2003, 233–36).

focus. We want to explore how racial-ethnic minority scholars of the Bible within the United States[2] may cross the "color line" to form a coalition or an alliance to transform the discipline of biblical studies.[3] The title *They Were All Together in One Place?* is meant to convey precisely such focus and objective. A reflection on its choice, its allusion and implications, is thus in order.

The title represents, first of all, a deliberate reference to Acts 2:1b: the main clause of the temporal-spatial description—"When the day of Pentecost arrived, they were all together in one place"—that begins the narratorial introduction to the narrative unit of Pentecost in Acts 2:1–42 (2:1–4). This brief description identifies various components of the story: the timing of the events about to unfold, the day of Pentecost; the composition of the group in question, the just reconstituted group of Jesus' twelve disciples (see 2:14); and the location of this group at this point, an undisclosed place in Jerusalem. It is within this gathering, then, that the bestowal of the Spirit, promised by Jesus for the time after his resurrection and ascension, takes place. Upon its reception, through "tongues of fire," this group of "Galileans" (2:7) begin to speak and to be understood in many "tongues," bringing about a mixture of amazement, perplexity, and even ridicule among the assembled crowd, which consisted of Jews "from every nation under heaven living in Jerusalem" (2:5). The title, therefore, makes a connection between the coming together of Jesus' disciples for their newly appointed mission and the coming together of minority scholars in their newly assumed undertaking.

At the same time, the title does constitute a deliberate variation on this narratorial description: a concrete identification of time, characters, and space has been transformed into a query involving metaphorization and inversion. The connection established, therefore, between the two coming-togethers should be

---

2. Native Americans are not represented in this conversation for two main reasons. First, there is a serious shortage of Native Americans scholars in biblical studies, which is a situation that we very much lament; second, "minority" is an inappropriate term for Native Americans, because "minority" does not communicate the fact that their rights, including their land claims, existed prior to and independently of the U.S. government. As a result, most Native Americans prefer terms such as "indigenous peoples" or "First Nations," since these better communicate their sovereignty and rights to self-determination, especially, though not exclusively, over their traditional territories. See, e.g., Venne 1998, for which we are indebted to the generous recommendation of Andrea Smith.

3. After all, Du Bois ends *Dark Princess* with a letter from Princess Kautilya that the "Great Central Committee of Yellow, Brown, and Black is finally to meet" (1995, 296), and the meeting turns out to be a celebration of birth that alludes to the Magi's visit to the Christ child in Matthew's Gospel (2:1–11), with the bi-racial son of Princess Kautilya and Matthew Townes—an African American—playing the role of Du Bois's "Messenger and Messiah to all the Darker Worlds" and the child's adorers as "three old men: one black and shaven and magnificent in raiment, one yellow and turbaned … and the last naked save for a scarf about his loins" (1995, 311).

seen as a play, a sort of serious *divertissement*, on the phenomenon of speaking in new "tongues," as both sets of newly empowered groups proceed to do: the disciples of Jesus in this unit of biblical narrative by way of actual glossolalia and minority critics in this exercise in biblical criticism by way of scholarly cooperation. A word about the various elements of the variation is imperative.

First, by means of the metaphorical turn, the strategic character of the enterprise is foregrounded. Given the coming together of various groups in this project-volume, an expansive sense of "place" is at work, involving not a physical place as such but an academic or disciplinary venture. Consequently, the question of location is surfaced, since the groups themselves design and embark on a "place" of their own choosing. What, the project inquires, are the rationale and the purpose among minority critics for such a "place"?

Further, through the inversionist turn, the diverse nature of the enterprise is highlighted. Given the coming together of different minority groups in this project-volume, a convoluted sense of "place" is also at work, involving not a fairly homogeneous group of modern-day "Galileans" but rather a conjunction of highly diverging groups. As a result, the question of sameness or oneness is raised, since these groups already speak in different "tongues" as they pursue a new "tongue" in this "place" of their own. What, the project queries, are the realities and experiences behind minority critics in such a "place," both as individual groups and as a collective?

Lastly, by way of the interrogative turn, the problematic character of the enterprise is foregrounded. Given the coming together of various minority groups in this volume-project, a comparative sense of "place" is likewise at work, involving not only harmonious but also tensive relations. Consequently, the question of positionality, both between and among such different and new "tongues" is surfaced. What, the project inquires, are the horizontal relations among the minority groups, and what are the vertical relations, individually and collectively, vis-à-vis the dominant group?

Such are the type of questions that we, as minority biblical critics, address in this volume-project, as we pursue our goal of crossing the "color line" in order to work out a disciplinary coalition or alliance with transformation in mind. As a further step in this direction, we take up the following important topics of discussion for consideration in this introduction: We begin by reflecting on the historical and theoretical framework of minority criticism in general: the meaning of the term *minority* and why an alliance of racial-ethnic minority persons across the "color line" may be desirable and/or feasible. We continue by describing the historical and theoretical contours of biblical minority criticism: its origins, trajectories, challenges. We conclude by outlining the rhetorical dynamics at work in minority biblical criticism: its strategies, major and minor alike.

MINORITY CRITICISM: HISTORICAL AND THEORETICAL FRAMEWORK

WHAT TO MAKE OF "MINORITIES"? OR, WHAT DO "MINORITIES" MAKE?

According to many scholars, both the early framers and subsequent interpreters of the U.S. Constitution have generally presented citizenship as an abstraction or a disembodiment from particularity that is, in fact, a re-embodiment of the assumed white male—and, we should add, heterosexual and property-owning—norm (Holland 2001, 66–68). In fact, these seemingly different identity factors intersect and overlap each other in complex ways in the measurement of merited or unmerited citizenship. For instance, Aihwa Ong has discussed how a wage slave of African descent is understood to be the antithesis of a free (working) and (financially) independent (white) citizen and how the autonomous entrepreneurial citizen is a masculinist ideal (2003, 10–14). These interchanges and networks help explain why neither poor Irish immigrants on the East Coast nor Chinese immigrants on the West Coast were considered white and deserving of citizenship in the nineteenth century or why "welfare *mothers*" and "model minority" have been such powerful and popular stereotypes since the late 1960s.

These interlocking dynamics have, of course, immense implications for reading race *and* using race as a lens to read the Bible; they will also prove significant when we explore the dynamics of a racial-ethnic minority "alliance." We want to point out for now that "minority" is really less about number but more about power. While it may be true that, demographically or numerically, there has not been a "majority" race in the U.S. since the 1990s, "whites," as David Henry Hwang is quick to point out, "continue to control a wildly disproportionate amount of power" (1994, xi). Power is, in fact, the issue at stake when Immanuel Kant talks about a state of "minority" as a "*self-incurred* ... inability to make use of one's own understanding without direction from another" (1996, 17, emphasis original). In other words, "minority" signifies for Kant both a lack in and a need for maturity, which Kant understands basically in terms of independence and self-reliance. Kant's "minority" person or person in "minority" is, therefore, a minor who is inferior, immature, and, perhaps most of all, ignorant of his or her own independence. Of no less significance is the fact that Kant's reflection on and definition of "minority" is done in response to the question of the nature of the Enlightenment (1996).

Enlightenment is understood here as a progress from "minority" to autonomy, just as U.S. citizenship is often a process of becoming an economically independent white heterosexual male. Again, Ong has talked about the "ethnic succession" process, through which minority groups in the U.S., like the Irish, are supposed to be able to ascend to white status as they accumulate merits or capital gains—both economically through class mobility and morally by making social contributions and/or suffering injustice—through successive generations (2003, 2–5). Because of differences in language and/or appearance, however, not every racial-ethnic minority person or minority group can "pass" in or through this process (Omi and Winant 1994), though it is undeniable that economic gains have whitened or engendered a new "middle" or "upper middle" class among segments within these minority groups. The bankruptcy of the ethnic succession myth is believed by many to have led to "the politics of recognition" (Taylor 1994) by many minority groups in the U.S. in the recent decades. As certain minorities learn that no amount of accumulated merits or capital gains through successive generations will usher them into the mainstream, they begin to move from aiming for assimilation to insisting on being acknowledged and admitted as different (Rosaldo 1997).

If U.S. citizenship in general and the ethnic succession myth in particular find a parallel in Kant's reading of the Enlightenment as a maturing process of the "minority," the guild of biblical studies within the U.S. carries a similar set of dynamics when it comes to its membership. The academic rhetoric of objectivity, or the pretense that difference makes no difference, is itself premised on a particular set of differences in terms of race, gender, class, and sexuality. Michel Foucault, in his reading of Kant's musing on the Enlightenment, suggests that one may be able to oppose and affirm Kant at the same time (1997). More precisely, Foucault attempts to turn Kant's emphasis on "maturity" onto Kant's own understanding of or emphasis on "reason." Does one have the maturity or the courage to know, Foucault asks, the limits of Western or Kantian reason?

We would like to couple Foucault's simultaneous opposition to and affirmation of Kant's reading of the Enlightenment as a progress or progression out of "minority" with Du Bois's "double consciousness." Put differently, racial-ethnic minority scholars know how to not only be part of both the dominant and the minority culture but also use their simultaneous inside-and-outside location to credit and critique both cultures (Gilroy 1993, 1; Ang 2001, 4–5). We think feminist standpoint theorists are pointing to a similar thought with what they have called the "strong objectivity" of the marginalized (Hartsock 1998; P. Collins 2000; Harding 2004). The same may be true of Walter D. Mignolo when he refers to Rodolfo Kusch's work to talk about a "double consciousness" that he terms "border gnosis" (2000, 149–64). In short, the need of the "minorities" to know their own culture as well as that of their oppressors may lead to a theoretical and political practice that has particular transformative potential. "The most intense and productive life of culture," according to Mikhail Bakhtin, "takes place on the boundaries" (1986, 2).

Minority—or what bell hooks calls "marginality"—is a site that "offers the possibility of radical perspectives from which to see and create, to imagine alternative, new worlds" (1990, 341). Instead of understanding "minority" as "immaturity" as Kant does, we would, therefore, suggest that minority persons can turn the undeniable power differential that they suffer into springboards for new interpretations and critical interventions. Like Kant, however, we do read "minority" in terms of a struggle against oppressive authority (including the authority of assumed epistemology or methodology, as Foucault proposes), although this struggle is neither "self-incurred" nor individualistic. We do so as a group or as a community, and we may even attempt to do so by going across various communities of color. For our purposes here, it is also worth pointing out that Kant considers submission to a book or to a master to be symptoms of "minority" or "immaturity" (1996, 17). When it comes to the Bible, Kant's examples of "unreasonable" authority may also be combined as one; that is to say, the Bible is for many a canonical book of mastery, power, and domination. If Kant is on target in naming the various forms of power, he is off base in linking "minority" with willing submission. As one will see in the pages of this volume, "*minority* biblical criticism" may well involve readings that go along with as well as go against the "good book."

Understanding "minority" as a "double consciousness" that enables a vantage point for potential transformation of and against oppression can also be linked to the idea of "minority" as "selvage." Joseph Roach, writing about the racial dynamics of Louisiana as part of what he calls the "circum-Atlantic world," discusses "selvage" as "frontier" (1996, 177–80). Although literally referring to "the edge of a fabric [that is] woven thickly so that it will not unravel," Roach exegetes the term figuratively to imply a perimeter, a margin, or a boundary (1996, 177). Racial-ethnic minority scholars, given their need to negotiate between their own culture and the culture of the dominant society, can certainly be read—in the words of bell hooks—as "living ... on the edge" (1984, ix). What we appreciate about the image of a selvage is that it communicates positively how minority criticism may be a seam at which different worlds—not only between the dominant and the minority but also among various minorities—meet. The kind of intercultural interweavings—or series of stretching, folding, and blending—being signified here are both multilayered and multidirectional. Selvage bespeaks, then, a multiplicity that goes beyond a mere double. Its series of folds also imply the strength of perseverance as well as an ongoing creativity. If we may adapt what Mary Louise Pratt says about language to race/ethnicity—after all, for most Latino/as and many Asian Americans, these two issues are intimately linked—we can state that

> the [minority] person is not someone who translates constantly from one language or cultural system into another, though translation is something [minority] subjects are able to do if needed. To be [a minority] is above all to live in more than one [system], to be one for whom translation is unnecessary. The image for [minority] is not translation, perhaps, but *desdoblamiento* ("doubling"), a multiplying of the self. (2002, 35)

Minority as selvage becomes not only a site to resist and transform the center, but is itself a dynamic center of continuous self-expressions and definitions. While one cannot deny the power differential that confronts minorities, one also should not concede to the common but mistaken conception that there is only a singular center and that it belongs entirely to those of the dominant culture.

MAKING SENSE OF MINORITY ALLIANCE

As our beginning reference to Du Bois indicates, the suggestion that a minority person or community cross the "color line" among racial-ethnic minorities is hardly new, even if Du Bois's own crossing tended to take place within an international frame (think here also of Martin Luther King and his 1967address "Beyond Vietnam"). A very similar gesture has been made within biblical studies, when R. S. Sugirtharajah urges in the "postscript" to the first edition of his *Voices form the Margin* that Latin Americans, Africans, and Asians dialogue among each other for not only mutual challenge and correction but also as "partners in a common cause" (1991, 443).

The first reason given by Sugirtharajah makes sense, of course. Notwithstanding the argument of feminist standpoint theory mentioned earlier as well as the limits of a visual (over?)emphasis within hermeneutics (Punday 2003, 120–21), reading as looking out from a certain site or location does tend to imply a likelihood to forget and/or a difficulty in seeing one's own place. Conversations with other racial-ethnic minority groups within the U.S. might have helped Du Bois, for example, to see the problem of arguing for the rights of African Americans on the basis of "early" arrival (1903, 186–87). Likewise, Asian Americans like the original "Siamese twins" should have known better than to own over twenty slaves on the eve of the Civil War, especially since their tour organizer, P. T. Barnum, had begun his cultural or racial exhibition or exploitation with an African American woman rumored to be both over a hundred years old and a former nurse to George Washington (Okihiro 2001, 71–74). What we want to focus on is rather Sugirtharajah's second reason, particularly within the national frame of the U.S. Are there good and compelling reasons for minority scholars within the U.S. to go across the "color line" to become "partners in a common cause" with other minority communities of color?

We hope our opening attempt to make sense of the word *minority* has already signaled something about our desire for an alternative vision and practice, and not just for a demographic change in getting racial-ethnic minorities recognized as legitimate biblical scholars. There are plenty of examples within the history of the U.S. that relations among minorities are not exempt or immune from turning into competitions for domination. If minorities want to avoid duplicating domination over another minority culture in ways that are reminiscent of their own experience with the dominant culture, we must push and cross the boundaries to get in touch and, hopefully, come to some understanding with other minority identities. R. Radhakrishnan, for example, reaches across the "color line" among minorities and refers to Lani Guinier's "like minds, not like bodies" to talk about how a minority coalition may avoid the unnecessary and time-consuming process of reinventing the wheel to focus instead on "imagin[ing] a relational world that has retired once and for all the model of 'the winner take all' and the cultural politics of conquest" (2001, 261–62).

Similarly, cultural exchange is necessary if "cultural diversity" or "multiculturalism" does not turn into what David Dabydeen describes as a "beehive" situation where different cultural groups are each confined to their own "cells" and thus devoid of communication, interaction, or cross-fertilization with other groups (1991). Such a "beehive" situation is not only undesirable but also infeasible in the U.S. We will give but two examples. First, Korean American merchants often find themselves running their small businesses in African American neighborhoods (Chang 1994; Park 1997, 41), and so-called "Koreantowns," such as the one in Los Angeles, have gradually become "much more Latino oriented" (Suh 2004, 38). Second, one may look at how the history of Chinese coolies and African slaves worked together in Cuba, resulting in not only a Chinatown in Havana or santería in Cuban music but also a generation of Afro-Chinese Cubans (M. González 2004, 68; Yun 2008). Just as some feminist theorists want to talk about a self that is both dependent and independent of others (Kaminsky 1993, 68–69) or certain cultural studies scholars about the balance between prioritizing the local/national and the global/translational (Wilson and Dissanayake 1996), racial-ethnic minority group identity and minority affinity need not be mutually exclusive emphases. In contrast, as Gloria Anzaldúa suggests, in the act of disrupting boundary or inhabiting "borderland," a *mestiza* also increases her capacity "to stretch … horizontally and vertically" (1987, 79). One way to parse this horizontal and vertical capacity, we would propose, is to parse it in terms of building coalition.

Stretching this capacity across racial-ethnic minority lines is especially significant because the dominant society of the U.S. has long practiced the strategy of "divide and conquer" when it comes to its minority cultures.[4] The most obvi-

---

4. As it is often the case with dominant ideology, there can be internal contradictions that actually help certify and fortify control. Without dismissing necessarily that such contradictions may also become openings for resistance, contradictions within an ideology can function to demonstrate the arbitrary power of the dominant to make even opposing or contradictory decisions according to its whims and wishes. It is worth pointing out, therefore, that alongside the "divide-and-conquer" strategy, the dominant culture may *at times* also lump all the racial-ethnic minority groups together as if they were all one and the same. Thus, when the California State Supreme Court used the term "Black" in 1854 to bar certain people from equal citizenship and right, the term referred not only to "Negroes" but also to all who were not white (Edwards 2003, 36). According to Gary Y. Okihiro, the Chicago Exposition in 1893 not only pitted via architecture and layout the "orderly" (European) White City against the chaotic Midway Plaisance but also collapsed various racial-ethnic minority groups that were present at the Plaisance as "all barbaric … children in their ignorance" (cited in Okihiro 2001, 37, 63). Similarly, Glenn Omatsu would talk about a "one-sided class war" against various poor communities of color in the 1970s (1994, 33–37). Such *occasional* lumping together of different racial-ethnic minority

ous example is arguably the creation of the so-called "model minority" stereotype since the mid-1960s for Asian Americans. This "racial myth" not only prevents Asian Americans who are still needy from asking for and acquiring assistance but also "shames" other minority groups into submission, pits one minority group against others, and/or denies the existence of racial oppression in the U.S.[5] Aside from the "model minority" setup, one can cite numerous deployment of this "divide-and-conquer" strategy. For instance, when playwright Hwang and actor B. D. Wong complained in 1990 against the casting of white actors for Asian or Eurasian roles in the Broadway hit *Miss Saigon*, the play's producer, Cameron Macintosh, immediately pointed to two prominent African American actors, Morgan Freeman and Denzel Washington, and their "cross-casting" roles in other stage plays to illustrate and/or defend the industry's casting practice as "color blind" (Shimakawa 2002, 43–48). Richard Delgado and Jean Stefancic have insightfully pointed out that "divide-and-conquer" is effective, since it can promote "exaggerated identification" with whites by one minority group at the expense of other minority groups, on the one hand, and provide token "proofs" for whites to deflect the charge of racism, on the other (2001, 71–73). Instead of letting this divisive strategy work to create interminority rivalries like the recent extreme but nevertheless real example of Kenneth Eng's piece on "hating Blacks" in the San Francisco based "newsweekly," *AsianWeek* (2007), perhaps it is more helpful if minority groups come together and form an alliance, or what Antonio Gramsci conceives in terms of a "bloc" (2000, 189–221). This suggestion is akin to what Abdul R. JanMohamed and David Lloyd hope to accomplish with what they call "minority discourse," or the dialogues and hence collaboration among different minority cultures and groups (1990).

---

groups points again to the need and potential for alliance, although one must be careful not to erase or understate the differences that do exist among different minority groups.

5. The idea of situating Asians between whites and other peoples of color—and thus the "ideal" location as a buffer—is not new, even though the construction of the "model minority" is. As early as 1846, Thomas Hart Benton was already suggesting that Asians or the "Yellow" race was "a race far above the Ethiopian, or Black—above the Malay, or Brown (if we must admit five races)—and above the American Indian, or Red; it is a race far above all these, but still, far below the White" (cited in Okihiro 2001, 44; see also 36, 47–48; Nguyen 2002, 30–31). Ronald Takaki would therefore talk about how Chinese labor was brought into the South to serve as both a punishment and a model for black workers who might dare to strike (1989, 94–99). With the construction of the "model minority" myth, Asian Americans have been effectively excluded from affirmative action programs, thus creating, yet once more, jealousy and competition among the minority groups. According to one report, for instance, Asian Americans actually had a lower success rate in landing teaching jobs in law schools than blacks and Latino/as (13.42% vis-à-vis 21.89% and 29.89%, respectively) when affirmative action was first initiated in many hiring practices between 1990 and 1993 (Hom 2001, 86). Our point here is how the "model minority" thesis works as part of the divide-and-conquer strategy of the dominant society.

The affirmation by JanMohamed and Lloyd that solidarity across differences is possible because of the shared experience of domination is important, but I think it is equally important to exegete what the verb "shared" means. In addition to experiences that are the same or similar—or what Ong refers to as a "striking continuity … between perceptions, policies, and practices" of racism against diverse racial-ethnic minority and indigenous communities in the U.S. (2003, 72–73)—we would propose that we can also understand "shared" in terms of how racialization of one minority group may take place through those of other minority groups. We would go further to suggest that what makes divide-and-conquer effective as a strategy is inseparable from the ways racialization of different minority groups work together and intersect each other. Thus, as Kandice Chuh suggests, "differences do not exist independently of each other. Rather, they converge and conflict and thus participate in each other" (2003, 148).

For instance, Grace Kyungwon Hong has argued that the experience of internment by Japanese Americans and of segregation by African Americans, though undeniably different, are nevertheless linked by the way the state structures U.S. society by ownership of private property (1999). Matt S. Meier and Feliciano Rivera also published a 1942 report that attempted to establish the "criminal tendencies" among Chicano youth on the basis of their "Indian"—and hence "Oriental"—heritage (1974, 127–33). Citing Rudyard Kipling's "East is East and West is West, and never the twain shall meet," this report bluntly states that "the Indian … is evidently Oriental in background—at least he [*sic*] shows many of the Oriental characteristics, especially so in his [*sic*] utter disregard for the value of life" (1974, 128). Criminality is thus established for Chicanos in this report by racializing other groups, namely, Asians, through the curious circuit of "Indians."[6]

Around the time of the publication of the book by Meier and Rivera, Frank Chin and Jeffrey Paul Chan also suggested not only how the racialization of the Asian American male as lacking masculinity must be read in conjunction with the excessive masculinity that the dominant culture associates with black studs and

---

6. One should not forget, of course, that Columbus thought he had reached Asia—or, the "Indies"—when he arrived at the Americas, so he called the people he encountered in the so-called "New World" "Indians," as in Asians. The idea that Native Americans were once Asians has a long history, and both were linked as descendants of the biblical Shem. See Okihiro 1994, 18–22. Of course, these links that a racist society creates can also become grounds for resistance. For a brief comparison of the Japanese American internment and the Indian reservation, see Shimakawa 2002, 78–79. Even if it is appropriate that we do *not* "lump" Native Americans into a part of this volume on "minority criticism," we would like to point out that there are indeed many points of convergence between indigenous and racial-ethnic minority groups in this country, not least of which may be "the connection between the Indian wars of the American West and the military campaigns in Cuba, Puerto Rico, and the Philippines" (Okihiro 2001, 66–67).

Latino machos, but also how these differentiating stereotypes lead to hostilities among minority groups (1972, 68). As Viet Thanh Nguyen correctly identifies, Chinese American intellectuals such as Chin and Chan themselves often end up, in a most ironic fashion, duplicating but displacing these dominant representations onto Chinese American women (femininity/maternity as obstructions to masculine development) and African American men (excessive masculinity as dangerous and violent) to claim or "Americanize" their Asian American masculinity (2002, 87–91, 94–95).

These examples show that just as race may intersect with other key "identity factors" such as gender, class, or sexuality, racialization of one minority group in these various "keys" may also be worked out in relation to the racialization of other minority groups (Koshy 2004, 64). As Jenny Sharpe explains, a comparative understanding of racism is essential, since it is often through a larger typology that contradictions can be created, and hence ideological alibis provided (1993, 127–28; see also Guillory 1993, 11–13). Reading the struggles of Asian Americans vis-à-vis those of African Americans has helped Neil T. Gotanda, for instance, to articulate a process of racializing Asian Americans as "being foreign" in relation to one that racializes blacks as "being inferior" (2001). While we must be careful about generalizations, delineating some theoretical convergence and divergence in the racialization processes of various minority groups would necessitate *and* facilitate the forging of a coalition, both intellectually and politically.[7]

Creating an alliance among racial-ethnic minority groups is, however, much more than a defensive reaction to the dominant society's divide-and-conquer strategy and history. We have already mentioned how alliance work may (1) challenge and change the agonistic ethos that seems to govern interracial-ethnic interaction in the U.S. and (2) defy and diversify a carefully contained "multiculturalism" that is reduced to "an image of living-apart-together" (Ang 2001, 14). In addition, alliance work across racial-ethnic minority lines—or making other

---

7. To our knowledge, not as much theoretical work has been done yet on Latino/a racialization. While some initial work has been done (e.g., Suárez-Orozco and Páez 2002, 20–29), such work has not been done vis-à-vis the racialization processes of other racial-ethnic minority groups within the U.S. In light of all the furor around "Latino gangs" as well as "illegal immigrants" in general and migrant workers across the U.S.-Mexico border in particular, we would like to suggest "illegality" or "illegitimacy" as a distinctive and distinguishing key in Latino/a racialization. In her study of "American crime fiction," Rachel Adams has, for example, suggested that Mexico is often associated with crime and lawlessness (2007). Although we are not including Native Americans as a "minority" group, we would also like to point to the trope "vanishing Indians" as a key in the racialization of indigenous people in this country (see, e.g., Jones 1988; Okihiro 2001, 40). Others have, of course, provided alternative views and emphases on how various racial-ethnic groups have been racialized in the U.S. For Stephen Jay Gould, for instance, blacks have been seen as "submissive and obsequious," "Mongolians" as "tricky, cunning, and cowardly," and Native Americans as "proud" and primitive (1996, 78). Notice how Gould also makes no mention of Latino/as in his "cataloguing" of these groups' racialization.

racial-ethnic minorities instead of whites one's major conversation partners—has, as Tat-siong Benny Liew and Vincent L. Wimbush propose, the potential of displacing, diversifying, or multiplying established loci or centers of conversation (2002, 30–31). According to Liew and Wimbush, what we are calling "minority biblical criticism" may also lead to rethinking and perhaps even a reinvention of race-ethnicity (2002, 31–33).

Junot Díaz, the award-winning Latino writer whose prose is deeply influenced by and reflective of black rap and hip hop, laments that "[g]roups of color rarely write across to each other; they write for themselves or white people" (cited in Ch'ien 2004, 218). Stating that this kind of conversation across communities of color is "a second level of complexity that writers of color have to step into," Díaz goes on to comment on his friendship since childhood with an *Asian American* rap artist, Bert Wang, and states that "[w]e dream up communities we never belong to" (cited in Ch'ien 2004, 218, 227). In other words, crossing racial-ethnic minority lines helps highlight the arbitrariness of race-ethnicity and hence may create a space to confound dominant racialization processes by forming an alliance that comes close to being a new racial-ethnic group.[8] To quote Paul Gilroy:

> [N]o single culture is hermetically sealed off from others. There can be no neat and tidy pluralistic separation of racial groups in this country. It is time to dispute with those positions which, when taken to their conclusions, say "there is no possibility of shared history and no human empathy." We must beware of the use of ethnicity to wrap a spurious cloak of legitimacy around the speaker who invokes it. Culture, even the culture which defines the groups we know as races, is never fixed, finished or final. (1992, 57)

---

8. Although Roach is focusing on African slaves and Native Americans in the context of the Atlantic rim in the eighteenth and nineteenth centuries, his comment that liaisons between these marginalized groups posed a menace different from miscegenation between whites and a nonwhite group (1996, 125–26) is still worth pondering. JanMohamed and Lloyd provide a helpful window to this threat when they recount the negative feedback they received from one of the National Endowment of the Humanities (NEH) reviewers of their proposal to have a conference on "minority discourse." The reviewer states: "I cannot but feel that a conference that would bring together in a few days of papers and discussions specialists on Chicano, Afro-American, Asian-American, Native-American, Afro-Caribbean, African, Indian, Pacific Island, Aborigine, Maori, and other ethnic literature would be anything but diffuse. A conference on ONE of these literatures might be in order; but even with the best of planning, the proposed conference would almost certainly devolve into an academic tower of Babel. It is not at all clear that a specialist on Native-American literature, for example, will have much to say to someone specializing in African literature" (cited in JanMohamed and Lloyd 1990, 3). Putting aside for the moment the question of whether Native Americans and Africans have anything to say to each other (but see Forbes 1993 and hooks 1992), the decision and desire of racial-ethnic minority critics to converse with each other rather than with the dominant culture threatens to not only displace this center but also to dismantle the construction of a "beehive multiculturalism" that we mentioned earlier.

What Patricia Hill Collins says about black feminist intellectuals is true also of racial-ethnic minorities in general: "the challenge lies in remaining dynamic, all the while keeping in mind that a moving target is more difficult to hit" (2000, 41). Minority alliance is one such move or movement, because it has the effect of both claiming and challenging racial-ethnic minority identity simultaneously. As one expression of what Gramsci calls the "bloc," it is also comparable to what Homi Bhabha calls a "cultural front" (2003, 31; see also 2007, 190–93). To destabilize and transform hegemony, Bhabha suggests that one must go beyond pre-given political identities and imagine, narrate, or create an alliance that implies a new, different, and provisional collective subject. Such a cultural front implies for Bhabha an identity that is not only interconnected but also incomplete; as such, it not only promotes the constructed character of identity in general and racial-ethnic identity in particular (see also Holland 2001, 171–76) but also provides for Bhabha a potential for a global or cosmopolitan rather than a national citizenship. Bhabha's transnational frame is, of course, significant, especially in light of Sharpe's sharp critique that racial-ethnic minorities within the U.S. must not forget—in their protest against exclusion and desire to claim national membership—the neocolonial hegemony that the U.S. exercises around the world (1993). For our purposes here, we would like to remind ourselves that Bhabha's "cultural front" is a logical extension rather than a radical transformation or deviation for racial-ethnic minority group identities in the U.S. That is to say, interconnected and incomplete identities are always already true of African Americans, Asian Americans, and Latino/a Americans, since all of them are not only racialized but also *panethnic* identities (Lipsitz 2001, 299–301, 308).

As the earlier term *selvage* implies, minority identities are patched together; they are patchwork "like a quilt, pieced together over time by many hands out of odds and ends" (Roach 1996, 191–92). Michael Omi and Howard Winant suggest, in their reading of the so-called "Los Angeles riot" of 1992, that the incident helps bring to surface cleavages not only between different racial-ethnic minority groups but also within each minority group (1993, 106–7). In addition to differences in work status, class, and length of residence in the U.S., Omi and Winant note how these factors may also intersect difference in ethnicity. Thus, they talk about the division between Chicanos and those with roots from Central America among Latino/as, or between "[s]olidly middle-class Japanese Americans, largely working-class Filipinos, generally low-income Southeast Asians, and Chinese Americans and Korean Americans whose class positions vary significantly" (1993, 106).[9] While Omi and Winant are silent about African Americans, this

---

9. In the case of Latino/as, it is worth pointing out that many have suggested *mestizo* or *mestizaje* as characteristic of Latin America identities (J. González 2001a: 157; Gruzinski 2002). In other words, mixing across racial-ethnic lines is not something that Latino/as experience only in the U.S. For example, Severo Sarduy, in the final "Nota" of his novel *De donde son los*

community of color is also no less panethnic. One only has to think about someone like Audre Lorde, whose parents were Caribbean immigrants. The debate
over Barack Obama's "authenticity" as an African American because his father is
a first-generation immigrant from Kenya also demonstrates that heterogeneity of
African America can and should not be limited to class.

Racial-ethnic minority identity in the U.S.—whether African American,
Asian American, or Latino/a—is always already a form of coalitional invention as
a consequence of and response to minoritization, and thus theoretically amenable
to the permeability and negotiation that are required in the minority conversation, association, and perhaps even alliance being envisioned here. This is not to
say, of course, that minority coalition is easy or without its own share of pitfalls
and dangers. We should be clear, for instance, that while minority alliance may
help destabilize African American, Asian American, and/or Latino/a American
identity, it does not exactly "solve the problem" of racial-ethnic relations, whether
with whites or between communities of color. After all, "minority criticism" does
not have any guarantees against essentialization, commodification, and/or ghet-
toization (see also Sugirtharajah 2003, 166–72).

This is especially so if minority coalition or criticism fails to be vigilant
against the temptation to understate differences and power differentials that do
exist both between and within different minority groups. The fact that racialization of one minority group takes place in relation to the racialization of other
minority groups means not that we are simply structurally equivalent but that
racial-ethnic minority groups exist in dynamic and shifting relations of interde-
pendence, contradictions, and competitions. For instance, in South Central Los
Angeles around the time of the Rodney King incident, African Americans there
tended to be the jobless poor as opposed to the working poor there made up by
Latino/as. To make matters worse, Asian Americans had something to do with
that difference, because many store owners preferred to hire or exploit Latino/as
who might be more willing to work for less because of their immigration status
(Chang 1994, 13; Oliver, Johnson, and Farrell 1993, 122–24).

Commenting on the difference and power differential within African American communities, Patricia Hill Collins refers to the "love and trouble" tradition
that black women express toward black men and goes on to suggest that this tradition or tension aptly represents "a rejection of binary thinking" (2000, 152).
We would like to propose that Collins's suggestion is also appropriate and advan-
tageous to think about relations across racial-ethnic minority line. After all,
racial-ethnic minorities in the U.S.—going back to Du Bois's "double consciousness"—are also amenable to accepting "the both/and conceptual stance" that

---

cantantes, comments that Cuban culture is constituted by or of Spanish, African, and Chinese
cultures (1993, 235). The relevance of Sarduy's comment to our project should require no further comments.

Collins highlights for and in black feminist thought (2000, 152). To put it another way, minority alliance or criticism must be a conversation without necessarily the aim of reaching consensus or overcoming difference.

To return to our earlier suggestion that alliance may help transform the ethos of domination that tends to govern racial-ethnic relations, we agree that "[t]he ability to occupy [a] space of unlikely affinity is in fact the heart of the democratic ideal" (Cheng 2001, 193). In sum, associating without affinity, or conversing without consensus, is precisely what we need to honor and practice. Along the lines of what we have suggested with Collins's comment about African Americans, we would like to extend Lorde's remark about women to relations across racial-ethnic minority lines:

> Advocating the mere tolerance of difference between women is the grossest reformism. It is a total denial of the creative function of difference in our lives. Difference must be not merely tolerated, but seen as a fund of necessary polarities between which our creativity can spark like a dialectic. Only then does the necessity for interdependency become unthreatening. Only within that interdependency of different strengths, acknowledged and equal, can the power to seek new ways of being in the world generate, as well as the courage and sustenance to act where there are no charters.... It is not our differences which separate women, but our reluctance to recognize those differences and to deal effectively with the distortions which have resulted from the ignoring and misnaming of those differences. (1984, 111, 122)

Lorde's statement captures not only the need to acknowledge and honor—and engage—difference but also the nature of coalition across difference to be necessarily dynamic and strategic. That is to say, there is no fixity in either how we understand another racial-ethnic minority culture or how we understand the purposes and directions of minority coalition. At this moment, perhaps we should be more modest and admit that minority coalition or criticism may have more to do with taking a better look at the processes of racial-ethnic problems than "solving" those problems. For this purpose of "understanding," reading a canonical text from the past that continues to impact or have effects in the present, like the Bible, is particularly insightful and instrumental. At the same time, if one is to mine the processes of racial-ethnic problems, minority biblical criticism must not satisfy itself with alternative readings of the Bible that can be easily appropriated for amusement or embellishment but must pay attention to the historical, socioeconomical, and political processes that racialize and minoritize certain groups of people in a society.

EXAMINING AND PREPARING THE GROUND

According to Mignolo, "[a]lliances, in the last analysis, are not established by languages or traditions only, but by common goals and interests in the field of forces established by and in the coloniality of power" (2000, 143). We hope our immediately preceding discussion on the creative and coalitional characteristics of each racial-ethnic minority group in the U.S. will move us from goals and interests to the specific contexts within which alliance across racial-ethnic lines will have to take place. In addition to suggesting that such attempts at conversations and alliance make good sense and are but a logical extension of racial-ethnic minority identity in the U.S., we would like to propose that the ground has also been prepared for this kind of work.

First, the intersections between race-ethnicity and other identity factors such as class, gender, and sexuality mean that there may be many unexpected twists and turns when it comes to relations among racial-ethnic minority groups across color lines. If the dominant society uses these intersections to generate conflicts (such as blacks as sexual predators against Asians as asexual), these same intersections may also turn out to become bases of alliance (since both Asians and blacks are racialized as sexually "deviant," though in opposing terms or directions).[10] Likewise, a Vietnamese American worker in the garment industry may have more in common with a Latina household maid or an African American cabdriver than a Japanese American Ivy Leaguer. In other words, the relations of these intersections across racial-ethnic minority lines are precarious, unstable, and can be used as fertile ground for building allying as well as agonistic relations.[11] The best argument that the field is ready for this kind of minority alliance lies, however, in the fact that numerous convergences and alliances have taken place in our past. If minority alliance is but a logical extension of racial-ethnic minority identity in the U.S., it is also but a continuation or an expansion of historical forces that have brought minorities and that minorities have brought together.

There are many examples that we can cite here, so we must limit ourselves to only a few. Okihiro has pointed out that, in the history of the U.S., blacks, Latinos, and Asians have joined each other as "plantation" workers, as these minority populations have all been exploited as cheap migrant labor to build the master's economy for the master's profits and to maintain through that process white

---

10. It will be wrong of us if we fail to point out here the most obvious link between race-ethnicity and sexuality: the lives and contributions of black, Asian American, and Latino/a queer.

11. To follow up on the earlier reference to *Miss Saigon*, the controversy surrounding the box office hit further illustrates the complexity and possibility of intersectional and interracial-ethnic minority politics. Perhaps partly due to the financial success of *Miss Saigon*, two lesbian and gay activist groups ended up choosing to use it as their annual fund-raiser in 1991. As a result, these two groups found themselves protested by not only Asian American lesbian and gay activists but also lesbian and gay activists of other communities of color. One such supporter who crossed the minority color line is Lorde, who refused to accept an award given by one of the two groups (the Liberty Award of the Lambda Legal Defense and Education Fund) to be in solidarity against the representations of Asians and Asian Americans in *Miss Saigon*. For a more detailed account of these events, see Yoshikawa 1994; Shimakawa 2002, 53–56.

supremacy (1994, 29, 45). Instead of—or, more accurately, *in addition to*—emphasizing Asian coolies and African slaves as competing or substitution systems, Okihiro discusses (1) how the two systems are similar; (2) how blacks and Asians intermarried as a result of comparative and comparable racisms, whether when both were used as slaves on board Europeans ships in the Indian Ocean and in colonies since the sixteenth century (including the then British colonies of Massachusetts and Pennsylvania in the late eighteenth century) or in the southern states of the U.S. before 1942 because of racial segregation and antimiscegenation laws; and (3) how Chinese coolies were not only also shipped to Peru and Cuba but their work there also became the "inspiration" and the proof that led to the coolie system in the U.S. in the nineteenth century (1994, 38–53). Put differently, Okihiro suggests that Asian American history cannot be divorced from the African slave trade but also that it actually came at least partly by way of Latin America. Okihiro also emphasizes that, even when Asian coolies were used to discipline blacks and depress wages simultaneously in the latter part of the nineteenth century, some African Americans—such as Frederick Douglass and Blanche K. Bruce—were able to see through the racist politics and spoke in support of rather than in discrimination against Asian laborers (1994, 48).

Whether it is the Japanese-Mexican Labor Association in California in 1903, the protest against the establishment of "Oriental schools" for Japanese children in the early 1900s, the Brotherhood of Sleeping Car Porters in the 1930s, the wartime propaganda against Japanese Americans and their internment in the 1940s, or the formation of the African-Korean American Christian Alliance in the 1990s, we have an ample supply of historical precedents of not only parallel but also conjoining struggles by African Americans, Asian Americans, and Latino/a Americans (Okihiro 1994, 54–63, 158).

Okihiro's work not only points helpfully to historical precedents of minority alliance, but it is itself also a reflection of a growing tendency within the larger world of literary/cultural studies and/or ethnic studies to emphasize association and conversation across racial-ethnic minority lines. Again, it must be acknowledged, as evidenced by our beginning reference to Du Bois, that minority dialogue has a long history, even or especially if it took place beyond the national limits of the U.S. We said "especially" because, as we have also mentioned earlier, there is a growing scholarly emphasis on transnationalism, and hence a blurring of "area studies" and ethnic studies in this age of globalization (Ong 1999; Chuh and Shimakawa 2001; Spivak 2003). Without implying in any way that "cultures" remain static in various locations nor denying the need of racial-ethnic minorities to "claim" the U.S. as one "home" (Stack 1996), the increasing engagement between "area studies" and "ethnic studies" should also take into consideration that "area studies" are themselves crossing area or racial-ethnic lines. Latin American studies, for example, have been engaging South Asian subaltern studies more and more since the 1990s (Mignolo 2000, 184–87).

Back to ethnic studies within the U.S., the earlier intent to address conflicts between Korean Americans and African Americans in the late 1990s (K. C. Kim 1999; J. K. Kim 2000) have given way at the beginning of the twenty-first century to more general attempts to compare and/or connect African American and Asian American studies (Prashad 2001; D. Y. Kim 2005; Raphael-Hernandez and Steen 2006), Latino and Asian American studies (De Genova 2006), and the three racial-ethnic minority groups that we are also putting together in this volume (Lee 2004; Pulido 2006).[12]

Whether it is historical precedents of the past or scholarly trends of the present, both of these factors circle back to feature not only the readiness but also the reasons and the needs for minority conversations, associations, and alliance in this moment in time. As George Lipsitz suggests, our time of globalization calls for a new form of power analysis and a different form of sociopolitical activism, and minority coalition across the color line is one good way to help address both (2001). Back in the early 1970s, in the aftermath of Stonewall, Black Panther leader Huey P. Newton commented that the gay liberation movement was most radical, because Stonewall was in large measure the result of an alliance between African American and Latino/a transsexuals (Lee 2004, 6). We are glad to see that scholars in the larger literary/cultural and ethnic studies world are currently working hard to continue this radical tradition, and we would like to see and do the same within the discipline of biblical studies.

Minority Biblical Criticism: Historical and Theoretical Contours

All three minority groups come to biblical interpretation with differences and with similarities. Central to all, at various times in our histories, has been the claim that the Bible is the word of God. This designation gave weight to the authority of the text and to its efficacy in the adherence to it. This claim to the

---

12. To avoid an impression of an unproblematic linearity, one should keep in mind here a couple of early texts that seek to promote conversation and association across African Americans, Asian Americans, and Latino Americans, such as Okihiro 1994; Chang and Leong 1994. Since we gave an example from theater performance when we discussed the dominant strategy to divide and conquer, let us point out here that performance artists/theater activists of racial-ethnic minority groups have also been using the stage to perform, produce, and promote minority coalition. Examples include Ping Chong (whose play *Chinoiserie* has an African American woman assuming the role of Vincent Chin's mother to signify Chin's murder as a continuation of U.S. racism); Anna Devean Smith (who impersonates multiple characters, including Asian American and Latino/a as well as black, in her one-person but multivoiced and multicultural monologue performance about the Rodney King beating, *Twilight: Los Angeles, 1992*); and the collaboration between Culture Clash (a Chicano performance group), Theatre Lab (a Latina group), and the 18 Mighty Mountain Warriors (an Asian American group) that leads to a performance piece titled "Close Encounters of the Third World." For more on these performers and performances, see Cheng 2001, 169–95; Shimakawa 2002, 129–62.

text gave it a totemic dimension that enhanced its attraction. Since this text was associated with whites who had hegemonic powers in the U.S., oppressed groups often perceived that, to gain that power, they would have to gain access to this text and give allegiance to it. Interestingly, it was African, Asian, and indigenous notions of deity and authority that infused these notions of the meaning or sense of "word of God" associated with the text.

All three groups initially came to this country under different conditions and circumstances. Africans came here in chains as enslaved people (Bennett 2007; Franklin 2000). Asians came here as immigrants and as indentured servants to work in the frontier (Novas 2004). Latinos/as came initially as conquerors and empire builders. They also came with knowledge of and often under the guidance of "the Book" and its institution, the church. Both African and Latinos/as have hybrid experiences in relation to intermingling with the indigenous people in the land, which impacted, in turn, the ways in which they related to the dominant groups and to each other. All three groups have been impacted by the ravages of white supremacy as practiced in the U.S. While the degree of impact might differ, the commonality of being raced and subjugated to racialist discourses and policies have, to varying extents, impacted how members of the groups see themselves, the other groups, and their relation to the tasks of biblical interpretation.

In no way is this schematic an attempt to utilize essentialist categories in defining and contouring these groups, since such a move would rob one of the richness and diversity within the groups (Anderson 2001; Gilroy 1993; González 2001b). Rather, it is an attempt to show some of the differences in experiences that impacted these groups in their entry into and sojourn in the U.S. It is also a claim that it is out of these experiences that one comes to collective consciousness and to differing rules of reading. Similarly, the conversion to Christianity and engagement of the Book were also intertwined with the ways in which biblical interpretation for these groups served as both a means of assimilation and a means of resistance to oppression.

The initial response to the Bible by enslaved Africans in the U.S. was, as Wimbush argues, one of rejection and suspicion (1991). In his *The Talking Book: African Americans and the Bible* (2006), Allen Callahan discusses how African Americans had mixed views of the text. Some saw it as the "Good Book," while others saw it as the "Poison Book." The former view was based on the belief that this Book would get one closer to God. The latter view was based on the materials in the Book that were used as sources of oppression of enslaved Africans, such as the household codes of Eph 6:5–8 and the endorsement of slavocracy in many texts, such as the parables of the talents (Matt 25:14–30) and of the vineyard and tenants (Luke 20:9–19) in the Gospels (see Smith 2007). As the period of enslavement of Africans in the U.S. was most formative in their experience, the use of the text as a source of manumission was noticeable in the speeches of abolitionists. As time went on, however, and as distance to the times of enslavement grew wider, the proslavery texts in the Bible became viewed as less offensive to some black interpreters of the Bible. For instance, Renita Weems (1991) talks about how Hagar is identified with by black women who see her as abused by Abram. On the other hand, T. D. Jakes, in a sermon on the Hagar texts in Gen 16 and 21 entitled "Hagar's Baby: What Others Call a Mistake God Calls Great," engages the text by removing the objectionable parts of the story, especially the enslavement and rape of Hagar. Rape is now called a "mistake." So, the turning to the text for both liberation and accommodation still exists.

Liew has argued for situating Asian American biblical studies within the context of and in dialogue with Asian American studies (2002; 2008). He also looks at how biblical themes are taken up into artistic works and the literature of Asian American artists. In so doing he explores the range of peoples included under the nomenclature "Asian American" and the ways in which these groups have interacted with the text. While these groups are often divided along national designations of hyphenated-Americans, their experiences in the U.S. become the lens through which they read the text. Thus Uriah Kim, for example, uses his conversion to Christianity as a Korean American to explore the submerged character Uriah the Hittite in 2 Sam 11. Similarly, Mary Foskett utilizes her experience of having been adopted in a transracial situation as a way of reading Moses' adoption and Paul's use of the metaphor of adoption. In other words, the ways in which people have been treated in the U.S. become the hermeneutical frame for interpreting the text.

Segovia has developed an ongoing typology for interpreting Latino/a academic approaches to the biblical text, both among scholars in other theological disciplines and among biblical critics themselves (1994). Among the former, the variety of strategies identified include: configuring a canon within the canon—using an external criterion, such as what is liberative for Latino/a women, as the measure of evaluation; subscribing to the traditional fundamental principle at work in liberation hermeneutics—adopting the perspective of the poor or oppressed as privileged and indispensable; and having recourse to Latino/a experience as a point of entry into the text—establishing a critical correspondence between the reader in context and the text in context. Among the latter, he has traced how Latino/a critics avail themselves of the wide methodological repertoire at work in contemporary criticism, variously adapting such methods from the standpoint of and toward the ends of Latino/a reality and experience. He has also advocated for ideological analysis not only of the biblical texts but also of modern and postmodern scholarly readings of such texts as well as of the readers behind them.

Bailey has explored U.S. Afrocentric biblical interpretation growing out of responses to various forms of oppression in the U.S. (2000). His schema details works that actively search for Africans in the text, counteract white supremacist readings, use black cultural modes of interpretation, and employ ideological concerns. An example of this entails a look at the dissertations of several African American New Testament scholars. There appears to be an attempt at "redeeming Paul," given the ways in which Pauline and Deutero-Pauline statements, seen as being pro-slavery, worked in the subjugation of enslaved Africans. It thus appears that there is a sense of race consciousness behind these works, even though it could not be raised to the conscious hermeneutical level at the time of writing. In all of these explorations of cultural biblical interpretations, there are conscious attempts to demonstrate how these forms are not monolithic and are not to be seen in isolation from their contexts and from those of their peoples in this country.

One of the difficulties in exploring these forms of racial-ethnic interpretation is the recognition that the numbers of scholars engaging in these endeavors are small. As Liew notes (2002), many of the writers on Asian American biblical scholarship are not trained in biblical studies. Some are in other fields of religion, and others are trained in cultural studies. The same is true of Latino/a American biblical interpretation, where the number of critics trained in the discipline is small but where many theological voices do write on the Bible. In addition, there is the awareness that most of those scholars who come from these racial-ethnic groups and who have degrees in biblical studies were not trained in doing such forms of criticism. Many of us were not even allowed to explore the text from these vantage points while we were in coursework or dissertation modes in graduate programs. While the situation is somewhat changing during the present century, such was not the norm in the preceding decades, much less the preceding century. Thus the engagement and development of racial-ethnic biblical interpretations require a retooling, both in terms of methods and in terms of questions asked of the text. In so doing one becomes more aware of how racial-ethnic Eurocentric biblical scholarship has been (Kelley 2002). For example, one comes to understand how the de-Africanization of Egypt and the making of Israel into a proto-European group were integral to the enhancement and development of white supremacy and the marginalization of other groups (Bailey 1991; Du Bois 1946; Miller 1997).

One sees similarities in approaches and strategies between these groups as one looks at attempts to engage the traditions of the biblical text and the ways in which they have been used as harmful or liberatory agencies. Howard Thurman begins his monumental work *Jesus and the Disinherited* (1996) by describing his meeting with Gandhi on a trip to India. Thurman was asked how, given the ways in which Christianity has been used against blacks in the U.S., they could remain Christian. In answering this question, he goes to the Gospels and argues for a "religion of Jesus," which he spells out in the volume and which is different from the ways in which oppressors have used the text. This is similar to the work of a U.S. scholar long involved in Latin America, Jorge Pixley, as he contours the exodus event with liberation struggles in Latin America and critiques the "One man Hero" model presented in the biblical text as not being helpful in current-day liberation struggles (1987). This is a "canon within the canon" approach, working with the experiences and approaches of the common people. This view complements that of Patricia Hill Collins, as she discusses the role of the black intellectual (2000).

As with most identity critical scholarships, the works begin with essentialized views of the task and the group. The debates of who can do such scholarship, who is "in"—in other words, does one have to come from that particular racial-ethnic group to engage in such criticism?—went on in those early stages, similar to what is currently going on in sexual orientation interpretations (Guest 2005). Thus, there was discussion as to whether one needed to be a member of the particular racial-ethnic group to engage in biblical criticism from this perspective. Similarly, in the early stages of the current development of scholarship from these perspectives, the view was one of focusing on the group primarily from an androcentric focus. This tendency was promoted since the academy first began to train men from these groups and has been slow in the training of women. Even to this day, there is only one U.S. Latina scholar with the terminal degree in Hebrew Bible. This training primarily of men coupled with the patriarchal nature of not only the biblical materials but also the racial-ethnic cultures from which we have come helped to account for this contouring of these forms of scholarship. As the number of women scholars has increased, so has the engagement of the traditions from their perspective and the broadening of the dimensions of such racial-ethnic scholarship.

Another facet in the development of these racial-ethnic forms of interpretation was the relationship of these modes to those developments in the areas outside of the U.S. from which the groups came. In other words, how do these interpretations relate to what is happening in biblical scholarship on the continents of Africa, Asia, and Latin America and in the Caribbean and West Indies? Is there connection between what is being done in Chinese and Indian biblical scholarship in the homelands with what is being done in the U.S. by Asian American scholars? As Sugirtharajah talks about the use of indigenous Asian religious texts for sources in forming postcolonial interpretations of the biblical text, especially in regard to translation (1996), should the same be going on in the U.S.? Or should the interpretation be directed more by what happens to oppressed minorities in the U.S. as a focus or lens for interpretation?

Similarly, how do these forms of racial-ethnic interpretation interact with and learn from each other? Liew (2008) argues that Asian American biblical scholarship must be a form of internal dialogue among Asian American biblical scholars so as to create/leave a tradition of interpretation. Should the same also be the model for interaction among these groups? Robert Allen Warrior long ago leveled a challenge to black and other liberation theologies that claim the exodus narrative as a starting point (1995). As a Native American, he sees the "God of Liberation" being integrally tied in the text to the "God of Dispossession." Thus, as a member of a conquered group, he cannot read Joshua without misgivings. He then asks, Why is it that others who have been "othered" do not read with the Canaanites in the text? While most black theologians dismissed this challenge, it seems a most appropriate form of engagement and one that should be taken seriously (Bailey 2005). As the three racial-ethnic groups now have program units within the Annual Meeting of the Society of Biblical Literature, the attempts to have cross-fertilization and dialogue are growing. This dialogue, however, must be expanded to include members from other racial-ethnic groups whose numbers of biblical scholars have not grown to the point of critical mass to become institutionalized within the Society. Thus, questions of exile and landlessness can be engaged, and the groups can learn from each other. By the same token, there needs to be more engagement within the guild of those of us in the diaspora with groups from the homeland.

One of the difficulties in this sharing of work in the development of racial-ethnic biblical interpretation is the differences in experiences of these groups in this country, as noted above. In employing a hermeneutic of suspicion in the development of these forms of reading, what is the focus of the suspicion? What part or parts of the canon resonate with these different groups? With whom in the text does one identify, especially on the national or ethnological level? Do these groups valorize Israel and the early church to the exclusion of the Canaanites, Moabites, Ammonites, Gentiles, and so on?

How is class viewed in the development of these interpretations? Are the portrayals of deity "given a pass" in these interpretations? How do these forms of interpretation not duplicate the problems of black, liberation, and Asian theologies, namely, embracing patriarchy and marginalizing women embedded in the ideologies of the text? Can these methodologies play a constructive part in the negotiating and healthy resolution of tensions that exist between Asian, black, Latino/a communities in the U.S.? What are the "canons within the canon" of these groups, and how do they intersect and overlap? How do these methods of interpretation travel between the academy and the church?

Finally, as queer studies and its various mutations dealing with issues of sexual orientation develop, racial-ethnic biblical studies has to give voice to these concerns within the various groups as well as to challenge hetero-centrism within the various groups, just as we need to be vigilant and challenge patriarchy in our traditions. We have to make space for all members of the community to find safe space and credible voices in these groupings. We have to grow to see the multivalent readings that grow from such branching out and inclusivity. While most of us come to the task with confessional backgrounds and, in many instances, confessional influences on our scholarship, we must use such cultural criticism to challenge the oppressive ideologies embedded within the texts and traditions from which we come. We must also challenge queer and gendered readings and methodologies of biblical interpretation regarding their eclipsing of issues of race and ethnicity in the text, in the histories of interpretation, and in their own constructions.

Minority Biblical Criticism: Rhetorical Dynamics

The rhetorical dynamics of minority criticism may be approached in terms of major critical strategies. Four such strategies can be readily delineated: (1) interpretive contextualization, or puncturing objectivity and universality; (2) border transgressionism, or expanding the area of studies; (3) interruptive stock-taking, or problematizing criticism; and (4) discursive cross-fertilization, or taking the interdisciplinary turn. A number of comments are in order regarding this outline. To begin with, these models are presented as neither self-evident nor indispensable. They represent, rather, taxonomic constructions based on empirical observation over time of studies produced by minority critics; as such, they can be readily replaced, in part or in toto, by a different system of classification, should such a system be deemed more appropriate or more useful. Similarly, these models are not presented as self-contained and mutually exclusive formations, unique unto themselves. They are construed, rather, as interrelated and interdependent and thus deployable in a variety of combinations. In addition, each model is presented as encompassing a number of concrete strategies, or tactical maneuvers, also imbricated in one another and employable with one another. Lastly, this delineation of grand strategies and tactical procedures is by no means presented as exhaustive. It constitutes, rather, but a first step toward a taxonomy and theorization of such moves in minority criticism.

PUNCTURING OBJECTIVITY AND UNIVERSALITY

A major strategy in minority criticism consists in foregrounding contextualization at the level of interpretation or reception alongside its continued pursuit at the level of composition or production. Such contextualization involves a twofold angle of inquiry, both highly interrelated and interdependent: on one side, analysis of social-cultural location, with a focus on material matrix as well as discursive production; on the other side, unpacking of ideological-political agenda, along any number of axes, within any given social-cultural framework. This strategy minority criticism adopts, directly or indirectly, in the face of and in reaction to dominant criticism. As such, it counters a received model of contextualization as a task to be pursued in resolute fashion with regard to the past, the world of production, but to be avoided with unyielding determination with respect to the present, the world of consumption. In effect, minority criticism sees such opening and drawing of a critical curtain of silence as profoundly ambiguous and ultimately contradictory.

Such critical silence yields two basic postures: on the one hand, principled adherence, based on traditional claims to social-cultural abstraction and ideological-political impartiality in scientific research; on the other hand, pragmatic subscription, opting for (absolute) reticence in practice while questioning in principle any such claim to ideological-political neutrality or social-cultural transcendence. Consequently, the gaze uncast by dominant criticism upon itself, whether theoretically denied or pragmatically bracketed, emerges as paramount for minority criticism, as it seeks to construct and to theorize itself. In thus relativizing itself in relation to the established model of inquiry, minority criticism might appear on the surface as mortally undoing itself. So, indeed, will it be perceived from the perspective of dominant criticism, whose reaction will range from outright dismissal, with characterization of the whole enterprise as fatally biased and compromised, to effective marginalization, with classification of all such work as of interest and benefit only to the group(s) in question.

From its own perspective, however, minority criticism sees itself as ultimately relativizing, and hence mortally undoing, dominant criticism as well, insofar as it presses the question of location and agenda as applicable to and inescapable in all situations, not only at the periphery but also at the center. What minority criticism does thereby is to extend in logical fashion the driving principle of contextualization: the dictum that a cultural product from another time and/or place has to be situated and retrieved within its own context of production. This dictum, it argues, applies to any cultural product in any time and/or place and is thus relevant to both the realm of composition and that of interpretation, even when a claim to the contrary has been lodged by the interpretive tradition itself. In so doing, minority criticism need not argue that only through such placement and positioning in context can there be correct understanding and accurate recovery. It could well argue instead that what contextualization yields is fuller understanding and broader re-creation, through always involving a diversity of views as well as a diversity of conflicts in such views. In the end, therefore, for minority criticism any claim to universality and objectivity emerges as itself subject to contextualization, localized and ideological.

This first grand strategy of rupturing the objective-universal optic may be seen as encompassing a variety of tactical procedures.

1. Relentless Denuding/Investing. A first maneuver of interpretive contextualization involves intensive critical gazing on dominant criticism, seeking to move past the screen of silence erected on the foundations of objectivity and universality. This tactical procedure sets out deliberately to cut through such self-imposed reticence by searching around and ferreting out the submerged context and perspective of dominant criticism. This may be seen, therefore, as a variation on the classic exclamation of exposure captured in the tale of "The Emperor's New Suit" by Hans Christian Andersen: a child, upon seeing the emperor pass by, supposedly arraigned in the finest and costliest of garments, bursts out piercingly, "The emperor is naked!" Thus, minority criticism, when confronted by self-imputed scientific nakedness, cries out, "The emperor is clothed to the hilt!" Such epistemic denuding may or may not lead to a corresponding investing: the exposure may stop with the moment of unmasking as such or may go on to give a full description of the actual clothing worn by the emperor.

2. Appealing to Contextual Enlightenment. Another maneuver tied to interpretive contextualization is the use of context as point of entry into the reading of a text. In this tactical procedure direct insight is drawn from the material matrix and/or discursive production in order to render the text, as the claim would have it, more comprehensible and more effective. This claim need not be totalizing

in nature: it need not argue that without such contextualized light-shedding the meaning and impact of the text would remain altogether elusive. In fact, it is invariably relativizing in tone: it argues for distinctive and significant insight as a result of such contextualized light-shedding, without excluding similar such insights from other locations and/or agendas. As a result, a contextual reading may be advanced as special or even unique, but such a distinction would not be denied of other readings in their own right. In other words, such a reading would not be presented as requiring privileged access and yielding a privileged rendition. Indeed, any such claim would prove highly ironic, insofar as it would ironically duplicate the exclusivistic character of scientific reading in reverse fashion—privileged not as universal but as contextualized.

3. Retrieving the Religious-Theological. A third maneuver in league with interpretive contextualization consists in the recovery and accentuation of religious and theological frameworks. The curtain of silence drawn around location and agenda by dominant criticism includes the religious-theological realm as well. Such reticence may be seen as a direct result of the project of liberation undertaken by historical criticism in the nineteenth century: interpretation to be wrested away from the domain of the church, with its use of scripture as a timeless warrant for unproblematic appropriation in church dogma and life, and entrusted instead to the realm of the academy, via approach to scripture as a time-bound remnant in need of decipherment before application. In rummaging around the site of interpretation, however, minority criticism leaves no stone unturned, including that of underlying religious-theological constructions and relations. This tactical procedure amounts to a reverse process of liberation, away from the standard sanitization of the religious-theological in dominant criticism. In so doing, minority criticism is determined to do to its analysis of the present what it carries out in its analysis of the past, viewing such religious-theological frameworks as highly significant and highly influential for consumption as well as for production. The strategy may be limited to simple acknowledgment or proceed to active engagement.

EXPANDING THE AREA OF STUDIES

A second major strategy in minority criticism is to push aside and move past the established boundaries of the discipline. Such expansionism proceeds along different lines: amplifying the parameters of critical embrace and/or amplifying the modality of critical approach. It may thus involve the object of study, the reach or scope of the discipline, bringing about the incorporation of material heretofore altogether bypassed or effectively marginalized within the lens of analysis. It may also affect the mode of inquiry, the approach or framework of the discipline, leading to a transformation of method and theory in the lens of analysis. This strategy minority criticism also carries out, directly or indirectly, in the light of and in opposition to dominant criticism. In so doing, it takes on the received set of delimitations placed upon the craft of interpretation, bringing a (varying) charge of exclusionism against dominant scholarship. Such a practice of inclusion/exclusion is invariably cast in ideological terms through the argument that the omission(s) and silence(s) in question work to the advantage of dominant voices and the detriment of voices of the Other. This strategy allows minority criticism, therefore, to relativize the ways in which the discipline has been traditionally configured and exercised. This second grand strategy of breaking through disciplinary boundaries similarly reveals a number of tactical procedures.

1. Breaking Spatial-Temporal Models. A first maneuver adopted in border transgressionism is to call for a redrawing of the geographical and/or historical boundaries of the field. One such move has to do with the given spatial borders of antiquity as the proper context for biblical antiquity and research, on the grounds that the field as envisioned views and approaches the biblical texts as more closely related to an underlying vision of Europe. Dominant criticism, it is argued, embraces the texts as ultimately and fundamentally part of the Greek and Roman foundations of the West, separating them thereby from other areas and religions of contact and influence, such as the social-cultural frameworks of Africa or the religious frameworks of Hinduism and Buddhism. Another such move involves the set temporal borders of antiquity as the sole focus for biblical antiquity and research, on the basis that the field as visualized examines only the remains of antiquity. Dominant criticism, it is proposed, leaves out of consideration thereby the representations of antiquity and its remains, that is, the interpretations of the biblical texts and contexts and the interpreters behind them in modernity and postmodernity.

Through the first expansion, minority criticism portrays dominant scholarship as highly gravitational in aim, thus muddying the spatial or geographical constructions of antiquity by exposing their strong Western pull and raising the possibility of alternative contextualizations within antiquity itself. Through the second move, minority criticism depicts dominant scholarship as highly constructive in nature, thereby muddling any notion of antiquity as a temporal or historical reconstruction and exposing all criticism as a creative exercise in representation. While the first move stretches the discipline in largely cross-cultural fashion, away from an implicit European or Western center of gravity, the second does so in mostly transhistorical fashion, away from an explicit distantiation of antiquity as objectification.

2. Heightening the Discourse. A second maneuver followed in border transgressionism is to press for a revisioning of the methodological-theoretical repertoire informing and guiding the field. This move entails a turn toward interdisciplinary engagement and can proceed in various directions. In so doing, this tactical procedure follows the example of dominant criticism itself, given its earlier turn from traditional historical studies to literary studies and social studies in and since the 1970s, but along a different path altogether, full of complex twists and turns. Key in this regard is a recourse to the optic of minority dis-

course, with its focus on the problematic of race-ethnicity and its corresponding set of racialized and ethnicized constructions and relations—writ concretely as well as broadly.

To begin with, African American, Asian American, and Latino/a American critics can turn, respectively, to African American, Asian American, and Latino/a American studies for grounding and direction. All of these areas of studies—emerging explosively in the crucible of the 1960s, establishing solid footholds through the 1970s, and developing in variegated and convoluted fashion since the 1980s—provide ample material not only for criticism as such but also for all social-cultural dimensions and examinations of the groups in question. In addition, African American, Asian American, and Latino/a American critics can also refer to the other areas of studies besides their own. In other words, an African American critic can establish an ongoing conversation with Asian American and/ or Latino/a American studies and so on, mutatis mutandis. Thereby, a highly comparative optic can be established between and among the various groups—their trajectories and realities, their matrices and productions—for mutual refinement and support, especially given the parallel appearance, establishment, and maturation of these areas of studies. Lastly, African American, Asian American, and Latino/a American critics can further turn, beyond these areas of studies, to a more abstract consideration of minority studies as such. At this level, the problematic of race-ethnicity is pursued, in highly comprehensive fashion, by way of racial-ethnic studies and its corresponding focus on a variety of topics intimately related to race-ethnicity: migration, exile and diaspora; borders and borderlands between (nation-)states; minority and dominant groups; othering via ethnicization and racialization; the political economy of globalization. The result is a highly sophisticated grasp of the problematic with cross-cultural and transhistorical application.

3. Desacralizing the Text. A third maneuver flowing from border transgressionism is to call for a refashioning of stance or attitude toward the text on the part of the critic in the process of interpretation. This move may be seen as a direct reaction to what is by far the predominant position of dominant scholarship regarding proper critical demeanor: extracting and laying bare the findings of scholarly research, without any sort of engagement with or evaluation of such findings, least of all perhaps of a religious-theological nature, given the screen of silence imposed on all such aspects of interpretation for the sake of objectivity and universality. This move may thus be seen as well as a direct result of the strategy of recovering and accentuating religious-theological frameworks previously delineated under the umbrella of interpretive contextualization. Minority criticism may thus call for open and pointed dialogue with the text and its readings, providing in the process a set of social-cultural principles and commitments toward such a conversation and hence a set of criteria engagement and evaluation. In so doing, minority criticism may surface as well the religious-theological dimensions of interpretation, raising thereby the problematic of standing within

the Christian tradition, with a sense of the biblical texts as not only past and distant but also living and lived and thus a felt need to address the ramifications of texts and interpretations alike in the light of its own social-cultural location and ideological-political agenda. This tactical procedure moves the critical task beyond the traditional stance of textual sacrality, no involvement with the text on either principled or pragmatic grounds, toward a stance of textual desacralization, involvement with the text regardless of outcome, that is, whether by way of affirmation or critique.

Problematizing Criticism

A third major strategy for minority criticism consists in interrupting the normal process of interpretation by calling for critical conscientization, thus turning criticism upon itself in a quest for self-awareness and self-reflection. Such interventionism has to do with the identity and the role of the critic as critic and thus involves considered reflection upon personal as well as professional dimensions of criticism. This strategy minority criticism again unfolds, directly or indirectly, in the face of and in reaction to dominant criticism. As such, it counters an established vision of critical status and task in which the critic is assigned a twofold dimension: an indispensable medium, at once discoverer and guarantor, between past and present, production and reception; an unflinching crusader in a collective and cumulative quest for "truth," bound by exemplary disciplinary ideals of detachment and disengagement and unencumbered by social-cultural ties and interests of any sort.

Such conscientization moves in two directions, by no means mutually exclusive. On the one hand, it may veer toward questions of critical identity: background and motivation. Rather than engage in criticism in unreflective fashion, the critic pauses to ponder who s/he is as a critic, whence and why s/he does what s/he does as a critic. On the other hand, it may favor questions of critical role: procedure and objective. Instead of pursuing criticism in abstract terms, the critic halts to reflect on what it is that s/he does, how and to what end s/he does what s/he does as a critic. Both paths of questioning are closely interwoven: while the first type of intervention lays the ground for a circumscription of critical task, the second builds on the foundations of critical identity. In the end, regardless of emphasis, criticism takes on a different hue: not so much as a fairly straightforward academic process, impersonal and self-evident, yielding progressive scholarly evidence under a sense of joint critical endeavor; rather, as a highly convoluted scholarly discussion, immersed in differential relations and discursive frameworks of all sorts, yielding tensive and conflicting positions under a sense of critical engagement on and from all sides.

This third grand strategy of interrupting interpretation through conscientization may again be seen as encompassing a variety of tactical procedures.

1. Taking a Personal Turn. A maneuver deployed in interruptive stock-taking amounts to a focalization of the strategy of contextual enlightenment, delineated earlier under the banner of interpretive contextualization, through a personalization of the analysis of social location and ideological stance. This involves a shift—or, perhaps better, a tilt—from a more collectivist to a more individualist focus on material matrix and cultural production. Minority critics come to regard and to approach their identity and role as critics not only as members of minority groups but also as distinct members within such groups: in terms of location, different from other members, despite the similarities of membership, within the groups as constructed; in terms of agenda, espousing particular variations of visions and aims, within the overall spectrum of group aims and visions. Such differences and particularities minority critics seek to expose and theorize by foregrounding personal realities and experiences.

Thus, for example, while in some respects and for some occasions, a Latino/a American critic may concentrate on the Latino/a contingent as a group or on a particular national-origins segment within this group (say, Mexican American or Dominican American), in other respects and for other occasions, such a critic may choose to emphasize instead a specific trajectory, problematic, or position within the Latino/a formation in general, the national-origins segment in question or, indeed, any other subgrouping within them. Such a move would demand close attention to matters autobiographical across the board—not simply by way of enumeration, but rather with theorization in mind. Such a move would lead to critical dialogue with other members of the various groupings in question: critical comparison regarding trajectories, problematics, or positions. Such a move would further sanction a call for such self-analysis on the part of all critics, minority or dominant. To that extent, this tactical procedure would tear apart even more radically the curtain of silence drawn around the critical task in traditional criticism, extending analysis from the realm of production to the realm of interpretation.

2. Taking a Cultural Turn. Another maneuver invoked in interruptive stock-taking is to intensify the strategy of breaking spatial-temporal models, outlined earlier under the mantle of border transgressionism, by moving from the level of historiographical construction (a sense of the remains as represented) to that of disciplinary construction (a sense of the plurarity of traditions of representation). This entails not just moving beyond received geographical and historical confines of the discipline, therefore, but actually stepping outside such delimitations altogether by fashioning a more comprehensive vision of the discipline as discipline. Thus, minority critics come to regard their role as critics as much too constrictive, given their professional venue in the realm of the academy and its traditional focus on scholarly discourse—trajectories, paradigms, and disputations. Consequently, they begin to push instead for a vision of their task as taking in, beyond much-needed methodological and theoretical amplification within scholarly discourse, interpretive amplification as well: attention to and analysis of readings and readers of the biblical texts outside the academy. In so doing, minority critics

press—from within the academy and without abandoning the academic-scholarly tradition—for sustained and rigorous analysis of other traditions of interpretation, both within and without the religious realm.

In the process, minority criticism effects a twofold break: first, with dominant criticism, given its exclusive devotion, since the beginning of the discipline, to scholarly interpretation; second, with itself, as it moves beyond its own demand for contextualization at the level of interpretation within the discipline. The result is also twofold: (1) a broadly comparative analysis of the reception of the biblical texts within any given social-cultural context: placing scholarly interpretation alongside invocations of the texts across society and culture—from popular and devotional appropriations to social and cultural renditions (economics, politics; literature, the visual arts, film); (2) a similarly broad comparative analysis of the consumption of the biblical texts within the religious-theological framework in question: placing academic interpretation alongside the deployment of the texts across churches and practices—from dogmatic and theological formulations (doctrine, ethics) to institutional and liturgical appeals (polity, worship). This tactical procedure ultimately transforms the biblical critic from a strictly disciplinary practitioner into a cultural observer, with interest in and responsibility for the myriad of incarnations and uses thrust onto the biblical texts.

3. Taking a Global Turn. Yet another maneuver employed in interruptive stock-taking lies in expanding the maneuver of heightening the discourse, earlier set forth under the banner of border transgressionism as well, by moving beyond engagement with minority discourse to interaction with postcolonial studies. This involves a projection of minority criticism onto the global scene through the insertion of criticism into geopolitical formations and trajectories, with a focus on imperial center and colonial peripheries and hence on imperial-colonial frameworks and relations. In this process minority critics come to regard the categories "dominant" and "minority" as too limiting, given their emergence and signification within the parameters of a (nation-)state, where they reflect internal processes of ethnicization and realization at work. Minority critics thus reach beyond political formations and approach such categories in geopolitical dimensions, with a view of the (nation-)states in question as global powers and dependencies and of foreign affairs in terms of imperial-colonial constructions and relations.

Such expansion—involving perceptions, evaluations, and attitudes of the Other as global—has an impact on all domains of the critical task. To begin with, minority critics come to see their own reality and experience in the country as a result of underlying geopolitical forces and movements, which have a bearing on their material matrix and their cultural production. In effect, African American, Asian American, and Latino/a American critics begin to address their provenance, their passage, and their situation in the country in terms of their origins in or descent from Africa, Asia, and Latin America. In so doing, they further problematize the character of their country as a global power, not only a superpower but the hyperpower, and of its management of foreign affairs in terms of imperial-colonial constructions and relations. In addition, minority critics transfer the power of such geopolitical forces and movements onto the biblical texts and contexts, foregrounding their production within a variety of ancient imperial-colonial frameworks. Lastly, minority critics extend the influence of geopolitical forces and movements onto the dominant tradition of interpretation and its practitioners, given its historical development and continued operation within a variety of imperial-colonial frameworks in both modernity and post-modernity. Throughout, therefore, minority criticism approaches what transpires locally in dominant-minority relations and constructions of race-ethnicity as linked to what transpires translocally in postcolonial relations and constructions of geopolitical relations and constructions.

Taking the Interdisciplinary Turn

A fourth major strategy in minority criticism is to pursue sustained and systematic critical dialogue with scholarly discourses having to do with the problematic of identity. Such academic cross-fertilization may develop along different directions: in tandem, by engaging one such discursive framework; in combination, by reaching out to a couple of frameworks; or in unison, by striving to bring together as many as frameworks as possible at once. This strategy minority criticism similarly adopts, directly or indirectly, in the light of and in opposition to dominant criticism. As such, it sets itself apart from received attitudes toward interdisciplinary conversation in the various umbrella models at work in dominant scholarship.

Such distantiation takes place in different ways. Thus, for example, minority criticism distinguishes itself from traditional historical criticism, insofar as it seeks interaction with areas of study regarded as having a direct and crucial bearing on all aspects of biblical studies. In so doing, it underlines the stance of isolationism endemic in historical criticism, given its reluctance to engage in critical fashion developments within its own allied discipline of historical studies. From their perspective, minority critics find it hard to understand how historical critics can abstain from conversation with the trajectories and debates taking place in recent and contemporary historiography. Similarly, minority criticism differentiates itself from literary criticism and sociocultural criticism, insofar as it seeks interaction with areas of study that surface and address differential relations of power in society and culture, viewed as having a constant and key impact on all dimensions of biblical studies. In so doing, it accentuates the sense of innocence that often marks such criticisms, given their eschewal of power relations affecting identity as they engage their respective allied disciplines in the human or social sciences. From their point of view, minority critics find it difficult to comprehend how literary or sociocultural critics can pursue analysis of the material matrix or cultural production without explicit attention to developments and discussions in ideological and cultural studies.

Recourse to this fourth grand strategy has already been detailed in two respects: first, with regard to the maneuver of heightening the discourse, within the strategy of expanding the area of studies; second, with respect to the maneuver of taking a global turn, under the strategy of problematizing criticism. In the former case, the turn of minority critics to racial-ethnic studies was described: casting concerns and interests within the wider net, long-established and highly complex, of the race-ethnicity problematic. The task of criticism is here related not only to the primary issue of ethnic-racial constructions and relations but also to a set of concepts directly linked to it: migration, causes and consequences; the nation-state, dominant and minority groups; borderlands, diaspora, and exile. In the latter case, the appeal to postcolonial studies was explained: viewing concerns and interests against the broader framework, recent in origin but similarly complex, of the geopolitical problematic. Here too the task of criticism is joined not only to the overriding issue of imperial-colonial relations but also to a set of concepts closely tied to it: imperial expansionism, designs and discourses; colonial subordination, reactions and options; imperial-colonial rubbings—ambivalence, ambiguity, hybridity.

Three other such discursive frameworks should be mentioned as well, given their prominence in the academy: materialist studies, feminist studies, and queer studies. Thus, minority critics may variously latch their concerns and interests onto the following problematics: political economy, with its defining focus on constructions and relations around class; gender, with its central issue of masculine-feminine constructions and relations; political economy, with its defining focus on constructions and relations around social class; and sexuality, with its defining focus on constructions and relations around sexual orientation. In each case, again, a distinctive set of concepts follows in close association. To be sure, other scholarly discourses, such as disability studies and trauma studies, may be called upon by minority critics for fruitful engagement.

All such interdisciplinary ventures may, again, be pursued in single alliance or in group coalition. Minority critics may thus bring together biblical studies and, say, ethnic-racial studies or materialist studies. Minority critics may also seek the juncture of biblical studies with, say, both ethnic-racial studies and materialist studies. Ultimately, moreover, such interdisciplinary conversations may lead minority critics to pursue the ideal of intersectionality: the criss-crossing of manifold such constructions and relations of identity at once. Minority critics may thus press for invoking, at the same time, ethnic-racial studies, materialist studies, feminist studies, postcolonial studies, and queer studies—all in relation to biblical studies. Such a move would prove challenging in the extreme, given its demand for enormous theoretical sophistication and its call for enormous methodological savvy. Such a move would also signify a certain return to individualism, but an individualism now reconceptualized and reformulated on a radically different key: a social-cultural variation of individualism, with varying and shifting notions of centers and peripheries in identity at any one time and at all times. Such a move, lastly, would be considered applicable in both the social-cultural context of antiquity, the world of composition, and those of modernity and postmodernity, the world of interpretation.

The actual arrangement of these exercises in minority criticism could have followed a number of different options. The essays could have been readily listed according to the following criteria: (1) in alphabetical fashion, in line with the surnames of the authors; (2) divided into Hebrew Bible studies and early Christian studies, adhering to the central division in the canon; (3) in terms of minority groupings (African American, Asian American, Latino/a American), harping on the element of race-ethnicity; or (4) by order of preference in critical strategy, proceeding from the more to the less common procedure. All such arrangements would have been quite valid, providing different insights into the venture. The order of presentation adopted takes pedigree of critical strategy as its decisive criterion, moving from more established to more innovative procedures. This arrangement has a threefold aim: (1) to foreground the richness of theoretical orientations and methodological moves in minority criticism; (2) to bring out a sense of expanding critical exploration at this still-early stage among minority critics; (3) to serve as both point of entry into and point of departure for further work in minority criticism.

The result is as follows. The first section brings together essays engaged in "Puncturing Objectivity and Universality," a strategy with a long history among minority critics and the most common option by far in the volume. Given their number, the studies in this first section have been arranged by canon and, within the canon of the Hebrew Bible, alphabetically. The other three sections, then, feature studies that move minority criticism in different new directions. The second section, "Expanding the Field," addresses the object of study. The third, "Problematizing Criticism," pursues the question of critical standpoint. The fourth and final section, "Taking an Interdisciplinary Turn," deals with the issue of critical angle.

Following these studies in minority criticism, which together represent part 1 of the volume, there follows a series of critical assessments offered by a group of scholars who are based in disciplines other than biblical studies (theological studies; religious education; ethnic studies) and who formed part of the venture as interdisciplinary interlocutors from beginning to end; these constitute part 2 of the volume. A conclusion provides a critical reflection on central aspects of the venture, pointing out salient achievements as well as key lacunae, thus looking around at what has been done and ahead at what remains to be done, as the quest *Toward Minority Biblical Criticism* continues its path(s), at once well-established and ever-expanding.

Works Consulted

Adams, Rachel. 2007. At the Borders of American Crime Fiction. Pages 249–73 in *Shades of the Planet: American Literature as World Literature.* Edited by Wai Chee Dimock and Lawrence Buell. Princeton: Princeton University Press.

Aguilar-San Juan, Karin, ed. 1994. *The State of Asian America: Activism and Resistance in the 1990s.* Boston: South End.

Anderson, Victor. 2001. We See through a Glass Darkly? Black Narrative Theology and the Opacity of African American Religious Thought? Pages 78–93 in *The Ties That Bind: African American and Hispanic American/Latino/a Theologies in Dialogue.* Edited by Anthony B. Pinn and Benjamín Valentíin. New York: Continuum.

Ang, Ien. 1994. On Not Speaking Chinese: Postmodern Ethnicity and the Politics of Diaspora. *New Formations* 24:1–18.

———. 2001. *On Not Speaking Chinese: Living between Asia and the West.* New York: Routledge.

Anzaldúa, Gloria E. 1987. *Borderlands/La Frontera: The New Mestiza.* San Francisco: Aunt Lute Books.

Baker, Houston A., Jr., ed. 1982. *Three American Literatures: Essays in Chicano, Native American, and Asian American Literature for Teachers of American Literature.* New York: Modern Language Association.

Bailey, Randall C. 1991. Beyond Identification: The Use of Africans in Old Testament Poetry and Narratives. Pages 165–84 in Felder 1991.

———. 1994. They're Nothing but Incestuous Bastards: The Polemical Use of Sex and Sexuality in Hebrew Canon Narrative. Pages 121–38 in *Social Context and Biblical Interpretation in The United States.* Vol. 1 of *Reading from This Place.* Edited by Fernando Segovia and Mary Ann Tolbert. Minneapolis: Fortress.

———. 2000. Academic Biblical Interpretation among African Americans in the United States. Pages 696–711 in *African Americans and the Bible: Sacred Texts and Sacred Spaces.* Edited by Vincent Wimbush. New York: Continuum.

———. 2005. He Didn't Even Tell Us the Worst of It. *USQR* 59:15–24.

Bakhtin, Mikhail. 1986. *Speech Genres and Other Late Essays.* Translated by Vern W. McGee. Edited by Carol Emerson and Michael Holquist. Austin: University of Texas Press.

Bennett, Lerone. 2007. *Before the Mayflower: A History of Black America.* Chicago: Johnson.

Bhabha, Homi. 2003. Democracy De-realized. *Diagenes* 50:27–35.

———. 2007. Global Minorities Culture. Pages 184–95 in *Shades of the Planet: American Literature as World Literature.* Edited by Wai Chee Dimock and Lawrence Buell. Princeton: Princeton University Press.

Callahan, Allen Dwight. 2006. *The Talking Book: African Americans and the Bible.* New Haven: Yale University Press.

Chang, Edward T. 1994. Jewish and Korean Merchants in African American Neighborhoods: A Comparative Perspective. Pages 5–21 in Chang and Leong 1994.

Chang, Edward T., and Russell C. Leong, eds. 1994. *Los Angeles—Struggles toward
Multiethnic Community: Asian American, African American, and Latino Perspectives.* Seattle: University of Washington Press.

Cheng, Anne Anlin. 2001. *The Melancholy of Race: Psychoanalysis, Assimilation,
and Hidden Grief.* New York: Oxford University Press.

Ch'ien, Evelyn Nien-Ming. 2004. *Weird English.* Cambridge: Harvard University
Press.

Chin, Frank, and Jeffrey Paul Chan. 1972. Racist Love. Pages 65–79 in *Seeing
through Shuck.* Edited by Richard Kostelanetz. New York: Ballantine.

Chuh, Kandice. 2003. *Imagine Otherwise: On Asian Americanist Critique.*
Durham, N.C.: Duke University Press.

Chuh, Kandice, and Karen Shimakawa, eds. 2001. *Orientations: Mapping Studies
in the Asian Diaspora.* Durham, N.C.: Duke University Press.

Collins, Patricia Hill. 2000. *Black Feminist Thought: Knowledge, Consciousness,
and the Politics of Empowerment.* 2nd ed. New York: Routledge.

Dabydeen, David. 1991. On Cultural Diversity. Pages 97–106 in *Whose Cities?*
Edited by Mark Fisher and Ursula Owen. New York: Penguin.

De Genova, Nicholas, ed. 2006. *Racial Transformations: Latinos and Asians
Remaking the United States.* Durham, N.C.: Duke University Press.

Delgado, Richard, and Jean Stefancic. 2001. *Critical Race Theory: An Introduction.*
New York: New York University Press.

Du Bois, W. E. B. 1903. *The Souls of Black Folk: Essays and Sketches.* Chicago:
McClurg.

———. 1940. *Dusk of Dawn: An Essay toward an Autobiography of a Race Concept.*
New York: Harcourt, Brace & World.

———. 1946. *The World and Africa: An Inquiry into the Part Which Africa Has
Played in World History.* New York: International.

———. 1995. *Dark Princess: A Romance.* Jackson: University Press of Mississippi.
[orig. 1928]

Edwards, Brent Hayes. 2003. *The Practice of Diaspora: Literature, Translation, and
the Rise of Black Internationalism.* Cambridge: Harvard University Press.

Eng, Kenneth. 2007. Why I Hate Blacks. *Asian Week.* February 23.

Felder, Cain Hope, ed. 1991. *Stony the Road We Trod: African Americans and the
Bible.* Minneapolis: Fortress.

Forbes, Jack D. 1993. *Africans and Native Americans: The Language of Race and the
Evolution of Red-Black Peoples.* 2nd ed. Urbana: University of Illinois Press.

Forgacs, David, ed. 2000. *The Antonio Gramsci Reader: Selected Writing 1916–
1935.* New York: New York University Press.

Foucault, Michel. 1997. What Is Enlightenment? Pages 303–19 in *Ethics: Subjectivity and Truth.* Edited by Paul Rabinow. Translated by Robert Hurley et al.
New York: New.

Franklin, John Hope. 2000. *From Slavery to Freedom: A History of African Americans.* 2 vols. New York: Knopf.

Gilroy, Paul. 1992. The End of Antiracism. Pages 49–61 in *Race, Culture and Difference.* Edited by James Donald and Ali Rattansi. Newbury Park: Sage.

———. 1993. *The Black Atlantic: Modernity and Double Consciousness.* Cambridge: Harvard University Press.

———. 2005. *Postcolonial Melancholia.* New York: Columbia University Press.

González, Justo L. 2001a. *Acts: The Gospel of the Spirit.* New York: Orbis.

———. 2001b. Scripture, Tradition, Experience and Imagination: A Redefinition? Pages 61–73 in *The Ties That Bind: African American and Hispanic American/ Latino/a Theologies in Dialogue.* Edited by Anthony B. Pinn and Benjamín Valentín. New York: Continuum.

González, Michelle A. 2004. Who Is Americana/o? Theological Anthropology, Postcoloniality, and the Spanish-Speaking Americans. Pages 58–78 in *Postcolonial Theologies: Divinity and Empire.* Edited by Catherine Keller, Michael Nausner, and Mayra Rivera. St. Louis: Chalice.

Gotanda, Neil T. 2001. Citizenship Nullification: The Impossibility of Asian American Politics. Pages 79–101 in *Asian Americans and Politics: Perspectives, Experiences, Prospects.* Edited by Gordon H. Chang. Stanford: Stanford University Press.

Gould, Stephen Jay. 1996. *The Mismeasure of Man.* Revised and expanded edition. New York: Norton.

Gramsci, Antonio. 2000. *The Antonio Gramsci Reader: Selected Writings, 1916–1935.* Edited by David Forgacs. New York: New York University Press.

Gruzinski, Serge. 2002. *The Mestizo Mind: The Intellectual Dynamics of Colonization and Globalization.* Translated by Deke Dusinberre. New York: Routledge.

Guest, Deryn. 2005. *When Deborah Met Jael: Lesbian Biblical Hermeneutics.* London: SCM.

Guillory, John. 1993. *Cultural Capital: The Problem of Literary Canon Formation.* Chicago: University of Chicago Press.

Harding, Sandra, ed. 2004. *The Feminist Standpoint Theory Reader: Intellectual and Political Controversies.* New York: Routledge.

Hartsock, Nancy C. M. 1998. *The Feminist Standpoint Revisited and Other Essays.* Boulder, Colo.: Westview.

Holland, Catherine A. 2001. *The Body Politic: Foundings, Citizenship, and Differences in the American Political Imagination.* New York: Routledge.

Hom, Sharon K. 2001. Cross-Discipline Trafficking? What's Justice Got to Do with It? Pages 76–103 in Chuh and Simakawa 2001.

Hong, Grace Kyungwon. 1999. "Something Forgotten Which Should Have Been Remembered": Private Property and Cross-Racial Solidarity in the Work of Hisaye Yamamoto. *American Literature* 71:291–310.

hooks, bell. 1984. *Feminist Theory: From Margin to Center.* Boston: South End.

————. 1990. Marginality as Site of Resistance. Pages 337–43 in *Out There: Marginalization and Contemporary Cultures*. Edited by Russell Ferguson, Martha Gever, Trinh. T. Minh-ha, and Cornel West. New York: New Museum of Contemporary Art.

————. 1992. Revolutionary "Renegades": Native Americans, African Americans, and Black Indians. Pages 179–94 in idem, *Black Looks: Race and Representation*. Boston: South End.

————. 1996. *Yearning: Race, Gender, and Cultural Politics*. Boston: South End.

Hwang, David Henry. 1994. Foreword: Facing the Mirror. Pages ix–xii in *The State of Asian America: Activism and Resistance in the 1990s*. Edited by Karin Aguilar-San Juan. Boston: South End.

Inden, Ronald B. 2000. *Imagining India*. Bloomington: Indiana University Press.

JanMohamed, Abdul R., and David Lloyd, eds. 1990. *The Nature and Context of Minority Discourse*. New York: Oxford University Press.

Jones, Eugene H. 1988. *Native Americans as Shown on the Stage, 1753–1916*. Metuchen, N.J.: Scarecrow.

Kaminsky, Amy K. 1993. *Reading the Body Politic: Feminist Criticism and Latin American Women Writers*. Minneapolis: University of Minnesota Press.

Kant, Immanuel. 1996. An Answer to the Question: What Is Enlightenment? Pages 15–22 in *Practical Philosophy*. Edited and translated by Mary J. Gregor. New York: Cambridge University Press.

Kelley, Shawn. 2002. *Racializing Jesus: Race, Ideology, and the Formation of Modern Biblical Scholarship*. New York: Routledge.

Kim, Claire Jean. 2000. *Bitter Fruit: The Politics of Black-Korean Conflict in New York City*. New Haven: Yale University Press.

Kim, Daniel Y. 2005. *Writing Manhood in Black and Yellow: Ralph Ellison, Frank Chin, and the Literary Politics of Identity*. Stanford, Calif.: Stanford University Press.

Kim, Kwang Chung, ed. 1999. *Koreans in the Hood: Conflict with African Americans*. Baltimore: Johns Hopkins University Press.

Koshy, Susan. 2004. *Sexual Naturalization: Asian Americans and Miscegenation*. Stanford, Calif.: Stanford University Press.

Lee, James Kyung-Jin. 2004. *Urban Triage: Race and the Fictions of Multiculturalism*. Minneapolis: University of Minnesota Press.

Liew, Tat-siong Benny. 2008. *What Is Asian American Biblical Hermeneutics: Reading the New Testament*. Honolulu: University of Hawaii Press.

————. 2002. Introduction: Whose Bible? Which (Asian) America? *Semeia* 90–91:1–26.

Liew, Tat-siong Benny, and Vincent Wimbush. 2002. Contact Zones and Zoning Contexts: From the Los Angeles "Riot" to a New York Symposium. *Union Seminary Quarterly Review* 56:21–40.

Lipsitz, George. 2001. "To Tell the Truth and Not Get Trapped": Why Interethnic Antiracism Matters Now. Pages 296–309 in Chuh and Shimakawa 2001.

Lorde, Audre. 1984. *Sister Outsider: Essays and Speeches.* Trumansburg, N.Y.: Crossing.

Meier, Matt S., and Feliciano Rivera, eds. 1974. *Reading in La Raza: The Twentieth Century.* New York: Hill & Wang.

Mignolo, Walter D. 2000. *Local Histories/Global Designs: Coloniality, Subaltern Knowledges, and Border Thinking.* Princeton: Princeton University Press.

Mills, Charles W. 1997. *The Racial Contract.* Ithaca, N.Y.: Cornell University Press.

Mullen, Bill V., and Cathryn Watson, eds. 2005. *W. E. B. Dubois on Asia: Crossing the World Color Line.* Jackson: University Press of Mississippi.

Nguyen, Viet Thanh. 2002. *Race and Resistance: Literature and Politics in Asian America.* New York: Oxford University Press.

Novas, Himilce, and Lan Cao, with Rosmary Silva. 2004. *Everything You Need to Know about Asian American History.* New York: Plume.

Okihiro, Gary Y. 1994. *Margins and Mainstreams: Asians in American History and Culture.* Seattle: University of Washington Press.

———. 2001. *Common Ground: Reimagining American History.* Princeton: Princeton University Press.

Oliver, Melvin L., James H. Johnson Jr., and Walter C. Farrell Jr. 1993. Anatomy of a Rebellion: A Political-Economic Analysis. Pages 117–41 in *Reading Rodney King, Reading Urban Uprising.* Edited by Robert Gooding-Williams. New York: Routledge.

Omatsu, Glenn. 1994. The "Four Prisons" and the Movements of Liberation: Asian American Activism from the 1960s to the 1990s. Pages 19–69 in Aguilar-San Juan 1994.

Omi, Michael, and Howard Winant. 1993. The Los Angeles "Race Riot" and Contemporary U.S. Politics. Pages 97–114 in *Reading Rodney King, Reading Urban Uprising.* Edited by Robert Gooding-Williams. Routledge: New York.

———. 1994. *Racial Formation in the United States: From the 1960s to the 1990s.* 2nd ed. New York: Routledge.

Ong, Aihwa. 1999. *Flexible Citizenship: The Cultural Logics of Transnationality.* Durham, N.C.: Duke University Press.

———. 2003. *Buddha Is Hiding: Refugees, Citizenship, the New America.* Berkeley and Los Angeles: University of California Press.

Park, Kyeyoung. 1997. *The Korean American Dream: Immigrants and Small Business in New York City.* Ithaca, N.Y.: Cornell University Press.

Pixley, Jorge V. 1987. *On Exodus: A Liberation Perspective.* Translated by Robert R. Barr. Maryknoll, N.Y.: Orbis.

Prashad, Vijay. 2001. *Everybody Was Kung Fu Fightin: Afro-Asian Connections and the Myth of Cultural Purity.* Boston: Beacon.

Pratt, Mary Lousie. 2002. The Traffic in Meaning: Translation, Contagion, Infiltration. *Profession* Fall:25–35.

Pulido, Laura. 2006. *Black, Brown, Yellow and Left: Radical Activism in Los Angeles.* Berkeley and Los Angeles: University of California Press.

Punday, Daniel. 2003. *Narrative Bodies: Toward a Corporeal Narratology.* New York: Palgrave.

Radhakrishnan, R. 2001. Conjunctural Identities, Academic Adjacencies. Pages 249–63 in Chuh and Shimakawa 2001.

Raphael-Hernandez, Heike, and Shannon Steen, eds. 2006. *AfroAsian Encounters: Culture, History, Politics.* New York: New York University Press.

Roach, Joseph. 1996. *Cities of the Dead: Circum-Atlantic Performance.* New York: Columbia University Press.

Rosaldo, Renato. 1997. Cultural Citizenship, Inequality, and Multiculturalism. Pages 27–38 in *Latino Cultural Citizenship: Claiming Identity, Space and Politics.* Edited by William V. Flores and Rina Benmayor. Boston: Beacon.

Sarduy, Severo. 1993. *De donde son los cantantes.* Edited by Roberto González-Echevarría. Madrid: Ediciones Cátedra.

Segovia, Fernando F. 1994. Reading the Bible as Hispanic Americans? *NIB* 1:167–73.

Sharpe, Jenny. 1993. *Allegories of Empire: The Figure of Woman in the Colonial Text.* Minneapolis: University of Minneapolis Press.

———. 1995. Is the United States Postcolonial? Transnationalism, Immigration, and Race. *Diaspora* 4:181–99.

Shimakawa, Karen. 2002. *National Abjection: The Asian American Body Onstate.* Durham, N.C.: Duke University Press.

Smith, Mitzi. 2007. Slavery in the Early Church? Pages 11–22 in *True Commentary.* Edited by Brian K. Blount. Minneapolis: Fortress.

Spivak, Gayatri Chakravorty. 1996. *The Spivak Reader.* Edited by Donna Landry and Gerald Maclean. New York: Routledge.

———. 2003. *Death of a Discipline.* New York: Columbia University Press.

Stack, Carol. 1996. *Call to Home: African Americans Reclaim the Rural South.* New York: Basic.

Suárez-Orozco, Marcelo M., and Mariela M. Páez, eds. 2002. *Latinos: Remaking America.* Berkeley and Los Angeles: University of California Press.

Sugirtharajah, R. S., ed. 1991. *Voices from the Margin: Interpreting the Bible in the Third World.* Maryknoll, N.Y.: Orbis.

———. 1996. Textual Cleansing: A Move from the Colonial to the Postcolonial Version? *Semeia* 76:7–19.

———. 2003. *Postcolonial Reconfigurations: An Alternative Way of Reading the Bible and Doing Theology.* St. Louis: Chalice.

Suh, Sharon A. 2004. *Being Buddhist in a Christian World: Gender and Community in a Korean American Temple.* Seattle: University of Washington Press.

Takaki, Ronald. 1989. *Strangers from a Different Shore: A History of Asian Americans.* New York: Penguin.

Taylor, Charles. 1994. The Politics of Recognition. Pages 25–73 in *Multicul-turalism: Examining the Politics of Recognition*. Edited by Amy Gutmann. Princeton: Princeton University Press.

Thurman, Howard. 1996. *Jesus and the Disinherited*. Boston: Beacon.

Venne, Sharon Helen. 1998. *Our Elders Understand Our Rights: Evolving International Law Regarding Indigenous Peoples*. Princeton: Theytus.

Warrior, Robert Allan. 1995. A Native American Perspective: Canaanites, Cowboys, and Indians. Pages 287–95 in *Voices from the Margin: Interpreting the Bible in the Third World*. Edited by R. S. Sugirtharajah. Rev. ed. Maryknoll, N.Y.: Orbis.

Weems, Renita J. 1991. Reading *Her Way* through the Struggle: African American Women and the Bible. Pages 57–77 in Felder 1991.

Wilson, Rob, and Wimal Dissanayake, eds. 1996. *Global/Local: Cultural Production and the Transnational Imaginary*. Durham, N.C.: Duke University Press.

Wimbush, Vincent L. 1991. The Bible and African Americans: An Outline of an Interpretive History? Pages 81–97 in Felder 1991.

Yoshikawa, Yoko. 1994. The Heat Is on *Miss Saigon* Coalition: Organizing across Race and Sexuality. Pages 275–94 in Aguilar-San Juan 1994.

Yun, Lisa. 2008. *The Coolie Speaks: Chinese Indentured Laborers and African Slaves in Cuba*. Philadelphia: Temple University Press.

PART 1: STUDIES
SECTION 1: PUNCTURING OBJECTIVITY AND UNIVERSALITY

Reflections in an Interethnic/racial Era on Interethnic/racial Marriage in Ezra

Cheryl B. Anderson

In Ezra 9–10, certain "foreign women" (*nāšîm nokriyyōt*) who are married to Jews and the children from such marriages are expelled from the community. Such marriages are condemned as acts of faithlessness and an undesirable mixing of "the holy seed" (*zéraʿ haqqōdeš*). Although the book of Ezra and its intermarriage ban are traced to the postexilic period (539–333 B.C.E.), reading this text today as an African American woman reminds me of a more recent history of racial segregation and state-enforced prohibitions against interracial marriage (antimiscegenation laws). This essay's purpose is to explore the interpretive challenge posed by such a text to Christian communities that happen to be African American.

According to the normative reading of this text, the expulsion of the women and children is understandable as a way to establish and maintain the identity of that ancient community of faith. Therefore, if African American faith communities adopt the normative reading, we are identifying with Ezra and his community and supporting their decision to exclude the foreigners. Given our history, however, African Americans have more in common with those who are to be sent away in the text than with those who remain. Furthermore, accepting the apparent rationale means that excluding those who are different can be warranted, and critical questions about the group identity to be preserved and the impact on those excluded, as experienced in our own past, are obscured.

After presenting the striking similarities between the functions of an exclusionary policy, whether in the setting of the Persian Yehud or the antimiscegenation laws in the United States, this essay will suggest that African Americans need a different reading, one that resists the normative reading. More specifically, I will argue that such an intermarriage ban not only constructs a group religious identity in the biblical text; it also constructs differences in ethnicity/race, class, and gender that are similar to those used in the segregationist era and still have repercussions today. As a result, I will contend that the intermarriage ban in Ezra is a "cautionary tale." The ban highlights the need for a contemporary reading strategy that takes the social and historical context of the contemporary reading community as seriously as it does the social and historical context of the biblical text. Otherwise, the silencing of the marginalized groups in the text (women and children) continues to silence a marginalized group today (African Americans).

The Intermarriage Ban in Ezra

In Ezra 9, according to the wording in the New Revised Standard Version (NRSV), Ezra receives complaints from officials that members of the community, including the priests and the Levites, have not separated themselves from foreign women. Rather, they have taken as wives the daughters of "the peoples of the lands [*'ammê hā'ărāṣôt*] with their abominations." As a result, "the holy seed (*zéra' haqqōdeš*) has mixed itself with the peoples of the lands" (Ezra 9:1–2). Ezra is appalled by the news and, after a time of fasting and mourning, prays to the Lord (9:4–5). In his prayer, Ezra remembers God's condemnation of "the peoples of the lands" (*'ammê hā'ărāṣôt*) who had polluted the land and the divine prohibition against marrying these people (9:10–12). As articulated by Ezra, the purpose of the prohibition against intermarriage was to ensure that the people of Israel "may be strong and eat the good of the land and leave it for an inheritance to your children forever" (9:11–12). However, the people of God have intermarried, and Ezra says that "all that has come upon us" is due to "our evil deeds and our great guilt." Unless they stop these practices, according to Ezra, God may even destroy the remnant of the people that now remains (9:13–14). In the next chapter, a member of the community, Shecaniah, proposes to Ezra that they "make a covenant with our God to send away all these wives and children," and Ezra has the community swear to that effect (10:1–4). Ezra 10 provides the names of the men who had married foreign women, and in the last verse of that chapter we are told that these men sent away their foreign wives and their children (10:44).

Ezra is described as a priest and a scribe of the law who was appointed and funded by the Persian imperial authorities to return to Jerusalem, accompanied by others of those exiled who wished to go with him (Ezra 7:11–28). The date of Ezra's mission is disputed but is often set in 458 B.C.E., thus prior to Nehemiah's mission as governor (political administrator) of the province in 444 B.C.E. (Brueggemann 2003, 363). Ezra had both religious responsibilities (to teach the law of the Lord and to refurbish the temple) and political responsibilities (to administer the king's law). Therefore, Ezra and those who returned from Babylon during the postexilic period, referred to collectively as the *golah* community, had dual allegiances and responsibilities to God and the emperor (Berquist 199, 112; Marbury 2003). They sought religious reforms, and they also had to ensure that the required taxation revenues were generated and submitted to the Persian king.

The *golah* community consisted of the religious and political elite that had been deported to Babylon after the fall of Jerusalem in 587/586 B.C.E. They had returned to Jerusalem and Judah, now a province in the Persian Empire referred to as Yehud, after 539 B.C.E. Those deported to Babylon comprised only a small percentage of the population, possibly 10 percent (Washington 1994, 232). Consequently, the largest percentage of the people remained in Judah. That population, referred to as "the poorest people of the land" in 2 Kgs 24:14 and 25:12, may actually have benefited from the absence of the elite. If subsistence farmers had lands seized by the elite, they may have been able to regain them once that group had left (Gottwald 1985, 424). Furthermore, worship practices in Jerusalem had continued during that period, but those practices were not considered to be legitimate by the returning community (Brueggemann 2003, 364). Understandably, tensions arose between the *golah* community, those once exiled, and the people of the land when the former group returned and wanted to resume leadership. For example, the *golah* community began to rebuild the temple and, because they saw the project as their sole responsibility, refused to allow the people of the land to participate (Ezra 4:1–4). In many respects, the returned exiles considered themselves to be the "true" Israelite community, and all others were deemed "foreigners."

Considering this postexilic setting, the intermarriage ban can be thought of as demonstrating a need for boundaries to maintain Jewish identity within the Persian Empire and to avoid "religious and cultural assimilation" (Birch et al. 2005, 437). Nevertheless, a specific rationale for the intermarriage ban varies according to the specific group or groups thought to be excluded. Those considered to be foreigners could have been the descendants of the Judeans who had not gone into exile and were now deemed "lesser Jews" (Klein 1999, 740 n. 98; Brueggemann 2003, 369) or Samaritans (J. Collins 2004, 434). If these groups, in the elite's absence, had acquired (or regained) land previously owned by the returnees, intermarriage with these groups (and the possibility of inheritance) would have been a means for the *golah* community to take possession again.

The foreign women excluded by the ban may have been Persian. Persian authorities may have encouraged intermarriage between Persian women and men from leading families in the *golah* community as a way to solidify that group's allegiance to Persia (Johnson 1999). Because marriages with members of other local ethnic groups would have expanded the wealth and influence of the *golah* community beyond the borders of Yehud and outside of Persian control, an intermarriage ban with those groups even may have served Persian interests (Fried 2004, 211). It is at least plausible, then, that Persian authorities encouraged intermarriage between Yehudites and imperial families but not with members of any other ethnic groups. In general terms, the imperial administration would have preferred dealing with one identifiable and exclusive group in its province that was closely affiliated with it and loyal to it, as the *golah* appear to have been (Hoglund 1992, 244). Such marriages between Jewish and Persian families could well have occurred in the years between the arrival of the first returnees after 539 B.C.E. and Ezra's arrival in 458 B.C.E.

These various opinions as to which groups were excluded as "foreigners" and why such marriages became problematic in Ezra's era will be discussed in greater detail in the following section of this study. At this point, it is simply worth noting that the ban makes a distinction between a privileged group (those included within the community) and a nonprivileged group (those excluded from the community), and that distinction is justified as a divine command. Both of these features—a distinction and divine warrant for that distinction—feature prominently in the antimiscegenation laws of the United States.

Segregationist policies that resulted in the separation of groups by race existed either by law or by custom for most of this country's history and were challenged broadly during the civil rights era of the 1960s. As part of that earlier history, antimiscegenation laws were geared to prevent certain kinds of sexual mixing across racial lines and prohibited, among other things, a marriage between a white person and a black person, as those categories were defined by statutes. Such laws were in effect for nearly three hundred years (1691–1967), and Alabama, the last state to remove a provision banning interracial marriages from its state constitution, did so only in the year 2000 (Wallenstein 2002, 247). In the 1960s, the United States Supreme Court held in *Loving v. Virginia* (388 U.S. 1 [1967]) that such laws were unconstitutional. At an earlier stage of that legal process, a judge in Virginia had upheld the state's intermarriage ban, writing the following statement in his conclusions: "Almighty God created the races white, black, yellow, malay and red, and he placed them on separate continents. And but for the interference with his arrangement there would be no cause for such marriages. The fact that he separated the races shows that he did not intend for the races to mix" (Wallenstein 2002, 219).

The same features noted in Ezra's intermarriage ban are seen here: a distinction made between groups and divine warrant for those distinctions. I am not claiming that Ezra's policy was racist in the modern sense or that Judaism then or now is racist or that this ban is directly related to the segregationist policies of a different time and place. Rather, the concern here is that texts such as the intermarriage ban in Ezra, regardless of whether any foreign women were actually expelled in that historical setting, are biblical precedents that were used against African Americans in a much later time, with tragic consequences. Furthermore, my argument is that, if groups reading these texts today fail to recognize the underlying dynamics in these texts and in American history, the harmful effects continue. To begin the discussion, the next section will show that the group identity enforced by Ezra and those in our segregationist past also shaped notions of race/ethnicity, class, and gender.

Constructing Group Identity: The Persian Yehud and the Segregationist Era

As mentioned earlier, scholars think that the intermarriage ban in Ezra served to construct or strengthen the group's religious identity through the maintenance of specific boundaries. Opinions about the specific rationale for the prohibition in Ezra, as seen earlier, vary depending on which group or groups are targeted. In this section, three perspectives on the subject of intermarriage in this biblical text are presented and then compared to similar constructions in the segregationist past. When considered together, these three perspectives demonstrate that race/ethnicity, class, and gender are inherent aspects of group identity. Consequently, the various scholarly approaches to the intermarriage ban in Ezra can be seen as highlighting different aspects of group identity formation. Moreover, to fulfill the purpose of this reflection, I will demonstrate the ways in which these same categories—race/ethnicity, class, and gender—were used to consign African Americans to the excluded and marginalized group in the segregationist era.

RACE/ETHNICITY

Ethnic identity, as in Ezra-Nehemiah, is constituted around several elements, including myths of common ancestry and a narrative that combines both "fact and fiction" and "expresses something essential about the group" (Esler 2003, 414–15). As part of her work on the construction of Jewish identities, Christine Hayes defines identity "as a social and cultural construct" that is "a group's subjective sense of itself as being different from other groups" (2002, 7). Accordingly, she argues that Jewish ethnic identity is set up in opposition to Gentile, or alien, "others" (7). Through the concept of impurity, Hayes observes, the boundary between the Israelite and the alien is both inscribed and policed, but insufficient attention has been paid to differences in the types of impurity attributed to the alien (7).

The type of impurity is important to consider, according to Hayes. Two types of impurities (ritual and moral) create permeable boundaries that will allow some aliens to be incorporated into the community, but one type of impurity (genealogical) creates an impermeable boundary. Building on earlier studies in the field, Hayes distinguishes ritual impurity (Lev 12–15) and moral impurity (Lev 18 and 20)—which are remediable "by means of ritual procedures or moral reformation, respectively"—from genealogical impurity (Lev 7–8; 22–23). Hayes finds that "Ezra is the first to define Jewish identity in almost exclusively genealogical terms" and that he "advanced the novel argument that *all* Israel—not just the priestly class—is a holy seed distinct from the profane seed of the Gentiles" (2002, 10). Hayes summarizes the significance of Ezra's ban as follows:

> According to Ezra, genealogical purity is required of all Israelites to guard against "profanation" of the holy seed. Concomitantly, because holy and profane seed cannot be mixed, the boundary between Jew and Gentile was declared by Ezra to be impermeable. Intermarriage became impossible. Indeed, as a desecration of holy property, it was seen as a serious offense against God. (10)

Following Hayes, then, the intermarriage ban plays a role in developing and maintaining a Jewish ethnic identity. Yet when I consider this prohibition against intermarriage and the impermeable nature of the boundary established, I immediately think that it is constructing a racial, rather than an ethnic, boundary. Indeed, the New International Version (NIV) translates the literal "holy seed" in Ezra 9:2 as the "holy race." Nevertheless, Hayes rejects any argument that a "racial ideology" is reflected here and states that the rationale is not "purity of blood" but genealogical purity. She summarizes her argument by stating: "The genealogical purity promoted in Ezra-Nehemiah refers to biological descent from full Israelite parents, undergirded by the notion of Israel as a holy seed" (27). Furthermore, she contends that this genealogical purity is "not racially based but religiously based," because it results from "God's separation of the seed of Abraham to himself—an act that conferred on that seed a holy status" (230 n. 30).

Hayes seems to assume, as many do, that there is a basic difference between race and ethnicity. Race is thought to describe "differences created by imputed biological distinctions, but ethnicity refers to differences with regard to cultural distinctions" (Malik 1996, 174). Ethnicity then creates more fluid and permeable boundaries between groups, whereas race creates inflexible and impermeable ones (174–75). Critical race theory, however, teaches us that "race is nothing more, and nothing less, than ethnicity" (Zack 2006, 36). Race and ethnicity are not intrinsically different for at least two reasons. First, the concept of race being associated with "blood," as in the expression, "She has black blood," has been discredited. There are four major blood types, and they do not correspond to membership in a particular race (Zack 2006, 9). As a result, when race is discussed, it is essentially a discussion about genealogy. Second, the inflexible and impermeable qualities of race are challenged by the fact that boundaries between groups can change.

In the Persian Yehud, the marriages with groups that Ezra condemned had been considered valid before his arrival; therefore, the boundary that he labeled as impermeable had, in fact, been flexible and permeable. Likewise, in the segregationist era, the statutory definition of who was "black" changed over time and varied from state to state. For example, at one point in Virginia, a person was black only if he or she had one black grandparent, great-grandparent, or great-great-grandparent; at a later point, a person was black if there were any black ancestors at all—"known as the one drop rule of black classification because it is based on the myth that one drop of 'black blood' is sufficient to determine racial blackness" (Zack 2006, 11). Correspondingly, then, "a person is white if he or she has no black ancestry anywhere in the family history," and it "means that in order to be white, a person has to be purely white" (11). Consequently, purity of genealogy was required for membership in the privileged community in both the Persian Yehud and the segregationist era—even if we (mistakenly) think of intermarriage bans as constructing ethnicity in the former context and race in the latter. Hayes argues that the genealogical purity Ezra called for is "not racially but religiously based" because the "higher (and holy) status" of the Israelites comes from God (2002, 230 n. 30). In a similar vein, black Christians during slavery "were constantly told that their bondage to the white man had been decreed by God" (Smith 1972, 11). Here is a portion of a sermon preached in the mid-1700s by the Rev. Thomas Bacon of Maryland to a congregation of Episcopal slaves: "'Almighty God,' he declared, 'hath been pleased to make you slaves here, and to give you nothing by Labour and Poverty in this world.' Far from giving them any hope of earthly freedom, he said 'If you desire Freedom, serve the Lord here, and you shall be his Freemen in heaven hereafter'" (Smith 1972, 11–12). Similarly, Rev. Bacon told the black congregation that their masters and mistresses were "God's overseers" and that, if they did not serve these overseers faithfully, "God would punish them severely in the world to come" (12). We know that not all slaves accepted this message without question. To the contrary, a hermeneutic of resistance was developed that enabled them to challenge their subordinate status and the idea that their bondage was God's will.

As I reflect on the intermarriage ban in Ezra, I wonder how that tradition of resistance can be revived and sustained. We tend to read the text today as though we are included in the privileged community. However, our history clearly indicates that, as African Americans, we were excluded and dominated on the basis of our race/ethnicity under comparable criteria. Intermarriage bans in the Persian Yehud or the segregationist era serve the purpose of a privileged group; our history is of those who are disadvantaged by them.

CLASS

Willa Mathis Johnson explores the relationship between economics in the Persian Yehud and the intermarriage ban in Ezra. She argues that economic concerns are related to marriage in the ancient Near East because "marriage included financial exchanges," including land acquisition (1999, 3). Furthermore, Johnson points out that the *golah* community, having returned from exile, no longer owns the land, which is a traumatic occurrence because that land is intimately connected to their kinship patterns, sense of group identity, and their relationship to God (137–54). After demonstrating that, as a Persian colony, land ownership in Yehud would have been held primarily by the Achaemenid ruling elite, Johnson argues that upper-echelon Yehudite men could regain land by marrying Persian women from ruling families (147–49). However, Johnson acknowledges that intermarriage constitutes a "double edged sword" for the *golah* community, because that economic gain conflicts with the process of group identity formation in the postexilic period. She writes, "Even though intermarriage provided possible economic advantages, it presented a larger identity conflict. It worked at cross-purposes with the need often attributed to exiled peoples, that is, to close ranks and segregate as a means of establishing boundaries" (153).

In Ezra, the need to establish group boundaries seems to have been given priority over economic gain. The "ostensible message of Ezra 9–10," Johnson submits, "is the confession and conversion of the unfaithful Yehudites who had married interethnically but through repentance are united into one God-fearing ethnic entity" (1999, 261). In other words, religious faithfulness wins out over economic advantages and possible political repercussions from the imperial power. Indeed, as Gale Yee points out, Ezra's policies "undoubtedly offended the leading families of the women whose marriages were in jeopardy," and such "social destabilization in Yehud during a politically vulnerable time would not have pleased Artaxerxes I and his associates" (2003, 146). The displeasure of the Persian imperial authorities may even have been strong enough that Ezra was abruptly recalled to Babylon after being in Yehud only about a year (Yee 2003, 146; Blenkinsopp 1988, 179; Eskenazi and Judd 1994, 271).

Renouncing the foreign wives helped to reinforce group boundaries and religious identity, but a significant economic advantage was solidified as well. After the *golah* community had regained the land through earlier intermarriages (exogamy), now prohibiting marriages outside of that community (endogamy) would allow them to retain it and pass it on as an inheritance to their descendants. Simply put, "the elites practiced exogamy to obtain the land and endogamy to keep it" (Yee 2003, 145; Johnson 1995, 182–83; Berquist 1995, 118).

In addition to accumulating land, there were other economic advantages that the *golah* community obtained, and these advantages created class differences in Yehud. Initially, Persian resources supported both an upper class and the temple's activities. As Persian financial support lessened, however, the peasantry was called upon to contribute more toward the temple as well as the taxes and tributes required by the imperial authorities (Yee 2003, 142; Berquist 1995, 62, 113). Eventually, "[a]s Persia continued to deplete the resources of the colonies, the effects struck Yehud differentially, and the rich maintained their power while the poor grew markedly poorer" (Berquist 1995, 113–14). Nehemiah 5:1–13 describes a desperate situation, only about fifteen years after Ezra's mission, in which the elite had benefited financially from the poor, their own kin, who had to mortgage their lands, take out loans, and sell their sons and daughters in order to pay their debts to the elite. In this context, a class structure deepened. There was a division "between those who live solely by their own labor and those who drew on the uncompensated labor product of others" (Gottwald 1999, 10).

To make matters worse, Nehemiah's reforms would not have brought permanent relief. Although Nehemiah forces the nobles and officials to return the interest and security of defaulted debts (both property and people), the debts themselves were not forgiven (Boer 2005, 247). Plus, there were no systemic changes to the abusive economic system itself. Still remaining were "the elite monopoly of agricultural land, noncompensation for those who farmed it, stiff burdens on the peasantry to pay imperial taxes, costly tithes for the temple (Neh 10:32–39), and the priestly elite's exemption from having to shoulder any portion of Persia's taxation (Ezra 7:24)" (Yee 2003, 142–43; see Gottwald 1999, 9, 12–13). After the rebuilding of Jerusalem's city wall, Nehemiah repopulates the city with members of the *golah* community (Neh 7:5–73), thereby rendering the wall a symbolic barrier between the upper and lower classes (Yee 2003, 143). Berquist writes, "The rebuilt city exists for the urban elite and their cohorts from Persia; the outlying, unprotected countryside remains for the poorer inhabitants of the land" (1995, 114; see Yee 2003, 143).

Nehemiah, like Ezra, condemns intermarriage. Yet, unlike Ezra, Nehemiah does not demand the expulsion of the foreign wives and children (Neh 13:23–29). Consequently, both Ezra and Nehemiah consider intermarriage a sign of unfaithfulness, but only Nehemiah was concerned with the plight of the lower classes. Ezra does not address the issue. For my purposes, the significance of opposition to intermarriage in Ezra-Nehemiah is that it presents intermarriage as a moral issue at the same time when growing economic disparities between the rich and the poor do not receive the same degree of critique. Furthermore, the attention paid to intermarriages shows how "theological arguments masked the class issues involved in these marriages" (Yee 2003, 145). In the segregationist era, antimiscegenation laws were supported with theological arguments that masked the class issues involved with slavery and segregation. If nothing else, slavery created a class system where there was a clear demarcation between those who labored and "those who drew on the uncompensated labor product of others" (Gottwald 1999, 10). Similarly, intermarriage was considered to be a moral issue, but the economic exploitation of African Americans did not merit the same degree of scrutiny. Once again, the experience of African Americans is closer to that of the groups excluded from the *golah* community than to that of those included within it.

Gender

Gender, the oppositional characteristics attributed to males and females, features in the intermarriage ban. Most clearly, differences result from the expulsion of foreign females but not the expulsion of comparable males. Harold Washington observes that, although the boundaries set against outsiders by Ezra appear to be impermeable, they "prove to be quite permeable" (2003, 431). Specifically, the census in Ezra 2 lists male heads of households who are unable to prove their genealogy within the *golah* community, but there is no mention of their expulsion; some priests were excluded from office for that reason, but a process for reconsideration is given (Ezra 2:61–63; 8:33); and in Ezra 6:21 the Passover celebration includes some from outside the community "who had joined them and separated themselves from the pollutions of the nations" (Washington 2003, 431). The question has to be asked: Why were women not given these opportunities to be a part of the community? Furthermore, the Deuteronomic law referred to in Ezra 9:12 prohibits both foreign husbands and foreign wives (Deut 7:3). Why are only the wives (and their children) banned in Ezra 9–10? (431).

Using the analytical framework of Julia Kristeva, Washington argues that women are excluded because of "the particularly gendered vocabulary that denotes, on the one hand, the community's holiness (*zéra' haqqōdeš*, "the holy seed"; Ezra 9:2), and, on the other, the threatening contaminant (*niddâ*, '[menstrual] impurity'; Ezra 9:11)" (2003, 431). Since "seed" is a "male emblem of purity" and menstrual impurity is a "specifically female pollution," Washington submits, "[t]his language therefore unavoidably positions women as signifiers of the stranger within" (431). Following Kristeva's analytical framework, then, women are rendered the abject and the abject must be expelled. Furthermore, Washington notices that in Ezra 9:11 the description of the land of Judah as a "land unclean [*'ereṣ niddâ*] with the uncleanness of [*niddâ*] the peoples of the land" uses the term *niddâ* "to stigmatize the peoples of the land and their defilement as feminine in a manner unknown to the cultic legislation of the Pentateuch" (434).

The connection that Washington identified in Ezra between negative attributes ascribed to a people and negative ones ascribed to females is not a coincidence. Johnson found that references to "intermarriage as 'abominable' (Ezra 9:1, 11, 14) or as an act of infidelity which has the power [to pollute] the land with uncleanness are equivalent to depicting marriage to foreigners as pornographic (Ezra 9:2, 4, 14; 10:2, 6)" (1999, 58). She suggests that negative connotations of sexuality are implied in an additional way "because the Hebrew words (*nāšîm nokriyyōt*) utilized in Ezra 9–10 to denote foreign women (Ezra 10:2, 10–11, 14, 17–18, 44) are used syntactically in parallel constructions with terms to describe the strange, whorish, and harlotous wife elsewhere in the Hebrew Bible" (1999, 58). As a result, foreigners (the ethnically Other) are debased as well as female sexuality, "since the two were nearly synonymous" (1999, 58–59).

Without a doubt, associating a particular group (consisting of males and females) with sexual waywardness is a way to demean and dehumanize them so that actions taken against that group are justifiable. As Daniel Smith-Christopher surmises, references in Ezra to the foreigners as Canaanites, Amorites, Jebusites, Perizzites, and Hittites are anachronistic, because those groups did not exist in the mid-fifth century B.C.E. Consequently, he thinks that these terms "almost surely have become *stereotypically pejorative slurs* referring to those ethnic groups who have long since either disappeared or assimilated, but who were condemned *historically* as those unclean peoples 'justifiably' destroyed by Joshua in the legendary patriotic tales of the founding of the Davidic House" (1996, 126). That the term "Canaanites" became a "stereotypically pejorative slur" as Smith-Christopher describes may explain how it was used in a Tennessee court decision in 1871. In that decision, *Lonas v. State*, 50 Tenn (1 Heisk.) 287 (1871), the following statement was written in opposition to interracial marriage: "[Marriage] is an institution of God, and a very honorable estate.... 'Thou shalt not,' said Abraham, 'take a wife unto my son of the daughters of the Canaanites.'... The laws of civilization demand that the races be kept apart in this country" (Ross 2002, 263).

In the segregationist era, the dominant culture did not rely just on biblical laws to promote its policies. A powerful ideology was developed that characterized black men and women as hypersexual: black women were thought of as promiscuous "Jezebels" and black men as strong "bucks." In other words, black people were labeled a sexually deviant group in order to justify their exploitation and domination. Although other stereotypes arose over time, the association between blackness and deviant sexuality is, as Patricia Hill Collins describes it, "one lynchpin of racial difference in Western social thought" (2004, 27). Antimiscegenation laws were meant primarily to preserve the purity of the white race, but the rationales offered and the laws promulgated involved protecting the purity of white women, who, it was feared, might otherwise be ravaged by black men (Higginbotham and Kopytoff 2000). Differences in female-gendered characteristics, therefore, existed based on race and class. Middle-class white women were characterized as "pure, chaste, and innocent," in contrast to black women, who were viewed as sexually wanton Jezebels (K. B. Douglas 1999, 39).

In practice, though, antimiscegenation laws meant that white men were able to sexually exploit black women and avoid legal responsibility for any mulatto children produced. African American leaders—including W. E. B. Du Bois, Booker T. Washington, and Frederick Douglass—opposed antimiscegenation laws specifically because of the resultant harm to black women (Robinson 2003, 118–19). When Tamara Eskenazi considered the intermarriage issue in Ezra and Nehemiah, she found that "an opposition to foreign women, so easy to criticize from a distance, is at the same time an affirmation of women who belong to the group" (1992, 36). Presumably, *golah* men and women would have more potential mates if they could marry only within their own ranks. She then writes that "[r]ather than being simply a misogynous act, this dismissal of foreign wives is an opposition to some women in favor of others" (36). Her assessment of the intermarriage ban in the Yehud fits well the circumstances of the antimiscegenation laws of the segregationist period. They were ostensibly in favor of white women and functioned in opposition to black women.

According to the list in Ezra 10:18–44, only about 110 women were affected. It is unclear why that small number of women, out of a total population of about 20,000, would have been perceived as such a threat, or why expelling them would seem to solve the problem (Janzen 2002, 13). David Janzen, in his study of the intermarriage ban in Ezra, proposes that the expulsion of foreign wives in Ezra occurred as a "ritual act of social purification," a witch-hunt, that blamed these women for extant social crises (19–20). Janzen argues that, "in the ideology of the text, the nature of the community is to be separate (*bdl*) from all impure influences" and the women are expelled "not because of what they have done but because of who they are (impure) and who they are not (members of the exile community)" (96). In other words, the women become associated with foreign influences in their midst—when those influences actually came from regional trade practices and Persian military and fiscal control of Yehudite resources (116–

63). Janzen's thesis is that, by expelling this small number of foreign wives and their children, the community symbolically purged itself of foreign influence and affirmed its cultic identity as the people of God. Obviously, the presence of these women created anxieties for some members of the *golah* community and seemed to pose a threat to their dominance in the community (Brueggemann 2003, 372).

Even if the women were to be expelled, why did the children have to go as well, when, in a patrilineal system, the children would have belonged to the father? Johnson's answer is that "the children are the defiled seed made manifest" and their expulsion is required because "they repeat the topography of their foreign mothers" (1999, 272). In the same way, underlying the antimiscegenation laws was the fear that racial mixing would "result in the amalgamation of the two races, producing a mongrel population and a degraded civilization" (Wallenstein 1998, 70). One of the earliest antimiscegenation laws, a 1691 Virginia statute, banned intermarrying to prevent increases in mixed-race children, who were referred to as "that abominable mixture and spurious issue" (Wadlington 1966, 1192). Furthermore, just as the children took on the marginalized social status of the mother in Ezra, in the segregationist era the mixed-race children were slave or free, according to the condition of the mother (Wadlington 1966, 1191; Davis 1983, 12).

Inheritance rights may have been an incentive for excluding the children in Ezra. It is Shecaniah son of Jehiel, a member of the community, who proposes to Ezra that the foreign wives and children be sent away (Ezra 10:2), and his father, Jehiel, is listed as one of the transgressors (10:26). A possible scenario is that Shecaniah was Jehiel's son with an earlier wife, and Jehiel had subsequently married "a distant kinswoman with land," which would make it possible for one of her sons, fathered by Jehiel, to inherit her husband's estate (M. Douglas 2002, 11–12). As a result, Shecaniah and other sons from previous marriages would fear being disinherited. Mary Douglas admits: "[i]t is understandable that the elder sons would fear their half-siblings, and so we hear the demand that the children be sent away (in effect, disinherited), along with their mothers" (12; Fewell 2003, 61–62). Under similar circumstances in the segregationist era, that fear of disinheritance led some white offspring to claim that the white father's subsequent marriage to a nonwhite woman violated antimiscegenation laws. For example, a white father could have married a black woman—either in a different state that allowed such marriages or in that state if the woman's race had not been obvious. If the later marriage was contested, the antimiscegenation laws would mean that it was null and void. Under these circumstances, the woman's children would be considered illegitimate and ineligible to inherit any property from the father (or stepfather). Just such a case came before the Oklahoma Supreme Court in 1967, several weeks after the United States Supreme Court's ruling in the *Loving* case. In *Dick v. Reaves*, 434 P.2d 295 (Okla. 1967), the Oklahoma Supreme Court held that the second marriage was valid "regardless of the racial ancestry of either party" (Wallenstein 2002, 237).

The intermarriage ban in Ezra constructs a religious identity, but it also constructs identities based on gender. Likewise, the antimiscegenation laws constructed differences based on gender (as well as race). As seen previously, though, black men, women, and children were denied any privileges generated by the ban, and that should influence how the biblical text is read by such communities today.

Constructing Group Identity: Further Reflections

The intermarriage ban in Ezra is conventionally supported as a means of constructing religious identity during the period of the Persian Yehud. My premise is that such an exclusionary policy also constructs notions of race/ethnicity, class, and gender, similar notions of which were used against African Americans in the segregationist era and antimiscegenation laws. As people of faith, then, if we view the ban in Ezra favorably, we are basically ignoring the tragedy of such exclusion in our own past. Some might conclude, however, that since segregation laws have been repealed, it is appropriate to leave such laws and the hardships they caused in the past. Given the fact that the United States today is more racially and ethnically diverse than ever, some see a need to network with groups outside the African American community, thinking that it would be divisive to focus on the historical black-white binary. Yet this past can be the thread that connects various groups together across racial and ethnic differences.

Yee, for example, found that the elite male constructions of females as Other in the Hebrew Bible parallel those of Asian American women at various historical stages of American popular culture as "the diabolically villainous Dragon Lady, the exotic hooker Suzy Wong, the seductive and coy geisha, and the Mongol slave girl" (2003, 159). In the Hebrew Bible and the United States, she notes, "[i]nstead of real Asian or Israelite women, we have ideological constructs that masked specific historical and socioeconomic subtexts" (159). In the same way, Patricia Hill Collins found that European interest in colonial expansion depended on characterizations of women in the territories to be conquered as "hot-blooded Latinas, exotic Suzy Wongs, wanton Jezebels, and stoic native squaws" (2004, 30). From a postcolonial perspective, therefore, racial-ethnic communities could use insightful analyses of their pasts to forge social and political alliances. Acknowledging our pasts does not necessarily mean that deeper divisions between communities of color will result.

The segregationist past and antimiscegenation laws also need to be considered in today's context because they continue to affect us in often unacknowledged ways. Two examples illustrate this: racial self-identification and the privilege of privacy.

First, allowing individuals to choose their own racial identification would seem to counter the imposition of a racial-ethnic identity that occurred in Ezra and the segregationist era. Beginning with the 2000 census, individuals are now able to check all races that apply to them. In that year, about seven million Americans indicated that they were members of "two or more races" (Zack 2006, 2). Racial self-identification, though, has been a controversial issue. For many African Americans, it is a reminder of the educational and economic advantages afforded mixed-race African Americans with lighter skin tones in the segregationist past, and they think that these individuals are trying to distance themselves from the African American community. There is also the fear that racial self-designation will undercut the avenues of legal redress based on race that were established during the civil rights era. A possible solution might be to think of racial self-designation on various institutional forms as a personal choice. Nevertheless, selections on those forms should not prevent a person from also "being black," where race becomes a political choice, that is, a commitment to struggle against economic injustice and the marginalization of racial-ethnic communities (Guinier and Torres 2002).

Second, choosing a marriage partner is thought to be a private matter today, but in the Persian Yehud and the segregationist era it was a public matter, since others outside the relationship could determine which relationships were acceptable and forbid unacceptable ones. It is only after the *Loving v. Virginia* Supreme Court decision in 1967, therefore, that "marriage between people of different racial identities became a private matter" (Wallenstein 2002, 231). Such a transition from "public" to "private" should remind us that privacy is socially constructed and a privilege not given to everyone. For instance, same-sex relationships, for the most part, remain public matters that are categorized as deviant and subjected to governmental intervention and control. To that extent, such relationships are not granted the privilege of privacy. In contrast, U.S. Senator Strom Thurmond, a white male, maintained a segregationist political platform, although when he was twenty-two he fathered a child with a fifteen-year-old African American domestic worker in his home (Lubin 2005, 151). Thurmond "could enter the public sphere because he was accorded the privilege of keeping his intimate affairs private" (151). Even today, African Americans do not have this level of privacy. The high incarceration rates for African American males, the high percentages of African American children in the foster care system, and the recognition within the community that police departments have "created" an offense for us, a DWB (Driving While Black), indicate that our actions and relationships are treated as public and not private matters. The segregationist era has officially ended, but black lives are still often categorized as deviant and subjected to governmental intervention and control.

To take into account the history of segregation and its continuing legacy when reading biblical texts such as Ezra, African American people of faith must have a different reading strategy—a hermeneutic of resistance. Resistance is appropriate because the dominant culture's interpretation of texts often erases that history and avoids dealing with the impact such texts have on people of color. An interpretive paradigm for the reading strategy could be "intersectionality." Intersectionality is a term used in critical race theory, and it refers to the ways in which race, class, and gender (including sexuality) function and interact with one another in society. For example, intersectionality implies that the disadvantages of race, class, and gender have to be nuanced in order to recognize that "a poor black person suffers greater racism than an affluent black person, and her race may make it more difficult to overcome poverty" (Zack 2006, 50–51; see P. H. Collins 2004, 11). A liberationist reading of Ezra 9–10, then, would actively engage the intersections of race, class, and gender both inside and outside the text.

Engaging these dynamics inside the text also means analyzing the intersection of the text itself (intrinsic analysis) and its social and historical settings (extrinsic analysis) (Yee 1995; 2003). Such a reading would then involve looking at an intersection outside the text—that is, between those readings from the text and the social and historical context of the African American community of faith. At that point, a hermeneutic of resistance, given the segregationist past, would require us to question whether the intermarriage ban in Ezra is the only biblical model for dealing with the Other. Similarly, is its depiction of God demanding such separation the only biblical depiction of God's nature? Alternative models in the Hebrew Bible that allow foreigners to be incorporated are available (Smith-Christopher 1996, 117–42). Also, qualities of God that emphasize loving, merciful, and just human-divine relationships, rather than the dominance, bullying, or shaming communicated in Ezra, have "genuine transformative potential" (Johnson 1999, 287–98). Space limitations prevent me from developing these alternative treatments of the foreigner and the divine more fully. My point, however, is simply this: African American communities will not even seek out these competing biblical traditions if they just acquiesce and read Ezra 9–10 in the traditional manner.

"Contemporary forms of oppression," Patricia Hill Collins observes, "do not routinely force people to submit. Instead, they manufacture consent for domination so that we lose our ability to question and thus collude in our own subordination" (2004, 50). Correspondingly, forgetting our ability to question is the result of forgetting our past. Ultimately, then, the intermarriage ban in Ezra is a cautionary tale that reminds us of the damage caused if we ignore our past (and our present) when we open the Bible. The ban is also a call to conscience, because it models the ways in which those with privilege in any time period create systems that exclude others without considering fully the negative repercussions (McClenny-Sadler 2003). From a liberationist perspective, the book of Ezra teaches us the importance of a critical and contextual reading strategy. After all, how we read affects how we live.

WORKS CONSULTED

Berquist, Jon L. 1995. *Judaism in Persia's Shadow: A Social and Historical Approach*. Minneapolis: Fortress.

Birch, Bruce C., Walter Brueggemann, Terence E. Fretheim, and David L. Petersen. 2005. *A Theological Introduction to the Old Testament.* 2nd ed. Nashville: Abingdon.

Blenkinsopp, Joseph. 1988. *Ezra-Nehemiah: A Commentary.* OTL. Philadelphia: Westminster.

Boer, Roland. 2005. No Road: On the Absence of Feminist Criticism of Ezra-Nehemiah. Pages 233–52 in *Her Master's Tools? Feminist and Postcolonial Engagements of Historical-Critical Discourse.* Edited by Caroline Vander Stichele and Todd Penner. SBLGPBS 9. Atlanta: Society of Biblical Literature.

Brueggemann, Walter. 2003. *An Introduction to the Old Testament: The Canon and Christian Imagination.* Louisville: Westminster John Knox.

Collins, John J. 2004. *Introduction to the Hebrew Bible.* Minneapolis: Fortress.

Collins, Patricia Hill. 2004. *Black Sexual Politics: African Americans, Gender, and the New Racism.* New York: Routledge.

Davis, Angela Y. 1983. *Women, Race and Class.* New York: Vintage Books.

Douglas, Kelly Brown. 1999. *Sexuality and the Black Church: A Womanist Perspective.* Maryknoll, N.Y.: Orbis.

Douglas, Mary. 2002. Responding to Ezra: The Priests and the Foreign Wives. *BibInt* 10:1–21.

Eskenazi, Tamara C. 1992. Out from the Shadows: Biblical Women in the Postexilic Era. *JSOT* 54:25–43.

Eskenazi, Tamara, and Eleanore P. Judd. 1994. Marriage to a Stranger in Ezra 9–10. Pages 265–85 in Eskenazi and Richards 1994.

Eskenazi, Tamara C., and Kent H. Richards, eds. 1994. *Second Temple Studies 2: Temple Community in the Persian Period.* JSOTSup 175. Sheffield: Sheffield Academic Press.

Esler, Philip F. 2003. Ezra-Nehemiah as a Narrative of (Re-invented) Israelite Identity. *BibInt* 11:413–426.

Fewell, Danna Nolan. 2003. *The Children of Israel: Reading the Bible for the Sake of Our Children.* Nashville: Abingdon.

Fried, Lisbeth S. 2004. *The Priest and the Great King: Temple-Palace Relations in the Persian Empire.* Biblical and Judaic Studies 10. Winona Lake, Ind.: Eisenbrauns.

Gottwald, Norman K. 1985. *The Hebrew Bible: A Socio-literary Introduction.* Philadelphia: Fortress.

———. 1999. The Expropriated and the Expropriators in Nehemiah 5. Pages 1–19 in *Concepts of Class in Ancient Israel.* Edited by Mark R. Sneed. SFSHJ 201. Atlanta: Scholars Press.

Guinier, Lani, and Gerald Torres. 2002. *The Miner's Canary: Enlisting Race, Resisting Power, Transforming Democracy.* Cambridge: Harvard University Press.

Hayes, Christine E. 2002. *Gentile Impurities and Jewish Identities: Intermarriage and Conversion from the Bible to the Talmud.* New York: Oxford University Press.

Higginbotham, A. Leon, Jr., and Barbara K. Kopytoff. 2000. Racial Purity and Interracial Sex in the Law of Colonial and Antebellum Virginia. Pages 81–139 in *Interracialism: Black-White Intermarriage in American History, Literature, and Law*. Edited by Werner Sollars. New York: Oxford University Press.

Hoglund, Kennth G. 1992. *Achaemenid Imperial Administration in Syria-Palestine and the Missions of Ezra and Nehemiah*. SBLDS 125. Atlanta: Scholars Press.

Janzen, David. 2002. *Witch-Hunts, Purity and Social Boundaries: The Expulsion of Foreign Women in Ezra 9–10*. JSOTSup 350. Sheffield: Sheffield Academic Press.

Johnson, Willa Mathis. 1995. Ethnicity in Persian Yehud: Between Anthropological Analysis and Ideological Criticism. Pages 177–86 in *Society of Biblical Literature 1995 Seminar Papers*. SBLSP 34. Atlanta: Scholars Press.

———. 1999. The Holy Seed Has Been Defiled: The Interethnic Marriage Dilemma in Ezra 9–10. Ph.D. diss. Vanderbilt University.

Klein, Ralph W. 1999. Ezra. *NIB* 3:663–747.

Lubin, Alex. 2005. *Romance and Rights: The Politics of Interracial Intimacy, 1945–1954*. Jackson: University Press of Mississippi.

Malik, Kenan. 1996. *The Meaning of Race: Race, History, and Culture in Western Society*. New York: New York University Press.

Marbury, Herbert R. 2003. The Separatist Rhetoric of the Ezra-Nehemiah Corpus: Its Political, Cultic, and Economic Significations. Ph.D. diss. Vanderbilt University.

McClenny-Sadler, Madeline. 2003. Cry Witch: The Embers Still Burn. Pages 117–41 in *Pregnant Passion: Gender, Sex, and Violence in the Bible*. Edited by Cheryl A. Kirk-Duggan. SemeiaSt 44. Atlanta: Society of Biblical Literature.

Robinson, Charles Frank II. 2003. *Dangerous Liasons: Sex and Love in the Segregated South*. Fayetteville: University of Arkansas Press.

Ross, Josephine. 2002. The Sexualization of Difference: A Comarison of Mixed-Race and Same-Gender Marriage. *Harvard Civil Rights-Civil Rights Law Review* 37:255–88.

Smith, H. Shelton. 1972. *In His Image, but...: Racism in Southern Religion, 1780–1910*. Durham, N.C.: Duke University Press.

Smith-Christopher, Daniel L. 1994. The Mixed Marriage Crisis in Ezra 9–10 and Nehemiah 13: A Study of the Sociology of the Post-Exilic Judaean Community. Pages 243–65 in Eskenazi and Richards 1994.

———. 1996. Between Ezra and Isaiah: Exclusion, Transformation, and Inclusion of the "Foreigner" in Post-Exilic Biblical Theology. Pages 117–42 in *Ethnicity and the Bible*. Edited by Mark G. Brett. Leiden: Brill.

Wadlington, Walter. 1966. The Loving Case: Virginia's Anti-Miscegenation Statute in Historical Perspective. *Virginia Law Review* 52:1189–1223.

Wallenstein, Peter. 1998. Race, Marriage, and the Supreme Court from Pace v. Alabama (1883) to Loving v. Virginia (1967). *Journal of Supreme Court History* 1998:65–86.

———. 2002. *Tell The Court I Love My Wife: Race, Marriage, and Law—An American History*. New York: Palgrave Macmillan.

Washington, Harold C. 1994. The Strange Woman of Proverbs 1–9 and Post-exilic Judaean Society. Pages 217–42 in Eskenazi and Richards 1994.

———. 2003. Israel's Holy Seed and the Foreign Women of Ezra-Nehemiah: A Kristevan Reading. *BibInt* 11:427–437.

Yee, Gale A. 1995. Ideological Criticism: Judges 17–21 and the Dismembered Body. Pages 146–70 in *Judges and Method*. Edited by Gale A. Yee. Minneapolis: Fortress.

———. 2003. *Poor Banished Children of Eve: Woman as Evil in the Hebrew Bible*. Minneapolis: Fortress.

Zack, Naomi. 2006. *Thinking About Race*. 2nd ed. Belmont: Thomson Wadsworth.

Exile in the Hebrew Bible:
A Postcolonial Look from the Cuban Diaspora

Francisco O. García-Treto

Colonial Origins, Exilic Reality

As I approach the autobiographical reflection with which this essay begins, two elements of my experience immediately come to the foreground: my bilingualism and the bilingual education and culture that nurtured it; and my condition as an exile, which has caused me to live with the constant echo of another reality, with the memory of another place, enriching and subverting my accommodation to my present life.

"When I was a child," says Paul, "I spoke as a child." In all likelihood Paul, as I imagine him, could have added "in two languages" (at least), and I can certainly say the same of myself. I grew up in pre-Castro Havana as the son of a Cuban Presbyterian minister. My father was born in Cuba in 1899, at the end of years of bitter national struggle for Cuba's independence from Spain, which ended with the U.S. intervention in 1898, traditionally called the Spanish-American War in the U.S. My grandparents, grateful for the end of years of a conflict that had exacted a heavy toll on the civilian population, gave their first baby the name Francisco de la Paz (Francisco of the Peace). That peace also inaugurated a *pax Americana* that in many and various ways shaped the sociocultural and political context in which I was born and in which I grew up. In particular, the U.S. Protestant mission churches and schools became a major influence in the life of my parents, as they were to be in mine. My father, a convert to (American-sponsored) Protestantism from Roman Catholicism, a young carpenter who eventually desired to become a minister, studied at *La Progresiva*, the flagship Presbyterian school in Cuba, and then in Georgia before graduating from the *Seminario Evangélico de Puerto Rico*, as most Cuban ministers of his generation did.

There was a great advantage in learning English, and those who could speak it well, as my father did, found it a real advantage to their advancement within the church. The same was true in the world of business and industry, where young Cubans who aspired to white-collar positions with American companies knew that learning English was an essential step in their preparation. I very early assimilated my parents' conviction that bilingual education—that is, learning both Spanish and English—was the key to my future. From kindergarten to fifth grade, as a pupil at the *Central Methodist School* (*sic*!) in Havana, I laid the solid foundations of my bilingualism, beginning to learn English in the company of Dick, Jane, Sally, and Spot, the characters in the Scott-Foresman series of readers then in use in American (U.S.) schools. I must confess that those modern, colorful readers left a deeper impression on my memory than the Cuban books from which I was concurrently learning Spanish. My sixth-grade to high school (*bachillerato*) sojourn as a boarding student at *La Progresiva* was interrupted by a year in Princeton, New Jersey, where my father pursued a year of study at the Princeton Theological Seminary and I the tenth grade at Princeton High School. In a real sense, my parents were right. All of this facilitated my coming to the States to study (Maryville College and Princeton Seminary), eventually to receive the degrees that qualified me for remaining here as a college professor. When I left Cuba for college in the U.S., my father gave me his leather-bound copy of the King James Version of the Bible—the gift of an American evangelist for whom he had served as a translator during a preaching campaign in Cuba—along with a New Testament and Psalms in Spanish.

I regard all of this as a personal success story, but also as one that from another perspective takes on a very different meaning. Like the young men in the first chapter of Daniel, I found success in a project that was not entirely mine, nor my parents', but that can be fairly attributed in large part to the centripetal attraction of the metropolis for the colonies and for the colonized. From Dick and Sally to Faulkner and Hemingway, my education included a heavy emphasis on elements from another culture, in a manner similar to that of those Hebrew boys of whom the king said, "Let them be taught the literature and language of the Chaldeans," so that at the end of their education "they could be stationed at the king's court" (Dan 1:4).

Another overriding fact of my personal experience is my permanent displacement from the land of my birth and from the city where I grew up. Along with many other Cubans since the revolution and the resultant estrangement between Cuba and the U.S., I have become part of a diaspora, a people who live elsewhere, remembering a world that no longer exists except in memory. In particular, the city of my youth, Havana, has become the centerpiece of that memory. My now-lost Havana is one of those cities of memory that, like Jerusalem, become powerful symbols particularly in the mind of those who count their loss as a pivotal point in their lives. In contemporary exilic Cuban literature, Havana often appears comparable to the tragic figure that, in the opening of the book of Lamentations,

> weeps bitterly in the night,
> with tears on her cheeks;

among all her lovers
she has no one to comfort her;
all her friends have dealt treacherously with her,
they have become her enemies. (Lam 1:2)

In these pages I propose to comment on those two defining facts of my personal experience, bilingualism and exile, as they have come to be part of my perspective on reading and on teaching the Bible.

Diaspora Doubletalk

A distinctive characteristic of diaspora, and of the colonial context in which diasporas arise, bilingualism is part of my own experience, as well as of that of my Hispano/Latino/a and particularly Cuban counterparts in the United States. In this, I differ from most of my (Anglo-American) students and even from many of my academic colleagues who are not Hispanic, who do not have another language at the level of interaction of true bilinguals. Phenomena such as "code switching" or the use of "Spanglish" are part of my daily experience (even in worship) and are not limited to the familiar and vernacular in a city such as San Antonio. Most of the modern Cuban literature I read, for example, is in some sense bilingual: produced by authors, whether in the island or in its diaspora, for whom Spanish-English bilingualism, in different varieties and for many reasons (colonialism prominently among them), is an essential medium. In Cuban and Cuban American literature, bilingualism serves a wide range of purposes. It seems useful here to mention and to illustrate two of those uses and what they contribute to my reading of a bilingual text such as Daniel.

First, openly and substantially bilingual literary texts—very different from texts that use occasional words from the "other" language as convenient devices to suggest an atmosphere or the flavor of another culture to a monolingual reader—presuppose a bilingual reader, for whom the meaning of the bilingual play goes well beyond the dictionary meaning of the words in the "other" language. Social and political relations in colonized situations can be effectively conveyed in this way. I cite as an example Guillermo Cabrera Infante's novel *Tres Tristes Tigres*, where bilingualism is used in a variety of ways to inscribe the colonized ambiance of prerevolutionary Havana. The novel's opening "Prólogo" purports to be the obsequious show-opening speech of the master of ceremonies at *Tropicana*, Havana's famous night-club, which begins in a mixture of Spanish and English sentences seemingly mirroring each other, as it mirrors the mixed audience of Cubans and Americans addressed by the M.C. Cabrera Infante uses the (mis)translations and malapropisms spoken by this character to good effect, as for example when he says, in Spanish, that he is going to offer "una traducción literaria" (a "literary," not a "literal," translation of his English spiel), or when, toward the end of a speech loaded with racially tinged sexual innuendos, he adds, "Y ahora ... and now ... señoras y señores ... ladies and gentlemen ... público que sabe lo que es bueno ... Discriminatory public..." (1999, 27). The use of "discriminatory" where the correct translation of "que sabe lo que es bueno" would have been "discriminating" is another deliberate and telling bilingual (mis)take.

Another literary use of bilingualism, that is, its use to represent the "other," in this case the (North) American as he looks to Cubans, can be seen in the bilingual tour de force in *Tres Tristes Tigres*, called "The Tale of the Walking-stick" ("El Cuento del Bastón"), where two American characters, Mr. and Mrs. Campbell, narrate a touristic mishap caused by Mr. Campbell's insensitivity to, and suspicion of, the "natives" as thieves during a visit to Havana. Cabrera Infante tells the tale first as "history," that is, as a straightforward account of what happened, then repeats it in a hilarious version in which Mr. and Mrs. Campbell speak in the stilted and distorted Spanish of people thinking in English and attempting to translate word for word, a language full of wrong grammatical constructions, barbarisms, and lexical mistakes obvious to a Spanish speaker. "Miel," Mr. Campbell quotes his wife, "esto es el Trópico," literally (mis)translating "Honey, this is the Tropics" into a pastiche that recalls the punch lines of many Cuban jokes lampooning the "Americanos." I cite these examples from *Tres Tristes Tigres* to illustrate two of the ways in which a bilingual author can use bilingualism to communicate the fraught and sometimes toxic relationship between colonizer and colonized.

William Luis's insightful *Dance between Two Cultures: Latino Caribbean Literature Written in the United States* includes a discussion of Oscar Hijuelos's *The Mambo Kings Play Songs of Love*, the Pulitzer Prize-winning novel, later made into a movie and a Broadway musical (Luis 2001, 188–214). Hijuelos, a Cuban-American, wrote the novel in English, but as Luis points out—notably when he discusses the song (bolero) "Beautiful Maria of My Soul," a central element in the novel's plot—it is an English intersected and influenced by Spanish (2001, 199–203). The bolero's English lyrics appear, for example, in the crucial scene where the Castillo brothers—the Mambo Kings—perform it at the Mambo Nine Club in New York, with Desi Arnaz in the audience, a circumstance that leads to their appearance in an episode of *I Love Lucy*, as well as at the end of the novel when Eugenio, the son of one of the brothers, recalls the incident during a visit to the retired Desi Arnaz. The Spanish lyrics appear, handwritten on a slip of paper, by the elbow of César Castillo's body when he is found in the room of the Hotel Splendour, where he dies alone at the end of the long flashback that provides the novel's structure. Luis compares both versions—as well as the different English and Spanish lyrics produced for the movie—and finds it impossible, by analyzing the subtle errors and mistranslations present in both, to determine whether Hijuelos wrote the song in English and translated it into Spanish or vice versa. In my opinion, Luis reaches a judgment about the song that is valid for a much broader scope of literature written by bilingual authors when he observes,

More likely than not, both the Spanish and the English are originals and both are translations. When composing the song, Hijuelos may have been writing in Spanish but thinking in English, or if he composed it first in English, he was also thinking in Spanish. Both languages are native and foreign to him. When he employs one language, it contains traces of the other. One signifies the other and both occupy the same space. These observations highlight the tension and mediation that take place when two cultures come together, and point toward the essence of Latino culture and literature written in the United States. (2001, 203)

In other words, for a truly bilingual author, no matter which of the two languages he or she writes in, Luis's cultural "tension and mediation" are not an accidental event but an existential condition.

My bilingual condition has made me particularly sensitive to an already-mentioned phenomenon of the Hebrew Bible: the bilingualism of some of its books. Every commentary on Daniel, for example, will duly note that the book begins in Hebrew, switches to Aramaic at 2:4, and continues in that language until it switches back in chapter 8 to conclude in Hebrew. What none of the commentaries does is explain this phenomenon in a fully satisfactory way—in particular, given our predisposition to look no further than the "scissors and paste" compositional or redactorial schemes of a past generation of biblical scholarship, much less in a way that brings meaning out of the obvious and clearly intentional choice of the author to present bilingual readers with a bilingual text.

John Collins's Hermeneia commentary summarizes four kinds of theoretical explanations that have been offered for Daniel's bilingualism. Three of them depend heavily on composite authorship or redaction: (1) the book was composed in Hebrew, later translated into Aramaic, and even later, when parts of the Hebrew became lost, restored by including the Aramaic translation of the lost parts; (2) the book was composed in Aramaic but had its beginning and end translated into Hebrew to facilitate the book's inclusion in the canon; (3) alternatively, an older Aramaic composition was incorporated later into the Hebrew final form. Collins lists first another option, that a "single author composed the work in two languages," which he immediately dismisses: "Various reasons are suggested for this, none very convincing" (1993, 12). Nonetheless, Collins comes close to where I want to look for an understanding of the bilingualism of Daniel when he says that "both the author and the audience were presumably [Hebrew/Aramaic] bilingual" and places the author or redactor of Daniel in the Maccabean period, a time when Israel's colonized status was painfully in evidence. Could it be that the bilingualism in Daniel can come to be read more as an intentional device used by a bilingual author to address a bilingual audience about the specific conditions of cultural "tension and mediation" in which they found themselves? Could it be that it is self-referential to the condition of Hebrews who, like Daniel, carried the proud burden of being well-educated bilinguals, capable of serving the Seleucid court, along with the attendant danger of assimilation and loss of their national and religious identity? It is the "Chaldeans" at court, as is well known, who in

Dan 2:4 begin to carry out their responsibility to the king by answering "in Aramaic," thus introducing the long Aramaic section of the book.

Much more needs to be done in order to flesh out this suggested direction for an understanding of the bilingual character of Daniel, particularly in reconstructing the culture of precisely the sociopolitical class of Hebrews that the book addresses, but my personal experience tells me that the effort will be illuminating. Recently, Hugh S. Pyper has generously made available to me his unpublished paper, "Daniel Writes Back: Hybridity, Language and Identity in the Book of Daniel," which begins by asking the right question, "Can postcolonial theory help us to read the book of Daniel?" I agree with Pyper that indeed it can, due in large part to the resonances Daniel raises in my mind because of my own experience from the days of my childhood and youth, when learning to speak English was a central goal of my Cuban upbringing, to my ambivalent bilingualism of today.

THE EXILE LOOKS BACK

Published in a 1999 volume of *Biblical Interpretation*, Archie C. C. Lee's "Returning to China: Biblical Interpretation in Postcolonial Hong-Kong" influenced my choice of a topic for this section of my essay. Lee's explicit goal was "to construct a new framework for biblical studies from [the] context of postcolonial Hong-Kong" (1999, 156). A new generation of Asian biblical scholars, Lee says, is starting "to conceive a different approach to the Bible, because of not only a new context of reading, but also a radically different cultural-political location of the reader" (156). Facing a new historical moment brought about by the end of 150 years of British rule and a return to Mainland Chinese control, Lee claims for himself a "highly hybridized" Hong Kong identity, "culturally Chinese and yet pragmatically British ... [with] ... both a sense of identification with China and an unexplainable fear of being national Chinese" (157). From his social location as a resident of contemporary Hong Kong, Lee reads Trito-Isaiah in a manner that finds insight into the well-known questions of conflict among the fifth-century B.C.E. returnees to Jerusalem from Babylonian exile and between the returnees and those who remained in Jerusalem, and also of "the predominantly unsympathetic attitude toward those 'remnants' in Jerusalem in the Hebrew Bible" (157). I will not recapitulate Lee's arguments, which lead him to reject a simple opposition between the returned exiles and the "people of the land" and to

> contend that the exilic community is not homogeneous and that it does not only define its identity over against the community left behind in the land. There are those among the returnees who emphasize an openness both to the world outside and to Jerusalem at home. Their intention to incorporate both the new experience and the old tradition in an integrative and creative way opens up a future for the faith of Israel—it is postcolonial imagining that affirms the coloniality and marginality of the present, as well as the centrality of the Jerusalem temple. (172)

In his appreciative response to Lee, found in the same issue of *Biblical Interpretation*, Fernando Segovia raises a crucial question that more directly informs my purpose. After stating his sympathy for the reading strategy, the stance "regarding the critical role and the value of hybridity in questions of identity" (1999, 196) and the interpretive analysis present in Lee's article, Segovia asks, "Why engage in such interpretive analysis to begin with? Why bring the Bible and Hong Kong together? Is it for the exhilaration of the exercise itself or is there a more profound and unarticulated theological agenda at work here?" (196)

Segovia's question looms large in my agenda. To counteract the fallacious construct of the "universal and informed reader," which Segovia has so clearly identified and often spoken of, what is needed—and, in particular, what is needed from the standpoint of minority biblical scholars—is a diverse variety of readings, each one shaped and nuanced by the social status, the cultural baggage, and the historical experience of each reader.

Since our intent is to look at our task as scholars of the Bible as one of consciously reading, for ourselves, for our students, and for our scholarly and/or ecclesiastical audiences as "minority" scholars (Hispanic/Latino/as in my particular case, more specifically as a Cuban), we must of course begin by defining ourselves individually in terms of the self-identities we have defined for ourselves, in terms of the historical experiences and the cultural resources that have shaped those self-identities and that continue to shape us. The plurals in those terms stem from my conviction that, notwithstanding our solidarity as minorities in the U.S., each one of us is rooted in a very different part of the historical-cultural-national continuum. For reasons that will become clear, for example, I tend to use the category of "exile" where a Mexican-American colleague might prefer to give emphasis to "borderlands." We have much to learn from each other, and much to teach our audiences, but we will do it from individual and different perspectives.

I argue that as a Cuban who has been in the U.S. for well over forty years, whose college and graduate degrees were earned here, who was naturalized as a U.S. citizen more than thirty years ago, and whose career as a college professor has been exclusively carried on in the U.S., I belong to a group that labels its still somewhat ambiguous self-identity more exile than immigrant, more Cuban than hyphenated-American. All four of those terms apply, of course, but I hold a decided preference for the first of each pair. I sympathize, for example, with José Kozer, a Cuban poet of my generation (both leaving Havana for the U.S. in August 1960, when he was twenty and I twenty-three), who expresses his deep ambivalent feelings about exile:

"Exile," that chic word, that lousy word. It means an expulsion. You leave the womb as you leave Eden, as you leave the Island [Cuba]. And live burdened by a vivid awareness that death has a hold on you; you meditate daily on death having a hold on you. That is exile. The bitch bites you in many different places.... There is more. The bitch bites, and one of the bites takes you away from where you were born. What can you do? Get the hell out. It makes you richer; it makes you poorer.... After thirty-seven years of "exile" (OK, I'll use the lousy word), the balance is positive. I gained in freedom, in experience, in "modernity." And, to my definite advantage, the tongue I speak gained, too, becoming enriched by contact with English and with the different varieties of Spanish in Spain and Latin America. What more can a "poet" ask for? (2001, 209)

For Cubans, however, exile is much more than the result of the coming to power of Fidel Castro in 1959. One can say that exile has been a central theme of Cuban national and cultural formation from the very beginning. Those of us who grew up in the island learned early—as part of our formative education—to read and memorize the poetry of the likes of José María Heredia or José Martí, political exiles from their native land who wrote and published their work among and for other exiles from Cuba (largely in the U.S.) during the struggles to achieve independence from Spain in the nineteenth century. Take as an example the small collection published in New York City in 1858 under the title *El Laúd del Desterrado* (*The Exile's Lute*), which opens with Heredia's "Himno del Desterrado" ("The Exile's Hymn"), one of the staples of my earliest literary education (Montes-Huidobro 1995). When I perused this book recently, I was surprised to find that two of the other exiled poets represented had actually used Ps 137, "By the rivers of Babylon...," one of the signature works of the Babylonian exile, in their works: Miguel Teurbe Tolón as an epigraph for his "Cantar de las Cubanas" (35); and Pedro Santacilia, who paraphrases the entire psalm in his "Salmo CXXXVII de David" (80), contextually equating Cuba with "Jerusalén amada" (beloved Jerusalem) and Spain with "los hijos de Edom" (the sons of Edom) in the bitterly angry ending.

I fall naturally, in a way, in this tradition, not only when I locate myself in the contemporary Cuban diaspora for whom exile from the *patria* (fatherland) is a historical reality, but when I use that location as a standpoint from which to reflect on the biblical exile and its literary products as a target for interpretation. I also propose that the works of certain writers of the Cuban exile can help me in this endeavor, by opening to me the emotional tone and the feelings represented in their art, with which I inevitably resonate, particularly when it speaks to me of the experiences of our diaspora.

As a minimal example of method, I propose to look at some aspects of the first two poems (chapters) in the book of Lamentations—an early product of the Babylonian exile—with the help of a passage from contemporary Cuban author Daína Chaviano's *El hombre, la hembra y el hambre* (the punning title means *Man, Female, and Hunger*).

LAMENTATIONS 1–2

If I am pressed to put a description of the Hebrew Bible in a single adjective, I can make a good case for choosing "exilic" as that adjective. The exile is, without question, the central theme in the production and in the content of the Hebrew Bible. The Babylonian exile raised crucial theological questions about the historical experience that brought about the expatriation of a large portion of Jerusalem's elites and served as the setting where much of the text that was going to become the Hebrew Bible found its trajectory towards definitive form. The postexilic Persian and Hellenistic periods provided the context for the production of more texts, eventually to become canonical, which notwithstanding their differences share themes, concerns, and attitudes shaped by the exilic agendas. The Hebrew Bible is, above and beyond what other and more ancient traditions it contains, an exilic/postexilic text in much more than a simply chronological sense. It also embodies a set of reactions to the colonial dynamics in which its production was enveloped, to the tensions between the communities of those who went to Babylon and those who remained in Jerusalem, and later between those who returned and the "people of the land." The literature ranges widely from the genres of lamentation to apocalyptic, from ideologically shaped historiography to liturgical poetry, but it revolves around a center defined by the unthinkable catastrophes of the loss of a city, the destruction of a temple, and the fall of a dynasty. It also ranges emotionally from numb despair and anger in the face of horrible loss, to hopes of return and rebuilding, to the realization that indeed "you can't go home again," and to various forms of accommodation to life, in the homeland as well as in diaspora, in subjection to imperial powers—in short, to exile, whether external or internal, in all of its dimensions.

Lamentations 1 and 2 constitutes a stark cry of horror at the destruction of Jerusalem, a poetic tour de force in which the ruined city, empty of its leaders and looted of its treasures of palace and temple, is represented by the powerful image of the Daughter Zion. The use of this image is not unique to Lamentations, but rather frequent in the Hebrew Bible, as a recent study by Mary Donovan Turner points out. The sensitive recent readings of Tod Linafelt and Kathleen M. O'Connor and the older but seminal study by Alan Mintz help us to understand this figure as a personification of the ravaged city as a desolate woman. O'Connor describes her in these words:

> Inheriting the personified city from ancient Near Eastern texts, and Daughter Zion from the book of Jeremiah, the poet(s) of Lamentations chooses not just any female image but that of a fallen and abandoned woman. She is a woman who is "raped and defiled" but who has survived "as a living witness to pain that knows no release" (Mintz 1982, 3). Her violation corresponds to the violation of the sacred temple; both sacred, intimate places are penetrated by a despoiler. From the narrator's perspective, she has caused her own pain by sexual liaisons that express betrayal and violence. Yet the central feature of her pain is only hinted at so far—her separation from and loss of her children (Linafelt 2000, 43–58). In all this she has no comforter. (Turner 2003, 23)

Linafelt makes the illuminating choice of interpreting Lam 1 and 2 as "literature of survival," that is, as literature that, besides demonstrating "a commingling of life and death," also "demonstrate[s] the strong desire ... to make present to the reader the pain and suffering of survivors" (Linafelt and Beal 1999, 45). While Lam 1 and 2 include elements of both the presentation of pain and of the interpretation of pain, the two must be clearly distinguished—and for Linafelt, "The extent and significance of each have been given very uneven treatment in modern critical interpretation. Biblical scholars have tended to focus on the *interpretation* of pain, and not surprisingly they have done so primarily by explaining pain and suffering as resulting from the guilt of the sufferer" (43). By "refocusing" the interpretation of the chapters in question on the *presentation* of pain, Linafelt seeks to incorporate in his reading a "sobering corrective," derived from the work of Terrence Des Pres, "to the view that suffering can, or even must, be absorbed into a system of meaning (whether theological or otherwise)" held by "biblical scholars, who seem overeager to make the move from the fact of pain to the recognition of guilt and subsequently to repentance" (43).

My personal perspective as an exile leads me to agree wholeheartedly and to side with the Daughter Zion, who, as O'Connor shows in her masterful reading, actually interrupts the narrator's harangue, based in chapter 1 at first on a simplistic theory of "suffering comes from sin," which blames the victim for the abuse suffered (2002, 21). The first interruption comes in 1:9b, when the Daughter of Zion addresses God: "O LORD, look at my affliction, for the enemy has triumphed!" and in 11b, where she again interrupts the narrator, "Look, O LORD and see, how worthless I have become!" and immediately broadens her appeal to a human audience in the eloquent plea of verses 12–16. She has sinned, yes, but God has inflicted punishment "on the day of his fierce anger," a circumstance that raises its own problems. Has God gone too far in punishment? Addressing God and asking him to acknowledge responsibility for her suffering, she seems, in chapter 2, to have persuaded the narrator to her point of view, even though

> There is no response to Zion's petition. God does not speak. God does not comfort, restore health, return children, or bring life back to any semblance of order or of human dignity. In [these] poem[s], God is silent. Daughter Zion is left with her tears, surrounded by devastation, alone without her children.... But she has gained a witness, an advocate, and a companion in her suffering who sees, who pays attention, and who takes into consciousness the immeasurable, overwhelming power of her suffering. In the narrator Zion has found a comforter. (O'Connor 2002, 43)

DAÍNA CHAVIANO

In recent decades the Cuban exile has produced a rich, many-textured, and multiform literature, a production of which at least some parts serve as "literature of survival" and which I find serves to feed my own connection with my history, my culture, and my identity. I want to propose that in that literature may be found tools for my reading the Hebrew Bible—not necessarily the *interpretive* tools of theology, but certainly the tools of *presentation* and of its counterpart *reception*, which help to make my reading more compelling and powerful as *my* reading. To illustrate, let me return to Daína Chaviano's novel mentioned above, *El hombre, la hembra y el hambre*.

Chaviano belongs to a younger Cuban generation, having been born in 1957 and therefore grown up under the revolution. She graduated from the University of Havana in 1980, having majored in English language and literature, and left Cuba in 1991 to live in the United States. Her novel is the first of a cycle (three already published, one more in preparation) revolving around the decay of Havana and the variety of hungers the inhabitants of the city suffer, especially during the so-called *Período Especial* (special time period) that followed the implosion of the Soviet Union. One of the results of the constant struggle to stave off starvation (and to preserve minimum standards of personal hygiene), given the unavailability of the most basic staples except to those who could pay for them with dollars and the presence of numerous first-world tourists willing to pay in dollars or barter for prostitution, is the appearance of the *jineteras*, women who for the most part would not have become prostitutes except for their desperate situation. Another constant theme is the effort to leave the island, sometimes through schemes such as marrying a foreigner, but mainly by the desperate—almost suicidal—recourse to sailing away to the north on small boats, makeshift rafts, truck tires, or anything that could be hoped to float.

Claudia, the central character in Chaviano's novel, is a graduate of the University, an art history major who lost her job in the National Museum when she realized, and complained, that her boss was selling paintings from the museum's collection to foreign buyers. Unemployed, and having to provide not only for herself but for her small child, she experiences hunger and privation as she gravitates inexorably toward prostitution. Claudia, quite clearly, *is* in a sense Havana, whose decaying, crumbling, and crowded buildings house a mass of human misery, just as the Daughter Zion of Lamentations is ruined Jerusalem and its people. For example, Claudia has a "magical-realist" trick of suddenly finding herself walking in the past of the city, or in the city of the past, sometimes accompanied by Muba, a long-dead African slave woman who has taken her under her tutelage, or by some other symbolic figures. There is much more in this rich novel than I can possibly mention here, but I must comment on one brief chapter, an "Interludio," as Chaviano titled it, that I find crucial for my reception of this painful presentation of "Daughter Havana."

Every Cuban schoolchild, of my generation as well as Chaviano's—or I am sure, Elián González's—got to know José Martí, the visionary and patriot who inspired the Cuban rebellion against Spain, first as a storyteller and poet through his *La Edad de Oro* (*The Golden Age*), a magazine for children that he published and wrote during his exile in New York in 1889. Only four issues appeared, but collectively they have become a canonical text of Cuban moral formation and idealism. In the third issue of *La Edad de Oro*, Martí published "Los Zapaticos de Rosa" ("The Rose-Colored Shoes"; 2001, 221–29), a sweetly sentimental poem in which Pilar, a richly attired little girl spending a day at the seaside with her parents, with spontaneous generosity gives her brand-new rose-colored shoes to a dying consumptive child whose indigent mother has brought her to the beach from their dark hovel "so she'll see the sun, and sleep." Chaviano's "Interludio" ("Interlude") in the novel is constructed as a trope on "Los Zapaticos de Rosa," in which verses from the poem are interwoven with an account of Claudia's walk along the *Malecón*, Havana's famous seawall boulevard, now a place where tourists go to pick up *jineteras*. The first words in her "Interlude" are a quotation of Martí's opening verses in "The Rose-Colored Shoes": "There's bright sunshine and a foamy sea, and fine sand"; however, where Martí continues with Pilar innocently wanting to go out and show off her new feathered hat, Chaviano's line continues "and the Cuban women go out to flaunt the new clothes the tourists have given them" (1998, 155, translation mine). Claudia walks "oblivious to the presence of other women who, like her, only seek to survive until some miracle should allow them simply to go on living" (155).

The superposition of the innocent verses on a scene of degradation and despair makes a profound impression on this reader, an impression deepened when the "translucent shade, a presence of another century," of José Martí appears, only to be shocked into sorrowful anger, "as he asks himself, bitterly, where the dreams of those flowering young women have gone" (155). When we remember the canonical primacy of Martí's idealism in the moral formation of all Cubans, the scene carries some of the weight of the narrator's change of attitude in Lam 1 and 2. In the end of Chaviano's "Interlude," Martí repudiates the most famous of his verses, the magnanimous ending of "La Rosa Blanca" ("and for the cruel one who tears out my living heart, I grow not thistles nor weeds: I grow a white rose") as he tosses to the wind the sheets of paper containing his work to be carried out to sea, some to be lost in the direction of the Florida Straits, some brought back by the currents to the shore, where they "remain, wearing out on the rocks and growing old under the immutable sky" (155).

Juxtaposing Lamentations and Chaviano

When I read Lam 1 and 2, the pain at the loss of Jerusalem expressed by that long-lost Judean poet touches mine as it interacts with my very identity, shaped by the loss of the city and the culture of my youth and reflected in works such as Chaviano's. There is a pain in exile and in the loss it entails that defies all explanation or justification, a pain susceptible only to presentation, not to interpretation, to use Linafelt's terms. I find it more difficult, for example, to identify with Walter Brueggemann's suggestion that "the theme of exile" can be used to "redescribe" the "loss of the white, male, Western, colonial hegemony, which is deeply displacing for us" (2001, 10), even though I find his startling standpoint illuminating.

Conclusion

First, a recapitulation. My bilingualism, a sign of colonially based hybridity, illuminates for me the production of parts of the Hebrew Bible, such as the book of Daniel. That illumination is mediated by my acquaintance with Cuban literature in which bilingualism is central to the work. My juxtaposition of Lamentations with a text of the Cuban exile focuses on my emotional resonances with the loss caused by exile from "the City," be it Jerusalem or Havana, even to the choice of a victimized and defiled "Daughter City" as a central figure whose suffering puts into question the fairness or applicability of former values. Such literature, and my personal experience of the historical conditions that nurtured its production, is for me a window into texts that remain opaque for all of us because of historical distance, but more so for students for whom exile is at best only real as a metaphor.

Second, some pedagogical suggestions. I simply want to suggest "catalog descriptions" of two courses that I would, as a next step, like to teach, perhaps as adult education courses in a church context. I think there will be difficulties because of the lack of translations—and the impossibility of translations for some—of many of the Cuban texts I would want to use, but in a bilingual city such as my adopted San Antonio, they are not insuperable. First, in "Exilic and Postexilic Literature: A Postcolonial Look," postcolonial theory will provide the framework for a reading of representative selections from works of the exilic and postexilic period, to see how new insights appear into such "problems" as the bilingualism of Daniel. Comparison will be made to recent and contemporary works from writers of the Cuban diaspora. Second, in "The Exile Looks at the City," exilic and postexilic selections from the Bible where the loss of Jerusalem, and Jerusalem in memory and hope, are given literary expression in images such as the Daughter Zion in Jeremiah and Lamentations, or the Heavenly Bride in Revelation will be read against the background of recent and contemporary Cuban literature with similar themes.

Works Consulted

Brueggemann, Walter. 2001. Cadences Which Redescribe: Speech Among Exiles. *Journal for Preachers* 17:10–17.

Cabrera-Infante, Guillermo. 1999. *Tres Tristes Tigres*. Barcelona: Seix Barral.

Chaviano, Daína. 1998. *El hombre, la hembra y el hambre*. Barcelona: Planeta.

Collins, John J. 1993. *Daniel*. Hermeneia. Minneapolis: Fortress.

Des Pres, Terrence. 1976. *The Survivor: An Anatomy of Life in the Death Camps*. New York: Oxford University Press.

Hijuelos, Oscar. 2005. *The Mambo Kings Play Songs of Love*. New York: Harper.

Kozer, José. 2001. The Bite of Exile. Page 209 in *ReMembering Cuba: Legacy of a Diaspora*. Edited by Andrea O'Reilly Herrera. Austin: University of Texas Press.

Lee, Archie C. C. 1999. Returning to China: Biblical Interpretation in Postcolonial Hong-Kong. *BibInt* 7:156–73.

Linafelt, Tod, and Timothy K. Beal. 1999. *Ruth and Esther*. Berit Olam. Collegeville: Liturgical Press.

Luis, William. 2001. *Dance between Two Cultures: Latino Caribbean Literature Written in the United States*. Nashville: Vanderbilt University Press.

Martí, José. 2001. *La Edad de Oro*. Edited by Eduardo Lolo. Miami: Universal.

Mintz, Alan. 1982. The Rhetoric of Lamentations and the Representation of Catastrophe. *Prooftexts* 2:1–17.

———. 1984. *Hurban: Responses to Catastrophe in Hebrew Literature*. New York: Columbia University Press.

Montes-Huidobro, Matías, ed. 1995. *El Laúd del Desterrado: Edición crítica*. Houston: Arte Público.

O'Connor, Kathleen M. 2002. *Lamentations and the Tears of the World*. Maryknoll, N.Y.: Orbis.

Segovia, Fernando F. 1999. Postcolonialism and Comparative Analysis in Biblical Studies. *BibInt* 7:192–96.

Turner, Mary Donovan. 2003. Daughter Zion: Giving Birth to Redemption. Pages 193–204 in *Pregnant Passion: Gender, Sex and Violence in the Bible*. Edited by Cheryl A. Kirk-Duggan. SemeiaSt 44. Atlanta: Society of Biblical Literature.

"They Could Not Speak the Language of Judah": Rereading Nehemiah 13 between Brooklyn and Jerusalem*

Jean-Pierre Ruiz

Introduction: Reading Nehemiah in Brooklyn

Let me begin with a confession of sorts: I never read Ezra or Nehemiah in semi-nary, and it is probably a good thing that I did not and that my professors in biblical studies courses ignored this material altogether.[1] When I returned from Rome after seminary studies there, my bishop assigned me to serve as parochial vicar at the Church of Our Lady of Loreto on Sackman Street, on the border between the Brownsville and East New York sections of Brooklyn. I had never heard of the place, so, just a few days after arriving back in New York, I looked it up on the map and made my way there together with a seminary classmate from La Crosse, Wisconsin, who was staying with my family for a few days before taking up his own first pastoral assignment. When my classmate and I arrived at the rectory that stands beside this run-down Italian Renaissance-style build-ing and sat down with the pastor to make our acquaintances, the first words out of the pastor's mouth took the form of a question: he wanted to know what in the world I could possibly have done to deserve an assignment to that forgotten corner of the diocese. As my classmate and I drove around the neighborhood later that afternoon, we continued to be haunted by the very same question.

When I arrived at Our Lady of Loreto, which was founded in 1893 as a non-territorial parish to serve Italian immigrants, the church had become (and now continues to be) home to a mostly Hispanic (Puerto Rican and Dominican) and

---

* I extend my thanks to my graduate assistants Louis Maione and Richard Omolade for the time and energy they contributed to the research for this essay.

1. The neglect of Nehemiah in the seminary classroom might be justified in view of the fact that this book does not have a high profile in the liturgy. Appearing only rarely in the Roman Catholic *Lectionary for Mass*, it is used only once in the three-year Sunday lectionary cycle: Neh 8:2–4a, 5–6, 8–10 is the first reading for the Third Sunday in Ordinary Time in Cycle C.

African American congregation, with notable exceptions that included three of the neighborhood's remaining Italian matriarchs—Marie Disco, Margaret Giangone, and Filomena ("Fannie") Di Napoli—who were everyone's honorary godmothers, grandmothers, and great-grandmothers. The first issue of the Roman Catholic Diocese of Brooklyn's weekly newspaper *The Tablet* (4 April 1908) carried a front-page story (with a photograph) about the dedication of the Church of Our Lady of Loreto. Italian American Cardinal Anthony Bevilacqua, Archbishop-Emeritus of Philadelphia, was baptized at Our Lady of Loreto because his family was unwelcome at the territorial parish in which they lived: prejudice against immigrants is nothing new!

Through whatever twist of chance or of providence—and possibly even a little of both—it was at Our Lady of Loreto that I got around to reading Ezra and Nehemiah for the first time, and in ways that my seminary courses in biblical studies could never have taught me. Our Lady of Loreto was one of the founding members of East Brooklyn Churches (EBC),[2] an affiliate of Saul Alinsky's Industrial Areas Foundation (IAF) (Alinsky 1946). After getting its feet wet and its hands dirty in the hard work of community organizing during the late 1970s and early 1980s with small-scale and relatively easy victories such as food-store cleanups and the installation of street signs, EBC took on the much more formidable task of building thousands of affordable single-family, owner-occupied homes (Boyte 1989, 82–83). Taking up the controversial idea of building developer and *New York Daily News* columnist I. D. Robbins, that home ownership could generate community pride and stable neighborhoods in ways that high-rise rental housing could never achieve, this ecumenical organization launched a project that was dubbed the Nehemiah Plan on the basis of a sermon preached by the Reverend Johnny Ray Youngblood, the pastor of EBC member St. Paul's Community Baptist Church (Freedman 1993, 332; Boyte 1989, 83). The words of Nehemiah became a rallying cry taken up even by the likes of New York's irascible mayor Ed Koch: "You see the trouble we are in, how Jerusalem lies in ruins with its gates burned. Come, let us rebuild the wall of Jerusalem, so that we may no longer suffer disgrace" (Neh 2:17).[3] The response of the repatriated Jews of Yehud echoed across the centuries from Jerusalem to Brooklyn: "Then they said, 'Let us start building!' So they committed themselves to the common good" (2:18).

In *Commonwealth: A Return to Citizen Politics*, Harry Boyte quotes EBC lead organizer Michael Gecan, who explained that "[t]he story connected our work to something real, not something bogus.... It got it out of the 'housing' field and the idea that you have to have a bureaucracy with 35 consultants to do anything.

---

2. When a synagogue became a member in 1988, East Brooklyn Churches became East Brooklyn Congregations, retaining EBC as its acronym.

3. Except as otherwise noted, citations from the Bible are taken from the New Revised Standard Version.

It made it a 'nonprogram,' something more than housing" (1989, 83; Terkel 2003, 233–42). As EBC leader Celina Jamieson emphasized, "We are more than a Nehemiah Plan. We are about the central development of dignity and self-respect" (Boyte 1989, 83). Despite ongoing opposition and considerable foot-dragging on the part of New York City government, several thousand Nehemiah homes have been built in Brooklyn since the 1980s, and the project became a model for the rehabilitation of blighted urban areas across the United States (Freedman 1993, 307–44).[4] As for EBC, it demonstrated what could happen when such unlikely partners as the Lutheran Church Missouri Synod, St. Paul's Community Baptist Church, and Roman Catholic parishes (such as Our Lady of Loreto) founded by immigrants of earlier generations and now home to more recent arrivals could come together to do something more than just read the Bible. Reading Nehemiah together in Brooklyn inspired the EBC's member congregations to do what was necessary to rebuild their community.

During the three years I spent at Our Lady of Loreto before going back to Rome to pursue doctoral studies, I never actually discovered what I might or might not have done that resulted in my being appointed as parochial vicar there fresh out of seminary. Even so, I did learn a great deal about community organizing and the politics of biblical interpretation from people like the Reverend Johnny Ray Youngblood, Mike Gecan, Stephan Roberson, Alice McCollum, Sister Immaculata Kennedy, Father John Powis, and Edgar Mendez—EBC leaders and IAF organizers who "committed themselves to the common good," knowing that the houses they helped build were only as strong as the community that organized, strategized, and mobilized to get them built. On 1 October 1982 at the groundbreaking for the first Nehemiah homes, several years before I arrived in East New York, Reverend Youngblood addressed a gathering of some

---

4. In an article in the 31 July 1996 issue of the *New York Beacon*, published shortly after the death of I. D. Robbins and his cousin Lester, Bernice Powell Jackson wrote: "I. D. Robbins was a New York City builder whose vision of a single-family home for all Americans became a reality for some 2,800 poor families in Brooklyn and the South Bronx. The tragedy is that the political, financial and contracting worlds kept that dream from becoming a reality for many thousands of poor Americans across the nation. The Robbins cousins were successful builders who were convinced that simple row houses were the key to the vitality of the cities and to the nurturing of families. I. D. Robbins figured that a family earning $20,000 a year could own a $40,000 home, which he believed he could. When the Industrial Areas Foundation learned of Mr. Robbins' dream, they brought together 36 congregations in one of Brooklyn's poorest neighborhoods, East New York. These churches put up $8 million for a revolving fund for construction and without federal assistance began to build homes in Brownsville.... these three bedroom, brick houses sold for $39,000. They were built on large tracts of cleared, city-owned land, with foundations for whole blocks being poured at one time. They were 18 feet wide and 32 feet deep, with front and back yards and full basements. Mr. Robbins believed these were the answers to many of the city's problems which he blamed on high density, high-rise government-subsidized housing projects" (Jackson 1996, 8).

six thousand members from forty-two member churches and declared: "Contrary to popular opinion ... we are not a 'grassroots' organization.... Grass roots grow in smooth soil. Grass roots are tender roots. Grass roots are fragile roots. Our roots are deep roots" (Freedman 1993, 339).

Rereading Nehemiah: Walls Built of Words

It was not until many years later that I returned to reconsider Nehemiah, indirectly prompted to do so by a curious convergence of circumstances that got me to thinking about twenty-first-century walls and fences (Ruiz 2005, 122–30). The first such prompting came by way of Samuel P. Huntington's article, "The Hispanic Challenge" (2004a), excerpted from his *Who Are We? The Challenges to America's National Identity* (2004b). That article begins:

> The persistent inflow of Hispanic immigrants threatens to divide the United States into two peoples, two cultures, and two languages. Unlike past immigrant groups, Mexicans and other Latinos have not assimilated into mainstream U.S. culture, forming instead their own political and linguistic enclaves—from Los Angeles to Miami—and rejecting the Anglo-Protestant values that built the American dream. The United States ignores this challenge at its peril. (2004a, 31)

Huntington's article concludes even more ominously:

> Continuation of this large immigration (without improved assimilation) could divide the United States into a country of two languages and two cultures.... A few stable, prosperous democracies—such as Canada and Belgium—fit this pattern. The transformation of the United States into a country like these would not necessarily be the end of the world; it would, however, be the end of the America we have known for more than three centuries. Americans should not let that change happen unless they are convinced that this new nation would be a better one. Such a transformation would not only revolutionize the United States, but it would also have serious consequences for Hispanics, who will be in the United States but not of it. Sosa ends his book, *The Americano Dream*, with encouragement for aspiring Hispanic entrepreneurs. "The Americano dream?" he asks. "It exists, it is realistic, and it is there for all of us to share." Sosa is wrong. There is no Americano dream. There is only the American dream created by an Anglo-Protestant society. Mexican Americans will share in that dream and in that society only if they dream in English. (2004a, 44–45; see Sosa 1999)

Whether by free association or by some other caprice of intertextuality, reading the end of Huntington's anti-immigrant rant led me to reread the end of Nehemiah with different eyes, a text I found just as unsettling as Huntington's:

> In those days also I saw Jews who had married women of Ashdod, Ammon, and Moab; and half of their children spoke the language of Ashdod, and they could

not speak the language of Judah, but spoke the language of various peoples. And I contended with them and cursed them and beat some of them and pulled out their hair; and I made them take an oath in the name of God, saying, "You shall not give your daughters to their sons, or take their daughters for your sons or for yourselves. Did not King Solomon of Israel sin on account of such women? Among the many nations there was no king like him, and he was beloved by his God, and God made him king over all Israel; nevertheless, foreign women made even him to sin. Shall we then listen to you and do all this great evil and act treacherously against our God by marrying foreign women?" And one of the sons of Jehoiada, son of the high priest Eliashib, was the son-in-law of Sanballat the Horonite; I chased him away from me. Remember them, O my God, because they have defiled the priesthood, the covenant of the priests and the Levites. Thus I cleansed them from everything foreign, and I established the duties of the priests and Levites, each in his work; and I provided for the wood offering, at appointed times, and for the first fruits. Remember me, O my God, for good. (Neh 13:23–30)

These verses did *not* make it into Reverend Youngblood's sermon at St. Paul Community Baptist Church, the sermon that inspired EBC lead organizer Mike Gecan to dub the organization's housing initiative the Nehemiah Plan (Freedman 1993, 332).

This is not the first time that the controversy over marriage with "foreign women" (*nashim nokriyot*) comes to the surface in Ezra-Nehemiah, nor is it the first instance in Ezra-Nehemiah where tensions flare up between the returnees from exile and the inhabitants of the land. These tensions boil to the surface as early as Ezra 3, when Jeshua and his fellow priests and Zerubbabel and his kin "set out to build the altar of the God of Israel, to offer burnt offerings on it, as prescribed by the law of Moses the man of God" (Ezra 3:2). In the following verse we read: "Despite their fear of the peoples of the land, they replaced the altar on its foundations and offered holocausts to the LORD on it, both morning and evening" (Ezra 3:3 NAB).[5] In Ezra 4:4 the lines are drawn between the "people of the land" (*'am-ha'arets*), whose opposition to the rebuilding of the temple by the returnees renders the "people of Judah" (*'am-yehudah*) afraid to build.

The matter of exogamous marriage by the priests and Levites among the returnees is the focus of Ezra 9–10. There the Ezra memoir reports:

The officials approached me and said, "The people of Israel, the priests, and the Levites have not separated themselves from the peoples of the lands with their

---

5. Curiously, the NRSV translation of this verse suggests that fear of the inhabitants of the land was the reason for which Jeshua and Zerubbabel set up the altar as they did: "They set up the altar on its foundation, because they were in dread of the neighboring peoples, and they offered burnt offerings upon it to the LORD, morning and evening" (on the text of Ezra 3:3, see Williamson 1985, 41.)

abominations, from the Canaanites, the Hittites, the Perizzites, the Jebusites, the Ammonites, the Moabites, the Egyptians, and the Amorites. For they have taken some of their daughters as wives for themselves and for their sons. Thus the holy seed has mixed itself with the peoples of the lands, and in this faithlessness the officials and leaders have led the way." When I heard this, I tore my garment and my mantle, and pulled hair from my head and beard, and sat appalled. (Ezra 9:1–2)

The solution Ezra imposes on the priests and Levites requires them to "separate [themselves] from the people of the land and from foreign wives" (Ezra 10:11), and the book ends with a listing of the names of those who sent away their "foreign wives" (10:44). It would be more accurate to say, with H. G. M. Williamson and other commentators, that the narrative breaks off at the end of Ezra 10 without actually concluding (Williamson 1985, 159). On the unity of Ezra-Nehemiah, Williamson maintains "that there is good reason to approach Ezra and Nehemiah as two parts of a single work and that this work is to be regarded as complete as it stands" (xxiii). While an exploration of the question of whether Ezra-Nehemiah should be considered "complete as it stands" would be well beyond the scope of this essay, the widely maintained position that affirms the original unity of Ezra-Nehemiah is presupposed here. Joseph Blenkinsopp offers a "reasonable guess" that the sudden ending of the Ezra narrative may indicate the failure of Ezra's mission (as a result of his opposition to exogamous marriage) and his recall by his Persian superiors "after a stay of no more than a year" (1988, 179).

In Neh 13:1–3, the reading of "the book of Moses" builds walls of words that fix exclusionary boundaries even more effectively than walls of stone:

On that day they read from the book of Moses in the hearing of the people; and in it was found written that no Ammonite or Moabite should ever enter the assembly of God, because they did not meet the Israelites with bread and water, but hired Balaam against them to curse them—yet our God turned the curse into a blessing. When the people heard the law, they separated from Israel all those of foreign descent.

This restriction (based on Deut 23:4–7, which recalls Num 22–24) provides Nehemiah with further ammunition against Tobiah, the Ammonite official who opposed the rebuilding project from the beginning (Neh 2:19) and against whom Nehemiah acts in 13:8, ejecting Tobiah's furnishings from the room in the temple that had been prepared for him by the priest Eliashib while Nehemiah himself was away from Jerusalem consulting with King Artaxerxes (13:4–9). The reference to Deut 23:4–7 provides Nehemiah with the legal basis for acting against his opponent. Blenkinsopp points out that the reading "from the book of Moses" is rather selective inasmuch as Neh 13 makes no mention of the restriction against genitally mutilated males (Deut 23:1), against "those born of an illicit union"

(Deut 23:2), or even of the less restrictive legislation regarding Edomites and Egyptians (Deut 23:7–8) (1988, 351).

We are introduced to Tobiah in Neh 2:10, where, together with Sanballat the Horonite, he is said to oppose Nehemiah's mission "to seek the welfare of the people of Israel."[6] As soon as Nehemiah rallies the people, "Come, let us rebuild the wall of Jerusalem, so that we may no longer suffer disgrace" (Neh 2:17), an exhortation that follows his covert inspection of the wall by night (2:15–16), the project is said to meet with opposition from Sanballat the Horonite and Tobiah the Ammonite official (*ha'ebed ha'ammoni*) and Geshem the Arab, of whom Nehemiah says "They mocked and ridiculed us" and in response to whose opposition Nehemiah makes exclusive claims: "The God of heaven is the one who will give us success, and we his servants are going to start building; but you have no share or claim or historic right in Jerusalem" (Neh 2:20; Blenkinsopp 1988, 226–27; Williamson 1985, 192–93).

While a number of recent studies have devoted attention to the matter of marriage with "foreign women" in Ezra and Nehemiah,[7] far less attention has been devoted to the specific issue at stake in Neh 13:23–24: Nehemiah's violent reaction to the returnees who married women of Ashdod, Ammon, and Moab, half of whose children "spoke the language of Ashdod, and they could not speak the language of Judah, but spoke the language of various peoples" (on the text of Neh 13:23–24, see Williamson 1985, 393). Clearly, the troublesome matter of intermarriage between *Yehudim* and "women of Ashdod, Ammon, and Moab" has to do with much more than purity or with concern over land tenure and inheritance of real property. Here Nehemiah regards the inability of a significant number of the children of such "mixed" marriages to speak Yehudite to be a dangerous symptom of assimilation, underscoring the important links between language and group identity.

Disturbed that so many of the children of the *Yehudim* do not speak *Yehudit*, Nehemiah resorts to verbal and physical abuse: "I contended with them and cursed some of them and beat them and pulled out their hair" (Neh 13:25). Elsewhere in the Hebrew Bible, *Yehudit* is used to designate a language in 2 Kgs 18:26, 28. During the Assyrian siege of Jerusalem, Hezekiah's officials beg the Rabshakeh, "Please speak to your servants in the Aramaic language [*Aramit*], for

---

6. On the identity and background of Sanballat the Horonite and Tobiah the Ammonite, see Blenkinsopp 1988, 216–19. Blenkinsopp suggests that "Tobiah belonged to a distinguished Jerusalemite family with close ties to the high priesthood and the aristocracy, and at the time of Nehemiah's mission he was the Persian-appointed governor of the Ammonite region" (219; Smith-Christopher 1994, 258–59).

7. See the chapter by Cheryl B. Anderson in this volume; see also Berquist 1995, 117–19; Douglas 2002, 1–23; Eskenazi and Judd 1994, 266–85; Esler 2003, 413–26; Hayes 2002, 27–34; Klawans 1998, 391–415; Smith-Christopher 1994; 1996, 122–27; Olyan 2004, 1–16; Washington 1994, 217–42; 2003, 427–37; Yee 2003, 143–46.

we understand it; do not speak to us in the language of Judah [*Yehudit*] within the hearing of the people who are on the wall," but the Rabshakeh ignores their plea and addresses the inhabitants of the besieged city in *Yehudit*. The same term is used in the Isaianic parallel (36:11, 13) and also in the Chronicler's account of the siege (2 Chr 32:18). As for the offending language in Neh 13, "Ashdodite" (*Ashdodit*), Blenkinsopp notes: "There have been several guesses, all inconclusive, as to the language in question: a residue of the Philistine language—about which, unfortunately, we know next to nothing; an Aramaic dialect; perhaps even Phoenician, given the political and commercial Phoenician presence in the coastal area" (363). He thinks little of the suggestion by E. Ullendorf that *Ashdodit* "was simply a current designation for any unintelligible foreign language (as in our expression, 'It's all Greek to me')," inasmuch as this hypothesis "overlooks the actual issue, which is Jewish-Ashdodite marriages" (363; Williamson: 398; Ullendorf: 125–35). Indeed, as Blenkinsopp explains, "What was really at stake was not so much speaking a foreign language as the inability to speak Hebrew" (1988, 363).

For many commentators, at this point exegetical analysis of the issues at stake gives way to broad generalizations and unrestrained guesswork. Daniel L. Smith-Christopher observes that, when dealing with the intermarriage issue in Ezra and Nehemiah, "contemporary commentators are frequently unsettled from typical 'scholarly reserve'" (1996, 122). For example, Williamson suggests: "For a religion in which Scripture plays a central part, grasp of language is vital; one might compare the importance of Arabic for Islam. When religion and national culture are also integrally related, as they were for Judaism at this time, a knowledge of the community's language was indispensable; indeed, it was one of the factors that distinguished and sustained the community itself" (1985, 397). With regard to the indication in Neh 13:24 that *half* of the offspring of the mixed marriages spoke the language of Ashdod and could not speak *Yehudit*, Williamson finds this indication "curious" and wonders whether some fathers were "more conscientious about teaching their children their own language than others for whom the children's education was considered an entirely maternal concern? Or was it a question of age, a knowledge of Hebrew coming only as the children began to mix outside the immediate confines of the home?" (398). The text of Nehemiah offers us no information that would make it possible to resolve this question. For his part, Blenkinsopp opines, "In view of the dominant influence of the mother in the formative years, it is not surprising that many of the children spoke her language, though why the other half did not remains unexplained" (1988, 363). He adds: "Language has always been an important ingredient of national identity: whether Gaelic in Ireland or Welsh in Wales or, more to the point, Hebrew during the Bar Kokhba rebellion and in Israel during the modern period" (363).

Even though Blenkinsopp does not linger very long over Neh 13:24, his observation about the relationship between language and group identity deserves further attention. This is confirmed when we consider the six features that John

Hutchinson and Anthony D. Smith identify as characteristics that establish the distinctiveness of ethnic groups (1996, 6–7; Esler 2003, 414): (1) a common proper name to identify the group; (2) a myth of common ancestry; (3) a shared history or shared memories of a common past, including heroes, events, and their commemoration; (4) a common culture, embracing such things as customs, language, and religion; (5) a link with a homeland; and (6) a sense of communal solidarity. Reading Neh 13:24 calls particular attention to the first and fourth characteristics, that is, the proper name by which the group is distinguished (either prescriptively or diagnostically) from other groups and the language that distinguishes the group from other groups.

With regard to the first characteristic, a common proper name for the group, Ezra 4:4 identifies the returnees as "people of Judah" (*'am-yehudah*), and this identification stands in marked contrast to the designation of their opponents in disparaging terms as "people of the land" (*'am-ha'arets*). This designation, as Gale Yee points out, was deployed as part of the strategy by which the immigrants established ideological distance between themselves and the members of the Judean population who had not been taken into exile (2003, 144–45). In Neh 13:23 the returnees are identified as *Yehudim*, and Nehemiah objects to their intermarriage with Ashdodite, Ammonite, and Moabite women.

With regard to language as a distinctive group characteristic, Neh 13:14 describes the distinctive language of the *Yehudim* as *Yehudit*: the group is identified according to the language spoken by its members, and the language is identified as the language that is held in common by members of the group. On one level, it could be said that Nehemiah feared that the loss of Judean language among the children of the Yehudites would lead to the dissipation of a distinctively Yehudite identity in the very next generation. Yet the vehemence of his response to the practice of intermarriage suggests that much more was at stake. As Yee demonstrates, neither the practice of intermarriage by the immigrant community nor Nehemiah's violent reaction against it is merely a matter of ethnic identity.

She suggests that "[o]ne of the earliest economic issues faced by the immigrants was land tenure and gaining control of the principal means of production in Yehud from the natives" (2003, 143). Yee agrees with Mary Douglas, who explains that intermarriage was one of the strategies by which the immigrants acquired access to land: "marriage was the obvious way for the new arrivals to insert themselves into the farming economy" (Yee 2003, 144; Douglas 2002, 11). Reading this in the light of social exchange theory, which attends to how agents weigh the costs and rewards that result from entering into particular relationships, Yee suggests that by intermarrying "the immigrant political and cultic elites exchanged or parlayed their high status as imperial agents in order to gain access to the land as a means of production through noncoercive means. The natives exchanged their land to 'marry up' into the ranks of the returning elite, their ethnic kinsfolk who had good connections with the Persian authorities" (144).

Thus the practice of intermarriage by the immigrants should not be understood as a practice that had assimilation as its aim. Yee regards Neh 13:23–30 as evidence that

> the *golah* community continued to intermarry for socioeconomic reasons, particularly into ethnically foreign families. For Nehemiah, such intermarriages meant the threat of foreign influence on Yehud's internal affairs during a time of economic depletion by the Persian Empire. Land tenure was also an issue. If women could inherit during the postexilic period, land could be transferred from the Jerusalem elite into ethnically foreign hands through marriages with foreign wives. Furthermore, since the temple was crucial to the economic affairs of Yehud, intermarriage with foreign women among the priestly class, in particular (Neh 13:28–29), could permit unwelcome or detrimental influence on these affairs from the outside. (146)

For Nehemiah, the Persian-appointed governor of Yehud, the problem of intermarriage was complicated by the fact that the children born of these marriages were learning the languages of their mothers. Discussing the intermarriage issue in Neh 13 in the course of his analysis of the roles of Ezra and Nehemiah as governors of Yehud during the reign of Artaxerxes I (465–423 B.C.E.), Jon L. Berquist notes that here

> The more specific problem is that the children of such marriages speak only the language of their mothers (Neh 13:24); without a knowledge of Hebrew or Aramaic they would not be capable of assuming leadership positions within the community. Nehemiah then offers a comparison to Solomon's problems of dissipating alliances developed on the basis of intermarriage; thus Nehemiah indicates that the problems may involve foreign complicity within issues of colonial policy (Neh 13:25–27). (1995, 117–18)

Dismissing the hypothesis put forward by many scholars that concern over ethnic purity lies at the heart of the intermarriage issue, Berquist suggests instead that the prohibition against intermarriage was intended to "solidify political control and economic security within the ruling stratum of Jerusalem society" (118) and to guard against outside interference in the internal colonial affairs of Yehud. Thus, for Nehemiah the fact that "half of their children spoke the language of Ashdod and could not speak the language of Judah" (Neh 13:24) is an alarming symptom of the deeper problem of the fast-moving erosion of the immigrant community as a distinctive group. The assimilation signified by the loss of the group's distinctive language among the children of the immigrants implied a loss of group cohesion and threatened "a further depletion of already scarce resources through dissipation into a widening social circle" (118). Nehemiah's violent reaction to the exogamous marriages of his fellow immigrants thus represents an act of antiassimilationist resistance, an act that was as vehement as it was futile.

"Losing a language," Alejandro Portes and Rubén Rumbaut declare, "is also losing part of one's self that is linked to one's identity and cultural heritage" (2001, 144). The emotional impact of the loss of a shared language across generations is captured vividly in the complaint of a thirty-two-year-old Cambodian woman who laments, "I have a niece living in East Boston who knows only English. I cannot talk to her because I don't speak English.... Those children act and talk like Americans. They eat American food like pizza and McDonald's ... and they say to their parents, 'I don't want to live with you; I want to move in with a roommate'" (144).

The intersections between language, ethnic identity, and colonization remain as complex for immigrants in the twenty-first century C.E. as they were during the fifth century B.C.E. (Nanko-Fernández 2006, 267–69). For Latin American immigrants to the United States and for their children, Nehemiah's outburst against the intermarrying immigrants and their Ashdodite-speaking children sounds frighteningly familiar, echoing in Samuel Huntington's nativist rhetoric, "There is no Americano dream. There is only the American dream created by an Anglo-Protestant society. Mexican Americans will share in that dream and in that society only if they dream in English" (2004a, 45). This is nothing new. President Theodore Roosevelt insisted: "We have room for but one language here, and that is the English language, for we intend to see that the crucible turns our people out as Americans, and not as dwellers of a polyglot boarding house; and we have room for but one sole loyalty, and that is loyalty to the American people" (Portes and Rumbaut 2001, 113). Roosevelt's remarks at the beginning of the twentieth century are reflected in the workings of U.S. colonial expansion, when the Spanish-American War resulted in the extension of U.S. sovereignty over Cuba and Puerto Rico. In 1920, a Department of War's Annual Report boasted, "The people of Porto Rico [sic] are American citizens. Perhaps the most important factor in their complete Americanization is the spreading of the English language. Diligent efforts along this line are being made and with very satisfactory progress" (Cabán 1999, 131).

In their important study of the immigrant second generation in the United States, Portes and Rumbaut explain:

> Immigrants arriving in a foreign land face a significant dilemma, one whose resolution lies at the very core of the process of acculturation. On the one hand, the languages that they bring are closely linked to their sense of self-worth and national pride. On the other hand, these languages clash with the imperatives of a new environment that dictate abandonment of their cultural baggage and learning a new means of communication. Language assimilation is demanded of foreigners not only for instrumental reasons but for symbolic ones as well. It signals their willingness to seek admission into the circles of their new country, leaving past loyalties behind. Precisely because a common language lies at the

core of national identity, host societies oppose the rise of refractory groups that persist in the use of foreign tongues. (2001, 113)

With respect to language assimilation, Portes and Rumbaut point to research that supports the dominant scholarly view that the process typically takes three generations:

Adult immigrants in the United States typically combine instrumental learning of English with efforts to maintain their culture and language. They also seek to pass this heritage to their children.... The instrumental acculturation of the first generation in the United States is followed by a second that speaks English in school and parental languages at home, often responding to remarks in those languages in English. Limited bilingualism leads, almost inevitably, to English becoming the home language in adulthood. By the third generation, any residual proficiency in the foreign language is lost since it is supported neither outside nor inside the home. (114)

Yet other research has begun to challenge this assumption, pointing especially to the persistence of Spanish among Latino/a children regardless of generation (Arriagada 2005; Alba et al. 2002). Research also shows that linguistic assimilation is significantly affected by intermarriage (Alba et al. 2002, 471, 478–79). In one important study of mother-tongue shift to English, Gillian Stevens reports, "children of two foreign parents are most likely to learn a parent's non-English language; those with one foreign parent are less likely; and those with two native-born parents least likely" (1985, 81). Stevens reports that with almost half of the children in the study belonging to ethnically heterogamous backgrounds, "Few of these children learned a parent's non-English mother tongue." Stevens thus concludes that non-English languages are disappearing through mother-tongue shift in large part because of ethnic intermarriage" (81). This recalls the situation described in Neh 13, where Nehemiah complains that ethnic exogamy is resulting in mother-tongue shift among the children of Yehudites who have married Ashdodite, Ammonite, and Moabite women, so that half of their offspring "could not speak the language of Judah."

The complex and ongoing history of the U.S. colonization of Puerto Rico sheds important light on the tangled intertwinings of language, identity, and colonization. After Puerto Rico became a U.S. possession in 1898, in the wake of the U.S. war against Spain, the island's new colonial masters engaged in the ideological Americanization of the island, with policies that aimed at "fostering loyalty to the U.S. colonial project" (Negrón-Muntaner 1997, 259). In 1907, Education Commissioner Martin G. Brumbaugh spelled it out in the following terms: "The first business of the American Republic, in its attempt to universalize its educational ideals in America, is to give these Spanish-speaking races the symbols of the English language in which to express the knowledge and culture which they already possess" (as cited in Cabán 1999, 131). The Americanization of the Puerto Rican population went hand in hand with the disparagement of the language that had been spoken by the inhabitants of the island during its four centuries as a colony of Spain. The American Commissioner of Education said that Puerto Ricans lack

> [t]he same devotion to their native tongue or to any national ideal that animates the Frenchmen, for instance, in Canada or the Rhine provinces.... A majority of the people do not speak pure Spanish. Their language is a patois almost unintelligible to the natives of Barcelona and Madrid. It possesses no literature and little value as an intellectual medium. There is a bare possibility that it will be nearly as easy to educate these people out of their patois into English as it will be to educate them into the elegant tongue of Castile. Only from the very small intellectual minority in Puerto Rico, trained in Europe and imbued with European ideals of education and government, have we to anticipate any active resistance to the introduction of the American school system and the English language. (Wagenheim and Jiménez de Wagenheim 1994, 111)

The English language was the medium, and Americanization was the unmistakable message. Puerto Rico's new colonial masters correctly recognized that it was the disempowered *criollo* elites that would mount the most vocal opposition to the use of English as the real and symbolic instrument for expressing the island's new status quo as a U.S. territory. In 1930, Victor Clark wrote:

> English is the chief source, practically the only source, of democratic ideas in Porto Rico. There may be little that they learn to remember, but the English school reader itself provides a body of ideas and concepts which are not to be had in any other way. It is also the only means which these people have of communication with and understanding of the country of which they are now a part. (Cabán 1999, 133)

For the vast majority of the Puerto Rican population, mastery of English was positively associated with upward economic mobility, so that, according to a 1930 study published by the Brookings Institution,

> An opportunity to learn English, no matter how imperfectly and adequately, is one of the magnets that draws the children of the poorer classes to the public schools. To tens of thousands of disinherited in Puerto Rico, a knowledge of that language seems to promise—perhaps fallaciously—a better economic future. Popular willingness to make sacrifices for the schools is in some degree due to this pathetic faith. (Negrón-Muntaner 1997, 263)

More than a century after Puerto Rico became a U.S. possession, the island's ambivalent colonial betwixt-and-betweenness in the economic and political spheres continues to surface in polemics over language. As Frances Negrón-Muntaner explains in a study of language and nationalism in Puerto Rico,

> Although in the United States Puerto Ricans are legally "first"-class citizens, they are often perceived as a racialized minority group and treated as such. On the other hand, in Puerto Rico Puerto Ricans are second-class citizens of the United States with little decision-making power, but islanders tend to think of themselves as an autonomous region and/or a separate country. (1997, 281)

Bluntly declaring that "language nationalism is a farce," Negrón-Muntaner is duly critical of moves that sought to impose a Puerto Rican monolingual "essence," efforts that borrowed from the rhetoric of the "English only" movement in the United States to agitate for a linguistic nationalism that would establish Spanish as the wall of words that would enforce a cultural border between the island and the United States (281). In that vein, Nehemiah might well have found common cause across the centuries with Severo Colberg Ramírez, who insisted, "Vamos a ver quiénes son puertorriqueños 'de a verdad,' quiénes los son a medias y quiénes menosprecian el hecho de haber nacido aquí y haberse criado con el español como vernáculo" ("We will see who the 'real' Puerto Ricans are, who are only halfway, and who looks down on having been born here and being raised with Spanish as their native tongue"; as cited in Negrón-Muntaner 1997, 280).

Negrón-Muntaner maintains that "[n]ative command of Spanish does not signify or contain Puerto Ricanness" (1997, 281). Indeed the English/Spanish binaries and the hard-and-fast linkages of language and ethnic identity collapse before the realities of transnationalism and globalization, conditions that nourish bilingualism and that result in such linguistic betwixts-and-betweens as Spanglish/*inglañol* (see Stavans 2003, 1–54; Sandoval Sánchez 1997, 189–208; Lao 1997, 169–88). What, then, of the identification of *Yehudim* with *Yehudit*? How might a Nuyorican Spanglish-speaker from Our Lady of Loreto reread Neh 13? How might a twenty-first-century Brooklynite find words to lend to the Ashdodite-speaking offspring of ethnically mixed marriages whose own betwixt-and-betweenness in fifth-century B.C.E. Jerusalem led Nehemiah to curse their fathers? Afro-Puerto Rican poet Tato Laviera can help (Álvarez Martínez 2006, 34–35). In a poem entitled, "my graduation speech," he confesses:

> I think in Spanish
> I write in English
> ....
> tengo las venas aculturadas
> escribo en Spanglish. (1979, 17; as cited in Álvarez Martínez 2006, 29)

In another poem Laviera protests that he is neither assimil*ated* (English) nor asimil*ado* (Spanish), underscoring tensions between assimilation and resistance, between language and ethnic identity, that resonate eloquently across the centuries between Brooklyn and Jerusalem, from the margins of the global metropolis to the colony at the fringes of the Persian Empire (Álvarez Martínez

2006, 34–35). In a distinctively Puerto Rican idiom that attests to the linguistic *mestizaje/mulataje* that is itself the legacy of more than five centuries of colonization, he is, as the title of the poem itself proclaims, "asimilao":

assimilated? qué assimilated,
brother, yo soy asimilao
así mi la o sí es verdad
tengo un lado asimilao

....

but the sound LAO was too black
for LATED, LAO could not be
trans*lated*, assimilated,
no, asimilao, melao,
it became a black
spanish word but
we do have asimilados
perfumados and by the
last count even they
were becoming asimilao
how can it be analyzed
as american? así que se
chavaron
trataron
pero no
pudieron
con el AO
de la palabra
principal, dénles gracias a los prietos
que cambiaron asimilado al popular asimilao. (Laviera 2003, 54)

WORKS CONSULTED

Alba, Richard, John Logan, Amy Lutz, and Brian Stults. 2002. Only English by the Third Generation? Loss and Preservation of the Mother Tongue among the Grandchildren of Contemporary Immigrants. *Demography* 39:467–84.

Alinsky, Saul. 1946. *Reveille for Radicals*. Chicago: University of Chicago Press.

Álvarez Martínez, Stephanie. 2006. ¡¿Qué, qué?!—Transculturación and Tato Laviera's Spanglish Poetics. *Centro Journal* 37:25–46.

Arriagada, Paula A. 2005. Family Context and Spanish-Language Use: A Study of Latino Children in the United States. *Social Science Quarterly* 86:599–619.

Berquist, Jon L. 1995. *Judaism in Persia's Shadow: A Social and Historical Approach*. Minneapolis: Fortress.

Blenkinsopp, Joseph. 1988. *Ezra-Nehemiah: A Commentary*. OTL. Philadelphia: Westminster.

Boyte, Harry. 1989. *Commonwealth: A Return to Citizen Politics*. New York: Free Press.

Cabán, Pedro A. 1999. *Constructing a Colonial People: Puerto Rico and the United States, 1898–1932*. Boulder, Colo.: Westview.

Chambers, Edward T., and Michael A. Cowan. 2003. *Roots for Radicals: Organizing for Power, Action, and Justice*. New York: Continuum.

Douglas, Mary. 2002. Responding to Ezra: The Priests and the Foreign Wives. *BibInt* 10:1–21.

Eskenazi, Tamara C., and Eleanore P. Judd. 1994. Marriage to a Stranger in Ezra 9–10. Pages 265–85 in Eskenazi and Richards 1994.

Eskenazi, Tamara C., and Kent H. Richards, eds. 1994. *Second Temple Studies 2: Temple Community in the Persian Period*. JSOTSup 175. Sheffield: Sheffield Academic Press.

Esler, Philip F. 2003. Ezra-Nehemiah as a Narrative of (Re-invented) Israelite Identity. *BibInt* 11:413–26.

Freedman, Samuel G. 1993. *Upon This Rock: The Miracles of a Black Church*. New York: Harper Collins.

Gecan, Michael. 2000. Recasting Identity in Ruth and Hindu Indo-Guyanese Women. Pages 167–79 in *Religion, Culture, and Tradition in the Caribbean*. Edited by Hemchand Gossai and Nathaniel Samuel Murrell. New York: St. Martin's.

Hayes, Christine E. 2002. *Gentile Impurities and Jewish Identities: Intermarriage and Conversion from the Bible to the Talmud*. New York: Oxford University Press.

Huntington, Samuel P. 2004a. The Hispanic Challenge. *Foreign Policy* 141:30–45.

———. 2004b. *Who Are We? The Challenges to America's National Identity*. New York: Simon & Schuster.

Hutchinson, John, and Anthony D. Smith., eds. 1996. *Ethnicity*. Oxford: Oxford University Press.

Jackson, Bernice Powell. 1996. The Right to a Home. *New York Beacon* 31 July.3.29:8.

Klawans, Jonathan. 1998. Idolatry, Incest, and Impurity: Moral Defilement in Ancient Judaism. *JSJ* 4:391–415.

Lao, Agustín. 1997. Islands at the Crossroads: Puerto Ricanness Traveling between the Translocal Nation and the Global City. Pages 169–88 in Negrón-Muntaner and Grosfoguel 1997.

Laviera, Tato. 1979. *La Carreta Made a U-Turn*. Houston: Arte Público.

———. 2003. *AmeRícan*. 2nd ed. Houston: Arte Público.

Nanko-Fernández, Carmen M. 2006. Language, Community, and Identity. Pages 265–75 in *Handbook of Latina/o Theologies*. Edited by Edwin David Aponte and Miguel A. De La Torre. St. Louis: Chalice.

Negrón-Muntaner, Frances. 1997. English Only Jamás but Spanish Only Cuidado: Language and Nationalism in Contemporary Puerto Rico. Pages 257–85 in Negrón-Muntaner and Grosfoguel 1997.

Negrón-Muntaner, Frances, and Ramón Grosfoguel, eds. 1997. *Puerto Rican Jam: Essays on Culture and Politics.* Minneapolis: University of Minnesota Press

Olyan, Saul. 2004. Purity Ideology in Ezra-Nehemiah as a Tool to Reconstitute the Community. *JSJ* 35:1–16.

Portes, Alejandro, and Rubén G. Rumbaut. 2001. *Legacies: The Story of the Immigrant Second Generation.* Berkeley and Los Angeles: University of California Press.

Ruiz, Jean-Pierre. 2005. Of Walls and Words: Twenty-First Century Empire and New Testament Studies. *USQR* 59:122–30.

Sandoval Sánchez, Alberto. 1997. Puerto Rican Identity Up in the Air: Air Migration, Its Cultural Representations, and Me Cruzando el Charco. Pages 189–208 in Negrón-Muntaner and Grosfoguel 1997.

Smith-Christopher, Daniel L. 1994. The Mixed Marriage Crisis in Ezra 9–10 and Nehemiah 13: A Study of the Sociology of the Post-Exilic Judaean Community. Pages 243–65 in Eskenazi and Richards 1994.

———. 1996. Between Ezra and Isaiah: Exclusion, Transformation, and Inclusion of the "Foreigner" in Post-Exilic Biblical Theology. Pages 117–42 in *Ethnicity and the Bible.* Edited by Mark G. Brett. Leiden: Brill.

Sosa, Lionel. 1999. *The Americano Dream: How Latinos Can Achieve Success in Business and in Life.* New York: Penguin.

Stavans, Ilan. 2003. *Spanglish: The Making of a New Language.* New York: Harper Collins.

Stevens, Gillian. 1985. Nativity, Intermarriage, and Mother-Tongue Shift. *American Sociological Review.* 50:74–83.

Study of Islam Section of the American Academy of Religion. Online: http://groups.colgate.edu/aarislam/response.htm.

Terkel, Studs. 2003. *Hope Dies Last: Keeping the Faith in Difficult Times.* New York: New Press.

Ullendorf, E. 1968. C'est de l'hébreu pour moi. *JSS* 13:125–35.

Wagenheim, Kal, and Olga Jiménez de Wagenheim, eds. 1994. *The Puerto Ricans: A Documentary History.* Princeton: Markus Wiener.

Washington, Harold C. 1994. The Strange Woman of Proverbs 1–9 and Post-Exilic Judaean Society. Pages 217–42 in Eskenazi and Richards 1994.

———. 2003. Israel's Holy Seed and the Foreign Women of Ezra-Nehemiah: A Kristevan Reading. *BibInt* 11:427–37.

Williamson, H. G. M. 1985. *Ezra, Nehemiah.* WBC 16. Waco, Tex.: Word.

Yee, Gale A. 2003. *Poor Banished Children of Eve: Woman as Evil in the Hebrew Bible.* Minneapolis: Fortress.

What Does Manzanar Have to Do with Eden? A Japanese American Interpretation of Genesis 2–3

Frank M. Yamada

What does Manzanar have to do with Eden? More precisely, can the internment experience of Japanese Americans in the 1940s provide an interpretative lens through which one can read the etiological tale found within Gen 2–3? On the surface, one would expect that the connection between these two texts, one historical and one mythological, would be tenuous at best. Scholars and novelists who have written about the internment of 120,000 Japanese and Japanese Americans during World War II agree that it was a troubled time in U.S. history, illustrating the failures of the American government in an atmosphere of war hysteria. Issues of civil liberties, racial injustice, and human survival punctuate the anecdotal and scholarly literature that is written on this topic. The story of Adam and Eve in the garden of Eden, however, is traditionally assumed to be an account of humanity's fall from grace, the "original sin" that leads to alienation between Creator and creation, between the divine and the human. So what possible connection can there be between these two apparently unrelated but formational narratives?[1]

I will argue that the connection between these two texts is not only justified but produces a reading of the biblical material that scholars have often failed to see. The rationale for reading the Edenic narrative in connection with internment stories has become more compelling with recent studies in the Pentateuch and exilic/postexilic literature. Scholarship on the Pentateuch suggests that an ethos of exile and displacement are appropriate contexts for understanding the Genesis material. Though traditions and sources within this material predate the Babylonian captivity, the final shaping of the Pentateuch likely happened within the Persian period. Hence, one could propose that the experience of another displaced people, in this case Japanese Americans during World War II, would

---

1. I use the term "narrative" here intentionally. Hayden White has documented and exposed the difficulties within the literary form of historiography—a type of history writing that relies on narrativity (1978; 1987).

provide an intriguing intertext with the biblical narrative, suggesting textures and themes that would resonate with an exilic or postexilic identity and ethos.[2] I will argue that when one reads these two texts together, significant thematic convergences emerge, particularly the themes of survival in the midst of adversity and authority's exercise of power for the sake of self-preservation. The first theme is not present in the scholarly literature on Gen 2–3, even when this idea is pervasive throughout Israel's literature and narrative self-understanding and would be a natural way of thinking for repatriating exiles during the Persian period. Reading Gen 2–3 in this way suggests that the experience of Japanese Americans can impact the interpretative possibilities within the text. Thus, my reading of the Eden narrative is an attempt to take seriously Fernando Segovia's charge to recognize the "flesh and blood" reader in biblical interpretation (1995, 57).

INTERPRETATIONS OF GENESIS 2–3

Christian interpretations of Gen 2–3 have traditionally focused on themes such as "the fall" or "original sin." According to this reading, one that is heavily influenced by Paul and later interpretations from Christian theologians such as Augustine and the Reformers, Adam and Eve, humanity's primordial parents, are created immortal in a garden of paradise and perfection. They are given a command by the Lord God not to eat the fruit from the tree of the knowledge of good and evil. The serpent in the garden, who is usually depicted as an evil being, even Satan, tempts the woman. Eve takes the fruit and eats it along with her husband. This disobedience, which is the original sin, results in shame and a cursed human condition. Shortly after, the couple is expelled from the garden. Paradise is lost.[3]

This traditional interpretation of the Edenic narrative, as many modern scholars have recognized, has gaps and incongruities (see, e.g., Bechtel 1995; Fretheim 1994). The obvious problem is that "sin" terminology is not present in the narrative itself, and later traditions in the Hebrew Bible make little or no reference to Gen 2–3 when describing human beings as sinful or rebellious. One would imagine that, if sin and disobedience were dominant interpretations of the Edenic tradition in ancient Israel, other biblical writers would have drawn on this metaphor to understand Israel's failings and shortcomings.[4] Within the Edenic story itself, there are certainly consequences for disobedience in Gen 3. The nar-

---

2. Daniel Smith (1990) uses the Japanese American internment along with the study of many other displaced peoples in his examination of the exilic and postexilic period.

3. For a survey of Christian, Jewish, and Muslim understandings of Gen 2–3, see Kvam et al. 1999. For a summary of the Christian use of this text, see Barr 1993; Pagels 1988.

4. Fretheim (1994, 146) overstates his case when he says, "It is uncommon for the Old Testament to refer to any Genesis text." He rightly points out, however, that the paucity of reference to Gen 2–3 in the Hebrew Bible does not mean that the text lacks importance in Israelite thinking.

rative develops in a particular direction, with the disobedience acting as a turning point in the story.[5] While readers have exerted much interpretative energy to explain the dynamics surrounding the humans' actions, interpreters have not usually focused on the problematic nature of Yahweh's command and the fact that Yahweh's threat—death as punishment—is never carried out. The interpretations that emphasize sin and disobedience take for granted the just nature of the Lord's decree, something that the present interpretation will show to be problematic. Another difficulty with the traditional interpretation of Gen 2–3 is that it assumes that evil comes into the world when human beings acquire knowledge when they eat the fruit. Hence, in this worldview, knowledge is not power; it is the root of all evil. When one considers the problematic characterization of Yahweh's authority in this passage, the withholding of knowledge takes on a more ominous tone.

Biblical scholars, trained in the methods of historical criticism and comparative ancient Near Eastern studies, have suggested that the traditional readings of Gen 2–3 are not based in a close examination of the text itself or in ancient Israelite understandings of the text but are a later Christian or Jewish theological understanding of the story (see, e.g., Kvam et al. 1999; Barr 1993). Such scholars have emphasized that the biblical narrative must be understood within the sociohistorical context from which it emerges. Thus, Gen 2–3 has been understood as a Yahwistic narrative, a J text that is part of the epic tradition, which was written during the early monarchy. Within such interpretations, human initiative is portrayed as open rebellion to the gracious deity/king. Throughout the Yahwist's primeval history, the benevolence of Yahweh allows for the continuation of human life (von Rad 1972, 153). When human beings seek to take fate into their own hands—an act that sovereign authority will often understand as rebellion—bad things happen: human beings are expelled from the garden in shame (Gen 3); brother kills brother (Gen 4); and the earth is filled with violence (Gen 6:5).

This understanding of Gen 1–11, however, does not take into account the problematic aspects of Yahweh's characterization throughout the primeval history, including Gen 2–3.[6] Why would Yahweh ban the human beings from the tree of knowledge? After the human couple fails to comply, Yahweh is threatened by the possibility that the human beings might become immortal and subsequently removes them from the garden. How are these actions consistent with graciousness? One could argue just as easily from the text that Yahweh's actions betray divine paranoia. Yahweh prevents human access to knowledge and life, punishing those who would take the initiative to seek wisdom and live. The deity within the

---

5. Phyllis Trible's important discussion of this text emphasizes the consequences of disobedience within the Edenic narrative (1976, 72–143).

6. Roger Whybray (1996) has argued that God acts immorally within Gen 2–3 and in other texts from the Hebrew Bible. In the Eden story, Yahweh seeks to preserve his privileged status of immortality. See also Carmichael 1992.

J source does show certain acts of kindness to the human beings: clothing the human beings after the garden incident (3:21) and marking Cain to protect him from retributive violence (4:15). It is also clear, however, that Yahweh acts in ways that reveal the deity's capricious authority.

Other scholars have proposed that Gen 2–3 is a myth, similar to other myths found within the ancient Near East. Within this understanding, the etiological stories of the Edenic narrative help to explain certain aspects of human life: why women hate snakes (3:15); why snakes live on the ground; why there is pain in childbirth; why the ground is hard to work; and so forth. One of the recurring interpretations among biblical scholars is that Gen 2–3 is a story about human maturation (Gunkel 1997, 4–40; Meyers 1988, 72–94; 1993; van Wolde 1989; Bechtel 1995). In this interpretation of the text, when the human beings eat from the fruit of the tree of knowledge they are enlightened, realizing what it means to be fully human. Even if such knowledge is painful, it is, nevertheless, necessary for a proper and mature understanding of the world. The knowledge that life is painful reflects a more mature understanding of humanity's complicated place within the created order.

Scholars who highlight this theme often draw parallels to the Epic of Gilgamesh, an ancient Mesopotamian myth, to support their interpretation. In this well-known story, a primordial human creature, Enkidu, runs wild with the animals and refuses civilization. A temple prostitute is sent to seduce Enkidu. She has intercourse with the creature. After the encounter, Enkidu attempts to return to the animals but finds that they run away in fear from him. The prostitute declares to Enkidu that he has received a new wisdom: a carnal/sexual knowledge. In the process, he has become fully human.[7] Note the parallels in the story to Gen 2–3: (1) prior to human sexual differentiation,[8] the human creature is naïve and exists among the animals; (2) when the human acquires knowledge, there is an enlightenment that is painful to the human; and (3) the acquisition of knowledge, though painful, is necessary for the being to become fully human. Therefore, in a comparative ancient Near Eastern reading of Gen 2–3, the progression in the narrative moves from innocence or naiveté to complex if not painful human maturity through the acquisition of knowledge.

While this interpretation of the Genesis text is compelling, fixing some of the problems that the traditional interpretation creates, it also has limitations. Such interpretations have tended to deemphasize the role that disobedience plays in this narrative and tends to ignore or minimize the arbitrary command of the

7. For a good summary of the mythical themes within the Gilgamesh Epic, see Jacobsen 1976, 193–219.

8. Trible argues that the differentiation of human gender categories, and hence the beginning of sex, does not occur until after the creation of woman. Thus, ha'adam is considered to be an androgynous human creature prior to the creation of Eve (1976, 94–105).

deity. The reason for this is obvious. If the major theme of the narrative is human maturation, then eating the fruit of knowledge cannot be seen as disobedience or a step backward but must be seen as advancement, indeed, the fundamental advancement in a myth about human development. Disobedience and human insubordination, however, do play a significant role in Gen 2–3, since it is the consequences of disobedience that cause Yahweh to expel the human couple from the garden. Moreover, humanity's access to knowledge causes the deity to fear more significant ramifications: the humans might eat from the tree of life and become immortal like the gods (Gen 3:22). I will address how this theme of human disobedience and insubordination works within my interpretation below. For now, however, it is sufficient to point out that the interpretation that stresses human maturation, while providing an important etiological understanding of Gen 2–3, is ultimately lacking, because it fails to deal adequately with the role that both the divine command and human disobedience play in the narrative.

To summarize, traditional interpretations of Gen 2–3 have overemphasized themes such as the fall or original sin, even when these themes are absent from the text itself, and no interpretative tradition within the Hebrew Bible appropriates this understanding of the Edenic narrative. Biblical scholars, emphasizing the historical-critical or ancient Near Eastern comparative methodology, have surfaced other themes: human maturation and Yahweh's grace in spite of human rebellion. While these themes provide an intriguing read of this creation narrative and address the difficulties in the traditional interpretation of Gen 2–3, they often fail to account for the conflicted characterization of Yahweh, the problematic divine command, and the role of human disobedience.

I would add that both the traditional and the scholarly interpretations of Gen 2–3 minimize or rationalize a central crux within the story. Yahweh's command has been broken, a crime that is punishable by death within the narrative (Gen 2:17). There is, however, no death in this passage. The human beings disobey the Creator, but they do not die. Instead, the deity removes the human beings from Eden so that they cannot eat from the tree of life and become immortal! This development in the story is surprising. It is no wonder that interpreters both modern and ancient have put forth much interpretative energy to make sense of this discrepancy by spiritualizing, rationalizing, or ignoring death in the story.[9] The interpretation that I offer below suggests that this lacuna is a key element in the text for the reader, pointing to humanity's ability to survive in spite of the arbitrary command from a threatened authority figure. Thus, my interpretation

---

9. For a thorough discussion of how different interpreters deal with death in this passage, see Whybray 1996, 91–98. Whybray rightly notes that the phrase *mot tamut* ("you shall surely die"), in conjunction with *beyom*, suggests a "death sentence which, although it may not be executed precisely within twenty-four hours, will be executed swiftly, and is the consequence of a specific criminal act" (91).

emphasizes the theme of human survival in the midst of adversity and hostile authority. Before I put forward my own interpretative thoughts on Gen 2–3, which are formed by the experience of the Japanese internment, let me quickly sketch some of the issues and themes that come from that experience.

THE EXILE OF A PEOPLE: THE JAPANESE INTERNMENT OF WORLD WAR II

A qualification is in order. My understanding of the Japanese and Japanese American internment, certainly not the only understanding, is necessarily shaped by my experience as a Sansei: a third-generation Japanese American. I grew up in a predominantly white, upper-middle class suburb in Southern California. I converted to Protestant Christianity when I was in college and proceeded to do my master's and Ph.D. work in biblical studies at a Protestant seminary in the northeastern United States. Neither of my parents was interned, though my father's family was evacuated, like most of the Japanese and Japanese Americans on the West Coast during World War II. The FBI arrested my paternal grandfather like many other Issei, first-generation Japanese American men. My father's family, with several other Japanese families, was permitted to move to a "safe zone" on an abandoned farm in Keatly, Utah. Ironically, though they had more freedom than the families who were interned in camps, their living conditions were almost as poor, and they were not always as well-protected from the surrounding community, where war hysteria had taken hold. Like most Japanese families who were evacuated, my father's family lost almost everything that they had owned. Though my parents were not interned, most of my relatives and friends in the Japanese American community are connected to the experience of the internment in a direct way. Moreover, the internment was a profoundly significant event in Japanese American history and had a decisive effect on Japanese American identity in the second half of the twentieth century, particularly for those Japanese Americans who lived on the West Coast of the United States. It was the critical, defining moment for many within Japanese American communities.[10]

Having now situated myself as an interpreter, let me move forward by painting some broad strokes concerning the dynamics in and around the Japanese internment. The internment of Japanese and Japanese Americans during World War II was and continues to be the pivotal event in Japanese American consciousness. On 19 February 1942, in response to Japan's bombing of Pearl Harbor, Franklin D. Roosevelt signed Executive Order 9066, which allowed for the imprisonment of over 120,000 people of Japanese ancestry, a large number

---

10. Literary and scholarly treatments on the internment are too numerous to list. Some representative discussions include: Daniels 1981; 1993; Nagata 1993; Okihiro 1999; and Inada 2000. The autobiographical works of David Mura have also shaped the present author's understanding of the internment and Japanese American identity (1992; 1996).

of them American citizens by birth. They were moved into isolated camps throughout the western United States because of racist policies on the part of high-ranking officials such as Lieutenant General John L. DeWitt and Secretary of War Henry L. Stimson. Many within the government believed that people of Japanese ancestry posed a threat to national security. The Japanese and Japanese American people were imprisoned solely on the basis of race and ethnicity without due process of law.

The U.S. government later admitted wrongdoing in an official report of the Commission on Wartime Relocation and Internment of Civilians, a commission that was created by Congress. The report reads:

> The promulgation of Executive Order 9066 was not justified by military necessity, and the decisions which followed from it ... were not driven by analysis of military conditions. The broad historical causes which shaped these decisions were race prejudice, war hysteria, and a failure of political leadership. Widespread ignorance of Japanese Americans contributed to a policy conceived in haste and executed in an atmosphere of fear and anger at Japan. A grave injustice was done to American citizens and resident aliens of Japanese ancestry who, without individual review or any probative evidence against them, were excluded, removed and detained by the United States during World War II. (Daniels 1981, 5)

Even though the government officially apologized, it took almost forty years for redress to become a reality. This unfortunate series of events left an indelible mark on the Japanese American community and its identity. The already difficult tension between the preservation of cultural identity and integration into American culture was made increasingly difficult through the internment experience.

Within the camps, the different Japanese American communities and generations were torn. Some believed that complying with the government was the best strategy for survival. For these the best way out of the camps was for the internees to show their loyalty and commitment to America.[11] Others, however, believed that resistance and civil disobedience was more appropriate.[12] This disagreement

---

11. Japanese American expressions of loyalty to the United States during the internment are well documented. The Japanese American Citizens League (JACL) was a predominantly Nisei (second-generation) organization. During the internment, the JACL encouraged detainees to answer affirmatively on two crucial questions within the War Relocation Authority's (WRA) questionnaire. Question 27 asked those within the camps whether or not they were willing to serve in the U.S. military. Question 28 asked internees if they would swear allegiance to the U.S., disavowing loyalty to the Japanese emperor. The highly decorated 442nd Regiment and the 100th Battalion are examples of all-Japanese American troops that volunteered for the war (Takaki 1998, 400–404).

12. Some Japanese Americans resisted the camps and the subsequent draft into the armed forces (Daniels 1993, 58–71). John Okada, in his fictional piece *No-No Boy*, looks at the damag-

within the Japanese American community continues to be a painful topic.[13] After the camps, the response of most Issei and Nisei, first- and second-generation Japanese Americans, was unanimous—silence. Also, many, though not all, Nisei came out of their camp experience vowing to be doubly American. This conflicted patriotic response was hard to understand for their later, more Americanized Sansei children, who grew up during the 1960s and 1970s with the rhetoric of civil rights deeply engrained in their consciousness. A Nisei author, Yoshiko Uchida, describes this dynamic in *Desert Exile*:

> Today some of the Nisei, having overcome the traumatizing effects of their incarceration and participated in a wide spectrum of American life with no little success, are approaching retirement. Their Sansei children, who experienced the Vietnam War, with its violent confrontations and protest marches, have asked questions about those early World War II years.
>
> Why did you let it happen? They ask of the evacuation. Why didn't you fight for your civil rights? Why did you go without protest to the concentration camps? They were right to ask those questions, for they made us search for some obscured truths and come to a better understanding of ourselves and of those times.... They are the generation who taught us to celebrate our ethnicity and discover our ethnic pride....
>
> It is my generation, however, who lived through the evacuation of 1942. We are their link to the past and we must provide them all ... we can remember, so they can better understand the history of their own people. As they listen to our voices from the past, however, I ask that they remember they are listening in a totally different time; in a totally changed world. (1982, 147)

I would suggest that all of these responses to the events surrounding the internment share a theme of survival and community preservation. The nationally

---

ing effects of the WRA's questionnaire and the consequences for those who answered negatively on both the issue of the draft (question 27) and forswearing allegiance to the Japanese emperor (question 28). Others within the camps sought to dissent by renouncing their U.S. citizenship (Nagata 1993, 13–14).

13. Tensions around issues of loyalty and dissent during World War II arose in the Japanese American community when a quotation from Mike Masaoka was proposed as one of several inscriptions for the National Japanese American Memorial in Washington, D.C. Masaoka, a leader in the JACL during World War II, advocated complete loyalty to the U.S. government during the internment. The JACL allegedly supplied the FBI with information about Japanese American community members. His quotation was part of the JACL superpatriotic creed: "I am proud that I am an American citizen of Japanese ancestry, for my very background makes me appreciate more fully the wonderful advantages of this nation. I believe in her institutions, ideals and traditions; I glory in her heritage; I boast of her history; I trust in her future" (cited from Daniels 1993, 20). Though the memorial board voted to keep the inscription, the arguments over its inclusion resurfaced old wounds within the Japanese American community around these issues.

decorated heroism of the 442nd Regiment and the 100th Battalion, both all-Japanese American military units, on the one hand, and the "No-No Boys," who refused to disavow loyalty to the Japanese emperor and serve in the U.S. military, on the other, represent examples of the conflicting and conflicted responses of a community that was struggling to preserve its identity in the midst of unjustified war hysteria. Even the silences and hyper-patriotic responses to be doubly American were survival strategies. It was a response motivated not only by the survival instincts of those who endured the camps, but as many Nisei would repeat as a mantra, they did it *kodomo no tame ni*, "for the sake of the children."[14] Hence, the survival and persistence of the Japanese American community after World War II was difficult and conflicted, and represented the internal and external contradictions of living in a country that perceived the Japanese as a threat.

Hence, the internment of Japanese and Japanese Americans in the 1940s has at least two persistent themes that relate to the present study of Gen 2–3. One theme points to the paranoid response of a government that used its authority to exercise control over its Japanese American subjects. The U.S. officials and agencies misused their power to imprison more than 120,000 people of Japanese descent, because they perceived these "others" to be a threat to national security.[15] Within this environment of fear and suspicion, arbitrary laws and legislation were created in order to maintain the status quo. In spite of this situation, the Japanese American community was able to survive, even thrive, in the midst of a hostile environment. Thus, the second theme points to the problematic and conflicted survival strategies of the Japanese and Japanese American people. These prominent themes, which emerge out of the historical experience of Japanese Americans, have significant points of intersection with the Eden story. It is to this other formative (hi)story that I now I turn.

THE GARDEN AND EXILE: A JAPANESE AMERICAN READING OF GENESIS 2–3

I will focus my interpretative thoughts on themes that emerge from the story of Eden when read inter(con)textually[16] with the Japanese American experience of

---

14. See Takaki's discussion of this phrase and its social significance (1998, 179–230, 357–405).

15. The post-9/11 ethos has created a similar environment of fear and paranoia in the name of national security, which has affected the lives of many Muslims. See the website from the Study of Islam Section of the American Academy of Religion, which was created in response to the issues that arose following 9/11.

16. Jean Kim and Uriah Kim both use the term "intercontextual" to describe their mode of culturally informed biblical interpretation. My use of the term "inter(con)textually" has a dual purpose. First, as I stated above, I am reading Gen 2–3 intertexually with the Japanese internment. Second, the blurring of context and text points to the ways that a reader's location or social context creates new interpretative possibilities.

internment as described above. Consistent with my exploration of the Japanese American internment, I will look specifically at the characterization of Yahweh's problematic authority in Gen 2–3 and the theme of human survival in the midst of a life of adversity. This last idea is all but absent in the traditional and scholarly interpretations of Edenic narrative, even though, as I will argue, such a theme makes perfect sense, given the context of exile within which significant editorial shaping of the Genesis and pentateuchal literature occurs.

Genesis 2–3 is an etiology that describes certain facets of human existence within creation. It helps to answer questions about human origins: how human beings were created; why human beings are ashamed of being naked; why women hate snakes; why the soil seems to resist human labor; why women have pain in childbirth; and why human beings cannot attain immortality. By combining this type of story within a series of genealogies or *toledot* formulas in the book of Genesis, the final editors or shapers effectively tie human history back to an original set of parents, indeed back to creation itself. The J narrative immediately follows the phrase, "These are the generations of the heavens and the earth" (2:4a). Hence, Israel's primordial ancestors are tied back to the very beginning of creation. In this way, Gen 2–3 serves as a family story of origins that not only traces Israel's ancestry back to the beginning but also reminds them of the realities of human existence. It is a formative story that shapes readers' perceptions of identity. That Gen 2–3 is an etiology is well-established. The question, however, remains: What does this story describe about human existence? I will explore this more below.

The environmental setting of the Eden story is not initially described as a garden paradise but as a barren desert land (Kennedy 1990, 4–5; Yee 2003, 69). One of the purposes of this narrative is to depict the creation of humankind. Hence, the emptiness of the land carries a certain meaning, namely, that the land is lifeless prior to the creation of the human beings.[17] The wording in the text suggests that the original state of the land is inhospitable for life. Water comes up from the ground (2:6), but no plant or herb grows, and no one is present to work the ground (2:5). The Garden of Eden does not exist until after Yahweh Elohim creates *ha'adam*: "Yahweh Elohim planted a garden in Eden, in the east; and there he set the human whom he had fashioned" (2:8). Thus, the garden is a work of the deity's own making.

---

17. I agree with Westermann, who argues against von Rad that the aridness of the land is not symbolic of primordial chaos. The language of the text points to the "lifeless earth of the desert" (1984, 199).

Similarly, the internment camps were located "at desolate, faraway sites where no one had lived before and no one has lived since" (Daniels 1993, 66).[18] Takaki, utilizing the experiences of internees, describes the setting for the camps:

> Most of the camps were located in remote desert areas.... "No houses were in sight, no trees or anything green—only scrubby sagebrush and an occasional low cactus, and mostly dry, baked earth." They looked around them and saw hundreds of miles of wasteland, "beyond the end of the horizon and again over the mountain—again, more wasteland." They were surrounded by dust and sand. (1998, 395)

These concentration camps,[19] which the U.S. government authorized and the War Relocation Authority organized and maintained, were situated in isolated, uninhabited areas in order to minimize the perceived threat of a concentrated Japanese population. The camps were "safe" locations and provided the U.S. government with the illusion of control over issues of national security. However, to the Japanese Americans who lived behind the barbed wire, under the watchful surveillance of armed military guards, these secured lands were prisons. They were sites of captivity that prohibited the Japanese Americans from access to American public life. Ironically, Manzanar, a camp that was located in an isolated area of California, is Spanish for "apple orchard." When the Japanese Americans arrived at the site, however, no fruit or trees were left. What remained of this *manzanar* was the dust, the wind, and the harsh natural elements. Thus, the WRA and the war department turned this windy desert area into a human dwelling by an act of force, creating Manzanar—an orchard of the U.S. government's making—out of the dust and barren land.[20]

What does Manzanar have to do with Eden? My original question has become pregnant with meaning. How does a garden (or an orchard) emerge in the middle of the desert? How do humans maintain life in a garden not of their own making? When is a desert a garden, and when does a garden/orchard become a prison? In order to explore these questions, one must first look at the characterization of authority that maintains the right to make gardens in the desert.

---

18. The ten internment sites were "Topaz in Utah, Poston and Gila River in Arizona, Amache in Colorado, Jerome and Rower in Arkansas, Minidoka in Idaho, Manzanar and Tule Lake in California, and Heart Mountain in Wyoming" (Takaki 1998, 395).

19. The U.S. government preferred to call the camps "relocation centers" to avoid comparison with the Nazi death camps of World War II. While it is certainly the case that the Japanese Americans were treated more humanely, I agree with those like Kitano and Daniels, who designate these sites as concentration camps (Kitano and Daniels 1995, 65–66).

20. I thank Fernando Segovia and Francisco García-Treto for the insight about the irony inherent in the name Manzanar (personal communication). Manzanar was a thriving farming community in the early twentieth century, until water was diverted from this location to supply the growing population in the Los Angeles area.

YAHWEH'S AUTHORITY: ARBITRARY COMMAND, CONTROL, AND THE THREAT OF HUMANITY

When the Edenic narrative is placed in conversation with the Japanese American experience of internment, certain aspects of authority become prominent. Yahweh is perceived as a threatened deity/ruler who exercises control over the subjects in the garden by barring access to knowledge and life through an arbitrary command. The characterization of Yahweh as a king or political ruler is well-established, especially among interpreters who stress a materialist approach to the text (Yee 2003, 67–79; Kennedy 1990). Throughout the story, Yahweh Elohim's characterization is set over against the description of the humans. As the plot progresses, the distance between deity/king and humanity/subject becomes increasingly pronounced (Yee 2003, 69). One can detect this distance in Yahweh's prohibition not to eat from the tree of knowledge. Scholars have long debated the meaning of this tree.[21] The story makes clear, however, that the tree has at least two functions in the story. First, the tree becomes the locus for obedience/disobedience because of Yahweh's arbitrary imperative not to eat from it (2:17). Regardless of the nature of the fruit, the function of the tree is tied directly to the deity's prohibition and humanity's response (Trible 1976, 87). Second, the tree of the knowledge of good and evil functions initially as a way to distinguish between the divine and the human. As the serpent later makes clear, this knowledge has the potential to make the human beings like the gods, "knowing good and evil" (3:5). Yee states the social significance of this divine/human differentiation:

> The ruling elite hold the monopoly on wisdom, and according to their ideology, the ignorance of the peasant is part and parcel of the created social order. Should the peasant obtain a greater critical knowledge of the real state of affairs governing his life, it would constitute a danger to the elite's tight political control. (2003, 70)

Hence, "knowledge" in this passage is under the direct control of Yahweh Elohim. The deity's command functions in this passage to maintain distance between the divine and human realms. The text does not give an explicit reason for the command; thus, the prohibition not to eat from the tree of knowledge is arbitrary. Yahweh's motivation only becomes clear later in the text, after the human beings disobey the command. In this etiology, authority uses its power to maintain distance between the gods and humans.

Moreover, the story's focus on the command is made clearer through the character of the serpent. The serpent's comments to Eve question the veracity of Yahweh Elohim's command and threat: "Did God really say, 'You shall not eat

---

21. There has been much discussion on the meaning of the tree of knowledge. For a complete discussion, see Westermann:241–45; Wallace:115–32; and Barr:57–72.

from any tree of the garden?'" (3:1). After the woman reiterates the divine command, the serpent contends, "You will surely not die" (3:4). Given the fact that
Yahweh Elohim's power in the story is analogous to that of a king/ruler, the serpent represents "perceived and actual dangers to the state" (Yee 2003, 72). That is,
the serpent's character has a symbolic function in that it represents anything that
questions the legitimacy of the ruling authority, including that authority's right
to control access to knowledge through an arbitrary command.[22] Furthermore,
in a story world where a command becomes the focal point of the plot, human
actions or inactions are characterized within the limited framework of obedience/
disobedience to the state. Human beings can either comply or rebel within such
parameters. Characters must take sides, and the authority perceives as a threat
any statement or action that questions the integrity of the command.

The motivation for Yahweh Elohim's prohibition becomes clear after the
humans eat from the tree of knowledge. After spelling out the consequences for
disobedience in 3:14–19 to all parties involved, Yahweh Elohim makes a statement that reveals the deity's sense of danger and threat. The ruler of the garden
acknowledges that the human beings, by obtaining knowledge of good and evil,
have become like the gods. God now fears that the human beings will become
immortal: "lest he [the human] put forth his hand and take also from the tree
of life, and eat, and live forever" (3:22). This phrase provides the reader with the
first indication of Yahweh Elohim's motivation for prohibiting the humans to eat
from the tree of knowledge. The initial command functioned to create distance
between the divine and the human, barring the couple's access to knowledge. This
final declaration makes clear that Yahweh's primary motivation for keeping the
human beings without knowledge was to prevent them from becoming immortal.
That is, God seeks to maintain social order—to preserve the division between the
human and divine realms. The human beings have become unsafe because they
have transgressed the boundary between the gods and humanity. Thus, Yahweh
Elohim's final statement in the Edenic scene reveals the deity's threatened status.
The human subjects have become dangerous, and their subordinate status must be
preserved. Hence, Yahweh Elohim clothes them with skins, a symbolic reminder
that they are human and not divine,[23] and drives (*wayegaresh*) them from the
garden. God exiles the human beings because they represent a threat to the divine
realm. Cherubim with flaming swords guard the garden to prevent any further

---

22. Yee suggests different possibilities for the specific meaning of this threat, including
Kennedy's proposal that the snake represents the danger of an informed peasantry rebelling
against the state (Yee 2003, 72–73; Kennedy 1990, 8–9).

23. Scholars often view Yahweh Elohim's clothing of the humans as an act of grace or
mercy (von Rad 1972, 96–97; Brueggemann 1982, 50; Trible 1976, 134). Robert Oden, however,
has argued persuasively that clothing in the ancient Near East is a symbol that firmly distinguishes humans from the gods (1987, 104; followed also by Yee 2003, 76).

attempts by the humans to transgress their status. Though the human beings have been exiled from the garden, the divine control over issues of life remains.

Hence, Yahweh Elohim is characterized within the Eden story as an authority figure who rules by control. The deity attempts to maintain social order through an arbitrary command and, when the threat of the humans becomes too great, removes the couple by forceful exile. The primary motivation for the ruler's behavior is based on fear and the threat of the other. Within this context of divine suspicion, the human beings' actions become suspect, and the range of options for human initiative is restricted to obedience or disobedience: a yes or no to the divine imperative.

HUMAN SURVIVAL OUTSIDE THE GARDEN

My second observation revolves around what I see to be the most significant plot twist within the Edenic story: the fact that the human beings do not die. One of the most problematic and overinterpreted details in Gen 2–3 occurs when Yahweh commands the first human, "You may surely eat from every tree in the garden; but from the tree of the knowledge of good and evil you shall not eat, for in the day that you eat of it you shall surely die" (2:16b–17). The plot thickens in Gen 3 when the serpent, whom the narrator describes as "cunning," comes and counsels Eve about the very fruit that Yahweh has said not to eat. When the serpent asks Eve if they may eat of every tree, the woman repeats Yahweh's command that they shall not eat from the tree in the middle of the garden or they will die (3:3). The serpent declares, "Surely you will not die," and proceeds to tell Eve that the fruit will open their eyes, giving them knowledge of good and evil.

The surprising twist in this text does not revolve around the human beings' disobedience to Yahweh's command, though such actions have inevitable consequences. Nowhere in this story does it suggest that human beings were made perfect or sinless. In fact, an ancient Near Eastern or Israelite audience would have assumed that human beings are fallible and prone toward rebellion against the gods.[24] Nor is it surprising that humans experience shame and painful consequences from knowledge. This fact is something that the audience of Gen 2–3

---

24. In the ancient Near East and in ancient Israel, the concept of human fallibility and rebellion against the gods was well known. In Mesopotamian flood narratives such as the Epic of Gilgamesh and Atrahasis, the gods destroy humankind because they are noisy and rebellious. A Sumerian proverb from the early second millennium B.C.E., Man and His God, reads, "Never has a sinless child been born to its mother." Examples abound in the biblical text as well. For example, in Ps 51 the psalmist states, "Indeed, I was born guilty, a sinner when my mother conceived me" (51:5). It is important to point out that nowhere in the Genesis text are we given an indication to think that humanity is in an original sinless state, that the disobedience in the garden is a sin that moves humanity from perfection to imperfection. In fact, the easier, less-forced interpretation would be to assume that the narrator assumes that humans will bite on the

would know well about human existence. Life is filled with pain and suffering. The surprise comes when, after the primordial parents eat, they do not die. Yahweh's command is clear. If the humans eat the fruit of the tree of knowledge, they will most certainly die. The emphatic nature of this command is made clear with the use in Hebrew of the infinitive absolute and imperfect in combination (*mot tamut*). The humans eat the fruit, but they do not die. In fact, the plot has not unfolded according to the command of Yahweh, but according to the prediction of the serpent. When the man and woman eat of the fruit of knowledge, their eyes are opened, and they do not experience death. Many interpreters, in an allegorical-like fashion, try to figure out ways to preserve death in this text, for example: spiritual death, death of innocence, and the human couple's eventual physical death.[25] The less-forced reading of the story, however, would be to say that there is no death in Gen 2–3. Yahweh, after cursing the snake to live a life upon its belly, simply spells out the consequences of the humans' actions: women will have pain in childbirth, and the ground will be cursed, growing thorns and thistles while yielding its produce with difficulty. Death is not proclaimed as a consequence of or punishment for eating from the tree of knowledge. The human beings do not die but survive even after they have broken the divine command.

The canonical context of this passage points further to the surprising nature of this turn of events. The final shape of this story puts it immediately after the Priestly creation story, in which the divine command of Elohim brings about an ordered world. God speaks and things happen. In Gen 1:3, Elohim says, "Let there be light," to which the narrator concludes, "and there was light." The creation story of Gen 1 points to an ordered creation that obeys the voice of its Creator. Thus, the opening of the book of Genesis unfolds like a cosmic liturgy of call and response. Within this narrative context, humanity's disobedience to the command of Yahweh, while not a surprise to the reader, acts as a foil to the unfolding of events within Gen 1. What is shocking, however, is that the deity's words do not come to pass, as they do with cyclical regularity in Gen 1 with the word of Elohim. Yahweh had said that death would result from eating the fruit of the tree of knowledge, but, when the humans eat from the tree, they do not die.

In fact, the Yahwist creation story itself suggests that even Yahweh is not prepared for the human beings' course of action. Genesis 3:22 reads, "Then the LORD God said, 'The human has become like one of us, knowing good and evil; and now, he might put forth his hand and take also from the tree of life, and eat, and live forever.'" As stated above, Yahweh's words suggest that the deity is threatened by the possibility that the humans could become immortal. Yahweh

---

snake's temptation all along, especially since the quest by humans for immortality and to be like the gods is also a prominent theme in other ancient Near Eastern myths.

25. For examples of how interpreters deal with death in Gen 2–3 within postbiblical Jewish literature, see Kvam et al. 1999, 43–45.

now perceives the humans as a threat to the security of the divine realm. Thus, Yahweh sends the humans forth from the garden and blocks the entrance with a cherub, wielding a flaming sword so that they cannot return. The garden was kept secure by the deity's command. When the command failed, however, the ruler of the garden banishes the humans from their home, barring access to their former way of life. Yahweh is a god who creates exile, a reality that Israel knew all too well. In spite of the fact that death had been pronounced upon the human couple and they have been exiled from Eden, in the end they do not die as Yahweh had proclaimed but continue to live their lives away from the center. Yahweh seems unprepared for this turn of events. The human beings continue to survive, albeit outside of the garden.

Looking further at the larger canonical and narrative context of Gen 2–3, one can trace how the theme of human survival in the midst of adversity continues to develop. Chapter 4 begins, "The man knew his wife Eve, and she conceived and bore Cain." The original human family, who managed to live even when Yahweh had announced their death, produces future generations of the human family. It is significant that Adam and Eve's first action outside of the garden is to make more humans. Not only does the human family fail to die, but they continue to live and multiply. In addition, the first event after the garden scene is tied directly to the series of curses that result from Adam and Eve's disobedience. One aspect of the woman's curse is that she will have pain in childbearing. Her first act outside of the garden is to give birth to a son, Cain. Similarly, Adam's curse mentions difficulties with agriculture. The narrator makes clear in Gen 4:2 that Cain was a "tiller of the ground." These thematic ties between Gen 2–3 and Gen 4 suggest that the human family continues to live even after such activities have been cursed with pain and suffering as announced by Yahweh in Gen 3:15–19.

The etiological/genealogical stories found within Gen 2–3, which trace humanity's roots to the beginning of creation, describe how the human family has an almost stubborn ability to survive even when death has been announced. Human beings continue to live, even when their lives are marked with the knowledge that life is filled with pain, suffering, and conflict. One of the consequences of human disobedience in Gen 2–3 is that human beings are set against God, each other, and the created order. Human beings must disobey their Creator in order to acquire the knowledge of being human. When they attain this knowledge, they are forcefully barred from immortality and their garden realm. Human beings resort to blame when things go wrong (3:12–13). Snakes are set against women (3:15), and the ground is cursed on account of the humans. This series of consequences paint a picture of human existence as being full of conflict, resulting in a life that is painful and full of suffering. The Cain and Abel story in Gen 4 continues this theme. In spite of this painful knowledge, however, human beings continue to live, even thrive in their life of adversity. They survive, make more humans, and continue to fill the earth.

As the story progresses, this theme is prominent within Israel's epic tradition and canonical story. When the human beings multiply and violence fills the earth, Yahweh cleanses the world through a flood, a cosmic reversal moving the created order back into the watery chaos (see Gen 1:2). Noah's family shows its ancestral lineage to their Edenic parents by surviving the re-creation of the world through the building of an ark. Later Israelite traditions also testify to the theme of human survival in the midst of adversity: through the exodus, the wilderness, into a new land, all the way through the Babylonian exile. Surviving adversity is part of what makes Israel, Israel. Even the name Israel, which is given to Jacob their ancestor in a folk etymology, means "one who strives with God" (Gen 32:28). Surviving adversity is also, as the story in Eden suggests, what makes humans, human. Like the Japanese Americans who were exiled within their own land but continued to survive, some would say even thrive, in an untidy world filled with the painful knowledge of life in North America, so too the Israelites persisted and continued to live even when death was proclaimed for them in a land that was not their home.

THE CONTEXTUAL NATURE OF DISOBEDIENCE

In closing, I must address the question of how disobedience functions in the Edenic narrative. As suggested above, the traditional reading of Gen 2–3 has taken this small but crucial theme and made it central, creating a doctrine of original sin. On the other hand, biblical scholars who support the human maturation interpretation tend to minimize this feature of the story. Disobedience does play a key role in Gen 2–3, because human noncompliance to the divine command leads to Adam and Eve's expulsion from the garden. Their actions are also what help Adam and Eve become aware of the knowledge that life is painful. That human disobedience plays a key role in the Edenic narrative is not disputable.

I would argue, however, that the meaning and function of human rebellion in Gen 2–3 depends on the context in which obedience/disobedience is assumed. Interpreters have often sided with Yahweh in this text without questioning the ethical consequences of such an interpretation in different contexts. When interpreters align their perspective with the divine point of view, human disobedience, which is usually equated with sin, creates a rift between God and humanity. Human beings are blamed for the resulting alienation from God, and life is full of suffering because of Adam and Eve's sin. The humans have created this painful reality through their disobedience (von Rad 1972, 101–2; Fretheim 1994, 148). Humanity's inability to conform to the divine imperative results in social disorder and chaos. Within such interpretations, human beings should maintain their "rightful" place, and Yahweh the king is justified in punishing those who transgress Yahweh's command. When translated into the social realm, the meaning of this text is clear. Human beings should not seek to transgress their place within society. One must learn to rely on the benevolence and wisdom of the king. When humans act autonomously, even if their desire is to acquire knowledge, bad things happen. It is no wonder that scholars have long argued for the early monarchy as being the historical context for this Yahwistic narrative. The danger of this position, however, is that such interpretations produce meaning structures that function to reinforce the logic of the status quo, contributing to cultures of violence against people who are considered as other in the system.[26] Divine authority and social order are given preference over the particularities of human experience. Disobedience is a threat to social order, and, thus, ruling authority is justified in suppressing humanity's initiative, especially in the name of state security.

Moreover, when one considers that the final shape of the Pentateuch was completed in the postexilic period, the logic of reading through a promonarchial lens does not make as much sense. Those who were in exile would have had a much more ambivalent view of kingship. Both the Israelite and Judean monarchies ultimately failed, a point that the Deuteronomistic History emphasizes. Moreover, the most visible sign of royal authority in exile was either a Babylonian or Persian king. One would expect that myths that involved the characterization of Yahweh as king would also be reframed or reinterpreted within a context where royal authority was capricious and potentially harmful to its citizens, especially if the exile was sanctioned by divine authority. Within an exilic context, the logic of obedience/disobedience breaks down. When the deity has made a decision about the fate of a nation, the options left to the human subjects are limited and problematic. How does one accept the fate of an exilic punishment and still remain loyal to the God who has decreed a people's alienation?

When one puts the Edenic narrative in conversation with the Japanese and Japanese American internment, a more complex picture of disobedience emerges. As my reading of Gen 2–3 suggests, Yahweh is characterized as a deity who is threatened by the human beings' acquisition of knowledge and life. When Yahweh's arbitrary command not to eat from the tree of knowledge is broken, the ruler of the garden exiles the human beings. As I argued above, when a suspicious governing authority gives an arbitrary command, the options for the ruled subjects become limited between the constrained polarity of obedience/disobedience. As the experience of Japanese Americans suggest, this harsh reality results in difficult consequences for whatever way of life the human subjects choose.

---

26. Cheryl Anderson, in her recent book *Women, Ideology, and Violence* (2004), contributes to the growing literature on biblically inscribed violence and violent cultures. She argues that the biblical material, specifically the legal material, contributes to cultures of violence against women. Anderson's work contributes to this area of study by showing the ways in which these cultures of violence affect the arenas of both gender and race/ethnicity simultaneously. Anderson builds off the work of Harold Washington, who has written on how violent cultures are reinforced through the biblical material, specifically cultures that exhibit violence against women (1997; 1998).

One must either decide between the harsh realities of a life that is not human—a life without knowledge or wisdom—or face the penalty for noncompliance in an atmosphere of divine suspicion. For those who were interned during World War II, the dualism took the form of compliance with the U.S. government's imprisonment or further punishment for noncooperation.

Hence, when readers take up the point of view of displaced peoples in the garden story, a different set of meanings surface. Within a setting of mistrust and control, marked by the arbitrary command of a suspicious ruling authority, the primordial parents must decide between a denial of their human existence and the consequences of a life in exilic noncompliance. The first humans choose to transgress the boundaries that Yahweh Elohim had created for them. They choose to survive in a life that would now be marked with suffering and painful existence. In our present day, the governing authorities in the U.S. justify much of their actions through the rationale of national security. An environment of suspicion and fear has been created and reinforced through the Patriot Act and recent legislative movements on immigration.[27] Thousands of people, especially those of Arab descent or Muslim persuasion, have been imprisoned or harassed, forced to make a choice within the constrained duality of community preservation and loyalty to the United States. In this historical setting, siding with a ruling authority's point of view can have devastating consequences for the human subjects involved.

WORKS CONSULTED

Anderson, Cheryl. 2004. *Women, Ideology, and Violence: Critical Theory and the Construction of Gender in the Book of the Covenant and the Deuteronomistic Law.* JSOTSup 394. London: T&T Clark.

Barr, James. 1993. *The Garden of Eden and the Hope of Immortality.* Minneapolis: Fortress.

Bechtel, Lyn M. 1995. Genesis 2.4b–3.24: A Myth About Human Maturation. *JSOT* 67:3–26.

Brueggemann, Walter. 1982. *Genesis.* IBC. Atlanta: John Knox.

Carmichael, Calum M. 1992. The Paradise Myth: Interpreting without Jewish and Christian Spectacles. Pages 47–63 in *A Walk in the Garden: Biblical, Iconographical and Literary Images of Eden.* Edited by Paul Morris and Deborah Sawyer. JSOTSup 136. Sheffield: Sheffield Academic Press.

Daniels, Roger. 1981. *Concentration Camps, North America: Japanese in the United States and Canada During World War II.* Malabar: Krieger.

———. 1991. The Conference Keynote Address: Relocation, Redress, and the Report: A Historical Appraisal. Pages 3–9 in *Japanese Americans: From Relo-*

---

27. For responses to Islamophobia in the post-9/11 aftermath, see Zine 2003.

cation to Redress. Rev. ed. Edited by Roger Daniels, Sandra C. Taylor, and Harry H. L. Kitano. Seattle: University of Washington Press.

———. 1993. *Prisoners without Trial: Japanese Americans in World War II*. New York: Hill & Wang.

Fretheim, Terence E. 1994. Is Genesis 3 A Fall Story? *Word and World* 14:144–53.

Gunkel, Hermann. 1997. *Genesis*. Translated by Mark E. Biddle. Macon, Ga.: Mercer University Press.

Inada, Lawson Fusao, ed. 2000. *Only What We Could Carry: The Japanese American Internment Experience*. Berkeley: Hayday.

Jacobsen, Thorkild. 1976. *The Treasures of Darkness: A History of Mesopotamian Religion*. New Haven: Yale University Press.

Kennedy, James M. 1990. Peasants in Revolt: Political Allegory in Genesis 2–3. *JSOT* 47:3–14.

Kim, Jean. 2004. *Woman and Nation: An Intercontextual Reading of the Gospel of John*. Biblical Interpretation Series 69. Leiden: Brill.

Kim, Uriah Y. 2005. *Decolonizing Josiah: Toward a Postcolonial Reading of the Deuteronomistic History*. The Bible in the Modern World 5. Sheffield: Sheffield Phoenix.

Kitano, Harry H. L., and Roger Daniels. 1995. *Asian Americans: Emerging Minorities*. 2nd ed. Englewood Cliffs, N.J.: Prentice Hall.

Kvam, Kristen E., Linda S. Schearing, and Valarie H. Ziegler, eds. 1999. *Eve and Adam: Jewish, Christian, and Muslim Readings on Genesis and Gender*. Bloomington: Indiana University Press.

Meyers, Carol. 1988. *Discovering Eve: Ancient Israelite Women in Context*. New York: Oxford University Press.

———. 1993. Gender Roles and Genesis 3:16 Revisited. Pages 118–41 in *A Feminist Companion to Genesis*. Edited by Athalya Brenner. FCB 2. Sheffield: Sheffield Academic Press.

Mura, David. 1992. *Turning Japanese: Memoirs of a Sansei*. New York: Anchor.

———. 1996. *Where the Body Meets Memory: An Odyssey of Race, Sexuality, and Identity*. New York: Anchor.

Nagata, Donna K. 1993. *Legacy of Injustice: Exploring the Cross-Generational Impact of the Japanese Internment*. Critical Issues in Social Justice. New York: Plenum.

Oden, Robert A., Jr. 1987. *The Bible without Theology: The Theological Tradition and Alternatives to It*. San Francisco: Harper & Row.

Okada, John. 1979. *No-No Boy*. Seattle: University of Washington Press.

Okihiro, Gary Y. 1999. *Storied Lives: Japanese American Students and World War II*. Seattle: University of Washington Press.

Pagels, Elaine. 1988. *Adam, Eve, and the Serpent: Sex and Politics in Early Christianity*. New York: Random House.

Rad, Gerhard von. 1972. *Genesis*. Rev. ed. OTL. Philadelphia: Westminster.

Segovia, Fernando F. 1995. Toward a Hermeneutics of the Diaspora: A Hermeneutics of Otherness and Engagement. Pages 1–32 in *Social Location and
Biblical Interpretation in the United States*. Vol. 1 of *Reading from This Place*.
Edited by Fernando F. Segovia and Mary Ann Tolbert. Minneapolis: Fortress.

Smith, Daniel L. 1990. *The Religion of the Landless: The Social Context of the Babylonian Exile*. Bloomington: Meyers-Stone.

Study of Islam Section of the American Academy of Religion. Online: http://
groups.colgate.edu/aarislam/response.htm.

Takaki, Ronald. 1998. *Strangers from a Different Shore: A History of Asian Americans*. Rev. ed. Boston: Backbay.

Trible, Phyllis. 1976. *God and the Rhetoric of Sexuality*. OBT. Philadelphia: Fortress.

Uchida, Yoshiko. 1982. *Desert Exile: The Uprooting of a Japanese American Family*.
Seattle: University of Washington Press.

Wallace, Howard N. 1985. *The Eden Narrative*. HSM 32. Atlanta: Scholars Press.

Washington, Harold C. 1997. Violence and the Construction of Gender in the
Hebrew Bible: A New Historicist Approach. *BibInt* 5:324–63.

———. 1998. Lest He Die in Battle and Another Man Take Her: Violence and the
Construction of Gender in the Laws of Deuteronomy 20–22. Pages 185–213
in *Gender and Law in the Hebrew Bible and the Ancient Near East*. Edited by
Victor H. Matthews, Bernard M. Levinson, and Tikva Frymer-Kensky. JSOT-
Sup 262. Sheffield: Sheffield Academic Press.

Westermann, Claus. 1984. *Genesis 1–11: A Commentary*. Translated by John J.
Scullion. Minneapolis: Augsburg.

White, Hayden. 1978. *Tropics of Discourse: Essays in Cultural Criticism*. Baltimore:
John Hopkins University Press.

———. 1987. *The Content of the Form: Narrative Discourse and Historical Representation*. Baltimore: John Hopkins University Press.

Whybray, Roger N. 1996. The Immorality of God: Reflections on Some Passages
in Genesis, Job, Exodus and Numbers. *JSOT* 72:89–120.

Wolde, Ellen van. 1989. *A Semiotic Analysis of Genesis 2–3: A Semiotic Theory and
Method of Analysis Applied to the Story of the Garden of Eden*. Studia semitica
neerlandica. Assen: Van Gorcum.

Yee, Gale A. 2003. *Poor Banished Children of Eve: Woman as Evil in the Hebrew
Bible*. Minneapolis: Fortress.

Zine, Jasmin. 2003. Dealing with September 12th: The Challenge of Anti-
Islamophobia Education. *Orbit* 33:3. Online: http://www.oise.utoronto.
ca/orbit/anti-racism_sample.html.

"She Stood in Tears Amid the Alien Corn": Ruth, the Perpetual Foreigner and Model Minority[1]

Gale A. Yee

One of the joys of reading a biblical text from my own social location was learning about the history of my people here in the States. I immersed myself into the vast field of Asian American studies. Even as it was an immensely satisfying experience, especially as I inserted my family's story into the larger narrative of the Chinese in America, it was also sobering. Our immigration history is one of bitter hardship and oppression. As I looked for a biblical text to explore through Asian American eyes, I found one that readily lent itself to such a reading. One can safely say that, of the books of the Hebrew Bible, the book of Ruth has captured the attention of many scholars interested in feminist and multicultural interpretations of the text.

The book conjoins issues of gender,[2] sexuality,[3] race/ethnicity, immigration (Honig 1999), nationality, assimilation, and class (Boer 2003) in tantalizing ways that allow different folk to read their own stories into the multivalent narrative of Ruth and Naomi. It is particularly apt for the purposes of this volume on minority criticism that the book of Ruth is the only biblical text bearing the name of a female Gentile,[4] a non-Jew, and a foreigner. The multicultural perspectives on the book of Ruth are a veritable global village: African-South African female (Masenya 1998; 2004), South African Indian female (Nadar 2001), Batswana female

---

1. The main title is from John Keats, "Ode to a Nightingale," st. 6.

2. The feminist bibliography on Ruth is large. For good starting points, see Brenner 1993; 1999a; Levine 1998; Kates and Reimer 1994. One of the earliest feminist commentaries makes Ruth into a proto-liberated woman who works for a living: "Ruth said to Naomi, I must not sit here with folded hands, nor spend my time in visiting neighbors, nor in such of amusement, but I must go forth to work, to provide food and clothes, and leave thee to rest.... It was evident that Ruth believed in the dignity of labor and of self-support" (Stanton 1993, 39).

3. Although this essay focuses primarily on race/ethnicity, I want to acknowledge the various readings of the homoeroticism in the book of Ruth: Duncan 2000; Alpert 1996; Jordan 1994; Exum 1996; Brenner 2005.

4. Bearing the title of a male Gentile is the book of Job.

(Dube 1999; 2001), Kenyan female (Kanyoro 1997), Mexican American male (Maldonado 1995), Costa Rican female (Foulkes 2003; Nayap-Pot 1999), Cuban American male (De La Torre 2000; García-Treto 2001), Hindu Indo-Guyanese female (Gossai 2000), Latin American female (Cavalcanti 1989), Brazilian male (Mesters 1985), Palestinian female (Raheb 2003), Hong Kong Chinese male (P. Lee 1989) and female (Kwok 2005; Wong 1999), Taiwanese female (Chu 1997), mainland (PRC) Chinese female (Kuo 1994), Thai and Philippine females (Gallares 1994, 104–11; see also Sakenfeld 1999b; 2003), Myanmar female (Win 2000), New Zealand *Pakeha* (non-Maori) female (McKinlay 1999; 2004; Dawson 2001), Native American female (Donaldson 1999), African American womanist (Weems 1988, 23–36; Kirk-Duggan 1999; Travis 2000; Williams 1989), European female immigrants (Erbele-Küster 2002), German rural women (Silber 1999), Eastern European foreign workers in Israel (Brenner 1999b), and African women suffering from HIV/AIDS (van Dyk 2002).

In this essay I enter into this global conversation by reading the book of Ruth as an Asian American biblical scholar of Chinese descent. I argue that the construction of Asian Americans historically as the "perpetual foreigner" and "model minority" can shed light on the various, often conflicting interpretations and readings about Ruth the Moabite. The portrayal of Ruth as the model emigrée is similar to the construction of Asian Americans as the model minority. Their depictions in both cases are used for propagandistic purposes, casting them simultaneously as the perpetual foreigner in the lands in which they live.

THE ASIAN AMERICAN AS THE PERPETUAL FOREIGNER

Asian American racialization involves two specific and related stereotypical configurations. The first is that of the perpetual foreigner (Tuan 1998; Ancheta 2000, 44; Wu 2002, 79–129; Bow 2003, 489), which lurks behind the seemingly harmless question white people constantly ask Asian Americans: "Where are you from?" (See Ang 1994 for the Chinese Dutch equivalent.) Notice that this question is usually not asked of African Americans. When I tell whites that I am from Chicago, they are not satisfied. Predictably, they follow up with: "Where are you *really* from?" Sometimes I inform them directly that I am a Chinese American. At other times, I cheekily play with and deflect their interrogation: I now live in Boston; I was born in Ohio, and I have lived in Canada and in Minnesota. The dance of the seven veils performed by white America to uncover my ethnicity is symptomatic of their assumption that I do not really belong in this country.

Asian American intellectuals have criticized the U.S. discourse on race as being circumscribed by the conflicts between blacks and whites (Wu 2002, 79–129; Ancheta 2000, 1–18). They point out that in the black/white binary, the experiences of Asian Americans (as well as Latino/a and Arab Americans) fall through the cracks, since racial bigotry can vary qualitatively among different racial and ethnic groups. Asian Americans experience the process of racialization

differently than African Americans.[5] Although both groups have suffered hor-
rendously under white racism, the markers for determining the Other rest on
different axes. For African Americans, the axis is *color*, white versus black. For
Asian (and Latino/a and Arab) Americans, it is *citizenship*, American versus foreigner (Ancheta 2000; Tuan 1998, 8; S. C. Miller 1974).

Because of the focus on racial color (being black), as well as a shared history
of slavery, African Americans do not identify themselves by their national origins, such as Nigerian American or Ghanan American, much less by their African
tribal origins, such as Mandingo American or Ashanti American (Ebron and
Tsing 1995, 131; Bruner 1996). In contrast, Asian Americans hail from ethnically
and culturally distinct Asian nations and have different immigration histories to
and ethnic conflicts with white America. They therefore consistently describe
themselves in terms of their national or ethnic origins: Chinese American, Japanese American, Korean American, and so forth. With respect to citizenship in
the U.S, these ethnic demarcations have often been a matter of great importance
in the conflicted history of U.S.-Asian relations. During World War II, Chinese
Americans consciously distinguished themselves from Japanese Americans to
prevent being interned with them.

Institutional and cultural racism found in the legal system, government
policy, and so forth has traditionally constructed what it means to be American and hold power in terms of white, male, European descent—particularly
Anglo-Saxon Protestant descent—to the exclusion of Other groups. After long
and difficult struggles, women and blacks were enfranchised as American citizens with the right to vote. Evinced by the ubiquitous experience of being asked
"Where are you from?" Asian Americans have not been fully assimilated into the
collective consciousness of what it means to be American.[6] Even though many,
like my family, have been here for generations, the perception of being aliens in
their own land is one that Asian Americans find difficult to shake off. They continue to be seen as more Asian than American.

The notion of Asian Americans as the perpetual foreigner intensified during
certain overlapping periods of economic, military, and political conflicts in U.S.-
Asia relations. The U.S. government and businesses exploited Chinese peasants as
cheap labor at various points of American history (e.g., for building the transcontinental railroad, to replace blacks on Southern plantations after emancipation,

---

5. I am using as a springboard here the discussion of racial formation in Omi and Winant
1994, 52–76. For them, racialization is the extension of racial meaning to a relationship, social
practice, or group.

6. Brought home in a very public way during two winter Olympics when Chinese American skater Michelle Kwan failed to win gold. The MSNBC headline in 1998 read "American
beats Kwan," when Kwan finished second to teammate Tara Lipinski. In 2002, the *Seattle Times*
described Kwan's loss to teammate Sarah Hughes, "American outshines Kwan, Slutskaya in skat-
ing surprise."

as strikebreakers for New England textile mills (for histories, see Chang 2003; Takaki 1989; 1993). Incensed by the competition, however, whites violently harassed and oftentimes killed Chinese laborers and their families. They eventually lobbied Congress to pass the Chinese Exclusion Act in 1882, barring Chinese from entering the U.S. and becoming citizens. This act was not repealed until 17 December 1943, when the U.S. wanted the Chinese as allies during World War II against Japanese aggression. Nevertheless, Chinese Americans were still racialized as the foreign Asian enemy.

Collapsing diverse Asian groups into the foreign Other, white Americans did not always distinguish Chinese Americans from the Japanese (during World War II), the Koreans (during the Korean War), and Vietnamese (during the Vietnam War). In 1982, the economic downturn in the Detroit automobile industry fueled the rage of two white men who killed the Chinese American Vincent Chin, scapegoating Chin as one of the Japanese automakers who cost them their jobs (Zia 2000, 55–81). During the Cold War, the U.S. recruited Chinese scientists and engineers to strengthen American defense systems, only to nurse suspicions later that some Chinese were passing nuclear secrets to mainland China. The unfounded accusations against the Taiwanese American Wen Ho Lee during the late 1990s continued to demonstrate that simply looking like the enemy means that you are (Chang 2003, 236–60, 359–64). The Chinese American architect Maya Lin, who won the national contest to design the Vietnam Memorial, was condemned as a "gook" (a derogatory term for the Vietnamese) by U.S. veterans. Chinese American identity is thus inescapably linked with other Asian ethnic and national identities for whom it is mistaken.

The perpetual-foreigner syndrome takes on a different permutation nowadays in the politics of U.S. multiculturalism, which "in its reliance on symbolic representations of diversity, only serves to oversimplify and essentialize the diversity of racial and ethnic groups in the United States" (Louie 2004, 97). Chinese Americans are expected to put their Chinese "culture" on display. This culture becomes objectified and measurable, taking the form, for example, of speaking and writing Chinese, using chopsticks, immersing oneself in the *Analects* by Confucius, celebrating Chinese New Year, enjoying Jackie Chan movies, and perhaps even taking kung fu lessons.[7] Chinese American females might feel compelled to "go native" and to slip their heftier American bodies into *cheongsams*, those form-fitting Suzie Wong-type dresses with the slit up the side.

When such traits of Chineseness become essentialized as visible hallmarks of authenticity, Chinese Americans are put in a double bind. As perpetual foreigners they are tagged as not being American enough. Alternatively, they are expected to exhibit on demand their knowledge and culture of China, about which many, whose families have lived in the U.S for generations, know little.

---

7. Except for reading *The Analects*, I have dabbled in all of the above.

The commodification of Chinese identity in U.S. multicultural politics presumes that this identity is "out there," just waiting to be discovered.

When placed on a continuum of being more or less authentically Chinese, many American-born Chinese sometimes experience ambivalence in the presence of those who seem to be "more" Chinese, such as those who have a Chinese accent or have recently come from China:

> While on the one hand Chinese Americans, under assimilationist models, should identify with their U.S. roots, the realities of racial politics cause them to remain perpetual foreigners. Chinese Americans have always been told that "home" is in the United States but that their "roots," and therefore a missing piece of their identity is somewhere in China. (Louie 2004, 104)

Eventually, some American-born Chinese, such as myself, might actually visit China to find that missing piece that will ostensibly transform one into an "authentic" Chinese. Actually finding that piece is another matter. Although the stigma of perpetual foreigner assumes that I do not belong in the U.S., I discovered that I did not belong in China either, as my recent year-long experience teaching in Hong Kong starkly revealed (Yee 2006).

I faced several challenges during my time in Hong Kong that I did not have to face in my twenty years of undergraduate and graduate teaching in the U.S. First were the obvious personal and cultural dislocations I experienced as a Chinese American who had never been west of San Francisco, going ashore in a Hong Kong Chinese context. (Asian Americans often refer to newly arrived immigrant Asians as FOBs or Fresh Off the Boats. In a sense I was the FOB counterpart in Hong Kong, although it would be more accurate to say that I was a FOP, Fresh Off the Plane.) Second was a linguistic dislocation, since my three weeks of Mandarin study (which was not good to begin with) were completely forgotten in the largely Cantonese-speaking culture. I taught in English, a dislocation for my students. There was also a gender dislocation. The Department of Religion at the Chinese University of Hong Kong was primarily composed of men. Only one other female colleague, untenured, taught in the department, while more than half of the faculty in my home institution, the Episcopal Divinity School, are female, and all are tenured. Finally, there were what I can only describe as ideological dislocations in that I came as a feminist, with strong social views on racism, class exploitation, American imperialism and colonialism, and fundamentalistic readings of the biblical text. All of these strong positions are formed by and in reaction to my U.S. context. For a third-generation Chinese American who grew up in the urban slums of Chicago's South Side (Yee 1997), Asian forms of theologizing, such as Waterbuffalo Theology (Koyama 1974; 1998), seemed to come from another planet and were just as alien. Minimally knowing the language, the history, and the culture in Hong Kong made me like Ruth the Moabite, a woman "who stood in tears amid the alien corn."

My experience of being a foreigner both in the U.S. and in China is typical of many American-born Chinese who visit China in search of their "roots." Just as Chinese Americans are not American enough for whites in the U.S., they are not culturally Chinese enough with respect to China.[8]

The Asian American as the Model Minority

Besides being pigeonholed as the perpetual foreigner, Asian Americans simultaneously labor under the model-minority stereotype (Wu 2002, 39–77; R. G. Lee 1999, 145–79; Osajima 2000; Cho 1997). After a century of blatant racial discrimination and slander,[9] Asian Americans are singled out as a group that has successfully assimilated into American society, becoming financially well-off and achieving the American dream. This stereotype is often part and parcel of those essentialist traits that "real" Chinese individuals are assumed to have. Traditional Chinese values and attributes are said to include respect for elders, strong family ties, intellectual giftedness, a hard-work ethic, a focus on higher education and a striving to achieve, mathematical and scientific ability, and so forth.

My experiences as a model minority were much more conflicted. For example, when my family moved from the inner city to a white neighborhood, the Catholic grade school I attended had "homogeneous" groupings. In descending order, group 1 comprised the most intelligent and talented, and group 4 was regarded as the "dumb-dumb" group. I was put in the latter. Even at the young age of ten, I saw that the individuals in group 1 were all white and that group 4 contained the racial and ethnic students and those white who were regarded as "trash." With respect to the assumption that Asians are good in math, I withdrew from college algebra three times before I flunked the course and had to change my major from psychology to English literature because there was no way that I could pass the required statistics course. When I took the GRE I barely made it on the scale for mathematical ability. In the range of 300–800, I received something like 320.

---

8. See especially Louie 2004, who examines issues of Chinese identity through an in-depth ethnographic study of the In Search of Roots program, sponsored by the PRC (People's Republic of China) and certain Chinese American organizations. The intent of this program is to bring young Chinese Americans to the villages of their ancestors to learn about the greatness of Chinese "culture." The underlying motive of the PRC is to encourage Chinese American economic investment in China, their true "homeland." Louie draws conclusions for Chinese identity from the PRC perspective, especially in its agenda for the In Search of Roots program and how this agenda is negotiated and often subverted by the Chinese American students who participate in it. See also Ang 1994, 2–3.

9. In the popular media, see the fears about the "Yellow Peril," Fu Manchu and Dragon Lady, Ming the Merciless from the planet Mongo, documented in R. G. Lee 1999, 106–44.

The model-minority stereotype is a gross generalization of disparate Asian immigrant populations that vary in terms of ethnicity, immigration history, linguistic facility, education, and economic class (Cheng and Yang 2000). Camouflaged by the notion of model minority are the unexpressed questions, Model of what? and Model for whom? (Wu 2002, 59). On the one hand, the phrase "model minority" could imply that Asian Americans are exemplary, despite the fact that they happen to be "colored" and, as such, still inferior to the dominant white society. This understanding is hardly flattering to Asian Americans. On the other hand, the phrase could mean that Asian Americans are exemplary and other racial and ethnic groups should take after them. The model-minority stereotype then becomes more of a critique and a denigration of other racial groups rather than a compliment to Asian Americans.

It is no accident that articles hailing Asian Americans as the "superminority" and the "whiz kids" emerged particularly during the Cold War of the 1950s and the racial conflicts of the 1960s:

> The narrative of Asian ethnic assimilation fit the requirements of Cold War containment perfectly. Three specters haunted Cold War America in the 1950s: the red menace of communism, the black menace of race mixing, and the white menace of homosexuality. On the international front, the narrative of ethnic assimilation sent a message to the Third World, especially to Asia where the United States was engaged in increasingly fierce struggles with nationalist and communist insurgencies, that the United States was a liberal democratic state where people of color could enjoy equal rights and upward mobility. On the home front, it sent a message to "Negroes and other minorities" that accommodation would be rewarded while militancy would be contained or crushed. (R. G. Lee 1999, 146)

Asian Americans are held up as living proof that racial minorities can succeed in America presumably by the sweat of their brow, not by civil rights demonstrations or protests. Using the model-minority stereotype as a weapon, whites tell blacks and Latinos/as that "Asian Americans do not 'whine' about racial discrimination; they only try harder" (Wu 2002, 44). The supposed accomplishments of Asian Americans divert attention away from the fact that racial discrimination is a structural feature of U.S. society, produced by centuries of systematic exclusion, exploitation, and disregard of racially defined minorities (Omi and Winant 1994, 69). Blame for any social disparities falls on the other racial minorities, who "whine" about racial discrimination. White construction of the model-minority stereotype has as its antithesis their racist construction of other groups, such as blacks, as the "deficient" or "depraved" minority.

The model-minority stereotype buttresses the dominant ideology of the U.S. as a just and fair society, in which all its citizens compete on a level playing field. All foreign immigrants and racial minorities who have worked hard and played by the rules can be readily assimilated and succeed economically. White America judged and rewarded Asian Americans not by the color of their skin but by the content of their character.[10] Significantly, some Asian American students have espoused the stereotype as a means of upward mobility and white approval. These students are primarily immigrants who have bought into the ideology of white America as the land of opportunity and dismissed any racial episodes as the isolated acts of single individuals. American-born Asians, however, are more likely to be wary of the model-minority stereotype and view any racial incidents as part of a larger social problem (Tuan 1998, 8).

Following the model-minority stereotype can backfire on Asian Americans (Wu 2002, 67–77). The perception of Asian American success in higher education often rebounds in anti-Asian attitudes. White students become threatened by and resent the growing number of Asian students in classrooms. They fear that so-called hordes of Asian students distort the grading curve, and many refuse to register for sections containing a large Asian critical mass. The zero-sum perception that Asian American gains denote white American losses often results in violence, as the Detroit death of Vincent Chin demonstrates. The Michigan Congressman John Dingell angrily accused "little yellow men" for the economic hardships of Detroit automakers, rather than placing the blame on the fact that domestic cars are not as skillfully made or as fuel efficient as Japanese imports (Zia 2000, 58).

The perpetual-foreigner and the model-minority stereotypes work in tandem to construct contradictory images of Asian Americans in general and Chinese Americans in particular. As perpetual foreigners, they become a secondary caste that can be exploited and used. They are perceived as aliens in their own land, even though their citizenship often goes back several generations. When they ostensibly excel as model minorities through industry and entrepreneurial talents, they become a threat to be contained or destroyed. These two stereotypes make more complex the nature of U.S. race relations, which have usually operated under a black/white binary. Rather than functioning on the color axis, racial discrimination against Asian Americans operates on the axis of citizenship, casting Asian Americans as the perpetual foreigner. Colluding with this stereotype is the pigeonholing of Asian Americans as the model minority, which at times benefits them compared to other ethnic groups while simultaneously obscuring the countless ways in which they are marginalized and victimized by racism. It is through these two lenses that I view the book of Ruth.

THE BOOK OF RUTH

The social matrixes in the book of Ruth are rich. They include male/female, husband/wife, mother/son, mother-in-law/daughter-in-law, owner/overseer/

---

10. My apologies to Dr. Martin Luther King.

laborers, mother's house/father's house, native resident/foreigner, and so forth. These relations are forged through marriage, friendship, widowhood, sexual attraction, economic and labor arrangements, immigration, and political amity or enmity. As the wealth of global interpretations of Ruth attests, the story is a "mine or mosaic of social relations, where readers can take their pick" (Dube 2001, 68). With the plurality of different readers comes a plurality of differing, often antithetical, interpretations. Juxtaposed to the more positive readings of the book, as an enchanting bucolic story about female empowerment and romantic heterosexual love, are others that see a more ambiguous and unsettling narrative.[11] I follow the lead of other people of color and allow the ambiguity of the text to favor a reading against the grain (Maldonado 1995; Donaldson 1999; Kwok 2005; García-Treto 2001; Wong 1999; see also: Fewell and Gunn 1990; Levine 1998; Linafelt and Beal 1999). The usual optimistic and romantic readings of Ruth obscure issues of ethnicity, economic exploitation, and racist attitudes about the sexuality of foreigners that are evident in the text. Refracting the story of Ruth through the prism of the Asian American experience, I argue that, in its own way, the ideology of the text constructs Ruth the Moabite as a model minority and perpetual foreigner.

GĒR AND NOKRÎYÂ IN RUTH

The book of Ruth uses two words to describe foreigners: *gēr* and *nokrîyâ* (see van Houten 1983; Rendtorff 1996; Snijders 1954; Bennett 2002; Begg 1992; Spencer 1992). A *gēr* is a foreigner who has immigrated into and taken up residence in a society in which she or he has neither familial nor tribal associations. Although granted some protection under the Holiness Code and Deuteronomic Code, the *gēr* is not a full-fledged member of the Israelite community but, rather, someone of different and lower status. Ruth is not called a *gēr*. The term is used to describe Elimelech's sojourn to Moab with his family (Ruth 1:1). However, because Ruth takes advantage of the laws about gleaning for the poor, the *gēr*, and the widow (Lev 19:9–10, 23:22; Deut 24:19–22), the text implies that Ruth is a *gēr*.

When Ruth encounters Boaz's kindness for the first time, she falls on her face and exclaims: "Why have I found favor in your sight, that you should take notice of me, when I am a foreigner [*nokrîyâ*]?" (Ruth 2:10). The text has Ruth acknowledge in direct speech her status as a foreigner in Judah. The connotation of *nokrî* is generally negative, highlighting the person's otherness and separateness from the dominant culture (Rendorff 1996, 77; Begg 1992, 829). We will see that the

---

11. Alta and Pete van Dyk (2002, 15–24) classify these differing readings under four categories: (1) reading with the grain of the text (positive); (2) a romantic reading (even more positive); (3) a feminist perspective (against the grain); (4) "a man, trapped by the slyness of two women." See also Masenya 1998, 82–85.

negativity of the *nokrî* is particularly underscored by the fact that Ruth was a Moabite, one of Israel's traditional hated enemies. If Ruth was written during the time of Ezra and Nehemiah, the use of *nokrîyâ* in the mouth of Ruth is significant. Intermarriage between the exiles and foreign women (*nāšîm nokrîyôt*, Ezra 10:2, 10; Neh 13:26) was severely condemned. Note that the nemesis of Lady Wisdom is the Foreign Woman[12] in the book of Proverbs, whose author shares Ezra's and Nehemiah's Persian period ideologies (Yee 2003, 143–65). Some interpret the marriage of Boaz to the *nokrîyâ* Ruth as a critique of Ezra's and Nehemiah's policies against foreign marriages (LaCocque 2004; Matthews 2004; Bush 1996; see overviews in Larkin 1996, 18–25; Sakenfeld 1999a, 1–5). Others argue for an earlier context for the composition of Ruth, perhaps as an apology for David to remove the taint of Moabite descent (Gow 1992). I maintain, however, that, whatever the date, the negative connotations of Ruth's foreignness implied in *nokrîyâ* are not completely erased in the book.

RUTH AS A MODEL MINORITY

In the construction of Ruth as the model minority, her Moabite ancestry is of prime importance. Ruth is not simply from any foreign nation but from Moab, whose entanglements with Israel have been antagonistic. According to Gen 19:37, the Moabites were the spawn of a drunken incestuous encounter between Lot and his eldest daughter. Numbers 25:1–3 blames the idolatry of Israelite men who "yoked" themselves to the Baal of Peor on the bewitching sexuality of Moabite women. The seer Balaam, hired by the king of Moab to curse the Israelites, ends up blessing them and cursing Moab instead (Num 22–24). Moab, along with Ammon, refused to offer bread (*leḥem*) and water on Israel's journey from Egypt and was thus denied admittance to the assembly of God, even down to the tenth generation (Deut 23:3–4). The irony is that Elimelech and his family must emigrate from Bethlehem (House of Bread) to Moab because of a famine in Judah.[13] But this flight comes at a great cost: the patriarch and his two sons die in Moab, leaving three impoverished widows and a threatened patriline.

The deeper the enmity between Moab and Israel, the greater the valor in Ruth's resolve to embrace the latter and its God. Her rejection of Moab and its negative links with Israel transforms her into the Jewish convert par excellence. In rabbinic interpretation, Ruth was the daughter of a Moabite king when she

---

12. <*'iššâ zārâ*>, which parallels *nokrîyâ* in Prov 2:16; 5:20; 7:5. See also 5:3, in which *nokrîyâ* parallels <*ēšet ra'*>, "evil woman," in 6:24, and *zônâ*, "harlot," in 23:27.

13. Moab had reasonably good agricultural land, which was productive even when other parts of Palestine were hit by famine. According to 2 Kgs 3:4, King Mesha of Moab bred sheep and used to deliver 100,000 lambs and the wool of 100,000 rams to the king of Israel (see M. Miller 1997).

rejected her homeland and its false deities "to become a God-fearing Jewess— loyal daughter-in-law, modest bride, renowned ancestress of Israel's great king David" (see Darr 1991, 72; Caspi and Havrelock, 1996, 85). Ruth's ḥesed (generosity, compassion, and love) toward her mother-in-law in accompanying Naomi to a strange land and in supporting her by gleaning is recognized by Ruth's future husband and provider. Boaz exclaims that the Israelite God, under whose wings she has sought refuge, will fully reward Ruth (2:11–12). If the book was written as an apology for the Moabite ancestry in David's line (see 1 Sam 22:3–4), Ruth the faithful convert purges the line of any foreign stain.

Indeed, Ruth is not only the model convert but also an exemplar for the Jewish people. According to André C. LaCocque, "[Ruth's] 'heroism' is to become more of a Judean than those who are Judean by birth! Retrospectively, one can say that her fidelity toward the people and their God provides a lesson to those who should have been her teachers" (2004, 24–25). LaCocque further adds that the central theological message of the book is the meaning of ḥesed, which Ruth epitomizes for the people: "A non-Judean shows the way to the Judeans, precisely in an era where the respect for the letter had become the very condition of membership in the Second Temple community" (28).

In her article "Ruth, the Model Emigrée," Bonnie Honig criticizes readings that turn the book into "a kind of nationalist narrative that Ruth's story does not only nor unambivalently support" (1999, 51). She outlines the two problems for the present discussion that inhere in the concept of the model emigrée. According to Honig, dominant readings of Ruth fall into two categories that correspond to the two major responses to immigrants. On the one hand, immigrants are welcomed for what they can bring to a nation, whether it is diversity, talents, energy, novel cuisines, or a rekindled sense of national pride that had attracted the immigrants in the first place. On the other hand, immigrants are dreaded because of what they will do to the nation (burden the welfare system, weaken the common heritage, and so forth) (54). Ruth's decision to leave her natal land for Israel reconfirms Israel's identity as the chosen people, a people worthy of being chosen. Nevertheless, Ruth's relocation does not mean that Israel is now borderless land, embracing all foreigners, even the hated Moabites. "Israel is open only to the Moabite who is exceptionally virtuous, to Ruth but not Orpah" (55–56).

The construction of Ruth as the model emigrée is similar to the model-minority stereotype of Asian Americans. Ruth is held up for propagandistic purposes, either to expunge any contamination of Moabite descent for David or to critique Ezra and Nehemiah's policies against intermarriage. She thus reveals what a virtuous foreigner can teach the nation. As model minorities, Asian Americans supposedly exemplify traditional values, such as respect for elders, industry and hard work, and family loyalty. Similarly, Ruth incarnates the quality of ḥesed in her overwhelming devotion to her mother-in-law, her willingness to support her by diligently gleaning in a strange man's field, not resting "even for a moment" (2:7), and in her conversion to another God. As Ruth the Moabite teaches Judeans the meaning of *ḥesed*, Asian Americans educate Others on how to be "good" minorities who know their place in a white society. Nevertheless, just as Asian Americans remain perpetual foreigners in the land of their birth, Ruth's disappearance in chapter 4 after the birth of her son leads one to question whether Ruth has been successfully assimilated as a foreigner into Judean society or ultimately abandoned once she preserves the male lineage (Levine 1998, 85).

RUTH THE PERPETUAL FOREIGNER

The flipside of the model-minority stereotype for Asian Americans is that of the perpetual foreigner. This Janus-like phenomenon is also apparent in the book of Ruth. Just as Asian Americans are consistently perceived as being more Asian than American by the dominant white society, so is Ruth continually called Ruth the Moabite, rather than Israelite, even after her immigration (1:22; 2:2, 6, 21; 4:5, 10). Ruth seems to lose this qualifier after she finally gives birth to a son (4:13), but it comes at the cost of not being recognized as his mother (4:17).[14] Naomi's ultimate incorporation back into the community is manifested by her displacement of Ruth as Obed's mother. This displacement implies that the revitalization of this community and the continuation of the patriline toward David's monarchy depend not only on Ruth's exemplary character but also on her marginalization as a foreigner (Honig 1999, 73–74).

As Chinese Americans were economically exploited for cheap labor, particularly during the 1800s and early 1900s, so is Ruth's foreign labor exploited by both Naomi and Boaz. Jack M. Sasson (1989, 124) and Athalya Brenner (1999b, 158–62) argue that 1:16–17, which is usually read as Ruth's tender pledge to Naomi, is actually a verbal contract in which Ruth submits her person to the wishes of her mother-in-law. The "love" that Ruth has for Naomi (4:15) can connote the relationship between an inferior to her or his superior, such as the one between a vassal and his lord (Moran 1963; Thompson 1977; Ackerman 2002; see also Dube 2001, 77). This interpretation would explain, for example, why Ruth alone goes out to glean and why she easily acquiesces to Naomi's dangerous proposal to seduce Boaz on the threshing floor. She might have had little choice in the matter.

Issues of class, especially as they intersect with ethnicity and gender in Ruth, are also underscored in a perceptive analysis by Roland Boer. In Marxist fashion, Boer notices who owns the means of production, namely, the land, and who

---

14. Although space constraints limit my discussion, issues of surrogate motherhood and its exploitation of poor and ethnic women looms here, as it does in the Sarah and Hagar story of Gen 16. Also on the horizon is the practice of white Americans adopting female Chinese babies abandoned at birth. It remains to be seen whether or not these babies will be fully accepted as "Americans" or also tagged as perpetual foreigners in spite of having white adoptive parents.

actually works it in the book of Ruth. The economic gulf between Boaz, as owner of the land, and Ruth, as foreign gleaner of the land's leftovers, is wide. For Boaz does not work in the fields as do his reapers or his overseer, but, rather, he commands them. "In other words, he lives off the surplus labour of those who do work" (Boer 2003, 79–80). His seeming munificence toward Ruth (2:8–9, 14–16) is that of one who has more than enough already. He can afford to dole out a little something for Ruth. In this regard, Boaz's injunction to Ruth not to work in another man's field (2:8) may be motivated more by economic rather than personal interests. Boaz has already been told that Ruth "has been on her feet from early this morning until now, without resting even for a moment" (2:7). She continues the grueling work of gleaning until evening and then she beats out an *ephah* of barley (2.17), which weighs somewhere between 30 and 50 pounds (Bush 1996, 133). Boaz knows good foreign help when he sees it, and his so-called generosity can be read as offering inducements to keep Ruth's productiveness for his own benefit. Although Boaz does not acquire economic capital from Ruth's labor, he certainly reaps much social capital and prestige in the Israelite community as a benefactor of widows. We will see shortly that Boaz will eventually acquire land as economic capital through Ruth's person. Ruth continues to toil in his field "until the end of the barley and wheat harvests" (2:23). Boer quips, "This is hardly benevolence, but more like pure exploitation" (2003, 83).

Naomi does not work in the fields either. She too lives off the labor of Ruth the foreigner, whose actions she directs: urging Ruth to continue the nonstop work of gleaning, instructing her to make herself attractive to seduce a man in the middle of the night, and ultimately taking Ruth's child as her own. Some justify Naomi's absence in the field to her old age or the fact that she still grieves the loss of her husband and sons. Others think she is hard at work in the invisible domestic sphere while Ruth works outside the home. However, within the economics of the text, Naomi is more aligned with Boaz than with Ruth, especially when kinship intersects with ownership of the means of production. As related kin, Naomi and Boaz are complicit regarding "that piece of land" (4:3) that belonged to Naomi's husband, Elimelech. Another kinsman has a better claim to redeem this land, but Boaz is able to trump this claim by means of Ruth's body. "On the day you acquire the field from the hand of Naomi, you are also acquiring Ruth the Moabite, the widow of the dead man, to maintain the dead man's name on his inheritance" (4:5). By her kinship with Boaz and by strategically using Ruth to preserve the lineage of her husband, Naomi ultimately dislocates Ruth as Obed's mother.

Marxist feminists have often noted the deficiency in Marxist theory in not fully incorporating into its theorizing on class women's productive labor and their reproductive (or sexual) labor in the continuation of the species (Hartmann 1997; Barrett 1988, 8–41). These labors interconnect most clearly in the person of Ruth. Exhausting herself by working the land for Boaz and Naomi, Ruth also becomes the reproductive means by which Boaz and Naomi profit economically. In Boaz's case, Ruth becomes the stumbling block that prevents the land from falling into

the hands of Mr. So-and-So, who cannot marry Ruth and beget a son through her
without jeopardizing his own inheritance (4:6). Through Ruth, Boaz is thus able
to enlarge his landholdings. And Ruth's birth labors in producing a son secure
Boaz's patriline and Naomi's economic place in the community.

Other aspects of Ruth's sexual exploitation in the text work hand-in-hand
with Ruth's foreignness. Foreign women in the Hebrew Bible have a long tradition of erotic allure and sexual insatiability. Witness Madame Potiphar, Delilah,
the queen of Sheba, Solomon's foreign wives, Jezebel, the whore of Babylon, and
the Foreign Woman in Proverbs. These women bring about the downfall of men
through their sexuality. Asian American women also suffer under similar exotici-
zation by white American males in the images of Suzie Wong, Madame Butterfly,
the submissive lotus blossom, the seductive geisha, the Mongol slave girl, and the
treacherous Dragon Lady (Uchida 1998; Yoshikawa 1999). Catering to the sexual
fantasies of white men, the flourishing global trafficking of Asian women's bodies
is built on such stereotypes (Brock and Thistlethwaite 1996). Male domination
and colonial supremacy coalesce here in the sexual depiction and exploitation of
the foreign woman.

Lingering over Ruth is the notorious tradition of the Moabites as the perverse
progeny of incest, whose women sexually seduced the Israelites away from Yhwh
(Num 25:1–3). Ruth is particularly vulnerable to sexual harassment and violence
in the fields by the male farmhands, who may regard her as "easy," because she is
a Moabite, one of "those" women (see Carasik 1995; Shepherd 2001). To protect
his industrious worker and keep her working in his field, Boaz shields Ruth from
these "attentions" by ordering his men to keep their hands to themselves (2:9).

The reputed carnality of foreign women injects greater ambivalence into
the narrative of Ruth and Boaz on the threshing floor (Ruth 3). Biblical commentaries are rife with speculation on whether Ruth and Boaz "did it" that night.
If intertextual parallels are drawn between Lot's daughters (Gen 19) and Tamar
(Gen 38), Ruth did indeed "do it" with Boaz (Fisch 1982; Fuchs 1997; van Wolde
1997). All three stories involve a threat to the patriline because of the death of a
male. The fiancés of Lot's daughters are killed in the destruction of Sodom. God
slays Er and Onan, leaving Judah's lineage in jeopardy. Elimelech and his sons die
in Moab. In all three stories, women take the initiative to restore and continue the
lineage. Further, foreignness is attached to all three. Lot's daughters become the
progenitors of the Moabites and Ammonites. Tamar is most likely a Canaanite,
and Ruth is a Moabite. All three adopt sexually unorthodox means to achieve
their purposes. Lot's daughters collude in an incestuous encounter with their
father. Tamar pretends to be a hooker at the side of the road. Ruth marshals her
charms to seduce Boaz on the threshing floor. All three take advantage of the
men's inebriation from too much wine.[15] Certainly, Lot's daughters and Tamar

---

15. Wine is implied in Gen 28:12–13, since it is the festive time of sheep shearing.

succeed in having sex with their targeted males, becoming pregnant with sons as a result. If the story of Ruth follows the same literary pattern, Ruth and Boaz consummated their union on the threshing floor, issuing in the birth of David's grandfather.

Whether Ruth and Boaz had sex that fateful night should not distract us from the economic urgency that compelled Ruth the foreigner to go to the threshing floor in the first place. Here I am in complete agreement with Katherine Doob Sakenfeld (who does not think the couple "did it") that:

> No woman should have to do something so socially unacceptable in Israelite culture as to approach a man in the dark of night, at risk of discovery and public humiliation, and possibly severe legal penalties in order to put food on her family's table for the longer term. This is not a slightly adventurous tryst. It is a desperate act by a desperate person. (2002, 174)

While some white feminists may be appalled at the notion that the key to a woman's happiness is the Cinderella story of finding and seducing a rich man who will become her patron, for many destitute women in the Third World such a hope is often one of the few options available (see Kanyoro 1997, 373). Sakenfeld relates a story about a young impoverished Filipina who was recruited to go to a wealthy foreign country as a "dancer." In response to her pastor's suspicions that she was destined for the Asian sex trade, the girl pointed to the book of Ruth: "Ruth put herself forward attractively to a rich man in hopes that he would marry her and take care of her family. I am doing the same. Hopefully a rich man from that country will choose me to marry and will look after me and my family. God made things turn out right for Ruth and God will take care of me too" (1999b, 221). The adverse consequences of global capitalism were brought home to me recently in Hong Kong, where it is not uncommon for Filipina domestic help (whose working conditions are often deplorable) to seduce the male head of household and sometimes engineer a divorce in order to better her situation. In these cases, as in the book of Ruth, economic survival often forces impoverished women to acts they would never do otherwise, literally spending their lives "in tears amid the alien corn."

CONCLUSION

Seen through the eyes of the dual Asian American experiences of being a model minority and perpetual foreigner, the book of Ruth holds in dialectical tension the positive and the more ambivalent interpretations of the story.

On the one hand, the book of Ruth is a (fairy)tale about a devoted widow who rejects her homeland and her idols to accompany her mother-in-law to a new country. In this scenario, Ruth becomes a model emigrée (gēr)—a model convert—who teaches the chosen people the true meaning of God's covenantal ḥesed.

She is an exemplar of female empowerment, initiative, hard work, family loyalty, and upward mobility. And to top things off, she does get the guy in the end.

On the other hand, Ruth is also the perpetual foreigner—a *nokrîyâ*—whose consistent label of Moabite implies that she, not unlike Asian Americans in the U.S., is not fully assimilated in the text's consciousness of what it means to be Israelite. Ruth's foreignness is the linchpin in the economics of the text. It sets her apart from those characters who do not work in the book but who appropriate her labor and her body. Chinese American labor contributed to the building of a nation, but their efforts went unacknowledged.[16] So also does Ruth's labor in the field and especially in giving birth to Obed play a major role in strengthening the Davidic line and the formation of the state, but she too disappears at the end. The insidious economic picture that surfaces in the book of Ruth is that the Israelites—in the persons of Naomi and Boaz—are those who do not work, who exploit and live off the surplus labor of the foreign Other. Naomi assimilates into the world of Israelite men, the landowners who possess the means of production, while the foreign female worker, Ruth, vanishes when her body is exhausted. Ruth's story thus becomes an indictment for those of us who live in the First World who exploit the cheap labor of developing countries and poor immigrants from these countries who come to the First World looking for jobs.

Works Consulted

Ackerman, Susan. 2002. The Personal Is Political: Covenantal and Affectionate Love in the Hebrew Bible. *VT* 52:437–58.

Alpert, Rebecca. 1996. Finding Our Past: A Lesbian Interpretation of the Book of Ruth. Pages 91–96 in Kates and Reimer 1996.

Ancheta, Angelo N. 2000. *Race, Rights, and the Asian American Experience.* New Brunswick, N.J.: Rutgers University Press.

Ang, Ien. 1994. On Not Speaking Chinese: Postmodern Ethnicity and the Politics of Diaspora. *New Formations* 24:1–18.

Barrett, Michèle. 1988. *Women's Oppression Today.* Rev. ed. New York: Verso.

Begg, Christopher T. 1992. Foreigner. *ABD* 2:829–30.

Bennett, Harold V. 2002. *Injustice Made Legal: Deuteronomic Law and the Plight of Widows, Strangers, and Orphans in Ancient Israel.* Grand Rapids: Eerdmans.

Boer, Roland. 2003. Terry Eagleton: The Class Struggles of Ruth. Pages 65–86 in idem, *Marxist Criticism of the Bible.* New York: T&T Clark.

Bow, Leslie. 2003. Making Sense of Screaming: A Monkey's Companion. Pages 487–97 in *Screaming Monkeys: Critiques of Asian American Images.* Edited by M. Evelina Galang. Minneapolis: Coffee House Press.

---

16. See the famous picture of the white men posing at the completion of the transcontinental railroad, with not a Chinese face in sight.

Brenner, Athalya, ed. 1993. *A Feminist Companion to Ruth*. Sheffield: Sheffield Academic Press.

———, ed. 1999a. *Ruth and Esther: A Feminist Companion to the Bible*. FCB 2/3. Sheffield: Sheffield Academic Press.

———.1999b. Ruth as a Foreign Worker and the Politics of Exogamy. Pages 158–62 in Brenner 1999a.

———. 2005. The Three of Us: Ruth, Orpah, Naomi. Pages 99–119 in *I Am … Biblical Women Tell Their Own Stories*. Minneapolis: Fortress.

Brock, Rita Nakashima, and Susan Brooks Thistlethwaite. 1996. *Casting Stones: Prostitution and Liberation in Asia and the United States*. Minneapolis: Fortress.

Bruner, Edward M. 1996. Tourism in Ghana: The Representation of Slavery and the Return of the Black Diaspora. *American Anthropologist* 98:290–304.

Bush, Frederic W. 1996. *Ruth, Esther*. WBC 9. Waco, Tex.: Word.

Carasik, Michael. 1995. Ruth 2,7: Why the Overseer Was Embarrassed. *ZAW* 107:493–94.

Caspi, Mishael Maswari, and Rachel S. Havrelock. 1996. *Women on the Biblical Road: Ruth, Naomi, and the Female Journey*. Lanham, Md.: University Press of America.

Cavalcanti, Tereza. 1989. The Prophetic Ministry of Women in the Hebrew Bible. Pages 118–39 in *Through Her Eyes: Women's Theology from Latin America*. Edited by Elsa Tamez. Maryknoll, N.Y.: Orbis.

Chang, Iris. 2003. *The Chinese in America: A Narrative History*. New York: Viking.

Cheng, Lucie, and Philip Q. Yang. 2000. The "Model Minority" Deconstructed. Pages 459–82 in *Contemporary Asian America: A Multidisciplinary Reader*. Edited by Min Zhou and James V. Gatewood. New York: New York University Press.

Cho, Sumi K. 1997. Converging Stereotypes in Racialized Sexual Harrassment: Where the Model Minority Meets Suzie Wong. Pages 203–20 in *Critical Race Feminism: A Reader*. Edited by Adrien Katherine Wing. New York: New York University Press.

Chow, Rey. 2002. *The Protestant Ethnic and the Spirit of Capitalism*. New York: Columbia University Press.

Chu, Julie Li-Chuan. 1997. Returning Home: The Inspiration of the Role Dedifferentiation in the Book of Ruth for Taiwanese Women. *Semeia* 78:47–53.

Darr, Katheryn Pfisterer. 1991. *Far More Precious Than Jewels: Perspectives on Biblical Women*. Louisville: Westminster John Knox.

Dawson, Jenny. 2001. The Power of Women's Friendship. *In God's Image* 20.1:39–40.

De La Torre, Miguel A. 2000. Cubans in Babylon: Exodus and Exile. Pages 73–91 in *Religion, Culture, and Tradition in the Caribbean*. Edited by Hemchand Gossai and Nathaniel Samuel Murrell. New York: St. Martin's Press.

Delgado, Richard, and Jean Stefancic. 2001. *Critical Race Theory: An Introduction*. New York: New York University Press.

Donaldson, Laura E. 1999. The Sign of Orpah: Reading Ruth Through Native Eyes. Pages 131–44 in Brenner 1999a.

Dube, Musa. 1999. The Unpublished Letters of Orpah to Ruth. Pages 145–50 in Brenner 1999a.

———. 2001. Divining Ruth for International Relations. Pages 67–80 in *Postmodern Interpretations of the Bible: A Reader*. Edited by A. K. M. Adam. St Louis: Chalice.

Duncan, Celena M. 2000. The Book of Ruth: On Boundaries, Love, and Truth. Pages 92–102 in *Take Back the Word: A Queer Reading of the Bible*. Edited by Robert E. Goss and Mona West. Cleveland: Pilgrim.

Dyk, Alta C. van, and Peet J. van Dyk. 2002. HIV/AIDS in Africa: Suffering Women and the Theology of the Book of Ruth. *OTE* 15:209–24.

Ebron, Paulla, and Anna Lowenhaupt Tsing. 1995. From Allegories of Identity to Sites of Dialogue. *Diaspora: A Journal of Transnational Studies* 4.2:125–51.

Erbele-Küster, D. Dorothea. 2002. Immigration and Gender Issues in the Book of Ruth. *Voices From the Third World* 25.1–2:32–39.

Exum, J. Cheryl. 1996. Is This Naomi? Pages 129–74 in idem, *Plotted, Shot, and Painted: Cultural Representations of Biblical Women*. Sheffield: Sheffield Academic Press.

Fewell, Danna Nolan, and David M. Gunn. 1990. *Compromising Redemption: Relating Characters in the Book of Ruth*. Louisville: Westminster John Knox.

Fisch, Harold. 1982. Ruth and the Structure of Covenant History. *VT* 32:425–37.

Foulkes, Irene. 2003. The Book of Ruth and a Group of Prostitutes in Costa Rica. Pages 86–87 in *Feminist Interpretation of the Bible and the Hermeneutics of Liberation*. Edited by Silvia Schroer and Sophia Bietenhard. New York: Sheffield Academic Press.

Fuchs, Esther. 1997. Structure, Motifs and Ideological Functions of the Biblical Temptation Scene. *Biblicon* 2:51–60.

Gallares, Judette A. 1994. *Images of Faith: Spirituality of Women in the Old Testament*. Maryknoll, N.Y.: Orbis.

García-Treto, Francisco. 2001. Mixed Messages: Encountering *Mestizaje* in the Old Testament. *Princeton Seminary Bulletin* 22.2:150–71.

Gossai, Hemchand. 2000. Recasting Identity in Ruth and Hindu Indo-Guyanese Women. Pages 167–79 in *Religion, Culture, and Tradition in the Caribbean*. Edited by Hemchand Gossai and Nathaniel Samuel Murrell. New York: St. Martin's Press.

Gow, Murray D. 1992. *The Book of Ruth: Its Structure, Theme and Purpose*. Leicester: Apollos.

Hartmann, Heidi. 1997. The Unhappy Marriage of Marxism and Feminism: Towards a More Progressive Union. Pages 97–122 in *The Second Wave: A*

Reader in Feminist Theory. Edited by Linda Nicholson. New York: Routledge.

Honig, Bonnie. 1999. Ruth, the Model Emigrée: Mourning and the Symbolic Politics of Immigration. Pages 50–74 in Brenner 1999a.

Houten, Christiana van. 1983. *The Alien in Israelite Law*. JSOTSup 107. Sheffield: JSOT Press.

Jordan, June. 1994. Ruth and Naomi, David and Jonathan: One Love. Pages 82–87 in *Out of the Garden: Women Writers on the Bible*. Edited by Christina Buchmann and Celina Spiegel. New York: Fawcett.

Kanyoro, Musimbi R. A. 1997. Biblical Hermeneutics: Ancient Palestine and the Contemporary World. *Review and Expositor* 94:363–78.

Kates, Judith A., and Gail Twersky Reimer, eds. 1994. *Reading Ruth: Contemporary Women Reclaim a Sacred Story*. New York: Ballantine.

Kirk-Duggan, Cheryl A. 1999. Black Mother Women and Daughters: Signifying Female-Divine Relationships in the Hebrew Bible and African-American Mother-Daughter Short Stories. Pages 192–210 in Brenner 1999a.

Koyama, Kosuke. 1974. *Waterbuffalo Theology*. Maryknoll, N.Y.: Orbis.

———. 1998. Waterbuffalo Theology—After 25 Years. *PTCA Bulletin* 11.2:5–9.

Kuo, Sui May. 1994. Ruth the Moabitess. *In God's Image* 13.1:53–56.

Kwok Pui-Lan. 2005. Finding A Home For Ruth: Gender, Sexuality, and the Politics of Otherness. Pages 100–121 in idem, *Postcolonial Imagination and Feminist Theology*. Louisville: Westminster John Knox. Repr. from pages 135–54 in *New Paradigms for Bible Study: The Bible in the Third Millennium*. Edited by Robert M. Fowler, Edith Blumhofer, and Fernando F. Segovia. New York: T&T Clark International, 2004.

LaCocque, André C. 2004. *Ruth: A Continental Commentary*. Translated by K. C. Hanson. Minneapolis: Fortress.

Larkin, Katrina J. A. 1996. *Ruth and Esther*. Old Testament Guides. Sheffield: Sheffield Academic Press.

Lee, Peter K. H. 1989. Two Stories of Loyalty. *Ching Feng* 32.1:24–40.

Lee, Robert G. 1999. *Orientals: Asian Americans in Popular Culture*. Philadelphia: Temple University Press.

Levine, Amy-Jill. 1998. Ruth. Pages 84–90 in *The Women's Bible Commentary*. Edited by Carol A. Newsom and Sharon H. Ringe. Expanded ed. Louisville: Westminster John Knox.

Linafelt, Tod, and Timothy K. Beal. 1999. *Ruth and Esther*. Berit Olam. Collegeville, Minn.: Liturgical Press.

Louie, Andrea. 2004. *Chineseness across Borders: Renegotiating Chinese Identities in China and the United States*. Raleigh-Durham, N.C.: Duke University Press.

Maldonado, Robert D. 1995. Reading Malinche Reading Ruth: Toward a Hermeneutics of Betrayal. *Semeia* 72:91–109.

Masenya, Madipoane. 1998. *NGWETSI*. (BRIDE). The Naomi-Ruth Story from an African-South African Woman's Perspective. *JFSR* 14.2:81–90.

———. 2004. Ruth. Pages 86–91 in *Global Bible Commentary*. Edited by Daniel Patte. Nashville: Abingdon.

Matthews, Victor H. 2004. *Judges and Ruth*. NCBC. Cambridge: Cambridge University Press.

McKinlay, Judith E. 1999. A Son Is Born to Naomi: A Harvest for Israel. Pages 151–57 in Brenner 1999a.

———. 2004. Reading Rahab and Ruth. Pages 37–56 in idem, *Reframing Her: Biblical Women in Postcolonial Focus*. Sheffield: Sheffield Phoenix Press.

Mesters, Carlos. 1985. *Rute: Una historia da Biblia*. São Paolo: Ediçoes Paulinas.

Miller, Max. 1997. Ancient Moab Still Largely Unknown. *BA* 60:194–204.

Miller, Stuart Creighton. 1974. *The Unwelcome Immigrant: The American Image of the Chinese, 1785–1882*. Berkeley and Los Angeles: University of California Press.

Moran, William L. 1963. The Ancient Near Eastern Background of the Love of God in Deuteronomy. *CBQ* 23:77–87.

Nadar, Sarojini. 2001. A South African Indian Womanist Reading of the Character of Ruth. Pages 159–75 in *Other Ways of Reading: African Women and the Bible*. Edited by Musa W. Dube. SBLGPBS 2. Atlanta: Society of Biblical Literature.

Nayap-Pot, Dalila. 1999. Life in the Midst of Death: Naomi, Ruth and the Plight of Indigenous Women. Pages 52–65 in *Vernacular Hermeneutics*. Edited by R. S. Sugirtharajah. Sheffield: Sheffield Academic Press.

Omi, Michael, and Howard Winant. 1994. *Racial Formation in the United States: From the 1960's to the 1990's*. 2nd ed. New York: Routledge.

Osajima, Keith Hiroshi. 2000. Asian Americans as the Model Minority: An Analysis of the Popular Press Image in the 1960s and 1980s. Pages 449–58 in *Contemporary Asian America: A Multidisciplinary Reader*. Edited by Min Zhou and James V. Gatewood. New York: New York University Press.

Raheb, Viola. 2003. Women in Contemporary Palestinian Society: A Contextual Reading of the Book of Ruth. Pages 87–93 in *Feminist Interpretation of the Bible and the Hermeneutics of Liberation*. Edited by Silvia Schroer and Sophia Bietenhard. New York: Sheffield Academic Press.

Rendtorff, Rolf. 1996. The *Ger* in the Priestly Laws of the Pentateuch. Pages 77–88 in *Ethnicity and the Bible*. Edited by Mark G. Brett. Leiden: Brill.

Sakenfeld, Katherine Doob. *Ruth*. 1999a. IBC. Louisville: John Knox.

———. 1999b. The Story of Ruth: Economic Survival. Pages 215–27 in *Realia Dei: Essays in Archaeology and Biblical Interpretation in Honor of Edward F. Campbell, Jr. at His Retirement*. Edited by Prescott H. Williams Jr. and Theodore Hiebert. Atlanta: Scholars Press.

———. 2002. At the Threshing Floor: Sex, Reader Response, and a Hermeneutic of Survival. *OTE* 15:164–78.

——. 2003. Ruth and Naomi: Economic Survival and Family Values. Pages 27–48 in *Just Wives? Stories of Power and Survival in the Old Testament and Today.* Louisville: Westminster John Knox.

Sasson, Jack M. 1989. *Ruth: A New Translation with a Philological Commentary and a Formalist-Folklorist Interpretation.* 2nd ed. Biblical Seminar 10. Sheffield: Sheffield Academic Press.

Shepherd, David. 2001. Violence in the Fields? Translating, Reading, and Revising in Ruth 2. *CBQ* 63:444–63.

Silber, Ursula. 1999. Ruth and Naomi: Two Biblical Figures Revived among Rural Women in Germany. Pages 93–109 in Brenner 1999a.

Snijders, L. A. 1954. The Meaning of *Zar* in the Old Testament. *OtSt* 10:1–110.

Spencer, John R. 1992. Sojourner. *ABD* 6:103–4.

Stanton, Elizabeth Cady. 1993. *The Woman's Bible.* Edited by Maureen Fitzgerald. Boston: Northeastern University Press.

Takaki, Ronald. 1989. *Strangers from a Different Shore: A History of Asian Americans.* New York: Penguin.

——. 1993. *A Different Mirror: A History of Multicultural America.* Boston: Little, Brown.

Thompson, J. A. 1977. Israel's "Lovers". *VT* 27:475–81.

Travis, Irene S. 2000. Love Your Mother: A Lesbian Womanist Reading of Scripture. Pages 35–42 in *Take Back the Word: A Queer Reading of the Bible.* Edited by Robert E. Goss and Mona West. Cleveland: Pilgrim.

Tuan, Mia. 1998. *Forever Foreigners or Honorary Whites: The Asian Ethnic Experience Today.* New Brunswick, N.J.: Rutgers University Press.

Uchida, Aki. 1998. The Orientalization of Asian Women in America. *Women's Studies International Forum* 21:161–74.

Weems, Renita J. 1988. *Just a Sister Away: A Womanist Vision of Women's Relationships in the Bible.* San Diego: LuraMedia.

Williams, Dolores S. 1989. Breaking and Bonding. *Daughters of Sarah* 15.3:20–21.

Win, Su Mo Mo. 2000. The Concept of *Hesed* in Ruth 1:1–22. *In God's Image* 19.2:10–14.

Wolde, Ellen van. 1997. Intertextuality: Ruth in Dialogue with Tamar. Pages 426–51 in *A Feminist Companion to Reading the Bible: Approaches, Methods and Strategies.* Edited by Athalya Brenner and Carole Fontaine. Sheffield: Sheffield Academic Press.

Wong, Angela Wai Ching. 1999. History, Identity and a Community of *Hesed*: A Biblical Reflection on Ruth 1:1–17. *AJT* 13:3–13.

Wu, Frank. H. 2002. *Yellow: Race in America beyond Black and White.* New York: Basic Books.

Yee, Gale A. 1997. Inculturation and Diversity in the Politics of National Identity. *Journal of Asian and Asian American Theology* 2:108–12.

———. 2003. The Other Woman in Proverbs: My Man's Not Home—He Took His Moneybag with Him. Pages 135–58 in *Poor Banished Children of Eve: Woman as Evil in the Hebrew Bible*. Minneapolis: Fortress.

———. 2006. Yin/Yang Is Not Me: An Exploration Into an Asian American Biblical Hermeneutics. Pages 152–63 in *Ways of Being, Ways of Reading: Constructing Asian-American Biblical Interpretation*. Edited by Mary F. Foskett and Jeffrey K. Kuan. St. Louis: Chalice.

Yoshikawa, Mako. 1999. *One Hundred and One Ways*. New York: Bantam.

Zia, Helen. 2000. *Asian American Dreams: The Emergence of an American People*. New York: Farrar, Straus & Giroux.

PAUL AND ETHNIC DIFFERENCE IN ROMANS

Jae Won Lee

Paul uses kinship language to identify both Jewish and non-Jewish Christ believers as members of one community defined in terms of likeness to Christ. According to him, both are children of God, co-heirs with Christ (thus brothers and sisters of Christ), and brothers and sisters of one another. However, in order for both Jewish and non-Jewish Christ-believers to affirm that they belong to this community, do they have to forfeit their ethnic identity?

Numerous Western interpreters have answered affirmatively. In the name of equality, they have universalized Paul's statement that in Christ "there is neither Jew nor Greek" so that ethnic identity is irrelevant. Yet who uses this logic of identity, and who imposes it on whom? Subtly, this has meant that Western identity exercised hegemony because Western identity was the norm from which ethnic identity was considered irrelevant.

As a Korean American woman who empathizes with *minjung* theology, I draw an analogy between the way "Gentile" Christianity deprived "Jewish" ethnicity of its specificity and the way the universal discourse and imperialistic moves of Western Christianity suppressed Korean ethnic, historical, and cultural values. This does not mean, however, that I associate personal and collective Korean American experiences more with first-century Jews than with ethnically unspecified Gentiles, because under certain circumstances (e.g., Galatians) other groups also suppressed Gentiles. Thus, when Asian Americans make correlations with first-century Christ-believers, we should avoid analogies that are too simple. Like Paul, we stand among Jews and Gentiles, unable to identify definitively with either. Additionally, identity in minority communities is complicated by the intersection of ethnicity with class, gender, nation, and empire.

In Second Temple Judaism, Jewish identity stood in polarity with Gentile (pagan) identity. Since the second century, Christendom has largely replaced this by a polarity between Christian and Jewish identity. This move has associated Jewish identity with *pagan* identity, resulting in a Christian/Jewish (pagan) polarity. Further, Korean Christianity's exclusivism toward non-Christians has replicated Western Christianity's exclusivism toward Jewish (pagan) difference.

These shifting identities demonstrate that the "other," like ethnicity, is a historical, social construct (Hall 1997, 16, 19; Segovia 1995, 290–92).

Zealous to identify with Western/American Christianity, Korean/Korean American Christianity failed to recognize that the latter is not the "same" as the former and has never been treated as equal. Endeavoring to imitate the universalism of Western Christianity, Korean/Korean American Christianity has assimilated to, and has been deeply colonized by, Western cultural imperialism. This has occurred to such an extent that many Korean/Korean American Christians have slight awareness of the ways in which a Western "universal" identity, which is not "ours," has suppressed Korean/ Korean American identity (Min 1999, 151–59).

Korean/Korean American Christianity is characterized predominantly by a personal faith centered on a worldly-otherworldly dichotomy. Particularly, Paul's discourse on justification by faith, his comments regarding God's impartiality toward Jews and Gentiles, and his alleged spirit-flesh dualism have been interpreted as integral elements of an apolitical, ahistorical, and acultural Christian faith. As such, faith has been understood as having little to do with differences in class, gender, race, and empire.

However, Paul's discourse is capable not only of being used for the denial of difference; it is also capable of undergirding ethnic identity. Do Paul and the Pauline movement actually represent the universalistic move that later Christianity pronounced particularly against Judaism? What interpretive moves have been made concerning Paul's discourse with respect to the formation of the early Christian identity in order to derive from it the universalistic claim of later Christianity, including moves by dominant Pauline scholarship? Answers to these questions need to take seriously the impact of the universal claim of Christianity as "racially inclusive" upon minority groups who struggle with how to claim their ethnic identities in their self-understandings and practices of Christian identity (Buell and Johnson Hodge 2004, 235–51).

This essay joins an emerging challenge within Pauline scholarship to take "ethnicity" as a central issue for early Christ-believers in relation to other Jewish and Greco-Roman social groups. I interrogate the historical and hermeneutical consequences of interpreting Paul's discourse as a universalistic move toward eradication of ethnic particularities among Christ-believers. To do so, I deal with issues involving the "strong" and the "weak" in Rom 14:1–15:13, focusing especially on Paul's politics of difference insofar as it pertains to matters of ethnicity and insofar as it demonstrates the relevance of my contextual approach for the relationship between ethnicity and marginality.

Paul and Ethnicity: What Is at Stake?

Universalism: The Hermeneutics of the "Strong"

The dominant stream supporting Christian universalism views Paul as a pillar for overcoming ethnic identities by adopting a universal identity. The dichotomy between Jewish and Christian identity has been closely allied with interpretations of Paul. Although some scholars have already challenged this construal, far more remains to be done. I join the enterprise with the thesis that Paul's politics of difference as attested in Rom 14–15 does not obscure but rather upholds ethnic particularity.

One may think that taking ethnicity seriously in biblical studies is a recent phenomenon among scholars from minority groups acclimating to current trends in contextual interpretation. However, ethnicity is already implicated in the insistence of dominant scholarship that ethnicity is irrelevant, thus disparaging attention to ethnicity in minority interpretations (Kelley 2002). Dominant interpretation has attempted to transcend ethnicity by making Christianity "all inclusive," thus ethnicity-neutral (Buell and Johnson Hodge 2004, 236–37). Allegedly, ethnicity is irrelevant to normative, historical, objective, value-free criticism; a corollary is that ethnic concerns constitute the idiosyncrasies of a few ethnic scholars.

Surprisingly, the "New Perspective" on Paul with its revisionary view toward Judaism has contributed little to shifting the universalizing paradigm. Granted, E. P. Sanders made valuable contributions to "the foundations for a reading which neither slanders Judaism nor slanders Paul by making his account of Judaism a slander" (Boyarin 1994, 47). However, Sanders's version of Paul's "exclusivistic universalism" makes ethnicity "indifferent," especially in relation to Jewish practices of circumcision, special days, and special food (Sanders 1983, 113–14). Sanders argues that Paul's principle of "tolerance" toward Jewish law did not work in actual interaction between Jews and Gentiles. Concerning the Antioch incident in Gal 2:10–14, Sanders states: "If Jewish and Gentile Christians were to eat together, one would have to decide whether to live as a Jew or as a Gentile.... The Antioch incident would seem to show that, if Jews were present, Paul would expect them not to observe the Jewish dietary laws" (177). Thus, Sanders presents Paul as a Jew who "viewed it as the only behavior in accord with the truth of the gospel to live as a Gentile" (178). For Sanders, "Gentileness" is not only oppositional to "Jewishness" but is nonethnic "Gentileness." Jewish particularity functions as a foil against Gentile Christian inclusivism. As Denise Kimber Buell and Caroline Johnson Hodge critically remark, "The understanding of ethnicity or race as 'given' operates as a foil for a non-ethnic, all-inclusive Christianity" (2004, 236). By contrast, I would argue that Rom 14:1–15:13 expects Jews to continue their ethnic practices.

James Dunn presents Paul as attacking a "nationalistic or racial" understanding of the Jewish covenant (1990, 186). He assumes that Paul understood Jesus' death and resurrection as the fulfillment of the covenant that transcends ethnic boundaries. Dunn's use of "nationalistic" reflects the dominant nonethnic construal of Paul's Gentile Christianity, a position that implies that (Jewish) ethnicity is inferior vis-à-vis (Christian) universalism.

I discern a hermeneutical circle running through the mainstream. It views itself as universal, transcending ethnic particularities. Questions of ethnic particularity supposedly violate universality. This perspective also entails a value judgment: the universal is inclusive and good; the particular is limited and weak. Yet the claim of being inclusive denies the ethnic identities of minority groups and hampers their equal participation in sociopolitical, economic, and academic realms. To state this in Pauline terms, the "strong" (dominant biblical criticism) exclude the "weak" (minority criticism) by judging the "weaknesses" (ethnic particularities) from the ideological perspective of the strong. The hermeneutics of the strong dominates the hermeneutics of the weak while disguising its exclusive tendency, that is, the hegemony of identity, in its claim for universality. Iris Marion Young captures this well:

> The irony of the logic of identity is that by seeking to reduce the differently similar to the same, it turns the merely different into the absolutely other. It inevitably generates dichotomy instead of unity, because the move to bring particulars under a universal category creates a distinction between inside and outside.... Because the totalizing movement always leaves a remainder, the project of reducing particulars to a unity must fail. Not satisfied then to admit defeat in the face of difference, the logic of identity shoves difference into dichotomous hierarchical oppositions: essence/accident, good/bad, normal/deviant. (1990, 99)

Alternative Voices

Over against such a universalism, Daniel Boyarin foregrounds a hermeneutical question that deserves special mention. He stands against Western Christian universalism, "which deprives those who have historically grounded identities in those material signifiers of the power to speak for themselves and remain different" (1994, 233). Boyarin assumes, however, that "Paul was motivated by a Hellenistic desire for the One, which ... produced an ideal of a universal human essence, beyond difference and hierarchy" (7). He persistently argues that Paul's universalism of "neither Jew nor Gentile" is meant to erase not only Jew-Gentile difference but all cultural specificities. Yet Boyarin's reading equates Paul's universalism far too much with post-Pauline Western Christian imperialist universalism.

To begin with, although Boyarin considers Paul's writing as inner-Jewish cultural discourse, he sees Paul as if he were a devotee of a new religion separate from

Judaism. Accordingly, he sets the question of "Jewish difference" in Paul in the framework of the later debate between Jews and Christians, though Christianity at Paul's time was still characteristically Jewish. Therefore, Boyarin identifies Pauline universalism with Western Christian universalism. Second, Boyarin identifies the contemporary question of Jewish difference with Paul's Jewish difference. He clearly reflects an essentialist understanding of "difference" in his statement that "the quintessentially 'different' people for Paul were Jews and women" (1994, 17). Boyarin imposes this agenda on Paul's dealing with difference, since for him the question is "*not* the relative statuses of Jewish and gentile Christians but the statuses of those—Jews and others—who choose not to be Christians" (9, emphasis original). Third, Boyarin disallows the possibility that Paul approached the question of Jew-Gentile difference contextually in particular community situations. Rather, Boyarin states: "I suggest that for the logic of Paul's theology, which was complete in its entirety from the first moment of his revelation, there was not the slightest importance to the observance of such rites for Jews or gentiles" (111).

If Boyarin's interpretation is actually that of later Christianity as a dominant religion, then ironically he denies a first-century Jew, Paul, the right to speak for himself from his own context. In the end, addressing the present question of identity and difference, Boyarin offers a proposal over against Paul's solution as he perceives it: "A dialectic that would utilize each of these as antithesis to the other, correcting in the 'Christian' system its tendencies toward a coercive universalism and in the 'Jewish' system its tendencies toward contemptuous neglect for human solidarity might lead beyond both toward a better social system" (1994, 235). My reading of Rom 14:1–15:13 is that in Romans Paul dealt with the first part of Boyarin's statement, whereas he dealt with the second part in Galatians, if the word "Gentile" is substituted for "Christian."

Recently, other scholars have challenged the dominant hermeneutics of universalism by focusing on the hermeneutics of suspicion, the politics of interpretation, and different interpretive modes. Sze-kar Wan suggests a differentiated Asian American diasporic hermeneutics. In dialogue with Fernando Segovia and Boyarin, Wan recognizes "the shared commonality in diasporic hybridity" (the inevitable impact of colonizers on the colonized without the colonized assimilating to the colonizers). At the same time, he raises the question of ethnocentrism in Segovia's emphasis on "otherness" (which I cannot differentiate from Wan's "power differential"). Further, against Boyarin's description of diasporic identity as "a state of permanent powerlessness," he asserts that minority groups cannot practice "self-emptying of power … [because it] is practicable only if we have something to empty of" (2000, 118). Wan rightly identifies issues of power affecting ethnic minority groups but still detects "ethnocentricism" in emerging minority interpretation. Ironically, this resonates with a typical critique from dominant biblical scholarship. Wan's alternative to both "the universalization of the dominant cultural values and hierarchy" and "ethnocentric insularity" is "hybridity" (109). "[Hybridity] could be a kind of common ground for universal discourse between former colonizers and the colonized and between the colonized themselves" (110).

Wan questions whether Segovia's diasporic hermeneutics of otherness and engagement allows "for dialogue across cultural and ethnic lines" (2000, 113). Although Wan perceives Segovia's intercultural criticism as pertinent to the relationship between the text as a culturally conditioned "other" and the reader also as a culturally conditioned "other," the importance of the reader's role in interpretation, and the significance of the reader's engagement with other readers, Wan contests "the common agenda of liberation" as the ground for engagement: "One group's liberation could … become another's oppression" (112–14).

In response, I interject some suggestions from Iris Marion Young. Young challenges "an ideal of justice that defines liberation as the transcendence of group difference." This amounts to "assimilation." She proposes instead an "emancipatory politics of difference," which affirms group difference (1990, 157). Affirming difference involves revisioning equality. Although liberation as the ideal elimination of difference, especially privileged differences, is important in the history of emancipatory politics, a politics of difference, not the assimilationist ideal, needs to be promoted. Young posits that "a positive self-definition of group difference is in fact more liberatory" (157). She affirms that:

> Groups experiencing cultural imperialism have found themselves objectified and marked with a devalued essence from the outside, by a dominant culture they are excluded from making. The assertion of a positive sense of group difference by these groups is emancipatory because it reclaims the definition of the group by the group, as a creation and construction, rather than a given essence. (172)

Against Boyarin's "state of permanent powerlessness," Wan protests, "Now that we have learned to speak and write like our white teachers, we are told we should develop and construct our own narratives, or, in Boyarin's terms, divest ourselves of power and the basis for that power, neither of which we have, even now" (2000, 119). Christine Di Stefano responds similarly to the postmodern deconstruction of the self. She asks: "Why is it, just at the moment in Western history when previously silenced populations have begun to speak for themselves and on behalf of their subjectivities, that the concept of the subject and the possibility of discovering/creating a liberating 'truth' become suspect?" (1990, 75).

Although I agree with Wan that for ethnic minority groups to take a permanent status of powerlessness is to weaken what is not yet strong, I am wary of Wan's basis for power. Is it an assimilation to the ground of the power of the strong, rather than resistance against the postmodern imposition of a decentered self and meekness regarding the coherence and truth of their claims upon minority?

Finally, in an important article dealing with the "eruption of the issue of ethnicity on the global scene," Fernando Segovia summarizes the task facing minority biblical scholars as follows:

First and foremost, a re-reading and re-interpretation of the biblical texts from outside the Western context, with a focus on such issues as the following: the self-construction of the early Christian groups; their construction of the "other"—of all those outside the boundaries of the group—and of the relationship vis-à-vis such "others"; their construction of the political realm and of their relationship to this realm, whether at the imperial level or at the local level; their visions of a different world, a world in which peace and justice prevail. (2000, 176)

In this essay I make a commitment to such a task by a rereading of Rom 14:1–15:13. This text has been used to marginalize ethnic particularity in the discussion of early Christian identity. The dominant interpretation supports Paul's so-called universal position toward ethnicity. My contribution below translates Segovia's emphasis on "from outside the Western context" into a challenge to the tendency to universalize Paul in Western interpretations. I read against the universalized interpretation from my Asian American hermeneutical perspective in conversation with other voices dealing with ethnicity in Paul. I relate my rereading to Segovia's call for the biblical investigation of "the self-construction of the early Christian groups" and "their construction of the 'other.'"

The discourse about the "strong" and the "weak" in Rom 14:1–15:13 is among the earliest cases that provide us with opportunities to scrutinize both *us* versus *them* constructions in early Christian groups and the problems in dominant scholarship today. Thus, I intend to show that the discourse about the "strong" and "weak" not only reflects issues of ethnicity in marginalized groups in first-century Rome but can also be extended to include a discussion of the hegemony of and resistance to dominant biblical criticism (the "strong") over biblical criticism practiced by ethnic minority scholars (the "weak"). The terms the "strong" and the "weak" are problematic in that they imply binary opposition. Yet, as Korean scholar Yang Geun Seok's assessment of the current geopolitical reality under the wave of universalizing globalization shows, such terms are justified because they recapitulate the desperate personal and corporate reality of the socially weak (2005, 15–16).

ROMANS 14–15

In his innovative proposal, Mark Nanos suggests that the "weak" in Rom 14–15 are not Christ-believers but members of the Jewish community (1996, 103–65). In my view, the address in 1:6–8, which clearly identifies the recipients as those who belong to Jesus Christ, is implicated in Paul's exhortation against judging in 14:4. As people who abstain from eating certain foods, the weak judge those who do eat, and Paul directly admonishes them. This indicates that the weak are among the addressees, and in 1:6–8 they are identified as Christ-believers. Moreover, one can hardly construe the status of Gentile Christians in Rome as socially strong enough to be dominant over the larger Jewish community, as Nanos's construct requires.

Another of Nanos's primary arguments rests on Rom 14:1: they are weak "in faith" (*ton de asthenounta tē pistei proslambanesthe*). To be weak in faith here means for him that these people are not Christ-believers (1996, 103–19). I return to this text below, but for the moment suffice it to say that it is more likely that *tē pistei* modifies the main verb, *proslambanesthe*, rather than the participle, *asthenounta*. Instead of describing weakness in terms of faith, the verse exhorts the addressees to receive the one who is weak as a part of their faith (read not "the one who is weak in faith" but "receive in faith the one who is weak").

Nanos correctly points to Paul's references to non-Christ-believing Jews as "brethren." Further, I agree that to regard Paul's argument as meaning that Jewish practice can be disregarded would make the logic self-contradictory in that Paul appeals to the weak and the strong not to judge each other. Nanos assumes that if the weak are Christ-believing Jews, then they would be required to give up Jewish practice, which in turn would mean that they would be judged for their Jewishness. This, however, is the assumption I contest. To the contrary, Paul values difference for both Jewish and Gentile Christ-believers. Thus, when he argues that "we who are many are one body in Christ" (12:5), he advocates oneness with difference that does not disregard the distinctiveness of either Jews or Gentiles.

Neil Elliott has recently expressed dissatisfaction with interpretations of Romans that imply that Paul is mediating between non-Jewish and Jewish Christ-believers in conflict. Without identifying any such interpretations, he generalizes nevertheless that they rely on "unhistorical and prejudicial characterizations of Judaism" in presuming that Jewish Christ-believers adhere to the boundary markers of Jewish identity and that these alone create social tensions with non-Jewish Christ believers. He further avers that such interpretations misconstrue Paul's use of *ta ethnē* by making it an ethnic category on the same level as "Jews." For him, this is a category mistake in that Paul uses *ta ethnē* to refer to the nations who will join Israel in worshiping the God of Israel. As such, the term expresses no specific ethnic identity, because it embraces a host of ethnic identities such as Syrians and Bithynians (Elliott 2007, 181–83).

Commendably, Elliott points instead to the way Roman imperial power shapes cultural identities to inscribe Roman ethnic identity as superior to others. In this connection, I agree that as monotheists the recipients of Romans were marginalized over against the dominant Roman construct of the social order. Not only were they monotheists; they also were committed to a Christ who had been crucified. The status of those committed to Jesus is related to his crucifixion in that death on a cross was usually reserved for insubordinate slaves and subversive foreigners (Hengel 1977, 13–20, 34–38; Marcus 2006, 78–79, 86–87).

In light of Elliott's focus on the dominance of the Roman imperial construct of identity, both groups in Rom 14–15 are marginalized with respect to the dominant social order. Yet, over against the ideology of Roman superiority, Elliott curiously claims that there were no "Gentiles" in the first century of our era and does not deal with the situation in Rom 14–15 as involving conflict related to ethnic identity. To claim that no ethnic group carried the title "Gentiles" occasions no objection from me. However, in Elliott's move to the ideology of Roman supremacy, does he not close his eyes to specific tensions between *hē peritomē* ("the circumcision") and *hē akrobustia* ("the foreskin") with which Paul does deal (Rom 2:25–29; 3:30; 4:9–12)? Joel Marcus correlates *peritomē* and *akrobustia* with the "weak" and the "strong" by suggesting that they originated as ethnic slurs: Gentile Christians in Rome labeled themselves the "strong" and their opponents the "weak"; Jewish Christians called themselves *peritomē* and their opponents *akrobustia* (1989, 67–82). Robert Jewett also analyzes this language of *peritomē* and *akrobustia* in terms of contests of honor and shame (1995; 2006, 232). Further, in Rom 3:30 *peritomē* and *akrobustia* are reiterations of *Ioudaioi* and *ethnē* in 3:29. Do not these tensions and equivalences in Rom 2–3 between circumcision and uncircumcision as well as Jews and Gentiles anticipate the conflicts in Rom 14–15 between the weak and the strong?

Granted, *Gentile* is not an ethnic identity that people claim for themselves. Rather, it is an in-group's label for an out-group, and in this sense on at least three occasions it is a designation imposed by Paul on a group that is opposite and analogous to "Jews." One of these, already noted, is in 3:29, where the Gentiles (*ethnē*) are juxtaposed to the "Jews" (*Ioudaioi*). The same juxtaposition occurs in 9:24, while in 9:30 the *ethnē* stands over against *Israēl*. Furthermore, there is sufficient group identity of the *ethnē* in Rome that Paul can address them as such (11:13) and urge them not to *boast* over the natural branches. What can this boasting be but the kind of tension played out in Rom 14–15? Without these tensions, Elliott could be correct in asserting that references to the *peritomē* and *ethnē* in 15:8–9 are Paul's allusions in Israel's Scripture to the nations who join Israel eschatologically in worshiping Israel's God: "Christ has become a servant of the circumcised on behalf of the truth of God in order that he might confirm the promises given to the patriarchs, and in order that the Gentiles might glorify God for his mercy." However, after the reiterations for the strong to accommodate to the weak, to please the neighbor in order to build up the other, to live in harmony with one another, and to welcome one another, then the christological argument in 15:8–9 with respect to the *peritomē* and the *ethnē* is a part of the reiterated exhortations for reconciliation between two groups (see Reasoner 1999, 136).

Elliott also appeals to Mark Reasoner's work on the weak and the strong in Rom 14–15 as locating Paul's discussion within the ideological context of the elite in Rome. It is commendable to locate this discussion in a context where the strong are associated with power and social status and the weak with powerlessness and shame in lower social strata. Elliott's appeal to Reasoner notwithstanding, even though the latter does not limit the weak only to people of Jewish origin nor the strong to people with only a Gentile identity, Reasoner suggests that the abstinence from meat and wine that characterizes the weak was likely motivated by Jewish concerns (1999, 63, 131, 137–38, 201–2, 210, 214–15; see Segal 1990, 234–36). In particular, Paul's use of *koinon* in 14:14 implies issues of Jewish cultic purity (Reasoner 1999, 131, 136, 201). Elliott shows that tensions between Roman citizens and foreigners complicate the tensions in Rome. Nevertheless, evidence for tensions between those identified by circumcision and those identified by foreskin is abundant.

Further, I distance myself from Elliott's claim that interpretations of Romans that deal with ethnic tensions reinscribe "unhistorical and prejudicial character-izations of Judaism." I hope to show that my reading of Paul's politics of difference in terms of equality with difference is historical, while avoiding at the same time a prejudicial characterization of Judaism.

In dealing with Rom 14:1, to which I referred above, Reasoner, like Nanos, construes the dative phrase *tē pistei* with the substantive participle *ton asthe-nounta*, so that he translates "the weak in faith." Further, he takes the *hos pisteuei* ("one believes") of 14:2 to be the counterpart of the dative phrase *tē pistei* (1999, 65). In spite of the prevalence of this view, both construals are dubious. It is far more probable that *tē pistei* modifies the verb *proslambanesthe*, a point to which I shall return shortly. True, it is possible for the dative *tē pistei* to modify *asthe-nounta* in connection with the verbal quality of the participle. However, if *tē pistei* is attributive in connection with the substantive use of the participle, the repeti-tion of the article would be expected: *ton asthenounta ton tē pistei*. The absence of the article is an initial indication for *tē pistei* to be construed with *proslambanes-the*: "Accept in faith the one who is weak."[1]

Moreover, when Reasoner finds the counterpart of *tē pistei* (14:1) in *hos pisteuei* (14:2), he has literally gone too far, since such a counterpart appears immediately after the verb *proslambanesthe*: *mē eis diakriseis dialogismōn* ("not for quarrels over opinions"). Paul juxtaposes two ways of relating to the one who is weak. Negatively put: "Do not accept the one who is weak for quarrels over opinions"; put positively: "Accept in faith the one who is weak."

In addition, given the line of argument, the full meaning of *proslambanesthe* should be emphasized: "Accept in faith the weak one as a *helper*." On its own, *pro-slambanesthe* can mean "to take to oneself as one's helper or partner" (LSJ). Such a meaning for 14:1, however, is supported by the parallel in 15:7–9, with which 14:1 forms an *inclusio*. Romans 15:8 presents Jesus as a *diakonos* ("helper") of the circumcision, and on this christological basis Paul urges the Roman community to accept one another. Thus, *proslambanesthe* in 14:1 likely implies accepting each other as partners.

---

1. The same dative expression *tē pistei* occurs in Rom 4:19, where it modifies a participle of the same verb *astheneō*. In that case, however, the participle is not substantival but circum-stantial. In 4:20 and 11:20 *tē apistia* and *tē pistei* modify finite verbs in parallel with what I am arguing for 14:1. In the undisputed Pauline Epistles, the dative *tē pistei* appears seven times apart from its use with prepositions, and, with the exception of 4:19, in the other occurrences it modifies finite verbs.

Buell and Johnson Hodge argue that, in spite of Paul's moves toward egalitarianism, he maintains the ethnic priority of Israel over the nations (2004, 235–51).
Such a stance would present an obstacle to my interpretation of ethnicity in Paul
in terms of equality with difference. They argue that Paul preserves the categories
"Greek" and "Judean" while uniting them under Abrahamic ancestry, but only in
the hierarchy of "to the Judean first, then to the Greek" (238). They argue further
that for Paul to be "in Christ" is a Judean identity (247).

Buell and Johnson Hodge correctly point to Paul's advocacy of the God of
Israel and his use of Abrahamic ancestry to include Gentiles in the people of God.
Yet, three factors raise the issue of whether "first" and "then" should be construed
as hierarchical. First, there is Paul's assertion of equality before God on the basis
of monotheism (e.g., 3:29). Second, Paul proclaims that this God is also the Creator (1:20, 25; 8:19–23), which is to say that God has a history *prior to* Israel's
election. Third, "to the Judean first, then to the Greek" is not Paul's only comment
on sequence. The first reference to sequence appears in 1:16: "[The gospel] is the
power of God for salvation … to the Judean first and also to the Greek." This text
seems to substantiate Buell and Johnson Hodge's claim with respect to hierarchy.
On the other hand, this is but the first occurrence of a topic that keeps reoccur-
ring. A striking inversion arises when Paul deals with the problem of evil in 2:9:
"Tribulation and distress are upon the life of every human being who does evil,
the Judean first, and also the Greek." Granted, the next verse reverses this verdict
with respect to doing good. Nevertheless, if hierarchy means priority in punishment, it is a bizarre hierarchy.

Even more startling is the inversion in 4:10–12. Paul first claims that Abraham was justified before he was circumcised. He then questions why Abraham
was circumcised. In his answer he asserts that Abraham is first the ancestor of
the Gentiles who have faith like the faith of Abraham. The purpose of circumcision, then, is to make him also the ancestor of the circumcised who have like
faith. Instead of taking the Abrahamic heritage in terms of "to the Judean first
and also to the Greek," Paul here inverts it in terms of "to the Gentile first and
also to the Judean."

We have little knowledge of what contact Paul had with traditions about
Abraham, but traditions were in existence in his time that considered Abraham to
be the ancestor of the whole human race, like Adam and Eve, and Noah. During
Second Temple Judaism, at the same time that traditions such as those represented
in Pss. Sol. 9:9–11, Jub. 22:16–18, 4 Macc 6:17–22, and the Damascus Document
(CD 12:11) appealed to Abraham as the progenitor of Israelites exclusively, other
traditions such as 1 En. 90:33 make Abraham the ancestor of all nations. Whereas
Jacob is the ancestor of Israel, Abraham, especially through Hagar and Keturah, is
considered to be the ancestor of the entire Mediterranean world. It is well known
that 1 Macc 12:21 claims that the Spartans are descendants of Abraham. Josephus
asserts that Abraham's sons through Keturah founded colonies in Troglodytis,
Arabia, and Libya. Further, he cites Polyhistor, who is citing Cleodemus Malchus,

to claim that Abraham's sons by Keturah were the ancestors of Assyria and Africa. Ishmael's twelve sons gave their names to Arabian tribes (*Ant.* 1 §§220–221, 238–241; 12 §§225–226). Similarly, Eusebius, citing Polyhistor, who cites also from Cleodemus Malchus and Demetrius, derives the Assyrians, Africans, the people of Carthage, and Moses' wife Zipporah from Abraham through Keturah (*Praep. ev.* 9.20; 9.29.1–3). Thus, God's promise to Abraham that he would be the ancestor of multitudes found fulfillment not only in Israel but also in the Gentiles. Paul's arguments that Abraham is ancestor of Gentiles and also ancestor of the Jewish people who have faith like his (Rom 4:11–25; Gal 3:7) resonate with such traditions. These traditions and Paul's inversions of "to the Judean first and also to the Greek" challenge an Abrahamic hierarchy as Buell and Johnson Hodge understand it.

ONENESS WITH DIFFERENCE

In support of my claim that Paul advocates a politics of difference with equality, I return to the details of Rom 14:1–15:13. Paul's repeated use of *krinein* in connection with *kyrios* has rarely received adequate attention. *Krinein* occurs eight times in the passage, and, in connection with Paul's exhortation not to welcome one who is weak for "disputes over opinions" (14:1), such frequency indicates that judging is part of the disputes.

Paul first moves rhetorically from his addressees to an imaginary interlocutor: "Who are you to pass judgment [*krinōn*] on another's servant [*allotrion oiketēn*]? It is before his own [*idiō*] master that he stands or falls. And he will be upheld, for the Master is able to make him stand" (14:4). Relationships of difference and identity are expressed by *allotrios* (difference) and *idios* (identity). The RSV translation is misleading in that it can imply that the servants belong to different masters. However, those who abstain and those who eat have the same master. Each servant has a different relationship with the master. Their identities are different, but both have the same status before the one Lord.

In Rom 14:6–9 *kyrios* functions to unite differences in a common framework without dissolving the differences. Living for oneself stands over against living for the honor of the Lord. Those who eat do not eat for themselves; rather, they eat in honor of the Lord. Similarly, those who abstain do not abstain for themselves; rather, they abstain in honor of the Lord. If eating or not eating were matters of indifference, Paul could have said so. Yet, eating or abstaining does matter to those who eat or abstain in honor of the Lord. In their equal relationship with the Lord, difference remains. Jews remain Jews; Gentiles remain Gentiles. The identity derived from honoring the Lord does not abrogate ethnic-cultural identity, and one identity is not absorbed into another. Because Paul couches his argument in terms of living and dying, matters of eating or abstaining are not minor concerns. They are matters of living and dying in honor of the Lord.

Further, Paul grounds the different but equal identity of living or dying to the Lord on Christ's death and resurrection. This establishes an unconventional mutuality between Lord and servants. Christ died and lived again so that he might be Lord of those who live or die to the Lord (14:7–9). In light of the conventional domination of master over slave in Roman antiquity, the mutuality expressed here is startlingly subversive (Georgi 1991, 97).

To be sure, Paul introduces a universal perspective in 14:10: "We must all stand before the judgment seat of God." This universalism, however, requires no sacrifice of particularity. Rather, each is accountable to God (14:12). Certainly, one does not live to oneself, but, in living to the honor of the Lord, one does not cease to be oneself.

Paul underscores the point that both Jews and Gentiles are accountable for their difference before God's judgment and reinforces it with: "Then let us no longer pass judgment on one another" (14:13). Immediately he moves to how this can be put into practice. A simple answer is "mutuality" (*allēlous*).[2] Yet the answer is not simple, since relationships always involve power, and the relationships in Rom 14–15 reflect unbalanced power. The "strong" group is in a position to cause pain for the "weak" (14:15). They are even capable of "destroying the work of God" (14:20), which is the marginalized hybrid community of both Jews and Gentiles. For Paul, the strong are the ones who jeopardize the community (see Nanos 1996, 96–103).

At this juncture Paul engages again in wordplay with *krinein*. Paul's admonition concerning judging is not directed toward both the weak and the strong, as in 14:3, but only to the strong. Moreover, he no longer employs a negative prohibition but now a positive imperative: "But rather *discern* [*krinate*] never to put a stumbling block of hindrance in the way of the other" (14:13). Practicing mutuality means an adjustment of the dominant group toward the subordinate group.

Paul's shift to the first-person singular (only here in 14:1–15:13) likely makes reference to his personal position: "I know and am persuaded in the Lord Jesus that nothing is unclean [*koinon*] in itself; but it is unclean for anyone who thinks it is unclean" (14:14). Given the use of the diatribe style, it could be taken as a paradigmatic "I." In any case, the strong recognize a position on food as an issue of purity for the weak.

With 14:20 this text has misleadingly been taken as evidence that Paul advocates freedom from the law and, therefore, that Jewish laws are irrelevant. Significantly, from 14:15 on the rhetorical force is directed toward the strong. Paul's reminder of the priority of justice, peace, and joy in the Holy Spirit in the kingdom of God is aimed primarily at the strong (14:17). On the basis of the

---

2. Brigitte Kahl notes that the Greek for mutuality (*allēlous*) derives from a doubling of the word for "other" (*allos–allos*) and that in Galatians it involves a movement down to the level of the lowly and excluded (2000, 47).

priority of God's kingdom, the community is urged to pursue "what makes for peace and mutual upbuilding" (14:19–20) instead of causing the other to stumble. Paul's metaphor of "building up" is closely tied to his attempt to construct a new identity for members of the community. Instead of reinforcing one group over the other, Paul offers a household built of both Jews and Gentiles—a "bridge identity" (on this term, see Ferguson 1998, 95–113). The bridge identity is built on radical mutuality: "the things of peace and upbuilding one another" (14:19).

The brunt of practicing mutuality falls on the strong. Paul acknowledges their claim ("all things are clean") but does not make that the issue. What surpasses this claim is the wrong (kakon) committed by eating when it makes the other stumble (14:20). Thus, Paul exhorts the strong to change their practice. He also exhorts the weak not to judge the strong but does not encourage them to change their practice (see Nanos 1996, 96–103). "The 'strong' are Paul's target," Nanos argues, "and the entire paraenesis is concerned with convincing them to accept the 'weak' without 'judging their opinions,' and further, to accommodate the sensibilities of the 'weak' by modifying their behavior to mirror that of the 'weak,' even as Christ had" (147). Regarding the dispute between the weak and the strong, E. P. Sanders concludes that "[Paul] judged one form of behavior to be wrong. The wrong form was living according to the law" (1983, 178; also Dunn 1988, 811; Watson 1991, 205–6). This contradicts, however, the evidence that Paul asks the weak to change their attitude but not their practice.

For Paul, to accommodate to the practice of Jewish Christians does not require Gentiles to change their conviction. It requires rather a change of practice. In 14:22 Paul supports the faith of the strong in terms of their relationship with God, but he urges them to change their practice so as not to undermine the faith of the weak in terms of their relationship with God.[3] In 14:23 Paul obviously has the weak in mind when he uses the term ho diakrinomenos (Dunn 1988, 828). Yet the verse also makes it clear that the weak are not encouraged to change their conviction with respect to their practices. To the contrary, for them to change eating practices to comply with the practices of the strong is identified as lack of faith (hoti ouk ek pisteōs)—in fact, it is sin (hamartia).

In Rom 15:1 Paul uses the epithet "strong": "We who are strong [oi dynatoi] are in debt to bear the weaknesses of the weak [hoi adynatoi]." He hardly invented the terms but used labels current in the community (Marcus 1989, 67–81; Reasoner 1999, 56). Moreover, these antonyms betray a power relationship of dominance and subordination. In this case Paul does not advocate a mutuality that

---

3. Against Dunn: "The 'stronger' the faith (that is, the more unconditional the trust), the less dependent is it on observance of particular traditions; the 'weaker' the faith, the more dependent" (1988, 827). I fully agree with Nanos's incisive critique of such traditional interpretations (1996, 85–95), while holding reservations with respect to his identification of the strong and the weak as Gentile Christians and non-Christian Jews.

involves reciprocal accommodations of each group to the other. Rather, because the power dynamics are unequal, Paul calls on only the strong to practice radical mutuality by solidarity with the weak. Such behavior enables them to deconstruct the relationship of dominance and subordination.

Further, Paul grounds the practice of solidarity with the weak in the praxis of Christ: "For Christ did not please himself" (15:3). Precisely this same kind of orientation, not to please oneself, to which Paul testifies in Christ, is his prayer for the community (*to phronein en allēlois kata Christon Iēsoun*, 15:5). The unity of the community for Paul is not harmony based on "diplomatic magnanimity" (Segal 1990, 236) or rational pluralism (Tomson 1990, 236–58), but "oneness-in-difference" (Kahl 1999, 57–73) based on an orientation of solidarity with the weak. This orientation depends on the radical welcome of Paul's address-ees by Christ: "Christ has welcomed you for the glory of God" (15:7). The next two verses not only elaborate this basis for radical mutuality in Christ but could well be taken as a summary of Romans: "For I tell you that Christ has become a servant of the circumcised on behalf of the truth of God in order that he might confirm the promises given to the patriarchs, and in order that the Gentiles might glorify God for his mercy" (Rom 15:8–9). For the first time in the discussion of the weak and the strong, the terms *peritomē* and *ethnē* surface. The two terms serve as reiterations of "weak" and "strong," and they confirm that a major part of the problem of the strong and the weak is Jewish-Gentile difference.

CONCLUSION

This essay resists a universalizing reading of Paul, as if Paul establishes principles that are everywhere always valid. Rather, Paul's argument is embedded in the concrete sociohistorical context of Romans. Although I cannot elaborate my argument here, I have shown elsewhere that in the concrete sociohistorical context of the Antioch incident in Galatians, Paul reverses the dynamics of who accommodates to whom. There, power relationships install Jewish Christians as dominant and Gentiles as subordinate, and Paul resists attempts to compel the Gentiles to accommodate to the Jewish Christ-believers (Gal 2:1–14).

I reiterate that distinct dynamics involved in different situations mean that we cannot draw principles from Paul that are valid everywhere for all times. Nevertheless, I wish to mention how these texts from Paul may have implications for the situation of Korean and Korean American Christianity.

One of my concerns is the division of my homeland, where for over half a century citizens of the two Korean nations have demonized each other as subjects of irreconcilable conflicting ideologies. Not only have such ideological battles been fought by political powers, but churches have given their support. According to this way of viewing things, the only solution to the division of Korea is for one political entity to become dominant enough to subdue the other, to coerce a unity of sameness. Today, some new voices are resisting the ideology of domination of one political force over another. Something like the radical mutuality that Paul advocates in Romans, that is, unity with difference, has emerged on the horizon.

Not altogether surprising, similar ideological conflicts divide Korean and Korean American congregations. It is unfortunate that they are reproducing power struggles that have emerged in Western, especially American, churches between people who designate themselves and their counterparts as "progressive" or "evangelical" or "conservative." Furthermore, undesirable cultural and generational conflicts divide more Korean/Asian (less American) identity and less Korean/Asian (more American) identity among Korean/Asian American communities, churches, and academic institutions, when especially it becomes more urgent for an ethnic minority group to stand firm in the emerging intercultural solidarity of others. Here too it seems helpful for people who are involved in such struggles to seek an orientation grounded in the practice of Christ, which is not to serve themselves but to welcome the other. Such welcoming seems to me to be possible when we pursue oneness with difference.

Works Consulted

Boyarin, Daniel. 1994. *A Radical Jew: Paul and the Politics of Identity*. Berkeley and Los Angeles: University of California Press.

Buell, Denise Kimber, and Caroline Johnson Hodge. 2004. The Politics of Interpretation: The Rhetoric of Race and Ethnicity in Paul. *JBL* 123:235–51.

Di Stefano, Christine. 1990. Dilemmas of Difference. Pages 63–82 in *Feminism/Postmodernism*. Edited by Linda J. Nicholason. New York: Routledge.

Dunn, James D. G. 1988. *Romans 9–16*. WBC 38B. Dallas: Word.

———. 1990. *Jesus, Paul and the Law*. Louisville: Westminster John Knox.

Elliott, Neil. 2007. Political Formation in the Letter to the Romans. Pages 179–90 in *Character Ethics and the New Testament*. Edited by R. Brawley. Louisville: Westminster John Knox.

Ferguson, Ann. 1998. Resisting the Veil of Privilege: Building Bridge Identities as an Ethico-Politics of Global Feminism. *Hypatia* 13.3:95–113.

Georgi, Dieter. 1991. *Theocracy in Paul's Praxis and Theology*. Minneapolis: Fortress.

Hall, Jonathan. 1997. *Ethnic Identity in Greek Antiquity*. Cambridge: Cambridge University Press.

Hengel, Martin. 1977. *Crucifixion in the Ancient World and the Folly of the Message of the Cross*. Philadelphia: Fortress.

Jewett, Robert. 1995. Honor and Shame in Pauline Theology: A Preliminary Probe. Unpublished paper.

———. 2006. *Romans*. Hermeneia. Minneapolis: Fortress.

Kahl, Brigitte. 1999. Gender Trouble in Galatia? Paul and the Rethinking of Difference. Pages 57–73 in *Is There a Future for Feminist Theology?* Edited by D. Sawer and D. Collier. Sheffield: Sheffield Academic Press.

————. 2000. No Longer Male: Masculinity Struggles Behind Galatians 3:28? *JSNT* 79:37–49.

Kelley, Shawn. 2002. *Racializing Jesus: Race, Ideology and the Formation of Modern Biblical Scholarship*. London: Routledge.

Lee, Jae Won. 2007. Justification of Difference in Galatians. Pages 191–208 in *Character Ethics and the New Testament*. Edited by Robert Brawley. Louisville: Westminster John Knox.

Marcus, Joel. 1989. The Circumcision and the Uncircumcision in Rome. *NTS* 35:67–81.

————. 2006. Crucifixion as Parodic Exaltation. *JBL* 125:73–87.

Min, Anselm Kyungsuk. 1999. From Autobiography to Fellowship of Others: Reflections on Doing Ethnic Theology Today. Pages 135–59 in *Journeys at the Margin: Toward an Autobiographical Theology in American-Asian Perspective*. Edited by Peter C. Phan and Jung Young Lee. Collegeville, Minn.: Liturgical Press.

Nanos, Mark. 1996. *The Mystery of Romans: The Jewish Context of Paul's Letter*. Minneapolis: Fortress.

Reasoner, Mark. 1999. *The Strong and the Weak: Romans 14:1–15:13 in Context*. SNTSMS 103. Cambridge: Cambridge University Press.

Sanders, E. P. 1983. *Paul, the Law, and the Jewish People*. Minneapolis: Fortress.

Segal, Alan. 1990. *Paul the Convert: The Apostolate and Apostasy of Saul the Pharisee*. New Haven: Yale University Press.

Segovia, Fernando F. 1995. The Text as Other: Towards a Hispanic American Hermeneutic. Pages 276–98 in *Text and Experience: Towards A Cultural Exegesis of the Bible*. Edited by Daniel Smith-Christopher. Sheffield: Sheffield Academic Press.

————. 2000. *Decolonizing Biblical Studies: A View From the Margins*. Maryknoll, N.Y.: Orbis.

Tomson, Peter. 1990. *Paul and the Jewish Law: Halakha in the Letters of the Apostles to the Gentiles*. Minneapolis: Fortress.

Wan, Sze-kar. 2000. Does Diaspora Identity Imply Some Sort of Universality? An Asian-American Reading of Galatians. Pages 107–31 in *Interpreting beyond Borders*. Edited by Fernando F. Segovia. Sheffield: Sheffield Academic Press.

Watson, Francis. 1991. The Two Roman Congregations: Romans 14:1–15:13. Pages 203–15 in *The Romans Debate*. Edited by Karl Donfried. Peabody, Mass.: Hendrickson.

Yang, Geun Seok. 2005. Globalization, Intercultural Hermeneutics and Mission. *International Journal of Contextual Theology in East Asia* December (December):7–26.

Young, Iris Marion. 1990. *Justice and the Politics of Difference*. Princeton: Princeton University Press.

PART 1: STUDIES
SECTION 2: EXPANDING THE FIELD

Ancient Ethiopia and the New Testament: Ethnic (Con)texts and Racialized (Sub)texts

Gay L. Byron

Introduction: Reading My Way through the Trajectories and the Struggle

Early Christian literature was generated in a variety of ethnic (con)texts and geographical locales that invariably gave rise to different worldviews and expressions of what it meant to be "Christian." Generally, when examining the origins and trajectories of early Christianity, New Testament scholars emphasize the major cities of the Roman Empire in such a manner as to assume that the Roman Empire was the *only* empire that had anything to do with the formation of the New Testament and early Christian communities (Robinson and Koester 1971; Koester 2000; Duling 2003). Even when scholars attempt to critique the privileging of certain worldviews, orientations, and voices in the Roman Empire (e.g., Bauer 1996; Ehrman 2003; Horsley 1998; Wimbush 1995), there is still an overwhelming predisposition to focus the interpretation of the New Testament within a prescribed set of historical and geographical contexts that preclude any real engagement with peoples and places beyond the contours of *the empire*, especially those cities related to the travels of Paul. As an African American biblical critic, I am concerned with this imbalanced preoccupation with the Roman Empire, especially in light of the fact that Rome was only *one* of the four great kingdoms of the ancient world, alongside Persia, China, and Axum (Munro-Hay 1991, 17). Indeed, the Axumite Empire (modern Tigray), which flourished from the first through the sixth centuries c.e., was a leader in international trade and commerce in the ancient world, with its own political, cultural, and economic systems. Axum also had a strong Christian presence and a variety of religious texts, which have generally not been included for analysis in studies of the New Testament and early Christianity (Henze 2000, 22–43; Munro-Hay 1991, 196–213; 2002, 231–335; Pankhurst 2001, 18–42). One way to avoid this imbalanced emphasis on the Roman Empire is to broaden the geographical lens through which early Christian writings are understood and to include sources and insights from African (specifically Ethiopian) civilizations, such as the Axumite Empire.

In previous writings I have discussed the factors that prompted my interest in the places and peoples south of the Mediterranean (2002, 3–8; 2003; 2005). I was fascinated by the number of references to Egyptians, Ethiopians, and blacks in early Christian writings and equally frustrated by the ways in which many scholars—for the most part white[1]—have concluded that such references were sporadic or inconsequential for understanding the development of early Christianity (2002, 6).[2] Furthermore, it became apparent to me that inclusion and critical analysis of narratives about Ethiopian and black women had escaped the purview of many of the important sourcebooks dealing with women in the Greco-Roman world (2002, 8). Further, although womanist scholars have produced many valuable studies and have identified the hermeneutical significance of texts related to women in both the Old Testament and the New Testament, they have generally not focused on "Ethiopian" or "black" women in biblical or extrabiblical writings (Weems 1988; 1992; 1995; Martin 1990; 1991; Redding 1999; Venable-Ridley 1997).[3] This lack of attention to the haunting and troubling references to Ethiopian and black women in early Christian writings[4] led me to theorize about ethnopolitical rhetorics (that is, discourses about the symbolic representations of ethnic and color "othering") in Greco-Roman literature in general (2002, 17–51) and early Christian literature in particular (55–129).

I am now at a point, however, where I realize that solely focusing on ethnicity, even if it is with the intent of uncovering the ideological, political, and patriarchal aspects of early Christianity, does not adequately account for the limited trajectories that define the scope of New Testament scholarship. As I continue to reflect on my role as a biblical critic and clergyperson, it is becoming clear to me that my various communities of accountability have given rise to my com-

---

1. In this essay, I will refer to scholars with Anglo-European racial and ethnic origins as "white" unless they identify themselves otherwise. The nomenclature used to refer to whites varies in the literature from "European-American" (Patte 1995), to "Anglo-European" (Donaldson 1996, 10), to "European" (Sugirtharajah 1996b, 9), to "white" (Redding 1999, 456). For an excellent article dealing with the complexities and responsibilities associated with racial difference, see Ramsay 2002, 11–27.

2. Notable exceptions include: Wimbush 1992; Wicker 1990; Brakke 2001; Aubert 2002.

3. One notable exception is the story of Miriam and her Cushite sister-in-law, Zipporah (Num 12:1–16; Exod 2:1–10), in Weems 1988, 71–83.

4. See, for example, from the Acts of Peter: "I saw you sitting on a high place, and before you a great assembly; and a most evil-looking woman, who looked like an Ethiopian, not an Egyptian, but was all black, clothed in filthy rags. She was dancing with an iron collar about her neck and chains on her hands and feet.... And immediately a man who looked like yourself, Peter, with sword in hand, cut her all to pieces, so that I gazed upon you both, both on you and on the one who was cutting up the demon, whose likeness caused me great amazement." For this and other texts like it, see Byron 2002, 17, 94–103.

mitments and have challenged me to provide a synthetic critical analysis of early Christianity that is not apologetic of its African origins and influences and is not ashamed of the ways in which "Scripture" still holds salvific meaning for those who confess faith in Jesus Christ (Byron 2003; Torjesen 2005, 103–7). Moreover, the wider global transformations affecting persons in the U.S. have challenged me to expand my conversation partners and to appeal to a broader range of texts and traditions in my scholarly endeavors (Byron 2005, 95–96; Wicker 2005, 8). Thus, I am now much more interested in delving into the vast body of literature "beyond the boundaries of the world of Western Christianity" (Torjesen 2005, 106) as a key exegetical strategy for exploring the worlds that gave rise to what have become known as "lost Christianities" (Ehrman 2003).

Indeed, a growing number of New Testament scholars have already taken up the important work of identifying race and racism in biblical narratives (Felder 1982; 1989b; 2002; Nash 2003), analyzing the racist foundations upon which the guild of biblical studies has been established (Kelley 2002; Coates 2005), and isolating the intersections between ethnicity and the Bible (Walters 1993; Brett 1996; Wan 2000; Johnson Hodge 2007; Braxton 2003) and extrabiblical writings (Buell 2005; Byron 2002). Cain Hope Felder, for example, was one of the first New Testament scholars to analyze the "racial motifs in biblical narratives." Beginning with his acknowledgment of the methodological problems associated with this topic, Felder describes the implications of two broad processes related to racism: sacralization in the Old Testament and secularization in the New Testament (1989b, 37–48; 2002). Shawn Kelley (2002), assuming a completely different starting point from Felder's, goes back to the period of Enlightenment to demonstrate that the very foundations of the guild of biblical studies were shrouded in the "racialized discourses" of three influential philosophical movements (Hegelianism, Heideggerianism, and Romanticism). Most recently, Delmon Coates, drawing upon the work of Kelley, also argues for a critique of the "methodological tyranny" imposed by biblical fundamentalism and historical criticism. With respect to ethnicity, Mark Brett's collection of essays was one of the first to deal with various aspects of ethnicity and the Bible. James C. Walters, Sze-kar Wan, and Brad Braxton (2003) have all utilized ethnicity as a conceptual lens for understanding Paul's discourses about Jews and Gentiles. Denise Kimber Buell takes on the challenge of reflecting on both race and ethnicity for the purpose of understanding ethnoracial discourses as early Christian strategies of self-definition (Buell 2005, esp. 35–62).

In addition to this, biblical scholars from various underrepresented racial and ethnic minority groups[5] are continuing to produce a vast array of studies

---

5. The Society of Biblical Literature (SBL) Committee on Underrepresented Racial and Ethnic Minorities in the Profession (CUREMP) was constituted to assess the status and encourage the participation of underrepresented racial and ethnic minorities, usually understood as

from their respective social and cultural locations ranging from collections of essays (Felder 1991; Wimbush 2000; Liew 2002; Bailey 2003; Segovia 2000b), to analyses of different biblical texts that perpetuate gender disparities in the church (Felder 1989b, 139–49; D. Williams 2004), to interpretations of key African figures in the Bible such as Simon of Cyrene (Sanders 1995; Buckhanon Crowder 2002) and in later monastic writings such as Ethiopian Moses (Wimbush 1992; Byron 2002, 115–20), to assessments of the presence of blacks in the biblical and extrabiblical writings (Copher 1993; Bailey 1991; Hood 1994), to rhetorical and ideological readings of women in the Hebrew Bible (Weems 1995; Yee 2003), to studies about biblical law (Anderson 2004; Bennett 2002), to readings of Pauline texts (Martin 1991; Redding 1999; Braxton 2002), to proposals for cultural readings of the Bible (Blount 1995; Segovia 1995a; 1995b), to an overall assessment of the aims of African American biblical scholarship (Brown 2004), and to, most recently, a commentary of the New Testament from an African American perspective (Blount et al. 2008).[6] Given this wealth of material dealing with various aspects of race and ethnicity as it influences the reading and teaching of the Bible, I am confident that the time is right for an additional level of scholarly inquiry that may go even further toward expanding our understandings of the theoretical trajectories through early Christianity.

When it comes to the Bible, African American women generally find themselves reading their way through the struggle (Weems 1991). I am no exception (Byron 2005). Likewise, other racial and ethnic minorities also find themselves interpreting biblical texts *en la lucha* (Isasi-Díaz 1993)—in the midst of struggle (Segovia 1994; 1996, 484–92; Liew 2002; Dube 2001). But imagine what might happen if *all* biblical interpreters acknowledged *their* "struggles" and identified with those who struggle—not only for life, throughout this world, but also for voice within the guild of biblical studies. Ann Holmes Redding draws this point into sharp focus with the following reflection:

> Whenever I begin to work on a topic that carries such ideological weight as the household codes in the New Testament, I am haunted by the words of a professor of church history from my seminary years. This professor, who was—not incidentally—a white male, said to our class, "Don't trust the work of Black scholars on slavery: they are too subjective." Since then I have often pondered

African American, Caribbean, Asian, Asian American, and Latino/a, in all professional areas of biblical studies. The Committee focuses its efforts in areas of mentoring and networking, opening the Society to greater participation by minorities and calling attention to the ways in which the Society speaks to and about racial and ethnic minorities. See http://www.sbl-site. org/SBLcommittees_CUREMP.aspx. For a thorough discussion about racial and ethnic biblical scholars, see Segovia 1996; Bailey 2000.

6. This list and the one in the previous paragraph are by no means exhaustive. They are only representative of the rich collection of scholarly studies that are now in circulation.

the vast extent of scholarship by white males that would, on these grounds, also be rendered suspect; *we all have a stake in the scholarship we do*. (Redding 1999, 456, emphasis added)

Some white colleagues are already beginning to declare their stakes and acknowledge the ways in which interpreting biblical texts is loaded with many "ethical" and "political" challenges (e.g., Patte 1995; Schüssler Fiorenza 1999; 2000; G. West 1996; Buell and Johnson Hodge 2004; Wicker 2005). But there is still much more work to be done.

For my part, in this essay I will examine the story of the Ethiopian eunuch in Acts 8:26–40, calling attention to the ethnic (con)texts of Axum and the racialized (sub)texts that permeate many discussions about the pericope, especially those dealing with text-critical methods. By utilizing postcolonial and critical race and ethnicity theories, I will demonstrate what is at stake for *all* interpreters of the Bible, not just those of us who are considered "racial and ethnic minorities."

Ethnic (Con)Texts: The Axumite Empire and Its Sources

Postcolonial Biblical Criticism

During the past two decades, postcolonial biblical critics have introduced a fresh wave of interpretive insights into biblical studies (e.g., Boer 2001; Donaldson 1996; Dube 2000; Kwok 1995; Liew 1999; Moore and Segovia 2005; Segovia 2000b; Sugirtharajah 1998b; 2002).[7] Concerned with the tendency among biblical scholars to neglect the imperialism inherent in biblical texts, the colonized readings of biblical texts, and the other subtle silences, ellipses, or gaps that discourage accessing or understanding the rich cultures and traditions that inform the stories in biblical texts, postcolonial biblical scholars have challenged the presuppositions and interpretive methods of traditional biblical interpretation (or "colonial" biblical interpretation). Although the term "post(-)colonial" has been the subject of much debate over the years (Sugirtharajah 1998b, 15; Moore 2000, 182; Segovia 2000c, 133–35), one thing is clear: postcolonial studies take seriously the reality of empire, nation, ethnicity, migration, and language (Sugirtharajah

---

7. Moore and Segovia identify three major "clusters" of interpretation with respect to postcolonial biblical criticism (2005, 5–10): (1) contextual hermeneutics evidenced in the works of Prior (1997), Sugirtharajah (1998a; 1998b), Dube (2000), Segovia (2000c, 3–53), Segovia and Tolbert (1995a; 1995b); (2) the "X and empire" approach practiced by biblical critics (e.g., Horsley 1997; 2003a; 2003b; Carter 2001); and (3) the studies that include a thoroughgoing engagement with the field of extrabiblical Postcolonial Studies (e.g., Gallagher 1994; Donaldson 1996) or utilize theoretically fluent interdisciplinary approaches exemplified in the works of Boer (2001), Runions (2001), and Liew (1999).

1998b, 16).[8] Moreover, this hermeneutical stance (Moore 2000, 183)[9] invites new opportunities for exploring the intersections and discontinuities between gender, race, and class in ancient writings and among contemporary biblical interpreters (Donaldson 1996, 8–10; Dube 2000; 2005; Kwok 1995, 79; Liew 2005).

For my purpose of demonstrating the necessity of examining sources from the ethnic (con)texts of ancient Ethiopia, I will use the "postcolonial optic" suggested by Fernando F. Segovia, who outlines a three-dimensional framework for applying postcolonial theory to contemporary biblical criticism (1998; 2000c; 2005, 24). What is most compelling about his framework is the way in which the different levels of biblical analysis (the ancient texts, the interpretation of such texts, and the readers themselves) are isolated and problematized so that texts, traditions (especially the Western imperial tradition of the last five hundred years), and interpreters are held accountable for the complex and often elusive ways in which they are ideologically complicit in the colonializing impulse.

Before going any further, I need to emphasize that my postcolonial focus on the Axumite Empire and its sources should not be viewed in an *additive* sense— that is, as if it were an optional mass of geographical information added to an already well-conceived map of the ancient world (Moore 2000, 187–88; Moore and Segovia 2005, 7). As Moore and Segovia observe, the focus on "empires" is already a common enterprise for the traditional biblical scholar who tends "to peer through that lens intermittently" with a "succession of empires" approach (8; Segovia 1998, 57), or the postcolonial biblical critic who "gazes through it unrelentingly" with an "X and empire" approach (8; e.g., Carter 2001; Horsley 1997; 2003a; 2003b).[10] With both of these approaches, when it comes to New Testament studies, the Roman Empire is the central (and only) frame of reference.[11] I depart from these approaches by reflecting on the Roman Empire only to the extent that it intersects with the history, culture, socioeconomic, and political conditions of the Axumite Empire, thus focusing on primary sources written by "outsiders" (in

---

8. The early theorists who set the stage for postcolonial studies include Edward Said (1978; 1993), Gayatri Chakravorty Spivak (1985; 1988; 1990; 1996), and Homi K. Bhabha (1992; 1994).

9. Stephen Moore indicates "postcolonial criticism is not *a* method of interpretation (any more than is feminist criticism, say) so much as a critical sensibility attuned to a specific range of interrelated textual and historical phenomena" (2000, 183).

10. Moore and Segovia emphasize that few of the authors of this "X and empire" trajectory of postcolonial biblical scholarship evince any interest in affixing the label "postcolonial" to their projects (2005, 8).

11. As Segovia observes with respect to a lacuna in postcolonial studies, "whenever the imperial-colonial formation is understood in broad terms, the world of the Roman Empire is unfailingly invoked as a prime, even ideal, example of this phenomenon" (2005, 72–73)." Segovia is concerned with unexamined assumptions about the Roman Empire and its privileged place as the "prototype" for future formations of empire, especially in the West.

this case, Greek and Latin authors) and primary sources generated by "insiders" (in this case, ancient Ethiopians) within the Axumite Empire. In this regard, my focus on empire differs from the many studies that are being produced among New Testament scholars in that I view the Axumite Empire as a *necessary* frame of reference for the task of reconstructing Christian origins.

The postcolonial biblical critic R.S. Sugirtharajah also offers several useful insights for framing my exploration of the Axumite Empire. Sugirtharajah asserts that postcolonial criticism will foreground so-called "marginal elements" in biblical texts and, in the process, subvert "traditional meanings." He understands postcolonial criticism as a means for engaging in "archival exegesis" so that narratives and voices that have been subjected to "institutional forgetting" can be memorialized (Sugirtharajah 1996a, 25). This notion of institutional forgetfulness is critical when it comes to understanding the ancient Ethiopians. Edward Gibbon, for example, in *The Decline and Fall of the Roman Empire*, summed up the prevailing view about ancient Ethiopians: "Encompassed on all sides by the enemies of their religion the Ethiopians slept near a thousand years, forgetful of the world, by whom they were forgotten" (1910, 176). The persistence of this motif in both ancient sources and modern studies is partly explained by the fact that the kingdom of Axum (modern Tigray) has been one of the least studied and most widely misunderstood kingdoms of antiquity. Although it was considered one of the four great empires of the ancient world (alongside Persia, Rome, and China), scholars have only recently begun to acknowledge its religious, political, cultural, and economic significance (e.g., Burstein 1997; Henze 2000; Munro-Hay 1991).[12]

Many biblical critics acknowledge the relevance of ancient Ethiopia—especially scholars of the Hebrew Bible and others specializing in Ethiopian studies who analyze the relationship between Ethiopia and the Old Testament (Ullendorff 1968; Cowley 1988; Fisher 1974; Hidal 1997; Sadler 2005) and pseudepigraphal works, such as the "Ethiopic Book of the Cock" (Piovanelli 2003). Others have provided translations and commentaries of the book of Enoch, which survives in its entirety only in manuscripts preserved in ancient Ethiopic (Geʿez; see E. Isaac 1983; Nickelsburg and VanderKam 2004). Most recently, scholars are analyzing the hermeneutical complexities involved in reading the Bible in various contemporary African contexts (McEntire 2000).[13] Scholars of the New Testament,

---

12. Axum has received considerable attention among archaeologists especially because of the obelisks (or stelae) located there. See, for example, Munro-Hay 1989, describing the work of Dr. Neville Chittick of the British Institute in Africa during the 1970s.

13. Within the context of a Protestant seminary in Ethiopia, Mark McEntire analyzes the interpretations of Alan Boesak and Itumeleng J. Mosala of South Africa and Modupe Oduyoye of Nigeria. He also includes the responses of the students at the Mekane Yesus Seminary in Addis Ababa who registered cautious and even dissenting comments about the methods introduced.

though not as numerous, have also generated several critical studies dealing with the relationship between ancient Ethiopic sources and the study of the New Testament (e.g., Hofmann 1967; Metzger 1977; Montgomery 1934; Zuurmond 1989; 1995). Yet, despite Cain Hope Felder's efforts, in collaboration with Ephraim Isaac, to explore the origins of Ethiopian civilization (Isaac and Felder 1984),[14] generally scholars of the New Testament have not devoted sufficient attention to understanding the culture, history, politics, and religions of the Ethiopians who dwelled in Axum. A full analysis of this background is beyond the scope of this essay, but a brief overview of Axum, and its language and sources, is in order.

THE AXUMITE EMPIRE: HISTORY, LANGUAGE, AND SOURCES

The Axumites developed a civilization of considerable sophistication that wielded its powerful influence from the first through sixth centuries C.E. The architecture, coinage, and inscriptions attest to an empire with a number of urban centers and a well-developed economic, military, and political presence in the ancient world (Munro-Hay 1991, 166–79, 214–32). The city of Axum dominated the ivory trade along the Nile Valley and through Ethiopia's main Red Sea port at Adulis (located in modern Eritrea). Both of these cities are discussed in the writings of some of the sea travelers who captured valuable details about the material culture of this empire.

The first mention of Axum occurs in a first-century C.E. document known as *The Periplus [Geography] of the Erythrean Sea*. This document was written around 70 C.E. by an anonymous Greek sailor living in Egypt (*Periplus* 4–5; Burstein 1997, 79–82).[15] Included in this sea guide are notes on trade and other items of interest, such as the description of Adulis, Axum's most important commercial center. The author of *The Periplus* also describes the many imports into the Axumite Empire, mentioning, among other things, sheets of soft copper, small axes, a little wine from Italy, gold and silver plates for the king, military cloaks, iron and steel from India, and cotton cloth from Egypt. These articles of trade reflected the empire's contact with the outside world, mainly cities throughout the Mediterranean, Egypt, and India. Its widespread influence in the eastern Mediterranean–Red Sea regional economy made this empire a major force in international affairs.

At its greatest extent, Axum was able to unify the several principalities of north Tigre and, toward the end of the third century C.E., to include parts of western Arabia in the empire (Adejumobi 2000, 233). The empire also controlled shipping in the Red Sea around 360 C.E., after it conquered the kingdom of Meroë

---

14. See also Felder's research on the Queen of Sheba (1989a); see also Ullendorff 1956.

15. The dating of this text, ranging from the first to the third century C.E., is subject to debate. Most scholars agree that a first-century date is most probable (Pankhurst 2001, 23; Munro-Hay 1991, 17).

(Burstein 1997, 97–100; Welsby 1996, 196–205). One cannot, therefore, overlook the hegemonic presence of this empire in northern Ethiopia (Munro-Hay 1991, 33–39; Marcus 2002, 5). On the other hand, the Axumites, as a result of their contacts with foreigners, did not escape the widespread Hellenistic and Roman influences.

One of the best examples of such influences can be found in the numismatic evidence from this region. Coins were produced in Axum in gold, silver, and bronze; their size, weight, and value signaled their design for foreign trade (Munro-Hay 1991, 180–95; 1993; Pankhurst 2001, 26–28). Initially, the coins were inscribed in Greek, the *lingua franca* of the time, but there are later examples of inscriptions in the local language, Geʻez, which apparently indicated that the currency was intended primarily for circulation only within the Axumite region. In addition to its coinage, Axum was also one of the principal sources of gold for the Roman Empire in late antiquity. Another sailor by the name of Cosmas, in his *Christian Topography*, includes valuable information about the Red Sea basin, and he also describes the gold and salt trade of the Axumites (*Cosmas* 52–54; Burstein 1997, 91–93).[16]

The language spoken in Axum, Geʻez, was a Semitic language first written in Sabaean or South Arabian letters. Most scholars conclude that Geʻez is the literary language developed in the fourth century C.E. for the translation of ancient Christian texts in Ethiopia (Lambdin 1978; Ullendorff 1968, 44). Though it ceased to be spoken as the vernacular language in ancient Ethiopia during the sixth century C.E., it is still used today for liturgical purposes in the Ethiopian Orthodox Church. Most manuscripts written in Geʻez comprise a wide range of literature, including not only biblical, religious service books, homilies, commentaries, and works on theology, but also writings on ecclesiastical and civil law, lives of saints, local and foreign history, and medicine (Haile 1993; Ricci 1991). One of the most important inscriptions in Geʻez describes how the Axumite King Ezana suppressed a rebellion by a nomadic tribe known as the Blemmyes (Burstein 1997, 87–88).[17] This inscription, which is still standing in Axum today, is recorded in Greek, Geʻez, and South Arabian.[18]

Scholars often dismiss the value of Ethiopic sources (particularly the literary sources) by concluding that the material is "late" (generally thirteenth or fourteenth century or later) and thus irrelevant for any form of analysis (Davies 1987). Added to this situation is the overall consensus among scholars that most of the extant information about ancient Ethiopians is "legendary" and thus unreliable for critical historical or exegetical purposes. One account, which continues

---

16. See *The Christian Topography of Cosmos, An Egyptian Monk*, 52–54.

17. For a more detailed description of the Blemmyes, see Byron 2002, 82–84.

18. For a full discussion of the various inscriptions in Axum, see Munro-Hay 1991, 221–32; 2002, 231–301).

to cause scholars to raise questions about its historical reliability, documents how Christianity came to Ethiopia (e.g., Zuurmond 1995, 147—discussed later in this essay). In this story, two Syrian merchants[19]—Aedesius and Frumentius—survive a shipwreck and eventually end up in the court of the Ethiopian emperor Ezana (325–350 c.e.). According to the church historian Rufinus, Frumentius was instrumental in governing the kingdom and supporting the establishment of Christianity:

> While they lived there and Frumentius held the reins of government in his hands, God stirred up his heart and he began to search out with care those of the Roman merchants who were Christians and to give them great influence and to urge them to establish in various places conventicles to which they might resort for prayer in the Roman manner. He himself, moreover, did the same and so encouraged the others, attracting them with his favor and his benefits, providing them with whatever was needed, supplying sites for buildings and other necessaries, and in every way promoting the growth of the seed of Christianity in the country. (Burstein 1997, 95)[20]

Frumentius later traveled to Alexandria, where he was subsequently named the first bishop of Ethiopia by Athanasius and given the name Abba Salama. By the time of Ezana's death in 350 c.e., Christianity was the official religion of the Axumite Empire.[21]

This fourth-century c.e. text, although considered "legendary," is one of the earliest records about the beginnings of Christianity in Ethiopia and may offer valuable clues for understanding the cultural and social interactions between "Greeks," "Romans," and "Ethiopians" in late antiquity. It also opens a window onto the widespread commerce, complex political relationships, and fascinating historical and ecclesial background of the ancient African civilizations that are included in biblical narratives.

Once again, a postcolonial optic challenges me to focus on such "legendary" texts and traditions. Because of the prescribed parameters and trajectories for understanding the New Testament and early Christianity, biblical scholars generally have not considered the diverse cultural and literary milieu that influenced the formative years of Christianity. R. S. Sugirtharajah deals with this omission by calling for a wider hermeneutical base that incorporates Indian, Buddhist, and Hindu influences (1998b, 108). He argues for "moving beyond the Mediterranean milieu" (1998b, 107–11) by paying attention to the Indian presence in

---

19. Some scholars describe the two merchants as "two boys"; see E. Isaac 1968; Yamauchi 2004, 175–76.

20. See Rufinus, *Historia Ecclesiastica* 1.9 (PL 21:478ff).

21. It is reported that, prior to his conversion to Christianity, Ezana worshiped gods identified with such Greek deities as Zeus, Poseidon, and Ares (Munro-Hay 1991, 196–209).

the Mediterranean world. Most instructive for my purpose of highlighting the Axumite Empire and its sources is his critique of the deep-seated Eurocentric bias that precludes any serious engagement of texts not supplied by Greco-Judeo traditions:

> The tendency of biblical scholars to impose Christianity as the interpretative template has often blurred their vision. They have successfully promoted the belief that the New Testament writings were the product exclusively of Hellenistic and Hebraic thinking. When looking at the New Testament period and the literary productions which emerged at that time, biblical scholars maintain a deep-seated Eurocentric bias, asserting that anything theologically worthwhile can only be supplied by Greco-Judaeo traditions.… In thus failing to widen their hermeneutical base, these scholars also invent a Christianity successfully insulated from any contact with Indic religions. (Sugirtharajah 1998b, 107)

Although I do not intend to follow Sugirtharajah's comparative religions approach, I am persuaded by his appeal to move beyond the Mediterranean milieu with respect to understanding the literary and cultural productions of early Christianity—in my case, by exploring the Axumite Empire and its sources.

SUMMARY

Postcolonial biblical criticism opens the way for utilizing the ethnic (con)texts of the Axumite Empire as a viable point of departure for reexamining stories about Ethiopians in early Christian writings, especially Luke's story about the Ethiopian eunuch in Acts 8:26–40. By ethnic (con)texts, I mean sources (literary, epigraphic, numismatic, etc.) that extend beyond the Mediterranean milieu and emphasize the diverse literary and cultural expressions of early Christianity. However, postcolonial biblical criticism does not account for the many racialized (sub)texts associated with this text that occur in commentaries and other forms of analysis generated by biblical scholars. The chief limitation of the postcolonial optic, in my view, is its implicit assumptions about race and ethnicity. As Moore and Segovia accurately observe, early discussions about postcolonial biblical criticism did not take into consideration critical race and ethnic theory (2005, 5).[22] But given the ways in which postcolonial biblical critics muse about the plight of persons in the two-thirds world, Native North Americans, and other racial and ethnic minorities in the West due to oppressive imperial systems of domination (e.g., Dube 2000; 2005: Donaldson 1996; Segovia 2000b), it seems that postcolonial theories and race and ethnicity theories would be natural conceptual partners

---

22. Moore and Segovia acknowledge "a significant lacuna in the original round of papers, insofar as there had been no piece on racial and ethnic theory, again a most important preoccupation for both biblical and postcolonial criticisms" (2005, 5).

for interpreting biblical texts. Yet, as one looks over the contents of many of the postcolonial studies that have emerged in the past two decades, this is clearly *not* the case.[23] Now, part of the reason for this may be the sheer "newness" of both of these disciplines within the guild of biblical studies, so that the necessary "time" for cross-fertilization has simply not elapsed. However, as Liew observes, it is more likely that the scholars who appeal to race/ethnicity as an interpretive category have neglected postcolonial theory because of the "late" arrival of postcolonialism "on the larger academic scene" and because of their "anxiety" or "hesitation" to trust whether "postcolonialism's tendency to (over)emphasize textuality, hybridity, and multiplicity is not a fragmentation of, or even a flight from, politics" (2005, 129). In the next section I will use the conversion story of the Ethiopian eunuch in Acts 8 to discuss the racialized (sub)texts that are a very real component of biblical scholarship.

RACIALIZED (SUB)TEXTS: THE CASE OF ACTS 8:26–40

CRITICAL RACE [AND ETHNICITY] THEORIES: THE "HERMENEUTICAL DILEMMA" REVISITED

There is no shortage of books dealing with the topic of race. Legal theorists[24] such as Derrick Bell (1992) and Patricia J. Williams (1991; 1998), geographers such as Ruth Wilson Gilmore (2002),[25] literary critics such as Toni Morrison (1992) and Ishmael Reed, and scholars of religion such as Cornel West (1993) and Michael Dyson (1996) all conclude in one way or the other: *race matters!* Yet, biblical scholars have been slow to appeal to critical race and ethnicity theories (Liew 2005, 128), although it is obvious in many cases that race is an important frame of reference (e.g., Bailey 1996; Felder 1982; 1989b; 1991) and an almost inescapable mode of discourse for many biblical interpreters (Kelley 2002, 216).

William H. Myers nearly two decades ago described "the hermeneutical dilemma of the African American biblical student" when it comes to utilizing what he calls "the Eurocentric approach to biblical interpretation" (1991, 47)—a dilemma whose resolution, he insists, must come primarily from African American biblical scholars (49–50).[26] Myers does not offer any type of constructive

---

23. *Pace* Liew (2005, 125), who argues that "race/ethnicity and postcolonialism are conceptually connected with, or maybe even embedded in, each other."

24. See Crenshaw 1995 and Delgado and Stefancic 2001 for excellent reading related to the "critical race theory" movement that emerged in the mid-1970s as a number of lawyers, activists, and legal scholars realized that new theories and strategies were needed to resist the subtler forms of racism that were gaining ground in the post–civil right era.

25. I thank Jim Lee for informing me of Ruth Wilson Gilmore's compelling research.

26. Myers asserts: "The result of the Eurocentric approach is the exaltation of one cultural worldview over all others. In addition, the approach tends to lock the interpretive task in the

theory per se on the topic of race and ethnicity. Rather, he presents a kind of position paper for the purpose of carving out *interpretive space* for the African American biblical scholar—something that was still needed as he wrote in 1991 (see Bailey 2000). While some may conclude that this is a type of "essentialism" based on some intuitive understanding of African American experience (Liew 2005; see also Delgado and Stefancic 2001, 56–58), I believe it is more an honest acknowledgment of the "stony road" that has been traveled by Myers and many other African American biblical critics. It is now time, however, to revisit this hermeneutical dilemma.

As noted earlier, African American Cain Hope Felder was one of the first New Testament scholars to examine racial motifs in biblical writings. He concluded: "We do not find any elaborate definitions or theories about race in antiquity" (1989b, 37). Felder, like most scholars who deal with the topic of race in the Greco-Roman world, followed the important scholarship of Frank M. Snowden. Based on his extensive research on "blacks in antiquity," Snowden asserted that "there is no color prejudice in antiquity" (1970; 1983). Since that time, as I noted in my introduction, things have changed considerably. Nevertheless, Snowden's seminal scholarship has remained the unrelenting foundation upon which biblical scholars, church historians, and others exploring theoretical matters related to race and antiquity begin and summarily end their research (e.g., Kelley 2002, 26; Goldenberg 2003).[27] I have already called into question Snowden's findings (2002, 4–5, *passim*; 2004); moreover, Benjamin Isaac, professor of ancient history at the University of Tel Aviv, in his book entitled *The Construction of Racism in Classical Antiquity*, has identified what he calls "prototypes of racism" or "proto-racism" in Greco-Roman antiquity (2004, 5, 15, 36–38). Using a geographical approach, Isaac examines specific groups (e.g., Syrians, Phoenicians, Egyptians, Parthians, Persians, Gauls, Germans, and Jews) for the purpose of isolating the effects of Greek and Roman imperialism as manifested in ethnic prejudice and stereotypes. Although he does not analyze Ethiopians, his research now offers an incisive challenge for those who have been relying on the findings of Snowden.[28]

---

past (e.g., in debates over authorial intent) while evading key contemporary issues like racism or intercultural dialogue" (1991, 41).

27. For a more detailed discussion of my concerns about Snowden's research, see Byron 2002, 4–5. I have likewise raised these concerns in two public forums: an SBL panel reviewing *Racializing Jesus* (Kelley 2002), November 2003; and a lecture entitled "The Theoretical Challenge of Interpreting the 'Gendered' Other in Early Christian Literature," sponsored by Union Theological Seminary, New York Theological Seminary, and The World Christian Movement, 25 March 2004.

28. Isaac does not include a systematic discussion of the attitudes towards black Africans (or Ethiopians) for the following reasons (2004, 49–50): (1) "They did not form much of an actual presence in the Greek and Roman worlds.... [F]ew of them lived among the Greeks and Romans and no country inhabited by Blacks was ever part of the Greek and Roman empires."

When white biblical scholars deal with the topic of race (and such engagement has occurred only since the mid-1990s), it is usually as a means of critiquing
the larger institutional forces or systems that have made it possible for contemporary racism to influence the interpretation of biblical texts (e.g., Kelley 2002;
Buell and Johnson Hodge 2004). These scholars are actually calling attention to
the racialized (sub)texts that permeate modern and postmodern interpretations
of the Bible, exposing the cultural biases of the interpreters under review. Yet they
fail to acknowledge their own cultural biases or other *subjectivities* at work in
their interpretation of biblical texts (Bailey 1998).

Toni Morrison, in *Playing in the Dark: Whiteness and the Literary Imagination*, contends that "the contemplation of the black [or Africanist] presence is
central to any understanding of our national (or American) literature and should
not be permitted to hover at the margins of the literary imagination" (1992, 5).
Likewise, for biblical scholars, discussions about race, ethnicity, blacks, Africans,
or any other "Africanist presence"—or indeed any other cultural or ethnic subjectivities—should not hover at the margins of the biblical scholar's imagination
but move to the center of the interpretive process. These racialized (sub)texts, as
I will demonstrate in the next section, are a key component of the "hermeneutical dilemma" (Myers 1991) or "hermeneutical problem" (Fuchs 1964) facing *all*
biblical critics.

INTERPRETATIONS OF ACTS 8:26–40

The story of the Ethiopian eunuch in Acts 8:26–40 has received much analysis
among biblical interpreters. From the standard commentaries about salvation
history (Fitzmyer 1998), to the conversion motif that demonstrates that Christianity could extend to the ends of the earth (Gaventa 1986; Martin 1985), to
the many attempts on the part of African American biblical scholars to understand the historical, literary, and textual implications of the text for the lives
of contemporary African Americans (Martin 1989; Smith 1994; 1995; Carson
1999), this text continues to beg for new readings that would provide insights
onto the "forgotten" and misunderstood land of ancient Ethiopia. In this section, I discuss five interpretations of Acts 8:26–40 in order to define and assess
a sample of "racialized (sub)texts" in contemporary scholarship with respect to
this pivotal conversion story in the Lukan narrative structure of Acts: Joseph
Fitzmyer (1998); Beverly Roberts Gaventa (1986); Clarice J. Martin (1989); R.
Cottrel Carson (1997); and Edwin M. Yamauchi (2004, 161–81, 205–13). None
of these scholars utilizes critical race and ethnicity theories for interpreting this

(2) Although "mentioned fairly frequently in some sources, this was usually as representative of
peoples living near the edge of the world." (3) "For some authors, they are clearly mythical and
this study deals only with people whom the Greeks and Romans actually experienced" (49–50).

text, and none of them identifies explicitly his or her racial-ethnic background in these commentaries.

White biblical scholars such as Fitzmyer and Gaventa are apparently free to interpret Acts 8:26–40 without the constraints of "identity politics" or explicit "racialized discourses." Both of these scholars deal with the Ethiopian's identity only for the purpose of clarifying whether he was a Jew or Gentile. They make salient observations about the geographical provenance of the Ethiopian and draw upon critical research generated by reputable scholars dealing with "blacks in antiquity" (especially Gaventa), but they do not comment on how this biblical passage provides an opportunity for reflecting upon contemporary concerns related to race in churches and the larger society. They have locked the interpretive task in the past (Myers 1991, 41) and made themselves "transparent" or "invisible" in the interpretive process (Liew 2005, 119, 127).[29]

African American biblical scholars such as Martin and Carson explicitly deal with the "ethnographic identity," "geographical provenance," "politics of omission," and "liberative" hermeneutical strategies that are key for understanding this text from Acts. Martin does this much more explicitly than Carson, who uses a "safe" text-based approach to uncover the "paradigmatic outlook" (1997, 70) that holds sway among New Testament text critics. By the end of her article, Martin clearly defines what has prompted her "hermeneutics of suspicion" with respect to this text: "Racial minorities and women in particular have challenged epistemological, analytical and interpretive constructs in modern academic discourse which render them invisible" (1989, 122). Although Carson does not explicitly discuss the racialized (sub)texts operating among the various New Testament text critics he examines, it is clear that he wants to expose the authoritative figures, biased presuppositions, and abstract assumptions that have given certain manuscript traditions more credence and validity than others among New Testament text critics.[30] His remarks about the need to incorporate findings generated from methods other than textual criticism is, in my view, critical. Text criticism has usually escaped the purview or critique of many of the recent hermeneutical perspectives that have emerged over the past several decades among biblical scholars. I will discuss this point more fully later in this essay.

Japanese American Yamauchi, as a historian of ancient cultures who also seems "free" of the strictures of race and ethnicity, simply sets the record

---

29. Using the research of Richard Dyer, Tat-Siong Benny Liew observes that "whiteness operates through invisibility (Liew 2005, 119; Dyer 1988, 44–45).

30. For example, when he discusses the conclusions and inconsistencies of Williston Walker regarding the baptism of the Ethiopian eunuch, Carson says: "Strangely while Walker asserts that baptism 'was always accompanied by a confession of faith,' his 'paradigmatic outlook' does not allow him to see the inconsistency of implying that the eunuch's baptism did not originally contain such a confession" (1997, 70).

straight![31] He wants to make it clear that the Ethiopian eunuch was *not* from Ethiopia. In the attempt, however, he inadvertently demonstrates his racialized understanding of the scholarship of African American biblical interpreters (2004, 205–13) by focusing on a very narrow and early group of biblical scholars who were laying the groundwork for the more innovative studies that are now available. He does not discuss the many provocative and critical works that have been published by a new generation of biblical scholars.[32] In his effort to demonstrate that the Ethiopian eunuch was *not* from Ethiopia, and given his apparent working assumption that material from late antiquity is irrelevant for biblical interpretation, Yamauchi ignores the Axumite inscriptions and other sources (such as biblical translations in Geʻez) as relevant material for interpreting Acts 8:26–40. While it is true that the Axumite Empire and Geʻez sources may have no direct connection with Meroë, the assumed home of the eunuch who was the treasurer for *Kandakē*, it is clear that there was some type of exchange or interaction between these kingdoms (2004, 176).

Summary

Given my reading of the racialized (sub)texts related to Acts 8:26–40, I now conclude that this text is a *locus classicus* for exploring the intersections between postcolonial biblical criticism, race and ethnicity theories, and ideological readings of biblical texts. All of these rubrics provide a frame of reference through which I can now see how Acts 8:26–40 is more than a story about an *Ethiopian* who is being idealized in a sophisticated discourse about ethnicity (2002, 109–15). Indeed, the ethnopolitical rhetoric about this Ethiopian *black* man is worth identifying and analyzing, especially given the ways in which it calls attention to the ascetic influences reflected in the text and the ways in which it idealizes this virtuous "black man" as humble, silent, illiterate, and passive—effectively, representing the extremes to whom Christianity could extend. The implications for such an ideal figure for contemporary African American males and constructions of progressive black masculinities is significant (Byron 2006; Byrd and Guy-Sheftall 2001).[33] Moreover, such ancient constructions of ethnopolitical rhetorics are still wreaking havoc in contemporary discourses about blacks (and other racial and

---

31. Yamauchi, who was born in Hawaii, does not explicitly state his ethnic background in his scholarly works. In a biographical narrative, however, he discusses both of his parents' connections to Okinawa, Japan; his father emigrated from Japan, and his mother, though born in Hawaii, spent her childhood in Okinawa. See Yamauchi 1998, 192.

32. For important collections of essays, see Felder 1991; Wimbush 2000; Bailey 2003; for monographs, see Braxton 2002; Byron 2002; Buckhanon Crowder 2002; D. Williams 2004; and the many studies discussed in the introduction of this paper.

33. For provocative discussions about black masculinities, see Mutua 2006; Stecopoulos and Uebel 1997; Carbado 1999; Byrd and Guy-Sheftall 2001.

ethnic minorities) in the U.S. and are often embedded (or encoded) in religious and political sermons, speeches, and other forms of mass communication (Byron 2002, 126–29). But, of course, there is much more going on with this Ethiopian.

As R. Cottrel Carson has documented extensively, the fact that the Ethiopian was a *eunuch* was of extreme significance for the author of this text (1999, 94–124; see also Liew 2005, 142–43). Moreover, given Donaldson's challenge to engage in a "multiaxial" reading of biblical texts (1996, 8; see also Kwok 1995, 79)[34]—that is, as I understand it, a reading that exposes and explores the multiple intersections of race and ethnicity, gender and sexuality, class and status, imperialism and colonialism, privileged and marginalized, language and text, and the list could go on and on—it is clear that there is much interpretive potential in this text. The ideological implications of these racialized (sub)texts offer a wealth of information about the ways in which race and ethnicity impact the interpretation of biblical texts, especially texts that explicitly deal with black persons or geographical locales in Africa (Kelley 2000, 214–15). These "racialized (sub)texts" point to the need for a more engaged analysis of this text that challenges the principles and methods informing the area of text criticism, a subspecialty that has traditionally escaped scrutiny of postcolonial biblical critics or racial and ethnic minorities in the West. These (sub)texts also point to how *context* and specifically the (con)texts of ancient Ethiopia should receive more attention with respect to text-critical scholarship.

(Con)Text-Critical Scholarship: Ancient Ethiopia and the New Testament

Bruce M. Metzger was one of the first text-critical scholars to conduct research on ancient Ethiopic writings and their relevance for interpreting the New Testament. In *The Early Versions of the New Testament*, he examines both Western and Eastern versions of the New Testament, including Latin, Gothic, Slavonic, Syrian, Coptic, Armenian, Georgian, and Ethiopic (1977). Metzger concludes that "one of the most pressing *desiderata* is the preparation of a critical edition of the Ethiopic New Testament" (231). To my knowledge, no such critical edition has come to fruition, though several of the books of the New Testament are now available (e.g., Zuurmond 1989a; 1989b; 2001; Hofmann 1967). In his book *Reminiscences of an Octogenarian*, Metzger describes the extensive research he conducted on sixty-five Ethiopic manuscripts in order to determine the presence or absence of the longer ending of the Gospel of Mark (16:9–20) (1997, 167–68; Metzger and

---

34. Both Laura Donaldson and Kwok Pui-lan make their appeal for a "multi-dimensional perspective" or "multi-axial frame of reference" in terms of combining postcolonial studies with feminist studies. Neither engages race and ethnicity theory in their work, although Donaldson does acknowledge the importance of race in an earlier work (1992).

Ehrman 2005, 120). Metzger clearly sees the value of Ethiopic manuscripts, but, as Carson has noted in his study of Acts 8:37 (discussed above), Metzger depends on "a traditional reading of the principles of text criticism" (1997, 61; see Metzger 1975, 359), which invariably leads him (and his editorial team) to omit verse 37 from the Greek New Testament.

The principles of text criticism have been developed to guide the biblical critic through the science and art of evaluating textual evidence for the purpose of determining the most reliable, pure, or original reading of a text. Kurt and Barbara Aland have summarized the twelve basic rules for textual criticism (1989, 280–81; see Metzger and Ehrman 2005, 205–49),[35] all of which indicate the need for a systematic method for gaining control of the plethora of sources and traditions that inform the various books of the Greek New Testament. Unfortunately, there is very little methodological space for actually *using* text-critical data for understanding the social and cultural history of early Christianity. I will briefly revisit this point after looking more closely at scholarship related to the Ethiopic version of the New Testament.

Rochus Zuurmond, of the Universiteit van Amsterdam, has also provided critical scholarship related to the Ethiopic version of the New Testament (1995, 142). He states that research into the text of the Ethiopic (Ge'ez) New Testament (Eth) has mainly centered on seven topics: (1) When, where, and why did this version originate? (2) Has there been one translation only, or have there been several independent attempts to translate? (3) It is obvious that the Ethiopic version, as we know it from the extant manuscripts, has been revised several times. When and on which basis were these revisions made and can they be traced in the manuscript tradition? (4) Have all the books of the Ethiopic New Testament basically the same history of transmission, or are there significant differences? (5) Was the earliest Ethiopic text of the New Testament translated from the Greek or from another language (in particular, Syriac)? (6) If the *Vorlage* was Greek, to which type of Greek text did it belong? (7) Finally, given a reliable critical edition, what is the value of the Ethiopic version for textual criticism of the Greek New Testament?

Zuurmond provides a detailed historical discussion of these topics with many important references and summarizes the current state of research. With respect to the first question, he concludes the following:

> The Eth originated book by book, possibly at first even pericope by pericope, in the *kingdom of Axum* [emphasis mine] in the course of the fourth and fifth centuries, for the use of a Christianized population that did not understand Greek. Some details, however, are still disputed. Whether the charming story

---

35. Metzger and Ehrman also include discussions about the "reactions against classical textual criticism" (2005, 210–14) and some "alternative methods of textual criticism" (218–31).

of the little brothers, Frumentius and Edesius, as reported by Rufinus is historically reliable—I doubt it—is not very important. Frumentius is named by Athanasius and his adversaries as "bishop of the Axumites" in the mid-fourth century. It is possible that at least parts of the New Testament in Geʻez existed at that time. Early in the sixth century Ethiopia was a Christian nation. By that time the clergy must have had access to a complete Bible in their own language. (1995, 147)

Zuurmond goes on to note the limitations of the Ethiopic version of the New Testament, but overall he implies that this material has potential value for textual criticism of the Greek New Testament:

> Like other versions Eth should be used with much caution in reconstructing the underlying Greek. In addition, a gap of about half a millennium separates the actual translation(s) from the earliest MSS. No one knows what happened to the text during that period. From the twelfth century onward there is ever-increasing confusion, caused by the influence of Arabic texts. For the Gospels we have a few MSS of the thirteenth century of earlier. In the rest of the NT the earliest MSS come from the fourteenth century. If a critical edition is able to overcome these handicaps, considerable value remains. (154; see also Davies 1987)

Using Metzger and Zuurmond as examples, when ancient Ethiopic (Geʻez) sources have been explored by New Testament scholars, it is usually for the purpose of validating the Greek text by focusing mainly upon the Ethiopic version of the New Testament (Eth) with little or no attention devoted to examining the background or context of the text. Although it seems that such background information is important (see question 1: When, where, and how did this version originate?), very little effort has been made to understand the *kingdom of Axum*—as (con)text—by New Testament text-critical scholars.

Bart D. Ehrman acknowledges the potentially "myopic" endeavor of text criticism (Metzger and Ehrman 2005, 280–81; see also Ehrman 1995).[36] He notes in his discussion of "manuscripts and the social history of early Christianity" how some text critics are beginning to recognize the value of variant readings because they recognize how "changes that scribes made in their texts sometimes reflect the socio-historical contexts within which they worked ... contexts that are otherwise but sparsely attested in our surviving sources" (Metzger and Ehrman 2005, 281; see also Ehrman 1993; Epp 2004). This development among text critics opens up yet another window for (con)text-critical scholarship that illuminates the potential value of the Ethiopic version of the New Testament.

---

36. N.B. This section in Metzger and Ehrman is based on Ehrman's research (1995); this discussion was not included in the previous version (Metzger 1992).

Conclusion: (Con)texts, (Sub)texts, and the Politics of *Recognition*

I opened this essay by naming some of the trajectories and struggles that have led me to expand the interpretive lens through which I read and teach the Bible. Given the recent emergence of many studies dealing with "empire" and the continuous stream of scholarship utilizing postcolonial theory for the interpretation of biblical texts, I suggest it is *necessary* for New Testament scholars to broaden their geographical frame of reference by considering the ways in which the Axumite Empire and its sources might bring to light a whole new set of possibilities for understanding the New Testament and early Christianity. But this geographical expansion and awareness is not enough. As I have demonstrated through my case study of Acts 8:26–40, biblical scholars render racialized readings of this text whether they realize it or not. These racialized (sub)texts are embedded in the "politics of interpretation," which invariably affects all biblical interpreters, even the most objective and theoretically fluent. Such racialized (sub)texts generally come to light when dealing with texts related to the "Africanist presence" in the Bible.

While some African American scholars have identified their "hermeneutical dilemma," "struggles," or "what's at stake" when they interpret biblical texts, these admissions have not been framed, for the most part, as a conceptual point of departure for interpreting biblical texts. In other words, these scholars have not enlisted the (sub)texts of contemporary race and racism as a theoretical tool for interpreting the Bible. And even for those who have (e.g., Kelley 2002), it is usually for the purpose of isolating the racist attitudes from modernity that still influence the reading and teaching of the Bible. But there still remains the issue of the racialized (sub)texts in the ancient texts themselves (B. Isaac 2004), which leads to raising questions about the ethnic (con)texts from which ancient texts were generated and recognizing that the Axumite Empire and its sources offer fertile ground for exploration.

Using a postcolonial optic, I have demonstrated that critical theories about race and ethnicity should inform *all* aspects of interpretation: the ancient texts and (con)texts; the interpretations of these texts; and the interpreters themselves. Once we are able to *recognize* the various ethnic (con)texts in antiquity, the racialized (sub)texts that are embedded in the interpretations of ancient texts, and the hermeneutical struggles that all interpreters face in acknowledging what is at stake, then, hopefully, interpretations of texts dealing with ancient Ethiopia and the New Testament (e.g., Acts 8:26–40) will shift from the "politics of omission" to the "politics of *recognition*."

Works Consulted

Adejumobi, Saheed A. 2000. Ethiopia. Pages 231–42 in *African History Before 1885*. Vol. 1 of *Africa*. 3 vols. Edited by Toyin Falola. Durham, N.C.: Carolina Academic Press.
Aland, Kurt, and Barbara Aland. 1989. *The Text of the New Testament*. Grand Rapids: Eerdmans.
Anderson, Cheryl. 2004. *Women, Ideology, and Violence: Critical Theory and the Construction of Gender in the Book of the Covenant and the Deuteronomistic Law*. JSOTSup 394. London: T&T Clark.
Aubert, Jean-Jacques. 2002. La Pertinence de la Négritude: Moïse L'Éthiopien. Pages 27–40 in *Histoire et Herméneutique: Mélanges offerts Gottfried Hammann*. Edited by Martin Rose. Geneva: Labor et Fides.
Bailey, Randall C. 1991. Beyond Identification: The Use of Africans in Old Testament Poetry and Narratives. Pages 165–84 in Felder 1991. Minneapolis: Fortress.
———. 1996. "They Shall Become as White as Snow": When Bad Is Turned into Good. *Semeia* 76:99–113.
———. 1998. The Danger of Ignoring One's Own Cultural Bias in Interpreting the Text. Pages 66–90 in Sugirtharajah 1998b.
———. 2000. Academic Biblical Interpretation among African Americans in the United States. Pages 696–711 in Wimbush 2000.
———, ed. 2003. *Yet With a Steady Beat: Contemporary U.S. Afrocentric Biblical Interpretation*. SemeiaSt 42. Atlanta: Society of Biblical Literature.
Bauer, Walter. 1996. *Orthodoxy and Heresy in Earliest Christianity*. Mifflintown, Pa.: Sigler.
Bell, Derrick. 1992. *Faces at the Bottom of the Well: The Permanence of Racism*. New York: Basic Books.
Bennett, Harold V. 2002. *Injustice Made Legal: Deuteronomic Law and the Plight of Widows, Strangers, and Orphans in Ancient Israel*. Grand Rapids: Eerdmans.
Bhabha, Homi K. 1992. Postcolonial Criticism. Pages 437–65 in *Redrawing the Boundaries*. Edited by S. Greenblatt and G. Gunn. New York: Modern Language Association of America
———. 1994. *The Location of Culture*. London: Routledge.
Blount, Brian K. 1995. *Cultural Interpretation: Reorienting New Testament Criticism*. Minneapolis: Fortress.
Blount, Brian K., Cain Hope Felder, Clarice J. Martin, and Emerson Powery, eds. 2008. *True to Our Native Land: An African American New Testament Commentary*. Minneapolis: Fortress.
Boer, Roland. 2001. *Last Stop before Antarctica: The Bible and Postcolonialism in Australia*. Bible and Postcolonialism 6. Sheffield: Sheffield Academic Press.
Brakke, David. 2001. Ethiopian Demons: Male Sexuality, the Black-Skinned Other, and the Monastic Self. *Journal of the History of Sexuality* 10:501–35.

Braxton, Brad R. 2002. *No Longer Slaves: Galatians and African American Experience.* Collegeville, Minn.: Liturgical Press.

———. 2003. The Role of Ethnicity in the Social Location of 1 Corinthians 7:17–24. Pages 19–32 in Bailey 2003.

Brett, Mark G., ed. 1996. *Ethnicity and the Bible.* Leiden: Brill.

Brown, Michael Joseph. 2004. *Blackening of the Bible: The Aims of African American Biblical Interpretation.* Harrisburg, Pa.: Trinity Press International.

Buckhanon Crowder, Stephanie. 2002. *Simon of Cyrene: A Case of Roman Conscription.* New York: Lang.

Buell, Denise Kimber. 2005. *Why This New Race: Ethnic Reasoning in Early Christianity.* New York: Columbia University Press.

Buell, Denise Kimber, and Caroline Johnson Hodge. 2004. The Politics of Interpretation: The Rhetoric of Race and Ethnicity in Paul. *JBL* 123:235–51.

Burstein, Stanley, ed. 1997. *Ancient African Civilizations: Kush and Axum.* Princeton: Markus Wiener.

Byrd, Rudolph P., and Beverly Guy-Sheftall, eds. 2001. *Traps: African American Men on Gender and Sexuality.* Bloomington: Indiana University Press.

Byron, Gay L. 2002. *Symbolic Blackness and Ethnic Difference in Early Christian Literature.* London: Routledge.

———. 2003. Biblical Interpretation as an Act of Community Accountability. *USQR* 56:55–58.

———. 2004. Review of David M. Goldenberg, *The Curse of Ham: Race and Slavery in Early Judaism, Christianity, and Islam. Christian Century* 121.18:55–56.

———. 2005. The Challenge of "Blackness" for Rearticulating Global Feminist New Testament Interpretation. Pages 84–101 in *Feminist New Testament Studies: Global and Future Perspectives.* Edited by Kathleen O'Brien Wicker, Althea Spencer Miller, and Musa W. Dube. New York: Palgrave.

———. 2006. Images of Masculinity in the Pauline Epistles: Resources for Constructing Progressive Black Masculinities, or Not? Pages 101–20 in Mutua 2006.

Carbado, Devon, ed. 1999. *Black Men on Race, Gender, and Sexuality: A Critical Reader.* New York: Routledge.

Carson, Cottrel R. 1997. Acts 8.37: A Textual Reexamination. *USQR* 51:57–78.

———. 1999. "Do You Understand What You Are Reading?": A Reading of the Ethiopian Eunuch Story (Acts 8:26–40) from a Site of Cultural Marronage. Ph.D. diss. Union Theological Seminary.

Carter, Warren. 2001. *Matthew and Empire: Initial Explorations.* Harrisburg, Pa.: Trinity Press International.

Coates, Delman L. 2005. And the Bible Says: Methodological Tyranny of Biblical Fundamentalism and Historical Criticism. Pages 97–100 in *Blow the Trumpet in Zion: Global Vision and Action for the 21st-Century Black Church.* Edited by Iva E. Carruthers, Frederick D. Haynes III, and Jeremiah A. Wright Jr. Minneapolis: Fortress.

Copher, Charles B. 1993. *Black Biblical Studies: An Anthology of Charles B. Copher*. Chicago: Black Light Fellowship.

Cowley, Roger. 1988. *Ethiopian Biblical Interpretation: A Study in Exegetical Tradition and Hermeneutics*. New York: Cambridge University Press.

Crenshaw, Kimberlé Williams. 1995. Mapping the Margins: Intersectionality, Identity Politics, and Violence against Women of Color. Pages 357–83 in *Critical Race Theory: The Key Writings That Formed the Movement*. Edited by Kimberlé Crenshaw, Neil Gotanda, Gary Peller, and Kendall Thomas. New York: New Press.

Crocker, P. T. 1986. The City of Meroë and the Ethiopian Eunuch. *Buried History* 22:53–72.

Davies, D. M. 1987. The Dating of Ethiopic Manuscripts. *JNES* 46:287–307.

Delgado, Richard, and Jean Stefancic. 2001. *Critical Race Theory: An Introduction*. New York: New York University Press.

Donaldson, Laura E. 1992. *Decolonizing Feminisms: Race, Gender, and Empire-Building*. Chapel Hill: University of North Carolina Press.

———. 1996. Postcolonialism and Biblical Reading: Introduction. *Semeia* 75:1–14.

Dube, Musa W. 2000. *Postcolonial Feminist Interpretation of the Bible*. St. Louis: Chalice.

———. 2001. *Other Ways of Reading: African Women and the Bible*. SBLGPBS 2. Atlanta: Society of Biblical Literature.

———. 2005. Rahab Is Hanging Out a Red Ribbon: One African Woman's Perspective on the Future of Feminist New Testament Scholarship. Pages 177–202 in *Feminist New Testament Studies: Global and Future Perspectives*. Edited by Kathleen O'Brien Wicker, Althea Spencer Miller, and Musa W. Dube. New York: Palgrave.

Duling, Dennis C. 2003. *The New Testament: History, Literature, and Social Context*. 4th ed. Belmont, Calif.: Wadsworth.

Dyer, Richard. 1988. Whiteness. *Screen* 29:44–64.

Dyson, Michael. 1996. *Race Rules: Navigating the Color Line*. Reading, Mass.: Addison-Wesley.

Ehrman, Bart D. 1993. *Orthodox Corruption of Scripture: The Effect of Early Christological Controversies on the Text of the New Testament*. New York: Oxford University Press.

———. 1995. The Text as Window: Manuscripts and the Social History of Early Christianity. Pages 361–79 in *The Text of the New Testament in Contemporary Research: Essays on the Status Quaestionis*. Edited by Bart D. Ehrman and Michael W. Holmes. Grand Rapids: Eerdmans Press.

———. 2003. *Lost Christianities: The Battles for Scripture and the Faiths We Never Knew*. New York: Oxford University Press.

Epp, Eldon. 2004. The Oxyrhynchus New Testament Papyri: "Not without Honor Except in Their Hometown"? *JBL* 123:5–55.

Felder, Cain Hope. 1982. Racial Ambiguities in the Biblical Narratives. Pages 17–24 in *The Church and Racism*. Edited by Gregory Baum and John Coleman. Concilium 151. New York: Seabury.

———. 1989a. Ancient Ethiopia and the Queen of Sheba. Pages 22–36 in Felder 1989b.

———. 1989b. *Troubling Biblical Waters: Race, Class, and Family*. Maryknoll, N.Y.: Orbis.

———, ed. 1991. *Stony the Road We Trod: African American Biblical Interpretation*. Minneapolis: Fortress.

———. 2002. *Race, Racism, and the Biblical Narratives*. Minneapolis: Fortress.

Fisher, M. C. 1974. Some Contributions of Ethiopic Studies to the Understanding of the Old Testament. Pages 71–86 in *The Law and the Prophets: Old Testament Studies Prepared in Honor of Oswald Thompson Allis*. Edited by J. H. Skilton. Nutley, N.J.: Presbyterian & Reformed.

Fitzmyer, Joseph A. 1998. *The Acts of the Apostles: A New Translation with Introduction and Commentary*. AB 31. New York: Doubleday.

Fuchs, Ernst. 1964. The New Testament and the Hermeneutical Problem. Pages 111–45 in *New Frontiers in Theology, II: The New Hermeneutic*. Edited by J. M. Robinson and J. B. Cobb. New York: Harper & Row.

Gallagher, Susan VanZanten, ed. 1994. *Postcolonial Literature and the Biblical Call for Justice*. Jackson: University Press of Mississippi.

Gaventa, Beverly Roberts. 1986. *From Darkness to Light: Aspects of Conversion in the New Testament*. Philadelphia: Fortress.

Gibbon, Edward. 1910. *The Decline and Fall of the Roman Empire*. New York: Dutton.

Giday, Belai. 1992. *Ethiopian Civilization*. Addis Ababa: Privately printed.

Gilmore, Ruth Wilson. 2002. Fatal Couplings of Power and Difference: Notes on Racism and Geography. *The Professional Geographer* 54:15–24.

Goldenberg, David M. 2003. *The Curse of Ham: Race and Slavery in Early Judaism, Christianity, and Islam*. Princeton: Princeton University Press.

Haile, Getatchew. 1993. Ethiopic Literature. Pages 47–54 in *African Zion: The Sacred Art of Ethiopia*. Edited by Roderick Grierson. New Haven: Yale University Press.

Henze, Paul B. 2000. *Layers of Time: A History of Ethiopia*. New York: St. Martin's Press.

Hidal, Sten. 1997. The Land of Cush in the Old Testament. *Svensk exegetisk årsbok* 41–42:97–106.

Hofmann, Josef. 1967. *Die Äthiopische Übersetzung der Johannes-Apokalypse*. CSCO 55–56. Louvain: Secrâetariat du CSCO.

Hood, Robert E. 1994. *Begrimed and Black: Christian Traditions on Blacks and Blackness*. Minneapolis: Fortress.

Horsley, Richard A., ed. 1997. *Paul and Empire: Religion and Power in Roman Imperial Society*. Harrisburg, Pa.: Trinity Press International.

———. 1998. Submerged Biblical Histories and Imperial Biblical Studies. Pages 152–73 in Sugirtharajah 1998b.

———. 2003a. *Jesus and Empire: The Kingdom of God and the New World Disorder*. Minneapolis: Fortress.

———. 2003b. *Religion and Empire: People, Power and the Life of the Spirit*. Minneapolis: Fortress.

Isaac, Benjamin. 2004. *The Construction of Racism in Classical Antiquity*. Princeton: Princeton University Press.

Issac, Ephraim. 1968. *The Ethiopian Church*. Boston: Sawyer.

———. 1983. 1 (Ethiopic Apocalypse of) Enoch: A New Translation and Introduction. Pages 5–89 in vol. 1 of *Old Testament Pseudepigrapha*. Edited by James H. Charlesworth. 2 vols. Garden City, N.Y.: Doubleday.

Isaac, Ephraim, and Cain Hope Felder. 1984. Reflections on the Origins of the Ethiopian Civilization. Pages 71–83 in *Proceedings of the Eighth International Conference of Ethiopian Studies* 1. Addis Ababa: Institute of Ethiopian Studies.

Isasi-Díaz, Ada María. 1993. *En la lucha: A Hispanic Women's Liberation Theology*. Minnepolis: Fortress.

Johnson Hodge, Caroline. 2007. *If Sons, Then Heirs: A Study of Kinship and Ethnicity in the Letters of Paul*. New York: Oxford University Press.

Kelly, Shawn. 2000. Race. Pages 213–19 in *Handbook of Postmodern Biblical Interpretation*. Edited by A. K. M. Adam. St. Louis: Chalice.

———. 2002. *Racializing Jesus: Race, Ideology and the Formation of Modern Biblical Scholarship*. London: Routledge.

Koester, Helmut. 2000. *History and Literature of Early Christianity*. Vol. 2 of *Introduction to the New Testament*. 2nd ed. New York: de Gruyter.

Kwok Pui-Lan. 1995. *Discovering the Bible in the Non-biblical World*. New York: Orbis.

Lambdin, Thomas O. 1978. *Introduction to Classical Ethiopic (Ge'ez)*. HSS 24. Missoula, Mont.: Scholars Press.

Liew, Tat-siong Benny. 1999. *The Politics of Parousia: Reading Mark Inter(con)textually*. Biblical Interpretation Series 42. Leiden: Brill.

———, ed. 2002. *The Bible in Asian America. Semeia* 90–91.

———. 2005. Margins and (Cutting-)Edges: On the (Il)Legitimacy and Intersections of Race, Ethnicity, and (Post)Colonialism. Pages 114–65 in Moore and Segovia 2005.

Marcus, Harold G. 2002. *A History of Ethiopia Updated Edition*. Berkeley and Los Angeles: University of California Press.

Martin, Clarice J. 1985. The Function of Acts 8:26–40 within the Narrative Structure of the Book of Acts: The Significance of the Eunuch's Provenance for Acts 1:8c. Ph.D. diss. Duke University.

———. 1989. A Chamberlain's Journey and the Challenge for Interpretation for Liberation. *Semeia* 47:105–35.

———. 1990. Womanist Interpretations of the New Testament. *JFSR* 6:41–61.

———. 1991. The *Haustafeln* (Household Codes) in African American Biblical Interpretation. Pages 206–31 in Felder 1991.

Mutua, Athena, ed. 2006. *Progressive Black Masculinities.* New York: Routledge.

McEntire, Mark. 2000. Cain and Abel in Africa: An Ethiopian Case Study in Competing Hermeneutics. Pages 248–59 in *Bible in Africa: Transactions, Trajectories, and Trends.* Edited by Gerald O. West and Musa W. Dube. Leiden: Brill.

Metzger, Bruce M. 1975. *A Textual Commentary on the Greek New Testament.* Corrected ed. New York: United Bible Societies. [orig. 1971]

———. 1977. The Ethiopic Version. Pages 215–56 in idem, *The Early Versions of the New Testament: Their Origin, Transmission and Limitations.* Oxford: Clarendon.

———. 1992. *The Text of the New Testament: Its Transmission, Corruption, and Restoration.* 3rd ed. New York: Oxford University Press.

———. 1997. *Reminiscences of an Octogenarian.* Peabody, Mass.: Hendrickson.

Metzger, Bruce M., and Bart D. Ehrman. 2005. *The Text of the New Testament: Its Transmission, Corruption, and Restoration.* 4th ed. New York: Oxford University Press.

Montgomery, James A. 1934. The Ethiopic Text of Acts of the Apostles. *HTR* 27:169–205.

Moore, Stephen D. 2000. Postcolonialism. Pages 182–88 in *Handbook of Postmodern Biblical Interpretation.* Edited by A. K. M. Adam. St. Louis: Chalice.

Moore, Stephen D., and Fernando F. Segovia, eds. 2005. *Postcolonial Biblical Criticism: Interdisciplinary Intersections.* London: T&T Clark.

Morrison, Toni. 1992. *Playing in the Dark: Whiteness and the Literary Imagination.* Cambridge: Harvard University Press.

Munro-Hay, Stuart. 1989. *Excavations at Aksum: An Account of the Research at the Ancient Ethiopian Capital Directed in 1972–4 by Dr. Neville Chittick.* London: British Institute in Africa.

———. 1991. *Aksum: An African Civilisation of Late Antiquity.* Edinburgh: Edinburgh University Press.

———.1993. Aksumite Coinage. Pages 101–16 in *African Zion: The Sacred Art of Ethiopia.* Edited by Roderick Grierson. New Haven: Yale University Press.

———. 2002. *Ethiopia, the Unknown Land: A Cultural and Historical Guide.* New York: St. Martin's Press.

Myers, William H. 1991. The Hermeneutical Dilemma of the African American Biblical Student. Pages 40–56 in Felder 1991.

Nash, Peter T. 2003. *Reading Race, Reading the Bible.* Minneapolis: Fortress.

Nickelsburg, George W. E., and James C. VanderKam. 2004. *1 Enoch: A New Translation.* Minneapolis: Fortress.

Pankhurst, Richard. 2001. *The Ethiopians: A History.* Malden, Mass.: Blackwell.

Patte, Daniel. 1995. *Ethics of Biblical Interpretation: A Reevaluation*. Louisville: Westminster John Knox.

Phillipson, David W. 1998. *Ancient Ethiopia: Aksum: Its Antecedents and Successors*. London: British Museum Press.

Piovanelli, P. 2003. Exploring the Ethiopic Book of the Cock, an Apocryphal Passion Gospel from Late Antiquity. *HTR* 96:427–54.

Prior, Michael. 1997. *The Bible and Colonialism: A Moral Critique*. Biblical Seminar 48. Sheffield: Sheffield Academic Press.

Ramsay, Nancy. 2002. Navigating Racial Difference as a White Pastoral Theologian. *Journal of Pastoral Theology* 12:11–27.

Redding, Ann Holmes. 1999. Not Again: Another Look at the Household Codes. Pages 455–63 in *Eve and Adam: Jewish, Christian, and Muslim Readings on Genesis and Gender*. Edited by Kristen E. Kvam, Linda S. Schearing, and Valarie H. Ziegler. Bloomington: Indiana University Press.

Reed, Ishmael, Shawn Wong, Bob Callahan, and Andrew Hope. 1989. Is Ethnicity Obsolete? Pages 226–35 in *The Invention of Ethnicity*. Edited by Werner Sollors. New York: Oxford University Press.

Ricci, Lanfranco. 1991. Ethiopian Christian Literature. Pages 975–79 in vol. 3 of *The Coptic Encyclopedia*. Edited by Aziz S. Atiya. New York: Macmillan.

Robinson, James M., and Helmut Koester. 1971. *Trajectories through Early Christianity*. Philadelphia: Fortress.

Runions, Erin. 2001. *Changing Subjects: Gender, Nation and Future in Micah*. Playing the Texts 7. Sheffield: Sheffield Academic Press.

Sadler, Rodney Steven, Jr. 2005. *Can a Cushite Change His Skin? An Examination of Race, Ethnicity, and Othering in the Hebrew Bible*. New York: T&T Clark.

Said, Edward. 1978. *Orientalism: Western Conceptions of the Orient*. London: Penguin.

———. 1993. *Culture and Imperialism*. New York: Knopf.

Sanders, Boykin. 1995. In Search of a Face for Simon the Cyrene. Pages 51–63 in *The Recovery of Black Presence: An Interdisciplinary Exploration. Essays in Honor of Dr. Charles B. Copher*. Edited by Randall C. Bailey and Jacquelyn Grant. Nashville: Abingdon.

Schüssler Fiorenza, Elisabeth. 1999. *Rhetoric and Ethic: The Politics of Biblical Interpretation*. Minneapolis: Fortress.

———. 2000. *Jesus and the Politics of Interpretation*. New York: Continuum.

Segovia, Fernando F. 1994. Theological Education and Scholarship as Struggle: The Life of Racial/Ethnic Minorities in the Profession. *Journal of Hispanic/Latino Theology* 2:5–25.

———. 1995a. Cultural Studies and Contemporary Biblical Criticism: Ideological Criticism as Mode of Discourse. Pages 1–17 in Segovia and Tolbert 1995b.

———. 1995b. Toward Intercultural Criticism: A Reading Strategy from the Diaspora. Pages 303–30 in Segovia and Tolbert 1995b.

———. 1996. Racial and Ethnic Minorities in Biblical Studies. Pages 469–92 in Brett 1996.

———. 1998. Biblical Criticism and Postcolonial Studies: Toward a Postcolonial Optic. Pages 49–65 in Sugirtharajah 1998b.

———. 2000a. *Decolonizing Biblical Studies: A View from the Margins*. Maryknoll, N.Y.: Orbis.

———, ed. 2000b. *Interpreting beyond Borders*. Bible and Postcolonialism 3. Sheffield: Sheffield Academic Press.

———. 2000c. Notes toward Refining the Postcolonial Optic. Pages 133–42 in Segovia 2000a.

———. 2005. Mapping the Postcolonial Optic in Biblical Criticism: Meaning and Scope. Pages 23–78 in Moore and Segovia 2005.

Segovia, Fernando F., and Mary Ann Tolbert, eds. 1995a. *Social Location and Biblical Interpretation in the United States*. Vol. 1 of *Reading from This Place*. Minneapolis: Fortress.

———. 1995b. *Social Location and Biblical Interpretation in Global Perspective*. Vol. 2 of *Reading from This Place*. Minneapolis: Fortress.

Smith, Abraham. 1994. Do You Understand What You Are Reading? *Journal of the Interdenominational Theological Center* 22:48–70.

———. 1995. A Second Step in African Biblical Interpretation: A Generic Reading Analysis of Acts 8:26–40. Pages 213–28 in Segovia and Tolbert 1995a.

Snowden, Frank M., Jr. 1970. *Blacks in Antiquity: Ethiopians in the Greco-Roman Experience*. Cambridge: Harvard University Press.

———. 1983. *Before Color Prejudice: The Ancient View of Blacks*. Cambridge: Harvard University Press.

Spivak, Gayatri Chakravorty. 1985. Can the Subaltern Speak? Speculations on Widow-Sacrifice. *Wedge* 7–8:120–30.

———. 1988. *In Other Worlds*. New York: Routledge.

———. 1990. *The Post-Colonial Critic: Interviews, Strategies, Dialogues*. London: Routledge.

———. 1996. *The Spivak Reader*. Edited by Donna Landry and Gerald Maclean. New York: Routledge.

Stecopoulos, Harry, and Michael Uebel, eds. 1997. *Race and the Subject of Masculinities*. Durham, N.C.: Duke University Press.

Sugirtharajah, R. S. 1996a. From Orientalist to Post-Colonial: Notes on Reading Practices. *Asia Journal of Theology* 10:20–27.

———. 1996b. Textual Cleaning: A Move from the Colonial to the Postcolonial Version. *Semeia* 76:7–19.

———. 1998a. *Asian Biblical Hermeneutics and Postcolonialism: Contesting the Interpretations*. Maryknoll, N.Y.: Orbis.

———. ed. 1998b. *The Postcolonial Bible*. Sheffield: Sheffield Academic Press.

———. 2002. *Postcolonial Criticism and Biblical Interpretation*. Oxford: Oxford University Press.

Torjesen, Karen Jo. 2005. Response (to Gay L. Byron): Paradoxes of Positionality as the Key to Feminist New Testament Studies. Pages 103–7 in *Feminist
New Testament Studies: Global and Future Perspectives*. Edited by Kathleen
O'Brien Wicker, Althea Spencer Miller, and Musa W. Dube. New York: Palgrave.

Ullendorf, Edwards. 1956. Candace (Acts VIII. 27) and the Queen of Sheba. *NTS*
2:53–56.

———. 1968. *Ethiopia and the Bible*. London: Oxford University Press.

Venable-Ridley, C. Michelle. 1997. Paul and the African American Community.
Pages 212–33 in *Embracing the Spirit: Womanist Pespectives on Hope, Sal-
vation, and Transformation*. Edited by Emilie M. Townes. Maryknoll, N.Y.:
Orbis.

Walters, James C. 1993. *Ethnic Issues in Paul's Letter to the Romans*. Valley Forge,
Pa.: Trinity Press International.

Wan, Sze-kar. 2000. Collection for the Saints as Anticolonial Act: Implications of
Paul's Ethnic Reconstruction. Pages 191–215 in *Paul and Politics*. Edited by
Richard A. Horsley. Harrisburg, Pa.: Trinity Press International.

Weems, Renita J. 1988. *Just a Sister Away: A Womanist Vision of Women's Relationships in the Bible*. San Diego: LuraMedia.

———. 1991. Reading Her Way through the Struggle: African American Women
and the Bible. Pages 57–77 in Felder 1991.

———. 1992. The Hebrew Women Are Not Like the Egyptian Women. *Semeia*
59:25–34.

———. 1995. *Battered Love: Marriage, Sex, and Violence in the Hebrew Prophets*.
Minneapolis: Fortress.

Welsby, Derek A. 1996. *The Kingdom of Kush: The Napatan and Meroitic Empires*.
London: British Museum Press.

West, Cornel. 1993. *Race Matters*. Boston: Beacon.

West, Gerald O. 1996. Reading the Bible Differently: Giving Shape to the Discourse of the Dominated. *Semeia* 73:21–42.

Wicker, Kathleen O'Brien. 1990. Ethiopian Moses (Collected Sources). Pages
329–48 in *Ascetic Behavior in Greco-Roman Antiquity: A Sourcebook*. Edited
by Vincent L. Wimbush. Minneapolis: Fortress.

———. 2005. Introduction. Pages 1–15 in *Feminist New Testament Studies: Global
and Future Perspectives*. Edited by Kathleen O'Brien Wicker, Althea Spencer
Miller, and Musa W. Dube. New York: Palgrave.

Williams, Demetrius K. 2004. *An End to This Strife: The Politics of Gender in African American Churches*. Minneapolis: Fortress.

Williams, Patricia J. 1991. *The Alchemy of Race and Rights*. Cambridge: Harvard
University Press.

———. 1995. The Ecclesiastical Context of the New Testament. *NIB* 8:43–55.

———. 1998. *Seeing a Color-Blind Future: The Paradox of Race*. New York: Noon-
day Press.

Wimbush, Vincent L. 1992. Ascetic Behavior and Color-ful Language: Stories about Ethiopian Moses. *Semeia* 58:81–92.

———, ed. 2000. *African Americans and the Bible*. New York: Continuum.

Yamauchi, Edwin M. 1998. An Ancient Historian's View of Christianity. Pages 192–99 in *Professors Who Believe: The Spiritual Journeys of Christian Faculty*. Edited by Paul M. Anderson. Downers Grove, Ill.: InterVarsity Press.

———. 2004. *Africa and the Bible*. Grand Rapids: Baker.

Yee, Gale A. 2003. *Poor Banished Children of Eve: Woman as Evil in the Hebrew Bible*. Minneapolis: Fortress.

Zuurmond, Rochus. 1989. *Novum Testamentum Aethiopic: The Synoptic Gospels*. Stuttgart: Steiner.

———. 1995. The Ethiopic Version of the New Testament. Pages 142–56 in Ehrman and Holmes 1995.

PART 1: STUDIES
SECTION 3: PROBLEMATIZING CRITICISM

Toward Latino/a American Biblical Criticism: Latin(o/a)ness as Problematic

Fernando F. Segovia

Introduction

Participation in all-minority projects, such as "Reading and Teaching the Bible as African American, Asian American, and Latino/a American Scholars," proves, I find, at once highly attractive, highly convoluted, and highly challenging. Highly enticing, insofar as such ventures bring together critics from minority groups for discussion and planning without the presence and gaze of the dominant group. Highly complicated, since the minority critics engaged in such ventures represent population groups involving quite different geopolitical backgrounds, quite different historical trajectories into the country, and quite different material and discursive formations within the national scene. Highly demanding, insofar as such ventures bring to the fore, immediately and radically, a set of foundational yet controverted questions alien to the discipline, issues that have not traditionally formed part of the standard repertoire of biblical criticism and pedagogy and that the discipline finds itself, as a result, singularly unprepared to deal with in either theoretical or practical fashion. Such participation calls, therefore, for critical self-reflection—at some point along the line—on the part of subscribers to such projects. That is precisely the goal of the present study, and, by way of introduction, I should like to expand on these various dimensions of and reactions to these projects.

A Sense of Attraction

A sense of enticement is undeniable, and quite potent in fact, but requires careful nuancing. The omission of the dominant in these ventures I by no means look upon as an ideal in and of itself—a goal to be intensely pursued and a procedure to be firmly institutionalized at all times and in all places. Quite to the contrary, such a modus operandi I would regard as seriously defective on various counts. First, it would be highly artificial: all groups remain inextricably related in manifold and complex ways within any social-cultural context, and no dichotomous separation of any sort will serve to bring about substantial and effective change in such a situation. Second, it would prove highly counterproductive: any such social-cultural context requires the collaboration of all groups if conscientization regarding the problematic of power relations is to be surfaced and an alternative vision of human fulfillment for all to be adopted. Third, it would prove highly contradictory: a separatist mission would actually betray the calls for inclusion, for acknowledgment of human dignity and pursuit of social justice, invariably at the heart of minority claims and hence imitate the policies of exclusion invariably at work in dominant formations. Lastly, it would be highly reductionist: an exclusivist commitment would flatten tensions and contradictions both within the dominant group and the minority formations, resulting in a naive simplification of power relations at work in and across all groups.

Consequently, if a gathering away from the gaze and the presence of the dominant proves attractive, it is, to my mind, because such an arrangement allows for a space—fleeting and contrived as it may be—in which critics from minority groups can talk about themselves, about their relation to the dominant formation, and about their relations to one another in the shadow of the dominant, all without the ever-watchful supervision and ever-ready interventionism on the part of such a powerful and encompassing shadow. I see such ventures as highly attractive, therefore, as tactical moves—strategic moments for joint assessment, interchange, and planning. Ways in which minority critics can affirm a presence of their own and return the gaze upon the dominant; venues in which to reconceive, reformulate, and reorient the discipline toward dialogue among all critics and fruitful change for all critics.

A SENSE OF CONVOLUTION

The sense of complexity, strikingly in evidence from the start, bears closer scrutiny as well. At its core, beyond the myriad experiences and realities of the minority groups themselves, lie two determining factors having to do with the dominant formation. First, the absence of dominant representation creates a material and discursive vacuum to which minority critics are altogether unaccustomed and in which they find themselves without their usual political and epistemic bearings. Indeed, outside of such ventures, minority critics have no option but to deal with the dominant formation directly and without respite, making familiarity with and savvy amid the dominant a sine qua non for academic and professional survival.[1]

---

1. It is, after all, dominant critics who control the centers of learning and the professional organizations; who set the ethos, the driving values and goals, of all such venues; who stand guard over admission into the ranks of students and faculty or into the corps of leaders and officers; who pass judgment regarding ability and worth in the case of evaluation and promotion

These projects create a situation, therefore, where minority critics, although certainly aware of one another and sympathetic toward each other's causes, have not developed patterns for dealing with one another, either between or among groups. Second, even in absentia, the presence and gaze of dominant representation continue to make themselves felt keenly. More generally, through the inevitable discursive and material frameworks of the dominant within which such ventures take place. More pointedly, through the ethos of competitiveness wrought upon and imbibed by minority groups by means of a constructed zero-sum situation in which the scarcity of positions and resources allotted discourages cooperation and engenders distrust among them. In coming together on their own, consequently, minority critics not only lack a working blueprint for interaction but also bear within themselves an attitude of suspicion toward any such interaction.

When they do come together, moreover, minority critics further realize the forbidding complexity of the task before them. Suddenly, the variations and tensions experienced within the respective groups, intricate enough as they are, find themselves multiplied in multiple directions across the other groups. First, there is the question of provenance—a felt need for knowledge about all groups, the global frameworks and national contexts from which they come or to which they trace their origins. Second, there is the question of translation—a sharp need for information about the causes and modes of emigration as well as the paths and experiences of immigration. Lastly, there is the question of status—a keen need for knowledge about the social matrix and cultural production of all groups, both through time and at present. In other words, such ventures require, as minority critics come to realize soon enough, a sophisticated comparative grasp of global histories and relations, of the circumstances and narratives of migration, and of minority problems and backgrounds. All such expertise, moreover, duly set against and integrated into the reality and experience, the perceptions and policies, of a controlling center, in itself always in transition as well.

A SENSE OF CHALLENGE

The sense of demand, altogether inescapable and rather overwhelming, also merits proper unpacking. The invocation of classifications such as "African Americans," "Asian Americans," and "Latino/a Americans" as well as the appeal to categories such as "minority" (under which the three groupings are subsumed) and "dominant" (signifying "Euro-Americans" of all stripes) straightaway insert the problematic of identity in general and of race-ethnicity in particular into a

---

or of exposure and responsibilities; who shape the contents, modes, and means of knowledge transmission in teaching and learning or of knowledge dissemination in presentations and publications; and who exercise close vigilance, directly and indirectly, over matters of recommendation and employment or recognition and advancement.

field of studies that has not conceived of itself in such terms, whether in common parlance or critical analysis, and that has not drawn upon the discourse of race-ethnicity to examine the texts and context of antiquity. It is fair to say that, while the discipline lay exclusively in the hands of European and Euro-American scholars, as was the case from its inception in the early nineteenth century through the mid-1970s, the problematic of race-ethnicity did not emerge as a central, or even minor, topic of interest or analysis, whether at the level of criticism or antiquity.

What it meant for a critic to be, say, "German" or "French" or "British", "European" or "American," was not a point of discussion or contention. In fact, given the ethos of the discipline, such considerations would have amounted—unless understood strictly as the application of ancient findings to contemporary contexts, a task, however, generally assigned to pastoral, moral, or theological studies—to a serious violation of the denial of identity inherent in its conceptualization and exercise. Given a scholarly ethos where neutrality and objectivity reigned as supreme values—or, to put it differently, where subjectivity and perspective were not problematized, even in those rare instances when acknowledged as such—such reflections would have been regarded as extraneous, if not detrimental, to the scientific task of interpretation through historical contextualization. Who carried out such work remained ultimately immaterial. Similarly, in texts and contexts suffused with all sorts of racial descriptions and distinctions—from, say, "Hebrews" and "Canaanites" to "Jews" and "Gentiles"—the analysis of such representations did not involve explicit and sustained dialogue with the ongoing study of race-ethnicity. As a result, such scholarship remained throughout at a rather impressionistic level of research, often taking over stereotypes conveyed by the ancient sources themselves or imbibed from the contemporary social-cultural contexts of criticism.

This state of affairs would not undergo significant alteration until the entry into the discipline of scholars from outside the established domain, native critics from a rapidly expanding global Christianity in the non-Western world as well as minority critics from the presence of such global Christianity within the West. It would be the latter in particular who would first foreground the question of race-ethnicity in and across the discipline.[2] The introduction of this problematic would bring with it serious critical challenges. First, the optic itself demands critical dialogue with racial-ethnic studies and thus close interdisciplinary work involving a well-established and highly sophisticated critical framework. Second, the discourse

---

2. To visualize this point, one need only imagine the following scenario: a critical project bearing the title of "Reading and Teaching the Bible as German, French, and British Scholars" or "Reading and Teaching the Bible as European and Euro-American Scholars." Even today, any such venture would strike minority critics as altogether inconceivable, and no doubt rather humorous as well, even though such projects would also be regarded as long overdue and painfully necessary.

of race-ethnicity reveals two significant complications: on the one hand, a highly complex and constantly shifting trajectory, with conflicting directions and major turns throughout; on the other hand, a set of closely related terms and concepts that call for attention as well: racism and ethnocentrism; the nation, borders and borderlands, dominant and minority; migration, exile, and diaspora. Finally, the problematic calls for critical attention to critics themselves in order to address how the question of race-ethnicity is approached, delimited, and exercised within criticism itself, as in the case of reading and teaching the Bible as "minority critics."

A First Sortie

It is precisely with such reactions and such concerns in mind that I undertake the present study, no doubt the first of several along these lines. I find it necessary to address what it means for me to be considered and to present myself as a Latino/a scholar and to take part in such all-minority projects. In so doing, I should like to make it clear from the start, I seek but a path, not *the* way, and offer but an entry, not *the* gate. This question of what I would characterize as "Latin(o/a)ness" is thus one that I find imperative at this point, deeply immersed in such projects as I find myself at present and envisioning ever greater participation in such ventures in the future. At the same time, it is also a question, I would readily and happily grant, that admits of manifold points of entry and multiple lines of inquiry. In this initial sortie of mine, I shall proceed as follows: I will begin by surveying the notion of Latin(o/a)ness; go on to complicate such a vision of Latin(o/a)ness; and conclude by offering a vision for Latino/a criticism, its contours and aims, in the light of such surveying and complicating.

Surveying Latin(o/a)ness

A fundamental question raised by all-minority projects—and one that ultimately surfaces as well in single- or twofold-minority projects as well as in all-group projects with a focus on racial-ethnic matters and where participants are chosen and work together on the basis of this criterion, in full or in part—is what constitutes, what is signified by or attributed to, each perspective in question. To get at this question, it is worth considering the driving postulates behind such endeavors. Toward this end, I use a project such as "Reading and Teaching the Bible as African American, Asian American, and Latino/a American Scholars" as a representative example and point of departure. The title itself conveys key dimensions of this project, ultimately at work in all such projects in one way or another, which are then duly expanded in the grant proposal behind it.[3]

---

3. The grant proposal was submitted to and generously funded by the Wabash Center for Teaching and Learning in Theology and Religion (2003).

DRIVING POSTULATES

First, as indicated by the various components of the comparative clause, subscribers are selected and agree to participate not only in their capacity as biblical "scholars"—as critics with appropriate training and expertise in the discipline, but also on account of their provenance from and ties to specific racial-ethnic groups—as highly skilled and highly knowledgeable "African American, Asian American, and Latino/a American" critics. In such ventures, consequently, as the proposal further brings out, an overt and active connection between the scholar and a community emerges as paramount. Critics are regarded as at home both in the world of the academy, as members of scholarly communities, and in society and culture at large, as members of particular racial-ethnic communities. These latter communities, moreover, are said to possess their own ways of reading the Bible and, in so doing, to reveal "points of contact" as well as "points of divergence" with one another.

Second, as borne by the subject, such grounding in and belonging to community are seen as having an important bearing on the process of "reading" and "teaching" the Bible, and hence on the particular optic, the status and function, of these scholars as racial-ethnic critics. In these ventures, therefore, as the proposal goes on to make clear, a distinctive process and relation among population groups proves crucial: the racial-ethnic formations in question are characterized as "historically marginalized" by the main racial-ethnic formation, described as "majority-white." A relationship of power is thereby posited: these are minority groups vis-à-vis a dominant group.

Such social-cultural marginalization is further viewed as having far-reaching effects on the reading of the Bible by these groups as well as on criticism and teaching on the part of scholars from such groups. While the former ramifications are not pursued as such, the latter are. Two contrasting developments are outlined. On the one hand, approaches to the Bible on the part of these communities as well as analyses of such approaches by racial-ethnic critics are relegated to the periphery in scholarship and pedagogy, given the discipline's location in "predominantly white" programs and institutions. On the other hand, expertise in such ways of reading and in such critical discourses and pedagogical practices is deemed ever more pressing in the face of a country in profound demographic transition, in urgent need of a religious leadership that can "function in multicultural, multi-racial/ethnic, and multi-faith environments and communities."

Third, as conveyed by the comparative clause as a whole, great value is placed on having scholars from the various groups come together to discuss such optics in common, constituting them thereby as a broader set of critics (minority) in distinction to all other critics (majority). In these projects, as a result, as the proposal sharply emphasizes, various overriding objectives are established as fundamental in minority criticism, ultimately demanded by the concrete situations in which such critics find themselves within the academy and the profession. First, seeking to understand and to teach how the various racial-ethnic communities read the Bible and how scholars from such communities do criticism "in a way that does not understate our differences"—in face of the dominant strategy of dividing and conquering. Second, developing skills for surviving as single minority scholars, now and for the foreseeable future, within "predominantly white and/or multicultural classrooms"—against a background of institutional tokenism and branding. Third, rethinking the exercise and impartation of the discipline in the future, "collectively reconfigur(ing) biblical studies in revolutionary ways"—in view of the need for different ways of "producing and transmitting knowledge."

Given such postulates—community orientation, academic marginalization, minority objectives—at work in these endeavors, I return to my original question: What constitutes such African American, Asian American, and Latino/a American perspectives? Put differently now: What, in effect, lies behind such a sense of grounding in and belonging to community, of relegation to the periphery, of taking on a minoritarian agenda, in each case? This question I should like to approach, given the scope of this venue and its character as an exploratory investigation, in concrete rather than in general terms or in etic terms: as a Latino/a scholar rather than as a minority scholar or from the standpoint of African American or Asian American scholars. In what follows, therefore, I proceed to query that perspective that I am perceived to embody and that I willingly appreciate—the optic of Latin(o/a)ness. What, then, is signified by or attributed to a Latino/a American critical perspective?

Unpacking Latin(o/a) Critics and Criticism

This is a question, I would submit, with a twofold dimension, both closely related but analytically separable. On the one hand, there is an element of identity or locus at play: What constitutes Latin(o/a)ness among critics and teachers, that is, in interpreters and instructors? On the other hand, there is an element of praxis or agenda: What constitutes Latin(o/a)ness in criticism and teaching, that is, in interpretation and pedagogy? Needless to say, it is a question of enormous complexity, profound significance, and varied interpretation. I should like to pursue it by offering a working framework and then elaborating on it by way of concrete examples.

I begin with a seemingly obvious but nonetheless fundamental point, worth reiterating at the outset. The concept of Latin(o/a)ness, I would argue, is neither self-evident nor determinate—self-contained and unchanging; readily accessible to and intelligible by all; bearing the same force throughout, regardless of historical situation or social-cultural formation. It is, rather, a construct. As such, it is always formulated within particular historical and social-cultural contexts and advanced from particular standpoints and agendas, from which junctures it derives a meaning or set of meanings. The concept is thus always situated and ideological—variegated and shifting, pointed and political. Such meaning, moreover, is always subject to interpretation and debate, given the situated and ideological character of all reading and research. The concept is thus always evasive and fragile as well: differently perceived and defined, enmeshed in discussion and dispute.

In my own configuration of it, presented as an initial maneuver within a process of reflection on my status and role as a Latino/a critic, I would endow the concept with a twofold semantic dimension. These I would describe as a sense of identity and locus, of historical experience and present reality, and a sense of praxis and agenda, of appropriation and engagement. To expand on these, I find it useful to draw on classic biblical terminology from the Gospel of John: the extended familial metaphor of "birth" and "rebirth." Thus, I would offer a view of a Latino/a scholar engaged in Latino/a interpretation and pedagogy as someone who is both "born" (of "flesh and blood," as it were) and "reborn" as such (in "spirit and truth," so to speak). This proposal I would immediately qualify, however, by adding that I view neither conception as monolithic or universal: Latino/a critics do not share exactly the same "birth" or undergo precisely the same "rebirth." To flesh out this working principle, I offer three examples, proceeding from the more concrete to the more general.

The first example has to do with personal experience, the Latino/a critic as individual. I submit my own case. Even a cursory look at my record of research and instruction reveals a marked difference between my earlier years and my recent years in the academy and the profession. This shift, involving not punctiliar conversion but a process of ongoing transition, follows a shift in the discipline itself. It is a shift that revolves around the problematization of the critic-stance, no longer assumed as universal and neutral but as contextual and perspectival. Such conscientization on my part, actually involving a number of different and intersecting directions, includes a growing sense of Latin(o/a)ness and thus a sharpening sense of racial-ethnic grouping. This awareness was altogether absent from or remained structurally unintegrated in my beginning corpus, given its historical-redactional (e.g., Segovia 1982) or literary-rhetorical orientation (Segovia 1992). It was also completely missing from my given set of course offerings, which focused on biblical books and topics as well as on formalist-objectivist methods and theories, both literary and sociocultural in nature. Such awareness is decidedly at work in my subsequent corpus, in the form of contextual (Segovia 1995a; 1995b) or ideological inquiries (Segovia 2000). It is also evident in my current set of course offerings, with their focus on critical location as well as on ideological approaches to criticism.

The issue of Latin(o/a)ness brought out by this first example is whether Latino/a scholars are such from the beginning or must become such in the course of time. Following the working framework, an affirmative nod is in order only in the second direction. Let me personalize the discussion. To be sure, I was "born" a Latino critic, insofar as I was a member of such a constituted minority racial-ethnic grouping. At the same time, I was "reborn" a Latino critic upon consciously appropriating the community ties, marginalized status, and minoritarian agenda associated with such a designation. Thus, I would readily avow, I would not qualify as a Latino/a scholar in my initial phase in the academy and the profession, although "born" as such of "flesh and blood," but only in my later phase, as a result of a process of conscientization, whereby I was "reborn" as such in "spirit and truth." Indeed, my reaction to any description of myself in that beginning phase of my academic and professional life as a Latino critic would be one of disavowal—unacceptable as well as misleading.

The second example involves dominant-minority relations, the Latino/a critic as agent. I submit an unexpected scenario for consideration. On one side, let us imagine a Latino/a scholar who is a product of Latino/a reality and experience and thus a "born" member of this racial-ethnic grouping. This individual, let us further imagine, at no time foregrounds such reality and experience: this scholar exhibits no identification with Latino/a circles and shows no interest in Latino/a concerns and projects. In sum, a scholar with no conscientization whatever as a Latino/a critic and teacher. On the other side, let us imagine a dominant scholar from the majority racial-ethnic formation who, although not a product of Latino/a reality and experience, becomes thoroughly conscientized in this regard and hence "reborn" as such: this scholar demonstrates profound acquaintance with Latino/a causes and concerns and strong commitment to Latino/a circles and activities. This contrasting scenario, I would hasten to add, is by no means solely theoretical. I can think immediately of excellent examples in both regards, individuals for whom I have the greatest respect as scholars and whose inclusion in either camp I offer simply by way of concretization. In the first instance, my compatriot Moisés Silva comes readily to mind. Trained at the University of Manchester under James Barr, Silva has—in addition to expertise in Pauline studies—specialized in linguistics and hermeneutics (1983; 1990; 1994), yet has never identified himself, to the best of my knowledge, as a Latino critic and has never taken part in Latino/a endeavors. In the second instance, my colleague Sharon Ringe stands out. Trained at Union Theological Seminary under Raymond Brown, Ringe has—in addition to her work in Lukan studies and Johannine studies—distinguished herself in feminism and liberation (1985; 1992; 2002) and has allied herself openly and wholeheartedly with Latino/a criticism and ventures.

The question of Latin(o/a)ness raised by this example is whether either qualifies as a Latino/a scholar. In light of the working framework, the answer would have to be in the negative in both cases. The first scenario shows a "born" Latino/a scholar with no public record of conscientization regarding racial-ethnic grouping—a situation akin to my own public stance during the first phase of my career. The second scenario shows a dominant-group scholar with broad awareness of Latino/a reality and experience leading to public appropriation and engagement, thus a "reborn" Latino/a scholar—a situation not unlike the second phase of my career. Neither conception by "flesh and blood" by itself nor conception in "spirit and truth" by itself qualifies, therefore. Public reaction and evaluation in Latino/a circles here proves insightful. The first scenario tends to provoke a mixture of wonderment, passive disassociation, and inquiry—an attitude of letting things be alongside a search for explanations along other lines, such as theological conservatism or ecclesial commitment. The second scenario brings out a twofold reaction: on the one hand, should the individual prove a colleague in the struggle, with no claims to being "one of us," a sense of appreciation and acceptance; on the other hand, should the individual begin to speak and act as if "one of us," a sense of distantiation and rejection.

The third example has to do with interminority relations, the Latino/a critic as ally. I submit the context provided by the project on "Reading and Teaching the Bible as African American, Asian American, and Latino/a American Scholars." The scenario now evoked is one in which all participating scholars become intimately acquainted and stand in close solidarity with the other racial-ethnic groups. All acquire sophisticated competency in each other's origins, trajectories, and parameters; develop high proficiency in cultural and social studies regarding one another's groups; and gain considerable expertise in issues of biblical interpretation, academic as well as extra-academic, relevant to each group. All, moreover, stand in basic accord with each other's concerns and interests and play an active role in each other's venues and ventures. Such a scenario, I would note, is by no means outlandish but actually already underway. Could we all, then, claim representation in all such groups at once? Let me concretize the issue: Could Randall Bailey describe himself as an Asian American critic and a Latino/a American critic? Could Benny Liew do likewise as an African American and a Latino/a American critic? Could I do the same as an African American and an Asian American critic? Would any of us even wish to?

The question of Latin(o/a)ness arising from this scenario is whether minority critics from other racial-ethnic groups can ever qualify as Latino/a scholars, and vice versa. In line with the working framework, the answer would have to be in the negative. This scenario reveals keen conscientization on the part of other minority groups, all standing in a similar position of marginalization vis-à-vis the dominant formation, yielding ample knowledge of Latino/a reality and experience as well as public appropriation of and engagement with Latino/a concerns and endeavors, and hence a sense of "reborn" Latino/a critics. Yet such scholars, as products of other racial-ethnic groupings, would not be "born" as part of the Latino/a racial-ethnic formation. By itself, again, conception in "spirit and truth" would not suffice. In fact, public reaction and evaluation in Latino/a circles would run along the same lines as in the previous example: appreciation and acceptance of the colleague in the struggle; distantiation and rejection vis-à-vis the usurping individual. At the same time, it must be said, such a situation would be widely, if not universally, regarded as unthinkable: minority critics would eschew altogether, unlike dominant critics, any claim to represent other minority faces and voices.

TAKING STOCK

In sum, then, I would propose, in answer to the pending question, that what constitutes Latino/a American biblical criticism and pedagogy involves: first, the component of membership, of identity and locus, within such a community—a conception by "flesh and blood," signified or attributed; second, the element of conscientization, of praxis and agenda, from within such a community—a conception in "spirit and truth," appropriated and exercised.

COMPLICATING LATIN(O/A)NESS

This twofold configuration of Latin(o/a)ness represents a first but necessary step on my part in coming to terms with my own status and role as Latino/a biblical critic. Yet I find that this concept, as soon as formulated, threatens to come apart: its fragile and slippery nature as a construct readily exposed. Such instability I should like to approach by complicating the notion of Latin(o/a)ness from a variety of angles: first, by invoking the discourse of race-ethnicity; second, by drawing on the critical framework of Latino/a studies; lastly, by foregrounding key features of the Latino/a American community.

RACIAL-ETHNIC PROBLEMATIC

The preceding reflections have made reference to racial-ethnic groupings, to dominant and minority formations, to the meaning signified by or attributed to racial-ethnic categories. In them I have further sought to circumscribe a minority racial-ethnic perspective by appeal to provenance and conscientization. All such terms and concepts bring the discussion immediately into the critical terrain of racial-ethnic discourse and provoke a juncture between two well-established discursive frameworks, biblical studies and racial-ethnic studies, both with extensive academic pedigrees as well as highly complex and controverted histories. It is a juncture that cannot be averted or obviated, without falling into a merely impressionistic use of such notions and expressions, but that must be head-on. If such linguistic repertoire and conceptual apparatus are going to be invoked, and there is no alternative but to do so, then such deployment should be carried out with a measure of analytic specificity and clarity. For this purpose I draw on two recent expositions, historical as well as constructive, of ethnicity (Fenton 2003) and racism (Miles and Brown 2003). In discursive frameworks of such long-standing, involved, and conflicted nature, scholarly accounts of this sort prove invaluable tools in navigating the discussion and establishing a compass for proper and effective engagement. The same would apply, of course, of anyone based in racial-ethnic studies and wishing to enter into the forbidding world of biblical interpretation.

1. Categories as Related and Divergent. A first point to be acknowledged is that the categories highlighted in minority projects—race and ethnicity, prominently so (African, Asian, Latino/a); nation, more subtly (American)—constitute a set of closely related terms and concepts that bear, within the linguistic and semantic framework of the world of modernity, a common core of meaning with significant divergences at the edges (Fenton 2003, 13–14, 23–24). At the center, and ultimately derived from the linguistic and semantic framework of the world of Greek and Roman antiquity, these are "communities" that are, see themselves, or are seen by others as bound together by "descent and culture." While both components are essential, they vary in significance. Descent emerges as of greater importance: a belief in common origins or ancestry; culture proves of lesser importance: a sense of common beliefs (about the past and regarding identity) and practices (language, dress, customs). At the core, then, all three bear the sense of a "people." At the edges, different emphases come into play: race points to overall divisions of humanity based on physical appearance; ethnicity refers to subdivisions within the nation based on nonphysical appearance and regarded as foreign; and nation is associated with the political realm, as a state or state-like formation.

In describing critics as African American, Asian American, and Latino/a Americans and in emphasizing thereby their ties to racial-ethnic communities, I have had recourse to the modern ideas of race, ethnicity, and nation, with their set core of meaning and established variations from one another. Further, in describing a Latino/a critic as someone who is both a product of Latino/a reality and experience and an agent in appropriating and engaging such reality and experience, I have followed a basic identification of ethnie: advancing the core ideas of common descent and culture and seeking to identify the particular perspective of this subdivision within the country on the basis of social-cultural rather than biological characteristics. I have not, however, taken a position on whether the other two groups, African Americans and Asian Americans, stand for racial or ethnic formations. Traditionally, I should think, the balance would tilt in both cases toward the biological in both cases and hence a "racial" (Negroid; Mongoloid) nomenclature.

2. Categories as Compromised. A second point to be made is that this modern triad of related terms and concepts witnessed, in the course of the twentieth century, major disruption in two respects: first, with the demise of race as a viable category (and racial thinking as a credible framework); second, with the shift from primordialism to constructivism in the category of ethnicity. On the one hand, a multifarious assault—from a variety of academic fields and political organizations—took place, beginning in the 1930s but especially after the 1950s, against the modern conception of universal and hierarchical human divisions based on biological features, constituting real ancestral groupings and possessing common cultural characteristics, such as temperament and ability (Fenton 2003, 53–54). The result has been a steady movement in scholarly circles toward

the substitution of race by ethnie, with corresponding emphasis on the social and cultural rather than on the biological. On the other hand, there was a decided shift, above all after the 1970s, in the literature on ethnicity away from objectivization of the ethnie as a real group and toward subjectivization as a constructed group (Fenton 2003, 64–71, 73–75, 80–81). The result has been a growing scholarly approach to ethnic groups not as entities marked by inherent features (e.g., territory, language, membership, mentality) but as identities socially constructed by either the ethnic actors or the host states.

In arguing for the need to establish what it is that constitutes the African American, Asian American, and Latino/a American perspectives in criticism and in describing the Latino/a critic as a member of a particular community of descent and culture, I have employed throughout the expression "signified by or attributed to" with regard to the meaning conveyed by such categories. In so doing, I have reproduced the range of options offered by the problematic of primordialism (via the "signified by") and constructivism (via the "attributed to," internally or externally), without taking a position as such. Suffice it to say at this point that I would stand closer to the constructivist pole of the spectrum. At the same time, in the light of these discursive developments, I find that a more informed position may now be formulated regarding the more precise classification of the various groups as "racial" or "ethnic" formations. Indeed, the differentiations of modernity begin to vanish. First, "racial" loses its strict biological denotation, so that "racial" and "ethnic" become increasingly interchangeable as a result, with emphasis on nonphysical characteristics but with a nod in the direction of loose physical features in the case of "racial." Second, "ethnic" takes on an ascribed rather than an inherent quality, reflecting the influence of social and cultural production. Consequently, the groups in question may be better construed as variations on racial-ethnic hyphenation, with varying emphasis on the conjunction signified by the hyphen rather than any disjunction. Thus, the Latino/a designation for biblical criticism, given its "ethnic" classification, would simply favor the nonphysical features but not exclude the physical altogether.

3. Categories as Dialectical. A third point to keep in mind is the overall material context out of which this triad of related terms and concepts emerges: the phenomenon of migration, in itself brought about by the interrelated forces of production, trade, and warfare (Miles and Brown 2003, 19-22). Migration brings groups of people into contact with one another, surfacing the question of difference among them and giving rise to attempts to understand and relate to such others. As such, the triad is applicable transhistorically and transculturally, with different configurations at work at different times and in different places, such as the modern development in the West of a core of meaning with distinctive variations at the edges. Such interaction with the other yields images, beliefs, evaluations about the other—representations that are dialectical in nature, for in defining the other, the self constructs itself as well. Such interaction, moreover, involves power relations among the groups in question, given their different

positions vis-à-vis one another in society and culture—the dialectical representations of others and self establish exclusion and inclusion, inferiority and superiority. Within the context of the West, then, race and ethnicity have served as ways of defining other and self—strategic and ideological moves in the social construction of a hierarchical world. Thus, race has entailed a dialectical process of racialization in which meaning is attributed to certain physical or phenotypical features—skin color as primary—whereby individual human beings are grouped into discrete categories of persons taken to reproduce themselves biologically (Miles and Brown 2003, 99–103). Similarly, ethnicity has involved a dialectical process of ethnicization whereby meaning is attached to social and cultural characteristics, as a result of which individual human beings are assembled into discrete categories of persons thought to reproduce themselves biologically, culturally, and economically (Miles and Brown 2003m 96-99).

I have characterized African American, Asian American, and Latino/a American critics as minority scholars, who find themselves and their discourses relegated to the periphery in academia and who embrace a minoritarian agenda. I have also described the Latino/a critic as someone who, through a process of conscientization, espouses Latino/a causes and concerns and becomes active in Latino/a circles and activities. In so doing, I have adopted a dialectical approach to race and ethnicity, emphasizing the process of defining self and others within the nation (the United States), whereby individuals are racialized or ethnicized into groups of people, self-reproducing in character, on the basis of physical and/ or social-cultural features respectively. Given such a hierarchical construction of reality, it would be more accurate to speak of such groups as well as of the biblical critics from such communities not as "minority" but as "minoritized," in order to harp on the strategic and ideological dimensions of such social construction. In using *minority*, it is *minoritized* that I mean.

4. Categories as Enduring. A final point to be recognized is the enduring nature of the modern conceptions of race and ethnicity, as well as of the nation, despite their sustained demystification for quite some time now in academic circles and their consequent recasting as the result of social and cultural processes. Such continuance takes various forms: from common-sense usage, through academic perpetuation, to inverted resistance (Miles and Brown 2003, 88–96). First, such notions are pervasive in everyday discourse, upholding, in direct opposition to scientific findings, the existence of a limited number of discrete groups of people. With respect to race, such groups are affirmed on the basis of physical difference, which biological or phenotypical features are further associated with accompanying social or cultural characteristics, all biologically self-perpetuating. With regard to ethnicity, such groups are posited on the grounds of nonphysical difference, which cultural or social attributes are regarded as inherent and, along the lines of race as biologically self-perpetuating. Second, such concepts remain alive within scientific discourse itself, as for example in the study of race relations in the social sciences, whether unwittingly (taking over

uncritically the common-sense use of such terms) or wittingly (marking the problematic through the use of quotation marks); either way, terms and concepts are preserved thereby that are analytically useless. Lastly, such notions are not uncommonly taken over and turned into means of resistance by the groups so constituted, with an appeal to the biological or cultural characteristics in question as rallying points against the existing hierarchical construction of reality; ultimately, however, such a strategy keeps in use, once again, analytically useless concepts and terms.

In speaking of African American, Asian American, and Latino/a American scholars as racial-ethnic critics and in inquiring into the perspective that underlies Latino/a American biblical criticism, I appeal to categories whose viability has been severely eroded, if not altogether demolished, in racial-ethnic discourse and perpetuate thereby their presence and power in biblical criticism and pedagogy. Moreover, in subscribing to minority projects and agendas of all sorts, I take on such categories as tools of resistance in the discipline and the profession, continuing thereby their spread and influence in both regards. Given the processes of racialization and ethnicization at work in the nation, and operative in the discipline and profession of biblical studies as well as in theological centers of education throughout, I see no option. In so doing, however, it is imperative to affirm, radically so, that recourse to such terms and concepts and membership in such projects and agendas is effected from a constructivist standpoint and oppositional/transformative agenda. On the one hand, therefore, the selection of physical and/or nonphysical characteristics as the basis for group formation is viewed as a strategic and ideological undertaking, the result of dialectical processes of defining self and other within the nation. On the other hand, a recourse to and deployment of this resultant construction of reality by the other is regarded as a strategic and ideological maneuver of its own, which can be used to unmask the dialectical process of construction and question the social reality in place. All in the name of a transformation that can move beyond othering.

Latino/a Studies

In my reflections on surveying Latino(a)ness, I set out to examine the optic of Latino/a biblical interpretation and advanced a view of the Latino/a critic as someone with both provenance from and conscientization within the Latino/a American community. Such concerns and efforts situate me immediately within the critical parameters of Latino/a discourse and create a juncture between two standing scholarly frameworks, biblical studies and Latino/a studies. As in the case of racial-ethnic discourse, this is a juncture that cannot be bypassed or ignored but that calls rather for direct confrontation, in order to prevent impressionism with regard to such notions and expressions. If such linguistic terminology and conceptual wherewithal are going to be called upon, and again there is no option but to do so, then such deployment should be marked by a degree of analytic sophistication and sharpness. Toward this end, I draw on two recent overviews, at once historical and constructive, of Latino/a studies (Flores 2000; Luis 1997). Simply put, Latino/a studies takes into consideration the whole of Latino/a reality and experience in the United States—a presence that antedates the Anglo-American in numerous and sizable territories that eventually came to form the federal union as presently constituted, that is related in a uniquely distinctive fashion to the United States as the geopolitical center of "the Americas," and that thus defies standard classification and analysis as a contemporary example of a traditional social-cultural model, the immigrant group.

1. Latino/a Studies: Origins and Development. There is a marked difference between the early phase of Latino/a studies in the 1960s and 1970s and its later, and present, phase in the 1990s and 2000s. The beginning configuration was tied to national and international struggles for liberation and justice; took shape in the form of discrete groups and identities; and revealed a deeply nationalistic impulse. The present configuration stands at a distance from any such local or global pursuits; has been affected by postmodern reflections on identity; and involves a much greater sense of a pan-Latino/a phenomenon. This difference is pointedly signified by the nomenclature applied to this area of studies: its description as "Latino/a" is altogether absent from the initial phase and comes into play only in the subsequent phase.

What eventually comes to be characterized as "Latino/a studies" arises out of and remains closely connected to social movements among Latinos/as forged in the social-cultural turmoils of the 1960s. These are movements, in solidarity with other such movements both inside and outside the country, bent on combating oppression not only in their own case but wherever found and inspired by the liberation drives of the time. Movements, therefore, very much in tune with the struggle for civil rights and social rights at home and very much aware of the decolonizing struggles at work throughout Africa and Asia as well as the Caribbean and Latin America. Such movements become organized around the two main Latino/a contingents in the United States at the time: Mexican Americans throughout the Southwest and Puerto Rican throughout the Northeast. As such, the foundational academic developments in this regard are established regionally along the lines of "Chicano studies" and "Puerto Rican studies." Such social movements and discursive formations are largely conceived as bounded identities, subscribed to in unproblematic fashion by all members of the groups in question. Central to such identities, their governing visions and resultant practices, was the fervor of nationalism—the sense of a "nation" within the nation, under domination and injustice and hence in need of redemption.

By the 1990s the social-cultural context of both the country and the world has experienced a dramatic change. To begin with, the radical visions of the 1960s had yielded to conservative retrenchment at home and neocolonial hegemony abroad. As a result, the social movements emerging from and informed by such visions had lost their sense of vigor and expectation. In addition, the transformation of industrial capitalism into global capitalism, at work through the 1970s and 1980s, was causing large-scale economic changes throughout the non-Western world, including Latin America and the Caribbean, yielding severe population displacement and massive migration into the West, including the United States. Lastly, such immigration into the country, fueled by the need for cheap labor and the relaxation of the restrictive legislation of the 1920s, launches the third major wave of migration, laying the grounds for the profound change in demographics still at work. The consequences for the now-baptized Latino/a studies prove far-reaching: little sense of grounding in protest movements as umbilical cord for the discursive formation, accompanied by pronounced ignorance of the history of the movement and scant attention to transnational concerns; expansion beyond Mexican Americans and Puerto Rican Americans to include the whole of Latin America and the Caribbean, giving way to a pan-Latino/a presence; and serious challenges to and reformulations of unbounded group identities as well as nationalistic dreams.

Concluding Observation. Latino biblical criticism and pedagogy is, I would argue, a child of this latter phase of Latino/a studies. That is certainly the case with regard to origins. Indeed, previous approaches to the biblical texts had come out of other theological disciplines and were largely in tune with the spirit of the movement's early phase. It should also be the case with regard to exercise, up to a point. First, it should take into account the whole of contemporary Latino/a reality and experience—the pan-Latino/a phenomenon. Second, it should approach the question of identity in the light of postmodernist thinking—a fractured and porous formation. Lastly, and here I would go against the current, it should reestablish close ties with Latino/a communities, seeking detailed awareness of the history of this discursive framework and underlying social-cultural context, as well as with issues and causes of global impact, in full consciousness of such solidarity in the past.

2. Latinos/as: Inclusion and Exclusion. The question of nomenclature—what to call the population group I have been addressing as "Latinos/as" and who belongs within such a category—has been a highly convoluted and conflicted one. Here I simply raise the issue, altogether unavoidable, by way of recent discussions in Latino/a studies. A theoretical spectrum marked by the following poles proves helpful: at one end, objectivist demarcation accompanied by conceptual inflation or expansive application; at the other end, constructivist configuration accompanied by conceptual deflation or narrow delimitation. In these recent discussions, it should be noted, the objectivist-inflationary stance serves as point of reaction, and thus I begin with that end of the spectrum.

Objectivist-Inflationary Pole. This pole is ideally represented by Ilan Stavans and his concept, taken from earlier criticism, of "life in the hyphen" (1995, 7–30). It is an approach grounded in the "intellectual and artistic legacies" of Hispanic Americans and Latinos rather than on politics, demographics, or sociology (20). This is a position that defies proper precision, given its linguistic exuberance and intertextual somersaults; nonetheless, various constitutive components can be secured. Stavans sets the stage by laying out the multiplicity of names bestowed on or invoked by the group, singling out "Hispanic" and "Latino" as the two "favorites," and detailing their prevailing semantic connotations ("Latino" as the choice of liberals and common in the arts; "Hispanics" as the preference of conservatives and employed in a variety of fields). Then, while characterizing any such distinction as "artificial and difficult to sustain," he goes on to express his own preference for "Hispanics" as a "composite" term and his opposition to "Latinos" (26–27). Immediately thereupon, however, he reasserts the distinction, arguing that it is useless to go against consensus, and modulates it as follows: Latinos are citizens from the Spanish-speaking world living in the United States; Hispanics are citizens from the Spanish-speaking world living elsewhere. All Latinos are Hispanics, therefore; not all Hispanics, however, are Latinos.

Various further elements central to this distinction should be highlighted. First, Hispanics are such as a result of their language and culture of origins, and thus the term encompasses not only the world of (Spanish) Latin America but also that of Spain. As he puts it, the scope of "Hispanic civilization" is "outstanding" (1995, 27); it is this, I believe, that he has in mind when he refers to the term as "composite." As Hispanics who reside in the United States, Latinos too go back to this civilization; hence, their ranks include those who have come from Spain or (Spanish) Latin America. Second, it is this linguistic and cultural referent that distinguishes "Latinos" from all other population groups in the country: Anglo Saxons or other European immigrants, African Americans or Asian Americans. Third, within the United States, this civilization, long established and quite varied, encounters Anglo-Saxon "domination," from which it has traditionally experienced rejection and discrimination ("imperial and enslaving") and to which it has responded with silence or resistance (12). Fourth, recent decades, since the 1980s, have witnessed two critical developments: the different national formations of Latinos have begun to interact more closely as a working whole; the mode of oppositional confrontation vis-à-vis the dominant culture has begun to yield to cultural meltdown on both sides—Hispanization of the United States ("*gringos hispanizados*") and Anglicization of Hispanics ("Latinos *agringados*") (9, 13). Finally, in decidedly eschatological tones, Stavans envisions a time and a country beyond all such divisions: an era marked by "acculturation and miscegenation" and a land where "multiculturalism will sooner or later fade away," a "radically different" United States where there will be no need for Latinos "to inhabit the hyphen" (19). In this paradise to come, it would seem, Latinos will cease to be Hispanics and become, shall we say, USasians.

At this one end of the spectrum, therefore, a fairly objectivist and universalist definition of the group prevails, based on original language and culture: "Latinos" as a subgroup of "Hispanics," bringing together all individuals and formations from both Spain and (Spanish) Latin America. In addition, a civilizational transformation from clash to fusion is posited vis-à-vis U.S. culture and language, yielding a breathtaking and celebratory hyphenated living, en route to life-beyond-the-hyphen.

Central Range. This middle section of the spectrum is pointedly represented by William Luis and his metaphor of "a dance between two cultures" (1997, ix–xxii). It is an approach similarly grounded in the cultural tradition of Latinos, yet with close attention to the material context as well. This is a carefully elaborated and detailed position, partly developed in opposition to Stavans, whose stance he submits to extended critical analysis. While a distinction between Hispanic and Latino is preserved, the difference moves beyond a mere geographical division of a "Spanish" linguistic-cultural civilization. To be sure, a sense of overarching cultural framework is also maintained, but extended only to (Spanish) Latin America and not to Spain. Similarly, a geographical dimension remains present as well, but now subordinate to social-cultural context. Thus, a Hispanic is defined as born or raised and educated in Latin America and a Latino as born or raised and educated in the United States. These categories are not hard and fast but admit of fluidity: a Hispanic may, in the course of time, become a Latino, especially if arrival in the U.S. takes place at a young age (283).

Other key components of this division should be noted. Two of these account for the fundamental divisions advanced. First, the sharp separation between Spain and Latin America is established on the basis of geopolitics: the relation between the European motherland and the Spanish American countries has involved an imperial-colonial framework, along the lines of other such European frameworks, both in direct (political domination) and indirect fashion (neocolonial domination). Such a difference, Luis argues, against Stavans, cannot be readily amalgamated into any sort of unproblematic civilizational unity. To be Spanish American, therefore, is to stand in a legacy of Spanish European subjugation and exclusion: this is what Hispanics have in common vis-à-vis Spain. Second, the firm separation between Hispanics and Latinos is established on social-cultural grounds: while the relation between the U.S. and Latin America has involved geopolitics, so that all Hispanics stand vis-à-vis the U.S. within an imperial-colonial framework, for Latinos such a relation is immediate and focalizing. This difference, Luis adds, again against Stavans, cannot be obviated: it involves direct and intense domination and exclusion. To be Latino, consequently, is to stand in a legacy of minority formation: a material and cultural situation that a Hispanic can only assume with time in the country, since they not only lack the context of exclusion but also remain tied to their countries of origin for a considerable period of time.

Three other components develop the situation of Latinos within the U.S. Third, as a group, Latinos have much in common with other minority groups in the country, both culturally and materially, given the similar relation on the part of African Americans, Asian Americans, and Native Americans to the dominant culture, quite aside from the fact that many Latinos have African, Asian, and Native legacies. Fourth, as a group, given their growing numbers and influence,

Latinos find themselves presently engaged in an intricate "metaphorical dance" with the dominant Anglo-American culture, which implies a "coming together" that influences the way the two partners dance, "to the same tune in the same dance hall" (xv). Finally, this vision of the Latino-Anglo dance does carry eschatological connotations. Such dancing will ultimately change both partners. Indeed, since such dancing involves other partners and dances as well, the prospect of a different country is raised—a "postmodern and postcolonial" United States where "a new concept of *Latino*, race, and identity" will result (290).

Toward the middle of the spectrum, then, a more flexible (not as objectivist) and more restricted (not as universalist) circumscription of the group obtains, based on social-cultural origins as well as social-cultural context: "Latinos" as "Hispanics" or Spanish Americans who reside in the United States—either by birth or upbringing and education, or by immigration and consciousness. This definition, moreover, places the group firmly within a set of minority formations vis-à-vis the dominant group, but also as one partner among several in a set of dances leading to inevitable national transformation.

Constructivist-Deflationary Pole. This pole is well represented by Juan Flores and his appeal to the "latino imaginary" (2000, 191–201). It is an approach grounded in both the material matrix and the cultural production of Latinos. This is a carefully modulated and sophisticated position, offered in opposition to those of Stavans and Flores, but without much ado. Here, while the use of both terms, Hispanic and Latino, continues, with the latter as more common by far, no formal distinction is offered between them: while Stavans's proposal is characterized as complicating the issue beyond recognition, that of Luis is described as unusual and confusing, both questionable and removed from common usage (244 n. 2). Flores turns instead to the notion of a "Latino community" and proceeds to unpack the twofold semantic connotations of the term "community" in Spanish, *comunidad*. On the one hand, the base term *común* conveys those cultural aspects that the different constitutive groups have in common; such shared elements constitute the sense of the community in itself. On the other hand, the base term *unidad* signifies the bonds that bring the community together over and beyond such commonalities; these unifying elements represent the sense of the community for itself. While the former semantic level involves facts and figures, the latter concerns self-perception, self-conception, self-imaginings. The Latino "experience," therefore, includes but is not coterminous with self-consciousness. How the community is imagined admits of variations, and, in such versions of the community, it is imperative to examine both the mode (external or internal) and the goal (aims and consequences) of such projections.

A number of fundamental elements underlying this approach need to be foregrounded. First, from the very beginning the "Latino community" has played a major role within the "American community": not only has there been migration throughout from Latin America to the United States, but also the United States has taken over areas of Latin America. Latinos, therefore, constitute a long-standing and highly prominent dimension of the national scene, although largely overlooked as such.

Second, such migration and incorporation have been driven throughout by a situation of "hemispheric inequality" between Latin America and the United States. The latter, in effect, has advanced its economic and political agenda throughout the region and has, as a result, brought about dislocation and interventionism everywhere. Third, this relation of actual and active inequality has been replicated within the country as well, so that the above-mentioned overlooking of the Latino community emerges as symptomatic of the relations between the two communities: a vision of the American dream that is accompanied by exploitation and discrimination on the part of the American community and by a quest for justice and affirmation on the part of the Latino community. Fourth, a conjunction of material and cultural developments—an exponential rise in migration from Latin America as a result of globalization and the spread of postmodern approaches to identity—have brought about a much-changed concept of the Latino community: a highly diverse formation involving the whole of Latin America and a thorough deconstruction of the early nationalist models. As a result, the Latino community has been imagined from the inside from a variety of perspectives, in the light of "lived experience and historical memory" (197). Lastly, a mild sense of eschatological utopia is unmistakable as well: such a search for community is ultimately a "search for a new map, a new ethos, a new *América*" (203).

At this other end of the spectrum, consequently, a fairly constructivist and multilateral definition of the group prevails, based on social-cultural origins and context: "Latinos" as Latin Americans who have either migrated into or have been incorporated by the United States, who constitute a "community" within the American community, and who construct such a community in different ways, as a result of varying historical experiences and shifting identity factors. Furthermore, such a process of imagining the community is ultimately construed as a way of imagining a very different "American community" as well.

Concluding Observation. Latino/a biblical criticism and teaching should, in my opinion, find its home toward the constructivist-deflationary pole. In so doing, it needs to take into consideration the material and cultural context of the Latino/a community. First, its roots in and to Latin America—not simply as the diasporic presence of "Hispanic civilization" in the United States, but rather as the bearer of a legacy of domination by and struggle against Spain. Second, its historical presence in the United States—the result of expansionary policy westward and southward, through war and annexation, and of population movement northward, in the light of political and economic insertion. Third, its conflicted relationship to the United States—the driving relation of inequality at work not only in the hemisphere as a whole but also within the country itself, yielding domination and marginalization at home. It should also bear in mind the present configuration of the community: all-encompassing in terms of national origins;

multilayered in terms of identity; and generative of multiple self-representations in terms of the Latino imaginary. In the end, although I would still prefer the expression "U.S. Hispanic Americans," I would argue that the term "Latino/a" captures well all such dimensions of the country. Indeed, in a classic move of Spanglish, the term adopts the English adjective "Latin" from Latin America, adds a final vowel from Spanish (both "o" and "a" to signify gender), and produces the Spanglish Latino/a.[4]

LATINO/A AMERICANS: SALIENT COMPONENTS

In my own approach to the Latino/a community, I regard certain features as fundamental to the group as a whole at this point in time: its constitution as a pan-Latino phenomenon; its distinctive relation to the United States; and its variegated sense of identity.

1. All-Inclusive Configuration. All three theorists of Latino/a studies agree that, in the course of the last forty years, the community has undergone a dramatic demographic transformation, not only in numbers but also in composition, with far-reaching and mounting consequences. Having lived through such a change myself, from the beginning to the present, I could not agree more. Here I should like to expand on remarks previously made with respect to the changed nature of Latino/a studies.

In the mid-1960s, the Latino/a community consisted of two largely separate national groupings: in the western part of the country (from Texas, throughout the Southwest, to California), a large Mexican American presence; in the eastern part (throughout the major cities of the Midwest and the Northeast), a significant Puerto Rican presence. Their presence in the country was due to two basic reasons: (1) territorial acquisition—large portions of Mexico in the mid-nineteenth century, before and after the Mexican American War, and the island of Puerto Rico in the late nineteenth century, after the Spanish American War; (2) migration in search of work—from Mexico, across the border; from Puerto Rico, to the mainland. At this time, Cubans and Dominicans were only just beginning to arrive in noticeable numbers—the first signs of a totally unforeseen demographic tsunami to come. By the mid-2000s, the Latino/a community embraced representation from all regions and all countries of Latin America, and in ever greater numbers. Their presence in the country was due to two key global developments:

---

4. My reservation continues to be that the term "Latin" is hispanicized thereby to the exclusion of other "Latin" components of Latin America whose populations have also found their way into the country, such as Haitians and Brazilians. In appropriating the term Latino/a solely for the populations of Hispanic countries, the same rhetorical exercise of exclusion takes place as when citizens of the United States use the name of the hemisphere to refer to themselves, "Americans" alone.

(1) widespread political turmoil—years of instability and violence as a site of struggle between capitalism and communism during the Cold War; (2) severe economic crisis—first, on account of massive accumulation of external debt; then, in the wake of the turn to the economic principles of neoliberalism.

The result has been a thorough national diversification of the group as well as a decidedly hybrid Latin(o/a)zation of its members, who, while mindful of and appealing to national identity in the first instance, find themselves increasingly coalescing into a sense of Latino(o/a)ness, partly on external grounds (attitude from the center) and partly on internal grounds (sustained co-existence alongside and interaction with one another). In addition, beyond such integration of the various groups within the country, the pan-Latino phenomenon, a powerful sense of involvement is also evident on the part of the group not only in the home countries but also in Latin America as a symbolic entity, giving way thereby to what Flores has aptly characterized as a trans-Latino phenomenon (Flores 2000a, 208–9)—a pan-Latino presence with close, active, and interested ties to Latin America. This emergent phenomenon Flores goes on to describe as more than a diasporic community: an "ethnoscape" or "world tribe," given its circular existence (recurrent comings and goings) as well as a "delocalized transnation," insofar as the group sees itself as both part of the nation and part of other nations, and indeed part of a greater configuration of nations as well—the *other* America or Latin America.

2. Peculiar Relationship. All three theorists also agree that the relation between the Latino/a community and the United States has always been and continues to be marked by a sharp division in the possession and exercise of power, materially as well as culturally. Having experienced such a differential relationship myself, both outside and inside the country, I stand in firm agreement. This relationship—construed and deployed as such from the center of power; similarly grasped and received in the periphery of power—is dialectical in nature: U.S. society and culture as superior vis-à-vis Latin American and Latino/a society and culture. Outside the country, such a relationship has been characterized by geopolitical domination, involving material interventionism and cultural exclusion—telltale signs of a long-standing imperial-colonial framework within the hemisphere. Inside the country, such a relationship has been marked by political subordination, material exploitation, and cultural discrimination— unmistakable signs of a long-standing dominant-minority framework within the nation. On the one hand, the dominant-minority dimension brings the Latino/a community into close association with the African American and Asian American communities, both minority communities vis-à-vis the center. On the other hand, the imperial-colonial dimension bestows upon the Latino/a community a clear distinctiveness among such communities, given the tradition of direct involvement in Latin America on the part of the United States.

Against this background, the emerging sense of a pan-Latino community may be read in terms of minority reaction and strategy. First, given the diversification of the community in terms of national origins and the treatment of the new arrivals along the same lines as the old formations, all groups begin to come together as a community vis-à-vis a center that sees them as undifferentiated. Second, in so doing, the coalescing community seeks to organize, to marshal its strength, and to press for inclusion and justice as a group within the nation. Similarly, the emerging sense of a trans-Latino formation may be seen in terms of colonial reaction and strategy. First, in the face of political and economic upheavals at home, the various national groups take on an active role of support toward their countries of origin—transferring enormous amounts of cash and sending goods of all sorts. Second, in the wake of the pivotal role played by the United States throughout Latin America, with its imprint on such political and economic crises and its neglect of the Americas in its field of vision, the group seeks to mobilize, to flex its muscle, and to press for a different approach—forcing the hemisphere into the national imaginary, laying bare existing representations and judgments, and calling for inclusion and justice within the hemisphere.

　　3. Deconstructed Identity. All three theorists further agree, in varying degrees of emphasis, that the advent of postmodern approaches to identity has had a considerable impact on the self-conception of the Latino/a community. Having experienced the shift from modern to postmodern modes of discourse, professionally as well as personally, I could not agree more. Here, again, I expand on earlier observations regarding the path of Latino studies.

　　The driving force behind the foundational social movements of the 1960s, the Mexican American and Puerto Rican American struggles for civil rights and social justice, was nationalism. This rallying cry applied to both the national groups within the country and their countries of origin. Such nationalism involved a threefold platform: a sense of nation denied (annexation of historical homelands) and nation segregated (exclusion of internal groups); a call for unity in action (as *chicanos/as* or as *neoriqueños/as*); and a vision of nation affirmed (inclusion of internal groups) and nation regained (liberation of historical homelands). This project was well signified by the common slogans of "Viva la Raza!" and "Viva Aztlán!" or "Pa'lante, Siempre Pa'lante!" or "Viva Puerto Rico Libre!" respectively. Such nationalism was also construed in oppositional fashion: against an American community and an American nationalism that were seen as oppressive, internally as well as externally. These movements took on, therefore, the shape of an anticolonial struggle, very much in tune with the times, as the battles for decolonization raged across much of the non-Western world. This was a struggle, however, waged by groups that deemed themselves as internally colonized within the colonizing state. Such counternationalism involved, as the reverse side of nationalism, a monolithic and totalizing representation of the groups in question, in which all other dimensions of identity were subordinated to that of national origins. Consequently, the communities in question were constructed as discrete entities and all existing tensions within them suppressed. With the diffusion of postmodern thought, however, this modus operandi began to be called into question from a variety of perspectives, in line with similar developments across all other social movements and discursive frameworks.

Various formations within the Latino/a community began to articulate critiques of such engulfing nationalism and to theorize instead various positions of difference within the groups. These voices surfaced differences grounded in unequal relations of power within the community itself, involving issues of gender, sexuality, race and ethnicity, class—differences that shattered any facile notion of a unified and harmonious national community and that highlighted instead the many and conflicted layers of belonging within and relating to the community. From such contexts and perspectives, different conceptions of the community emerged in contestatory fashion. As a result, the traditional essentialized and fixed notions of identity were replaced by versions stressing multiplicity and fluidity, so that the very concept of a Latino/a community was problematized. At the same time, similar developments within the dominant society and culture were problematizing the standing concepts of American community and nationalism. In the process, the dialectical character of the struggle began to be reconsidered as well, now seen as much more complex and ambiguous, especially in the light of concomitant reflections on the concept of the nation and on relations between colonizers and colonized in postcolonial theory.

Concluding Comment. Latino/a biblical criticism and teaching should, as I envision it, take to heart the presence and ramifications of these various features ascribed to the Latino/a community. From the point of view of its all-inclusive configuration, I see two foci as imperative: a pan-Latino angle of vision, in conversation with all segments of the community, while highlighting and analyzing one's own particular context and perspective within the community; a trans-Latino angle, in touch with all of Latin America, while emphasizing and examining one's own country of origin and its specific problematic. In so doing, Latino/a biblical criticism and teaching would recapture the grounding in community of early Latino studies. From the perspective of its peculiar relationship to the United States, I regard two tasks as essential: first, remaining in close contact with other minority communities within the country, joining hands against political exploitation and discrimination; second, maintaining close ties with Latin America, waging battle against geopolitical interventionism and exclusion. In so doing, Latino/a biblical criticism and teaching would resume, on a different key now, the internationalist thrust at the heart of early Latino studies. From the point of view of its deconstructed identity, it should take into account at all levels of reflection the other dimensions of identity and avoid any claim to totalization, presenting itself but as one option, among many such other options and in critical interaction with them, within the imaginary of Latino/a biblical interpretation and pedagogy. In so doing, Latino/a biblical criticism and teaching would proceed with its task on a postmodernist key within a postmodernist world.

Immediately upon advancing the working principle of a Latino/a scholar engaged in Latino/a interpretation and pedagogy as someone both "born" and "reborn" as such, having membership within the Latino/a community and exhibiting conscientization from within the Latino/a community, I hastened to add that such conceptions, whether of "flesh and blood" (identity and location) or in "spirit and truth" (praxis and agenda), I regarded not as universal and monolithic but rather as multifarious and diverse. In so doing, I was calling into question, in principle, any idea of a fairly discrete, homogenous, and unified community and perspective. The preceding reflections on Latin(o/a)ness from the point of view of ethnic-racial discourse, of Latino studies, and of the contemporary Latino/a community confirm in every respect the fragility of any notion of Latin(o/a)ness. Any such proposal is perforce a construct and, as such, contextual, partial, ideological in nature. Mine, with its appeal to processes of generation, is no different. I have tried to account for this by presenting Latino/a "birth" and "rebirth" as fluid. In both respects, I would argue, the markers of differentiation at work prove quite numerous, quite profound, and quite divisive.

Latino/a Reality and Experience. With regard to "birth," markers include general issues of society and culture (status, origins, language, religion, education) as well as concrete issues of power relations (gender, race-ethnicity, political economy, sexuality, geopolitics). This division is by no means presented as exhaustive. It is also by no means advanced as a binomial, for the presence of power pervades all social and cultural dimensions and social-cultural distinctions permeate all power relations. It is, rather, a representative division predicated on degree of ideological explicitness solely for the purpose of analysis. Latino/a criticism is inevitably impacted upon by and must keep in mind all such markers.

Social-Cultural Markers. The Latino/a community is differentiated by legal status within the country. While many Latinos/as have been born in the country and are thus U.S. citizen by birth, many others have been born outside the country and find themselves in the U.S. as a result of migration, in varying modes: naturalized citizens; resident aliens; illegal aliens. The community is further differentiated by country of origin. At present, Latinos/as hail from every region of Latin America: North America (Mexico); Central America; the Caribbean; South America. Furthermore, they come from every country of the Americas and from any number of areas within each country. Language further distinguishes the community: some speak neither Spanish nor English well but are proficient in indigenous languages; others have command of only Spanish or English, with varying understanding of the other; and many engage in different modalities of Spanglish. Religion proves a significant community marker as well: overall, Latinos/as range from non-Christian to Christian; within Christianity itself, from pentecostal and evangelical, through historical or mainline Protestant, to Catholic—and any combination in between; outside Christianity: from indigenous, through African diasporic, to any number of others (spiritualism; Judaism; Islam)—and any mixture thereof. Lastly, Latino/a community is differentiated by educational level: some have little formal education; others have university and advanced degrees; many fall anywhere in between.

Power-Relations Markers. The community is riven throughout by deep and divisive fault-lines based on gender construction and relations (e.g., sexism and machismo, physical abuse and violence, employment discrimination), political economy and social class (e.g., exploitation of workers, disdain for undocumented, residential separation), racial-ethnic constructions and relations (e.g., discrimination on the basis of phenotypical and/or cultural characteristics), sexual orientation and relations (e.g., homosexual bashing, popular humor and ridicule, physical and psychological violence), and geopolitical orientation (e.g., contrasting political attitudes toward former and present imperial powers).

2. Latino/a Appropriation and Engagement. With respect to "rebirth," markers involve the context roundabout, the various historical contexts and trajectories, and the problematic of critical analysis as such. This division is presented not as mutually exclusive but, to the contrary, as highly imbricated and interdependent. Latino/a criticism is inevitably influenced by and must remain mindful of all these markers. To begin with, it must reflect on the present situation of the community within the United States, which involves: critical analysis of the country's material matrix and cultural production; critical analysis of minority life within such a matrix and production; and critical analysis of Latino/a life within both the minority and the dominant contexts. In addition, it must consider matters of historical import, including: the history of relations between the United States and Latin America; the history of relations within Latin America itself, among the various geographical divisions; and the history of relations within particular regions and specific countries. Finally, it must reflect on matters of theory and method regarding the critical frameworks to be invoked and the critical approaches to be deployed in such analysis of the situation at hand as well as previous situations, allowing in principle for multiplicity of points of entry and paths of inquiry.

My own "birth" and "rebirth" as a Latino in general and as a Latino critic in particular emerge thereby as not only highly circumscribed but also in need of critical pinpointing and evaluation. Any proposal on Latino/a criticism forthcoming from such positioning emerges perforce as limited and limiting—a strategic activation of the Latino imaginary. Highly unstable, but necessary nonetheless, if such a descriptor is to have, whether by bestowal upon me or my own assumption of it, any meaning at all.

Envisioning Latino/a Criticism

The preceding reflections on surveying and complicating Latin(o/a)ness have yielded a distinct yet ambiguous marker of identity and practice—readily bestowed and willingly assumed; specifically circumscribed in terms of origins and culture; carefully nuanced as diffuse and controverted; explicitly advanced as constructed and partial (situational, perspectival, nonexcluding). A marker, in effect, at once pressing and elusive—from the angle of material and cultural impact; laden and refracted—in terms of material and cultural diversity; signifying and open-ended—from the angle of material and cultural determinacy. Against this background, I should like to advance an outline of parameters and objectives that I see as both foundational and programmatic for my vision of Latino/a biblical criticism and teaching. Various specifications are in order here. First, the term itself, "outline," is used with deliberate intent: this is but an initial and working platform for the task ahead. Second, this platform is offered as by no means exhaustive but as representative—informing and guiding the task, but also open to expansion and refinement. Finally, the platform recapitulates points made in passing in the course of the preceding reflections on Latin(o/a)ness, while offering a number of further considerations as well—all in pointed but general fashion.

CRITICAL PARAMETERS

1. Range of Criticism. A first parameter addresses the question of critical scope. For me, to begin with, Latino/a criticism encompasses various worlds of interest: not only the world of antiquity, its texts and contexts, but also the worlds of modernity and postmodernity, their texts (the interpretations of biblical texts and contexts) and contexts (the sites of such interpretations). In this first point I have in mind the academic-scholarly tradition of reading, now stretched beyond its usual confinement to the realm of antiquity to include the study and representation of antiquity. Further, Latino/a criticism also includes for me various sites of interest: not only texts and contexts, throughout the various worlds in question, but also the faces and voices (the lives and visions of authors and interpreters) behind such texts and immersed in such contexts. In this second point I again have in mind the academic-scholarly tradition of readings, now extended from its usual confinement to texts and interpretations to include analysis of the scholars engaged in representing the past in the modern and postmodern periods. Lastly, Latino/a criticism further encompasses for me various reading traditions of interest: not only the academic-scholarly one, but also the gamut of other such traditions, such as the popular-cultural one or the political-statist one. With this third point I have in mind an expansion of the discipline to comprehend interpretations and interpreters of the biblical texts and contexts outside of the academic-scholarly tradition, with the same analytic rigor exercised in this tradition.

2. Character of Criticism. A second parameter deals with the issue of critical approach. Latino/a criticism must work, I believe, with a sense of construction in all realms of society and culture, and hence with a corresponding focus on the context, the perspective, and the ramifications of construction throughout. In

this regard my self-conception as a Latino critic involves the role of discoverer and artificer at once, indeed not only creative expositor but also critical evaluator. Latino/a criticism must also work, I would add, with a sense of society and culture as pluralist and conflicted, and thus have recourse to models and methods that allow for and theorize such multiplicity and conflict. My self-conception as a Latino critic in this respect calls for a view of society and culture as sites of struggle throughout. Latino/a criticism must further work, I would argue, with a commitment to theory and interdisciplinarity. It must have within its purview of critical inquiry a focus on the nature of disciplinary paradigms and pedagogical frameworks, a working acquaintance with social theory and cultural studies, and a working knowledge of the range of ideological standpoints and criticisms: feminism and gender; materialism and political economy; minority and race/ethnicity; sexuality and orientation; geopolitics and imperialism/colonialism. In this regard my self-conception as a Latino critic involves critical sophistication in any number of discursive frameworks.

3. Specifics of Criticism. A third parameter addresses the question of critical specificity, by which I mean the sort of discursive companions that would prove most helpful for its vision and task. First, as an exercise in biblical interpretation, I deem it imperative for Latino/a biblical criticism to work in cooperation with other minority strands of biblical interpretation. Here I have in mind, above all, African American and Asian American criticism, given their prominence, but with due attention as well to the concerns and interests of Native American criticism. From such discursive alliance comes a sense of criticism as part of a broader whole—a disciplinary pursuit.

Second, it is essential for Latino/a biblical criticism, as an exercise in a traditional discipline of theological studies or a standard area of religious studies, to remain in close conversation with Christian studies and/or religious studies: in particular, Latino/a religion and theology; in general, minority religion and theology. Such discursive dialogue produces a sense of criticism as: (1) in the first instance, part of a broader formation—a disciplinary pursuit, among other such pursuits, within a focal area of studies; (2) in the second instance, part of an encompassing formation—a disciplinary pursuit within a focal area of studies alongside other such focal areas of studies.

Third, it is crucial for Latino/a biblical criticism, as an exercise in Latino/a criticism, to stay in close contact with the analysis of race and ethnicity at a variety of levels: most concretely, Latino/a studies; more generally, minority studies; most broadly, ethnic-racial studies. Such discursive ties yield a sense of criticism, as a component of religious and theological discourse, as: (1) in the first instance, a form of cultural production among other such forms within the material matrix of the U.S.; (2) in the second instance, a strand of cultural production alongside other such strands within the material matrix of the U.S.; (3) in the third instance, a strand of cultural production alongside other such strands within any national or state matrix.

Finally, I deem it necessary for Latino/a biblical criticism, as an exercise in American criticism, to work in close association with national and global studies: most concretely, American studies; more generally, Latin American studies; most broadly, postcolonial studies. From such discursive connections flows a sense of criticism, as a component of religious and theological discourse, as a strand of cultural production: (1) in the first instance, within the material matrix of national provenance; (2) in the second instance, within the material matrix of national origins and hemispheric relations; and (3) in the third instance, within the material matrix of geopolitical studies.

CRITICAL GOALS

1. Critical Vision. As unfolded, the task of Latino/a biblical criticism appears daunting, even forbidding, given the breadth and the depth of its vision. At the same time, such a task, I would readily confess, is conceived and advanced as an utopian ideal. First, I see it as a useful mapping: a model of the whole, providing a sense of place, of direction, of relation as one pursues any one area of interest or proceeds in any one path of research. Second, it is also meant as an opportunity for collective work rather than individual action. Lastly, it is further meant as but one vision of the task: not as the one way of organizing and coordinating everyone's share but rather as one way of understanding and relating actual as well as potential avenues of development.

2. Critical Engagement. As laid out, the task of Latino/a biblical criticism calls for engagement throughout with all of its constitutive dimensions: from our sense of identity and praxis—our notions of descent and culture; through our conception and exercise of the discipline—our methodological approaches and theoretical frameworks, our disciplinary trajectories and discursive partners; to our involvement in society and culture—our local and global commitments and struggles.

3. Critical Purpose. As drawn, the task of Latino/a biblical criticism appears as radically situated and perspectival: emerging from a particular world of material and cultural exclusion; cognizant of a wider world in the throes of social and cultural devastation; and pledged to a world of freedom and justice, dignity and well-being, for all.

INITIAL CONCLUSION TO A BEGINNING SORTIE

From the start, I described the present study as but a first sortie; at the end, I should like to voice but a first conclusion. At some point along the line, I would insist, taking part in projects that foreground the problematic of ethnic-racial identity, its configurations and its relations and its consequences, demands self-reflection on the part of subscribers in the light of and with regard to the categories deployed and assumed in such projects. This is true whether the projects in question bring together members of a single minority group, members of two or more minority groups, or individuals from both minority and dominant groups. Here I have posed to myself the question of what it means to be thought of and to think of myself of as Latino/a critic. In so doing, I have offered a working definition, have undone in various ways such a definition as soon as offered, and have laid down a personal vision for the future. In all three respects my reflections I see, and hope that they are seen, as an exploratory sortie—in search and need of expansion, of correction, and of refinement.

WORKS CONSULTED

Fenton, Steve. 2003. *Ethnicity. Key Concepts.* Cambridge: Polity Press.

Flores, Juan. 2000. *From Bomba to Hip-Hop: Puerto Rican Culture and Latino Identity.* Popular Cultures, Everyday Lives. New York: Columbia University Press.

Luis, William. 1997. *Dance between Two Cultures: Latino Caribbean Literature Written in the United States.* Nashville: Vanderbilt University Press.

Miles, Robert, and Malcolm Brown. 2003. *Racism.* 2nd ed. Key Ideas. London: Routledge.

Ringe, Sharon. 1985. *Jesus, Liberation, and the Biblical Jubilee: Images for Christology and Ethics.* OBT 19. Philadelphia: Fortress.

Ringe, Sharon, and Wes Howard-Brooks, eds. 2002. *The New Testament: Introducing the Way of Discipleship.* Maryknoll, N.Y.: Orbis.

Segovia, Fernando F. 1982. *Love Relationships in the Johannine Tradition: Agapē/ Agapān in 1 John and the Fourth Gospel.* SBLDS 58. Chico, Calif.: Scholars Press.

———. 1992. *The Farewell of the Word: The Johannine Call to Abide.* Minneapolis: Fortress.

———. 2000. *Decolonizing Biblical Studies: A View From the Margins.* Maryknoll, N.Y.: Orbis.

Segovia, Fernando F., and Mary Ann Tolbert, eds. 1995a. *Social Location and Biblical Interpretation in the United States.* Vol. 1 of *Reading from This Place.* Minneapolis: Fortress.

———. 1995b. *Social Location and Biblical Interpretation in Global Perspective.* Vol. 2 of *Reading from This Place.* Minneapolis: Fortress.

Silva, Moisés. 1983. *Biblical Words and Their Meaning: An Introduction to Lexical Semantics.* Grand Rapids: Zondervan.

———. 1990. *God, Language, and Scripture: Reading the Bible in the Light of General Linguistics.* Grand Rapids: Academie Books.

Silva, Moisés, and Walter C. Kaiser. 1994. *An Introduction to Biblical Hermeneutics: The Search for Meaning.* Grand Rapids: Zondervan.

Stavans, Ilan. 1995. *The Hispanic Condition: Reflections on Culture and Identity in America.* New York: HarperCollins.

PART 1: STUDIES
SECTION 4: TAKING AN INTERDISCIPLINARY TURN

"That's Why They Didn't Call the Book Hadassah!": The Interse(ct)/(x)ionality of Race/Ethnicity, Gender, and Sexuality in the Book of Esther

Randall C. Bailey

Introduction

The book of Esther is fraught with problems and tensions. There is the timeless debate about the lack of mention of the deity in the book, which led to debates on whether it ought to be included in the canon. There is the problem of both Hebrew and Greek manuscripts having their differing lengths, ideologies, and theologies. There are the continued debates over date and authorship of the book. Those who argue for an early dating during the Persian period note the knowledge of the inner workings of the Persian court as depicted in the narrative (Levenson 1997). Those who argue for a late dating argue that the conflict with the Persians as depicted in the book does not conform to the historical setting of the period but more approximates the Greco-Roman period of colonization. There are debates over whether Esther is a pawn of Mordecai or a shaker and mover on her own right (see Crawford 1998 and Levenson 1997 for reviews of the literature in these regards). There are now appearing in postcolonial readings debates on the way one should view the violence in the book, especially the violence perpetrated against the indigenous people in the book (Masenya 2001; Wong 2004). While beneath the surface there has been an underlying reading of ethnicity in regard to the position of the Jews as *ethnos*, it is only recently that this discussion has been given attention in scholarly circles (Beal 1997; Craig 1995).

In this study I plan to explore ways in which ethnicity plays a part in the book on the narrative level, with examination as to how the range of questions in this area are conscribed by the race/ethnicity of the interpreters. I further intend to explore the ways in which gender and sexuality are utilized as signifiers for ethnicity and racialist politics of the narrator of the book. In this way, interse(ct/x)ionality will be explored as tools of oppressive ideologies. For purposes of clarity I choose to see this book as having been written during the Greco-Roman period, given its underlying critique of Greco-Roman lifestyles, the nature of the interethnic conflicts depicted in the book, and the negative critique of assimilationist ways practiced by certain characters in the narrative. Though much emphasis has been placed on utilizing the Greek texts for comparison for plot and characterization studies (Day 1995; Frolov 2002), I shall be restricting this narratological and ideological exploration to the Hebrew text.

ETHNICITY IN ESTHER

The book opens with an interesting geographical and ethnological notation. It reads, "This happened in the days of Ahasuerus, the same Ahasuerus who ruled over one hundred twenty-seven provinces from India to Ethiopia" (Esth 1:1). On the one hand, the only other references to India in the Hebrew corpus are in the apocryphal books of 1 Macc 8:8 and 1 Esdr 3:2. Besides Esth 8:9, the other references to the geographical span from "India to Ethiopia" are found in the Greek additions to the book of Esther. Thus, it appears that the notion of India as being the eastern border of empire comes from a late dating in the text, in other words, during the Greek rule of Syria Palestine. By the same token, the mention of Cush, Ethiopia, as the southwestern border, implying the ends of the earth, has been noted as one of the literary characteristics of the use of Cush in the Hebrew Bible (Bailey 1991) and in the Second Testament (Martin 1989).

While most commentaries gloss over these geographical locations (Beal 1997, 17; Levenson 1997, 44), if there is attention to the details of the verse, it is directed at the historical accurateness of "provinces" versus "satraps" and the number 127 (Levenson 1997; Fox 2001, 14–15). In other words, the historical reliability of the verse is challenged by seeing if the Persians really controlled such a large territory and, if so, whether there ever were 120 provinces or divisions in the Persian era. While these scholars conclude no, this does not convince such scholars of the error of taking the Persian Empire as the location of the historical setting and writing of the book. Rather, they suggest that this is just a detail of exaggeration.

Giving attention to this particular geographical expanse of "from India to Ethiopia," one immediately notes that it is a southern configuration. India to Ethiopia gives an array of territory concentrating empire and power in current-day nomenclature of Asia and Africa. It totally ignores Europe or northern territory. Could this be part of an anti-Greek polemic in the book, which calls attention to the past superiority of the south over the north? It is as if to say: this king controlled the highly honored parts of the ancient world; these northern empire people are late in development; there were vast empires before they came upon the scene. India and Ethiopia, thus, are not just geographical markers. They appear also to be racial-ethnic markers signifying (in the Gates sense) on Greece, since it was the southern countries, Egypt and Ethiopia, that were the standard of valuation for ancient Israel (Bailey 1991). Since neither of these nations plays heavily in Eurocentric biblical scholarship, one should expect that this detail in the narrative would be seen as extraneous, even to literary critics. These nations, in essence, get "written out," as Beal uses the term. By the same token, as Amin, Gilroy, and Said argue, the fixation with only Eurocentric inputs into history leads modern and postmodern scholars to ignore the other sources of data.

Ethnicity next raises its head in the composition of the guests to the royal banquet in Esth 1:3, those who come from the armies of Persia and Media and the officials from the other provinces. One is not sure if these were people indigenous to the provinces or colonial administrators from the empire sent to the colonies or a mixture (Berquist 1995, 54). In the letter sent in response to the refusal of Vashti to attend the king's banquet, however, we are informed that this is a multiethnic population within the empire, since it states, "he sent letters to all the royal provinces, to every province in its own script and to every people in its own language" (1:22). Interestingly, this designation of the empire being composed of multiethnic/racial groupings is also found in the decrees sent out by Haman calling for the destruction of the Jews (3:12) and in the oppositional one sent out by Mordecai and Esther (8:9). The mention that these groups maintained their own languages and scripts, and by implication their own cultures, suggests a situation where total assimilation was not expected. The issuance of laws requiring uniformity in adherence to patriarchal (Esth 1) and genocidal (Esth 3; 8) practices suggests these ethnic differences could remain in practice as long as the people also adhered to the oppressive practices of the empire. In other words, according to these laws, being ethnic is acceptable, as long as one does not use this as a way of counteracting the prevailing culture of the empire (see Marden and Mercer 1998).

It is unclear how the term "Jewish" is used in the book of Esther. While it appears to be an ethnic or national designation, it is not an identity that is readily apparent by looking at the individual, since Esth 2:10 states, "Esther did not reveal her people or kindred, for Mordecai had charged her not to tell." Evidently, the identity of her "people or kindred" is not an outward manifestation, since it is her lack of "telling" that keeps it a secret. This would suggest that in this book "Jewish" relates to a religious group, not a national or ethnically homogeneous group. While some scholars such as Fox and Paton interpret this injunction of Mordecai to Esther to have some basis in "anti-Semitism," such a designation speaks to modern notions of the concept, while at the same time ignoring the notion that ancient Persia, though not listed under the Shemite line in Gen 10, is in the general geographic vicinity of the nations listed there. Mordecai is reported by the narrator to use his being a Jew to explain his not bowing down to Haman (3:4). The question is whether this is a religious or a national defense on his part. Similarly, though Haman is upset with Mordecai's behavior, he decides to punish not only him but his "people/the Jews" (3:6). In this sense, they appear to be an ethnic group.

In speaking of this group to the king, however, Haman refers to this group as "a certain people scattered and separated among the peoples in all the provinces of your kingdom; their laws are different from those of every other people, and they do not keep the king's laws" (3:8). This stereotypical designation of this group is reminiscent of Homi Bhabha's understanding, "[t]o be amongst those whose very presence is both 'overlooked'—in the double sense of social surveillance and psychic disavowal—and, at the same time, overdetermined—psychically projected, made stereotypical and symptomatic" (1994, 236). In effect, Haman's charge against the Jews is that they have customs and laws different from others, which fits the previously noted acceptable definition of ethnic group, but then he implies that, because of these differences, they will not adhere to the policies of the empire. Thus, this "overlooked group" gets "overdetermined" stereotypically. The fixed nature of their presentation is thus determinative of their status and identity. Thus, they are identifiable by their customs and practices but not by their looks, since neither Haman nor the king knows Esther's ethnicity until she reveals it in Esth 7 (see Fenton 2003).

Ethnic conflict is signaled by the narrator in the introductions of Mordecai and Haman. The former is identified as "a Jew in the citadel of Susa whose name was Mordecai son of Jair son of Shimei son of Kish, a Benjaminite. Kish had been carried away from Jerusalem among the captives carried away with King Jeconiah of Judah, whom King Nebuchadnezzar of Babylon had carried away" (2:5–6). In this way he is identified with the nations of Israel and Judah. On the one hand, his genealogy is similar to that of King Saul as depicted in 1 Sam 9:1–2. On the other hand, the mention of the Babylonian exile and the first deportation would place him with the upper classes of the Judahites. In both designations Mordecai is identified with a failed king who gets bad press: Saul and a failed king who cannot sustain a revolt, Jeconiah. He is identified as a Jew, which is a term more appropriate during a time much later than the Babylonian exile.

Haman, on the other hand, is identified as son of Hammedatha the Agagite (3:1). This is an interesting notation, since Agag is mentioned in 1 Sam 15 as king of the Amalekites, against whom Saul is to go into battle and upon whom Saul is to commit genocide under the direction of YHWH. As the narrative goes, Agag gets killed at the altar by Samuel, since Saul had not carried out the ban, or *ḥērem*. While most scholars see in this introductory data the notion of the Amalekites as long-time enemies of the Israelites, they ignore the genocidal practices of Israel upon Agag and his people. This appears to be in line with the notion that, if YHWH says to do something, it must be okay. It is, however, this familial/ethnic identifier to which most scholars appeal in explaining Haman's plan to kill the Jews (Allen and Laniak 2003, 214–16; Beal 1997, 53; Davies and Rogerson 2005, 48; Laniak 1998, 73–74; Levenson 1997, 64–65). This appeal, however, is ironic for several reasons. First, in 3:5 it is Mordecai's continued refusal to bow down, not Mordecai's ethnic affiliation, that upsets Haman, since Haman has to be told about Mordecai's ethnic signifier. Second, Haman is not presented by the narrator as one acting out of his ethnic identity.[1] Finally, Mordecai is the one from the genocidal practicing group. As with most commentators, this irony goes "overlooked in the double sense" that Homi Bhabha notes above. On the one hand, Saul's genocidal activities are acceptable, while Haman's are to be frowned upon. This is part of the irony of how the book uses ethnicity and the ambiguity in the ethic being presented. In other words, the importance of ethnicity gets blurred by the ambiguity of the ethic of the characters.[2]

Part of the ambiguity in this regard is that Haman's plan to destroy the Jews—as described in his speech to the king in 3:9, "If it pleases the king, let a decree be issued for their destruction"—employs language used by YHWH, *'ābad*. In Deut 4:26 YHWH threatens Israel with destruction (*'abōd tō'wēdûn*) if they assimilate into Canaanite ways. In 7:20 YHWH calls for the destruction (*'ābōd*) of the Canaanites and in 12:2 (*'abēd tə'abdûn*) of their indigenous shrines. Similarly, YHWH calls for such destruction of the Amalekites in the speech put into Balaam's mouth in Num 24:20. In this way, Haman's speech and plan to destroy the Jews parallels that of YHWH's plans to destroy non-Israelites and Israelites who assimilate. While Levenson notes similarities of Haman's speech to that of Memucan in Esth 1 and translates the verb as "exterminate" (1997, 71), and while Fox sees the verb as "the substance of the scheme" (2001, 51), neither points to the ironic connection to divine speeches of the conquest injunctions in Numbers and Deuteronomy. To note such would require the acknowledgment on the part of scholars that the ethnic designations in the book are multivalent and ethically ambiguous.[3]

By the same token, the narrator also has Haman using *hišmîd* ("destroy") as part of his plan. The offense of the use of this word is that this is what YHWH proposed to do to Israel were they to worship other gods, as seen in Deut 9:8,

---

1. One would have to wonder, were it the case that Haman was presented as acting out of revenge for the genocide carried out on his people by Mordecai's ancestor, whether the reader would have a different view of him as character. The fact that he is presented through this signifier as one who does not have bad feelings for Mordecai and his people because of the treatment of his ancestors seems to function as a negative for him as character. In other words, he does not even know his own history. In this way he is portrayed as one like Pharaoh in Exod 1:8, "who knew not Joseph," in other words, one who does not even know "the history of how his royal family got so rich," at least as Genesis portrays it.

2. See Beal's discussion of his own identification with the Jews in the book and how this impacts his reading and Bal's charge that many writers collaborate with the ethnocentric leaning of the text in their use of psychologized readings of the characters (1999, 229 n. 31).

3. There is a confessional tendency to accept divine speech as ethically unquestionable and to construct corresponding language for these instances. Thus, while Levenson argues for translating *'bd* as "exterminate" in this instance, there is no such move among Bible translators for such language change in relation to the conquest narratives of Numbers and Joshua. It is the equivalent of the U.S. construction of "cavalry victory and Indian massacre" (see Warrior 2005; Bailey 2005).

19, and 25. Thus, Haman now is presented as taking on the divine prerogative of destroying Israel/the Jews for worshiping/not bowing down to other gods/him. In other words, though Haman represents an ethnic group that was to be annihilated by Saul, he is also presented as one usurping the divine prerogative.[4] While there is this reversal between human and divine prerogatives, here the reversal is that Haman is proposing to destroy the Jews because Mordecai would not bow down to him. Thus, the lack of religious significance to the act of bowing down in Esth 3, since Haman is a government and not a cultic official, militates against an interpretation that the Jews are remaining faithful to their religion by Mordecai refusing to bow down to Haman.

Finally, in the concluding chapters of the book, when the decree is issued permitting the Jews to defend themselves against "any armed force of any people or province that might attack them" (8:11), "their enemies" (8:13), and "those who had sought their ruin" (9:2), the only ethnic signifier is "the Jews." Interestingly, the generic terms presented in reference to these attacking "people" are void of any ethnic identification. While the ethnic identifier Jew remains prominent, not even "Persian" is noted for the others. One wonders whether only Jewish identity is to be honored or privileged by naming in this part of the book. One also wonders whether the designation "their enemies" moves ethnicity to a back burner, such that there is no "rational history" or intergroup engagement that might warrant the status of "enemy." Interestingly, Levenson addresses this by referring to these people as "the Gentiles" and arguing that the major focus here is the strengthening of Jewish identity (1997, 120).

Fox also refers to them as "Gentiles" and explains the text's excluding names of ethnic groups as a way of reinforcing that the ones killed were the attackers of the Jews. Most interesting in his argument is the enumeration of all the literary allusions in the chapters to the holy-war motif and conquest narratives of Numbers through Joshua. While he notes these genocidal references there in the text, he claims that the actions to "destroy ... kill ... annihilate ... plunder" mentioned in Esth 8–9 should not be interpreted in line with these past "historical" references (2001, 222–25). Similarly, Craig moves beyond his dis-ease with the actions, which he terms "massacres" by comparing them to Haman's plan (1995, 125). Thus, the privileging of one ethnic group over others is imbedded in the ideology of the text. This ideology seems to be embraced by commentators of the text, in the same ways in which Eurocentric translators of the Hebrew Bible have privileged Israelite/Judean/Jewish actions toward "the Other."[5]

---

4. Again the subtlety of this argument is not explored in the secondary literature, possibly because it could open the question of the ethic of such a "divine prerogative."

5. This is also seen on the translation level in instances such as Exod 7:11 where the word *ḥartummîm*, which LXX translates as *pharmakoi* and which is derived from the Egyptian *ḥry-tp*, is translated as "magicians" and not as "priests." On the one hand, Aaron the priest throws down

Beal dissents by saying, "the text raises further questions concerning the problematics of establishing identity-over-against, and plunges readers into a deep ethical maelstrom" (1997, 105). As Masenya and Wong have noted, these final chapters speak of violence against indigenous members of the empire who end up paying the price for conflicts of people at the top of the government. In essence, the colonial powers and their surrogates, be they ethnic/racial members of the colonizing group or from other groupings, often engage in and develop policies that lead to the physical extermination of the indigenous peoples. This raises both an ethnic and a class dimension to the struggles described in the text. The ethnic mention in the text only of the Jews and the anonymous "Others" lends credence to the critiques and concerns of these African and Asian exegetes.[6]

Thus, we see that the book treats ethnicity in several ways. While it is not phenotypical, it is tied to geographical or national determinants, as well as culture, most specifically language. It is also tied to lineage. It is the basis of inter-group conflict, but the lines of the conflict get blurred. While it relates to culture, it is not necessarily religio-cultural. Ethnicity also is given value not only by the narrator but also by the interpreter and plays an important part in the ways in which characters and plot are valued and evaluated by readers.

Interse(ct)/(x)tionality in Esther

There have been several organizing themes proposed for bringing unity to the narrative of Esther. Levenson has argued for banquets. Bal (1999) has argued for writing. Beal has argued for hiding. In this essay I wish to argue that sexuality is another organizing theme that is connected to constructs of ethnicity. Critical race theory has shown us that in situations of oppression people often belong to multiple oppressed groups and also that systems of oppression often reinforce each other (Delgado and Stefancic 2001, 51–55). While there has been attention to gender in exploring the book (Bal 1999; Kirk-Duggan 1999; Crawford 1998; Duran 2004; Masenya 2001; Wong 2004), not much attention has been paid to the role sex and sexuality play both in the portrayals of characters and in the movement of the plot. Thus, I shall explore the intersection of ethnicity, gender, and sexuality as ideological signifiers of the narrative.

One of the tools of ethnic critique offered by the narrator of the book of Esther is the use of sexuality and sexual practices to label characters negatively.

---

his rod and it becomes a snake. When the *ḥartummim* do the same thing, they are denied the designation "priest" (for further discussion of this phenomenon, see Bailey 1994, 8–9).

6. Interestingly, both these scholars arrive at different ways of addressing the concerns raised in this regard. Masenya takes a confessional approach, reconciling herself to the text, while Wong declares the text to be dangerous in this regard. It would be interesting to explore the role of race and racial history in these radically different ways of solving the problem.

The genesis of my awareness of this signifier was a Bible study I was asked to do for a United Methodist church-sponsored conference on the Black Church and HIV/AIDS whose theme was "Breaking the Silence." I was really asked to do a study on Esth 4:14, "For if you keep silence at such a time as this, relief and deliverance will rise for the Jews from another quarter, but you and your father's family will perish. Who knows? Perhaps you have come to royal dignity for just such a time as this." Now really, how does one do a Bible study for 90 minutes on one verse? I decided to look at who gets silenced in the book.

Having reviewed Nicole Duran's article on Esther in Kirk-Duggan's edited volume *Pregnant Passion*, I was aware that there were sexual issues embedded in the book, especially around the contest as to who would follow Vashti to the throne. I am ashamed to say that I had not, however, thought of this contest in terms of sexual abuse of teenagers until Duran pointed out this aspect of the story. On the one hand, the practice of sexual exploitation is so horrific that we as readers are defended against being troubled by its presence in the text by using the reading strategy of "not seeing what is there."[7] In this way, much of the sexual activity that I shall explore in this essay could be missed by the above-named reading strategy (Fish 1980).

On the other hand, another technique that is used to keep us from seeing the presence of sexuality in the text, especially in narratives, is what I term the art of cover-up translations. For instance, as a member of the Bible Translation and Utilization Standing Committee of the National Council of Churches, I once asked Bruce Metzger, the general editor of the NRSV, "When *regel* is clearly a reference to the male genitals in the Hebrew Bible, such as in Ruth 3, why did the NRSV still translate it as 'foot,' as opposed to 'penis'?" Metzger responded that the translation was not only for study but also for worship modes and that "you couldn't

---

7. When I drew attention to this aspect of Esth 2 in a Bible study at the local church where I attend, one person read the chapter as describing prostitution. Another felt that we should concentrate on the horrible killings at the end of the book and not on "the sex in chapter 2." I pointed out that the story speaks of sending virgin teenagers into the king's bedroom to decide if they were to become queen, so this is not prostitution nor just sex, but rather the sexual exploitation of teenagers. By the same token, a friend of my wife, who is a black professional woman, called me for help on a Women's Day sermon she was to give at her mother's church. She was dealing with Esther for the sermon. When I explored chapter 2 with her, she told me the twelve months of cosmetic and perfume training was a process of purification. This is a woman who deals with issues of child sexual abuse in her own professional sphere. She could not, however, "wrap her head around this as child sexual abuse." Given the horror of this possibility of reading, I understood all too well why the women, especially, want to gloss over this aspect of the story. To do otherwise might lead to the conclusion there are "problems" in the Bible. Not to read this way, however, encourages the churches to ignore problems of child sexual abuse in our communities. Much is at stake in these reading strategies. For a dogmatic response to these issues, see Vanhoozer 1998.

say 'penis' in the sanctuary."[8] Similarly, when Joshua sends the spies to Jericho and they go to Rahab's brothel, the text says, *wayyiškabû šām*: literally, "they lay there," or figuratively, "they had sex there," but the NRSV says, "they spent the night there." My recognizing of these cover-ups was in line with what the queer theorist Timothy Koch calls cruising, as a hermeneutical technique for seeing and exposing these aspects of the text. While his focus is on the homoerotic in the text, I was using the technique to unmask heteroerotic aspects of the text. Thus, I was prepared for the silencing of sex in the book of Esther, both by the defensive reading strategies, the tradition, and the translators. I was not, however, prepared for what else I found in the book as I began to explore it.

I shall now explore the ways in which the main characters in the book are sexualized as literary devices to portray them negatively. I shall explore the presentation of the king in chapters 1–2, Esther in chapters 2, 5, and 7, Haman in chapter 6, and Mordecai in chapters 2, 6, and 8.

SEXUALIZING KING AHASUERUS

As noted above, in Esth 1 we are introduced to a Persian king, Ahasuerus, who is king over 127 provinces from India to Ethiopia, quite an impressive empire. The text then tells us that this king has built an impressive palace and wants to show it off. This makes sense, for in 1 Kgs 10 we read of the Queen of Sheba being impressed not only with Solomon's wisdom but also his palace and servants and the like. In the instance of Ahasuerus, however, the narrator tells us that, "There were white cotton curtains and blue hangings tied with cords of fine linen and purple to silver rings and marble pillars. There were couches of gold and silver on a mosaic pavement of porphyry, marble, mother-of-pearl, and colored stones" (1:6). Fox's treatment of this description of the king's palace concentrates on the length of the sentence and the "*narrator's* wonder" (emphasis original) at the opulence and excess (2001, 16). In this he is following Clines (1984, 36). Levenson makes a similar claim (1997, 43, 45). Verse 7 goes on to describe the type of wine goblets being used at the banquet, and to be sure they are not jelly glasses. On the other hand, all this attention to fabrics, draperies, furnishings, floor coverings, and goblets seems to be turning this king into an interior decorator. It is almost as though the narrator is signaling the reader that the king is auditioning for a cast slot on "Queer Eye for the Straight Guy."

Lest one think I am making too much of this, we have to remember that these details are given to the reader with the explanation that the king is trying to impress his friends and associates, all of whom happen to be men. As the text states, for 180 days the king partied with his boys, "all his officials and ministers. The army of Persia and Media, and the nobles and governors of the provinces

---

8. I love telling this story while teaching Bible study in a sanctuary.

were present" (1:3)—not one woman mentioned in that group. He then invites *hāʿām*, which the NRSV translates as "the people," to join the party. Since verse 9 tells us that Vashti, the queen, holds a parallel party for the women, *hāʿām* in verse 5 must mean the army, another group of men. The narrator tells us they are drinking "without restraint, for the king had given orders to all the officials of his palace to *do as each one desired*."[9] It appears that this king is being eroticized, or, more specifically, queered,[10] by holding an all-male orgy with those who are drinking and doing whatever they desire. But let's not just jump to conclusions. Is there any other evidence for this reading in the text?

In verse 10 we read that, "on the seventh day, when the king was merry with wine, he commanded Mehuman, Biztha, Harbona, Bigtha and Abagtha, Zethar, and Carkas, the seven eunuchs who attended him," to bring Vashti to his party. As is the practice of most of my students, my initial readings of this verse skipped the list of men and went on to the next verse. While Fox does note the excess of the seven eunuchs, he seems not to be able to figure it out. As he states, "The affair seems to be formalized, with some significance as a state ritual, but this significance is lost to us." He goes on to suggest that it is just "pomp and circumstance" (2001, 20). Interestingly, however, as I read this passage for the AIDS workshop, I noticed that the text states that these seven eunuchs *attended* the king. In looking at the standard commentaries, none of them explores the meaning of the verb *šrt* in the text. What does it mean that the eunuchs "attend the king"? Clearly, it could not have a sexual meaning, because the rules of phalocentrism and androcentrism, which govern our reading and interpreting, understand eunuchs to be nonsexed, given their physical lacks. Or so I thought.

While *məšārēt* is used in P materials to deal with service in the tabernacle and in Chronicles for temple ministries, these were not the contexts of the eunuchs in Ahasuerus's court. What did strike me, however, was the use of this verb in 1 Kgs 1:4. When David was old and could not get warm,[11] they came up with the idea of getting a young, beautiful virgin, Abishag, to check him out, to see if he was still potent. As verse 4 states, *wattəšārətēhû wəhammelek lōʾ yədāʿāh*, "she *attended* him, but he did not know her." In his commentary on 1 Kings, DeVries states that Abishag becomes David's bed partner and translates this use of *šrt* as "waiting on

---

9. The only other time *rṣn* ("desire") appears in the book is in the description of the "self-defense" of the Jews, where they "struck down … slaughtering and destroying" their enemies in 9:5, where they "did as they pleased to those who hated them." The reversal of men drinking and doing as they pleased to slaughtering as they pleased speaks to ironic twists of plot and characterization.

10. It is most interesting to me that Jennings in his new book on homoeroticism in the Hebrew Bible sees the sex in Esther to be heterosexual only (2005, 185). His thesis to show homoeroticism in the Hebrew Bible to be a positive depiction could explain his not engaging these possible "queer" readings of Esther.

11. Note the euphemistic language in the translation.

his desires." This makes sense, since the text follows this verb with the statement that David still did not know, or have sex with, her. So this verb *šrt* has to do with sexual activity in 1 Kgs 1:4. While the NRSV translates it as "attends him," just like the case of the eunuchs and the king, could we say that the eunuchs have been "waiting on the king's sexual desires?"[12] Could this be why Vashti does not want to come to his party?

Beal writes on Esth 1:7 that "(t)he fact that seven eunuchs are sent to her on the seventh day, moreover, may suggest that this will be the impressive finale of the king's display (the ultimate act of hospitable exchange)" (1997, 21). Beal never engages *šrt*. His heterocentrist reading is signaled by his rubric of "proximity/distance," where he claims, "Within the sexual political order, beauty and pleasure are associated with objectification—to be one of the objects by which the subject secures power publicly" (19). He misses the eunuchs in this way, for he only understands them as signifiers who "pass between the sexes" (52). He thus sees them as representing "sexual ambiguity" and not as sexual beings. In this way Beal "writes the eunuchs out," which is his key construct for what happens to Vashti in the book.

But can we base our understanding of *šrt* solely on 1 Kgs 1:4? Well, thanks to word studies done by my students, we do not have to. (I told them I would give them a shout here!) The verb *šrt* appears also in 2 Sam 13. After Amnon rapes Tamar, the text tells us he loathed her greater than he had loved her. He has her thrown out by his servant who attends him. Here we have another aspect of cover-up translation, because *'ebed* is not found in this passage. The servant mentioned in this verse is a *na'ar*, the term for a teenage boy. The young boy throws her out, bolts the door, and the only ones left in the room are Amnon and his boy who waits on his desires, as DeVries translates the verb in 1 Kgs 1:4.

Returning to Esther, 2:2 states, "Then the king's servants who attended him said, 'Let beautiful young virgins be sought out for the king.'" In essence, there is to be a beauty contest to see who can sexually please the king best, and the one who sexes him the best becomes queen. Again not *'ebed* but *na'ar* is found in this verse. These are the ones who are "attending the king." As one of my students argued, they were saying, "Man, why don't you leave us alone and try a woman for a change?" While I did have to caution him on his heterocentrism, I did have to agree that his reading was in line with the narrator's point of view. Since Esther was written during the Maccabean period, this description of the king seems to be a negative caricature of sexual practices of the colonizers.[13] As Kelly Brown

---

12. While Berquist talks about the sexual excesses of Xerxes and sexual intrigue in his court, these are all heterosexual instances (1995, 91), and he does not speak to this verse.

13. While Foucault talks about the chase of the young boys by older men in the gymnasium (1990, 2:197–98), he later goes on to discuss the male same-sex sexual encounters with slaves (2:215–16).

Douglas in her use of Foucault tells us, the use of sex and sexuality as a signifier becomes a major tool of social control and manipulation of meaning. Similarly, I have argued that sexuality is often used as negative signifier for the "other" as a way of legitimizing Israelite oppression of such people (Bailey 1994b).

A final lynchpin in this reading is found in Esth 2:15–17, which reads, in part, as follows:

> When the turn came for Esther daughter of Abihail the uncle of Mordecai, who had adopted her as his own daughter, to go in to the king, she asked for nothing except what Hegai the king's eunuch, who had charge of the women, advised.... When Esther was taken to King Ahasuerus ... the king loved Esther more than all the other women; of all the virgins she won his favor and devotion, so that he set the royal crown on her head and made her queen instead of Vashti.

In other words, the way Esther wins the contest is to do exactly what Hegai, the king's eunuch, tells her to do. Now, how does he know what the king likes sexually? According to Rotten.com,

> Certainly loyalty and sterility were the eunuch's ticket into the harem. However, their lack of conventional sexual equipment did not always ban or exclude them from sexual activity. In fact, some eunuchs had an expressly sexual relationship with their masters. Homosexual slave owners, or especially those with pedophilic leanings, expressly enjoyed the effeminate or eternal boy look of slaves castrated before puberty. In fact, sometimes the manner of castration left the testicles crushed but not removed, precisely because it was hoped that the boy would retain erotic sensation (while losing his reproductive ability). (Rotten.com)

Thus, the narrator, in giving the reader this detail, hints at the sexual relationship between the king and either Hegai or other eunuchs, about which Hegai has knowledge.

As Wills argues, "The Jewish novels do not utilize slavery itself as a threat to the protagonist, a symbol of abject degradation, as do the Greek novels, but present individual slaves in much the same ways as do the ideal novels, slaves are in general faithful servants of the protagonists. Their will is identified with that of their masters" (1998, 127). He cites Orlando Patterson's work, which argues that not all slavery involves labor exploitation. Rather, there is a "relation of ritualized humiliation and dishonor (1982, 77–101). The irony here is that the ritualized humiliation on the narrative level is really of the foreign king, not the slave. As noted, this homoeroticizing of the king seems tied to the Maccabean struggles against the Greeks and their culture. It would appear that this sexual critique represents an intersectionality of sex, gender, and ethnicity as negative signifiers of the oppressor/colonizer/imperial powers. In essence, these sexual references to the king and his engagement in homoerotic behaviors are piled upon each other as a way of characterizing this king, who gets very bad press in the book as a whole. This form of signifying adds to the negative portrayal of the king.

SEXUALIZING ESTHER

While much ink has been spilled on arguing that the purpose of Ahasuerus wanting Vashti to be brought to his party was to show her off sexually,[14] there is almost no ink directed toward the sexual activities of Esther. Rather, there is a marked attempt to desexualize her as the model "good Jewish princess" (Cavalcanti 1989, 123–24). As will be shown below, the text seems to go to great pains to not only sexualize her but to present this as her major modus operandi.

As noted above, the king's boys suggest there be a beauty contest in the kingdom to find a new queen to replace Vashti. Young virgins are collected, given instructions in cosmetics and perfumes. Esther is entered into the contest by Mordecai. As the text then states,

> When the girl went in to the king she was given whatever she asked for to take with her from the harem to the king's palace. In the evening she went in; then in the morning she came back to the second harem in custody of Shaashgaz, the king's eunuch, who was in charge of the concubines; she did not go in to the king again, unless the king delighted in her and she was summoned by name. (2:13–14)

In essence, each girl is expected to have sex with the king, and the one who performs the best will win the contest. Clearly, this is a story of sexual exploitation of teenagers.[15] As the story continues,

> When the turn came for Esther ... to go in to the king, she asked for nothing except what Hegai the king's eunuch, who had charge of the women, advised.... the king loved Esther more than all the other women; of all the virgins she won his favor and devotion, so that he set the royal crown on her head and made her queen instead of Vashti. (2:15, 17)

In other words, Esther wins the contest by sexing the king better than anyone else. In this way she becomes commodified. This storyline exemplifies what Wolf argues as systems composed of "men who want objects and women who want to be objects" (1995, 421). Or at least, since the narrator never presents Esther as

---

14. See Fox for references and discussion of this type of interpretation (2001, 165).

15. While most of the questions about this book being included in the canon have centered around the lack of mention of God directly in the text, there is no questioning of the silence of God at this aspect of the story. Since it is characteristic of the deity to be portrayed as remaining silent at the sexual exploitation of women, such as Jephthah's daughter in Judg 11 and the Levite's concubine in Judg 19, perhaps this is why there is no questioning of this aspect of the story.

resisting the instructions of Mordecai or of Hegai, the reader gets the impression that she is a willing participant in this game.

In exploring 2:15 Beal cuts off (pardon the pun) part of the verse by stating, "she did not seek a thing, except what Hegai the keeper of the women said" (1997, 37). His concentration on Esther and her winning the contest keeps him from asking how Hegai knew what would please the king and from exploring the implications of the type of contest for the characterization of Esther.

Fox tips his hand in dealing with 2:15. He notes, "for Esther does not reject all beauty aids, but only avoids asking for more than she is offered. Her virtue is not abstinence from the heathen luxuries but self-effacing receptivity and passivity" (2001, 37). But the text states that she "asked for them." So, how is this passivity? Given his need to protect Esther, instead of engaging Hegai's relationship with the king, he refers to these people as heathens.[16] Levenson argues that her dependence on Hegai's "expertise" is a foreshadowing of her later dependence on another older man, Mordecai (1997, 63). But he draws no other parallel between these two men, whom he presumes to be old.[17]

Interestingly, Craig understands 2:15 to refer only to the clothes and jewelry Esther wore to see the king (1995, 94–95). He does connect this to the dress-up scene in Esth 5, but he does not see it as dealing with seduction either. His assumption is that it was her clothes that turned on the king, which might be the case, if the king was also a cross-dresser, I guess. In other words, Craig does not understand Hegai's instructions to have anything to do with what types of sexual acts she should perform. It seems, however, that the narrator is telling us straight up, no pun intended, that this is how Esther won the contest: she did what Hegai told her to do to please the king, and as a result *wattissŝā'-ḥēn*, she aroused (lit., she raised up favor in) him. In this way the narrator lets the reader know that Esther has "unusual sexual abilities and prowess." She is a contest winner. This sexualizing of her is not hidden by the text, though, as we have seen, it is virtually ignored in the secondary literature.

In 4:8 Mordecai tells Hathach the eunuch to tell Esther to go see the king and to make supplication. This is an interesting translation, since the verb *ḥnn* is used, which is related to the king's reaction to Esther's first night with him. This sexual connotation is reinforced by her reply to Mordecai that the king has not called for her to come to him in over a month (4:11b). After Mordecai threatens Esther if she does not follow his instructions, she calls for a fast for three days. She does not call for fasting and praying, just for fasting. In other words, it is not presented as a totally religious act. One could, however, see it as part of a strategy to lose weight so she would look good in that new dress that she puts on in 5:1. She then

---

16. In this signifier we see how the ethnic leanings of interpreters drive the commentary.

17. Jennings seems to follow this line of argument in his discussion of the eunuchs in Esther and their import to the narrative.

goes and stands outside the throne room so the king can see her through the window.

Her strategy works, for when the king sees her the text reads, *nāśa'â hēn ba'ênāyw.* While most English translations render this "she found favor with him," the Hebrew idiom for such a translation, *mṣ' ḥn,* does not get employed in the text. As noted above, the phrase literally means "she lifted up favor in his eyes," which reminds the reader of his sexual reaction to her during the contest (2:17b). In other words, he saw her standing out there looking good and favor rose up. He then extends the golden scepter that is in his hand (need we do a Freudian analysis of this?). She touches the *rō'š,* the head, of his scepter, whereupon he says, "Baby, you can have up to half of my kingdom." The use of cover-up translation thus reduces the chances of seeing the seduction motif. Given the negative view of sexuality among religious readers, viewing Esther as seductress does not come to most minds.[18] It appears, when Mordecai tells her to *ḥnn* the king, Esther decides once again to use her sexuality to achieve the objective, just as she had done to get the job of queen in the first place.

Esther is also portrayed as seductress in the scene in chapter 7 when she reveals the plan of Haman to destroy her people. Once the king hears of it, he goes out onto the balcony. When he returns, he sees that "Haman had thrown himself on the couch where Esther was reclining; and the king said, 'Will he even assault the queen in my presence, in my own house?' As the words left the mouth of the king, they covered Haman's face" (7:8). While the narrative concentrates on Haman's actions, one has to wonder why she went and lay down on the couch, once she exposed the plan to the king. Similarly, the note that Haman's face had to be covered raises questions as to what the king thought was really going on. While the king uses military terminology to describe Haman's actions, *kbš* ("to subdue or conquer"), the narrator's description of Haman falling on the bed on which Esther is reclining once again portrays her as seducer.

This presentation of the character Esther, who is a Jew acting like the non-Jews, both in the book and in other biblical books, namely, using sexuality to get what is needed, could explain why the book is called by her Persian name, Esther, as opposed to her Jewish name, Hadassah. It could be a signal from the community that there is some problem with her characterization, a point to which we shall have to return later.

---

18. When I have dealt with this passage in Bible studies in local churches and for the Balm in Gilead, an agency devoted to getting black churches to deal with problems of HIV and AIDS, I have had black women tell me, "I used to like Esther before you started talking, but now I have to rethink it." In other words, the subject of sex and sexuality is primarily viewed as a negative dimension of life, and, if Bible characters engage in it, even as a means of liberation, we are prepared to silence them. On the other hand, it is surprising that Berman's treatment of Esther as passing on the model of same-gender-loving people "coming out" misses all the homoerotic signifying in the text (Berman 2001).

Now let me quickly add that we must both decry the ways in which biblical narrators only allow women to function as seducers as a means to achieve national liberation and be cautious in our readings as to what is possibly going on in the text. We must also note that the same strategy of presenting a woman as seducing a man as a way of addressing a national enemy is used in Judg 4–5 with Jael and Sisera (Bal 1988, 65), in Judg 14 and 16 with Samson and the Timnite wife and with Samson and Delilah. While this paradigm of national struggle is thus utilized in the biblical text, we must be aware of its androcentric and misogynistic ideologies.

What is interesting to me is the ways in which interpreters either miss this aspect of Esther's characterization or go to great lengths to cover it up and explain it away. In these instances it appears that what is operative in these attempts is the ethnic commitments of the interpreter to see the Jews in the narrative in a totally positive light. In this way we see that that interpretation is generally guided by the ideological commitments of the interpreter.

Sexualizing Haman

There are two passages in the text that speak to Haman's homoerotic characterization in very interesting ways. In Esth 6 we get the story of the king not being able to sleep one night. He asks for the book of records, possibly thinking this would really put him to sleep. In the course of the reading, he discovers that Mordecai was never rewarded for thwarting the assassination attempt by the eunuchs as recorded in 2:21–23. At this time, Haman shows up, unannounced, at the king's bedroom. Unlike Esther's concerns in 4:11 that going before the king without being summoned could lead to death, Haman comes to the king's bedroom when he is supposed to be asleep. Is this a usual occurrence? While 3:15b presents the king and Haman as drinking buddies, his arriving at the king's bedroom when the king should be asleep raises questions as to the motivations of this character. Are they only to push his anti-Mordecai agenda, as his wife discusses with him (5:14; 6:4), or is something else happening? One clue to this being more than just a "state visit" is the narrator's notation that it is the "boys attending" the king who identify that Haman has arrived.

While commentators note that the king's question to Haman, "What should be done to one whom the king wishes to honor?" leaves out the reference to gədûlâ ("to promote"), which tricks Haman into thinking the king wants to honor him (Craig 1995, 146; Fox 2001, 178–80; Levenson 1997, 96), there is another ambiguity in this statement. The phrase posed to Haman is ḥāpēṣbîqārô. While this is generally translated as "wants to honor," it could also be translated as "desires his dearness." The only other reference to ḥpṣ in the book is in reference to the sexual activity with the virgins: 2:14 states that, after having sex with the king, each would return to the harem unless the king ḥāpēṣ bāh, desires her.

While *ḥpṣ* is usually followed by *l* plus the infinitive construct, there are several other passages that use the construction *ḥpṣ b*, as found in 6:6, 7, 9, and 11. In Gen 34:19 it describes Shechem's feelings for Dinah and his desire to marry her. In 1 Sam 19:1 it is used to describe Jonathan's feelings for David. In Deut 21:14 it is used for the law relating to "war brides." In all of these instances the sexual import of the idiom seems clear.[19]

In this regard, Haman thinks to himself, "Whose dearness would the king desire other than mine?" Since he has come to the king's bedroom at a time when the king ought to be asleep, expecting to be let in, so to speak, this seems like a reasonable interpretation/translation of the ambiguous phrase.

Interestingly, Haman's response is one of "let's play dress up." In other words, he suggests getting into the king's closet, so to speak, to wear clothes that the king has worn and to get into the king's saddle on a horse the king has ridden (6:7–9). While O'Connor notes the humor in this passage, she seems to miss the sexual innuendo. This sexualizing of the character is tied closely to the characterization of the king, as noted above. As Esther brings to mind Haman's ethnic identification as she tries to get the king to rescind his earlier decree, one sees that his attempt at being with the king in Esth 6 is as unsuccessful as his attempt to have Mordecai hung on the gallows.

Sexualizing Mordecai

One point that seems to go unnoticed in commentaries on 2:21–23 is that Mordecai discovers the plot to kill the king that is about to be carried out by two eunuchs. One has to wonder: Why is Mordecai hanging around with the eunuchs? Other than Esther, whom he is reported to have adopted, we do not hear of him having any other children or a wife.

By the same token, Mordecai is willing to participate in Haman's game of dress-up in Esth 6. This is ironic, since in 4:6–8 Esther sends Mordecai a change of clothes when he is outside the gates of the palace dressed in sackcloth and ashes. He refuses the change of clothes at that time, but now that the king's clothes are offered to him, he is ready to enter the game.

Finally, once Haman is killed, the king gives Mordecai the ring that he took back from Haman before Haman was killed (8:2). The king then gives Haman's house to Esther, but she gives it to Mordecai. Could this be so that he can make

---

19. While *yqr* does not appear in passages that are readily seen as sexual in context, it does appear in the law directed to wives in Esth 1:20. There the wives are instructed to give *yqr*, generally translated "honor," to their husbands. Given the use of the idiom of "desiring a man's dearness," one could wonder whether in this law the term is multivalent and women are instructed to have sex with their husbands. Given the varied understandings of what Vashti was speculated to be expected to do in coming to the king's party, this speculation is made even more tenable.

midnight runs to the king's palace, as Haman evidently used to do? Once Morde-cai accepts the royal office, we get the description of Mordecai appearing before the people "wearing royal robes of blue and white, with a great golden crown and a mantle of fine linen and purple, while the city of Susa shouted and rejoiced" (8:15). While Levenson explains this as Mordecai accepting regal status (1997, 116), the only other ones in the book whose clothes are described are women. Similarly, the only other ones in the book who wear, or are supposed to wear, a crown are Vashti, Esther, and possibly the horse,[20] depending on the view of the antecedent to "his" head in 6:8b. What is hilarious about this event is that the description of Mordecai's clothes matches the description of the king's drapes in the interior decorating noted in Esth 1. In other words, he comes out wearing the king's drapes. In essence, he is now fully "outed" as one of the king's boys, or pos-sibly the king's new boy, wearing the king's ring, a crown, and robes that match the drapes.

But how could this be? Mordecai is the hero of the book. As Mosala notes, Esther takes the risks, and Mordecai gets the job. Could it be that the narrator is not only using sexuality to negatively critique the Persians/Greeks but once again also negatively caricaturing the assimilationist Jews who get totally enmeshed in the colonizer's culture? Could this book be turning ethnicity on its head by saying that all of them, colonizer and neocolonizers, are equally problematic? Ethnicity that assimilates is not acceptable!

CONCLUSIONS

The above reading intersects gender, sexualities, and ethnicity as negative sig-nifiers for the four main characters in the book, but how does this speak to us today? As Audrey Lorde has argued, "in order to survive, those of us for whom oppression is as american as apple pie have always had to be watchers, to become familiar with the language and manners of the oppressor, even sometimes adopt-ing them for some illusion of protection" (1995, 532). In other words, we who have been living under genocidal conditions within this country need to be aware not only of how oppression has functioned against us in terms of race but also of how oppression operates in other spheres, especially since in the Afri-can American community there are people of varied sexualities and varied sexual orientations. We sometimes get so myopic in dealing with race oppression that we miss the interlocking nature of oppressions, especially as it relates to lesbian, gay, bisexual, and transgendered people. We even feel we have biblical warrant to oppress same-gender-loving people with holy hatred. Because of this Lorde further warns us,

---

20. Perhaps this is why the Hebrew uses *ṣhl* for their reaction, which is not only calling out shrilly, but used for the lusty neighing of stallions in Jer 5:8.

In the US there is a *mythical norm* which is usually defined as "white, thin, male, young, heterosexual, Christian, and financially secure." It is with this mythical norm that the trappings of power reside within this society. Those of us who stand outside that power often identify one way in which we are different, and we assume that to be the primary cause of all oppression, forgetting other distortions around difference, some of which we ourselves may be practicing. (534)

In essence, we need to be aware of the language of the text that sexualizes people as a means of "othering" them and not fall prey to endorsing or inscribing that discourse or those forms of discourse. We are invited into the book of Esther to identify with the plight of the Jews under Greek oppression and their struggle to survive in the face of genocide. We see this as speaking to our story. This text, however, is more complicated than that, for the initial introduction to the oppressor is a homoerotic tale that maligns the other and presents this as one of the major problems. Similarly, Esther's actions in the book are attributable to her continued use of her sexuality as a means to an end.

In the 2004 presidential election we heard much rhetoric around gay marriage and much heterosexist discourse coming from black pulpits and black televangelists. Bishop Eddie Long encouraged his flock to "vote for the one whose faith is like our faith." If our faith holds heterosexism as a major lynchpin, we can lose sight of the Hamans in the administration, at the expense of children being left behind and weapons of mass destruction being dropped on our communities. If our reading strategies are geared toward ignoring the sexualizing and sexual exploitation of women, we will turn our heads away from the teenaged virgins and Esthers in the book and in our midst. In essence, the biblical strategy advocated in this book is not to concentrate on socioeconomic policies of empire but rather to use sexuality as a way of discrediting the characters.

As Patricia Hill Collins helps us to understand, black constructs of masculinity are "hyper-heterosexual" in an attempt to define ourselves in relation to white masculinity, which we assume to be "heterosexual." Thus, the DL life becomes a way of lessening the threat to black masculinity, which sees same gender sexuality as "emasculation" (2004, 174).[21] She goes on to describe the construction of black gender ideology as representations of heterosexism as found in the white world. In other words, black men are depicted as less than strong/weak and black women as strong and domineering, the exact opposite of the fictive white constructs of gender ideology. Thus, the response to same-gender-loving individuals is out of reaction to the "new racism's" designs of black gender ideology (175–80). What is fascinating to me in her discussion of the constructions of black gender ideology is that this seems to be what is going on

---

21. The DL is a popular cultural term referring to "on the Down Low" and is used currently to talk about married men who are engaged in same-gender sex acts outside their heterosexual marriages. Previously, it referred to any secretive behavior, often in reference to illicit behaviors.

in the text of Esther: to show the king to be less than a man, within heterosexist terminology and constructs, and thereby to discredit him as a legitimate king; and to show Esther to be more "man" than the men in the book. While this is not the only ideological literary device used in the book to construct these characters, it is a pivotal strategy used by the narrator. Thus, Lorde's caution not to restrict our analysis to race but to expand it to interlocking natures of oppression can help us become resistant readers of this text. Similarly, as Spivak warns us, we as intellectuals must expose the oppressive components of various ideologies presented, either imperialist or liberationist readings.

In conclusion, Mieke Bal correctly argues that "[t]he eagerness to narrow history down to a narrative of war and political leadership is at least partly due to a number of 'centrisms.' Within those centrisms which include ethnocentrism, androcentrism, and theocentrism, [there] are also more subtle forms" (1988, 13). This essay has dealt with exploring the different ways in which ethnocentrism works in the book, both as a narrative device and as a marker of the ethnocentric leanings of the reader. By the same token, it has pointed to ambiguity in the depiction of both Persians and Jews as ethnic groups.

In addition, the essay has pointed to the interrelation of ethnocentrism with another such centrism, namely, heterocentrism, and the role it plays both in the telling of the story of Esther as well as in controlling our readings. First, I have argued in this regard that the narrator employs heterocentrism as a way of emasculating the king in chapters 1–2, Haman and Mordecai in chapter 6, and Mordecai in chapter 8. I have also argued that the narrative used heterosexism as a way of discrediting Esther, who acts like non-Israelite women such as Jael and Delilah in her seducing the king to get what Mordecai wants. Second, I have argued that we miss such heterocentrism because of cover-up translations. Third, I have argued that we miss it because of our heterocentrism and androcentrism, as regards our understanding of "king," and our ethnocentrism, as regards "Jew," thus rendering the narrator ineffective for non-Hebrew-language readers. As Kwok correctly argues,

> The Bible cannot be naively seen as a religious text reflecting the faith of the Hebrew people and early Christians. Instead, it must also be seen as a political text written, collected, and redacted by male colonial elites in their attempts to rewrite and reconcile with history and to reconceptualize both individual and collective identities under the shadow of the empire. (2005, 8–9)

It is hoped that this analysis of the book of Esther has contributed to going beyond a naïve, religious reading of the text to see the dangers in this book. Fourth, while some might wish to use my argument to show that the Bible is opposed to same-gender sex, I have argued that we, as people of the African diaspora who have been victims of similar strategies of gender and sexual ideologies as means of controlling us, should be wary of the happenings in this text. Thus, my bringing to our attention this ideological aspect of the text is to help us to learn to recognize it when it rears its ugly head and to resist it, not to endorse it.

WORKS CONSULTED

Ahmed, Sara. 1999. Home and Away: Narratives of Migration and Estrangement. *International Journal of Cultural Studies* 2:329–47.

Allen, Leslie C., and Timothy S. Laniak. 2003. *Ezra, Nehemiah, Esther.* NIBC. Peabody, Mass.: Hendrickson.

Amin, Samir. 1989. *Eurocentrism.* New York: Monthly Review.

Bailey, Randall C. 1991. Beyond Identification: The Use of Africans in Old Testament Poetry and Narratives. Pages 165–84 in *Stony the Road We Trod: African American Biblical Interpretation.* Edited by Cain Hope Felder. Minneapolis: Fortress.

———. 1994a. "And They Shall Know That I Am YHWH!": The P Recasting of the Plague Narratives in Exodus 7–11. *JITC* 22:1–17.

———. 1994b. "They're Nothing but Incestuous Bastards": The Polemical Use of Sex and Sexuality in Hebrew Canon Narratives. Pages 121–38 in *Social Context and Biblical Interpretation in The United States.* Vol. 1 of *Reading from This Place.* Edited by Fernando Segovia and Mary Ann Tolbert. Minneapolis: Fortress.

———. 2005. He Didn't Even Tell Us the Worst of It. *USQR* 59:15–24.

Bal, Mieke. 1988. *Death and Dissymmetry: The Politics of Coherence in the Book of Judges.* Chicago: University of Chicago Press.

———. 1999. Lots of Writing. Pages 212–38 in *Ruth and Esther: A Feminist Companion to the Bible.* Edited by Athalya Brenner. FCB 2/3. Sheffield: Sheffield Academic Press.

Beal, Timothy K. 1997. *The Book of Hiding: Gender, Ethnicity, Annihilation, and Esther.* New York: Routledge.

Berquist, Jon L. 1995. *Judaism in Persia's Shadow: A Social and Historical Approach.* Minneapolis: Fortress.

Berman, Joshua A. 2001. Hadassah and Abihail: The Evolution from Object to Subject in the Character of Esther. *JBL* 120:647–59.

Bhabha, Homi K. 1994. *The Location of Culture.* London: Routledge.

Boykin, Keith. 2005. *Beyond the Downlow: Sex, Lies, and Denial in Black America.* New York: Carol and Graf.

Cavalcanti, Tereza. 1989. The Prophetic Ministry of Women in the Hebrew Bible. Pages 118–39 in *Through Her Eyes: Women's Theology from Latin America.* Edited by Elsa Tamez. Maryknoll, N.Y.: Orbis.

Clines, David J. A. 1984. *The Esther Scroll.* JSOTSSup 30. Sheffield: Sheffield Academic Press.

Collins, Patricia Hill. 2004. *Black Sexual Politics: African Americans, Gender, and the New Racism.* New York: Routledge.

Craig, Kenneth. 1995. *Reading Esther: A Case for the Literary Carnivalesque.*
    LCBI. Louisville: Westminster John Knox.
Crawford, Sidnie Ann White. 1998. Esther. Pages 131–37 in *The Women's Bible
    Commentary.* Edited by Carol A. Newsom and Sharon H. Ringe. Expanded
    ed. Louisville: Westminster John Knox.
Davies, Philip R., and John Rogerson. 2005. *The Old Testament World.* 2nd ed.
    Louisville: Westminster John Knox.
Day, Linda. 1995. *Three Faces of a Queen: Characterization in the Books of Esther.*
    JSOTSSup 186. Sheffield: Sheffield Academic Press.
Delgado, Richard, and Jean Stefancic. 2001. *Critical Race Theory: An Introduction.*
    New York: New York University Press.
DeVries, Simon. 1985. *1 Kings.* WBC 12. Waco, Tex.: Word.
Douglas, Kelly Brown. 1999. *Sexuality and the Black Church: A Womanist Per-
    spective.* Maryknoll, N.Y.: Orbis.
Duran, Nicole. 2004. Who Wants to Marry a Persian King? Gender Games and
    Wars and the Book of Esther. Pages 71–84 in *Pregnant Passion: Gender, Sex,
    and Violence in the Bible.* Edited by Cheryl A. Kirk-Duggan. SemeiaSt 44.
    Atlanta: Society of Biblical Literature.
Fenton, Steve. 2003. *Ethnicity.* Key Concepts. Cambridge: Polity Press.
Fish, Stanley. 1980. *Is There a Text in This Class? The Authority of Interpretive
    Communities.* Cambridge: Harvard University Press.
Foucault, Michel. 1990. *The History of Sexuality.* Translated by Robert Hurley. 2
    vols. New York: Vintage Books.
Fox, Michael V. 2001. *Character and Ideology in the Book of Esther.* 2nd ed. Grand
    Rapids: Eerdmans.
Frolov, Serge. 2002. Two Eunuchs, Two Conspiracies, and One Loyal Jew: The
    Narrative of Botched Regicide in Esther as Text- and Redaction-Critical Test
    Case. *VT* 52:304–25.
Gates, Henry Louis, Jr. 1988. *The Signifying Monkey: A Theory of African Ameri-
    can Literary Criticism.* New York: Oxford University Press.
Gilroy, Paul. 1993. *The Black Atlantic: Modernity and Double Consciousness.* Cam-
    bridge: Harvard University Press.
Jennings, Theodore W., Jr. 2005. *Jacob's Wound: Homoerotic Narrative in the Lit-
    erature of Ancient Israel.* New York: Continuum.
Kirk-Duggan, Cheryl A. 1999. Black Mother Women and Daughters: Signifying
    Female-Divine Relationships in the Hebrew Bible and African-American
    Mother-Daughter Short Stories. Pages 192–210 in *Ruth and Esther: A Femi-
    nist Companion to the Bible.* Edited by Athalya Brenner. FCB 2/3. Sheffield:
    Sheffield Academic Press.
Koch, Timothy R. 2001. Cruising as Methodology: Homoeroticism and the Scrip-
    tures. Pages 169–80 in *Queer Commentary and the Hebrew Bible.* Edited by
    Ken Stone. Cleveland: Pilgrim.

Kwok Pui-Lan. 2005. *Postcolonial Imagination and Feminist Theology.* Louisville: Westminster John Knox.

Laniak, Timothy S. 1998. *Shame and Honor in the Book of Esther.* SBLDS 165. Atlanta: Scholars Press.

Levenson, Jon D. 1997. *Esther: A Commentary.* OTL. Louisville: Westminster John Knox.

Lorde, Audre. 1995. Age, Race, Class, and Sex: Women Redefining Difference. Pages 532–39 in *Race, Class, and Gender: An Anthology.* Edited by M. L. Anderson and P. H. Collins. 2nd ed. Belmont, Calif.: Wadsworth.

Marden, Peter, and David Mercer. 1998. Locating Strangers: Multiculturalism, Citizenship, and Nationhood in Australia. *Political Geography* 17:915–37.

Martin, Clarice J. 1989. A Chamberlain's Journey and the Challenge for Interpretation for Liberation. *Semeia* 47:105–35.

Masenya, Madipoane. 2001. Esther and Northern Sotho Stories: An African-South African Woman's Commentary. Pages 27–49 in *Other Ways of Reading: African Women and the Bible.* Edited by Musa W. Dube. SBLGPBS 2. Atlanta: Society of Biblical Literature.

Mosala, Itumeleng J. 1993. Implications of the Text of Esther for African Women's Struggle for Liberation in South Africa. *Semeia* 59:129–37.

O'Connor, Kathleen M. 2003. Humor in the Book of Esther. Pages 52–64 in *Are We Amused? Humour about Women in the Biblical World.* Edited by Athalya Brenner. JSOTSSup 383. London: T&T Clark.

Paton, L. B. 1908. *A Critical and Exegetical Commentary on the Book of Esther.* ICC. New York: Charles Scribner's Sons.

Patterson, Orlando. 1982. *Slavery and Social Death: A Comparative Study.* Cambridge: Harvard University Press.

Rotten.com. Eunuchs. Online: http://www.rotten.com/library/sex/castration/eunuch/.

Said, Edward. 1979. *Orientalism.* New York: Vintage.

Spivak, Gayatri Chakravorty. 1994. Can the Subaltern Speak? Pages 66–111 in *Colonial Discourse and Post-colonial Theory: A Reader.* Edited by Patrick Williams and Laura Chrisman. New York: Columbia University Press.

Vanhoozer, Kevin J. 1998. *Is There a Meaning in This Text? The Bible, the Reader, and the Morality of Literary Knowledge.* Grand Rapids: Zondervan.

Warrior, Robert Allen. 2005. Canaanites, Cowboys and Indians. *USQR* 59:1–8. Orig. published in *Christianity and Crisis* 49 (1989): 261–65.

Weems, Renita J. 1988. A Crown of Thorns (Vashti and Esther). Pages 99–110 in idem, *Just a Sister Away: A Womanist Vision of Women's Relationships in the Bible.* San Diego: LauraMedia.

Westermann, Claus. 982. *Genesis 37–50: A Commentary.* Translated by John J. Scullion. Minneapolis: Ausburg.

Wills, Lawrence. 1998. The Depiction of Slavery in the Ancient Novel. *Semeia* 83–84:113–32.

Wolf, Naomi. 1995. The Beauty Myth. Pages 417–22 in *Race, Class and Gender: An Anthology*. Edited by Margaret L. Anderson and Patricia Hill Collins. 2nd ed. Boston: Wadsworth.

Wong, Angela Wai Ching. 2004. Esther. Pages 135–41 in *Global Bible Commentary*. Edited by Daniel Patte. Nashville: Abingdon.

Queering Closets and Perverting Desires: Cross-Examining John's Engendering and Trans-Gendering Word across Different Worlds

Tat-siong Benny Liew

In "A Fire in Fontana," Hisaye Yamamoto writes briefly about her experience with segregated public restrooms in the South. She, a Japanese American, was generally able to "pass" and enter the ones labeled "white" without being challenged. Except once, Yamamoto recalls, a black cleaning woman in a "white" restroom gave her a long look. This, Yamamoto reasons, has to do with the fact that "the Negro woman had never seen a Japanese before" (1992, 368). James Kyung-Jin Lee, commenting on this restroom encounter as one in which Yamamoto's "racial identity is put into crisis in a racialized space that she cannot avoid," points out that the scene is made up of a series of misrecognitions by Yamamoto, including (1) her dismissal of her own racialization as a person of color in entering the "white" restroom; (2) her unawareness that what allows her to "pass" and pee in peace is the "invisibility" of her Asian-raced body in a black-and-white world; (3) her failure to see the irony of meeting a black woman in a segregated space that the latter can clean but never use; and (4) her mistaking of the black woman's knowing gaze as an act of ignorance (2004, 83–84).

Instead of racial binarism and segregation, Marjorie Garber writes about another system that confronts another group of people at the doors of public restrooms (1992, 13–15). For transvestites and transsexuals, the public restroom is a place of gender binarism and "urinary segregation" (Lacan 1977, 151). To "pass," Garber suggests, cross-dressers choose to (mis)read the signs on the doors of public restroom literally. Rather than pointing to male and female spaces, the stick figure in pants and the one in a skirt or dress signify for them a division by male and female clothing.

Perhaps not coincidentally, David L. Eng and Alice Y. Hom also begin their anthology on queer Asian Americans with a couple of misrecognition scenes in a public restroom (1998, 1). Both involve a white woman mistaking a masculine-looking Asian American lesbian in a women's restroom as a man. Eng and Hom explain that in both scenarios, "It is precisely mainstream stereotypes of an effeminized Asian American male (homo)sexuality that affect the ways in which the Asian American lesbian goes unseen and unrecognized" (1).

I begin with these scenarios to point to the multiple convergences of race, gender, and sexuality that must be recognized. Race, gender, and sexuality are not just analogous; they are entwined and imbricated with each other.[1] Kimberlé Williams Crenshaw calls this a "structural intersectionality"; intersections, for her, create a qualitatively different experience that cannot be understood in terms of any isolated identity factor or simple quantitative additions (1995).[2] If such convergences are present in deciding who should or should not enter a particular public restroom, they are also at work in legislating who may or may not have entry into the national space of the U.S. (Epps 2001; Luibhéid 2005, xiv–xvi; Somerville 2005).

The 1875 Page Law, for instance, disallowed Asian women from entering the U.S. for "lewd and immoral purposes" such as prostitution. One sees here already a coming together of racial-ethnic, gender, and sexual anxieties. Even when "immorality" is not stated, one can still see the convergence at work in the so-called Ladies Agreement of 1920, which barred Japanese brides from joining their husbands in the U.S. because of these women's presumably "threatening" childbearing rates. Similarly, when "national origin" was used to substitute "race" as a criterion for exclusion, the 1952 Immigration and Nationality Act simultaneously introduced "homosexuality" and "adultery" as explicit reasons to disqualify people who sought entry or citizenship. Supposedly all three factors concern the security of families in the nation as well as the national family, because "sexual deviants," with their "lack of emotional stability ... [and] ... weakness of ... moral fiber ... [make] them susceptible to the blandishments of the *foreign* espionage agent" (cited in Somerville 2005, 80; emphasis added). More recently, a 1993 campaign (Operation Hold the Line) invoked the particular threat of the "vestidas" (Mexican transvestite sex workers)—and their assumed association with HIV/AIDS—to underscore the need to "secure" the border with Mexico. Once again, hegemonic systems about race/ethnicity, gender, and sexuality converge to mark certain bodies as "emblem[s] of menacing excess and indeterminacy," and hence social chaos (Solomon 2005, 18).

---

1. This is not to deny that a lot of parallels exist between, say, Asian Americans and gays. Just to name one simple example, the dominant media has painted both groups as economically successful with higher-than-average disposable incomes. What get lost in analogies are the particularities of each identity group/factor as well as the interconnectedness and mutual implications that may exist between or among these identity groups/factors being analogized. For helpful critiques of analogic analysis or argument, see Joseph 2002, 80–94; Jakobsen 2003.

2. See also the work of another African American woman or womanist scholar, Audre Lorde (1998). My thanks to Randall C. Bailey for pointing me to Lorde's early but enduring text.

John's Jesus: A Transgendering Traveler?

John's Gospel tells of a Jesus who also trans-forms, enters into another world, and suffers the death of a criminal. One question that has long perplexed Johannine studies is the echoes or relations that exist between a female Wisdom and a male Word or Logos.[3] In the eyes of most feminist scholars, this Sophia-Jesus (con)figuration represents a regrettable process of masculinization, through which the male displaces or replaces the female and becomes (re)established as the norm (Levine 1990, 155; McKinlay 1996).[4] This complaint reminds me, however, of Garber's analysis of the 1982 film *Tootsie* (1992, 5–9). For Garber, seeing Dustin Hoffman's unemployed Michael Dorsey turning into a hugely successful Dorothy Michaels as yet another case of male preempting female results from a failure to see the whole picture. Rushing to look *through* Hoffman's character as Michael rather than Dorothy, (re)viewers end up not looking *at* and thus overlooking or even crossing out Michael/Dorothy's character as a cross-dresser. Garber goes on to suggest that this viewing or reading failure may have much to do with one's own rigid understanding of gender. Since gender is either male or female for most people, they are not equipped or prepared to see or read a transgendering character.[5]

If one follows the trajectory of the Wisdom/Word or Sophia/Jesus (con)figuration, what we have in John's Jesus is not only a "king of Israel" (1:49; 12:13–15) or "king of the *Ioudaioi*" (18:33, 39; 19:3, 14–15, 19–22), but also a

---

3. Representative works on this question spans over literally decades; see, for example, R. Brown 1966, cxxii–cxxv; A. Collins 1982; Scott 1992; and Conway 2003b, 175–79. Examples that point to connections between Sophia and John's Jesus include, among others: (1) their intimacy with God; (2) their role in creation; (3) their bridging function between God and humanity; (4) their search for human recognition; and (5) their roles as teacher, revelator, and host who provides food and drink.

4. While Ringe suggests a similar process of masculinization to be at work in the works of Philo, she is less forthcoming concerning the dynamics at play in John (1999, 29–45, 57). While her own reading focuses on the feminine or Wisdom-like qualities that are being emphasized in the Fourth Gospel (particularly John's understanding of community as accompaniment), she nevertheless proposes that the "masculinization" of the "beloved disciple" as a "son" in 19:26 is the Johannine community's nod to "a church increasingly marked by the patriarchalism and hierarchalism of the surrounding Roman society" (17). Not to be (dis)missed here is the curious reversal that Ringe seems to want to bring about: in contrast to a female Sophia being turned into a male Jesus, Ringe is advocating a switch of the "beloved disciple" from male to female. For alternative and more hopeful readings of this shift from or between a female Sophia and a male Logos/Jesus, see Rivera 2004, 198–203; Goss 2006, 550–51.

5. I am using "transgendering" here as an umbrella term that challenges all restrictive gender or engendering categories; thus, it covers various conceptions and practices of gender blending such as transvestism and transsexualism.

drag king (6:15; 18:37; 19:12).[6] Accordingly, this essay explores a different—even transgressive—reading strategy and the implications of reading John's Sophia/ Jesus less as female or male, but more as a transvestite. This is, in other words, an attempt to see or read otherwise and a desire to probe other "signs" that may be present in the text of John, particularly those that concern and overlap with race/ethnicity and sexuality.

THE TEXT OF THE GARMENT AND THE GARMENT OF THE TEXT

This reading is in my view plausible given not only John's emphasis on progressive revelation (13:7; 14:25–26; 16:12–14), but also scholars' ready admission of John's Jesus as an enigmatic figure (Berenson Maclean 2003, 48). According to Stephen D. Moore, for example, there is a contradiction between Jesus' speech and Jesus' person (1994, 59).

FROM JACOB TO VIEWING FLUIDITY

After the prologue in which Wisdom/Word is introduced (1:1–18), Jesus spends some time with the Baptizer and the Baptizer's disciples (1:19–42). Then he goes to Galilee, attends a wedding in Cana, and stays a few days at Capernaum (1:43–2:12). After several interactions in Jerusalem (2:13–3:21) and the Judean countryside (3:22–36), Jesus decides to return to Galilee by way of Samaria (3:27–4:4).

Many Johannine scholars have elaborated on the pivotal role Jacob plays in the exchange between Jesus and the Samaritan woman (Neyrey 1979; Moloney 1993, 137–43, 150). Not only is the city of Sychar associated with Jacob's inheritance and Jacob's well forms the backdrop for and a topic of Jesus' conversation with the woman (4:4–11), but also the Samaritan woman will wonder aloud about the comparative greatness of Jacob and Jesus (4:12). Jesus, of course, will respond not only by comparing his eternal-life-giving and forever-thirst-quenching water with Jacob's provisional provision of a well (4:13–15) but also by trumping the worship that the woman has inherited from her ancestral fathers with the spiritual and truth-full worship of his Father (4:16–24).

In addition to expanding Jacob's significance for the first four chapters of the Fourth Gospel, Jennifer K. Berenson Maclean has helpfully reminded us that

---

6. Because of the anti-Jewish implications of translating the Greek *Ioudaioi* as "Jews," I will leave the word untranslated. For examples of attempts to struggle with the issue of John and anti-Judaism, see Rensberger 1999; Goodwin 1999; and Lea 1999. I will have more to say about the meaning and implications of this word in a latter part of this essay. Note that Michael Joseph Brown has recently concluded his assessment of African American biblical scholarship with a suggestion that transvestitism be used as a hermeneutics to inform one's reading of the Bible, although Brown fails in my view to flesh out his suggestion with theoretical arguments for or practical illustrations of such a hermeneutics (2004, 175–83).

Jacob's benefactory role is tied up with his dubious trickery and deception.[7] While Berenson Maclean uses that insight to make sense of John's negative depiction of the *Ioudaioi* as a deceptive and rebellious people and argue for Jesus' recreation of God's people—and thus Jesus' superior trickery and ultimate supplanting of the Hebrew "supplanter"—in John, I would like to spend more time than Berenson Maclean actually does on Jacob's acts of trickery.

After trading food and drink that he has prepared for Esau's birthright as the firstborn son (Gen 25:27–34), Jacob—under the instruction and with the help of his mother, Rebekah—tricks his father, Isaac, and receives the blessing that is meant for Esau with another offering of food and drink (Gen 27:1–40). Jacob's trickeries involve, therefore, both identity reversal and identity theft. More significantly for my purposes, Jacob's second trick is a physical masquerade. He puts on not only Esau's "best garment" but also hairy animal skins to cover up his own "smooth skin" (Gen 27:11–12, 15–16, 22–23, 27). Jacob is, in other words, an impersonator—and he does so with the help of costumes and prosthetics.

Jacob's disguise is undoubtedly related to John's portrayal of Jesus as the sacrificial Passover lamb (1:29; 19:12–18). Rather than equating Jacob's dress then with simply Jesus' tricky embodiment or putting on of human flesh and thus reading John single-dimensionally, one should be careful not to (dis)miss either the gender dynamics or the visual focus that is present in both Genesis and John. Later I will return to the Rebekah/Isaac or Mother/Father dynamics; let me note now that Jacob's success in deceiving Isaac has much to do with Isaac's poor eyesight (Gen 27:1). John's Gospel is, of course, full of references to seeing (1:14, 29, 32–34, 36, 50–51; 4:35; 6:2, 14, 40; 9:37–39; 11:45; 12:21, 39–42; 14:17; 15:24; 16:16–24; 19:35, 37; 20:8). Repeatedly, readers are invited to "come and see" (1:39, 46; 4:29; 11:34). In one of the signs—and hence centers of controversies—in John, a man who is born blind is able to see, while his neighbors and the Pharisees turn out to have trouble seeing (9:1–10, 39–41).

Among Johannine scholars, Colleen M. Conway is one who has done much to keep us from losing sight of gender dynamics in John's characterization (1999; 2003b).[8] She further titles her most recent essay with John's own visualizing language (2003a). The phrase Conway chooses is one spoken by Pilate in reference

---

7. Berenson Maclean points to the contrast between Jacob's trickery and Nathaniel's identity as a true Israelite without "guile" as well as Jesus' reference to himself as Jacob('s ladder)—in other words, the bridge between God and humanity—in Jesus' response to Nathaniel (1:45–51). Finally, she compares and contrasts Jacob's marriage arrangements with Leah and Rebecca (Gen 29) with Jesus' "sign" at a wedding in Cana (John 2:1–11).

8. John's gender consciousness is shown by the way he uses the word "woman" repeatedly (4:7, 9, 11, 15, 17, 19, 21, 25, 27–28, 39, 42; 20:13, 15) and the way he uses *anthropos* and *andros* synonymously to refer to a male, as evidenced by his use of *anthropos* to talk about circumcision (7:22–23) and "valid witnesses" (8:17). On several occasions, including the healing of the man born blind, different characters also refer to Jesus as an *anthropos* (9:11, 16, 24; 18:29; 19:5). As

to Jesus, "Behold the man" (19:5). Juxtaposing vision and gender, it captures well what Conway wants us to see, namely, John's complex construction of Jesus' masculinity. What Conway does not point out is that this call to see by Pilate actually follows a description of Jesus' headdress ("the crown of thorns," 19:5) and Jesus' garment ("the purple robe," 19:5) and that this same description is given not once but twice (19:2). Furthermore, Pilate will make a similar call, "Behold your king," in 19:14. My reading of Jesus' gender in John must involve then a good look *at* his (drag-)kingly appearance, or more precisely, a careful investigation of how his dress relates to his Jacob-like but Jacob-supplanting trickery or disguise. It is time, in other words, to address Jesus' dress.

FROM TEXTUAL TO TEXTILE DYNAMICS

Conway is correct that John gives us "no incontrovertible hint of [Jesus'] biological maleness" (2003a, 164).[9] She is also more or less correct that "the Gospel provides no description whatsoever of Jesus' body" (171).[10] What the Fourth Gospel does contain are several references to Jesus' clothing. In fact, these references are often made in places that are strategic to the turning of the Gospel's plot, particularly in its second half (11:1–21:25). I would propose that Jesus' clothing engenders a text or a story in which the clothes literally make the "man," or mark the protagonist's transgendering identity as Sophia/Jesus. Like clothing, Sophia/Jesus puts on a gender to conceal and reveal, and this cross-dresser's biology basically remains veiled throughout John's Gospel. Again, my goal here is to point out or look at rather than see through Jesus' gender uncertainty.

Let me begin by returning to Pilate's call to "behold" in 19:1–5, 14. While most have read the "crown of thorns" and the "purple robe" as the Romans' sarcastic, but John's ironic, display of Jesus' royalty, a crown of thorns was actually a stable item in ancient Greek weddings. During a feast at the house of the father of the bride, right before the bride could take off her veil, a child would wear a crown of thorns and offer bread from a sieve to the guests. According to Anne Carson, what this signifies is that "[t]he thorny and savage bride … is about to be salvaged for civilization … [a]nd that redeeming function is represented in the relation between leaky vessel (the sieve in which bread is carried) and the good gift of bread itself which ritual calls forth from the leaky vessel" (1999, 91). This ritual is therefore a centering act in more than one sense: it disciplines the bride,

---

one learns from contemporary literature on cross-dressing, drag kings and queens, as well as those who write about them, refer to them in the gender that they are performing.

9. Conway specifically mentions as her evidence here, in contrast to Luke (2:21), John's lack of any reference to Jesus' circumcision.

10. John does tell us that Jesus' (dead) body has no broken bones (19:31–37) and that his (risen) body carries scars of his wounds (20:19–20, 24–28).

and it directs everyone's vision toward the bride. Pilate's emphasis on vision, then, may have to do with unveiling a wild but now captured bride in a wedding as much as seeing a king.[11] Although Jesus displaces a bridegroom by providing wine in a wedding at Cana (2:1–11) and is compared by the Baptizer to a "bridegroom" (3:27–30), he ends up appearing as a drag-kingly bride in his passion.

In addition, we find Jesus disrobing and rerobing in the episode that marks Jesus' focus on the disciples with the coming of his "hour" (13:3–5, 12). This disrobing, as Conway points out, does not disclose anything about Jesus' anatomy. Instead, it describes Jesus washing his disciples' feet. As more than one commentator has pointed out, foot-washing was generally only done by Jewish women or non-Jewish slaves.[12] John is clear that Jesus is an *Ioudaios* (4:9, 22; 18:33–35; 19:40); what John is less clear about is whether Jesus is a biological male. Like a literary striptease, this episode is suggestive, even seductive; it shows and withholds at the same time.

At another strategic point of John's narrative (Jesus' crucifixion or glorification), John tells us that Jesus wears a "seamless" tunic under his clothes (19:23–24). Of course, John connects this detail with what he finds in the Hebrew scriptures, and some scholars have linked Jesus' seamless tunic to his priestly role (Brown 1970, 920–22) or church unity (Moloney 1998, 143–44, 146).[13] Adopting cross-dressing or transgendering as a reading position, however, I will note not only that clothing is strategic in the lives and practices of drag kings but also that "seamlessness" is actually a favored and treasured vocabulary of many theorists on transvestitism and queer sexuality (Halberstam 1998, 110; Sifuentes-Jáuregui 2002, 4; Gopinath 2005, 184; see also Schlossberg 2001, 6). After all, what cross-dressers hope for is that the gender they perform "become seamlessly their own" (Volcano and Halberstam 1999, 75). The fact that this seamless tunic is only revealed and removed from Jesus at his death further signifies that he has—ironically, despite his death from and in a sort of (over)exposure (11:45–50; 12:9–23;

---

11. Some may want to equate Jesus with the child rather than the bride because of his wearing of the thorny crown. I would argue that such a rigid reading or distinction fails to take into consideration how the child functions to present or represent the bride in ancient Greek weddings. Put differently, the child and the bride are in a sense interchangeable.

12. For example, Abigail is the one who washes David's feet in 1 Sam 25:41. In the *Odyssey*, upon his return home in disguise, Odysseus asks an old woman to wash his feet, instead of the young female maid who has been assigned to the task by Penelope (19.335–507). Note also that as many have suggested (D. Lee 2002, 197–211; Webster 2003, 92–94), John provides a parallel to this foot-washing scene with Mary washing Jesus' feet (11:2; 12:1–8). For one description of this foot-washing practice, see Plato, *Symposium* 175a. On the intersection of women and slaves in the Greco-Roman world, see Murnaghan and Joshel 1998.

13. In addition to linking the tunic to the priestly role or function to purify, Webster also makes a connection between the "linen towel" (*lention*) that Jesus picks up to gird himself (13:4) and the "linen wrappings" (*othonia*, 20:6–7) in the empty tomb to argue that the foot-washing scene should be read in the context of Jesus' death and resurrection (2003, 96, 108).

19:13–20)—always played a veiled role. Even when the tunic is removed, John discloses to us "no biological or anatomical certainty but [only] a space of desire and possibility" (Garber 1992, 88). It is revealing that John's Jesus uses a "cloak" (*prophasin*) to talk about a cover, an excuse or a rationalization of sin (15:22); clothing for John is something that helps and hinders at the same time what one sees. That is also why one finds in John an emphasis on seeing, but also a distrust of appearance (7:24; see also 2:23–24; 4:48; 20:29).

Larissa Bonfante, in her study of "nudity" in ancient Greek art, concludes that naked bodies of Greek male both display and define what is "heroic, divine, athletic, and youthful" (1989, 549). Since these virtues or qualities are found in neither women nor non-Greek men, their bodies are best and often covered (Henderson 1999, 21, 30). Of course, both Greek philosophers (Plato, *Republic* 452a–e) and historians (Herodotus, *Histories* 1.8–12; Thucydides, *History* 1.5–6) have explicitly articulated this association between shame and naked women or naked non-Greek men. Karen Bassi, extending Bonfante's work on nudity as costume to address actual vestimentary practice, suggests that in the Greek world ostentatious clothing is also associated with women and foreigners (1998, 105–15). With what she calls the "Pandora paradigm" (111, 130), Bassi relates Hesiod's comments about how the elaborate dress of the "first woman" created by Zeus serves to conceal the lies and deceits Hermes fashions within her (*Theogony* 573–583; *Works and Days* 54–78) to illustrate the seamless cultural (ideo)logic that elides women, excess, clothing, concealment, deception, and trickery. It is this same (ideo)logic that causes Solon to "strangely" forbid women from going outdoors with more than three garments (Plutarch, *Life of Solon* 21.4). Ironically, women's excessive concerns with excessive clothing simultaneously reveal and conceal at once their suspect "nature." No less ironical is the cultural assumption that women like clothes and women need clothes to cover their shame and their sham. Such a need is obviously magnified for women who cross-dress as men. Thus, one finds in Aristophanes' *Ecclesiazousae* the concern of male imperson-ators not to "expose even a glimpse of your body" (93–97).

Jesus' "seamless tunic" betrays, then, his drag-kingly concern to conceal his body in order to perform masculinity. Reading Jesus as a drag king may also help explain the puzzling statement about Peter's robing in John 21:7. If this meeting of Peter with his resurrected Lord is a classic *anagnorisis* or recognition scene (Cave 1988), one must remember that such recognition is prefaced by another rhetorical convention: that of likemindedness or *homophrosunē* (Zeitlin 1996, 293). Peter's concern to be clothed, read in this light, is because of his awareness of Jesus' love of and dependence on clothing, "seamless tunic" and otherwise.

FROM CLOTHING ENIGMA TO PASSING LINES

Besides clothing, cross-dressers also have to pay close attention to imperson-ate another's speech, or what Brad Epps calls "passing lines" (2001). The Fourth

Gospel happens to place as much emphasis on "hearing" as it does on "seeing" (3:8, 39; 4:42; 5:25, 28, 30; 8:43, 47; 9:27; 11:42; 12:27–30; 14:24; 16:12–15; 18:37).[14] I have pointed out elsewhere that John's Jesus is his Father's "ventriloquized voice" (2002, 206). More than once Jesus professes that "I have not spoken on my own" (12:49a) and confesses that "the word that you hear is not mine, but is from the Father who sent me" (14:24b–c; see also 7:16–18; 8:28–29). In addition to making the connection between clothing and women, Bassi has shown how the Greco-Roman world generally frowned upon "mediated speech" as feminine and suspect (1998, 42–98). What that world valued instead was direct and unmediated speech, which was supposed to be the form of communication between elite males.

In addition to being his Father's "ventriloquized voice," John's Jesus is known for double-talking, as he himself readily admits (16:25; see also 10:6). He does so sometimes with language that contains double meaning, such as "to be born from above and/or to be born again" (*gennēthē anōthen*, 3:3), or "running water and/or living water" (*hudōr zōn*, 4:10). Other times he uses a word in both its literal and metaphorical meaning, such as "temple" (2:19–21), "food" (4:31–34), "bread" (6:32–35), and "sleep" (11:11–14). John's Jesus can also lie: after telling his brothers that he would not go to Judea for the Festival of Booths, he turns around and goes there secretly (7:1–10). His language is so confusing to his hearers that, one time, some circle him and say, "Until when are you holding our soul in suspense? If you are the Christ, tell us straight" (10:24). Not shooting straight, like mediated speech, is a female characteristic in the Greco-Roman world. Both Aphrodite and Hera, for example, have been associated with beguiling talk (*Iliad* 3.405; 14.300). If mediated and deceptive speech speak women and Jesus is guilty of both, his speech pattern is pointing more and more to his visual deception as a cross-dresser.[15]

Finally, given the aforementioned connection between excess and women, one may also think about the excessive speaking on the part of John's Jesus (at least until he is arrested and turns quiet before Pilate, 19:8–10).[16] John's Jesus

---

14. The importance of both "seeing" and "hearing" in John is nicely presented with two sets of parallel scenes. First, right after a long chapter on the importance of "seeing" (the healing of the man born blind, 9:1–41), the next chapter has Jesus delivering speeches that contain a cluster of references to "hearing" (10:3–5, 16, 27). Second, in John 20, Jesus' resurrection is recognized through the "seeing" of the beloved disciple (20:8) and the "hearing" of Mary Magdalene (20:16).

15. Later, Pilate will also demand John's Jesus to be "straight" with him but ends up utterly frustrated by Jesus' ambiguous talk and obstinate silence (18:33–38; 19:6–11).

16. Jesus turns quiet after Pilate asks the question, "What is truth?" (18:38–19:10). With this silence, Jesus, the cross-dressing performer, becomes a mime. Jacques Derrida suggests that "[t]he mime ... manifests the very meaning of what he is presently writing: of what he *performs*. He enables the thing to be perceived in person, in its true face.... We are faced then with mim-

talks unashamedly about himself through his well-known "I am" sayings (6:35, 41, 48, 51; 8:12; 9:5; 10:7, 9, 11; 11:25; 14:6; 15:1), which Satoko Yamaguchi has helpfully associated with "female figures" such as Ishtar, Sibyl, Sophia, and Isis (2002, 51–65). In addition, he also talks incessantly with many long monologues. After the Prologue's "In the beginning was the Word" (1:1a), what one encounters in the Fourth Gospel is a form of logorrhea by Jesus. According to Maud W. Gleason (1995), ancient rhetoric, as a means to separate elite men from imposters, is also a way to fashion and perform masculinity. In that light, John's Jesus comes across as such a hyper performer of rhetoric, and thus masculinity, that he ends up betraying his imposter status. I am, in effect, suggesting that Jesus' rhetorical excesses are meant to represent the cross-dresser. John is indulging in such literary excesses that his Jesus is performing male transvestitism rather than masculinity. At the same time, Jesus' wordiness also demonstrates his belief in the force of the speech act, and thus the effect of performance in general. Performative acts, both speech and bodily, are productive—"All things through [(the) Word(s)] came to be" (1:3a). Like speech and with speech, transvestitism is able to produce a "realness" or "realness-effect" that is otherwise not there (Sifuentes-Jáuregui 2002, 4, 180).

Despite these hints of femininity that I have pointed to, I must emphasize that I am not trying to suggest that John's Jesus is "really" a female. Doing so would be committing Garber's criticism of rushing to look *through* John's Jesus without looking *at* him as a transvestite. Nor am I suggesting that John's Jesus is an androgyny or a "failed" man. What I am attempting is something that is in my view more radical. First, I want to suggest an illegibility or indeterminacy that displaces the male and/or female structure. Jesus' cross-dressing body in John is a truly porous and polysemous site/sight in which a collection or a range of gender meanings converge, collude, collide, and compete with each other. Second, instead of thinking of an essential core identity that is interior and immutable (in terms of gender or otherwise), I want to suggest that John's cross-dressing Jesus shows that a so-called "core" is but a(n significant) effect of bodily acts (Butler 1990). What this effects is not a premature celebration of freedom that one can be anything that one wants to be but a call to analyze and perhaps even challenge the discursive and material forces that discipline one's acts, practices, and identities.

---

icry imitating nothing.... this speculum reflects no reality: it produces mere 'reality-effects'" (1981, 205–6, emphasis original). In preparation for a later development of this essay, I will suggest that Derrida is hinting here that, like a transvestite, a mime deconstructs the idea of the origin(al). In that sense, one may read Jesus' silence as in fact his answer to Pilate's question about truth, namely, the need to look beyond "truth" to see the constructions being parodied in the person of a transvestite. Jesus is, in other words, giving up his speech intentionally, so Pilate can concentrate on Jesus' bodily performance as a border-crossing cross-dresser.

Copying, Copulating, and Incubating Desires

I have been suggesting that, although John constantly refers to the (con)figuration of Wisdom/Word or Sophia/Jesus through various debates over Jesus' origin, most Johannine readers have joined most Johannine characters in their inability to see and read John's transgendering dynamics, or the connection and transition among incarnation, im-personation, and cross-dressing. Although I will also suggest that I am making a differentiation between John's "intentions" (however defined) and what results from my adoption of a transgendering reading position, I do not think that such a differentiation would warrant approaching my reading with a "take-it-or-leave-it" attitude (Spivak 2002, 57). In addition to making a connection between teaching and impersonation, Jane Gallop further points out that impersonation is a "double structure" that is "both serious and comic" (1995, 5). This is especially so since impersonation or cross-dressing reflects the desires of the audience as much as those of the performer. If John specifies that his own purpose for writing the Fourth Gospel is to give life and admits that this purpose dictates his selection and deletion of materials (20:30–31; 21:25; see also 6:40; 10:10, 28), I will likewise insist that my selective reading of John aims to redress the wrongs that have been suffered by people who have not been gendered strictly as either male or female. Put differently, my reading or seeing otherwise hopes to give recognition and life to those who desire to live otherwise gendered or transgendered lives (Butler 2004, 2, 4, 8, 12, 29–30). Furthermore, I would like to suggest that approaching John from a transgendering reading position leads to several "category crises" that are theologically, ideologically, and politically significant.

"Category crisis" is a term that Garber uses to refer to how cross-dressing or transgendering may subvert gender as a category (1992, 9). As Halberstam (1998) argues, drag kings testify to the inability of the biological male to monopolize masculinity.[17] For Garber, however, the presence of cross-dressers further points to *other* "category crises" beyond that of gender (1992, 16–17, 90). In what follows, I would like to turn to four categories that turn into sources of "anxieties" in John: (1) an original and originating deity; (2) desire; (3) the question of absence and presence; and (4) the idea of family. Although in a way that is true to "category crisis," it will become clear that even these four are leaky categories that cannot be neatly contained.

---

17. While John affirms the material world by seeing Jesus as the Word who engenders all life and existence, John's opposition to any kind of biological determinism is implied in his emphasis on the spirit (3:6; 6:26–27, 63). For an argument that John actually transcends the material and spiritual division, see Moore 2003.

AN ORIGINAL/ORIGINATING FATHER

In contrast to Chevalier d'Eon, the famously controversial cross-dressing diplomat of eighteenth-century Europe who once penned and underlined that "*God has no regard for the appearance of persons*" (cited in Kates 1991, 186) but whose presence at church was deemed by church officials to be a distraction from God (181), Jesus' presence in John is consistently depicted as one who directs attention and remains attentive to the Father. Not only is Jesus sent by the Father (5:23, 36–38; 6:29, 44, 57; 7:16, 18, 29, 33; 8:16, 18, 42; 9:4; 10:36; 11:42; 12:44–45; 13:3, 20; 15:21; 16:5; 17:3, 8, 18, 21, 23, 25; 20:21), but he is also faithful as the Father's representative and spokesperson (3:34; 4:34; 5:30; 6:38–39; 8:26–29, 40, 54–55; 10:18; 12:49–50; 14:10, 24, 31; 15:15; 17:4, 14; 18:11).

While the Samaritan woman wants to know about the comparative "greatness" of Jacob and Jesus (4:12), we will later find a group of *Ioudaioi* calling Jesus a "Samaritan" (8:48) and similarly comparing the "greatness" of Jesus to that of Abraham (Jacob's grandfather) and the prophets (8:53). The context of this latter comparison is a series of episodes under the backdrop of various Jewish festivals (5:1–10:42; see Yee 1989). If the first four chapters have Jesus supplanting the supplanter Jacob as well as John the Baptizer (1:15, 26–27, 30, 35–37; 3:25–30; 4:1; see also 5:36; 10:40–42), this section of John will focus on Jesus supplanting Moses, who is also a pretender impersonating as Pharaoh's son.[18] In contrast to Abraham, whose role is limited to 8:31–59, Moses is the prophet who gives the law but becomes the bone of contention in every chapter and every festival of this section (5:39, 45–47; 6:30–35, 45–51, 58; 7:19, 22–23, 38, 42, 49, 52; 8:17–18; 9:28–29; 10:34–36). What makes Jesus greater than Moses and the law he gives is, of course, already hinted at in the Prologue (Hooker 1997, 71–74). Unlike Moses, whose request to see God ends up in only a glimpse of God's back(side?) in Exod 33, John's Jesus is the only one who "has ever seen God" (1:18; see also 1:45–51; 3:11–16, 32; 5:37; 6:46; 7:28–29; 8:16–19, 38, 54–55; 10:14–15; 12:44–46; 14:6–11; 15:20–25; 16:1–3; 17:20–25).[19] From this unique and exclusive perspective, John's Jesus is able to pronounce that he "can do nothing on his own, but only what he sees the Father doing; for whatever the Father does, the Son does likewise" (5:19).

---

18. In 12:37–41 we will find out that one of the prophets whom John's Jesus supplants—in addition to Moses—is Isaiah.

19. Notice how these passages in John often highlight Jesus' unique and greater vision in connection with or in contrast to Moses, as well as how these passages seem to cluster within the section of John under consideration (5:1–10:42). Webster delineates the contrast between Jesus and Jacob in John 4 in terms of source, the contrast between Jesus and Moses in John 6 in terms of quantity, and the contrast between Jesus' wine and other(s'?) wine in terms of quality (2003, 70). I should also point out, as Randall Bailey pointed out to me, that Jacob, whom John's Jesus seems or aims to supplant, has actually also claimed to have seen God in Gen 32:30.

Butler, using the "theatricity" of transvestitism as an example, has argued that, once gender is understood to be performative, the differentiation between copy and original also becomes problematic (1990, 31, 137–38). This is particularly pertinent given Jesus' own confession to be the Father's copy or copier in John. This confession does not, however, mean that the Father is the original, since Jesus obviously copies his copying act also from the Father. Jesus is, in other words, not imitating the Father as much as imitating the Father imitating. To adopt a statement by Garber on cross-dressing, "[t]he question of an 'original'… here is immediately put *out* of question. There is in the [world of John] nothing *but* gender parody" (1992, 338).

John's Jesus imitates the Father imitating. John's "maverick Gospel" (Kysar 1993) turns now into a Gospel of masquerade that centers on not one but two cross-dressers. Given the association between women and clothes in the Homeric tradition, it should come as no surprise that women are often portrayed as both makers and givers of garment. For instance, Athena has done this for Hera (*Iliad* 14.175–183), and Odysseus has received clothing from both Nausicaa (*Odyssey* 6.277) and Penelope (*Odyssey* 23.153–162). What, then, does it say about the Father if he is the one who sends Jesus to the world below and thus presumably the one who gives Jesus his fleshly garment as well as garment for his flesh? In the story of Jacob, it is also the mother who gives instructions to and demands obedience from Jacob in a plot to deceive the father (Gen 27:5–13). Rebekah, as a woman with balls, is in a sense also a transvestite.[20]

What gender parody or parody in general does with its emphasis on artificiality and replicability is what Garber has also called "the transvestite effect" (1992, 36). It challenges and disrupts all self-contained boundary, stable identity, unquestioned primacy as well as the idea of an omnipotent and original father or Father-God. The category crisis of gender has now turned elsewhere: what surfaces is an anxious crisis over one's certain knowledge about the divine. Thinking about mimicry, Homi K. Bhabha not only emphasizes its link to the visual but also cites Jacques Lacan's understanding of mimicry as a camouflage that brings about a "mottling" effect rather than just situating "against a mottled background" (1994, 85, 88). The same can be said of John's Jesus with his mimicry or cross-dressing act: it blends, blurs, and blotches in such a way that it actually breaks things, including the Father, up and breaks them down. What Sophia/Jesus reveals is that the Father or the vinedresser (15:1) also has a closet of other dresses, and what this closet reveals is a Father who is losing ground or who is no

---

20. Webster suggests that John's reservation about the law has to do with John's emphasis on eating Jesus' flesh and drinking Jesus' blood (6:53–56), since Lev 17:10–14 is explicitly against the drinking of blood (2003, 83–84). I wonder if John's reservation does not have to do with two other things: the association of the law with Moses as the embodiment of Wisdom/Word or Sophia/Jesus; and the prohibition against cross-dressing in Deut 22:5.

longer the ground. At or as "ground zero," his role as the original and originating Sender—despite John's rhetoric about God or the Father being "true" (3:33; 7:28; 8:26; 17:3)—is also a masquerade. Beyond Robert E. Goss's recent queer reading of John that God "comes out" in Jesus as a lover (2006, 548–49), the Father ends up outing himself in all sorts of way through the sending the Jesus.[21]

DESIRE

Not to be lost in this discussion is the closeted affair of how subjects/objects of desire become incestuous and transferable in John. As the Father's mirror (image), John's Jesus may be understood in terms of a metaphorical equation that reflects or sheds light on the Father. Jane S. Webster has suggested, in her discussion of Johannine metaphors, that metaphors literally mean "to carry out a change" and that it often involves a juxtaposition of two different things or ideas with a copula "is" (2003, 6). Derrida, in his reading of Hegel's reading of the Gospels, has wondered aloud about how this copula linking the Father and Jesus becomes a copulation between the Father and Jesus because of the penetrating language in John 14 (1986, 68–69).[22]

Moore has questioned Jesus' thirst or desire in John (2003). Referring to Jesus' request for a drink from the Samaritan woman (4:6) as well as Jesus' cry "I thirst" on the cross (19:14), Moore argues that Jesus, the supposed dispenser of living and forever-thirst-quenching water, is himself thirsty to be desired by the woman, desirous of fulfilling Hebrew scriptures, and—shall I say—literally dying to be with the Father (see also Webster 2003, 126–27). Moreover, Moore notes that the Father himself desires to be desired by both Jesus and those who are drawn to and attracted by Jesus (4:23; 6:39; 10:16–17). What Moore points to here is not just the doubling—or perhaps more accurately, the endless deferral and dissemination—of desire but also the exchange of desires. Put differently, one's desire to be the object of another desiring subject may go through a curious circuit. Jesus desires to be desired by others, because the Father desires to be desired by these others. As a result of Jesus' desire for the Father, the Father's desires become Jesus' own.

I will not go into how this exchange of desire is a Lacanian turn on Freud's Oedipus relations and how this turn is, for Lacan, centered on the child's desire for and hence identification with his *mother's* desires (see Borch-Jacobsen 1991,

---

21. Johannes Beutler (2002) has recently argued that John's purpose is to encourage people to come out of their hiding to confess Christ, in spite of the dangers that they will face in a hostile context. I am in effect suggesting that there is a different kind of "coming out" in the Gospel of John, and it concerns not the followers of Jesus but Jesus himself and the Father.

22. I believe the three instances Derrida refers to are 14:10, 11, 20. See also 10:38. I must thank Theodore W. Jennings Jr. for alerting me to this interesting reading by Derrida.

30–40, 197–239). Suffice it to say that not only does this exchange of desires place the Father's identity in question but also that the Father-Son dyad in John is always already interrupted by and dependent on the participation of a third party. One may, as a result, turn around Jesus' well-known statement in John, "No one comes to the Father except through me" (14:6c): Jesus himself needs others to cum with the Father. Keeping in mind Derrida's reading of John's language of penetration (1986, 68–69), Jesus' statement that "I in them [his followers] and you [the Father] in me" turns out to be quite a description.

What we find in John is a Jesus who longs to be "had" by the Father. Since the Father also has other desires that desire others, Jesus turns out to "be(come)" like the Father. Not only does he copy the Father's cross-dressing or imperson- ating behavior; he also copies the Father's desire and actually becomes the one who engenders children for the Father. The disciples in John are called "children of God" (1:12; 11:52) as well as addressed directly as "children" by Jesus (13:33; 21:5), who also describes them as "orphans" without his presence (14:18). Even more telling is Jesus' comparison of his disciples' experience of his departure and return to the pain and joy of a woman giving birth (16:21–22). Since Johannine logos or logics conceives a chain of copies from Father to Son to followers of the Son, this experience of childbirth is transferable from the followers back to both Jesus and the Father, or to Jesus' desire to give birth to children to satisfy the Father's desires.[23]

Things do not get less queer as one gets to the other parts of John's Gospel. It is noticeable that throughout the Gospel Jesus and his Father form a "mutual glorification society" (5:41; 8:50, 54; 12:28–29; 13:32; 17:1, 4–5). This constant elevation or stroking is nothing less than an exciting of the penis, or better yet,

---

23. For examples of how the disciples are to copy Jesus, see 6:57; 12:26; 13:12–16; 15:12, 18, 20; 20:17. Jesus' copying of the Father is clear from 5:19, but see also 5:17, 30; 15:9–10; 17:18, 22; 20:21. In addition to "telling," John also "shows" readers of this copy chain in terms of "sending." Just as Jesus sees and is sent by God, Mary Magdalene will see and be sent by the risen Jesus (20:11–20). Not to be lost in this discussion is also how John's Jesus is one who engenders in all three senses of the word. Besides birthing children, he creates the cosmos (1:3–4, 10) as well as providing a transgendering figure (of speech) for followers/readers to perform (16:25). While it is possible to read 19:34, where Jesus gets "poked" with blood and water coming out as a result, as copulation and childbirth, others have read it as referring to the cleansing power of the Holy Spirit (Webster 2003, 128–29) or as referring to sacraments of baptism and the Eucharist (Moloney 1998, 147–49). I want to acknowledge the "danger" associated with the incestuous implication being brought up here, especially how it might affect readers who have experiences of incest, whether directly or indirectly through the history of their loved ones. In the same way that "coming out" should not be universalized as a "positive" experience for all people at all times, I would say that disclosure or flashback of incestuous relations is also not universally "negative." On the latter, see Cvetkovich 2003, 83–117. I must thank James Kyung-Jin Lee for introducing me to Cvetkovich's provocative text and Frank M. Yamada for pushing me to think through this issue.

phallus. Its consistency is then explainable, since "we all know that after … an orgasmic dissemination or circulation, the phallus, like most penises, becomes limp" (Sifuentes-Jáuregui 2002, 159). Fast forwarding to the passion narratives, Conway observes that John's Jesus is a "quintessential man" because he "reveals no weakening to the passions that might undercut his manly deportment" (2003a, 175). If this is so, there is also something quintessentially queer here. During the passion, Jesus is not only beaten (18:22–23; 19:3) and flogged (19:1); his body is also nailed and his side pierced (19:18, 23a, 34, 37; 20:24–28). Oddly, John defines Jesus' masculinity with a body that is being opened to penetration.[24] Even more oddly, Jesus' ability to face his "hour" is repeatedly associated with his acknowledging of and communing with his Father (12:27–28; 14:12, 28; 16:10, 17, 28; 17:1–25; 18:11), who is, as Jesus explicitly states, "with me" (16:32) throughout this process, which Jesus also describes as one of giving birth (16:21–22). What I am suggesting is that, when Jesus' body is being penetrated, his thoughts are on his Father. He is, in other words, imagining his passion experience as a (masochistic?) sexual relation with his own Father. In addition to the coming together of Freud's pleasure and death principle (1961a), one discovers here that Jesus' copulating desires with the Father are facilitated through not only those who believe but also those who do not.

Absence/Presence

Starting with Freud's concluding choice of "a piece of clothing [that] covered up the genitals entirely"—an athletic support-belt that doubles as "bathing drawers"—to illustrate fetish as the simultaneous belief in and denial of castration (1961b, 156–57), Garber talks about (1) how athletic support-belts are actually often used by contemporary drag kings; and (2) how a cross-dresser himself or herself becomes a fetish, since both transvestite and fetish are at once signs of "lack and its covering over" (1992, 121). If transvestite and fetish are both signs of desire because what is absent or present is not readable, John's Jesus will also be a locus of others' desires as well as one who desires others.

I have already talked about how Jesus' disrobing in John does not disclose the body under the garments. Mark W. G. Stibbe has helpfully pointed to John's Jesus as equally elusive in spatial terms (1991). In addition to the game of masquerade, people, including both Johannine characters and readers, also find themselves playing several games of "hide-and-seek" with Jesus (1:38; 5:13–14; 6:15–25; 7:1–11, 30, 44; 8:20–22, 59; 9:12, 35; 10:39–40; 11:1–6, 46–57; 12:36; 18:4, 7; 20:15).[25]

---

24. Even before his arrest, John's Jesus has already characterized himself or his body as an entrance (10:7, 9) and a path to entry (14:6).

25. Let me venture to suggest that, given Jesus' elusiveness (his inclination to hide as well as his ambiguous gender/sexuality, as mentioned), one may find in John's Jesus a challenge to

Even as the Gospel comes to an end, we find Jesus absently present and eluding any final capture. Jesus is the superior supplanter because he supplants even the capture of death.[26] Left inside the empty tomb are only some linen wrappings and a facecloth or veil folded up in a separate place (20:5–7). Once again, one is reminded of the need to see Jesus in his clothing, but most of the time a closet of wrappings or clothes is all one sees. Somehow Jesus is always absent. Even when Mary Magdalene is finally able to see and recognize the resurrected Jesus, she is told that both of them have other places to go (20:11–18). John's cross-dressing and cross-bearing Jesus literally or literarily becomes a fetish, because his phantom-like elusiveness arouses desires; as Lacan suggests, desire cannot, by definition, be satisfied (1977, 287). The same is true of an unknown and unknowable "Father's house" he promises to his followers (14:1–3; see also 7:34–36; 13:33, 36–38): it is a space of undefined possibility and hence a locus of powerful desire.

The fact that Jesus is always absent or elsewhere means, however, that he will keep coming back (14:18–20, 28). After his brief encounter with Mary, we will see Jesus appearing three more times in 20:19–21:23. John's Jesus, in other words, keeps on traveling between or traversing worlds. One finds in John both a "deferral of detection" and a "deferral of denouncement" (Garber 1992, 209). As a result, John "ends" his Gospel acknowledging that he cannot write down every act and action of Jesus (21:25), since Jesus' story literally has no end.

It is, furthermore, important to note that, as a true transvestite, John's Jesus also comes back in other forms. Along with the deconstruction of the original/copy binarism that I mentioned earlier, Jesus' continual presence/absence through his multiple transformations explains the futility of the *Ioudaioi*'s attempt to ascertain Jesus' "real" identity. Jesus' many transformations include, of course, the coming of the Holy Spirit (7:39; 14:15–27; 15:26; 16:7; 20:22), but the absent Jesus also returns in and through those whom he has brought into being or engendered

---

the emphasis on "coming out" and being visible that is so prevalent among *white* homosexuals. What one finds instead is someone akin to the more "wily" queer that Silviano Santiago argues for (2002); see also Manalansan 2003; Sifuentes-Jáuregui 2002, 179. As Linda Schlossberg points out, people of color are aware that (racial-ethnic) readability can easily become (social) invisibility; in contrast, whites, who are used to the privilege of being (racially-ethnically) transparent or invisible and thus the unmarked "norm," tend to demand or come to visibility immediately when they feel threatened (2001, 5–6). Leticia Guardiola-Sáenz, Jim Lee, and Fernando Segovia have all wondered if I have been foregrounding my own commitments and stance enough in this paper. Partly because of the reasons given above, I have stubbornly decided to "copy" John's representation of an elusive Jesus and let this paper remain a "trickster" piece.

26. For more examples of John's Jesus as the supreme supplanter, note (1) the similarities between Jesus' mother and Jacob's mother but the dissimilarities between Jesus and Jacob in John 2:1–12 and Gen 27:1–40; (2) how he supplants all the other supplanters in healing the lame man in 5:1–9, since the lame man's hope to enter the healing water is previously surpassed or supplanted by others (5:7); and (3) how his own resurrection (20:1–10) compares and contrasts with that of Lazarus (11:41–44).

as God's children. That is partly what the disciples fail to understand in 16:16–22. We have already talked about the chain of copies from the Father to the Son to the(ir?) children, but let us look at the way Jesus links loving him to not only being loved by the Father, but also his new commandment to the disciples to love each other (12:27; 13:20, 34; 14:15, 20–21, 23; 15:12, 17).

What we have here is not only again the dissemination of desires but also the exchange, change, or changeling of various children. These children, including John's implied readers, are no longer just exchanged for the (homo)social and (homo)sexual bonding of the Father and the Son, but they are now themselves changed in a sense to become substitutes or copies of God's Son, and thus in effect channeling Jesus' absence into a sort of omnipresence.[27] The most telling figure in this regard is the disciple Thomas, who performs the "digital" experiment to ensure Jesus' identity (20:24–29). Aside from inserting a finger into Jesus and thus performing a form of penetration, Thomas is always marked by his nickname, "the Twin" (11:16; 20:24; 21:2). Since the "twin" of Thomas is never explicitly identified, one can read him as a twin or a (digital?) copy of Jesus, the Father and/or (an)other disciple(s). As Johannine readers are aroused to desire an ever-elusive Jesus, their unrealizable desires turn into—within John's logos and logics of desire—what René Girard calls "mimetic desires," or desires that are both fostered by and imitations of other(s') desires. If John's Father/Son dyad—as I have argued—incarnates change and drag, John's readers are attracted, drawn, or dragged by this twosome (6:44; 12:32) to change and be exchanged. John asks its readers, then, to perform a kind of pan-eroticism.[28] Jesus' closet in John is not only from above (3:31; 8:23); it is also bottomless.

---

27. In transvestite fashion, people can very much change and interchange in John. The man born blind becomes, after receiving his healing from Jesus, Jesus' shadow copy: like Jesus, his identity causes confusion (9:8–12); he is tried and persecuted (9:13–34); and he even utters a Yahweh-like simple but definitive "I am" (9:9; see also 8:58; 18:6). Just to give a postresurrection example, Peter will become a shepherd figure who will feed Jesus' sheep (21:15–17). Not only is this thrice commissioning of Peter by Jesus preceded by Jesus feeding his disciples (21:9–14); it is also followed immediately by a discussion of Peter's martyrdom (21:18–19). Given this narrative structure, one may well read Peter's death as his feeding of Jesus' sheep. In other words, just as Jesus gives his flesh and blood to be consumed to give life (6:53–56), Peter will end up doing something similar.

28. If one reads the phrase about Jesus being in the Father's bosom erotically (1:18), one will have to do the same with the parallel statement about the beloved disciple being in Jesus' bosom (13:23; see also 21:20). Likewise, if one—as Derrida implies—reads "I am in the Father, and the Father is in me" as mutual penetration (14:10–11, 20), one will have to do the same with the parallel language in reference to the disciples (14:20, 23; 17:21–23). The combination of ingestion and penetration language in 6:56 further points to the anthropological insight about food and sex being parallel issues of boundary building and/or breaking. The idea of ingestion (Webster 2003) and its attendant, digestion, also emphasize yet once more the many trans-formations that John's Jesus is capable of and associated with.

FAMILY

This pan-eroticism threatens to collapse the conventional category of and the categories within the family. Greco-Roman families are often depicted and understood in terms of three sets of unequal relations: husband and wife; parent and child; and master and slave. Since I believe I have already said much that touches on the husband-wife and parent-child relations, I will give but one example on the parent-child dyad. Shortly after describing the disciples as "orphans" without him and thus implying his own status as their parent (14:8), Jesus will compare the disciples' grief in losing Jesus with women in labor, whose joy upon seeing the baby is then compared to the disciples' joy in seeing Jesus again (16:16–22). Jesus the parent of the disciples thus suddenly also becomes a child of the disciples.

Let me now focus on master-slave to talk about how John's transgendering and changeling disturb the categorization and the categorical imperative of this superior-subordinate relationship. While John's Jesus maintains that servants cannot be greater than their masters in 13:16 and 15:20, he also declares between these two references that his followers will do greater works than he himself (14:12). He also performs the womanly/slavishly task of washing his disciples' feet in 13:1–11 and further transforms his disciples from being his "servants" to his "friends" in 15:15. What this transformation effects is a transgression of filiations and affiliations. Friends and families are now mix-up categories. Jesus' beloved disciple can, for example, replace Jesus and become the son of Jesus' mother (19:26–27). John has already pronounced in the Prologue that "children" can be born supernat(ur)ally through divine will and human belief (1:13). If the encounter between John's Jesus and Nicodemus indicates that one can be born anew or from above (3:3–8), his encounters with the *Ioudaioi* will further disrupt or dismiss biological lineage by implying that one's ancestry can be changed or determined by one's actions (8:39–47).

JESUS AT THE CROSSROADS

Issues of birth and family touch upon those of kinship, people, and nation, since "nation" is derived from the Latin *nasci*, or "to be born" (Somerville 2005, 75). Writing about another "princely imposter" in India whose disappearance/death and return/resurrection reminds me in different ways of both the Moses of Exodus and the Jesus of John, Partha Chatterjee points out that this "strange and universal history" (2002) must be read within the particular context of British colonialism and Indian nationalism. I would suggest that the same must be done with John's story, since John's Jesus is not only (as I argued) a cross-dresser but also (as we can all see) a cross-bearer.

More specifically, I would argue that Jesus' travels between the world above and the world below (3:31, 8:23) puts into crisis not only gender and sexuality but also race/ethnicity as well as Roman colonial and Jewish nationalist politics.

Hence what Garber calls "category crises" themselves intersect with what Anne McClintock calls the "articulated categories" of race/ethnicity, gender, sexuality, and class, since these "categories" or factors "come into existence *in and through* relation to each other" (1995, 5). After all, Jesus incarnates in John as an *Ioudaios* as well as a male (4:9, 20; 19:3, 14–15, 19, 21). In other words, drag can be performed in terms other than gender. One must therefore consider Jesus' incarnation in John as also a racial-ethnic drag. This is in a sense what Tina Chen does when she uses Butler's theory on performativity to talk about how Asian Americans might employ a politics of impersonation amid charges of imposture to not only deconstruct the binary categories of "fake" and "real," but also simultaneously critique and claim Asian American identities as both "truth" and "fiction" (2005).

Fortunately for me, excellent work has recently been done on John and border-crossing as well as the Roman Empire, especially by racial-ethnic minority scholars (Dube 2002; Guardiola-Sáenz 2002; Rivera 2004). According to the late Gloria Anzaldúa, borderland is the habitus of the "crossed," the queer, or "those who cross over, pass over, or go through the confines of the 'normal'" (1999, 3). What I want to do now is to tie together Jesus' cross-dressing, border-crossing, and cross-bearing in John. I will proceed to do so by focusing on what Jesus' migration and mimicry may mean to the colonized people of Israel or Israel's national family.

Ioudaioi and Israel

As part of his larger project to rethink early "Judeo-Christian origins" not in terms of an abrupt and early "parting of the ways" but a protracted "twin birth" in late antiquity, Daniel Boyarin (2002) has recently argued that John's pervasive use and negative portrayal of *Ioudaioi* as Jesus' opponents and persecutors (if not exactly executors) must be better investigated.[29] According to Boyarin, *Ioudaioi* refers to a group within but not representative of all of Israel; as a result, the Fourth Gospel's named attack of the *Ioudaioi* does not imply a disidentification with Jews or Israel on the part of John and John's community of Jesus-followers. More specifically, Boyarin sees the *Ioudaioi* as an "inner-group" of Israel originally made up of the elitist families that had been exiled to and then returned from Babylon.

After or perhaps during their experience of exile (and thus the mass movement of people whether out of another's or one's own choice), these elites

---

29. One must, however, always remember that, however *Ioudaioi* is defined, it is yet another leaky category in John. Boyarin himself points to the faith that some *Ioudaioi* express in Jesus after witnessing Lazarus's resurrection (11:45–46) to suggest that "*Ioudaioi* are not identical with those who reject Jesus" (2002, 238). One can read further to see not only how John presents their faith—unlike the fickle faith of some other *Ioudaioi* in 8:31–59—as a continuous or lasting one (12:17; see also 12:11) but also the coming to faith of a group of ambiguously identified "rulers" or "authorities" (12:42).

had—paralleling or prefiguring today's Hindutva movement that not only champions a "return" to an ethnically "pure" Hindu nation in India but also is heavily funded by diasporic Indians in the U.S.—become more restrictive and sectarian, or even monist and fundamentalist with their particular creedal confession. As the book of Ezra indicates, these families, upon their return to Judea, were given control of the then new temple-state as the "holy seed," and one of the first things they did was—in a way that is reminiscent of the *retroactive* enforcement of the antimiscegenation bill against white-"Mongolian" intermarriage in California in 1933—to drive out those who had intermarried with ethnic foreigners (Ezra 9–10). Boyarin indicates that it was around this same time, when the *Ioudaioi* started to rebuild the temple, that the Samaritan schism also took place (2002, 225). Although there might be limited ways for one to join this elitist class (not the least of which would be a wholehearted embrace of its creeds and rituals), those who had not been exiled to Babylon (the so-called "people of the land" or the *'am ha'ares*) largely and effectively became "second-class citizens" within Israel (228).[30] John's hostility against the *Ioudaioi* is, for Boyarin, an indication and reflection of this second-class perspective.[31]

---

30. Read within the context of the colonial dynamics of Ezra's time and the nationalist ambitions of the returnees, the "class" struggle between the *Ioudaioi* and the "people of the land" might be comparable to how Christian missionaries in the Pacific Islands and Asia at the turn of the twentieth century tended to be rather harsh on fellow American expatriates in these same locations in light of the latter's sexual laxity and hence failure to embody the "American/Christian" ideals, especially because the missionaries were generally from a more privileged background; see Clymer 1986. I think this comparison is particularly helpful in bringing out not only the imbricated nature of religious, racial, cultural, and class politics but also the thin line that separates anticolonial nationalism and colonizing imperialism. The thin line I have in mind here cuts more than one way. In addition to how anticolonial activities (Ezra) might parallel or duplicate colonial ideology and practice (U.S. missionaries), I am also thinking of how—in the case of both Ezra and early twentieth century U.S. activities in and over the Pacific—internal class difference might accompany or appear as anti-imperial critiques. See also Koshy 2004, 37–38.

31. Although Boyarin himself does not make this comparison, the way he describes John in the context of Ezra's racial-ethnic and nationalist project reminds me of José Rabasa's (1997) suggestion of the Zapatista rebellion as a "subaltern insurrection" that challenges the dominant Mexican nationalism for the sake of including the natives or indigenous people. While Boyarin sees John's *Ioudaioi* as an intersection involving both a geographical (in terms of its origin and power base in Judea) and religious (in terms of its creedal or confessional restriction) identification, his analysis points to the fluidity or fragility of racial-ethnic identities, particularly how they intersect with or are ruptured by location, whether understood in terms of geography, creed, and/or class or status. Although Boyarin highlights only geography and creed, one must remember here the "elitist" status of the *Ioudaioi* both before their deportation to and after their return from Babylon. Likewise, one must not forget Boyarin's reference to Seth Schwartz's work to discuss how the later Hasmoneans, with the territorial expansion from Judea into the Palestinian hinterland, were able to incorporate various mixtures of people into Israel and

John's *Ioudaioi* are certainly very protective of their class or status, since they are obviously always on the lookout for any kind of people movement that may disturb their "homeland security." They want to know who the Baptizer is as well as why he baptizes (1:19, 22, 25; see also 4:1–3). The Baptizer's immediate reference to the Messiah (1:20), however, may also reveal that the *Ioudaioi* have some nationalist yearnings, despite their tendency to misread and mislead or their inability to imagine a nation without them being in control. Are the Baptizer's interrogators known for having an interest in finding the Messiah? Their desires for familial belonging or racial-ethnic membership can be seen also in their debate with Jesus over Abraham and Moses (5:44–47; 6:31–33; 7:18–24; 8:30–59; 9:27–30). After all, even "first-class" Jews, in the context of Roman colonization, occupy at best what Kamala Visweswaran calls a "middleman minority" position (1997). This is what Jesus is implying when he chides the *Ioudaioi* as "hired hands" situated between the sheep and a wolf (10:11–13), particularly since John tells us ahead of time that Jesus is using a "figure of speech" here (10:6).

While the *Ioudaioi* may play a role and dress themselves up as "brokers" of the Roman Empire out of necessity, the exchange between them and Pilate in John clearly shows that they are resentful of Roman rule. They think Pilate's praetorium is defiling (18:28), and they do not appreciate Pilate's dismissive attitude toward their concerns. As a result, the *Ioudaioi* and Pilate are often involved in a kind of tense yet thinly disguised verbal confrontations. One sees this in Pilate's reluctance to try Jesus and, after questioning him (18:29–32), his reluctance to sentence Jesus (19:1–8, 12–16). Interestingly enough, Pilate's reluctance actually involves an element of fear that his words of bravado fail to conceal, at least not in the eyes of Jesus (19:8–11). One sees this underlying tension again in Pilate's decision to inscribe "Jesus of Nazareth, the king of the *Ioudaioi*"—and then to keep that inscription despite the protest of the *Ioudaioi*—on Jesus' cross (19:19–22).

Jesus' passing in(to) the world below reveals and critiques, then, the travesty or even the transvestite-like behavior of both the Roman governor and the *Ioudaioi*. He reveals the colonial anxiety that Pilate is trying to conceal, and he discloses the role-playing of the *Ioudaioi* to cross over to the good side of the Romans (even if they are in fact quite crossed with their colonial masters) and to cross out other, less powerful Israelites. Colonial dynamics are complicated, and the complexity of the *Ioudaioi*'s negotiations is arguably best seen in 11:45–53, where they see both the Romans and Jesus as threatening to their "place" within/

---

make them all "*in some sense* Jewish" (Schwartz 2001, 36; cited in Boyarin 2002, 227, emphasis Boyarin's). Related to this but turning back to the Persian period that Boyarin is focusing on, Randall Bailey has suggested that Moses, though an Egyptian, was incorporated and turned into an Israelite. Bailey's suggestion points to racial as well as ethnic tensions that might have existed not only within Israel but also between Israel and Rome (1995). I would like to thank here both Bailey and Gay L. Byron for pushing me to think through the idea of black presence in the Bible by providing both conversations and bibliographical recommendations.

and their "nation" (11:48).[32] Besides competition and tradition, the *Ioudaioi* also kill Jesus because they feel they have to keep things calm to avoid the (nervous) suspicion and the (preemptive) military action of the Romans.

Ezra on Intermarriage

Boyarin's informative and helpful reading of John's *Ioudaioi* is in fact not new. Almost a decade earlier, as my African American colleagues (particularly Byron and Demetrius K. Williams) reminded me, Obery M. Hendricks Jr. (1995) had already proposed in his dissertation at Princeton University an alternative reading of John's *Ioudaioi* as a class distinction. Since Boyarin's reading, an Asian American scholar, Jean K. Kim, has also read John "intertextually with Ezra-Nehemiah" (2006). While Kim does not refer to Boyarin or account for Jesus' location vis-à-vis the elitist returnees, she does point to the important question of gender and mixed marriages by focusing on Jesus' encounter with the Samaritan woman in John 4.[33]

Susan Koshy, writing about antimiscegenation laws against Asian Americans, correctly suggests that such laws are making simultaneously "race, sex, gender, and nation" (2004, 3). Such laws involve not only a restriction but also an education of racial-ethnic *and* sexual desires in defining national membership. The antimiscegenation laws found in Ezra thus simultaneously affirm and amend Michel Foucault's exposition on biopower. While Foucault is correct that technologies of sex help "anchor" racism, his observation on governmental intrusion into intimate relations as just a modern phenomenon is too "short-sighted" (1978; see also Burchell, Gordon, and Miller 1991).

Ezra's prohibition is symptomatic of an anxiety over miscegenation, and thus Jewish identity in general as well as the hegemony of the *Ioudaioi* in particular.[34]

---

32. Even though the NRSV translates this verse's "place" as "holy place," or the temple, the *Ioudaioi*, as the ones who rebuilt the temple, certainly understand their status or place as insepa-rably tied to the temple. For a recent postcolonial reading of John that focuses on this passage, see Moore 2006, 45–74.

33. For Kim, the Samaritan woman is an "object of transaction" who only serves to facili-tate the bonding or a "nationalist" alliance between Jesus and Samaritan males against Roman colonization (2006, 106–8). Her reading, as is true of her earlier work on John (2004), does not, in my view, pay enough attention to the contention between the *Ioudaioi* and the Romans.

34. Koshy has helpfully pointed out that antimiscegenation laws against Asian Americans were economically as well as culturally and racially motivated (2004, 2, 6–7). The same can be said of Ezra and the *Ioudaioi*, as one of the issues confronting the returnees must be rights of possession over the land. By outlawing mixed marriages, which had supposedly been practiced by the "peoples of the land" who had stayed in Judah, the *Ioudaioi* might have also found a convenient way to "recover" or "repossess" the land they had been exiled from and left behind. See, for instance, J. Collins 2004, 434 . By also conveniently "proving" those who were not exiled or racially-ethnically "foreign" as "sexually deviant" by virtue of their "mixed marriages," Ezra's

Not only does it establish and/or entrench racial-ethnic boundary by normalizing certain sexual and marriage practices, but it also points to a significant linkage between maternity and membership in a racial-ethnic community. With the law aiming primarily at foreign women and those born of them, both Jewish identity and *Ioudaioi* power become contingent on the social control of women. The law does, of course, place restriction on Jewish males, since their children are illegitimate if they are born of foreign women. The effect of the law is, however, to "guarantee" the hegemony of the *Ioudaioi* and the homogeneity of Jewish identity by identifying mothers—and hence female bodies and sexuality—as threats.[35] Since a foreign man can never become or beget a Jew by marrying a Jewish woman, the Jewish male has always already been affirmed as the principal arbiter of Jewish identity.[36] What is new about Ezra's prohibition is that it pinpoints the necessity for a mother to be racially-ethnically Jewish as well. By doing so, women are made responsible for not only (re)producing but also promoting or polluting Jewish identity.[37] In other words, Jewish women, unlike and under Jewish men who arbitrate Jewish identity, become custodians and guarantors of Jewishness.

With the anxiety over the preservation of Jewish identity against foreign infiltration explicitly presented as a woman question, women's "purity" becomes tied to the "purity" of nation, tradition, and race/ethnicity. What I am getting at is how nationalism, perhaps particularly in the context of colonialism and imperialism, engenders "woman" as the boundary marker of a racial-ethnic community, and does so to shore up both the masculinity and community of the *Ioudaioi*.

---

command against miscegenation ends up justifying and thus entrenching the superiority and authority of the *Ioudaioi* both materially and symbolically, and it does so in a way that does not foster marriages and thus alliance among these two subordinated groups. I am indebted to Kah-Jin Jeffrey Kuan for taking the time to talk me through my many questions related to Ezra-Nehemiah. Related to the economic question is Marion Grau's (2004) theological work on how a "trickster-like Christ," including a "transgendered Jesus" in Jean-François Lyotard's *Libidinal Economy* (1993), may subvert and transform economic neocolonialism. I will have more to say about how John's transgendering Jesus subverts or challenges the *Ioudaioi* in a later section.

35. One may also wonder if this emphasis on "foreign women" rather than "foreign men" has any implication on gender in general and the comparative desirability or assumed readiness for assimilation on the part of foreign females and males in particular. See Koshy 2004, 22–23, 42–44.

36. Ezra 9:12a does briefly mention the inappropriateness of giving a Jewish woman to marry a Gentile man, but its brevity clearly indicates that Ezra's major concern has to do with Jewish men marrying Gentile women. Note also that conversion to Judaism only became "possible" for Gentiles in the second half of the second century B.C.E., as evidenced by Aseneth's conversion in *Joseph and Aseneth*; see Cohen 1999, 168, 170, 171 n. 97, 265–68.

37. Some have suggested that Ezra's concern to oust foreign wives and mixed children has to do with his embracement of the matrilineal principle, thus mixed children born of a Gentile woman would be by definition Gentiles. The matrilineal principle, however, does not seem to be in operation until the time of the Mishnah. See Cohen 1999, 243–44, 261–68, 273–307.

Since a woman represents "home" in more sense than one, both her body and her sexuality become communal (read: male) property and come under communal (read: male again) discipline.

Not to be lost in my mention of women's sexuality is the heterosexual assumption of Ezra's prohibition. Ezra's obsessive concerns over foreign women, marriage, and children speak volumes on the gender and heterosexual normativity that are at work in dominant racial-ethnic and nationalist ideologies. Like many nationalist and imperialist movements today, the "purity" of nation, tradition, and race/ethnicity are tied not only to the racial-ethnic and sexual but also the *hetero*-sexual purity of the woman. Put differently and in the words of Koshy, what Ezra effects is to make "racialized heterosexuality" a founding principle in the genealogy of the Jewish "nation" (2004, 12). In fact, given the elitist position of the *Ioudaioi*, one can go beyond Koshy to suggest that Ezra's heterosexual marriage and family order are grounding a nationalist project on gender and class difference as well as racial-ethnic and sexual exclusion.[38]

Males of the "people of the land" are made responsible for miscegenation, and thus guilty of being unable to not only resist the temptation of foreign women but also regulate the sexual relations of "their own" women. In contrast, males of the *Ioudaioi*, as they return to Judah, are fashioning themselves as saviors or founders of a "reunified" nation or people who "revive" Israel's religiocultural traditions.

The Fourth Gospel reveals not only that the boundaries of race/ethnicity, gender, sexuality, and class are constructed in association and collision with each other but also that a liberating return from exile might also be accompanied by certain deep-rooted though oppressive understandings of class, gender, sexuality, family, and nation. Through an interlocking system of exclusions, a restrictive familial order becomes a founding and utopian model of a people or nation. Then as well as now, McClintock is on target when she asks regarding nationalism: "Can the iconography of the family be retained as the figure for national unity, or must an alternative, radical iconography be developed?" (1995, 386).

Reading John in light of Ezra means that Ezra's anxieties over gender, sexual, and racial-ethnic identity as well as purity hover over the meeting of Jesus and the anonymous Samaritan woman at the well, which has been known as a symbolic betrothal type-scene, in John 4 (Fehribach 1998, 45–81). This betrothal type-scene, when read within the context of Ezra in general and the comparison

---

38. What one witnesses here is a depiction of the *Ioudaioi* as establishing/engendering a Jewish identity through questionable means. What this sets up, then, is a clash between values that also often becomes the justification for colonial aggression: invading or intervening a local or indigenous culture because of the injustice found within that tradition. Note that my use of "tradition" in the singular is deliberate here, since colonial ideology/practice tends to deny the plurality or multiplicity within a local or indigenous culture.

between Ezra 9 and 2 Kgs 17 in particular, provides extra texture and nuance to the Samaritan woman's question, "How is it that you, a male *Ioudaios*, ask a drink of me, a woman of Samaria?" (John 4:9). This is especially so if one reads John's Jesus as Sophia/Jesus and at the same time keeps also in mind that the nemesis of Sophia in Proverbs is supposed to be none other than a "foreign" woman (Yee 2003, 135–58).

WHEN TRANSVESTITISM MEETS NATIONALISM

Comparing Ezra's prohibition against mixed marriage to a witch-hunt, David Janzen writes, "The ideology employed in a witch-hunt must convince the partici-pants that the witches are people who had only been *masquerading* as community members" (2002, 19–20, emphasis added).[39] What happens when one reads the encounter between Jesus and the *Ioudaioi* as a meeting between a masquerading traveler and a prevailing and almost all-pervading racial-ethnic and national-ist ideology that is not only masculinist and heteronormative but also keen on exposing and executing masqueraders?

The short answer is, of course, the *Ioudaioi* make sure that the cross-dress-ing boundary-crosser is nailed to a Roman cross. While Chatterjee's division of nationalist culture into a material and a spiritual domain (1993) is questionable in light of both Ezra and John, his problematization of nationalism as "a derivative discourse" of colonialism (1986) seems to be on target. Anticolonial nationalism might not only be elitist but also reproduce colonial inequalities in its own ways. Given the desires of the *Ioudaioi* for epistemological certainty and keeping the racial-ethnic, class, gender, and sexual hierarchies intact in their nation-build-ing project, Jesus' passing in(to) the world below confuses them and threatens to displace these hierarchies and pollute everything with the queering desires of a cross-dresser.

The category crises I scrutinized earlier turn out to be, I contend, threaten-ing to the *Ioudaioi* also because their masculinist and heterosexist nationalist project functions simultaneously to explain and safeguard their place within the Roman Empire. In other words, the more the *Ioudaioi* can establish the differ-ences between themselves and others (Jewish or otherwise) below them, the more they can assert their legitimacy and value within the Roman Empire. John's Jesus, therefore, foregrounds the complicities between Roman colonialism and Jewish

---

39. I am indebted to Cheryl B. Anderson for this reference. The transformation of the *Ioudaioi* from being the exiled and the hunted in Babylon to being the hetero-masculinist elit-ist hunters in Judea again indicates that the meanings of race/ethnicity, gender, and sexuality are relational rather than unchanging. Their transformation also indicates that these relations, though changeable like clothes in a sense, are regulated by geopolitical space and socio-political structure (Li 1998, 159). Conway also gives a fine analysis of the relational dynamics in Jesus' masculinity in John (2003a, 177–80).

nationalism rather than only their contestations, and he refuses to be complicit with the nationalist project of the *Ioudaioi* and its attendant racial-ethnic, class, gender, and sexual hierarchies. After all, Boyarin's archaeological work on the identity of the *Ioudaioi* reminds us that their return was sanctioned by imperial Persia; if so, their repressive nationalist project might also not necessarily or solely be an "internal" development (Hoglund 1992).

In contrast to an idealized "home" represented by a stable father and a pure wife/mother correctly traditioning the children about the inviolability of boundaries, Jesus' transgendered performance of a queer sexuality transgressively points to a queerness or an otherness that exists at the root and the pinnacle of Israel's traditions, which the *Ioudaioi* thought they authorize and control. The hegemonic nationalist (ideo)logic of the *Ioudaioi* is reconfigured into a queer Father who, as I have suggested, not only dwells above with Jesus in a closeted world of copiers that undercuts both "origin" and "authenticity" but also sends Jesus to traverse into the world below to engender a new logic of affiliation through action to replace the old logic of filiation by (pure) blood. Jesus' hypercorporeal performance ("the Word became flesh," 1:14) in both cross-dressing and crossing borders challenges the *Ioudaioi*'s nation-building project that stigmatizes miscegenation, normalizes racialized heterosexual marriage among Jews, and perhaps quarantines racial-ethnic and/or sexual difference to other worlds or territories.[40] As the ultimate supplanter, Jesus' mimicking and migrating acts in John—*pace* Kim 2004—dislodge the *Ioudaioi*'s nationalist idea(l)s of identity and belonging. In other words, John displaces the narration of nation put forth in Ezra. Jesus' new family or kinship is one that is neither heterosexually monogamous nor racially-ethnically "monotonous"; it is, instead, a transnational or even transworld alliance that exceeds not only the *Ioudaioi*'s version of a Jewish nation but also the very category of nation.

To adopt and adapt Chen's work on Asian American impersonation (2005), John's Jesus is a "double agent" whose allegiance to Jewish traditions and nationalism (at least the versions being put forth by the *Ioudaioi*) is divided. This doubled or varied allegiance on the part of John's Jesus is perhaps best shown by his presence in and detachment from the world (8:23; 15:19; 17:14–16; 18:36). It is no surprise, therefore, that the *Ioudaioi* find Jesus to be guilty of betrayal (see also Chen 2005, 8). This is especially so given the way Jesus exposes and subverts the *Ioudaioi*'s own pretentious pretension or imposture as Israel's "true" representa-

---

40. As Koshy's study on Asian Americans shows, antimiscegenation laws have a way to increase ironically the desirability of "alien" sexuality, even if interracial sexual relations have to take place underground or "extraterritorially" (that is, outside the boundaries of the U.S.); see Koshy 2004, 8, 10–14, 29–49.

tives and authoritative boundary patrollers.[41] In John, one finds in Jesus all kinds of desiring relations that defy and interrupt the normative racial-ethnic and nationalist idea(l)s of the *Ioudaioi*, including those with the Samaritans (John 4) and the Greeks (John 7).[42] Given Mary Douglas's (1966) suggestion that what is out of place is polluting, Alberto Sandoval Sánchez's statement that "migration is an awareness of death" makes good sense (1997, 190). This is even more so since John's cross-dressing Jesus is polluting everything by perverting and breaching all kinds of boundaries even before his body is nailed and pierced, and hence opened, defiled, and turned (more) defiling. Put differently, Jesus' passing or crossing simultaneously reveals the intensity and the impossibility of the *Ioudaioi*'s desire to "fix" identities and affinities in static categories.

JESUS' COMING OUT AND BEING OUT OF PLACE

John's Jesus, after pronouncing the need to be "born of water and spirit" to enter God's kingdom (3:5) and promising "living water" to spring up like a "fountain" (4:14) or flow like "rivers" (7:38) within those who believe, ends up spilling "blood and water" when his crucified body is poked open with a spear (19:34). This spilling out of what should belong inside the body is, of course, polluting, but instead of dwelling on the implication of spilling blood in light of various Jewish traditions, I want to spend some time on Jesus' spilling of water.

The importance of "water symbolism" in John is well recognized (Jones 1997; Ng 2001). What is seldom recognized is that water—as fluid and formless, and thus unbounded and polluting—is supposedly also the nature of women in Greco-Roman medical understanding (Carson 1999, 78–88). Feminine fluidity means that women are not only porous, leaky, and unreliable but also able to "transform and deform" (80). In other words, women pollute not only by breaking others' boundaries but also by literally changing their own form and taking on those of others. Women pollute since their moist and soft nature is also more susceptible to the assaults of wanton desires, erotic or otherwise. In short, women are wet and (thus) wild. I am suggesting that John's constant references to Jesus wanting water (4:7; 19:28), giving water (6:35), and leaking water (19:34) speak to Jesus' gender indeterminacy and hence his cross-dressing and other queer desires

---

41. I am borrowing here from Leslie Bow, who argues for the connection between the accusation of betrayal and the acts of subversion in the context of gender and sexual politics within Asian America (2001).

42. One can add to this Jesus' relations with women, Jewish and otherwise. If the episode about Jesus forgiving the adulterous woman (7:53–8:11) is "original," then Jesus' attitude toward women's sexuality is clearly different from that of the *Ioudaioi*. The same can be said if Jesus' discussion with the Samaritan woman about her multiple "husbands" (4:16–19) is literal rather than metaphorical; see Schneiders (1999, 117–48) for a metaphorical reading of this "marital" discussion.

that put out of place everything that the *Ioudaioi* treasure, particularly those that relate to their racial-ethnic, masculinist, and heterosexist nationalism.

Focusing on Jesus' spilling water at death also provides a link to read John in light of both Ezra and Genesis. Ezra's racial-ethnic and nationalist project through the removal of foreign women and mixed children is nothing but a replay of Sarah's decision to cast out Hagar the Egyptian slave-woman and her son, Ishmael, so Sarah's own son, Isaac, would be the sole heir to Abraham's property and to God's promise (Gen 16:1–15; 21:1–10). Like her earlier plan to secure God's promise of "nationhood" to Abraham through Hagar, Sarah's plan to get rid of Hagar and Ishmael also ends with an unexpected twist. God is at first approving of this second plan, but, upon hearing Ishmael's cry of thirst in the wilderness, God ends up providing a well of water in the wilderness for both Ishmael and Hagar so they can continue to live, though they do so now in separation from Abraham and Isaac (Gen 21:11–21). Jacob, in displacing his own older brother through (1) Esau's impetuous hunger for food and (2) Jacob's impersonation of Esau in offering Isaac both food and drink, is in fact duplicating Isaac's displacement of Ishmael, but ironically Jacob is now doing so against Isaac's will. What we find in John is, I contend, in effect a rewriting of these stories.

Jesus comes in disguise like Jacob, but the water that leaks out of his pierced body quenches not only the thirst of Israelites who believe but also the thirst of the banished children of Samaria (4:1–42), even the thirst of the whole world (3:16; 10:16; 11:50–52; 12:20–21; 19:19–20). In contrast to Jacob, who steals a birthright for himself, Jesus will come to offer birthrights to all who would believe (1:12). John's Jesus thus becomes the ultimate supplanter, who is greater than even Jacob and Abraham. His passing in(to) the world below brings for the *Ioudaioi* epistemological uncertainties and categorical crises. Their inability to ascertain and/or accept—borrowing Avery Gordon's vocabularies (1997, 5)—Jesus' "complex personhood" (6:41–42, 52; 7:21, 25–27, 32–36; 9:29–30) leads to their own identity crisis. For Juliet Mitchell, "hysteria sometimes presents not the negative of the sexual perversion but the negative of a perverse knowledge," which may lead to a "traditionless subject" (1992, 104). The "perverse knowledge" that Jesus (re)presents causes the *Ioudaioi* to experience a crisis of tradition, and finally a moment of hysteria, as they scream collectively for Jesus' death in exchange for Barabbas (18:38–40) and in denial of their God in favor of Caesar (19:12–15).

John's mapping of queering desires onto the Father's world above also extends the critique of (the) origin(al) that I discussed earlier to challenge the nationalist assumption that the diaspora is by definition only an imperfect copy of the original homeland (Gopinath 2005, 7). In the Fourth Gospel, the Father's world above is—alongside the queer identifications and pleasures—always already—like the world below—a site/sight of hierarchical relations and leave-taking. While there are signs that Jesus' disciples may outdo Jesus (14:12) and clear "proofs" that Jesus has outdone everyone else, there is no question that Jesus remains completely and absolutely under the authority of the Father. Jesus has no voice of his own

(7:16–18; 8:28–29; 12:49–50; 14:24) and does nothing on his own (5:16–21, 30). Whatever the Father speaks and commands, Jesus copies and obeys in turn (Liew 2002, 206–7). One of the Father's commands is, of course, Jesus' (semivoluntary or involuntary?) departure into the world below. That is to say, leave-taking and loss already occur under the Father and within the Father's world above. Given what I said before about Jesus' multiple entries into the world below (whether in the form of the Spirit or his disciples), one can even talk about multiple leave-takings and losses in the world above.

Does this mean that even Jesus cannot feel "being at home" despite his supposedly "homecoming" after his resurrection? In fact, given the multiple comings and goings between the two worlds that John seems to assume, one may further argue that, in John, the conventional assumption of a fixed point of origin or that of a single "home" is itself complicated and put into question. John's Jesus is, in the words of Anzaldúa, "[a] queer … who [doesn't] belong anywhere, not in the dominant world, nor completely in [his] own respective cultures" (1981, 209). Or, in a somewhat surprising quote that puts together nicely my own transgendering and postcolonial emphasis in this paper, Jawaharlal Nehru writes, "I have become a *queer* mixture of the East and West, out of place everywhere, at home nowhere" (1936, 597, emphasis added). Moving between worlds and as a transvestite, John's Jesus is a "trickster who practices subjectivity-as-masquerade, the oppositional agent who accesses differing identity, ideological, aesthetic, and political positions" (Sandoval 2002, 25).[43] With alternative desires and multiple "homes," he is able to explode traditions and effect all forms of transformations, cultural and otherwise.[44] One may even say that this boundary-crossing and cross-bearing cross-dresser is an early representation of what M. Jacqui Alexander (1997) calls

---

43. In the Fourth Gospel, one finds Jesus both participating in and pronouncing judgment against various festivals and practices of the *Ioudaioi* (2:13–18; 6:48–51; 7:19–24). One also finds him claiming openly a greater status than the Hebrew patriarchs such as Abraham, Jacob, and Moses (3:10–15; 5:16–18; 8:52–59; 10:29–39), as well as hiding elusively from people's attention and visibility (4:1–3; 5:13; 6:15; 7:1–10; 8:59; 10:40; 11:53–54; 12:36). These actions correspond ironically in a way to the four modes of resistance ("equal rights," "revolutionary," "supremacist," and "separatist") that Sandoval outlines in addition to or in separation from the "differential" mode of a "decolonizing queer" (2002, 25, 30–31). At least in the case of John's Jesus, these modes of resistance turn out to be not necessarily mutually exclusive.

44. On the other hand, by locating queering desires within the Hebrew tradition not only in the world above but also temporally "in the beginning" (1:1–18), John does not sanitize "home" or "origin" by displacing such desires and practices as Greek and/or Roman influence. Jesus is not what Manuel Guzmán refers to as "sexiles," or people who leave home/nation because of their sexuality (1997, 227 n. 2). By refusing to do so, I would contend that John also provides an alternative to the teleological and imperialist narratives that present a colonized person as being sexually oppressed at "home" until he or she finds sexual liberation and a queer identity in an imperial center (Solomon 2005, 20).

"an insurgent sexuality" that works against hegemonic (ideo)logic, both diasporic and nationalist.

Conclusion

I hope I have demonstrated in this essay that sexuality can be an interested and interesting intervention in biblical studies, particularly in convergence with issues of race/ethnicity, gender, and (post)colonialism. In addition to queering biblical traditions in this essay, I have argued against constructions of racial-ethnic identity that turn out to be hetero-masculinist, even or perhaps especially when such constructions are done in resistance to colonial power. To go against the multiple and intersecting forms of hegemonic (ideo)logic that operate within our own discipline of biblical criticism, I would suggest that biblical scholars—minority or not—must also read across more worlds, whether in terms of discipline, gender, sexuality, race/ethnicity, and/or nation. After all, John has come to a similar conclusion years ago: no single world can contain the Jesus (as) word (21:25).

Works Consulted

Alexander, M. Jacqui. 1997. Erotic Autonomy as a Politics of Decolonization: An Anatomy of Feminist and State Practice in the Bahamas Tourist Economy. Pages 63–100 in *Feminist Genealogies, Colonial Legacies, Democratic Futures*. Edited by M. Jacqui Alexander and Chandra Talpade Mohanty. New York: Routledge.

Anzaldúa, Gloria E. 1981. La Prieta. Pages 198–209 in *This Bridge Called My Back: Writings by Radical Women of Color*. Edited by Cherríe Moraga and Gloria E. Anzaldúa. New York: Kitchen Table.

———. 1999. *Borderlands/La Frontera: The New Mestiza*. San Francisco: Aunt Lute Books.

Bailey, Randall C. 1995. Is That Any Name for a Nice Hebrew Boy? Exodus 2:1–10: The De-Africanization of an Israelite Hero. Pages. 25–36 in *The Recovery of Black Presence: An Interdisciplinary Exploration*. Edited by Randall C. Bailey and Jacquelyn Grant. Nashville: Abingdon.

Bassi, Karen. 1998. *Acting Like Men: Gender, Drama, and Nostalgia in Ancient Greece*. Ann Arbor: University of Michigan Press.

Berenson Maclean, Jennifer K. 2003. The Divine Trickster: A Tale of Two Weddings in John. Pages 48–77 in vol. 1 of *A Feminist Companion to John*. Edited by Amy-Jill Levine with Marianne Blickenstaff. Cleveland: Pilgrim.

Beutler, Johannes. 2002. Faith and Confession: The Purpose of John. Pages 19–32 in *Word, Theology, and Community in John*. Edited by John R. Painter, Alan Culpepper, and Fernando F. Segovia. St. Louis: Chalice.

Bhabha, Homi K. 1994. *The Location of Culture*. London: Routledge.

Bonfante, Larissa. 1989. Nudity as a Costume in Classical Art. *American Journal of Archaeology* 93:543–70.

Borch-Jacobsen, Mikkel. 1991. *Lacan: The Absolute Master*. Translated by Douglas Brick. Stanford, Calif.: Stanford University Press.

Bow, Leslie. 2001. *Betrayal and Other Acts of Subversion: Feminism, Sexual Politics, Asian American Women's Literature*. Princeton: Princeton University Press.

Boyarin, Daniel. 2002. The *Ioudaioi* in John and the Prehistory of "Judaism." Pages 216–39 in *Pauline Conversations in Context: Essays in Honor of Calvin J. Roetzel*. Edited by Janice Capel Anderson, Philip Sellew, and Claudia Setzer. Sheffield: Sheffield Academic Press.

Brown, Michael Joseph. 2004. *Blackening of the Bible: The Aims of African American Biblical Interpretation*. Harrisburg, Pa.: Trinity Press International.

Brown, Raymond E. 1966. *The Gospel according to John I–XII*. AB29. Garden City, N.Y.: Doubleday.

———. 1970. *The Gospel according to John XIII–XXI*. AB29A. Garden City, N.Y.: Doubleday.

Burchell, Graham, Colin Gordon, and Peter Miller, eds. 1991. *The Foucault Effect: Studies in Governmentality*. Chicago: University of Chicago Press.

Butler, Judith. 1990. *Gender Trouble: Feminism and the Subversion of Identity*. New York: Routledge.

———. 2004. *Undoing Gender*. New York: Routledge.

Carson, Anne. 1999. Dirt and Desire: The Phenomenology of Female Pollution in Antiquity. Pages 77–100 in Porter 1999.

Cave, Terrence. 1988. *Recognitions: A Study in Poetics*. Oxford: Clarendon.

Chatterjee, Partha. 1986. *Nationalist Thought and the Colonial World: A Derivative Discourse*. Minneapolis: University of Minnesota Press.

———. 1993. *The Nation and Its Fragments: Colonial and Postcolonial Histories*. Princeton: Princeton University Press.

———. 2002. *A Princely Imposter? The Strange and Universal History of the Kumar of Bhawal*. Princeton: Princeton University Press.

Chen, Tina. 2005. *Double Agency: Acts of Impersonation in Asian American Literature and Culture*. Stanford, Calif.: Stanford University Press.

Clymer, Kenton J. 1986. *Protestant Missionaries in the Philippines, 1898–1916: An Inquiry into the American Colonial Mentality*. Urbana: University of Illinois.

Cohen, Shaye J. D. 1999. *The Beginnings of Jewishness: Boundaries, Varieties, Uncertainties*. Berkeley and Los Angeles: University of California Press.

Collins, Adela Yarbro. 1982. New Testament Perspectives: The Gospel of John. *JSOT* 22:47–53.

Collins, John J. 2004. *Introduction to the Hebrew Bible*. Minneapolis: Fortress.

Conway, Colleen M. 1999. *Men and Women in the Fourth Gospel: Gender and Johannine Characterization*. Atlanta: Society of Biblical Literature.

————. 2003a. "Behold the Man!" Masculine Christology and the Fourth Gospel. Pages 163–80 in *New Testament Masculinities*. Edited by Stephen D. Moore and Janice Capel Anderson. SemeiaSt 45. Atlanta: Society of Biblical Literature.

————. 2003b. Gender Matters in John. Pages 79–103 in vol. 2 of *A Feminist Companion to John*. Edited by Amy-Jill Levine with Marianne Blickenstaff. Cleveland: Pilgrim.

Crenshaw, Kimberlé Williams. 1995. Mapping the Margins: Intersectionality, Identity Politics, and Violence against Women of Color. Pages 357–83 in *Critical Race Theory: The Key Writings That Formed the Movement*. Edited by Kimberlé Crenshaw, Neil Gotanda, Gary Peller, and Kendall Thomas. New York: New.

Cruz-Malavé, Arnaldo, and Martin F. Manalansan IV, eds. 2002. *Queer Globalizations: Citizenship and the Afterlife of Colonialism*. New York: New York University Press.

Cvetkovich, Ann. 2003. *An Archive of Feelings: Trauma, Sexuality, and Lesbian Public Cultures*. Durham, N.C.: Duke University Press.

Derrida, Jacques. 1981. *Dissemination*. Translated by Barbara Johnson. Chicago: University of Chicago Press.

————. 1986. *Glas*. Translated by John P. Leavery Jr. and Richard Rond. Lincoln: University of Nebraska Press.

Douglas, Mary. 1966. *Purity and Danger: An Analysis of Concepts of Pollution and Taboo*. London: Routledge.

Dube, Musa W. 2002. Reading for Decolonization (John 4.1–42). Pages 51–75 in *John and Postcolonialism: Travel, Space and Power*. Edited by Musa W. Dube and Jeffrey L. Staley. Sheffield: Sheffield Academic Press.

Eng, David L., and Alice Y. Hom. 1998. Introduction, Q & A: Notes on a Queer Asian America. Pages 1–21 in *Q & A: Queer in Asian America*. Edited by David L. Eng and Alice Y. Hom. Philadelphia: Temple University Press.

Epps, Brad. 2001. Passing Lines: Immigration and the Performance of American Identity. Pages 92–134 in Sánchez and Schlossberg 2001.

Farmer, William R., ed. 1999. *Anti-Judaism and the Gospels*. Harrisburg, Pa.: Trinity Press International.

Fehribach, Adeline. 1998. *The Women in the Life of the Bridegroom: A Feminist Historical-Literary Analysis of the Female Characters in the Fourth Gospel*. Collegeville, Minn.: Liturgical Press.

Foucault, Michel. 1978. *The History of Sexuality*. Translated by Robert Hurley. New York: Vintage Books.

Freud, Sigmund. 1961a. *Beyond the Pleasure Principle*. Translated by James Strachey. New York: Norton. [orig. 1920]

————. 1961b. Fetishism. Pages 152–57 in *The Future of an Illusion, Civilization and Its Discontents and Other Works*. Translated by James Strachey. New York: Norton. [orig. 1927]

Gallop, Jane. 1995. Im-personation: A Reading in the Guise of an Introduction. Pages 1–18 in *Pedagogy: The Question of Impersonation.* Edited by Jane Gallop. Bloomington: Indiana University Press.

Garber, Marjorie. 1992. *Vested Interests: Cross-Dressing and Cultural Anxiety.* New York: Routledge.

Girard, René. 1985. The Politics of Desire in *Troilus and Cressida.* Pages 188–209 in *Shakespeare and the Question of Theory.* Edited by Patricia Parker and Geoffrey Hartman. New York: Methuen.

Gleason, Maud W. 1995. *Making Men: Sophists and Self-Representation in Ancient Rome.* Princeton: Princeton University Press.

Goodwin, Mark. 1999. Response to David Rensberger: Questions about a Jewish Johannine Community. Pages 158–71 in Farmer 1999.

Gopinath, Gayatri. 2005. *Impossible Desires: Queer Diasporas and South Asian Public Cultures.* Durham, N.C.: Duke University Press.

Gordon, Avery F. 1997. *Ghostly Matters: Haunting and the Sociological Imagination.* Minneapolis: University of Minnesota Press.

Goss, Robert E. 2006. John. Pages 548–65 in *The Queer Bible Commentary.* Edited by Thomas Bohache, Robert Goss, Deryn Guest, and Mona West. Norwich: SCM.

Grau, Marion. 2004. Divine Commerce: A Postcolonial Christology for Times of Neocolonial Empire. Pages 164–84 in Keller, Nausner, and Rivera 2004.

Guardiola-Sáenz, Leticia A. 2002. Border-Crossing and Its Redemptive Power in John 7.53–8.11: A Cultural Reading of Jesus and the *Accused.* Pages 129–52 in *John and Postcolonialism: Travel, Space and Power.* Edited by Musa W. Dube and Jeffrey L. Staley. Sheffield: Sheffield Academic Press.

Guzmán, Manuel. 1997. 'Pa' la escuelita con mucho cuida'o y por la orillita': A Journey through the Contested Terrains of the Nation and Sexual Orientation. Pages 209–28 in *Puerto Rican Jam: Rethinking Colonialism and Nationalism.* Edited by Frances Negrón-Muntaner and Ramón Grosfoguel. Minneapolis: University of Minnesota Press.

Halberstam, Judith. 1998. *Female Masculinity.* Durham, N.C.: Duke University Press.

Henderson, John. 1999. Smashing Bodies: The Corinthian Tydeus and Ismene Amphora (Louvre E640). Pages 19–49 in Porter 1999.

Hendricks, Obery M., Jr. 1995. A Discourse of Domination: A Socio-rhetorical Study of the Use of *Ioudaios* in the Fourth Gospel. Ph.D. diss. Princeton University.

Hoglund, Kennth G. 1992. *Achaemenid Imperial Administration in Syria-Palestine and the Missions of Ezra and Nehemiah.* SBLDS 125. Atlanta: Scholars Press.

Hooker, Morna D. 1997. *Beginnings: Keys That Open the Gospels.* Harrisburg, Pa.: Trinity Press International.

Jakobsen, Janet R. 2003. Queers Are Like Jews, Aren't They? Analogy and Alliance Politics. Pages 64–89 in *Queer Theory and the Jewish Question.* Edited by Daniel Boyarin, Daniel Itzkovitz, and Ann Pellegrini. New York: Columbia University Press.

Janzen, David. 2002. *Witch-Hunts, Purity and Social Boundaries: The Expulsion of Foreign Women in Ezra 9–10*. JSOTSup 350. Sheffield: Sheffield Academic Press.

Jones, Larry Paul. 1997. *The Symbol of Water in the Gospel of John*. Sheffield: Sheffield Academic.

Joseph, Miranda. 2002. Family Affairs: The Discourse of Global/Localization. Pages 71–99 in Cruz-Malavé and Manalansan 2002.

Kates, Gary. 1991. D'Eon Returns to France: Gender and Power in 1777. Pages 167–94 in *Body Guards: The Cultural Politics of Gender Ambiguity*. Edited by Julia Epstein and Kristina Straub. New York: Routledge.

Keller, Catherine, Michael Nausner and Mayra Rivera, eds. 2004. *Postcolonial Theologies: Divinity and Empire*. St. Louis: Chalice.

Kim, Jean. 2004. *Woman and Nation: An Intercontextual Reading of the Gospel of John*. Biblical Interpretation Series 69. Leiden: Brill.

———. 2006. Empowerment or Enslavement? Reading John 4 Intertextually with Ezra-Nehemiah. Pages 99–111 in *Ways of Being, Ways of Reading: Asian American Biblical Interpretation*. Edited by Mary F. Foskett and Jeffrey Kah-Jin Kuan. St. Louis: Chalice.

Koshy, Susan. 2004. *Sexual Naturalization: Asian Americans and Miscegenation*. Stanford, Calif.: Stanford University Press.

Kysar, Robert. 1993. *John: The Maverick Gospel*. Rev. ed. Louisville: Westminster John Knox.

Lacan, Jacques. 1977. *Ecrits: A Selection*. Translated by Alan Sheridan. New York: Norton.

Lea, Thomas D. 1999. Response to David Rensberger. Pages 172–75 in Farmer 1999.

Lee, Dorothy. 2002. *Flesh and Glory: Symbolism, Gender and the Theology in the Gospel of John*. New York: Crossroad.

Lee, James Kyung-Jin. 2004. *Urban Triage: Race and the Fictions of Multiculturalism*. Minneapolis: University of Minnesota Press.

Levine, Amy-Jill. 1990. Who's Catering the Q Affair? Feminist Observations on Q Paraenesis. *Semeia* 50:145–61.

Li, David Leiwei. 1998. *Imagining the Nation: Asian American Literature and Cultural Consent*. Stanford, Calif.: Stanford University Press.

Liew, Tat-siong Benny. 2002. Ambiguous Admittance: Consent and Descent in John's Community of "Upward Mobility." Pages 193–224 in *John and Postcolonialism: Travel, Space and Power*. Edited by Musa W. Dube and Jeffrey L. Staley. Sheffield: Sheffield Academic Press.

Lorde, Audre. 1998 *Sister Outsider: Essays and Speeches*. Freedom: Crossing.

Luibhéid, Eithne. 2005. Introduction: Queering Migration and Citizenship. Pages ix–xlvi in Luibhéid and Cantú 2005.

Luibhéid, Eithne, and Lionel Cantú Jr., eds. 2005. *Queer Migrations: Sexuality, U.S. Citizenship, and Border Crossings*. Minneapolis: University of Minnesota Press.

Lyotard, Jean François. 1993. *Libidinal Economy*. Translated by Lain Hamilton Grant. Bloomington: Indiana University Press.

McClintock, Anne. 1995. *Imperial Leather: Race, Gender and Sexuality in the Colonial Context*. New York: Routledge.

McKinlay, Judith E. 1996. *Gendering Wisdom the Host: Biblical Invitations to Eat and Drink*. Sheffield: Sheffield Academic Press.

Manalansan, Martin F. IV. 2003. *Global Divas: Filipino Gay Men in the Diaspora*. Durham, N.C.: Duke University Press.

Mitchell, Juliet. 1992. From King Lear to Anna O and Beyond: Some Speculative Theses on Hysteria and the Traditionless Subject. *The Yale Journal of Criticism* 5:91–107.

Moloney, Francis J. 1993. *Belief in the Word: Reading John 1–4*. Minneapolis: Fortress.

——. 1998. *Glory and Dishonor: Reading John 13–21*. Minneapolis: Fortress.

Moore, Stephen D. 1994. *Poststructuralism and the New Testament: Derrida and Foucault at the Foot of the Cross*. Philadelphia: Fortress.

——. 2003. Are There Impurities in the Living Water That the Johannine Jesus Dispenses? Pages 78–97 in vol. 1 of *A Feminist Companion to John*. Edited by Amy-Jill Levine with Marianne Blickenstaff. Cleveland: Pilgrim.

——. 2006. *Empire and Apocalypse: Postcolonialism and the New Testament*. Sheffield: Sheffield Phoenix.

Murnaghan, Sheila, and Sandra R. Joshel, eds. 1998. *Women and Slaves in Greco-Roman Culture: Differential Equations*. New York: Routledge.

Nehru, Jawaharlal. 1936. *An Autobiography: With Musings on Recent Events in India*. London: John Lane.

Neyrey, Jerome H. 1979. Jacob Traditions and the Interpretation of John 4:10–26. *CBQ* 41:419–37.

Ng, Wai Yee. 2001. *Water Symbolism in John: An Eschatological Interpretation*. New York: Lang.

Porter, James I., ed. 1999. *Constructions of the Classical Body*. Ann Arbor: University of Michigan Press.

Rabasa, José. 1997. Of Zapatismo: Reflections on the Folkloric and the Impossible in a Subaltern Insurrection. Pages 399–431 in *The Politics of Culture in the Shadow of Capital*. Edited by Lisa Lowe and David Lloyd. Durham, N.C.: Duke University Press.

Rensberger, David. 1999. Anti-Judaism and the Gospel of John. Pages 120–57 in Farmer 1999.

Ringe, Sharon. 1999. *Wisdom's Friends: Community and Christology in the Fourth Gospel*. Louisville: Westminster John Knox.

Rivera, Mayra. 2004. God at the Crossroads. Pages 186–203 in Keller, Nausner and Rivera 2004.

Sánchez, María Carla, and Linda Schlossberg, eds. 2001. *Passing: Identity and Interpretation in Sexuality, Race and Religion.* New York: New York University Press.

Sandoval, Chela. 2002. Dissident Globalizations, Emancipatory Methods, Social-Erotics. Pages 20–32 in Cruz-Malavé and Manalansan 2002.

Sandoval Sánchez, Alberto. 1997. Puerto Rican Identity Up in the Air: Air Migration, Its Cultural Representations, and Me Cruzando el Charco. Pages 189–208 in *Puerto Rican Jam: Essays on Culture and Politics.* Edited by Frances Negrón-Muntaner and Ramón Grosfoguel. Minneapolis: University of Minnesota Press.

Santiago, Silviano. 2002. The Wily Homosexual (First—and Necessarily Hasty—Notes). Pages 13–19 in Cruz-Malavé and Manalansan 2002.

Schlossberg, Linda. 2001. Introduction: Rites of Passing. Pages 1–12 in Sánchez and Schlossberg 2001.

Schneiders, Sandra M. 1999. *Written That You May Believe: Encountering Jesus in the Fourth Gospel.* New York: Crossroad.

Schwartz, Seth. 2001. *Imperialism and Jewish Society, 200 BCE to 640 CE.* Princeton: Princeton University Press.

Scott, Martin. 1992. *Sophia and the Johannine Jesus.* JSNTSup 71. Sheffield: JSOT Press.

Sifuentes-Jáuregui, Ben. 2002. *Transvestitism, Masculinity, and Latin American Literature.* New York: Palgrave.

Solomon, Alisa. 2005. Trans/Migrant: Christina Madrazo's All-American Story. Pages 3–29 in Luibhéid and Cantú 2005.

Somerville, Siobhan B. 2005. Sexual Aliens and the Racialized State: A Queer Reading of the 1952 U.S. Immigration and Nationality Act. Pages 75–91 in Luibhéid and Cantú 2005.

Spivak, Gayatri Chakravorty. 2002. Resident Alien. Pages 47–65 in *Relocating Postcolonialism.* Edited by David Theo Goldberg and Ato Quayson. Malden, Mass.: Blackwell.

Stibbe, Mark W. G. 1991. The Elusive Christ: A New Reading of the Fourth Gospel. *JSNT* 44:20–39.

Visweswaran, Kamala. 1997. Diaspora by Design: Flexible Citizenship and South Asians in U.S. Racial Formation. *Diaspora* 6:5–29.

Volcano, Del La Grace, and Judith "Jack" Halberstam. 1999. *The Drag King Book.* London: Serpent's Tail.

Webster, Jane S. 2003. *Ingesting Jesus: Eating and Drinking in the Gospel of John.* SBLAcBib 6. Atlanta: Society of Biblical Literature.

Yamaguchi, Satoko. 2002. *Mary and Martha: Women in the World of Jesus.* Maryknoll, N.Y.: Orbis.

Yamamoto, Hisaye. 1992. A Fire in Fontana. Pages 366–73 in *Rereading America: Cultural Contexts for Critical Thinking and Writing*. Edited by Gary Columbo, Robert Cullen, and Bonnie Lisle. Boston: Bedford. [orig. 1985]

Yee, Gale A. 1989. *Jewish Feasts and the Gospel of John*. Wilmington, Del.: Glazier.

———. 2003. *Poor Banished Children of Eve: Woman as Evil in the Hebrew Bible*. Minneapolis: Fortress.

Zeitlin, Froma I. 1996. *Playing the Other: Gender and Society in Classical Greek Literature*. Chicago: University of Chicago Press.

"Upon All Flesh": Acts 2, African Americans, and Intersectional Realities

Demetrius K. Williams

In the Acts of the Apostles, the second volume of Luke's two-volume work, the author seeks to expand further upon the theme of universalism adumbrated in the Gospel of Luke. Thus, for example, the genealogy ends with Adam, the universal progenitor of humankind (Luke 3:38–42); Mary of Bethany sits at Jesus' feet as an equal to the male disciples (10:38–42); and Jesus is open to those outside the people of Israel (7:1–10; 10:25–37). With the descent and outpouring of the Holy Spirit in Acts 2, the author continues the theme of universalism by means of the prophecy of Joel, through which it appears not only that the "last days" are inaugurated but also that the promise of a new age is dawning wherein the former barriers and divisions of race/ethnicity ("all flesh"), sex/gender ("sons and daughters"), young/old ("young men/old men"), and class/status ("male slaves and female slaves") are in the process of being eradicated. However, as the narrative unfolds, only the race/ethnicity category receives ample attention and articulation (i.e., the inclusion of Gentiles into the people of Israel).

This essay seeks to explore how an examination of Acts' treatment of the traditional categories of race, class, and gender through the Joel-prophecy paradigm can be instructive for understanding historically African Americans' rhetoric of "equality." This can be accomplished through showing how Acts itself presents a *deficient implementation of this model of inclusivity* represented by Joel's prophecy. This essay will suggest further that, while these categories are understood today as intersectional and interstructural, race/ethnicity has inevitably continued to prevail to the neglect and detriment of the others. In short, the amelioration of one category does not necessarily ameliorate or correct the others.

The approach of this investigation will be ideological. One aspect of this type of analysis is to pay close attention to the ideology of the text and the author's narrative strategies. This is important because this essay seeks to avoid replicating or reinscribing the perspective of the text or capitulating to the persuasive strategies of the author. In this way, it will be possible to uncover hidden tendencies in the narrative of Acts and to expose the discursive predispositions of the author.

Another aspect of such analysis, as defined by Fernando Segovia, is to view it as an element of cultural studies. Segovia describes such an approach to ideology within biblical studies as a mode of discourse focusing on "contextualization and perspective, social location and agenda, and hence on the political character of all compositions and texts as well as reading and interpretation" (2000, 41). This means that the interpreter himself or herself must be as forthright and honest as possible about his or her own social context and location as well as presuppositions, realizing that both text and interpreter have particular agendas. Suffice it to say in this regard that I am an African American, forty-something, married with children, heterosexual male trained both in New Testament and Christian origins and religious studies. I was reared in and continue to practice ministry (for twenty-five years) in the African American Baptist tradition (although I have provided service for other Protestant denominations over the years). In addition, I have been teaching in both university and seminary settings for over fifteen years. Finally, while much more perhaps can be said, let it suffice to say that an essential aspect of my agenda in this essay is to examine, explore, and evaluate how the Pentecost paradigm of Acts 2 has functioned in African American experience and interpretive tradition(s).

THE PENTECOST PARADIGM

There is a general consensus that the Pentecost account of Acts 2 is central to the overall development of the narrative. It has been said that, "No text in Acts has received closer scrutiny than Acts 2. Whole theologies and denominations have been built up around the Acts 2 accounts" (Witherington 1998, 128). To be sure, the account of the descent of the Holy Spirit on the day of Pentecost is a significant and pivotal event for Luke. Of particular note is that Luke made some structural parallels to his Gospel. For example, John the Baptist proclaims that the one who is coming "will baptize you with the Holy Spirit and with fire" (Luke 3:16). This is followed by Jesus' baptism and the descent of the Holy Spirit upon him (Luke 3:21–22), resulting in his inaugural sermon based upon Isaiah (61:1; 58:6; 61:2; that includes the important reference, "the Spirit of the Lord is upon me…"), which clarifies that God's promises in the prophets are being fulfilled in Jesus' ministry (Luke 4:16–30; Witherington 1998). These features are paralleled in Acts: Jesus promises the Holy Spirit to the disciples (Luke 24:49; Acts 1:5); then the disciples are filled with the Spirit, resulting in Peter's programmatic sermon (Acts 2:14–41), and they become witnesses proclaiming the gospel to the ends of the earth (thus fulfilling Jesus' prophecy in Acts 1:8). Whereas Jesus' ministry and message was to the people Israel, now the message of the disciples, while beginning with Israel, is to reach all nations (Gentiles). For this reason, Peter's quotation of Joel (2:28–32) in his sermon plays a significant role in the entire book: Joel's prophecy summarizes the nature of all that follows in the rest of the book and is paradigmatic for the ministry of the apostles (Talbert 1975, 195).

To be sure, Pentecost for Luke is *the* critical event that sets the stage for all that follows. Ben Witherington captures this well, "Without the coming of the Spirit there would be no prophecy, no preaching, no mission, no conversion, and no worldwide Christian movement" (1998, 129–30).

It can be argued, then, that Acts expects that the Pentecost narrative be read as indicating that the coming of the Holy Spirit represents a new order that is manifested as a leveling power that destroys position and privilege. The Spirit is poured upon "all flesh," not just to certain chosen individuals, which is a sign of the messianic age. Peter's speech does not initiate the worldwide Gentile mission but is presented essentially to ethnic Jews from all parts of the known world. However, Luke's use of ethnic Diaspora Jews indicates not only that they represent every nation but also that the Holy Spirit eventually should overcome all barriers to the gospel—language, ethnicity, class, and gender. In the apostles' mission to reach the world with the gospel, the activity of the Holy Spirit becomes evident throughout the narrative. The theology of the early Christian missionary movement expressed in Acts 2 is rooted in the experiences of the Spirit: Jew and Gentile, slave and free, women and men have access to and receive the Spirit (Schüssler Fiorenza 1989, 180–85). It is possible to argue that the theology of the Spirit in Acts 2 has significant parallels to the statement of Gal 3:28. The prophecy of Joel compares quite tellingly with the conceptual framework of Gal 3:28. To clarify this point, compare the two passages below.[1]

Acts 2:16–21	Gal 3:28
Prophecy	
This is what was spoken through the prophet Joel:	And the scripture, foreseeing that God would justify the Gentiles by faith, declared the gospel beforehand to Abraham, saying, "All the Gentiles shall be blessed in you." (Gal 3:8)
Fulfillment	
In the last days it will be, God declares,	But now that faith has come … in Christ Jesus you are all children of God through faith. (Gal 3:25)

---

1. This comparison was utilized before in another work to emphasize Paul's use of the Gal 3:28 paradigm (Williams 2004, 29–31), but here it is being used to expose Acts' use of a similar paradigm based upon the prophecy of Joel (2:28–32).

Abolition of Racial/Ethnic Barriers

| that I will pour out my Spirit upon all flesh | As many of you as were baptized into Christ have clothed yourselves with Christ. There is no longer Jew or Greek. |

Abolition of Sex/Gender Barriers

| and your sons and your daughters shall prophesy … | there is no longer male and female |

Abolition of Class/Status Barriers

| Even upon my slaves, both men and women, in those days I will pour out my Spirit; and they shall prophesy … | there is no longer slave or free, |

Statement of Universality of Salvation/Human Equality and Unity

| Then everyone who calls on the name of the Lord shall be saved. | for all of you are one in Christ Jesus. |

The comparison of these two isolated passages above, with the emphasis on the traditional categories of race/ethnicity, class/status, and sex/gender—thus bracketing in this study the element regarding young/old in Acts—reveals several notable parallels. First, there is a similar structure: (1) there is a statement related to the realization of "end times" promises and their fulfillment within the Christian community (*prophecy* and *fulfillment*); (2) this is followed by a statement regarding traditional societal barriers: race/ethnicity, sex/gender, and class/status; (3) finally, there is a statement on the universality of salvation/unity of humanity. Second, such structural parallels indicate that both paradigms are based upon the advent and experience of the Holy Spirit within the early community of believers. Both passages include a discussion of the presence of the Spirit within the community (Acts 2; Gal 3:2–3). Lastly, both passages include baptism: the "baptism in the Spirit" in Acts (1:4; 2:38—followed by "water" baptism at the end of Peter's Pentecost sermon, 2:37–42); presumably water baptism in Galatians (Gal 3:26–28 has been recognized as a "baptismal confession"). The sum effect of this comparison is that in both paradigms the old patterns of division and separation are being reconceptualized through the theology of the Holy Spirit. What was promised in the prophets (Joel 2:28–29; Ezek 39:29; Isa 43:18–19; 65:17)—namely, that the outpouring of the Holy Spirit not only initiates the "last days" but also the reconstitution of Israel and the soon-following openness of salvation to all nations (Gentiles)—is now becoming realized in the community of the baptized. Thus, armed with this new paradigm, Luke portrays how the early Christian missionaries sought to propagate this message in the Greco-Roman world.

Like Paul, who to a greater or lesser degree appropriated the vision of Gal 3:28 into his mission and message, Luke also appropriated and incorporated certain elements of the similar vision of Joel into his gospel message. However, it is important to examine and explore Luke's narrative presentation of the mission of the early church in Acts in order to determine more accurately how he may have understood and sought to implement this vision. A brief look at Paul's use of the Gal 3:28 paradigm will be instructive for an examination of Luke's perspective.

Luke's Use of Joel's Prophecy in His Narrative: Universalist Predictions, Unfulfilled Promises

It was noted above that both Gal 3:28 and Acts 2:16–21 have striking conceptual and structural parallels. In exploring Luke's use of Joel's prophecy in the development of his narrative, it will be helpful to examine and explore how his narrative hero, Paul, sought to employ the Gal 3:28 paradigm in his mission and message. In the examination of both paradigms below, it will become apparent even here that Luke and his champion of the gospel, Paul, share telling similarities in the application of their respective paradigms.

Paul and the Galatians 3:28 Paradigm

The short, formulaic statement in Gal 3:28 has certainly gained the attention of many New Testament scholars over the past few decades or so because it has come to occupy center stage in the debate over the role of women within early Christianity (MacDonald 1987, 14). Two primary proposals have been offered regarding its meaning for Paul: (1) it is a paradigm for a revolutionary social program that represents Paul's ideal for Christian relations; (2) Paul merely acknowledges the equal accessibility to God's grace but entails no revolutionary social agenda.

Other approaches concern the composition of the passage as either pre-Pauline or Pauline. In the latter position, the passage can be viewed as both a traditional and original formulation. It is argued that Paul altered the wording of this confession, which profoundly affected its ethical consequences. In its present form, the denial of social divisions in Gal 3:28 is Paul's "own original declaration" (MacDonald 1987, 15). Nevertheless, many interpreters would suggest that Gal 3:28 is not Paul's own novel creation but a quotation from early Christian baptismal liturgy: a pre-Pauline baptismal confession expressing "the theological self-understanding of the Christian missionary movement" (Schüssler Fiorenza 1989, 209). The radical equality of humankind through baptism into Christ is not a completely new invention of Paul. This notion existed already in earliest pre-Pauline Christianity. To be precise, the Hellenistic Christian mission acknowledged the societal-leveling quality of baptism apart from Paul (Scroggs

1972, 292; Schüssler Fiorenza 1989, 208–9). Before baptism into Christ, the world was divided into Jew/Greek, slave/free, and male/female, but through baptism these distinctions are removed. Regardless of whether one is convinced by either a pre-Pauline or Pauline composition of Gal 3:28, it will become apparent that Paul did not appropriate Gal 3:28 necessarily as his declaration for the equality of male/female or of master/slave.

While the reference to "male and female" and "slave or free" could have been a part of a traditional saying, Paul omitted the male/female pair of the saying in 1 Cor 12:13 because apparently women were exercising their "freedom in Christ." Thus, in 1 Cor 12:13 Paul does not talk about "all are one" (Gal 3:28), which could imply a notion of equality, but about the social unification of the community implied by Christian baptism. So in 1 Cor 12:13 he uses the image of "one body" and the language of "one Spirit" to emphasize such unity. Moreover, in Gal 3:28 Paul uses "neither ... nor" to formulate the pairs of opposites, while in 1 Cor 12:13 he uses the positive "whether ... or." Paul's intention here is not to emphasize the abolition of social differences but the unity of these different groups into one body (MacDonald 1987, 116).

Moreover, recognizing that several believers in his communities are also slaves and may gain the possibility of manumission, Paul addresses some of them directly in 1 Cor 7:21, stating, "If you can gain your freedom, by all means avail yourself of the opportunity" (Bartchy 1973, 155–59). He also reminds them: "you were bought with a price; do not become slaves of men" (1 Cor 7:23; Bartchy 1973, 121–26). Although Paul does not advocate the mass rebellion of slaves nor challenge directly the system of slavery (although he encourages Philemon to treat Onesimus "no longer as [if] he were a slave, but as a beloved brother," Phlm 16), he does encourage slaves to take the opportunity of manumission if it arises. *Yet he provides no practical program to achieve such goals.* This, however, is not of central importance to Paul. Thus he advises that slaves are not to fret: "In whatever state each was called, there let him remain with God (7:24, rsv)." In fact, "because the appointed time has grown very short" (rsv; that is, the nearness of the parousia), slaves should not necessarily be overly concerned with their status as such. Therefore, Paul says, "Were you a slave when called? Never Mind" (1 Cor 7:21 rsv). In this way, Paul was able to make concessions with respect to the social realization of the male/female and slave/free categories.

This indicates that the categories related to sex/gender and slave/free were the least important for Paul. As a matter of fact, the last two categories in Gal 3:28 "came along for the ride" (Scroggs 1972, 291), because only the Jew/Greek pair was most important for Paul. It was also *the only category that Paul worked out theologically to support a program for the social realization of this vision prior to the parousia.* His teaching on justification by faith in Romans, Galatians, and Philippians was formulated to articulate and support his vision that Jew and Greek are equal and have equal access to the covenant promises (for Gentiles, without recourse to the Jewish identity symbols of circumcision and the observance of certain parts of the law). This ideal was sustained in Paul's theology and praxis even to the point of open conflict (as in his debate with Peter in Gal 2). Thus, *Paul only fully worked out a sustained solution to the Jew/Greek question, not the woman and slave question.* In this way, Paul's use of Gal 3:28 shows that it is possible to utilize all the categories of the seemingly egalitarian paradigm to promote only one particular aspect, while at the same time domesticating other aspects that could suggest more radical implications.

ACTS AND THE JOEL-PROPHECY PARADIGM

From the review of Paul's use of the Gal 3:28 paradigm, it will become apparent in the following discussion of Acts that a certain pattern will emerge in Luke's use of the Joel-prophecy paradigm. The Joel-prophecy paradigm, as noted above, includes the categories of "all flesh," sons and daughters, old men/young men, male slaves and female slaves. However, it must be examined whether it is the author's intention in the narrative to provide examples for how these categories (excluding the "old/young" category for our purposes) have become actualized within the community of believers. Since "Luke believes that God is faithful to his plan and promised purposes and that one can see certain patterns in history that indicate the regularity of God's working" (Witherington, 1998, 129), one should expect to see in the unfolding of the narrative how these categories are being fulfilled. Such an exploration will now engage our attention.

"ALL FLESH"

The prophecy of Joel, in the context of the ancient prophet himself, speaks of the "last days" in which God would pour out the Holy Spirit upon Israel and restore its fortunes, but offer judgment to the Gentiles (Joel 3:1–21). Although the dates of Joel's prophetic ministry cannot be determined with precision, scholars believe that he may have lived in Judah during the Persian period (539–331 B.C.E.). The context of Joel's prophetic utterances concerns a locust plague that ravished the country, which Joel viewed as God's judgment upon God's people. Using this event as a warning and a call to repentance (1:2–2:27), Joel depicts the advent of the Day of the Lord in which "all flesh" would be endowed with his Holy Spirit, and accompanied also by judgments and blessings (2:28–3:21; Hicks 1977, 1101). In the context of Joel's prophecy, however, "*all flesh* meant primarily the Jews" (3:2, 17, 19–21; Ezek 39:29; Hicks 1977, 1104), while for Luke it included *all nations* (Acts 2:17). Thus, according to the context of the passage in Joel (3:2, 17, 19–21), Gentiles ("the nations") are not included and, in consequence, are condemned to judgment! Luke may have been sensitive to such a context because "the event recorded in Acts 2 is not really about the inauguration of the worldwide Gentile mission" (Witherington 1998, 140) but about the gathering of ethnic Jews from around the known world. Nevertheless, Luke's narrative intention is to show how the gospel spread from Jerusalem to the ends of the world, which quite naturally for him included the Gentiles.

As the narrative in Acts unfolds, moving from the dramatic Pentecost event, it contains several episodes recounting the community's successful mission to the Samaritans, the near-kinsfolk of the Jews, and the Gentiles. Acts, however, appears to have an *ethnocentric presentation* of the early history of the church, because the work of mission and evangelism is restricted to Palestinian or Hellenistic Jews. Luke recounts the missionary activity of figures such as Peter, Philip, Barnabas, and Paul and includes also a few "minor" missionaries such as Priscilla and Aquila and the Alexandrian Jew Apollos, whom they "instructed more accurately in the faith" (18:1–2, 24–26). Yet Luke never recounts the missionary activity or preaching of any non-Jewish convert. In this regard Liew declares, "This ethnic monopoly (a kind of 'glass ceiling' for Gentile followers?) may explain why Paul circumcises Timothy, who has a Greek father and a Jewish mother (16:13)…. What distinguishes him is that Paul desires to make him a missionary partner (16:3)" (2004, 422).

In addition, it may also be questioned whether Luke depicts the Holy Spirit as bestowed upon all converts *without distinction*. This is an important question to explore, because the narrative of Acts indicates that faith in Christ without having the Holy Spirit represents incomplete or partial integration into the community (see 8:14–17; 18:24–9:7; Liew 2004). The Holy Spirit in Acts, however, is unpredictable (González 2001, 108–9): while the Samaritans experience a delay between their baptism and their receiving of the Holy Spirit (8:16), the Ephesians receive the Holy Spirit closely following their baptism (19:5–6). As for the centurion at Caesarea, Cornelius, the Holy Spirit comes upon him and his household even before they are baptized (10:44–48; Liew 2004, 420–21), causing some scholars to term this event, "the Gentile Pentecost" (Witherington 1998, 134). However, of the Ethiopian convert in Acts 8 whom Philip baptizes, there is no mention of his reception of the Holy Spirit. Instead, the Spirit moves upon Philip as he and the Ethiopian are rising from the baptismal waters, transporting Philip to a new locale, Caesarea (8:38–40). Despite the argument proffered for this,[2] the situation remains problematic. According to Benny Liew's cultural reading of Acts,

---

2. Interestingly, contemporary scholarship has also mitigated the significance of the conversion of the Ethiopian eunuch by suggesting that Luke does not follow a strictly chronological order in the presentation of the events. Rather, he completes the "Acts of Philip" before moving to the next subject. In this line of argument, although the conversion of the Ethiopian appears in Acts 8 and that of Cornelius in Acts 10, the latter preceded the former (González 2001, 117–18; Haenchen 1971, 309–17). This explanation still does not eliminate the valid perception of Luke's valuing the conversion of a European, a Roman centurion, over a *black* African, an official of the Candace.

If faith in Christ is like obtaining a "green card" that grants entry and residency, the coming of the Holy Spirit is comparable to the "naturalization" process that (theoretically) turns a "green-card" holder into a citizen eligible for equal rights and benefits. Yet in Acts, the newcomer cannot decide if and when he or she would satisfy this requirement of integration or "naturalization" by receiving the Holy Spirit. The matter is simply beyond human control. (2004, 420–21)

If this is the case, the ethnic black's incorporation into Christ is *incomplete*, while the nonblack, (European) Roman centurion's is complete, because "[t]hroughout Acts, the presence of the Spirit is seen as the distinguishing mark of Christianity—it is what makes a person a Christian.... The Spirit, then, is the *sine qua non* for being a Christian, not merely a means by which one gets a spiritual booster shot subsequent to conversion" (Witherington 1998, 140). That the Ethiopian was one of the few characters who after conversion through water baptism was not filled with the Holy Spirit leaves one to ponder.

"Sons and Daughters"

Luke saw in the mission of Peter and the other apostles, the evangelists such as Philip and Stephen, and especially in Paul the fulfillment of Joel's prophecy that, with the coming of the Holy Spirit upon *all flesh*, "sons and daughters would prophesy." It turns out that it is only the sons of Israel who do so. It should not be surprising now that there is no mention either of non-Jews in this regard or of the "prophesying daughters." Although Acts (and the Gospel of Luke) is generally held to be one of the New Testament writings that is affirming to women, this may not necessarily be so. Beverly Roberts Gaventa, in the thought-provoking article "What Ever Happened to the Prophesying Daughters?" raises this question to explore Acts' promise-fulfillment tendency. One might expect, after having read Luke's Gospel and the prominence accorded Elizabeth and Mary and the numerous women who appear in it, to hear the voices of the sons *and daughters* as one reads through Luke's companion volume Acts. There are several women mentioned by name in Acts—such as Tabitha, Mary (mother of John Mark), Lydia, and Damaris—who are among the believers, but they are not given voice. However, the first woman who speaks in the narrative, Sapphira, speaks her first *and last* words (Acts 5:8). It turns out that "[t]he famous—or rather infamous—first words from a woman in Acts are her last!" (Spencer 1977, 58, cited in Gaventa 2004, 49).

Since the first words of a woman believer are her last, one reads on, seeking to find in the narrative an account of the prophesying daughters in fulfillment of Joel's prophecy. Finally, one encounters them: they are Philip's four unmarried daughters (21:9). Although the reader is told that they prophesy, not a word is heard from their mouths. Instead, we hear from Agabus who came down from Judea to warn Paul of the danger awaiting him in Judea: "Thus says the

Holy Spirit, 'so shall the Jews at Jerusalem bind the man who owns this girdle and deliver him into the hands of the Gentiles'" (Acts 21:11). Agabus gave this prophecy while Paul was in Caesarea at the home of Philip the evangelist and his four prophesying daughters. Yet it is not the prophesying daughters of Philip who speak, but Agabus who travels some distance to do so. Thus, Gaventa asks, "What ever happened to those prophesying daughters? Where did they go and why do we not hear them speak?" (2004, 49). Their absence is not only the problem of *prophecy and its apparent nonfulfillment* but also of the general problem of the presentation of women (men and presentations of masculinity[3]) in Acts (50). Luke does not picture women as independent missionaries and preachers (even Prisca/Priscilla must *accompany her husband*). Rather, women are depicted in Acts as support workers and patrons for the male apostles' missionary activity (Schüssler Fiorenza 1989, 161).

"Male Slaves and Female Slaves"

The final element of the Joel-prophecy paradigm addresses prophesying slaves, male and female. Although Luke does not recount episodes of prophesying male slaves, he does provide two accounts of female slaves that are given voice, although briefly, in the narrative. In the first case of Rhoda, a house-slave who has an encounter with Peter and whose *testimony* about him is initially rejected, Luke approaches this aspect of the paradigm through the medium of comedy (Acts 12:6–17). In the second account, Paul exercises a sprit of divination from an unnamed slave-girl who *speaks the truth* (prophesies?) about his mission and message (Acts 16:16–18), and Paul's actions land him and his companion Silas into prison (16:19–40). While both women are described as slaves in the narrative, the only one who speaks prophetically is the mantic slave-girl of Acts 16, and she is not within the circle of Christian believers.

In Acts 12:6–17 the story of Peter's miraculous escape from prison is recounted. After his escape by means of an angelic deliverer, Peter makes his way to the house of Mary, mother of John Mark, and stands outside the door of the house knocking; then the comedy begins.

This slave-girl, Rhoda, answers Peter's persistent knocking at the door, while the believers in the house continue in prayer for his release. While Luke does not identify directly Rhoda's owner (which is most likely Mary, otherwise why would Rhoda attend her door?), her status is apparent: she is called a *paidiskē* (Acts 12:13; the range of meaning includes "young woman," "servant," "slave,"

---

3. See Gaventa 2004, 56–58. According to Penner and Vander Stichele, "male characters circumscribe female identity in the text, developing the 'domestic' characterization of women whereby premium Roman imperial values are demonstrated for leadership" (2004, 198; see also D'Angelo 2002).

even "prostitute"). When Rhoda arrives at the door, she is amazed to find Peter on the other side and runs back into the house to inform the others that, in answer to their prayers, Peter is present outside the door. This is a part of the humor: the flighty *servus currens* ("running slave") is a stock convention of ancient comedy (Chambers 2004, 91–92). Instead of opening the door as would normally be expected, she leaves Peter on the street to inform those assembled inside that Peter is outside the door. They tell her that "she is out of her mind," that it cannot be Peter, that it must be his "angel." The slave-girl, Rhoda, insists to those in the house (her superiors) that it is Peter, but they refuse to accept the veracity of her statement. Like the women at the tomb, who report to the male disciples that Jesus has risen, the slave-girl's message is flatly rejected. It is only when the believers in the house are willing to relinquish customary thinking (trusting the *testimony* of a slave) that they themselves recognize the truth (Chambers 2004, 95).

For Kathy Chambers, then, the comedic treatment of Rhoda, the female house-slave, in this episode is Luke's attempt to challenge the cultural status quo. She reads Luke's comedic trope positively: "The good news for those seeking liberative readings from Acts 12 is that Rhoda's appearance ... confirms the import of the voice of women and slaves. Rather than reinforcing the status quo, Luke's play upon comedic conventions can be seen as challenging constructions of status and gender" (96).

The challenge of social conventions is not so convincing, if it is recognized that "Luke is not afraid of exalting a slave woman at the expense of a wealthy, slave-owning woman" (Arlandsen 1997, 196, cited in Chambers 2004, 93–94). However, as we shall see below, in the case of Paul and the pagan owners of the Pythian-inspired slave-girl of Acts 16, her status is exalted neither over Paul nor over her male slave owners, even if they are pagans (Chambers 2004, 94). Even more, Robert Price views Luke's treatment of women on the whole as an attempt to suppress not only their voices but also their leadership roles and visionary experiences. Price argues that in Luke's sources originally Rhoda most likely beheld the Risen Christ, but Luke changes all this into her having an encounter with Peter. For Luke, then, according to Price, "If she saw someone, it was not Jesus, only Peter. If she bore tidings of the resurrection to the eleven, they were secondhand, from men at the tomb, not from the Risen One himself" (2004, 103). Thus, while Luke includes several accounts of women in Acts, his goal, as some interpreters suggest, is to suppress the roles of women that conflict with his own treatment of the church and understanding of authority. Luke's treatment of the Pythian slave-girl in Acts 16 exposes another aspect of his double-edged treatment of women.

Acts 16 recounts Paul's and his companions' travels into the region of Europe. In Luke's presentation of their journey into this "new region," he includes some apparent conventions of ancient (biblical) history having to do with encounters with (sometimes "bad") female inhabitants and soon-to-be-conquered territory (for example, Rahab the "harlot" in Josh 1; Staley 2004, 186, following Dube Shomanah's description of the "land possession type-scene" in 2000, 118–21). Paul's encounter with Lydia in Philippi, the first convert of Europe, conforms neatly to this land possession type-scene, which involves: (1) a traveling hero journeying to a foreign land, (2) meeting with a woman, and (3) bonding with her (Staley 2004, 186; Dube Shomanah 2000, 120). All these elements pertain in Acts 16:11–15:1): Paul enters into Philippi (16:12), (2) meets Lydia (and other women) at a place of prayer and converts her and her household (16:15), and (3) Lydia compels him to stay at her house (and share table fellowship?, 16:15). If our focus is to discuss the mantic slave-girl, why do we speak now of Lydia?

According to Staley, both Lydia and the slave-girl serve the same ideological function for Luke: as a means of legitimating the ideological and territorial conquests of nascent Christianity. "But what is surprising about the Acts text," Staley observes, "is the fact that it is the only biblical account where the reader finds *two* women on the border—one who is clearly more positive than the other" (2004, 186, emphasis original). Luke uses the stories of Lydia and the Pythian prophetess also as a part of his rhetorical strategy: as positive and negative examples of Christian and non-Christian virtues. Lydia, the well-to-do Christian convert and patroness of Paul, is respectable and deferential (the "good girl"); the mantic slave-girl (*paidiskē*) who prophesies for the profit of her pagan owners, "openly proclaiming her message on public streets has no place in Luke's church, but only an inferior religious practice until she is ultimately defeated and discarded" (the "bad girl"; Matthews 2004, 132). Hence, when the slave-girl prophesies correctly and truthfully about Paul, she is eventually silenced,[4] not because she lies but because Paul becomes annoyed with her (the spirit, neither identified as *demonic* nor *evil* but clearly problematic for Paul, is exorcised but she is not offered salvation, 16:18). It becomes clear, then, that Luke's handling of the narrative of the Pythian prophetess creates a contrast to the Christian women like Lydia (and Christian women prophets). The independent Lydia is domesticated through her conversion and comes *under* the authority of Paul.

Luke's narrative strategy shows that, through conversion, high-standing women enter the sphere of authoritative male control and thus Greco-Roman social values are manifested and displayed for the reader (Penner and Vander Stichele 2004, 207). This explains that, while the Pythian slave-girl *speaks and tells the truth* about Paul and his companions *and is silenced*, the Christian women prophets in the narrative like the daughters of Philip do not speak (and *should not speak*) at all. This has led some interpreters to argue that *Luke tends to distance Christian women from prophetic roles* (Matthews 2004, 128; D'Angelo 1990,

---

4. Robert Price argues that in Acts 16 the voice being silenced is actually that of the authentic Christian women prophets of which Lydia was a part (1997, 225–34). Like the Pythian slave-girl, they are an annoyance and should be silenced.

451–53). On the whole, as far as the Acts narrative goes, while Rhoda provides *truthful testimony* about Peter's presence outside of Mary's house and is ridiculed, another female slave in Acts 16 *prophesies truthfully* about Paul and Silas and is silenced.

Luke's Use of the Joel-Prophecy Paradigm: The Inclusion of the Gentiles

The preceding background discussion of Paul's use of the Gal 3:28 paradigm helps now to expose what aspects of the Joel-prophecy paradigm were most important for Luke and why. As noted above, although Paul utilized a preformulated (pre-Pauline) paradigm that could be read as having egalitarian and universalistic implications, his appropriation of it was not to produce a practical program for the social actualization of each element. Paul used the paradigm because it provided a foundation for him to argue for the incorporation (inclusion) of Gentiles into the covenant promises of Israel—making them a part of a new community, a new Israel, composed of both believing Jews and Gentiles (see 1 Cor 1:24). For this reason, the other aspects of the Gal 3:28 paradigm were least important and could be mitigated and subsumed under his overall missionary program, which received both theological articulation (the doctrine of justification by faith) and practical actualization (the founding of Gentile communities of believers).

In the same manner, Luke's goals are very similar to those of his narrative hero, Paul. Luke utilized the Joel prophecy to support his theology: the bestowal of the Holy Spirit upon "all flesh" embraces all racial-ethnic diversity without regard to geographical location, language, or nationality, validating and incorporating Gentiles into the covenant promises and the people of Israel. Acts portrays the integration of non-Jews into the early Christian community by linking conversion with integration into a new community (Liew 2004, 420–21). In this way, he is quite in line with Pauline teachings on Gentile incorporation into the new covenant community. To be sure, the incorporation of Jews and Gentiles as the new Israel receives major treatment and attention in Acts. The lengthy narrative encompassing Acts 8–15 indicates a tense and extended struggle (Liew 2004, 420–21). Not surprisingly for Luke, Paul's mission to "the ends of the earth" in the second half of the narrative is particularly important for showing this.

As mentioned before, Luke certainly sought to accomplish other goals by the use of the Joel-prophecy paradigm: arguing that the messianic age (the "last days") with the return of prophecy has begun, initiating and justifying thereby the church's worldwide mission. However, as the narrative unfolds, Luke's discursive strategies and intentions indicate that he is not disposed to recounting either how the social categories of sex/gender or class/status are being impacted contra the status quo in the community of believers or how the promise of prophesying daughters and slaves are being fulfilled within the same. Instead, only ethnic

Jewish-Israelite males are portrayed as delivering public speeches and engaging in mission. According to Penner and Vander Stichele,

> The imperial atmosphere of masculine comportment and display, quintessential in the formation of the narrative flow, also reflects on Luke's own manly performance.... The speaking voice in Acts is clearly a powerful male-gendered voice, which finally, says something about Luke and the masculine image he projects through inscribing it on the narrative community and especially its leaders, with whom Luke seems to identify the most, given the role they play in proclaiming *his* gospel. (202, emphasis original)

On this view, Luke upholds the Roman values of *virtus* and *imperium*, which encompasses the virtues of social order and masculinity. Therefore, Luke does not depict women and slaves engaging in powerful speech and behavior contrary to Roman social values, showing just how closely he comports to elite male values.

For this reason, Acts provides a deficient model of inclusivity. While the Joel prophecy has the rhetoric of universalism, Luke does not articulate how all of the various categories mentioned are fulfilled or are to be realized, nor does he provide a programmatic model for how the entire paradigm is being actualized through his narrative. In the final analysis, the category of "all flesh" (reflecting racial-ethnic realities, as I have argued) was most important for Luke, because the idea of embracing all ethnic diversity was in accordance with the values and self-image of the Roman Empire: it, too, could embrace all ethnic diversity without demolishing Roman social convention or hierarchical ordering of society.

African Americans and Acts 2: Liberating Vistas, Limited Vision

As noted above, the Pentecostal account in Acts 2 is a signal event in Luke's narrative. To be sure, the Joel prophecy as read through the presentation of Acts 2 has bred several universalist and egalitarian readings in the effective history and appropriation of this passage, despite the ideological scrutiny and criticism of the preceding section. African American Christians in general have read Acts 2 (and Acts as a whole) as essential for addressing arguments of inferiority, human unity, racism, and segregation. Black women, on the other hand, found ammunition to justify their practice of ministry, while at the same time posing a challenge to sexism in the black church and racism in society. Important for African Americans also was Luke's presentation of the dynamic spirituality of the event: this should not be overlooked because such spiritual enthusiasm will be the basis for a new black-founded denomination. Nevertheless, the issue of race/ethnicity emerges as an ever-present reality for African Americans within the U.S. social landscape. For this reason, I hope to show how the African American interpretive tradition(s) can benefit from the preceding ideological examination of Acts.

ACTS 2, AFRICAN AMERICANS, AND THE ORIGINS OF MODERN PENTECOSTALISM

The African American Christian interpretive traditions utilized Acts 2 (see Acts 2:23–47; 4:32–37; 8:26–40; 10:34–36; 17:36) to advocate for many social and religious changes, but this text has been important in African American religious history for another reason: the experience of *glossolalia*, "speaking in tongues," which was early on called the "Latter Rain" movement but later became known as the "Pentecostal movement" (Williams 2007, 218–21). The Pentecostal movement in the modern era began with the preaching of W. J. Seymour, a self-educated, African American, traveling Holiness preacher originally from Louisiana. His itinerant lifestyle led him to Los Angeles, California, where he began preaching a revival in 1906. The revival that he and others initiated between 1906 and 1909 became known as the Azusa Street Revival, and it would have far-reaching implications for American spirituality.

While initiated by an African American preacher, the movement was an atypical interracial movement from which whites later withdrew (Lincoln and Mamiya 1990, 76–78; Cox 1995, 45–47). Nevertheless, as in the Acts 2 account, "the coming of the Holy Spirit" in this latter-day event was marked by the development of a new community: at Azusa, black, white, Mexicans, and Asians alike sang and worshiped together. So uncharacteristic was such "integration" for its time that Harvey Cox remarks, "The interracial character … on Azusa Street was indeed a kind of miracle. It was, after all, a time of growing, not diminishing, racial separation everywhere else" (1995, 58). While most whites' observations about the interracial nature of the movement in the early days of the movement were negative, one white preacher wrote in his diary: "The color line was washed away by the blood" (58). Such positive observations were rare by whites and would soon give way to the separatist ideology of the day, causing Seymour to rethink his understanding of tongues.

Seymour's and the movement's continued attacks from white preachers caused him to rethink the power of *glossolalia* alone as a force to eradicate racism and separatism. During the early years of the movement, he put central emphasis on "tongues" both as the clearest evidence of the baptism in the Holy Spirit and as an indication of the last days. However, discovering that individuals who spoke in tongues could still continue to practice racism convinced him that it was not tongues that was most important but "the *dissolution of racial barriers* that was the surest sign of the Spirit's Pentecostal presence" (Cox 1995, 62–63). White Pentecostals disagreed. Having become uncomfortable with the disgust of other whites who castigated them for "worshiping with niggers," early white Pentecostals opted to reject interracial fellowship and black leadership but keep the tongues. Disheartened by whites' behavior, Seymour began to teach that tongue-speaking was only "one of the gifts of the Spirit," if indeed a gift at all. In other words, he now argued, "If you get angry, or speak evil, or backbite, I care not how many tongues you may have, you have not the baptism with the Holy Spirit." The genuine fruit of the

Spirit, he now recognized, were "love, joy, peace," and so forth (Gal 5:22–25; Cox 1995, 63). What becomes increasingly evident in the African American Pentecostal experience is that what begins as an expression of spiritual dynamism becomes tempered by social realism: the need to challenge racist attitudes and social structures. Despite this reality, the impact of the Pentecostal movement cannot be understated because what resulted from it was the establishment of the first black denomination that did not have its roots in a white denomination.

The founder of the first black Christian denomination in America, Charles Harrison Mason, a former Baptist minister, had an experience of "sanctification" in 1893, formed a Holiness church in 1897, and called it the Church of God in Christ (COGIC). In 1907, while attending the Azusa Street Revival, he experienced *glossolalia*, and this experience would initiate the founding of the COGIC denomination in that same year. COGIC was also the first black denomination to commission and ordain white ministers. Since COGIC was the only incorporated Pentecostal body from 1907 to 1914, it was the only ecclesiastical authority to which whites could appeal. As a result, Mason ordained many white men who were initially recognized as COGIC ministers. However, these same men, on account of segregation, organized in 1914 what became the Assemblies of God, the largest white Pentecostal denomination, ending by 1924 the brief interracial cooperation of black and white Pentecostals (Lincoln and Mamiya 1990, 81).

The COGIC fellowship began, as with the Azusa revival under Seymour, with the hope of the dissolution of racial (but not gender![5]) barriers between believers. For whites, Pentecostalism has been significant for "tongues," not recognizing that for blacks it also should include the divine presence that brings all people together in reconciliation, creating a new community of unity and equality. This has been the particular contribution of African Americans to the various Pentecostal manifestations in America: in their reading of Acts 2, the Spirit *democratizes* human relationships, dissolving the old patterns of domination and separation through the egalitarianism of the Spirit. Although Luke, in Acts, did not to bear this out completely in his account of the early church, his vision inspired hope among African Americans. They believed that what was promised in Joel is to be realized in the community of the baptized.

ACTS 2, AFRICAN AMERICANS, AND RACE

The African American biblical interpretive tradition leaves little doubt that it read "all flesh" in Acts 2 as referring to racial-ethnic categories. A clear indication of

---

5. The COGIC church still does not ordain women at the jurisdictional level, but they can "take charge" of a church until a male elder is available (Lincoln and Mamiya 1990, 90). However, W. J. Seymour was open to women preachers and exhorters; for him this was evidence of the gifts of the Spirit in the last days.

this reality can be noted in the account of Zilpha Elaw, a woman preacher of the nineteenth century who used the Pentecost account to argue against notions of "black inferiority" and race prejudice: "The Almighty," she says, "accounts not the black races of man either in the order of nature or spiritual capacity as inferior to white; for He bestows his Holy Spirit on, and dwells in them as readily as in persons of whiter complexion" (quoted in Andrews 1986, 85–86). In similar manner, the African Methodist Episcopal (AME) Bishop Reverdy Ransom also underscores the notion of race/ethnicity in his reading of the Pentecost account (Wimbush 1993, 139). He argues: "There should be no race problem in the Christian State. When Christianity received its Pentecostal baptism and seal from heaven it is recorded that, 'there were dwelling at Jerusalem Jews, devout men, out of every nation under heaven [Acts 2:5–11a]" (see Ransom 1999, 337).

In their use of Acts 2, both Elaw and Ransom agree that it pertains to issues of race/ethnicity. Yet as the African American interpretive tradition shows, there were some who were not willing to broaden the Joel-prophecy paradigm to apply to issues of women's ministry and leadership roles within the church. If most African American males consistently viewed Acts 2 as applying to the racial situation in the U.S., African American women understood it as including the gender equality issue, for the passage also says, "*and your daughters shall prophesy.*" For several black women, and a growing number of black men, this means a leveling of the barriers against women in the gospel ministry (Mitchell 1991; Williams 2004).

Early on, black women recognized the impact of Acts 2 for validating their call to ministry. The first black woman on record to make a plea for the recognition of her ministry in Richard Allen's newly organized AME church, Jarena Lee, used Acts' quotation of the Joel prophecy as the opening caption to her spiritual biography, *The Life and Religions Experience of Jarena Lee* (Andrews 1986, 27). Although she did not offer an overt interpretation of the passage as it pertained to her call to ministry, we can be certain that its placement as the opening caption to her spiritual biography is evidence of its provocative influence upon her.

Julia A. J. Foote, a preacher in the AME Zion church of the nineteenth century, describes her call to ministry in her spiritual autobiography, *A Brand Plucked from the Fire* (1879) (Andrews 1986; Collier-Thomas 1998, 57–59). Using the Joel prophecy of Acts 2, she presented a potent argument for supporting women preachers. She strongly felt that her call and commission to preach came from the Holy Spirit, despite the fact that the minister of the AME Zion church in Boston opposed her conviction to preach and had her ousted from the church. When recalling that her appeal to the denominational governing body of the AME Zion church was ignored, she reflected, "There was no justice meted out to women in those days. Even ministers of Christ did not feel that women had any rights which they were bound to respect" (Andrews 1986, 207). These words were a clear reverberation of the Supreme Court's statement in the Dred Scott Case, which held that African Americans "had no rights which the white man was bound to respect" (Andrews 1986, 20). Thus, she offers an entire chapter entitled "Women in the Gospel." Here she describes the authorization of Acts 2 for her preaching. She argues:

> I could not believe that it was a short-lived impulse or spasmodic influence that impelled me to preach. I read that on the day of Pentecost was the Scripture fulfilled as found in Joel ii. 28, 29; and it certainly will not be denied that women as well as men were at that "time filled with the Holy Ghost." ... Women and men are classed together, and if the power to preach the Gospel is short-lived and spasmodic in the case of women, it must be equally so in that of men; and if women have lost the gift of prophecy, so have men. (Andrews 1986, 208–9)

Foote reads Acts 2 and the Joel-Prophecy as having universal implications, which should be seen as eliminating the barriers against women's roles in preaching.

Rosa A. Horn, an ordained minister in the Fire Baptized Pentecostal Church in the early decades of the twentieth century, also used Joel's prophecy to support women's preaching:

> Note that when God said ["]your sons and your daughters shall prophesy["] (preach) [,] that meant man and woman.... Did not the Lord say that He would pour out His spirit upon all flesh in the last days? ... When you see the women preaching in the pulpit, preaching in the house, preaching in the streets, preaching everywhere, these are some of the signs of the last days.... Surely the Lord has called the women, under the Law and under Grace and he uses them whenever he needs them. (Collier-Thomas 1998, 180–81)

For Horn, Acts 2 and the entirety of Scripture ("under law and under grace") confirms the contemporary activity of women in ministry. She also argues that biblical women were not only equal to men in leading godly lives but often excelled men in doing God's work (Collier-Thomas 1998, 180–81).

Combining Joel's prophecy and Jesus' commissioning of the apostles in Acts 1:8 to be witnesses to the world, Leontine T. Kelly, a bishop in the United Methodist Church, argues that these witnesses are both male and female. She states that all are called and empowered by God through the Holy Spirit. Joel announces this centuries before the emergence of the church: "Joel understood that new visions would be needed and it would take the Spirit upon all flesh: '... and your sons and your daughters shall prophesy, your old men shall dream dreams, your young men shall see visions: And also upon the servants and upon the handmaids ... will I pour out my spirit'" (Joel 2:28–29, KJV). Kelly, like many women before her, finds a basis for supporting her ministry in particular and for all women in general in Joel's prophecy (Mitchell 1991, 142).

The Pentecost presentation of Acts 2 was thus important in the African American religious tradition because it supplied a basis for the black church to argue for inclusive and just practices within the church and American society.

Although African Americans' appropriation has captured the liberating vistas of the Joel-prophecy paradigm, it has also had limited vision, because concerns about race/ethnicity have been for the most part privileged above the other concerns. As for African American women, however, they have argued for the most part that the black church could not argue, on the one hand, for racial equality and, on the other hand, deny equal opportunity for women in ministry. It has been the African American women's interpretive traditions that have sought to push the full universal implications of the Joel-prophecy paradigm. To be sure, African American women's historical experience has compelled them to consider the intersectional realities of race/ethnicity, class/status, and sex/gender.

ACTS 2, AFRICAN AMERICANS, AND INTERSECTIONAL REALITIES

The incomparable success of Luke's treatment of Pentecost and Joel's prophecy in Acts 2 can be seen in the fact that it has continued to exert powerful influence in Christian communities throughout history. From our examination it is clear that Luke did not intend to eliminate social roles and differences in the communities of believers. Baptism in Jesus' name and the bestowal of the Holy Spirit upon "all flesh" entails the creation of a new community that includes all people, but this unity does not demand an elimination of social hierarchy, gender constraints, or one's former status. In Luke's treatment of slaves and women, there is no hint of equality, but both groups are under the authority of an appropriate male leader of the household/assembly. Upon conversion into the community of believers, one's "allegiances/alliances may shift, but the fundamental power structure [imperial order] stays in place" (Penner and Vander Stichele 2004, 209). It appears, then, that, for Luke and others in the ancient world, unity does not necessarily deny hierarchy, even in the community of believers. To be sure, unity in antiquity almost never implied social equality. In the ancient Mediterranean world, appeal to *interdependent* hierarchy is ubiquitous and was an established way of conceiving any sort of social unity (Stowers 1988, 304).

Contemporary African American biblical and theological scholars and social theorists have come to recognize the interesting interplay/interdependence between notions of social hierarchy and the three traditional categories of race/ethnicity, class/status, and sex/gender (as well as others) in oppressing people of color (Collins 1990). Moreover, Rosemary Radford Ruether, a feminist theologian, coined the phrase "interstructuring" to describe the interrelated nature of race, class, and sex and was one of the first white/Anglo scholars to explore this phenomenon. She argues that, while racism and sexism have been closely interrelated historically, they have not been exactly parallel. They have been, however, "interstructural elements of oppression within the overarching system of white male domination" (1995, 116). She asserts further that "this interstructuring of oppression by sex, race, and also class, creates intermediate tensions and alienations—between white women and black women, between black men and white women, and even black men and black women. Each group tends to suppress the experience of its racial or sexual counterparts" (116).

Our examination of African American appropriation of Acts 2 above—particularly noting how black men traditionally focused on race and black women on race and gender—has only hinted at such tensions. Moreover, recent womanist/feminist theologians and biblical interpreters have emphasized that patriarchy/white racism involved and involves a pyramid of interlocking that takes different forms in different historical circumstances (Schüssler Fiorenza 1992, 47; St. Clair 2007, 56). For this reason paradigms that cannot hold within their orbit multiplicative/multidimensional oppressions are to be considered deficient, but not necessarily to be devalued. As noted above, although Luke provided a deficient narrative fulfillment of the Joel-prophecy paradigm, African American Christians found aspects of its universalist language appealing and helpful in their struggles for justice and equality outside and inside the churches. The caveat is that African American appropriation of Acts 2 has also been deficient in implementing the full implications of the paradigm. Recognizing not only the interstructuring of the tri-/multidimensional oppressions of patriarchy/white racism, but also the "intersectional" realities of the same oppressions may help to think of liberation in critical and holistic terms.

The recognition of the multidimensional experience of an individual—for example, being black/African American, female/male, privileged/poor, and so forth—has been spoken of as "intersectional" realities. The same individual might improve upon or advance sociopolitically in one category, while the others remain the same or possibly worsen. Such intersectional realities should be recognized even more as African Americans explore the Bible in search of healing models and paradigms of liberation. History has taught us that liberation from overt, institutional racism did not cause an avalanche that automatically eliminated other oppressions. As we have seen in both Paul and Luke as well as in the African American interpretive tradition(s), racial-ethnic categories of unity and inclusion could be used without addressing equally as forcefully sex/gender and class/status concerns. For better or for worse, it appears that African Americans must be aware of the nature of postmodern blackness, which recognizes the permanency of race as an essential category in identity formation, continually in reconstruction as African Americans inhabit widely differentiated social spaces and communities of moral discourse. Furthermore, it recognizes that African American life and experience transpires in differentiated socioeconomic spaces along divisions of education, income, and occupations. "In these multiples sites," Victor Anderson has observed, "African Americans are continually negotiating the various languages of race, class, gender, and sexuality" (1995, 11–12).

WORKS CONSULTED

Anderson, Victor. 1995. *Beyond Ontological Blackness: An Essay on African American Religious and Cultural Criticism.* New York: Continuum.

Andrews, William L., ed. 1986. *Sisters of the Spirit: Three Black Women's Autobiographies of the Nineteenth Century.* Bloomington: Indiana University Press.

Arlandsen, James M. 1997. *Women, Class, and Society in Early Christianity: Models from Luke-Acts.* Peabody, Mass.: Hendrickson.

Bartchy, S. Scott. 1973. *MALLON CHRESAI: First-Century Slavery and the Interpretation of First Corinthians 7:21.* SBLDS 11. Missoula, Mont.: Scholars Press.

Chambers, Kathy. 2004. Knock, Knock—Who's There? Acts 12:6-17 as a Comedy of Errors. Pages 89–97 in Levine 2004.

Collier-Thomas, Bettye. 1998. *Daughters of Thunder: Black Women Preachers and Their Sermons 1850–1979.* San Francisco: Jossey-Bass.

Collins, Patricia Hill. 1990. *Black Feminist Thought.* New York: Routledge.

Cox, Harvey. 1995. *Fire from Heaven: The Rise of Pentecostal Spirituality and the Reshaping of Religion in the Twenty-First Century.* Reading, Mass.: Addison-Wesley.

D'Angelo, Mary Rose. 1990. Women in Luke-Acts: A Redactional View. *JBL* 109:441–61.

———. 2002. The *ANHR* Question in Luke-Acts: Imperial Masculinity and the Development of Women in the Early Second Century. Pages 44–69 in *A Feminist Companion to Luke.* Edited by Amy-Jill Levine. FCNTECW 3. London: Sheffield Academic Press.

Duba Shomanah, Musa W. 2000. *Postcolonial Feminist Interpretation of the Bible.* St. Louis: Chalice.

Gaventa, Beverly Roberts. 2004. What Ever Happened to the Prophesying Daughters? Pages 49–60 in Levine 2004.

González, Justo L. 2001. *Acts: The Gospel of the Spirit.* New York: Orbis.

Haechen, Ernst. 1971. *The Acts of the Apostles: A Commentary.* Hermeneia. Philadelphia: Fortress.

Hicks, R. Lansing. 1977. The Book of Joel (Introduction and Notes). Pp. 1101–6 in *The New Oxford Annotated Bible with the Apocrypha: Revised Standard Version.* New York: Oxford University Press.

Levine, Amy-Jill, ed. *A Feminist Companion to the Acts of the Apostles.* FCNTECW 9. Cleveland: Pilgrim

Liew, Tat-siong Benny. 2004. Acts. Pages 419–28 in *Global Bible Commentary.* Edited by Daniel Patte. Nashville: Abingdon.

Lincoln, C. Eric, and Lawrence H. Mamiya, eds. 1990. *The Black Church in the African American Experience.* Durham, N.C.: Duke University Press.

MacDonald, Dennis R. 1987. *There Is No Male and Female: The Fate of a Dominical Saying in Paul and Gnosticism.* Philadelphia: Fortress.

Matthews, Shelley D. 2004. Elite Women, Public Religion, and Christian Propaganda in Acts 16. Pages 111–33 in Levine 2004.

Mitchell, Ella P., ed. 1991. *Women to Preach or Not to Preach? 21 Outstanding Preachers Say Yes.* Valley Forge, Pa.: Judson.

Navone, John. 1978. *Themes of St. Luke.* Rome: Georgian University Press.

O'Toole, Robert F. 1984. *The Unity of Luke's Theology: An Analysis of Luke-Acts.* Wilmington, Del.: Glazer.

Penner, Todd, and Caroline Vander Stichele. 2004. Gendering Violence: Patterns of Power and Constructs of Masculinity in the Acts of the Apostles. Pages 193–209 in Levine 2004.

Price, Robert. 1997. *Widow Traditions in Luke-Acts: A Feminist-Critical Scrutiny.* SBLDS 155. Atlanta: Scholars Press.

———. 2004. Rhoda and Penelope: Two More Cases of Luke's Suppression of Women. Pages 98–104 in Levine 2004.

Ransom, Reverdy. 1999. The Race Problem in a Christian State, 1906. Pages in 337–46 in *African American Religious History: A Documentary Witness.* Edited by Milton C. Sernett. 2nd ed. Durhan, N.C.: Duke University Press.

Ruether, Rosemary Radford. 1995. *New Woman, New Earth: Sexist Ideologies and Human Liberation.* Boston: Beacon.

Schüssler Fiorenza, Elisabeth. 1989. *In Memory of Her: A Feminist Theological Reconstruction of Christian Origins.* New York: Crossroad.

———. 1992. *But She Said: Feminist Practices of Biblical Interpretation.* Boston: Beacon.

Scroggs, Robin. 1972. Paul and the Eschatological Woman. *JAAR* 40:283–303.

Segovia, Fernando F. 2000. *Decolonizing Biblical Studies: A View From the Margins.* Maryknoll, N.Y.: Orbis.

Spencer, F. Scott. 1977. *Acts.* Readings: A New Bible Commentary. Sheffield: Sheffield Academic Press.

St. Clair, Raquel. 2007. Womanist Biblical Interpretation. Pages 54–62 in *True to Our Native Land: An African American New Testament Commentary.* Edited by Brian Bount et al. Minneapolis: Fortress.

Staley, Jeffrey L. 2004. Changing Woman: Toward a Postcolonial Postfeminist Interpretation of Acts 16:6–40. Pages 177–92 in Levine 2004.

Stowers, Stanley K. 1988. Paul and Slavery: A Response. *Semeia* 83/84:295–311.

Talbert, Charles H., ed. 1975. *Perspectives on Luke-Acts.* Edinburgh: T&T Clark.

Williams, Demetrius K. 2004. *An End to This Strife: The Politics of Gender in African American Churches.* Minneapolis: Fortress.

———. 2007. The Acts of the Apostles. Pages 213–48 in *True to Our Native Land: An African American New Testament Commentary.* Edited by Brian Bount et al. Minneapolis: Fortress.

Wimbush, Vincent L. 1993. Reading Texts through Worlds, Worlds Through Texts. *Semeia* 69:129–39.

Witherington, Ben, III. 1998. *The Acts of the Apostles: A Socio-rhetorical Commentary.* Grand Rapids: Eerdmans.

Part 2: Assessments

INCARNATE WORDS: IMAGES OF GOD
AND READING PRACTICES

Mayra Rivera Rivera

Truth did not come into the world naked, but it came in types and images.
The world will not receive truth in any other way.
Gospel of Philip

The world will not receive truth in any other way: truth will always be among us as signs and images—particular and embodied—that communicate only through interpretation. Sought by particular subjects, embodied and embedded in culture and society, interpretation unfolds into uncontrollable multiplicity. Whether or not truth (or revelation) is explicitly invoked, biblical hermeneutics elicits the question of truth—or at least inquiries about truthfulness—in interpretation. What is the relationship between particular interpretations and truth, between meaning and words, or between finite texts and God's word?

As a theologian in dialogue with biblical scholars, I have been intrigued by the effects of unuttered questions of truth and revelation in the methodologies deployed by biblical scholars, especially those interested in issues of race and ethnicity. What is the theology of racial and ethnic approaches to biblical interpretation? What kind of God is affirmed by their methodological choices? What kind of creation do they speak about?

In this essay I ponder these questions. I attempt to uncover some of the links between the methodological considerations related to textuality and interpretation, commonly discussed among biblical scholars, and cosmological views pertaining to the relation of created particularity and the divine.

Theology undergirds models of interpretation. Conceptions of the relationship between the texts, contexts, and readers are informed by theories of language and representation, the discussions of which have become common in biblical scholarship. But theories of language, and particularly of biblical interpretation, are also influenced by (and influence) broader cosmological visions, including ideas about the nature of the divine and its relation to finite words. Indeed, for ancient theologians the multiplicity of meanings flowing from scripture had everything to do with the unrestrained flow of divinity throughout creation. My interest in this essay is to foreground the theological implications of the practices of interpretation espoused in this volume and in the consultation that preceded it as sources for embodied cosmologies, investigating not only the images of divinity that undergird their worldviews but also what they imply for human relationships to other created beings and to the divine.

This discussion, which is visibly marked by postmodern and postcolonial theories, seeks to identify not only dominant ideas that the essays in this volume reject but, most importantly, the methodological principles they accept, which suggest specific visions of the relationship between particular words and bodies, social bodies, and the divine. Ideas about texts, histories, and subjectivity are implicit in these views of interpretation. I will argue that a relational hermeneutics that is embodied, apophatic, and open-ended calls for a thoroughly incarnate theological vision: where the divine infuses the particularity of bodies and words, both affirming finitude and luring it to transformation.

In Search for Naked Messages

The essays included in this volume participate in the postmodern critique of modern views of representation, specifically targeting methods of interpretation that assume the independence between texts and readers. Their specific strategies are also infused with concerns for representation in its political sense: not only are they concerned with the production of meaning through language, but also with the possibilities of participation in sociopolitical structures for marginalized communities. There is thus a profound critique of dominant modes of interpretation not only in terms of constructions of notions of language but also of subjectivity. The idea of the "universal man" is as problematic as that of the transparency of language.

Thus, I begin this discussion of ideas about textuality with a negative example: meaning splits off from words/matter—the former is imagined as stable and univocal; the latter changing and multiple. It is this very separation between meaning and words that secures the stability of the linguistic system, for with meaning firmly attached to a foundation unaffected by the instabilities of worldly existence, the success of reference can be guaranteed. In Fernando Segovia's analysis of the main paradigms of biblical interpretation, it is historical criticism that exemplifies the tendencies that I want to point to. Segovia argues that historical criticism approaches scripture as *means* to a greater truth. Signs are stable means to make reality fully present to consciousness, and scripture is assumed to possess a "univocal and objective meaning": a universal message that could be retrieved using the proper tools (2000). Interpretation is thus conceived as the extraction of meaning from texts—meaning that remains always separable from but accessible through words.

The idea of the existence of an essential meaning beneath or behind the biblical texts—a message untainted by and independent from the contingency and obscurity of its words and stories—is not exclusive to modes of interpretation that explicitly dismiss the impact of sociopolitical ideology in the biblical words. Its common logic is expressed in the very idea of translation, for instance, which depends on the confidence that some meaning is transferable from one language to another. It is indeed possible to resist the idealist tendencies of interpretation, giving explicit attention to the social location of present and past readers of texts and still regard the meaning of scripture as univocal and stable. Some liberationist strategies of interpretation display this tendency to look beyond the contingencies and tensions of the biblical texts to a univocal and universal message of liberation. As R. S. Sugirtharajah has argued, this has led some liberation theologies to make the Bible the ultimate authority, creating the impression that liberation is intrinsic to the Bible (2002).

When assumed uncritically, this view of meaning may lead to the illusion of accessing some pristine land of interpretative solace beyond the limitations imposed by particularity. This mindset haunts interpretations that, while accepting the uncertainties and multiplicity of biblical interpretation, construe the knowledge that they produce as a secondary knowledge. Primary knowledge was once available, it is assumed. However, having acquired the knowledge of good and evil and sadly banned from re-entering the garden of Eden, humans are imagined to be condemned to desire the fullness and security of the divine Truth that they can no longer touch. Immediate, full knowledge is no longer possible, but, even in its inaccessibility, the imaginary space of stable independent meaning continues to function as the guiding utopia of reading.[1]

In Christian theology, the foundation of determinate meaning has often been identified with God. This is a God imagined as an external reality, absolutely unaffected by creation. This is a God "for whom it would be unworthy to get mixed up in the squalor of our lives," as Ivonne Gebara describes it (1999). Just as God is conceived in his [sic] total independence from creation—even as he manifests himself in it—scriptural truth is detached from the contingency of its context, even if it is through its finite words that we gain access to truth. Revelation is in this view the removal of a veil that hides the totality of truth, its full presence. The logic of externality is only reinforced by modern notions of subjectivity and the concomitant illusions of pure objectivity. After the age of reason, "God's epistemological function passed to man, initially by means of the Cartesian cogito and subsequently by means of the Kantian transcendental subject" (Hart 1989, 29).

---

1. The pervasiveness and effects of the dream of full knowledge as it relates to the idea of full presence has taken center stage in the works of postmodern critics influenced by Jacques Derrida's attention to what he calls "logocentrism." As Gayatri Spivak describes it, in Derrida's use of the term *logocentrism* means "the belief that the first and last things are the Logos, the Word, the Divine Mind, the infinite understanding of God, and infinitely creative subjectivity, and, closer to our time, the self-presence of full consciousness" (1998, lxviii).

The external God and the modern man mirror each other. Heretofore a self-present interpreter (like God) stands in utter independence from the text being read and the context from which the interpretation springs.

In this worldview, words and contexts have a secondary status in relation to truth. This hierarchy is another expression of the Platonic dualisms that are deeply ingrained in Christian theology and in dominant Western thought, where all finite things are thought to have their truest reality outside of themselves. For Plato, according to John Peter Kenney, "true being" was "an epithet that belongs to that which 'is what it is' without alteration, cessation, or relativity." Thus, on this ontology, true being belongs to the eternal forms: "Those entities that exhibit complete predicative stability have the strongest claim to metaphysical preeminence, and this entails, in Plato's analysis, that they be transcendent of this world, qualified as it is by instability and flux" (1991, 7–8). Bodies, words, and contexts belong to the realm of created things that are changeable and are thus deemed inferior both ontologically and epistemologically. At the heart of dominant Western culture, meaning and being interlace. Daniel Boyarin describes the effects of this paradigm in textuality thus: "Words are bodies and meanings, souls" (2005, 132).

That which escapes or triumphs over materiality, bodies, and their particularities is deemed a more suitable foundation of knowledge.[2] Thus, locating scriptural meaning in the unchangeable truths behind the finite unreliable signs betrays the desire for a paradise of unmediated knowledge of God. In this world of uncertainty, God is the exception: a God who has withdrawn and can only be accessed through signs. As Hart puts it, "Whether in nature or scripture, these signs must be interpreted, yet only in ways which acknowledge that timeless truths wait behind them and can be separated from them" (1989, 4). The cosmological structure ordered by the external, unaffected divinity and the epistemological hierarchy are interdependent.

Resisting the tendencies to bypass the particularities and dynamism of bodies, words, and the societies in which they live entails a theological challenge to the subtending cosmological framework that splits divinity from creation, transcendence from immanence. These theological challenges shall be explicated, for, in the absence of an explicit discussion of the theological grounds of contextual interpretations, unconscious metaphysical presuppositions stay in place. Besides, I suspect that, unless we deconstruct the absolute externality and self-enclosed independence of God, the practices of contextual interpretation will continue to be relegated to the realm of lower truths always overshadowed by avowed disembodied universalities.

---

2. For Christians, only in Christ, both Word of God and God, is there a perfect coincidence of the sign and that which is signified, as of body and spirit.

To move away from the idealism that subordinates the particularities of words, stories, and bodies in search of disembodied truths does not entail being abandoned in a self-enclosed realm where words and readers are imagined as repetitions of determinable sociopolitical systems, just as the lack of appeal to an external God does not leave us with a world of God-less immanence. What is in question here is the assumed dichotomies between truth and contingency, meaning and relationality. The Enlightenment tendency to exile God from the world—limiting God to a self-contained outside realm where it cannot undermine but founds the power and stability of "natural laws" (the cosmology that we questioned above)—produced a thoroughly predictable mechanistic worldview in which things are self-enclosed and manipulable. We shall resist both reductions: of God and of cosmos. To assume that meaning is fully contained within unchanging self-enclosed texts reverses the logic of the externality of meaning but retains the subject-object structure that construes signs (and created things) as self-enclosed entities. In this case meaning is locked in self-enclosed changeless scripts. Thus conceived, interpretation aims at its own closure. This tendency is found, for instance, in the attempts to find a full and final message in the true "intentions of the narrative"—whether that message is one of liberation or oppression. In this hermeneutics, scripture is an object to be analyzed and stabilized: as dead letter, soul-less bodies, spiritless words.

Highlighting the significance of race and ethnicity in biblical interpretations entails an explicit turn to the material realities of bodies, texts, and contexts. However, this hermeneutical turn is not equivalent to reducing bodies to predictable characteristics, nor is it conceiving the Bible as a lifeless object. Situating bodies in their matrices of social relations, particularly those that define relations of race and ethnicity, seeks not merely to describe their social inscriptions but also to move beyond them, to affirm both their specificity and their potential for transformation in relations. Such modes of interpretation depend on a rejection of the epistemological split between words, contexts, and meanings, and thus of the hierarchical cosmology on which such epistemological structure rests.

Meaning in Relation

Contrary to what is generally believed, meaning and sense were never the same thing, meaning shows itself at once, direct, literal, explicit, enclosed in itself, univocal, if you like, while sense cannot stay still, it seethes with second, third and fourth senses, radiating out in different directions that divide and subdivide into branches and branchlets, until they disappear from view, the sense of every word is like a star hurling spring tides out into space, cosmic winds, magnetic perturbations, afflictions.

José Saramago, *All the Names*

The epistemological world that Saramago describes in this passage mocks the paradise of interpretative stability described in the previous section. Saramago names "sense" (*sentido*) what I have been calling "meaning." Indeed, I wonder if the very diffraction of "sense," as he describes it, threatens the stability of the distinction between "sense" and "meaning" (*significado*) that he proposes. However, the infinite radiations of Saramago's images do illuminate a postmodern vision of textuality toward which we now move. That this transition towards views of interpretation that emphasize dissemination and multiplicity invokes images of spring tides and cosmic winds already suggests the broader context of hermeneutics that flows from contemporary (post-Newtonian) worldviews—where ideas such as evolution, genetic mutations, psychic transferences, and so on have gradually replaced the more predictable systems of modern sciences.

Postmodern theories of language stress that meaning is never merely contained within words or signs or rests securely in an essential link between signifier and signified. Meaning is rather produced by complex relations between signs through processes of differentiation: signs only mean in relation to other signs; words acquire their meaning by virtue of their difference from other words. These relations between signs form the context within which words mean. Yet contexts do not constitute an alternative stable foundation for meaning: contexts are open and fragmented. Furthermore, words, like all signs, are repeated in different contexts where their meanings are displaced. Thus words are inherently polysemic: they are open to a multiplicity of interpretations. It is, of course, possible to claim that contexts and texts are closed, but such a claim is always already affected by the inherent uncontrollability of language.

In biblical scholarship an understanding of language that emphasizes the "polysemic nature of all signs" has led to an increased emphasis on the irreducible plurality of possible interpretations as part of the very nature of texts. In contrast with the tendency to search for meaning behind the text, approaches in literary and cultural criticism locate meaning either in the text—in its structures and word choices—and/or between the text and contexts, scriptures and readers (Segovia 2000, 14). Relationality is here broader and more complex, connecting not only the biblical texts to their ancient contexts but also readers to their (multiple) present contexts—and to the future communities to which interpreters seek to contribute. In contrast to the images of meaning residing in a pure external realm, here meaning is very much "mixed up in the squalor of our lives," hurling spring tides, winds, and perturbation throughout. And so is, I would argue, God.

To say that meaning is produced between texts, contexts, and readers is a deceptively simple statement for a very complex worldview. Contexts open infinitively and endlessly. Histories are multiple and conflicted, and potentially open to the new. Readers are no longer seen as passive recipients but rather as active—though not necessarily conscious—participants in the production of meaning. Attention to the role of the reader in the production of interpretations also highlights the multiplying effect of reading perspectives. The interpreter's participation does not imply that meanings (by interpreters any more than by authors) can be controlled: they will continue to branch out in different directions. The interpreter does, as Origen suggests, "labor diligently" as a "skillful farmer" and hope for fertile ground in which scriptural seeds will multiply. But rather than identical repetition, these seeds will yield infinitely varied vegetation. The power to bring forth lives somewhere between the farmer, the seeds, and the earth.

Interpretative power is not controlling power, and this affects authors as much as it affects texts. Emerging from worlds linked by endless ties of relations, texts are excessive, their meaning extending deep into their past and far into the future possibilities of interpretations. In the case of scriptures, the excessiveness is intensified when they are considered as a (potential) site of revelation: where the finite encounters the transformative energies of the divine-in-the-finite. (I will return to this point.) But, as historical objects, they are also fragmented. Where textuality is not unilaterally controlled by the intentions of the author or by an omnipotent unaffected God, texts are, as the world, internally multiple and potentially conflicted. This absence of a homogenizing and stabilizing force has been seen as a curse of a God offended by the arrogance of its creatures exemplified in the tower of Babel. But oppressed communities have long depended on the impossibility of total homogeneity and of closure for their very survival. For instance, it is significant that practices of linguistic displacements ("Spanglish" and "signifying") were discussed during our consultation as hermeneutical lenses for Latina/os and African Americans, respectively. What these linguistic practices bring to the fore is not merely that languages compete with the hegemonic one but also the mobilization of the internal fractures in the dominant voice by subaltern voices.

Attentiveness to the failures of power within hegemonic structures and texts also grounds hope of encountering nearly erased stories, traces of the past, and of those who had been rejected by history still found in the biblical texts. It is this hope that Hélène Cixous holds on to:

> The only chance remaining to the dead whose death we have stolen is the rock on which one day we may stumble. If we have no ear for what the rock, become naked, smooth, mute, tells us, then all that has been silenced and assassinated will die again. The ones who have died alone on the frozen boulder will die again for eternity ... if we do not lay our hand on the stone, so as to blindly read the tale of a solitary death. May the reader come forth, may the ear, the hand come forth to hear so much silence. (1994, 17)

For those seeking to respond to past injustices, speech can be a "testimony to the silence," as Victor Anderson argues (2001, 89). To blindly read the tale of solitary death, perhaps between the triumphalistic lines written by the victors, is to seek to turn the failure of hegemonic closure into a subversive strategy.

Deconstructive and postcolonial reading strategies seek to make visible the ruptures within the text that undermine the closure of meaning, interrupting, shaking the illusions of absolute coherence, completeness, and finality. Magnifying the volume of otherwise weak voices barely recorded in the text, or uttering the call for the erased others whose exclusion is necessary for, but foreclosed by, the text's dominant voice(s), are part of these strategies of interpretation. Misplacing another story—our story—in the text dramatizes not only the possibilities that ancient texts might mean today but also the iterability (and vulnerability) of texts: the condition of possibility of meaning that is also what allows it to be read in changing contexts—to be read differently.

This does not mean that the past can be accessed as such. To attend to past oppressions cannot bring about the resurrection of others, if that means to bring them back in full presence. Therefore, those of us who trace our history to those excluded in past colonial encounters are warned against the illusion of bringing our excluded (or even killed) ancestors back to life, to full presence. We are reminded of the impossibility of re-presenting them. Attempts to call back into existence a dead past, which characterized many nationalist projects, rely on the assumption that one can access the Other through representation and reappropriate her or him as a source of authentic identity and authority. What Victor Anderson observes in reference to the use of black sources for religious insight can be extended as a warning for all uses of testimonies from the past: "Preoccupation with distilling [from them] their clear, distinct, universal, and exceptional countercultural intentions and values put at risk ... their particularities, their historical creative testimonies to different worlds ... and creativity" (2001, 79). Instead of crossing over the limits of time, to be attentive to past encounters is to bear witness to others in the present and, perhaps, the future.

Interpretation will not produce its own closure, nor will it reduce the ambiguities of scripture. Without recourse to the externality of meaning firmly established in the being of an external God, its "Archimedean point of refuge," we will not be able to avoid "laboring, actively and critically, in the legacy of the biblical to articulate how the possibility of the very best is tied up with the risk of the very worst," from "engaging with the performative promise and threat of each and every text" (Sherwood and Caputo 2005m 232). The biblical interpretations in this volume seek wisdom (and revelation) in the midst of the messy realities of life: a light not overcome by shadows—not an absence of shadows.

A relational theory of interpretation—one that honors the past as it hopes for the future, that refuses to subordinate concrete realities to disembodied truths or reduce the ambiguities of revelation—calls for a relational worldview, one in which readers affect and are affected by texts in ways that ultimately "disappear from view." Relations between texts and their ancient contexts, between readers and their collectivities are, in this view, not only irreducible but part of the revelation brought forth by biblical interpretations. Not only shall we recognize the embeddedness of texts and readers in their contexts but also seek in interpretation to illuminate those relationships. Whether they uncover "cautionary tales" of the detrimental effects of segregation (Cheryl Anderson) or the "fusion of sex and ethnicity" in the production of negative stereotypes (Randall Bailey), these interpretations place relationships at the heart of revelation.

The potency of suppressed stories is only actualized in its relationship with the present. That is, we only see the past in relation to our present. Thus, rather than a retrieval of the past, interpretation responds to its call. This response is given from within the current contexts by those who turn their hearts to those calls. It is thus that current readers read themselves into the text. Rather than appropriating the texts as an object to be fully contained in consciousness, they offer themselves in their encounter with biblical texts. Thus the "methodological messiness borne out of the gnawing feeling" that James Kyung-Jin Lee describes in his essay for this volume.

In a tradition that has denied God desire, it is perhaps not surprising if confessing that desire infuses biblical interpretation is met with embarrassment: as a sign of an undeniable fall away from God into the depths of materiality and its passions. Perhaps this desire seems distant to the one expressed in the mystical theologies as ascent toward or union with the divine. The positive movement of contextual interpretations might look irremediable earthbound. But for those who seek divinity within creation and in the face of others, the desire for God leads us to multiple and diffuse places. This desire attempts to move beyond— beyond words without abandoning the words, beyond the world-as-it-is without escaping the world, beyond the limits of the self without ever detaching from it. As Laurel Schneider asks of queer interpretations of scripture: "Who is to say that that is not revelatory of something other than our own desire?" (2001, 213). And how can that boundary between God's desire and the desire for God, for the reign of God, be drawn?

The implication of the reader's desire in the reading is, of course, considered to be the case of all readers. But the readings of an "othered" subject "raise[s] the question of imagination and desire on the part of the interpreter more plainly precisely because such interpretations stretch the imagination and taken-for-granted conclusions about the whole text and its history" (Schneider 2001, 213). The singularity of each reader makes possible a unique event of revelation: a revelation of sociopolitical relevance, which is also divine. By revealing what has escaped the sociopolitical gaze, they also uncover the limits of what is otherwise claimed as universal.

Reading Identities

I am a little discouraged: I shall never have the strength nor the time to write something worthy of you. Would I do better to remain silent? I know that in a certain respect it is easier to speak of God than to speak of You.... I cannot speak of you with the ease that divine mathematics provides, because it is perfectly simple, because absolutely without any relation to me, which is the true benediction. With God, I never risk anything, either mistake, or an aside, or truth, and I do not make him take any risk…. This is really without relation to the torments that bring the need to speak to you absolutely non-absolutely, but absolutely faithfully.

Hélène Cixous, "(With) Or the Art of Innocence"[3]

The God that Cixous is describing in this passage is the external unaffected God to which I have been referring as the very foundation of ideas of interpretation that transcendentalize meaning and obscure the implications of readers in their interpretations. A God who is absolutely without relations is, for some of us, no more than a caricature of the God we risk speaking to. However, by invoking this caricature of God, Cixous draws our attention to a crucial point: the complexity of subjectivity is in stark contrast to it. Furthermore, with delightful irony, Cixous reverses a common tendency of many mystical theologies that dwell on the mystery and the torments of speaking about God and yet reduce the human Other—indeed all creatures—to quasi-mathematical categories. While, as it is often observed, modern subjectivity mirrored a self-enclosed God of mathematical certainties, today that mirror has shattered. The visions of subjectivity that emerge from perspectives that emphasize the development of personhood in its complex relations to context and power mock the absolute independence and coherence of the Universal Man—and of the God of which that Man was an image.

Refusing the Universal Man as a caricature of persons, the interpreters in this volume seek to foreground the embodied, socially located, and unavoidably interested readers of scripture. These are readers who belong to specific ethnic/racial groups and are in touch with the distinctive experiences of those groups. They are interested in particular peoples: in the significance of their bodily existence and in what those bodies have come to "represent" in our societies. But the specificity of the perspective thus described does not erase the complexities of speaking "absolutely non-absolutely, but absolutely faithfully" to and about the groups that we identify with and yet will never fully represent. The stories that we read into the biblical stories, our "communal" stories, are as multiple and as internally conflicted as the ancient texts being read, and so are our readings of them. Being alert, for instance, to the connections between the epistemic paradigms of transparency in the claims of "correspondence" between narratives in the text and our experience, or of the immediacy between the interpreter and her or his "community," is a consequential challenge faced by these interpretations.

Racial and ethnic readings of scripture are interested in deconstructing the ideological apparatus that supports (and is supported by) racism and ethnocentrism. They thus seek to refute the assumed correspondence between racialized

---

3. I am grateful to Krista Hughes for bringing this passage to my attention.

bodies and their stereotypical images. But they do so by deploying categories of race and ethnicity as "perspectives," or, as James Kyung-Jin Lee puts it, "telling the stories through the fiction of race." In doing so, the interpreter places herself in an ambiguous position, for she claims the power of the very structure of representation that it seeks to unravel.

Postcolonial critic Gayatri Chakravorti Spivak explores this problematic of representation as it affects what she calls the migrant (or minority) critic. "No perspective critical of imperialism can turn the marginalized other into a self," she argues. Notions of identity that fail to challenge the coherence of the "self," that assume its full correspondence with an Other (as the signifier to the signified), are inherently flawed. On the one hand, assuming the Other as a self can only be accomplished by suppressing the heterogeneity of the identity it "represents" under discretely defined categories, mirroring the very logic of hegemonic power. On the other hand, the strategy will always fail "because project of imperialism has always already historically refracted what might have been the absolutely other into a domesticated other that consolidates the imperialist self" (Spivak 1999, 130). Indeed, "It is the very kind of colonized-anthropo-logized difference the master has always happily granted his subordinates," as Trinh Minh-ha observes (1989, 101). Simply claiming this kind of othering as identity may even end up objectifying subjects, locking them in categories of cultural representation.

However, the deconstructive impulse that leads to challenge "the illusion of precision about race categories," as Fumitaka Matsuoka calls it (1998, 38–48), shall not obscure the significance of the subjects' relation to categories of race and ethnicity. While suspicious of the ontologizing logic that undergirds the notion of "correspondence"—the same logic that founds the logic of truth (and thus interpretation) as correspondence—we cannot escape, nor would we deny, the effects of the "fiction of race" (James Kyung-Jin Lee) in our subjectivity. We cannot accept the reduction of racialized subjects to the representations that the dominant system produces of them, nor can we entertain the fantasy of an essential identity outside body and culture, or external to power and resistance. We are partly the effects of those fictions and something more than the signs by which we name ourselves and others. Critique entails both naming and deconstructing the logic of the name to signal the excess that overflows the names and the mystery that they never illuminate.

In his discussion of the problem of theological method in African American religious studies, Victor Anderson argues for the need to respect the mystery that infuses its historical sources. He uses the phenomenological hermeneutics of Charles Long to "accent the opacity of religious insight into the study of black religion" (2001, 79). Using the metaphor of opacity, Anderson seeks to "transcend the Western epistemic paradigm" of transparency by highlighting the irretrievable aspects of experience, which are not the effect of cognitive failure but rather an identifying characteristic that affects both racial symbolism and theological method. He writes, "[I]f the relationship between the signified and the signifier is arbitrary, then the religious significations are open to changes, transformations, and reconstitution as the relationships are altered through the various exchanges of power" (88). History and experience are untotalizable, and taking into account their opacity opens theology to encounter the wide variety of its sources and their unresolved ambiguities.

Attention to the opacity of experience may also help us affirm the profound mystery that envelops human experiences—an aspect of subjectivity that shall never be obscured by emphasis on social construction. Rather than contrasting language about that divine with language about the human Other, we might allow them to come closer—to touch each other—so that respect for the divine mystery infuses our discourses about the created world (Rivera 2007). Anderson's use of a metaphor commonly deployed by Christians to focus on the mystery of the divine—"We see through a glass, darkly"—hints at this constructive possibility. Allowing the divine mystery to infuse our understanding of the created world at all levels entails developing a thoroughly incarnational theology as a ground for a truly embodied hermeneutics.

While the "torments" to speak about others that Cixous witnesses to are "really without relation" to absolutely-self-certain theologies, they are not unrelated to the struggles with language to which apophatic theologies witness. These theologies foreground the limits of their own language and representations. In contrast with the theologies that trust "the ease that divine mathematics provides," apophatic theologies fence off the temptation of "easy reference," of thinking that the name has the power to fully capture the One whom it names, considered as dangerous as "cheap grace" (Sells 1994, 11).[4] Like Cixous, they occasionally wonder: "Would I do better to remain silent?" But theology can never renounce names, images, symbols, logos. It is only through images that we can speak or even think about the ineffable. Even "apophatic" theologies write; they inscribe the very negation of the divine attributes that they affirm, thus rebelling against the idolatry of names or images. Negative theology both makes reference to the Other, to the name God, and appeals to that which "the name supposes to name beyond itself, the nameable beyond the name, the unnameable nameable ... as if it was necessary to loose the name in order to save what bears the name, or that towards which one goes through the name ... to loose the name is ... to respect it: as name" (Derrida 1995, 58). Through endless negations and denegations, renunciations and denunciations, negative theology attempts to address that which is beyond representation, while realizing that its speech can never escape the limits of representation.

Postmodern attention to the problematics of representation has led to a renewed interest in the insights of apophatic theology and to the infusion of self-

---

4. Dietrich Bonhoeffer coined the phrase "cheap grace" to refer to grace that does not entail discipleship.

conscious negations of the referentiality of theological language—indeed, of all language. This generalization of negation beyond the limits of theological language entails, as we have seen, not only a critique of conceptions of the divine mind as the unchanging foundation of meaning but also of the idea of a transcendental subjectivity as the modern substitute for theological foundationalism.

These critiques are crucial for ethnic/racial readings of scripture, not only for their deconstructive force but also because they offer valuable insights for rethinking subjectivity beyond the confidence of dominant Western models in the powers of representation. There are resonances between the dilemmas and strategies of negative theology just described and those of scholars of color. As I said before, these critics are challenged by the limitations and dangers of the language with which they seek to speak to/about others. While acknowledging the violent history of categories of exclusion, they desire to point to meaning beyond (but not outside) those categories. Never free from implication of language in the histories of exclusion and oppression they critique, they nonetheless seek transformation rereading and rewriting in the interstices of hegemonic discourses. Furthermore, like negative theologians, they must always attend to the links between God-talk and human-talk, for in reading scripture such a relationship is always at stake. However, the discussions of apophatic language frequently ignore questions of enfleshed differences and contextual subjectivities. Through their silence about systems of sociopolitical power—and their potent machines of representation—postmodern retrievals of apophatic theologies still risk reproducing the illusion of detachment between God/human relations and human/human relations.[5]

Resisting reductionist visions of persons (and thus of "the reader") entails developing models of subjectivity that foreground relationality and dynamism. I have argued elsewhere that the notion of relational transcendence—both incarnate and dynamic—can help us envision a subjectivity as both ineradicable from and irreducible to categories of gender, race, ethnicity, and so on (2007). The notion of relational transcendence links together freedom, indeterminacy, and dynamism with social specificity, embodiment, and history, as mutually imbricated axes of human development and transformation. Although as people living in societies permeated by racism and ethnocentrism, we will always be identified according to categories and those categories do affect who we might become, we are not reducible to them. No name or category can possibly describe all a person is. Not because we are absolutely separate from the system or from one another, but because of the complex and infinite relationality of creatures. The transcendence of the person is that which exceeds all systems. It is neither abstract nor otherworldly, but openness at the heart of relation.

---

5. A recent colloquium at Drew University entitled "Apophatic Bodies: Infinity, Ethics, and Incarnation" (September 2006) is a hopeful sign that this shortcoming might begin to be addressed.

Each aspect of a person's identity develops in relation to realities that transcend her particularity, but which she also transcends—community, country of origin, sexual identity. For instance, the realities of my own community—its past history, its language, the geography in which I feel most at home—all embrace me, not only as a past reality but as something that I continue to relate to, be transformed by, and transform. Yet I never grasp it, just as it never completely defines me. These transcending realities exist only in particular persons. That is, they are never fully present, as such, and never appear in isolation from other aspects of a person's life. Our encounter with the Other touches and is touched by realities that transcend us both. In each person different realities meet and transform each other in unique ways. The unique outcome of these multiple relations accounts for each person's "radical singularity," to use Spivak's phrase. This radical singularity, this transcendence, is a function of relations rather than separation. It is a relational transcendence.

A HERMENEUTICS OF HOPE

> Theology is truly a hermeneutic of hope.
> Gustavo Gutiérrez, "Theological Language: Fullness of Silence"

The goal of biblical interpretation, especially for readers concerned with issues of race and ethnicity, is not to stay locked in a system of representation. Both scriptures and the collectivities in relation to which they are read are seen as inextricable from sociopolitical matrices of power, yet they are ultimately untotalizable. From their complex webs of relations, interpreters seek openings to liberate readings and readers from the "fate of language that serves the exercise of power, control, and possession" (Soelle 2001, 63). The interpreters in this volume have not renounced the hope for transformation in which biblical interpretation may participate, the expectation that the texts may still yield blessings, new revelation—even truth.

Revelation is not to be imagined as the unveiling of what was already but as an opening for new worlds. This is consonant with the goals of postcolonial criticism as Homi Bhabha describes it: "If the epistemological tends towards a reflection of its empirical referent or object, the enunciative attempts to reinscribe and relocate the political claim to cultural priority and hierarchy" (1994, 177). In so doing, such criticism hopes for the transformation of "the present into an expanded and ex-centric site of experience and empowerment" (4). Or, as James Kyung-Jin Lee puts it, quoting John Edgar Wideman: "To start a story so that an old story can end." Truth is here inseparable from ethics. Revelation is not the acquisition of cognitive data or evidence but, as Juan Luis Segundo describes it, a "difference that makes a difference" (1993, 330)—a difference in relation. To seek that truth is not to subordinate culture and embodiment but to transcend without escaping.

In many of its Christian versions, transcendence depicts a rift between cosmos and God that equates God's transcendence with exteriority. In such views social transformation and divine transcendence belong to different realms. But this hardly exhausts Christian interpretations of the relation between God and the cosmos. Other voices proclaim visions of the cosmos as a divine reality and thus of transformation as the outcome of the unfolding of God in creation. Creation is figured as the "infinite in the garb of the finite." Far from resembling the homogeneously simple entity of classical theology, or the coherent image reflected on the mirror of the Universal Man, God is envisioned as a multiple singularity that relates without homogenizing. It is a physical matrix of complexity and differentiation where "every real thing ... is intrinsically and constitutively" linked "to every other" (Ellacuría, as cited in Burke 2000, 55).

Within this heterogeneity of life the event of revelation might occur: an event of a call and a response (Caputo 2006, 117). Between the call and the response, a reader allows herself or himself to be read, to enter into relation. Revelation does not have the force of an irresistible Truth or irrefutable evidence, nor is it extrinsic from the ethical demands of "this world." And thus the outcomes are not guaranteed. Indeed, the relational hermeneutics that we have been describing—issuing a multiplicity of readings in the encounters between the relational singularity of readers and texts—would be overwhelmed by a God who always had the last word. Instead of a controlling power to stop the multiplying flow of interpretation, God may be seen as the spirit of relations that cannot but continue to evolve and complicate truth: God with us and between us.

The truth of scripture is neither behind nor inside it, for it is not an object to be apprehended, nor is it ever independent from the words and bodies that participate in the revelatory event. The truth of scripture is "true with the truth of the event; it wants to become true ... to be transformed into truth" (Caputo 2006, 118). This truth might entail affirmation and frequently also negation. What is calling to become true might be the denunciation of scriptural claims, the suppression of voices or lives unaccounted for. In as much as it relates to the voices that shall yet be heard or lives that might still be saved, its truth shall become true in our relations. This will not come true once and for all but will always require participation in arduous processes of discernment fraught with uncertainties. Perhaps it is our blessing if the world does not receive truth in any other way.

Works Consulted

Anderson, Victor. 2001. "We See through a Glass Darkly": Black Narrative Theology and the Opacity of African American Religious Experience. Pages 78–93 in *The Ties That Bind: African American and Hispanic American/Latino/a Theologies in Dialogue.* Edited by Anthony B. Pinn and Benjamin Valentin. New York: Continuum.
Bhabha, Homi K. 1994. *The Location of Culture.* London: Routledge.

Boyarin, Daniel. 2005. Midrash and the "Magic Language": Reading without Logocentrism. Pages 131–39 in *Derrida and Religion: Other Testaments*. Edited by Yvonne Sherwood and Kevin Hart. New York: Routledge.

Burke, Kevin F. 2000. *The Ground beneath the Cross: The Theology of Ignacio Ellacuría*. Washington, D.C.: Georgetown University Press.

Caputo, John D. 2006. *The Weakness of God: A Theology of the Event*. Bloomington: Indiana University Press.

Cixous, Hélène. 1994. *Manna: For the Mandelstams for the Mandelas*. Translated by Catherine A. F. MacGillivray. Minneapolis: University of Minnesota.

Derrida, Jacques. 1995. Sauf le Nom. Pages 35–85 in *On the Name*. Edited by Thomas Dutoit. Stanford, Calif.: Stanford University.

Gebara, Ivone. 1999. *Longing for Running Waters*. Minneapolis: Fortress.

Hart, Kevin. 1989. *The Trespass of the Sign: Deconstruction, Theology, and Philosophy*. Cambridge: Cambridge University Press.

Kenney, John Peter. 1991. *Mystical Monotheism: A Study in Ancient Platonic Theology*. Hanover: University of New England.

Matsuoka, Fumitaka. 1998. *The Color of Faith: Building Community in a Multiracial Society*. Cleveland: Pilgrim.

Pinn, Anthony B., and Benjamin Valentin, eds. 2001. *The Ties That Bind: African American and Hispanic American/Latino/a Theologies in Dialogue*. New York: Continuum.

Rivera, Mayra. 2007. *The Touch of Transcendence: A Postcolonial Theology of God*. Louisville: Westminster John Knox.

Schneider, Laurel. 2001. Yahwist Desires: Imagining Divinity Queerly. Pages 210–27 in *Queer Commentary and the Hebrew Bible*. Edited by Ken Stone. Cleveland: Pilgrim.

Segovia, Fernando F. 2000. "And They Began to Speak in Other Tongues": Competing Modes of Discourse in Contemporary Biblical Criticism. Pages 3–33 in idem, *Decolonizing Biblical Studies: A View from the Margins*. Maryknoll, N.Y.: Orbis.

Segundo, Juan Luis. 1993. Revelation, Faith, Signs of the Times. Pages 328–49 in *Mysterium Liberationis: Fundamental Concepts of Liberation Theology*. Edited by Ignacio Ellacuría and Jon Sobrino. New York: Orbis.

Sells, Michael A. 1994. *Mystical Languages of Unsaying*. Chicago: University of Chicago Press.

Sherwood, Yvonne, and John D. Caputo. 2005. Otobiographies, Or How a Torn and Disembodied Ear Hears a Promise of Death. Pages 209–39 in *Derrida and Religion: Other Testaments*. Edited by Yvonne Sherwood and Kevin Hart. New York: Routledge.

Soelle, Dorothee. 2001. *The Silent Cry: Mysticism and Resistance*. Minneapolis: Fortress.

Spivak, Gayatri Chakravorty. 1998. Translator's Preface. Pages ix–lxxxviii in Jacques Derrida, *Of Grammatology*. Baltimore: Johns Hopkins University Press.

———. 1999. *A Critique of Postcolonial Reason: Toward a History of the Vanishing Present*. Cambridge: Harvard University Press.

Sugirtharajah, R. S. 2002. *Postcolonial Criticism and Biblical Interpretation*. Oxford: Oxford University Press.

Trinh, T. Minh-ha. 1989. *Woman Native Other*. Bloomington: Indiana University Press.

Teaching for Color Consciousness

Evelyn L. Parker

White supremacy is the foundational ideology that anchors all other ideologies (economic, political, and so forth) in the sociohistorical milieu of the U.S. since its founding. Like other ideologies, it provides "the frameworks of understanding through which men [*sic*] interpret, make sense of experiences and 'live' the material conditions in which they find themselves" (Hall et al. 1980, 33). White supremacy is a system of ideas, beliefs, values, and attitudes held by white women and men that determines their actions or practices consciously/unconsciously. It informs their self-understanding as a superior race to all other nonwhites. White supremacists act out of a belief of entitlement, power, and dominance. It is a political ideology that advocates social and political dominance for whites and frames both liberal and conservative political ideologies in the U.S. It is the ideology by which those with white privilege and power act toward African Americans, Asian Americans, Latino/a Americans, and other people of color. Such practices are evident in the exploitation and dehumanization of other women and men based on their racial-ethnic identity.

White supremacist relations of exploitation engage in "practices that are governed by the rituals in which the practices are inscribed, within the material existence of an ideological apparatus" (Althusser 1971, 42), which include the church, the family, educational institutions, political parties, literature, visual and performing arts, and communications media. White supremacy, as the foundational or framing ideology, exists in many apparatuses, and its practices are manifest in the actions of white individuals or beneficiaries of white privilege. Louis Althusser argues that all apparatuses, including the religious and the educational, contribute toward the same goal, such as that of the capitalist relations of exploitation (28). The educational institutions, for Althusser, are the silent yet dominant apparatus for inculcating the ideology of the ruling class and ultimately engaging in relations of exploitation with regards to the poor and working classes (31). In the U.S. the Christian church also engages in class formation through lived practices that favor and reproduce the ideologies of the ruling and middle classes, of which white supremacy is the substructure.

This understanding of white supremacy does not intend to oversimplify the complexity of the philosophy of ideology but acknowledges this complexity while focusing on practices regarding race-ethnicity and the interlocking dimensions of class, gender, and sexuality in the ideological apparatuses of the church and institutions of theological education as situated in the capitalistic society of the U.S.

White supremacy is the foundational or framing ideology in the U.S. that produces "meanings in the service of power" (The Bible and Culture Collection 1997, 274), meanings that are crystallized in "images, representations, categories through which men [sic] live in an imaginary way their real relation to their conditions of existence" (Hall et al. 1980, 33). Historically, this deeply engrained system of meaning, rituals, and practices is related to the imperialism, colonization, and genocide of Native Americans during the formative years of the United States. White colonizers used the Bible to sanction their actions toward Native Americans. They exploited and betrayed the hospitality of Native people, exterminated their families and incarcerated those who survived on government reservations. Many Native American children were acculturated in Christian boarding schools where the Bible was the primary form of literature. White Christian missionaries sought to dismantle the Native value system using Scripture to stress the sinfulness of the young Indian students (Kidwell, Noley, and Tinker 2001, 8).

The Bible has played a significant role in buttressing and legitimizing white supremacy among white children. During the nineteenth century, white Christian settlers used biblical texts to instill values and beliefs of superiority, particularly in their young white males. This is illustrated in the 1845 publication of *The Bible Boy Taken Captive by the Indians* by the American Sunday School Union in Philadelphia. The story, written by Herman Cope, tells of a little boy named Joseph Reed who lived with his parents on a farm on the western frontier, far from any populated settlement. His mother taught him reading basics using an old spelling book. When Joseph completed the spelling book, he read the family Bible each night after working all day in the woods. As Cope develops the story, he carefully presents Joseph as a boy who is hard-working and obedient to his parents.

Cope introduces biblical stories that Joseph read. Thus, "He read many times the history of Joseph, with which I hope you are all well acquainted" (1977, 7). Cope tells the reader that Joseph read all the "beautiful narratives of the Old Testament" until he had completed it. Most significantly, Joseph confesses his sins and is converted to Christianity through his reading of "the history of Jesus, in the New Testament" (8). Cope develops his own Christology through his character Joseph Reed while quoting Scripture. Quoting Isa 53:5, Cope writes:

> Joseph wondered, at first, that God would allow so great sorrow to come upon one who never in his life did any thing wrong, and who came from heaven on purpose to do good; but, as he read still further, he found that all these sufferings were permitted, in order that he might atone *our* sins. He read, that "He was

wounded for *our* transgressions, he was bruised for *our* iniquities; the chastise-
ment of *our* peace was upon him, and by his stripes we are healed."

We read that, as Joseph grew older, his understanding of the Bible increased as he
studies its "doctrines" and "poetry": "His whole mind enlarged ... and [he] was
obliged to study out all these things *himself*, without much assistance, so that he
became a much better thinker, and had a far stronger mind than those boys have,
who are always depending on others to teach them, and make every thing as easy
as possible for them" (1977, 14).

Cope moves from Joseph Reed's conversion experience to tell about his
encounter with Indians, while his parents are away on business and he was alone
on the family farm. Joseph was fourteen years old when "about eight or ten"
Indians came upon him as he read the Bible. "Joseph," he points out, "had heard
that the Indians had lately been doing some mischief among the white people"
(1977, 16–17). Cope contrasts the mischief and rudeness of the Indians with the
brave and fearless behavior of Joseph. The Indians gestured that he must go with
them. "Joseph," Cope writes, "knew it was of no use to resist, and so, commend-
ing himself to the protection of God, he walked courageously along between the
two Indians who were appointed to guard him" (18–19). Cope writes of a "youthful savage" named Light Foot, who was about the same age as Joseph and spoke
a little English, who provided for Joseph's needs. Light Foot chided Joseph as the
Bible Boy because he would recite chapter after chapter to Light Foot and explain
the meaning. Light Foot eventually helped Joseph escape captivity. A few years
later, Light Foot, whose heart was touched by Joseph's stories of Jesus the Savior,
found Joseph in the village where he helped him escape. Cope writes:

> As time passed on, he gave evidence that he had felt himself a sinner, and had
> fled to Jesus for salvation. He never appeared happier than when studying the
> Bible with Joseph, and, in the course of a few years, he went back to his own
> people, the Indians, as a missionary and was the means, by the blessing of God,
> of leading many among them to "know God, and Jesus Christ whom he has
> sent." (33–34)

Cope concludes the chapter highlighting Joseph's accomplishments as a "prosper-
ous merchant" who spent time promoting the Sabbath school in the village and
establishing others around the country. Cope writes:

> When asked why he felt so much attached to this institution, he would say,
> "Because it is designed to encourage and promote the study of a book, to which I
> owe all my happiness and prosperity in this world, as well as all my hopes of sal-
> vation in the next, — a book, which if faithfully studied, would banish ignorance
> and wickedness from the world; and fill it with light and peace of Heaven, that
> book is THE BIBLE." (34–35)

Cope's story, *The Bible Boy Taken Captive by the Indians*, illustrates how the Bible was used to inculcate white supremacy within the ideological apparatus of the Christian church. In this case the practice of storytelling using biblical texts serves to instill supremacist beliefs in white children during the early nineteenth century. Althusser's idea of the ideological apparatus is illustrated in the nineteenth-century Sabbath school in the Christian church on the U.S. western frontier. The literature of this institution intentionally promoted the superiority of the white boy over the inferior Indian boy, while contrasting the high moral character of the white boy with the savage and rude nature of the Indian boy.

Most Sunday school literature in the twenty-first century seeks to address such blatant racism, yet the subtle expressions of white supremacist ideals are still practiced in Bible study materials. The selection of Scripture for study in Sunday school and various Bible study series tends to establish hegemonic identities of the slave-master and the object-subject for racial-ethnic people. An example would be the choice of the book of Philemon for the first session in a Bible study series with the goal of helping participants reflect on their relationship with God and humankind. Such selection of Scripture for the first session of a Bible study series draws lines of power and privilege with regard to race, gender, class, and sexuality. The exception of such practices would be intentional consideration of these issues in the text in light of the goal of exploring relationships with God and humankind.

White supremacy as a foundational ideology in the U.S. is not limited to whites. This ideology also provides meaning and dictates behavior for all citizens, both those with white privilege and those who are marginalized because of color, class, gender, and sexual orientation. This ideology is embedded not only in white dominant groups but in racial and ethnic minorities as well. Prior to and following the civil rights movement of the 1960s, the price of success concretized into becoming an "honorary white," especially for blacks, which meant "assimilation as a social policy" (hooks 1989, 115). Blacks were lulled into a state of complicity while focused on getting a quality education, a job, and the means to obtain economic stability for oneself and one's family. Blacks were socialized to embody white supremacy, which was manifested when blacks exercised power over one another with actions supported by white supremacist beliefs and values (113).

Also, the Bible played a significant role in reinforcing white supremacist practices in black, Asian, and Latino/a churches through their use of white images of Jesus hung on the walls and the use of Sunday school literature with images and stories of white families. Children in racial-ethnic congregations concretely understood God to be a white male with a long white beard. In many instances this understanding of the God of the Bible was collapsed with the Santa Claus of the Christmas holiday. Moses, Abraham, Sarah, Mary the mother of Jesus, and all characters of the Bible are viewed as white. Some Protestant denominations have become aware of this problem in the publication of Christian educational materials and have developed guidelines for writing curriculum resources that are inclusive in terms of race-ethnicity and gender. However, although the extensive use of white images in church resources is no longer the standard, there are few resources that authentically reflect the experiences of racial-ethnic communities.

Historically, this deeply engrained system of meaning and practices is related to the imperialism, colonization, and genocide of racial-ethnic people. The drive to conquer and colonize, while rooted in economic and material greed, motivated the slave trade from Africa to North America. Africans were sold as chattel labor, bred like cattle, and regarded as savage brutes. Ephesians 6:5–9 helped to enforce egregious laws instituted to control enslaved Africans:

> Slaves, obey your earthly masters with fear and trembling, in singleness of heart, as you obey Christ; not only while being watched, and in order to please them, but as slaves of Christ doing the will of God from the heart. Render service with enthusiasm, as to the Lord and not to men and women, knowing that whatever good we do we will receive the same again from the Lord, whether we are slaves or free.

Scripture was also used to support unjust political, economic, and social policies among powerful and privileged people, who practiced a white supremacist ideology. The Bible is used to uphold governmental policies and legal structures of U.S. society, including the constitution, regarding Native Americans and enslaved Africans. Romans 13:1–2 was one of those texts of Scripture: "Let every person be subject to the governing authorities; for there is no authority except from God, and those authorities that exist have been instituted by God. Therefore whoever resists authority resists what God has appointed, and those who resist will incur judgment."

The white supremacist reading of Scripture can be connected to a number of laws. Prior to the civil rights movement, racial-ethnic minorities fearfully obeyed national and state Jim Crow segregation laws and the "separate but equal" mandate regarding accommodations. Executive Order 9066, issued by President Franklin D. Roosevelt, was the default mode of white supremacist action: after the bombing of Pearl Harbor, thousands of Japanese Americans were rendered to internment camps from 1942 until 1946. Similarly, during 2006 white supremacy ideologically influenced the formation of public policy regarding immigration laws in the U.S. A city ordinance in Farmers Branch, Texas, prohibits landlords from leasing to undocumented Latinos/as. With the ordinance English is also declared the official language. Hence, private businesses receive fines for advertising in Spanish. Interpretation of Scripture through the lens of white supremacist ideology has affected every aspect of life, even the institutional apparatus of theological education.

The ideology of white supremacy provides the context for teaching and learning biblical studies in seminaries and schools of theology in the U.S. The Bible has been used to buoy the white supremacy ideology, and the ideologies of the Bible are equally supported by white supremacy. Reading and interpreting the Bible is compounded when a nonwhite person teaches the Bible in North American institutions of theological education.

A white supremacist ideology causes systemic injustices in every aspect of this society. As such, several questions come to mind as I reflect on the studies in this volume. What must a biblical studies professor—Asian, Black, Latino/a—consider when she or he teaches the Bible in this milieu of white supremacy? What concerns must a white biblical studies professor address? What is the pedagogical potential of these essays for critical awareness and critical action about white supremacist motivated injustice? What pedagogical practices are suggested? How does pedagogy for color consciousness interlock with and broaden consciousness of gender, class, and sexuality when reading Scripture? How is pedagogy for color blindness related to pedagogy for color consciousness? How does pedagogy for color consciousness confront cultural colorism? These are some of the many questions I seek to answer in this essay. Teaching for color consciousness results in transforming the larger framework of meaning and practice that is rooted in the ideology of white supremacy. Teaching the Bible through the lens of race and ethnicity is a method of teaching for color consciousness whereby the supremacist assumptions about the Bible and the biblical characters are challenged and all who engage in the experience become "conscientized" people.

COLOR CONSCIOUSNESS

Color consciousness is awareness of the white supremacist ideology operative in U.S. society that dominates and oppresses African Americans, Asian Americans, Latino/a Americans, and other racial-ethnic people. The central aim of color consciousness is to assist people of color and whites with divesting of white supremacy. It is attentiveness to power dynamics within human relationships both on a familiar level and in institutional and governmental settings. It is the realization that in U.S. society decisions about every aspect of life—including access to the basics of food, clothing, and shelter—are determined by many whose practices usher from a white, capitalistic, and imperialist mindset. It pays attention to who has power and who does not, how that power is used, who benefits and who does not. It resists the ideological straightjacket of a white supremacist ideology and the epistemological constraints of white dominant culture. It identifies the ontological state of honorary whiteness of oneself and in others as egregious assimilation into a white supremacist ideology and works toward being fully human as an African American, Asian American, Latino/a American. Likewise, it is epistemological insofar as "critical consciousness and critical action sit at the core of a way of knowing, a way of meaning making" (Parker 2003, 26).

Color consciousness is also awareness of the complexities of race and ethnicity and the intersections of class, culture, gender, and sexuality. Those who operate out of a white supremacist mindset deny that people in this nation still experience race, class, gender, and orientation injustice. Consider the following fictive case study. A Latina biblical studies professor enters the classroom of a seminary situated in a southwestern city, where the Latino/a population is almost 60 percent of the city's total population and almost 40 percent of the state's population. However, her classroom does not reflect this demographic, but has less than 5 percent Latino/a, African American, and other racial and ethnic minorities. Many of her white students have never had a female professor with an earned Ph.D., much less an Afro-Cuban, dark-skinned woman with a heavy Spanish accent. The white students are in a state of cognitive dissonance, a place of anxiety caused by this incongruity of belief and practice, because their experience of one who holds authority and power to teach the Bible is both white and male. The students of color struggle with an unidentified uneasiness. Some are not sure about this new experience, because they have been socialized to believe that women cannot and should not teach the Bible, since "the Bible says so." Additionally, they have been socialized to believe that good teaching, like good health care and good legal representation, is delivered only by white teachers, doctors, and lawyers. This situation illustrates the intersectionality of race, gender, and class. Color consciousness requires that the Latina professor and her students enter into a teaching and learning relationship with their "eyes wide open" to this novel situation, that it is good and that it holds potential for an educational experience unlike those ordinarily experienced in higher education in the U.S.

Color consciousness is not simply a cognitive state of being or conscious intellectual activity but also a physical manifestation as well. Cognition is coupled with action, the knowing and doing among those who move away from false consciousness and into this new found rim of consciousness. The aim of critical thinking and critically making sense of the world is critical action or justice. A divested ideology of white supremacy is shown in transformative action. A student of color from the case study above who has rid herself or himself of a thinking process filled with stereotypes of people from African and Spanish ancestry and their authority to guide the exploration of Scripture is compelled to act in ways that can help others to experience color consciousness. The student might intentionally seek to learn more under the tutelage of that professor or other professors with similar social locations. The student will advocate for a more diverse racial and ethnic minority faculty and administrators. Additionally, the student will advocate for changes in policy that affect communities that are oppressed and for clergy women and racial-ethnic minorities oppressed by the unjust governance of ecclesial communities. Yet, to be honest, the power differential of students versus faculty, administration, and trustees who pledge money is obvious. A student who has divested herself or himself of white supremacy has little power to effect immediate change. However, the student does have the long-term potential for transforming the institution if the will to do so is kept alive.

The color consciousness that I have described is akin to Paulo Freire's idea of *conscientização* or conscientization, which is "learning to perceive social, political, and economic contradictions, and to take action against the oppressive elements of reality" (1993, 16). Conscientization is a corrective to that form of education that "banks knowledge" with students through a hegemonic relationship between the teacher and the students. The banking concept of education serves the interests of the oppressor, the dominant ideology. Conscientization enables the oppressed to become critical thinkers about their situation and critical engagers with dominant powers to correct injustices. In reflecting on the problem-posing method of education and thematic investigation, Freire offers a poignant understanding of the process of conscientization:

> Reflection upon situationality is reflection about the very condition of existence: critical thinking by means of which people discover each other to be "in a situation." Only as this situation ceases to present itself as a dense, enveloping reality or a tormenting blind alley, and they can come to perceive it as an objective-problematic situation—only then can commitment exit. Humankind *emerge* from their *submersion* and acquire the ability to *intervene* in reality as it is unveiled. *Intervention* in reality—historical awareness itself—thus represents a step forward from *emergence*, and results from the *conscientização* of the situation. *Conscientização* is the deepening of the attitude of awareness characteristic of all emergence. (90)

Freire understands education of this nature as "the practice of freedom—as opposed to education as the practice of domination" (62). It is a problem-posing education that liberates cognitive processes rather than the transferral of information. People are free to raise questions about their existential reality, and they develop their power to transform a once-perceived static world. Education as the practice of freedom affirms the ontological aspect of women and men as "in the process of *becoming*—as unfinished, uncompleted beings in and with a likewise unfinished reality" (62–65).

Freire's educational theory has greatly influenced bell hooks, whom I also use as a dialogue partner to talk about color consciousness. She appropriates Freire's concept of conscientization in her teaching philosophy. In a piece titled "Paulo Freire," in *Teaching to Transgress: Education as the Practice of Freedom*, hooks uses a method of dialogue between herself, Gloria Watkins, and her writing voice, bell hooks, as she discusses Freire's work. She clearly indicates how his work liberated her own thinking during a time when she "was beginning to question deeply and profoundly the politics of domination, the impact of racism, sexism, and class exploitation, and the kind of domestic colonization that takes place in the United States" (1994, 46). This testimony launched reflection on African Americans and white supremacy, education as the practice of freedom, as well as a strong critique of Freire's "phallocentric paradigm of liberation—wherein freedom and the experience of patriarchal manhood are always linked as though they are one and the same" (49). Her reflections and writing on pedagogy, as influenced by Freire and others, have continued for more than a decade. In the preface of her recent book

Teaching Community: A Pedagogy of Hope, she situates the subject of the book with a quote from Freire on the relationship of educational practice to the process of hope.

Pedagogy for Color Consciousness

What does a pedagogy for color consciousness look like? What is the pedagogical potential of the studies in this book for color consciousness? What pedagogical practices are suggested? What pedagogical strategies organize how one can teach through the lens of race and ethnicity? To be clear, a pedagogy for color consciousness works to dismantle white supremacy. It resists distortions of the existential experiences of people of color. It is critical thinking joined with critical engagement with the world for the sake of justice.

This volume contains essays that address minority biblical criticism from an African American, Asian American, and Latino/a American perspective. This form of biblical criticism falls under the rubric of ideological biblical criticism. An ideological reading of the Scripture is

> a deliberate effort to read against the grain—of texts, of disciplinary norms, of traditions, of cultures. It is a disturbing way to read because ideological criticism demands a high level of self-consciousness and makes explicit, unabashed appeal to justice. As an ethically grounded act, ideological reading intends to raise critical consciousness about what is just and unjust about … power relationships. (The Bible and Culture Collective 1997, 275)

The very nature of minority biblical criticism makes it a perfect match with a pedagogy for color consciousness in settings where Scripture is taught. The pedagogical aims are the same: to disrupt unjust power relationships caused by the domination of white supremacy. When teaching the Bible through this method, each teaching/learning setting becomes a *consciousness-raising group*. I borrow this phrase from bell hooks, which she uses in reminiscing about the feminist consciousness-raising that occurred during the early days of the women's liberation movement in her book *Feminism Is for Everybody: Passionate Politics*. These settings focused on women realizing "patriarchy as a system of domination, how it became institutionalized and how it is perpetuated and maintained" (2000, 7). Such environments are common among critical educators. But I do not want to appear naïve and suggest that teaching for critical consciousness is a simple political practice in our various settings of theological education, where ideological restraints are real. White supremacy is alive and well in theological education and attacks the critical and transformative educator in an overt and covert manner, which includes learner resistance, negative course evaluations, and negative peer-teaching reviews.

On a more practical level, critical pedagogy, notwithstanding pedagogy for color consciousness, is alien to our students' educational history. Prior to arriving in settings of higher education, our students have been in public and private schools that use banking methodology rather than problem-posing methods for teaching. They arrive in seminary and divinity schools socialized in learning content for the test. If their biblical studies teacher does not "teach for the test," most students are uncomfortable and develop ways to resist the teacher and the educational possibilities that critical pedagogy provides. Such phenomena are complicated when the social location of the professor is like that of the Afro-Cuban female biblical studies teacher described earlier.

The common pedagogical strategy for all the pieces in this book is critical questioning about race-ethnicity. Color consciousness moves students into awareness and action about injustice by teaching them to question reality on every level. What better way of learning to question than through interpretation of the biblical text. For many students, questioning Scripture is a new experience, if they have been taught the Bible through a banking teaching methodology. As indicated earlier, most racial-ethnic minorities have been taught to be good U.S. citizens through the banking model. Seminary students who come from congregations where the Bible is taught by the one-and-only-authority of the Bible, the senior pastor, are restrained from asking questions. The practice is to sit in the sanctuary or a setting where a large number of participants gather and become "filled with good teaching," like empty pitchers before a water fountain. The banking model of Bible study is popular among congregations of racial-ethnic minorities. This phenomenon is clearly an exercise of power in the teaching setting that merits intentional and systematic investigation. The point is this: students in theological education who come from such settings find it harder to learn to question the Bible than those who are not from such congregations. Given these contextual matters, these studies inspire three pedagogical strategies: a pedagogy of hospitality for learning to question; a pedagogy for mirroring hard realities; and a pedagogy for resisting colorism.

A Pedagogy of Hospitality for Learning to Question

All the contributions to this volume suggest the pedagogical strategy of teaching that empowers students to learn to question. Extending hospitality to questions is essential to a pedagogy for color consciousness. It is welcoming the stranger to questioning powers and structures of U.S. society to make her or his home in a place where asking why, how, and why not is normative. The power-wielding teacher that does not invite racial-ethnic minority students, or all students, for that matter, to question Scripture does not have a welcome doormat for them, inviting them to be at home in their classes.

I witnessed the gravity of such inhospitality when I was a fledgling teacher in a seminary located in the South. Arriving at that institution with my "pedagogical tricks" for critical questioning, I assumed every student was anxious for liberative learning. One of my African students would never respond to my hospitable gestures to use his experiences to critique the authors in reading assignments and engage his peers in rigorous dialogue. Seeing this pattern, I invited him to have a conversation with me. I wanted him to know he was sincerely welcomed to exercise his right to raise questions. During our dialogue he made it clear he knew what I wanted of him. The decisive moment came when he recited an African proverb that indicated his fear of raising questions because he had been punished for doing so in the past. When a stranger has experienced abuse like this student, she or he may find it difficult to feel at home with asking questions in the biblical studies classroom or any classroom in institutions of theological education that seek to practice such hospitality. Teachers are challenged with creating a hospitable space where the stranger is welcomed to "talk back" without fear of punishment and without fear of being hurt for speaking their own truths (hooks 1989, 1–2). Can the Latino/a, Asian, and African American student talk back in the strange land of the biblical studies classroom in settings of theological education? These studies offer a resounding yes! Racial-ethnic minority students are welcome to pose questions rather than be filled with answers from the dominant power of authority.

Additionally, racial-ethnic minority students and most majority students are strangers to models of education that resist maintaining the status quo for U.S. citizens. To be an American citizen means the stranger conforms to values and beliefs of the state and jettisons those of his or her community. The conditions of citizenship are to remain a stranger in this land. Students are more at home with banking educational models. They are strangers to educational models that welcome resistance to the dominant way of teaching and learning. A pedagogy for color consciousness welcomes racial-ethnic minorities to resist educational models that prevent them from thinking critically about their own existential realities, to resist the conditions of citizenship, and to resist being a perpetual stranger. Racial-ethnic minority students are welcome to produce knowledge and transform the prevailing white supremacist knowledge.

Gay Byron's essay welcomes students in biblical studies to form questions about the worldview of the Roman Empire, which has been privileged in New Testament interpretation. Students are invited to expand their horizon of meaning by considering and investigating other contexts, particularly ancient Ethiopia, as worldview for interpreting the New Testament. As such, students gain skills for problematizing the Roman Empire with respect to Paul's travels. Teaching Benny Liew's "Queering Closets and Perverting Desires" welcomes questions about *normative readings* of biblical texts, while inviting a "transgressive … reading strategy … [of] John's Sophia/Jesus … as transvestite" (254). This reading takes note of race-ethnicity and sexuality.

A Pedagogy for Mirroring Hard Realities

In light of the contextual situations that welcome questioning the biblical text, in the theological classroom the challenge is to use Scripture as a mirror to reflect back to students' hard realities in their contemporary setting and to call the learner to act for justice. By this I mean students are invited to discover hard realities about modern sociohistorical events through the biblical text.

Frank Yamada's interpretation of Gen 2-3 in light of the Japanese American internment is a resistant act forcing learners to see incongruity in popular versions of U.S. history. Even if a Japanese American student is not present in the class, all students should wonder about this egregious governmental decision. How is it similar and different from the Jewish Holocaust? How does the thesis of displacement connect with the contemporary experience of poor African Americans displaced due to events surrounding Hurricane Katrina? How does it impact undocumented persons from Mexico, Central America, and South America? Yamada's thesis invites critical questioning from many racial-ethnic readers of his essay, since his interpretation of Gen 2–3 mirrors contemporary history. Gale Yee's "She Stood in Tears Amid the Alien Corn" considers the book of Ruth in terms of the construct of the Asian American as the "perpetual foreigner" and "model minority." She provides a mirror for racial-ethnic students, particularly Asian Americans, who uncritically strive to be the ideal minority in U.S. society. She also raises awareness for students about the model minority myth that is perpetuated by white supremacist ideology. In similar fashion, Francisco García-Treto mirrors the hard realities of hybridity and being an exile in his "Aspects of Exile in the Hebrew Bible from the Perspective of the Cuban Diaspora." Here he offers a triple-sided mirror of the Hebrew text, contemporary Cuban literature, and testimony of his own experiences.

A PEDAGOGY OF RESISTANCE TO COLORISM

A pedagogy for color consciousness foregrounds issues of colorism in learners. "Colorism," I have argued, "is interiorized color consciousness among African Americans regarding skin color, shades of complexion, hair texture, and physical features" (2003). In this society it is discrimination and inequality based on skin tone and physicality. Katie Cannon and Emilie Townes are among several theologians who have written about colorism among African Americans. However, this phenomenon is not limited to African Americans but has been problematic for Asians and Latino/as as well, given the problem of the color line in the U.S. Within every racial-ethnic group, lighter skin tones are preferred over darker skin tones. The practice of miscegenation, where European Americans produce offspring with African, Asian, and Latino/a heritage, makes issues of colorism highly combustible within these racial-ethnic groups. Cheryl Anderson's study, "Reflections in an Interethnic/racial Era on Interethnic/racial Marriage in Ezra," gives insight for teaching about miscegenation. She explains the contextual situation of miscegenation both historically and currently, as she lays a foundation for her argument. In similar fashion, Jean-Pierre Ruiz's essay lifts up interethnic-racial marriage while focusing on language and ethnicity in Neh 13.

Colorism becomes gendered when African American and Latina American women with lighter skin tones and small hips are preferred over women with darker skin and fuller/rounder hips. Pop culture icon Jennifer Lopez received caustic comments from media pundits about her rounded, more African-looking, "big" hips. Asian American women with lighter skin tones and "Western eyes" are preferred to darker-skinned women with "Asian eyes." Su Yon Pak discusses the struggle for "Western eyes" among middle- and upper-class Korean American girls whose privilege allows them the costly surgery (2006, 15–42). Eyelid surgery among Asian girls and women signals the problem of colorism, gender, and class for the Asian American community.

Darder and Torres argue against essentializing skin color for the sake of addressing racism without a class critique. This critique holds merit when we consider how colorism functions among African Americans, Asian Americans, and Latino/a Americans. Colorism is often directly related to class (Parker 2003). Ethnographic data of African American teenagers illustrates how colorism and class interlocks in their self-understanding of racial identity. Lighter-skinned African American youth struggle with being labeled "mixed" and "rich," even though that is not their reality. At the same time, the peers of biracial teens assume that they are from wealthy households when this may not be the case (Parker 2003).

In the color-consciousness classroom, discourse about colorism is an opportunity for teaching and learning. The topic of colorism was difficult for the participants of the Wabash project. Discussion about the perceptions of skin color in our communities was uneven and voiceless. Perhaps this was reflective of the incendiary nature of colorism among racial-ethnic groups in this society. Perhaps it was reluctance to air dirty laundry about our racial-ethnic communities of origin. Nevertheless, teaching for color consciousness must include the topic of colorism.

Given the struggle with colorism among members within the project, the studies in this volume do not address this topic explicitly. However, discussion about the complexity of colorism within and without racial-ethnic groups can be spotlighted. As mentioned above, both the pieces by Anderson and Ruiz lend themselves to critical awareness about colorism. Teachers and students who come to Randall Bailey's essay become aware of the many complex issues of race, gender, and sexuality. Students cannot and should not avoid the issue of "passing" as they engage his interpretation of Esther. Passing, secretly posing as a member of another racial-ethnic group afforded by light skin tone and other physical features, is an aspect of colorism. Discourse on colorism enhances pedagogy in the color consciousness classroom.

Color Blindness vis-à-vis Color Consciousness

In this essay I have argued that white supremacy is the ideology that shapes the context for teaching and learning in schools of theological education in the U.S. I have also argued for a pedagogy for color consciousness, which is awareness of the ideology of white supremacy and commitment to resist and transform this form of knowing in the routines, practices, and institutions of society. My reflection on various contributions to this volume stimulated three possible pedagogical strategies. They are a pedagogy for hospitality for learning to question, a pedagogy for mirroring hard realities, and a pedagogy for resisting colorism. There is, however, another aspect of color consciousness that I wish to discuss, due to its relevance for the discourse in this essay: color blindness. So, how is color consciousness related to the belief in a color-blind society held by white liberals in dominant society and aware people of color? I raise this question because it is a popular perception among dominant and oppressed people in this nation who feel they have overcome racism and racial prejudice and operate out of a critical awareness about race and ethnicity.

A form of white supremacy is captured in the idea of color blindness. It is the conviction that all people are equal and should be treated equally regardless of their race and ethnicity. Liberals in the North American legal system believe in color blindness and unbiased principles of constitutional law. They argue that it is wrong for the law to take any note of race. Critical race theorists argue that the belief in color blindness only rectifies the extremely horrific and obvious racial harms:

> But if racism is embedded in our thought processes and social structures as deeply as many [critical race theorists] believe, then the ... routines, practices, and institutions that we rely on to effect the world's work—will keep minorities in subordinate positions. Only aggressive, color-conscious efforts to change the way things are will do much to ameliorate misery. (Delgado and Stefancic 2001, 21–22)

As mentioned above, thinking related to color blindness is a popular idea shared by black and white people in U.S. society as well as among those who would arbitrate constitutional law. In my research I have identified beliefs in color blindness among African American adolescent girls. One example is Kathy (a pseudonym), a twelfth-grader from the near west side of Chicago. Kathy became a recognized peer leader in her high school, although she had personal hardships of deceased parents, incarcerated brothers, and poverty. During an interview, I asked her about her commitments to the liberation of African Americans based on our prior conversation about black liberation. She replied, "I don't see color. So if I can help 'em, I'll help 'em. If I can't help 'em, I won't." With further probing I concluded that Kathy's language was consistent with the belief in a color-blind society. Her meaning-making system has assimilated the white supremacist ideology that one can act justly toward anyone without considering their race and ethnicity. "I don't see color" is an idiomatic phrase within many African American communities that suggests that race does not matter for them (Parker 2003, 82–83).

As I think back to the time of this interview, I remember Kathy's social location, the pain in her eyes, and her deep despair as she told me her story. Being authorized by teachers and administrators in her school to be a leader among her peers probably came with the cost of practicing color-blind justice. Her education to that point had not invited her into problem-posing, into critical reflection, on her reality. It is safe to assume that her education encouraged her to think about equality and justice without regard for problems of race, poverty, and hardship. She had not been invited to think about her troubles in relationship to systems, institutions, and the dominant mindset that makes decisions with respect to her troubles. Color blindness is incompatible with raising questions about one's reality and the reality of their loved ones.

Color blindness is a by-product of a white supremacist ideology with its beliefs and practices. Color consciousness is a by-product of critical awareness and critical transformation. Color blindness prohibits critical questioning. Color consciousness permits critical questioning. Color blindness masks authentic justice. Color consciousness unmasks authentic justice. Color blindness discounts the historical aspects of race and racism. Historical assessment is essential to color consciousness. Color blindness is ideologically rooted in the white dominant patriarchy. Color consciousness is rooted in communities that are rendered subordinate to the white dominant patriarchy. Pedagogy for color blindness is grounded in the banking model of education. Color consciousness is compatible with a pedagogy of posing problems. This comparison between color blindness and color consciousness intends to illustrate the incongruity of these two concepts. I want to be clear that color blindness is not an indication toward critical awareness and critical action. Rather, color consciousness indicates that progression. Also, such clarity allows the transition into concerns about teaching for color consciousness.

A pedagogy for color consciousness—which is awareness of the ideology of white supremacy and commitment to resist and transform this form of knowing in the routines, practices, and institutions of society—is the appropriate pedagogical model for the studies in this volume. The suggested pedagogical strategies and those that occur during the teaching event of biblical studies through the lens of race-ethnicity hold limitless possibility for teaching/learning in institutions of theological education.

Works Consulted

Althusser, Louis. 1971. *Essays on Ideology*. Thetford, Norfolk: Thetford Press.

Cope, Herman. 1977. *The Bible Boy Taken Captive by the Indians*. The Garland Library of Narratives of North American Indian Captivities 59. New York: Garland. [orig. 1845]

Darder, Antonia, and Rodolfo D. Torres. 2004. *After Race: Racism after Multiculturalism*. New York: New York University Press.

Delgado, Richard, and Jean Stefancic. 2001. *Critical Race Theory: An Introduction.* New York: New York University Press.

Freire, Paulo. 1993. *Pedagogy of the Oppressed.* New York: Continuum. [orig. 1970]

Hall, Stuart, Dorothy Hobson, Andrew Lowe, and Paul Willis. 1980. *Culture, Media, Language: Working Papaers in Cultural Studies 1972–79.* London: Center for Contemporary Cultural Studies, University of Birmingham.

hooks, bell. 1989. *Talking Back: Thinking Feminist, Thinking Black.* Boston: South End.

———. 1994. *Teaching to Transgress: Education as the Practice of Freedom.* New York: Routledge.

———. 2000. *Feminism Is for Everybody: Passionate Politics.* Cambridge: South End.

Kidwell, Clara Sue, Homer Noley, and George E. Tinker. 2001. *A Native American Theology.* Maryknoll, N.Y.: Orbis.

Pak, Su Yon. 2006. "'I''s Wide Shut: Eyelid Surgery as a Window into the Spirituality of Korean American Adolescent Girls." Pages 15–42 in Parker 2006.

Parker, Evelyn. 2003. *Trouble Don't Last Always: Emancipatory Hope among African American Adolescents.* Cleveland: Pilgrim.

———, ed. 2006. *The Sacred Selves of Adolescent Girls: Hard Stories of Race, Class, and Gender.* Cleveland: Pilgrim.

Storey, John. 2001. *Cultural Theory and Popular Culture: An Introduction.* Harlow, U.K.: Pearson Education; New York: Prentice Hall.

The Bible and Culture Collective. 1997. Ideological Criticism. Pages 272–308 in *The Postmodern Bible.* New ed. New Haven: Yale University Press.

The Difference That Damage Makes: Reflections of an Ethnic Studies Scholar on the Wabash Consultation

James Kyung-Jin Lee

Remembrance and Recognition

One of my family's great unofficial games often took place coming home from church services on Sunday afternoons. For my father, a Reformed Church minister, and my mother, Sunday morning was always a feverish moment of the week—my dad, deliberately ambling about the house or apartment obviously nervous about his sermon; my mom spending an hour in the shower, clearly nervous about Dad's anxieties. Many Sunday mornings, I was awakened by my parents' bickering at each other, barely hushed Korean-speak that they thought my brother and I could not hear. But by church's end, when worship service and Bible study and the intervening lunch (and for me and Ted, an impromptu baseball or football game) had finally ended, there was in the family Oldsmobile a sense of relief that was measured by the cheerful gossipy talk that my parents would engage in about the latest impropriety of one of the parishioners.

It would be during these late afternoons, on Sunday-jammed Northern Boulevard or Long Island Expressway, that our car sometimes crept next to another car full of Asian-looking people. My parents' chat would pause briefly, my brother and I would stop playing "territory" in the back seat, and we would all look port or starboard side. For a brief moment, probably no more than five seconds, there would be silence in the car save the humming of the engine, but we all knew what the silence meant. Finally, almost always, my mother would break the seemingly solemn moment and blurt out what all four of us had in our minds: "Han-guk-sa-ram-yee-yah?" which, roughly translated, would go, "Hey, I wonder if they're Korean." And, almost always, we could see that the occupants of the other car were staring right back at us, the kids' noses pressed against the windshield, the adults staring just a little too long for American comfort.

So powerful is this desire to be recognized as socially significant by recognizing another as oneself that it can sometimes occlude the larger determining forces that animate the gesture toward the window, the muffled silence that barely conceals the blurt of correspondence: they are like me! "You belong here, you must belong, or you must go," is a concluding refrain in Chang-rae Lee's widely celebrated first novel *Native Speaker* (1995) the terrible and terrifying imperative of U.S. assimilation that, for the promises of future success, demands of its immigrants the bleak fascism of uniform universalism now. We bristle at the provincial self-segregation of looking for our "own kind"; we wonder why the kids of color sit at the same table at schools; and, if we are Walter Benn Michaels, we view such "multicultural" practice as the beginning of the end of American *civitas* (1997; 2006). But rather than viewing such social clumping as intellectual mistakes, perhaps a more productive means of analysis is to ask what is at stake in this social activity, right or wrong. For far from being an a priori principle of social formation, the desire to see oneself in another, to be seen by another by a particular axis of identity, is an ethical response to the condition of alienation that perhaps is a mark of anyone's fundamental humanity but that those geographically displaced, culturally unmoored, and spiritually detached feel most acutely.

Is it any wonder, then, that ethnic studies has been, generally imagined, the search for what Vijay Prashad refers to as "something of a horizontal assimilation" (2001, x) with others also injured by the terms set by white supremacy? Should it be surprising that those in this volume seek to find bonds and attachment that exceed the language of scholarly affiliation and institutional sanction? Reading the Bible through the eyes and ears of "others" is nothing more than telling stories through the fiction of race, the great story of the United States that socially binds us as tightly as it enables; reading the Bible through the lens of race is nothing less than the crucial acknowledgment that damage does not produce victimization only but also the capacity, the urgency, as John Edgar Wideman puts it, to "[start] a story so that an old story can end" (2001, 3).

Literary criticism and biblical scholarship derive from the same ancestral root, and in both fields scholars attentive to the power of the word know all too well how stories—biblical or otherwise—are complicit in justifying human suffering that are sadly all too imaginable. To this extent, the writers in this volume are fully aware of the caveat of criticism, best summed up by that severe poet and critic Yvor Winters, "to protect us from something we have been foolish enough to love" (as cited in Booth 1988, 49). This consultation, which focused attention on questions of race and ethnicity, relentlessly pursued how and why readers of the Bible were foolish enough to love the narratives—to see ourselves in those narratives—that produce all kinds of human vulnerabilities that have led to countless premature deaths in the name of the divine, for the benefit of some communities over others, and how race was and continues to be, in both textual production and interpretation, the primary means of creating such vulnerabilities and fatalities.

Still, we write in order to listen; we look out the window to recognize ourselves in someone else. In ethnic studies, the urge and urgency to claim, to find voice, to belong, to insist on the right to be heard and be seen, generates a pal-pable politics that undergird our scholarly endeavors. We create typologies and allegories of suffering across time and space, and, in the midst of poststructural-ist and postmodern challenges to the idea of centrality as such, racial subjects demand to be placed, if only provisionally, at the center of analysis to make leg-ible just how much damage has been inflicted, how much pain we feel, even if we ourselves have not experienced it personally. To the dismay of some of our col-leagues who blanch at the seeming lack of scholarly rigor (or institutional rigidity, depending on your point of view), the methodological messiness borne out of the gnawing feeling that it just takes a lot more time and words and scale to explain what racism actually feels like and how it works so insidiously in our daily sto-rytelling, we write a rhetoric that claims at the same time our injury and agency, exposes power and offers resistance, and proclaims a mode of reading with politi-cal eyes, which also asserts our reading *as* political acts.

Whether these are readings that deploy analogical frames, between ancient and more contemporary contexts, which suggest a felt allegorical connection of suffering, such as interracial marriage and their social vicissitudes (Anderson), reflections on the condition of exile (García-Treto and Yamada), the situation of liminal characters as representative of the tendentious and often contradictory relation to structures of power (Yee), or challenges to cultural "centrism" mas-querading as universalism (Byron and Lee); whether these critical gestures point to a deliberate reading "against the grain" of conventional protocol, in effect, "queering" the texts by posing Jesus as cross-dresser (Liew) or cross-dressing metaphors of identity themselves—sexual markers become racial ones and vice versa (Bailey), or placing vernacular speech at the center of one's analysis against imperial lexicons (Ruiz), or "other" cultural traditions at the center of biblical hermeneutic in order to develop a more vibrant, complicate *episteme* (Segovia); whether one heightens the complexity of experience and the difficulties of "equal-ity" by highlighting the intersectionality (Williams) of human struggle; or even whether we move in the other direction by considering contemporary racial expe-rience as a primary source and the Bible as the determining narrative (Parker) or decentering the Bible as a primary source in order to better imagine God for the twenty-first century with all its fragmentation and contestations (Rivera): all of these readers and writers engage their work fully aware that the elevation of the experience of living and working in a raced body (after all, race is better imagined as a verb than as a noun) triggers an immediate, oftentimes visceral snort that suggests political readings as acts of defilement.

Yet we engage in our foolish criticism since we are still foolish enough to love that which we should be protected from; we are unafraid of this foolishness because it is also the beginning of critical wisdom. In a descriptive sense, we are "wild readers," readers who write beyond and sometimes against tolerable pro-tocols and are often viewed as crazy, an intellectual insanity in no small measure and at least a partial result of intolerable regimes of power and the people in and with power who wield it in the security of gates and borders. And in our critical craziness, we look to those in the shadows who might offer the brief solace that they forged a path of resistance to power that may or may not be usable models but are, at the very least, inspiring figures of a different kind of cultural logic.

THE WARFARE IMPERATIVE

Still, in the midst of this critical exuberance of "wild reading" hides a fetter. The field in which I primarily though not exclusively work, Asian American literary studies, has introduced, albeit unevenly, the insights of postcolonial, queer, feminist, psychoanalytic, and "postmodern" theory in the last ten years both to revive and recalibrate the terms of cultural resistance to the debilitating effects of various modes of oppression and, in so doing, suggest the extent to which that resistance generates a profound diversity of productivity. But as Viet Nguyen (2002) has suggested recently, what remains unacknowledged in such critical work are the often unwitting ways in which resistance to, say, capitalist exploitation can turn quickly into a negotiation and accumulation of "symbolic capital" in the form of a kind of academic "ethnic entrepreneurship." Correspondingly, Min Hyoung Song (2003) argues that the very terms of current debates in Asian American literary studies remain locked in a kind of cultural sentimentalism, which follow the deeper U.S. cultural logic to find better "agencies," whether these identities are ones of absolute refusal or provisional essentialisms.

Nguyen's and Song's correctives point to a nascent political unconscious in Asian American literature and its critical discontents: that undergirding "resistance" is the necessary—and by this I mean *both* productive and debilitating—allegiance to a U.S. political economy based primarily on warfare throughout the latter half of the twentieth century and into this new one. Indeed, warfare is the generative ethos through which social relations are reconstituted, even when no single bullet is fired: warfare determines the boundaries through which Asian Americans define themselves with regard to racial, gender, sexual, material, and "national" meaning. And because warfare emerges as the preeminent agency of state formation and legitimacy, I would like to suggest that rather than engage in criticism that looks for, or even problematizes, the imagined community of "Asian America"—or by extension, a community of implicitly or inherently "resistant readers"—we might confront how Asian American stories buttress, through such anxieties over belonging, our allegiance to long-standing economies of death, tether us to an imperative that we cannot cut. It is my hope that this meditation on the state of Asian American literary studies might also be useful for those engaged in the work of reading the Bible attentive to our particular racial and ethnic experiences and to the possible illuminations of race in the text itself.

"Where there is power, there is resistance," states Michel Foucault in perhaps the most banal of statements of this dialectic that has animated many discussions of Asian American literature over the last decade. "And yet, or rather consequently," Foucault goes on, "this resistance is never in a position of exteriority in relation to power" (1990, 95). It is this second part of his statement that has troubled many of us in the field, for in attempting to understand the banality of power, Foucault suggests—to our chagrin—that there is something rather banal in the forms and content of our resistance. In foregrounding resistance in Asian American literature, or more precisely, in our critical regard of Asian American literature, we have encountered the imbrication of these two banalities that undergird the most disparate of projects, whether in book monographs, journal articles, or class syllabi. Over the years, however, I have been less troubled by this Foucauldian formulation, and less worried about the banality of resistance, and definitely less concerned about finding exceptional spaces and moments that some of us have been calling oppositional or subversive. What Asian American literary studies has taught me is that there is a deep ethics—that is, a mode of relationality—involved in the way in which however we configure "Asian American literature." There is an implicit engagement with what we might call the "social," which, to paraphrase Avery Gordon, is an acknowledgment that within each act or movement of liberation and freedom are the ghostly presences of enslavement and domination. That power and resistance are banal twins, then, does not mean that we dismiss or discard but rather that we engage them ever more fully. Foucault brings us to this place of never being outside the space we must critique and invites to wonder how to live in the discursive prison house.

Kandice Chuh (1995) has written a powerful book that engages with these banalities and takes the paradox to its limit. Simply put, it is a polemic for Asian American studies to take seriously poststructuralism's critique of (our desire for) subjectivity, and to therefore undertake an intellectual practice of Asian American studies as "subjectless." Chuh reminds us of the constructedness of the categories around which our intellectual practices are mobilized and suggests that the very fictionality of terms such as "Asian American" can free us from the binds of normativity that, ironically, produced the oppositional categories and identities from which we write and speak. Chuh's critique of Asian American literary studies' subject offers a crucial opportunity to reanimate the debate of race and racism that we seem to have been taken for granted over the years. All of us know it, most of us teach it, but somehow—perhaps because of the neoconservatism of our day—we still have managed to teach our students wrongly.

And here it is, just as a refresher: race is the *effect*, not the cause of racism. Racism precedes race. To use Achille Mbembe's parlance, "race is nothing else but the spectral effects of racism."[1] And what then is racism? "Racism," according to Ruth Wilson Gilmore, "is the state-sanctioned and/or extra-legal production

---

1. Mbembe made this statement at a lecture delivered on 19 November 2003 in Austin, Texas (2003b). For a fuller elaboration on his deployment of Foucault's notion of biopower onto the subject of race and racism, see 2003a, 17–18.

and exploitation of group-differentiated vulnerabilities to premature death, in distinct yet densely interconnected political geographies" (2002, 261). And alongside Mbembe's and Gilmore's delineations of race and racism, we might even return to Foucault, who suggests that racism is fundamentally a relationship of war, an established link between my life and your death, that the destruction of the Other is fundamental to my happiness. Racism, and the production of race, is the precondition that makes killing—and in the twentieth century, industrialized killing—acceptable and necessary, and what makes mass destruction possible.

That racial violence does not occur because of one's identity but rather precedes or even determines the contours of identity compels those violently deemed "other" to embody in oneself the externalization of self and other of idealized certainty. "It is a peculiar sensation," writes Du Bois in his century-old formulation of "double consciousness," "this sense of always looking at one's self through the eyes of others, of measuring one's soul by the tape of a world that looks on in amused contempt and pity" (1996, 5). The critical tension in this sentence is in the phrase "measuring one's soul." Occupy the space of fractured subject, damaged soul, and the urge, once one develops such a vocabulary as Anne Cheng suggests, is to turn grief to grievance, suffering to speech, as quickly as possible (2001, 3). The voicing of racial injury, the articulation of how painful it is to live in a body determined by both extraordinary and mundane violence, pushes against and tries to hold at bay the seeming inexorability of our premature death, to claim life if for only a little bit longer. We sometimes call this grief turned to grievance justice, and we claim this justice as legitimate. But the critical tension nudging this claim for justice against the injury inflicted is in "measuring one's soul": to achieve an outcome that approximates the idea of social parity. And to stake our claims in this logic brings with it a perhaps unwitting partner, a kind of modern categorical imperative—of primary violence—that might produce effects that exceed what we would like to think when we write with the desire for justice.

It is this categorical imperative of warfare, the warfare imperative, that sent Du Bois to Ghana toward the end of his life. It is this imperative that propels the young Maxine in Kingston's final story of *The Woman Warrior* to find her voice by lashing out—through verbal and physical abuse—against another silent Chinese girl, only to fall sick and silent herself, a melancholy mirroring of suffering sustained through injury inflicted.[2] It is this imperative that has troubled Asian American studies from its inception, as it has struggled to tell the absurdly ironic narrative that the superlative success of Asian Americans—their economic mobility, their educational attainment, their depiction as "model minorities"—is the mark of their psychic and spiritual poverty, the source of injury that they

---

2. This scene takes place in the final story of *The Woman Warrior*; see 1989, 174-82.

experience and to which others are caught.[3] And it is this imperative, in perhaps our most terrifying but honest moments, as Lawrence Chua has written, that allows us to speak the language of grievance, "You hit me," only to follow up with the kernel of grief that refuses its translation into grievance: "Hit me harder" (1995, 11).

Herein lies the warfare imperative that I am suggesting is at the heart of Asian American literary studies, and perhaps at the center of our collective enterprise of literary and biblical criticism. Crucial to understanding a state of war is in looking at its boundaries, its restraints, that which helps us delineate warfare from other kinds of technologies, other states of existence. The restraints to warfare (i.e., the laws and customs of war) are what we might call "civilization": of concepts of human/inhuman; of one's behavior toward the enemy; and of the methods and means of destruction.

These are conversations that we have been hearing a lot about in recent years, yes? Terrorism, in official U.S. parlance, is warfare out of bounds, illegal war. Weapons of mass destruction are weapons out of bounds, those weapons deemed outside the contours of civilized warfare. (A caveat: these rules of war are procedures [banalities?] meant to alleviate the calamities of war short of the abolition of war.) It is a banal statement at this point to suggest that current conversations about the illegalities of mass destruction and the criminalities of terrorism (think here of Fox News's use of the term "homicide bomber") also implicitly frame discussions of "legitimate" forms of destruction and killing. At the very margins of

---

3. Those who have championed model minority discourse for over three decades have generally "discovered" an exceptional minority community living within U.S. cities during moments of political crisis over questions of race. Its triangulated nature is foregrounded to mitigate this crisis. The first time the model minority myth gained popularity took place in 1966, when a series of articles in *The New York Times* and *U.S. News & World Report* celebrated the quiet tenacity of Japanese and Chinese Americans at the same time that the civil rights movement was entering its most visibly radical phase. The very first sentence of the *U.S. News & World Report* article offers this as its salutary description of the Chinese American community: "At a time when Americans are awash in worry over the plight of racial minorities—One such minority, the nation's 300,000 Chinese-Americans, is winning wealth and respect by dint of its own hard work" (cited in Tachiki et al. 1971, 6). The barely concealed premise of the article, to render insignificant black demands of material redistribution for the social theft of the U.S.'s racial legacy, emerged "at a time" of the rise of Black Power movements to specify the terms of black freedom. Almost overnight, Asian Americans, long a menace to U.S. society, became its models. The "model minority" myth has reemerged since the 1960s during other moments of heated historical and political crisis: during the Reagan era that sought to demonize black women as "welfare queens"; over the question of the legitimacy of affirmative action policies during the 1980s and 1990s; and in the aftermath of the 1992 Los Angeles uprisings that purported to pit Koreans against blacks and Latinos. Scholarly work on the "model minority" myth is extensive, but some useful introductory pieces would be Osajima 2005 and, for a more theoretical meditation, Palumbo-Liu 1999.

warfare's legitimacy—civilization's ends—lies the authority of the sovereign, the state: to quote Giorgio Agamben, "The sovereign ... is the one who marks the point of indistinction between violence and right by proclaiming the state of exception and suspending the validity of law [and] the police are always operating within a similar state of exception" (2000, 104). Agamben continues: "What we have witnessed ... from the end of World War I onward is a process by which the enemy is first of all excluded from civil humanity and branded as a criminal; only in a second moment does it become possible and licit to eliminate the enemy by a 'police operation'" (106). Illegality, criminality, the rules of war, and police procedure: warfare is what we are dealing with when we engage Asian American literary studies—the mutable line between warfare and civilization puts the work of criticism into crisis, because, as Benjamin has taught us, fifty years ago by now, the state of exception is the rule (1989).

That warfare is an unavoidable social condition is exactly how, in the current age of transnationalism, U.S. military planners are operationalizing social relations today, as it has done throughout the twentieth century. Major Jerome M. Lynes, USMC, published a report in 1997 titled "Command and Control Warfare: An Operational Imperative in the Information Age," in which he agrees with Alvin and Heidi Toffler's assertion that "the way we make wealth is the way we make war and that in the future, the manipulation of information is the way we will make wealth" (Lynes 1997). From this statement, Lynes spends the next seventy pages arguing that "information superiority" has become the most crucial technology in warfare's arsenal to achieve war's end: victory. What is most striking in this remarkable document are the ethical issues that Lynes raises at the end of his report, curiously titled "Miles to Go Before I Sleep." I simply provide an abbreviated litany. I apologize for its length:

> Unanswered issues yet to be explored include how C2W will apply in the likely Military Operations Other Than War (MOOTW) challenges of the future. If the center of gravity in MOOTW is the civil populace, then C2W is a superb vehicle to "win hearts and minds." Central to this observation is determining what is the military's proper role in C2W aimed at a civil populace. Does the military lead or follow civilian agencies such as the Department of State? What of international organizations and non-governmental organizations such as the Red Cross? Can war be "conducted" by civil agencies? What are the legal ramifications of the non-consensual co-opting of the media to serve C2W? Where does propaganda, military public affairs, and deterrence based upon the moral aspects of C2W separate? Do they ever? Related to the above and yet unanswered are the links between C2W and recent ideas on the merging levels of war and the concurrent expansion of the battlefield. Effective C2W at the operational level likely will begin in peacetime. Does waging "information operations"—the doctrinal expression for C2W in peacetime—blur the distinction between peace and war? What can we make of merged levels, expanded battlefields, and no clear distinction of peace and war? What happens to our basic understanding of war? Is the

targeting of an adversary for "peacetime C2W" an act of war? What then of the distinction between combatant and noncombatant?

I quote these questions at length to suggest that, at the heart of the warfare imperative, is the work of a sovereign state as an exercise of what Mbembe has called "necropower": the state's authority to classify and control life and to kill, and in fact a condition wherein killing is not simply a means to an end or a way to survive against "the enemy" but a "primary and absolute objective" (2003a, 12). Agency and killing are inseparable. I quote these questions at length also to suggest that the lines of peace and war, combatant and noncombatant, guilty party and innocent victim, is simply that: a line, subject to shifting and changing, so that at one moment you are on one side of the line and in a flash you are on the other. Agency and killing in warfare are inseparable, because the right to kill (agency) can and will change.

We kill without firing a bullet. We cower beneath protective shields of our fictive innocence and hope that war will pass over us, but warfare demands that we enable others to kill, even against our intentions, in order that we might safely belong within the borders that we so desperately want to claim as ours too. We cannot but assent to this ideological hail, because it is this clarion call that allows us into the blinding light of visibility. Nowhere is this imperative more obvious than in one of Asian American literature's most canonical works: John Okada's *No-No Boy* (1979; originally published in 1957).

I will not rehearse here the manifold ways how we in Asian American literary studies have struggled to get our students *not* to read the novel simply as a fable of the Nisei's break from their Issei parents nor to read these generational differences as simply a matter of culture, but to read the situations of these characters with more complexity: the contradictory impulses of race and gender and class in the context of postwar, postinternment, and Cold War politics (Nguyen 2002); the "provisional reconstitution of Japanese American masculinity vis-à-vis Black subordination" (Helen Jun, unpublished paper); the contested construction of "Nikkei transnationality" (Chuh 2003); the necessary ideological ambiguity to abstract U.S. citizenship and its attendant opposition (Ling 1998). Most of our attention gets paid to the "no-no boy" protagonist Ichiro and to a lesser extent the veteran Kenji, for they form a chiasmic mirroring of one another's social death, masculinities damaged by the special ways in which the war dealt with these young men. By the end of the novel, the boorish veteran Bull, after precipitating the death of Freddie, another no-no boy, howls "like a baby." We cry with his inarticulateness and teach our students that the pain of this war brutally inflicted on interned Japanese Americans, soldier or civilian, veteran or no-no boy, can only lead us to whisper, with hope: never again.

More often, the figure of Emi gets left aside, cast as a one-dimensional figuration of U.S. patriotism par excellence, the Nisei woman who can show her damaged male counterparts how to survive in the postwar era. We bristle at her final solution, not simply because it feels too easy, but because it seems also a narrative of forgetting, one that reminds us of Gordon's critique of dominant U.S. culture, that "America is all innocence and clean slates and the future" (1997, 189). So despite Emi's earlier critique of the racism in the U.S. construction of legitimate citizenship, to which Japanese Americans bore the brunt of its contradictions, she offers the salve of love and forgiveness that for most of us is wholly insufficient and somehow worthy of dismissal:

> This is a big country with a big heart. There's room here for all kinds of people.... Make believe you're singing "The Star-Spangled Banner" and see the color guard march out on the stage and say the pledge of allegiance with all the other boys and girls. You'll get that feeling flooding into your chest and making you want to shout with glory. It might even make you feel like crying. That's how you've got to feel, so big that the bigness seems to want to bust out, and then you'll understand why it is that your mistake was no bigger than the mistake your country made. (Okada 1979, 95–96)

That is how you have got to feel. In our day, we hear this injunction so many times, whether in the form of tattered American flags on car windows or in Bush's binarism ("Either you're with us or you're against us") or on T-shirts that read "United We Stand."

The "bigness" in our chests to which we are all supposed to consent we can face in our scholarly moments with deep skepticism, to be sure. But are Emi's words not also the tacit narratives that many of our students write in hopes that in uttering these narratives they might get beyond their experiences of racial injury? Why is it that at the end of Asian American studies courses and other courses that confront questions of race and culture, inequality, and power, we encounter evaluations (the good ones, at least) that almost always have the following sentences: "Before this class, I had no idea of the extent of racism that Asian Americans [or others] faced." Why is it that it takes so much intellectual work to get our students to see, say, affirmative action *not* as an unfair policy against Asian Americans and whites? Why do the institutions in which we work, teach, and write develop "diversity" programs after an injury has occurred? Why do so many students of ours claim that in their *own* lives they did not really experience racism, only to remember weeks later about that brief incident on the street or on the school playground?

Given our own experiences in the classroom and beyond, I think it is all the more important to encounter Emi's "complex personhood"[4] in this passage, to

---

4. Complex personhood is a phrase coined by Avery Gordon, who writes as follows: "Complex personhood means that all people (albeit in specific forms whose specificity is sometimes everything) remember and forget, are beset by contradiction, and recognize and misrecognize themselves and others. Complex personhood means that people suffer graciously and selfishly

unpack for our students that underlying the "clean slate" narrative whose bigness "busts" out and overwhelms all other emotions is the deep terror that generates us to utter, sometimes without conviction and sometimes with all intention, the Pledge of Allegiance. That is how you have got to feel, because to feel differently would entail your encounter with the fact that all of us are already dead, that the state of permanent war is already and has always worked to blur the distinctions between combatant and noncombatant, peace and wartime, civil and military agencies. That is how you have got to feel, because to feel differently may compel you to see the world in ways beyond all recognition. And that recognition leaves you not with bigness, but a deep pit that eats away at you. That pit is the work of death, the work of warfare of which we are all victims and also, more often than we would like to admit, perpetrators.

Emi's injunction of "bigness" has its corollaries in many other instances in our field's pedagogical and scholarly foundations, the banality of our resistance that briefly occludes the ubiquity of our fear. In the field in which I primarily but not exclusively work, we struggle against so-called Asian American invisibility and then invoke endlessly the ghost of Vincent Chin and the sorrow songs of his mother ("I want justice for my son") and revile the state and federal governments for not locking up Ronald Ebens and Michael Nitz for many years. Vincent Chin teaches us that we need "better" laws (hate crimes legislation) that show us that the state really does care about Asian Americans, and in doing so we knowingly empower the state to shore up its prison-industrial complex. The women and men of *Sa-I-gu* lament the lack of police protection and criticize the government for not taking care of black people, so that Koreans became the "sacrificial lambs" in 1992.[5] But if we wonder if the police had been there, in Koreatown, and done its job, would that demand a new kind of allegiance over the ambivalences

---

too, get stuck in the symptoms of their troubles, and also transform themselves. Complex personhood means that even those called 'Other' are never never that. Complex personhood means that the stories people tell about themselves, about their troubles, about their social worlds, and about their society's problems are entangled and weave between what is immediately available as a story and what their imaginations are reaching toward. Complex personhood means that people get tired and some of them are just plain lazy. Complex personhood means that groups of people will act together, that they will vehemently disagree with and sometimes harm each other, and that they will do both at the same time and expect the rest of us to figure it out for ourselves, intervening and withdrawing as the situation requires. Complex personhood means that even those who haunt our dominant institutions and their systems of value are haunted too by things they sometimes have names for and sometimes do not. At the very least, complex personhood is about conferring respect on others that comes from presuming that life and people's lives are simultaneously straightforward and full of enormously subtle meaning" (1997, 4–5).

5. The paradigmatic film that suggests, if not outright advocates for, imprisonment and more stringent hate crimes legislation to confront such anti-Asian violence is Renee Tajima's *Who Killed Vincent Chin?* (1988). Dai Sil Kim-Gibson's video, *Sa-I-Gu: From Korean Women's Perspectives* (1993; "Sa-I-Gu" translates into "4.2.9," the date of the start of the violence),

of supposed police inaction? We teach our students that being the "solution" to America's race dilemma—the model minority—only poses new problems, but we still must write their letters of reference to law, business, medicine and grad school, and seminaries, because being a problem will only get you so far. The warfare imperative provides us with the fiction that, if we feel what we have got to feel, then we still believe we are alive, and that it is okay then to call the police when "trouble" happens, to write those letters of recommendation, and to preface our critique of the war in Iraq or the war on terror with "I know that Saddam Hussein and Osama bin Laden are bad men and I don't defend them, but...."

If our current state of war has taught me anything, it is simply to remind me of something that Lawrence Chua stated in 1995, shortly after Asian American studies scholars collectively wrung their hands in response to the Los Angeles uprisings. In his critique of Asian American cultural politics, Chua proclaimed, "I think we are ready to dispose of the innocence of the Asian subject" (1995, 10). Part of this critique of innocence that buttresses our claims to resistance has to do with revisiting the earliest formations of the term "Asian American." In 1969, the late Yuji Ichioka led a group of Los Angeles students, scholars, and other activists to form an antiwar group titled "Asian Americans for Peace." Somehow, although we have struggled to teach our students otherwise, over the last three decades that slogan got inverted: "Justice for Asian Americans." Certainly, at times these two utterances were coterminous, imbricated, and perhaps for institutional and academic purposes a political necessity. But the warfare imperative that is at the heart of Asian American literary studies teaches us that the line between combatant and noncombatant, peace and war, and innocence and guilt is not immovable and indeed is always moving.

Emi in *No-No Boy* understands this, and if we listen deeply to her words and look at her face, then we can perhaps hear the tremor in her voice and the terror behind her eyes that barely hides her necessary claim to the "bigness busting out," that at any moment she may once again be on the other side of the innocence divide, because race is nothing but the spectral effects of racism. This is not to denigrate the work of resistance, but simply to suggest that there is a complexity in the work of complicity as well, and that in fact there is a deep relationship between power and resistance. And if the task of reading the Bible alongside ethnic studies amounts to a critical gesture toward recognition, we must also recognize the deep pit in ourselves, the work of death and all its attendant economies and technologies, that constitutes our structure of feelings in our most radical and sometimes even pleasurable moments of our analytic labor, borne in this state of exception that is not an exception but the rule.

---

produced in the immediate aftermath of the 1992 Los Angeles uprisings, maintains and even enhances the idea of the Asian as innocent victim in the chaos of racial unrest.

DIFFERENT RECOGNITION AND THE RESPONSIBILITY OF READING

The experience of reading and listening to the papers delivered by this community of scholars over two summers in downtown Chicago opened up for me heretofore untrodden epistemological routes and provoked in me what Gordon calls an "electric empiricity," that is, evidence that is "barely visible, or highly symbolized" (1997, 50). It is, perhaps, a feeling that some in theological circles might call "revelation"; it is what Freud would call "uncanny." This "uncanny," or revelation, is precisely the work of transformation, that which for the moment exceeds our expectations certainly, but also surpasses our capacity to know exactly what we are doing, and what that doing actually does, except that somehow we are doing it out of a concern for justice (Gordon 1997; Derrida 1995). It is that place and moment borne of crisis—that which interrupts and disallows the reproduction of social formations—whether that crisis is one produced by racism, migration, economics, sexuality, or even the capacity for certain rhetorical, political, cultural projects to work or not to work. And where crisis occurs, there surplus emerges. And here I am not simply talking surplus value in a vulgar Marxist sense, but the surplus of people left behind in progress's march, as well as the surplus that comes back to haunt us in the ethereal but no less real instances of revelation, testimony, uncanny experiences, the reminder of the consequences of our necessary allegiance to an ethic of warfare. To account for such marks of historical trauma, we often repress the so-called private as simply that, or rather convince ourselves that something that we might call a spiritual journey can be divorced from the mundane horrors, the ordinary betrayals, which determine the ground of our social being.

But what the papers in Chicago and now here in this volume suggest, or rather remind us of, is that the so-called private is always shot through with the fact that, while we feel the trauma of history alone, our experience is already public, collective, even to those who would rather think history is past them or who would rather read something like the Bible with faith unfettered but also untested. What begins at first glance as partial readings from particular perspective, the visions seemingly constrained by dark reflections clouded with the legacy of differential treatment, points to an encounter with another's private suffering. It is in this process of listening to and responding to that suffering that we can utter with all modesty and honesty: your difference has changed us; private grief now demands a public response.

In place of the fiction of universalism, we offer the ethic of polyculturalism, perhaps a different kind of universalism that does not claim authority but rather attends to the complexity of stories built through relationship and solidarity. Instead of viewing hybridity—cultural, sexual, or otherwise—as defilement and scandal, we see these as starting points for new community building no less difficult but also no less "holy." And rather than foregrounding exile simply to register what has been lost, we remember that loss in order to provide strength for a journey in a new land, and perhaps to look for others who have been rendered homeless and to say, I have been here before, tell me your story, maybe in this commensality we redefine what it means to be abundant. These essays displace the politics of claim as the ground upon which recognition should be sought; they become unavailable for the warfare imperative. In many ways, deferring claim runs the risk of placing these articulations beyond all recognition. Or, rather, they point to a way of recognizing differently, to insist that our encounter with our own difference and the difference of others can and has changed us.

The problem with a politics of claim through simple recognition, as these papers insist, is that it enables a corresponding politics of disavowal. The writers of this volume, like I, yearn for the recognition of our complex humanity in difference, but they also gesture to the limits of being "seen." The criticism that urges recognition only claims an ethical innocence that in the long run is unsustainable, not only because of our tether to the warfare imperative but also because that warfare imperative is always moving the line that marks the innocent from everyone else. In Asian American studies, we have been in the business of *both* claim and disavowal, to speak loudly about our progressive politics while silencing (and perhaps whispering to one another) those deep complicities that enable our claims to justice. And this is where the work of reading race in our criticism provides us not with a solution or even a model, but simply a charge, a gift: a revelation, a witness, to the deep misery that pervades even our most pleasurable moments of social existence. The stories that Asian Americans tell of themselves and others, the stories that we find in ancient Hebrew, Greek, and other texts, narrate the experience of this paradox: they are shot through with obliterated persons that mark the very contours of our subjectivity, our capacity to know the world with their electric empiricity, and long after the body is gone, the corporeality of their lives remains. This is the responsibility of the flesh made word, and is this not the responsibility that is the gift of religion? Or, as Derrida has put it, "Religion is responsibility or it is nothing at all" (1995, 2).

We write, then, without possibility of escape from the warfare imperative. We do so out of a sense of critical honesty that the grief borne of vulnerability does not preclude the possibility of using the technologies that are killing us. This recognition, the recognition that refuses the lure of our fictional innocence, sullies our scholarly work, perhaps beyond redemption. During the two summers that punctuated the years of work that this consultation engaged in, nothing was more difficult or revelatory than this reluctant admission. But in willingly giving up the innocence of our reading, we, the members of the consultation, and with hope the readers of this volume, gain the fearlessness of the collective endeavor of learning how to write and live as people determined but not defined by our racial grief. Rather, we recognize damage and in so doing recognize that damage differently; we organize around a different categorical imperative than the one offered to us, with the terrible fullness of its vocabulary that beckons us to pledge allegiance.

We become, in the words of Toni Cade Bambara (1977), "unavailable for servitude" not because our conditions are more free but because we regard innocence as a bankrupt category, and in doing so we set ourselves free to recognize the difference not as an obstacle to recognition but the very means to new sight. We yearn to be seen, and, in that yearning, we look to difference and realize that that difference has changed us. There is no ontology to this different kind of recognition, just as there is none for our most utopian terms: freedom, justice, redemption. Instead, we practice conscientious objection to the warfare imperative that has made us and continues to inform who we are. The difference now is that we refuse to collaborate with it, become unavailable to servitude, and instead craft the difficult, critical practice to look at what is not only killing us but killing someone else.

This is of course not to say that claims to justice should remain unacknowledged. This is only to say that there is no measurable outcome to this work. There are no guarantees to either theory or practice. We desire that which we ceaselessly critique, because we realize that we start new stories not so much to end old stories but to end sad ones. And these languages embedded in our collective intellectual and spiritual archives invite us to see reading Asian American literature or reading the Bible as racial and ethnic scholars as the search for that shadow that walks in front of and back of us, that girds and trammels us on our path, that offers us the gift of responding to that shadow (the shadow of justice) that is nothing more and nothing less than the face of God. And in doing so, this ceaseless dialectic of critique and recovery, perhaps we will continue to look out that window and find ourselves watching someone else watching us, and wonder whether there is indeed a look of recognition in both our faces.

WORKS CONSULTED

Agamben, Giorgio. 2000. *Means without End: Notes on Politics.* Translated by Vincenzo Binetti and Cesare Casarino. Minneapolis: University of Minnesota Press.

Bambara, Toni Cade. 1977. *The Seabirds Are Still Alive.* New York: Random House.

Benjamin, Walter. 1989. Theses on the Philosophy of History. Pages 255–66 in idem, *Illuminations: Essays and Reflections.* New York: Schocken.

Booth, Wayne C. 1988. *The Company We Keep: An Ethics of Fiction.* Chicago: University of Chicago Press.

Cheng, Anne Anlin. 2001. *The Melancholy of Race: Psychoanalysis, Assimilation, and Hidden Grief.* New York: Oxford University Press.

Chua, Lawrence. 1995. The Postmodern Ethnic Brunch: Devouring Difference. *MUAE: A Journal of Transcultural Production* 1:4–11.

Chuh, Kandice. 2003. *Imagine Otherwise: On Asian Americanist Critique.* Durham, N.C.: Duke University Press.

Derrida, Jacques. 1995. *The Gift of Death*. Translated by David Wills. Chicago: University of Chicago Press.

Du Bois, W. E. B. 1996. *The Souls of Black Folk*. Introduction by Herb Boyd. New York: Modern Library.

Foucault, Michel. 1990. *The History of Sexuality*. Translated by Robert Hurley. New York: Vintage. [orig. 1978]

Gilmore, Ruth Wilson. 2002. Race and Globalization. Pages 261–74 in *Geographies of Social Change*. Edited by R. J. Johnston, Peter J. Taylor, and Michael J. Watts. Malden, Mass.: Blackwell.

Gordon, Avery F. 1997. *Ghostly Matters: Haunting and the Sociological Imagination*. Minneapolis: University of Minnesota Press.

Kingston, Maxine Hong. 1989. *The Woman Warrior*. New York: Vintage. [orig. 1976]

Lee, Chang-rae. 1995. *Native Speaker*. New York: Riverhead.

Ling, Jinqi. 1998. *Narrating Nationalisms: Ideology and Form in Asian-American Literature*. New York: Oxford University Press.

Lynes, Jerome M. 1997. "Command and Control Warfare: An Operational Imperative in The Information Age." Online: http://www.globalsecurity.org/military/library/report/1997/Lynes.htm.

Mbembe, Achille. 2003a. Necropolitics. *Public Culture* 15:11–40.

———. 2003b. On the Idea of Mass Destruction. Distinguished Visiting Lecturer Series. Humanities Institute, University of Texas at Austin. 19 November.

Michaels, Walter Benn. 1997. *Our America: Nativism, Modernism, and Pluralism*. Durham, N.C.: Duke University Press.

———. 2006. *How We Learned to Love Identity and Ignore Equality*. New York: Metropolitan Books.

Nguyen, Viet Thanh. 2002. *Race and Resistance: Literature and Politics in Asian America*. New York: Oxford University Press.

Okada, John. 1979. *No-No Boy*. Seattle: University of Washington Press. [orig. 1957]

Osajima, Keith. 2005. Asian Americans as the Model Minority: An Analysis of the Popular Press Image in the 1960s and 1980s. Pages 215–25 in *A Companion to Asian American Studies*. Edited by Kent A. Ono. London: Blackwell.

Palumbo-Liu, David. 1999. Model Minority Discourse and the Course of Healing. Pages 395–416 in idem, *Asian/American: Historical Crossings of a Racial Frontier*. Stanford, Calif.: University Press.

Prashad, Vijay. 2001. *Everybody Was Kung Fu Fightin: Afro-Asian Connections and the Myth of Cultural Purity*. Boston: Beacon.

Song, Min Hyoung. 2003. Sentimentalism and Sui Sin Far. *Legacy* 20:134–52.

Tachiki, Amy, et al., eds. 1971. *Roots: An Asian American Reader*. Los Angeles: Continental Graphics.

Wideman, John Edgar. 2001. *Hoop Roots*. Boston: Houghton Mifflin.

CONCLUSION

TOWARD MINORITY BIBLICAL CRITICISM:
A REFLECTION ON ACHIEVEMENTS AND LACUNAE

Fernando F. Segovia

This joint venture in minority biblical criticism—not only an exercise in such criticism but also a search for its meaning and implications, a point keenly conveyed by the prepositional phrase adopted as subtitle, *Toward Minority Biblical Criticism*—is, I would submit, groundbreaking. Indeed, I see it as a landmark point of reference for the conjunction between racial-ethnic studies and biblical studies. So I would argue not because it represents the first attempt in such discursive interdialogue and cross-fertilization, for it does not. In fact, various efforts have taken place in the course of the last two decades, ever since the publication of Cain Hope Felder's *Troubling Biblical Waters: Race, Class and Family* in 1989, which I would posit as point of origins in this regard, within the paradigm of ideological criticism. Rather, I would so argue because of its specific focus within the set of concerns encompassed by the problematic of race and ethnicity in racial-ethnic theory.

This set of concerns is expansive: (1) the signification of race and *ethnos* as categories of identity—origins, trajectories, debates; (2) the central phenomenon of migration—underlying causes, processes of emigration and immigration, resultant effects; (3) representations of the Other—racialization and ethnicization processes; (4) the concept of the nation and/or state—boundaries and borderlands, exile and diaspora, assimilation and resistance; (5) the development of dominant and minority groups—group formations and perspectives, vertical relations between such groups, horizontal relations among the latter groups. While distinctive in their own right, such concerns should be seen not as mutually exclusive but as closely intertwined. The present venture is thus focused on dominant-minority formations and relations in general and minority formations and perspectives in particular—within the realm of a specific (nation-)state, the United States of America (U.S.). As such, the volume represents, to my mind, a foundational point of entry into what minority criticism signifies and entails and an imperative point of departure for any such further work in the future.

By way of conclusion, I should like to offer a critical reflection on both salient markers of achievement and key lacunae in need of development. The reflection will address the following central aspects of the venture: the configuration of the roster of participants—the move from intragroup to intergroup discussions in minority criticism; (2) the deployment of rhetorical mechanics—the varying activations and combinations of critical moves from the repertoire of rhetorical dynamics in minority criticism; and (3) the interdisciplinary framework of discussion—the assessments of minority criticism from discursive perspectives outside biblical criticism. Two main aims lie behind this reflection. The first one is to situate minority criticism, the location and role of minority critics, as envisioned by and embodied in this venture, within the discipline and profession of biblical studies. The second is to set the stage for future work along these lines by highlighting what has been done and how, so as to foreground what needs to be done and how to go about doing so.

CONFIGURATION OF ROSTER OF PARTICIPANTS

A first salient marker of achievement has to do with the distinctive, indeed unique, composition, in terms of group representation, of the set of participants. The intent of the venture in this regard was twofold: inclusion—to conduct a joint exercise in criticism involving the major (most numerous) minority groups in the country; and parity—to level the field of discussion by involving equal numbers of scholars from the groups in question. From the point of view of participation, therefore, minority criticism is situated as broad-based and well-balanced. The quest for the location and role of minority critics in discipline and profession alike emplaces them as diverse yet equal partners, imbricated in and collaborative with one another.

In what follows, I shall expand on both of these aspects of the venture: inclusion and parity. This, in turn, will prepare the way directly for a consideration of key lacunae in need of further attention.

Various consultations and conversations have taken place among racial-ethnic minority critics over the last twenty years or so, beginning with the collection of essays edited by Cain Hope Felder and entitled *Stony the Road We Trod: African American Biblical Interpretation*, published in 1991. All such undertakings, however, have proceeded by way of intragroup discussions and agendas. As a result, one has witnessed the emergence of African American, Asian American, and Latino/a American traditions of biblical criticism in these two decades, each by now with a solidly established and rapidly expanding body of work. There has been, to my knowledge, but a single exception to this rule. This was a colloquy—held at Union Theological Seminary of New York in 2005, under the leadership of Tat-siong Benny Liew and Vincent L. Wimbush—that brought together a (limited) number of African American and Asian American critics under the title of "Encountering Texts, Encountering Communities: African and

Asian American Engagements with the Bible." In this colloquy Latino/a American representation was present, although only at the concluding gathering and by way of response to the proceedings; indeed, it was my honor and privilege to have served in that capacity. The present venture constitutes, therefore, the first time that these three minority groups have engaged in sustained conversations and embraced a major publication project together.

Moreover, equal representation was sought on the part of all three groups: four critics from each group, two with expertise in Hebrew Bible studies and two in early Christian studies. Such parity was sought in other respects as well. First, equal representation was also a goal in terms of gender: two female scholars and two male scholars from each group, with specialization in each field within each gender set. Unfortunately, this objective proved impossible in the case of the Latino/a American contingent, on two counts: the lack of a woman scholar in Hebrew Bible and the dearth of women scholars in early Christianity. Second, diverse representation—rather than equal, for obvious reasons—was also a goal in terms of national origins or descent: a broad presence of faces and voices from different subgroups within each group. Unfortunately, this objective proved impossible in all groups, given sheer lack of numbers. Despite such shortcomings, the present venture embodies a concerted effort at parity, and diversity, in representation among the three minority groups.

In both respects, then, in terms of inclusion as well as in terms of parity, the venture attained its objectives. Its driving question was properly pursued, What happens, and should happen, when African American, Asian American, and Latino/a American scholars, of manifold stripes, come together and envision their place and task in biblical criticism by themselves—not only without the presence and gaze of critics from the dominant society and culture but also in the face of such gaze and presence? While the accomplishments in this regard are notable, certain limitations are also obvious and telling.

To begin with, the project does remain very much of a national undertaking. Its focus lies exclusively on the U.S., as directly signified by the twofold, unhyphenated characterization of the groups throughout: Asian, African, and Latino/a *Americans*. To be sure, the sheer number and widespread influence of such critics, given the long history of migration in the country and the ever-increasing numbers from the non-Western world since the mid-1960s, makes the U.S. situation special. Nevertheless, a consideration of parallel developments elsewhere is indispensable. The U.S. is by no means the only country that has experienced migration since the nineteenth century, nor the only "developed" country that is undergoing migration from "developing" or "underdeveloped" (nation-)states at present. The question of minority interpretation of the Bible needs to be raised and pursued in comprehensive global fashion.

In addition, the project also remains glaringly wanting in terms of symbolic representation within the U.S. Its focus on the three most numerous groups leaves out of consideration other groups—above all the faces and voices, the trajectories and critiques, of Native Americans. Such omission, it should be noted, was done not by accident but by design, and for two reasons. First, the severe lack of Native American critics and the goal of equal representation among the participant groups made such presence highly problematic. Second, the crucial distinction regarding presence in the country between Native Americans, on the one hand, and the three groups as a whole, on the other hand, rendered such presence quite problematic as well. To wit: while African, Asian, and Latino/a Americans find themselves in the country largely by way of migration, whether "voluntary" or forced, Native Americans were already on the land that was to become the country, so that it was the country that migrated to them and took them over, in different waves of occupation and displacement.

Ultimately, however, this second line of reasoning proves highly problematic in its own right. The distinction regarding presence in the country is not as sharp as it would at first appear. In fact, a core number of Latinos/as also find themselves in the country because the country migrated to their lands as well, taking them over: Mexican Americans throughout the Southwest, as the eventual result of the Mexican American War and the Treaty of Guadalupe-Hidalgo (1848); Puerto Ricans both on the island and on the mainland, as the eventual consequence of the Spanish American War and the Treaty of Paris (1902). Further, there is much that brings the two sets of groups together, given extensive biological as well as cultural intermixing within the boundaries of the country, leading to claims to indigenous descent and culture on the part of members from all three groups and vice-versa. In the end, then, it is the first line of reasoning that prevails, although the decision does leave behind a keen sense of absence and frustration. The question of minority interpretation of the Bible needs to be surfaced and addressed in comprehensive national fashion.

In both respects, therefore, in terms of international consideration as well as intranational scope, the need for expansion, materially and discursively, is urgent. While the present collaborative venture among African, Asian, and Latino/a American critics does represent, without question, a significant achievement in minority criticism, a great deal remains to be done by way of comparative analysis both across the world and inside the country. Such is especially the case in light of the globalization and diversification at work in all theological disciplines, including biblical criticism, since the 1970s. These lacunae represent, without question, key areas for critical development in the future.

Deployment of Rhetorical Mechanics

A second salient marker of achievement involves the wealth of rhetorical mechanics in evidence across the entire set of exercises in interpretation. The outcome of the venture in this regard sets forth minority criticism as sophisticated and creative, approaching the multifaceted problematic of race-ethnicity in the production and reception of the biblical texts in multifarious and incisive ways. Not only is the range of options at the level of major strategy broad, but also considerable mixing is to be had at the level of supporting tactics. In terms of mechanics, therefore, minority criticism is situated as at once similar and plural: while a sense of togetherness, of sharing the same context, prevails in the face of dominant society and culture, a sense of latitude, of manifold approaches to and readings of texts, rules in matters of theory and method. The quest for the location and role of minority critics in both discipline and profession presents them as unified from and toward the outside and as diverse from and within the inside.

In what follows I shall undertake a close analysis of the actual mechanics at work in the essays—a theoretical and methodological account of major strategies adopted and supporting tactics deployed. I shall proceed in two steps. First, I shall consider whether a sense of minority criticism is entertained as such, going beyond the doing of criticism in an African American, Asian American, or Latino/a American vein. In this first step, the main question addressed has to do with definition and consequences: Is there any vision, explicit or inchoate, regarding what such criticism means and entails? Second, I shall trace how the various strategies and tactics are activated and interlaced. In this second step, a set of questions is pursued: What is the primary line of approach adopted? What combinations are carried out within this guiding framework? How are such combinations articulated and to what ends are they put to work? This analysis will set the stage directly for a surfacing of key lacunae in need of critical attention.

Puncturing Objectivity and Universality

Interethnic/racial Exclusions—Cheryl M. Anderson. Anderson, writing in an overt African American vein, provides no theoretical reflection on minority criticism as such, yet comments offered on marginalization in general and on the consequences of her approach for such groups and critics yield a definite sense of a shared minority enterprise on her part. One such indication comes through in her exposition of reading strategy: to take seriously the "social and historical context" of both the biblical text and the reading community, bringing them together in order to do away with any silencing of "marginalized groups" at either level. Thus, the identity of the marginalized reading community is essential but open-ended. A further indication emerges in her assessment of the traditional white-black binary at work in the country in light of a transformed multicultural scene: to look upon such historical legacy as a "thread" for making connections among racial-ethnic groups, so that a focus on the past of any one group can serve as rallying point for "social and political alliances" among the different groups. Consequently, the trajectory of the marginalized reading community is essential, not only for the group in question but also for all others as well. As her exposition of reading strategy and retrieval of historical consciousness demonstrate, for Anderson as an African American critic—but ultimately for critics from other minority groups also—it is the puncturing of objectivity and universality through contextualization of interpretation that becomes the primary critical strategy.

In this study Anderson brings the text of Ezra 9–10, with its expulsion of foreign women and their children from the Persian imperial province of Yehud, and the community of African Americans, with its history of racial segregation and antimiscegenation laws in the United States, to bear on one another. This she does in ideological fashion from beginning to end: the insight afforded into the text by African American experience is used, in a move of scholarly denuding/investing, as a basis for a sharp critique of dominant criticism. What established interpretation views as a positive exercise in constructing religious identity for a community of faith in danger, the African American optic reveals as a negative exercise in marginalization, ultimately involving the construction of racial-ethnic, gender, and materialist identities as well. This ideological reading bears a strong religious dimension as well: the light shed on the text by African American experience yields, in a move of textual desacralizing, an attitude of opposition rather than submission to the text. While established interpretation shows ready identification with this measure of identity construction, the African American optic turns to outright resistance. Clearly, for Anderson, biblical models have profound and long-lasting consequence for communities of faith; consequently, such models and consequences should be carefully evaluated by communities of faith.

The actual reading together of text and community involves back and forth movement, in which the text (contextualized) serves as point of departure and the community (contextualized) as critical angle. Thus, in reading Ezra 9–10, situated within a postexilic context of conflict between the returning elite from exile (the *golah* community) and the nonelite who had remained behind ("the peoples of the lands"), Anderson focuses on the expulsion from the (Jewish) community of foreign women married to Jews, along with the children from such unions, undertaken by Ezra for the sake of group purity and on the basis of a divine decree. Then, appealing to contextual enlightenment, she invokes what she regards as the parallel situation of African Americans, given their banishment from the (white) community, through policies of racial segregation and antimiscegenation, for the sake of group purity and on biblical (divine) authority. Anderson foregrounds what is at stake at both levels: the separation, on religious grounds, of a group deemed "nonprivileged," "different," and "foreigners" from the group that advances itself as "privileged" and "true"—in other words, marginalization. Behind such a measure of religious exclusion lie, she adds, in a turn to intersectionality, other strategies of exclusion: ethnic-racial—separation involving the drawing of impermeable genealogical boundaries; materialist—separation involving economic conflict between social classes; and gendered—separation involving male-female distinctions and sexual stereotypes.

Given such exposé and such ramifications, the problematic for minority interpretation is clear. How can African Americans, or any marginalized group, view such a measure of community construction and such a representation of

God as acceptable? Resistance, she counters, becomes the proper answer: Ezra 9–10 should be taken as a "cautionary tale." Indeed, while the world of formal segregation and antimiscegenation may be a thing of the past, the shadows of that time still endure, in no uncertain fashion, today, certainly among African Americans, but also enveloping other minority groups as well.

Bilingualism and Exile—Francisco García-Treto. García-Treto raises in self-conscious fashion the question of minority criticism. While he does not entertain the nature of such criticism directly or at length, he does address its implications for minority scholars. Two directives are specifically outlined: on the one hand, an explicit reading of the biblical texts "for ourselves, for our students, and for our scholarly and/or ecclesiastical audiences"—a reading that is offered and appropriated as partial; on the other hand, an explicit acceptance of a variety of readings for all texts, with due attention to "the social status, the cultural baggage, and the historical experience" of each reader—a reading that is aware of multiple partial readings. This twofold mandate as minority scholars García-Treto advances as a way to fulfill the imperative of counteracting the dominant construct of the universal and informed reader. Thus, the primary strategy adopted by him as a minority critic is that of puncturing objectivity and universality.

Toward this end, he argues, it is essential to engage in a process of self-definition, whereby the various definitions of identity at work in individual minority scholars—rooted as they are in different crossroads of "the historical-cultural-national continuum"—are acknowledged and surfaced. In keeping with this call, García-Treto's approach to bilingualism and exile in the Hebrew Bible is far more expansive on his status as interpreter than on his interpretation of the text. Contextualization is thus emphasized at the level of reception. His own self-definition he captures in double fashion: Hispanic-Latino generally and Cuban American specifically. Through the latter he specifies his modality, or crossroads, in the former, with two factors identified as lying at the core of his identity: the linguistic-epistemic condition of bilingualism and the social-cultural situation of exilic diaspora. Through both, his minority status is further concretized via a geopolitical or postcolonial reading, a global turn, given the history of imperial-colonial relations between the United States and Cuba. At one level, his bilingualism reveals involvement in a project not of his own making, with strong socioreligious overtones, marking colonial submission to the imperial design. At another level, his exile yields existence in a double world, a present reality and a past memory. Both levels of contextual enlightenment are brought to bear on the biblical text.

His identity as bilingual leads him to the book of Daniel. Bilingualism is unpacked as a site of mediation and tension: a means for accommodation and success, certainly, but also a weapon in social-political relations and in representing the Other. The application to the text is broad and open-ended: What does it really mean to read Daniel, and other books, as the product of a bilingual author speaking to a bilingual audience? Is the author dealing thereby with the problematic of mediation and tension in the community? His identity as exilic leads him to the Hebrew Bible in general and the book of Lamentations in particular. Exile is unpacked as different from immigration (involving expulsion and emotion) and as eschewing hyphenation (more Cuban than Cuban-American). The application to the text is both broad and pointed. Broadly, he asks in open-ended fashion, What does it really mean to read the Hebrew Bible as exilic, not only chronologically (product) but discursively (content)? Pointedly, he invokes Lam 1–2, which he classifies as an example of survival literature in its conveyance of suffering, and the figure of "Daughter Zion," which he describes as a personification of the ravaged Jerusalem—"a desolate woman" in search of comfort from a silent God. To grasp such decay and such pain, García-Treto argues, only a similar literature of survival proves helpful, and for this he turns to recent Cuban literature, to a novel of Daína Chaviano, with a corresponding depiction of Claudia as a personification of the devastated Havana—"a desperate woman" in search of food and the intertextual apparition of José Martí, the national poet, abandoning all hope in anger. For García-Treto, only the correspondence afforded by a literature of survival, emerging out of exile, can help in grasping the Hebrew Bible as an exilic literature of survival—a presentation beyond interpretation, forged in minoritization.

Language and Identity—Jean-Pierre Ruiz. One finds in Ruiz, who writes in distinctly Latino fashion, neither overt consideration of minority criticism, its character or ramifications, nor pointed hints in the argument—by way of reference, say, to reading strategy or to other minority groups—toward a vision of a common minority project. What one does find is extended attention to his own context of interpretation, thus subscribing to puncturing objectivity and universality as the primary critical strategy. This option for contextualization at the reception level remains focused throughout on the exposition of his own approach to the text. As such, there is no explicit ideological critique of established interpretation, except to mention, in passing, the inability of traditional criticism to foreground an issue that he views as central to the text under analysis: the linguistic problematic at work between dominant and minority groups.

From such contextual self-descriptions, a reading strategy may be outlined. Ruiz details two encounters with the books of Ezra and Nehemiah. The first happens indirectly by way of ministerial insertion into an ongoing intercommunity reading of Nehemiah from a perspective of religious social activism: a public juxtaposition of (1) the rebuilding project undertaken by Nehemiah in Jerusalem and (2) a housing reconstruction project organized by an alliance of religious congregations in Brooklyn in the 1980s (the Nehemiah Project). The second takes place directly through engagement with a highly negative evaluation of immigration from Latin America from the perspective of the eminent political theorist, Samuel P. Huntington: a personal linkage of (1) Nehemiah's attack on children unable to speak the language of Judah, the issue of marriage between Jewish men and non-Jewish women, and (2) Huntington's accusations against Latinos/as for failing to assimilate to Anglo-Protestant society and culture and creating instead two nations—with two languages and two cultures—within the country. Together, these encounters reveal a keen sense of the politics at work in biblical interpretation on the part of Ruiz. In response, he deploys a reading strategy en route to ideological critique: a bringing together of the text in context and the reader in context, with the latter as point of entry into the former as an exercise in contextual enlightenment. In this mutual engagement the flow emerges as sequential: from analysis of the reader to analysis of the text.

The focus in this study is on the relationship between language, identity, and colonization, more specifically, on boundaries of exclusion signified by "walls of words" meant to secure group identity, within the framework of imperial-colonial constructions and relations. In so doing, Ruiz has recourse to the strategy of taking a global turn, ultimately situating the Latino/a situation within a broad geopolitical mapping. On the part of the reader, two ongoing "walls of words" are invoked, both within the American Empire: (1) inside, Huntington's "anti-immigrant" rant in the face of a perceived "Hispanic" challenge and threat—the immigration of "Mexicans and other Latinos"—with a call to assimilate to national values in order to preserve the American identity of the community; (2) externally, the sustained project to Americanize Puerto Rico since its conquest during the Spanish-American geopolitical conflict (1898), with a call to adopt American values in order to become part of the national community. On the part of the text, it is the "wall of words" of Neh 13 that is examined, within the context of the Persian Empire: the "violent reaction" against the perceived threat of intermarriage with foreigners—involving the returning "people of Judah" and the local "peoples of the lands"—with a call against assimilation to foreign values in order to ensure the Jewish identity of the community.

Such considerations lead Ruiz to ideological critique at both levels. Toward this end, he resorts to heightening the discourse. To begin with, he contends, all such linguistic boundaries, with their promise of identity maintenance and community preservation, prove ultimately "futile" insofar as "linguistic *mestizaje/mulatez*" is inevitable. Beyond that, he views such linguistic mixture as decidedly positive and as grounds against any attempt to enforce linguistic essentialism on behalf of group and national essentialism. As a Latino minority critic, therefore, Ruiz declares himself on the side of the "betwixts and betweens" of identity and against all "hard-and-fast linkages" of essentialism, whether in the biblical text (versus Nehemiah) or in the reading community (versus assimilation inside or subordination outside).

Authoritarianism and Survival—Frank M. Yamada. There is no explicit consideration in Yamada of minority criticism as a problematic, either in terms of its character as critical exercise or its ramifications for minority scholars. The closest he comes in this regard, which does afford a key insight into his way of thinking, is to be found in the overall objective assigned to his reading strategy: taking seriously into consideration "the 'flesh and blood' reader" in interpretation.

For Yamada, therefore, a—if not *the*—driving force behind minority criticism becomes contextualization at the level of reception, with contextualization at the level of production taken for granted. Thus, his primary strategy centers on puncturing any pretension to objectivity and universality.

His proposal in this regard involves a bringing together, an "inter(con)textual reading," of the contextualized text and the contextualized reader, yielding analysis of both by way of close and sustained interweaving. In this study the goal of inter(con)textuality is pursued through a juxtaposition of Eden, the etiological tale of Gen 2–3, and Manzanar, the national tale of Japanese Americans during World War II. This exercise involves a twofold dimension: at a textual level, the surface development of the argument is clear: from the text, through the reader, to the text; at a contextual level, a fundamental claim is advanced, which allows in the end for a sharp ideological turn.

To begin with, then, a word about the interweaving of narratives. The first step represents an initial exercise in scholarly denuding/investing: foregrounding blind spots in established interpretation. Thus, traditional theological and scholarly readings of Gen 2–3 are described as unable to explain central features of the unit: the arbitrary nature of God's authority (the command not to eat from the tree and the sense of knowledge as evil) and the unexpected survival of humanity beyond disobedience (avoiding the threat of death as punishment). The second step constitutes an appeal to contextual enlightenment by way of a historical-political situation involving Yamada's own family and population group: the internment of Japanese Americans in concentration camps throughout the United States. This situation reveals for Yamada not only the arbitrary exercise of authority on the part of the U.S. government, in fear of the threat represented by a racialized Other, but also the determination of the Other to survive, in various and conflicting ways (accommodation, rejection, silence) in the face of hostility. The final step is twofold. It begins with a reading of the text in the light of such a situation: a view of God's authority as similarly capricious, fearing the human Other, and of human survival as equally tenacious, against all duress. It continues with a further exercise of denuding/investing: an exposé of traditional interpretation as signifying respect for authority and obedience.

A word also on the interweaving of contexts. Indeed, there is a more fundamental deployment of contextual enlightenment as well. In effect, Yamada posits a structural parallelism between text and reader: both Japanese Americans, as a group, and the Pentateuch, as a text, are marked by displacement and exile. This is a claim that moves beyond special insight and tends toward privileged insight. The result is an ideological reading in sharp resistance to traditional interpretation: against its acceptance of God's behavior as just, and against its rendition of human behavior as overreaching or immature. Consequently, dominant stances of capricious authority over others and mandated satisfaction with hierarchy, and their ramifications for society and culture at all times, are severely challenged from this racialized, minority perspective.

Ethnicity Foregrounded and Affirmed—Jae Won Lee. Lee does address the problematic of minority criticism, which she views and unpacks as in dialectical relation to dominant criticism. This dialectic involves two key claims. Articulated from the dominant point of view, they are as follows: (1) a denial of ethnicity, with a corresponding marking of this category as appropriate only to minority groups; (2) a devaluation of ethnicity, with a corresponding designation of it as "irrelevant," in the eyes of universal-objective criticism, and "idiosyncratic," peculiar to contextual-engaged criticism. Advanced from a minority point of view, Lee's critique is radical. First, the dominant dismissal and depreciation of ethnicity constitutes in itself not a universalizing but rather an ethnicizing move—the masquerading of a particular ethnicity as universal and superior with power in mind. Second, it is imperative for minority criticism to foreground ethnicity at all times—approaching it always, however, as a site of intersectional complexities ("class, gender, nation, and empire"). Without question, therefore, Lee's primary strategy aims at puncturing objectivity and universality, both via contextual enlightenment and via scholarly denuding/investing, and with a sense of the need for an interdisciplinary turn.

The reading strategy employed toward this end is chiastic: a beginning, succinct analysis of the reader in context; a central, careful reading of the text in context; a concluding, brief return to the reader contextualized, with specific applications in mind arising from the text contextualized. As reader, Lee presents herself as an Asian American critic in general and a Korean American critic in particular. As text, she focuses on Paul, specifically the ethnic dimensions behind the categories of "weak" and "strong" in Romans (chs. 14–15). The angle of inquiry throughout is ideological: exposé, critique, and revisioning of ethnic constructions and relations. The field of vision is ecclesial: the deployment of ethnicity in the religious tradition of Christianity—a further exercise, therefore, in retrieval of the religious/theological tradition.

Her context as reader is drawn broadly and sharply. Following the pattern of both early Christianity vis-à-vis Jewish Christianity and later Christianity vis-à-vis Judaism and "paganism," Western Christianity construed itself as universal vis-à-vis non-Western Christianity. In Korea, as in so many other places, Christianity set out to suppress local values in favor of its own nonethnic and superior values. Korean Christianity, like so many others, responded with zealous assimilationism, without problematizing such a merging of "universal" and "Western" in Christianity. As a result, Korean Christianity—and Korean American Christianity, by extension—absorbed uncritically the Western vision of a personal faith, removed from all matters social and cultural and hence having nothing to do with issues of "class, gender, race, and empire." Given such contextual enlightenment, Lee issues a clarion call: it is imperative for Korean and Korean American critics—and ultimately for all non-Western and minority critics as well—to move beyond such collusion by highlighting ethnicity throughout.

Given the use of the Bible as a charter in this regard, and in particular the driving image of Paul as the universalizing pivot in Christianity, a rereading of

Paul, Lee argues, is in order. This analysis is twofold: a denuding/investing of traditional Western interpretation and a re-visioning of Paul's own project of ethnic construction and relations. It is filtered through the discussion, taken as intra-Christian in nature, involving the "strong" and the "weak" in Romans. Paul, Lee proposes, has been cast by standard Western interpretation as advancing inclusion in the community through the elimination of ethnic differences. To the contrary, Lee counters, Paul espouses inclusion through affirmation of ethnicity. Further, ethnic relations within the community are handled differently in different contexts, with no universal measure in this regard: whereas in Galatians Paul favors Gentile Christians in face of dominant Jewish Christians, in Romans he favors Jewish Christian in face of dominant Gentile Christians. At the same time, one universal principle does prevail everywhere: "radical mutuality."

Lastly, for Lee this rereading of Paul has consequences for Korean and Korean American Christian readers. In effect, any domination of one side by another in conflict must be resisted in favor of the Pauline model of unity with difference and radical mutuality. Such is the case, Lee specifies, across a variety of ongoing situations: ecclesial disagreements regarding relations between the two Koreas; the division within Korean and Korean American Christianity between "conservative" and "progressive" churches; and the separation among Korean and Korean American Christians by culture and/or generation. Only then will the vision of Paul, and "the practice of Christ," come through as it should: "oneness with difference." Again, the universality of such a stance for all minorities can be readily visualized.

Perpetual and Exemplary Foreignness—Gale Yee. Yee does not discuss minority criticism as such, either in terms of character or ramifications, addressing instead her own status and role as an Asian American critic of Chinese descent. Nevertheless, from her delineation of this reader construct, it is possible to imagine a vision for a shared minority project. The introduction proves key in this regard. First, a foundational mode of reading is laid down: doing so from one's "social location." Second, a clear indication is also given regarding what such reading entails: self-immersion in the historical experience of the group in question (the story of Chinese immigration into the United States) as well as in the field of studies devoted to analysis of this group formation, both by itself and among other groups from the same geopolitical region (Chinese American studies and Asian American studies, respectively). Third, there is a distinct focus to this reading: attunement to the "hardship and oppression" encountered by the group(s). Lastly, there is a self-conscious realization of such a reading as partial: one among a host of interpretations involving a variety of reading approaches and social locations. Such reflections lend themselves readily to universalization for minority criticism: location as point of departure; theorization of location as imperative; foregrounding marginalization and oppression as fundamental; and realization of partiality as constitutive. They also reveal Yee's subscription to puncturing objectivity and universality as primary critical strategy.

This contextualization at the level of reception is marked by expansive appeal to contextual enlightenment and minimal attention to denuding dominant interpretation. The result is sharp ideological critique of her own location and agenda as a reader but minimal critique of the scholarly tradition. Thus, Yee does discard the "more positive readings" of the text, producing a standard nationalistic-romantic line of argumentation, in favor of "more ambiguous and unsettling" readings, advanced by "people of color." However, within this "reading against the grain," Yee's own interpretation appears as distinctive rather than privileged: an effort to shed light on the variety of "often conflicting interpretations and readings" by means of a racial-ethnic reading, but with no displacement or resolution in sight. This process of contextualization is also marked by a pointed use of heightening the discourse. This is filtered through the lens of Asian American theorizing, yielding two recurrent and related stereotypes of Asian Americans at work in the national dialectic of racialization: perpetual foreigner and model minority. Here interethnic differentiation plays a major role, at two levels: external and internal. First, Yee argues, such a representation of Asians breaks the mold of the traditional dominant-minority divide between "white" and "black": it is a dialectic ruled not by "color" but by "citizenship." Thus, Asian Americans in general and Chinese Americans in particular are marked by such constructs, unlike African Americans and Latino/a Americans and others. Second, she adds, such representation collapses the multiple ethnic and national variations among Asian Americans. Consequently, oppression becomes targeted or indiscriminate, as the occasion should warrant.

Yee interprets, therefore, self-consciously "against the grain," given her status and role as an Asian American critic—a "perpetual foreigner" and "model minority." The actual reading strategy adopted in this regard is strictly sequential: analysis of the reader in context as point of entry into analysis of the text in context. The study itself focuses on the book of Ruth, whose protagonist she sees as portrayed in the same racialized terms as Asian Americans: a perpetual foreigner and model minority. As perpetual foreigners, first of all, Asian Americans never fully qualify as "American" in dominant consciousness, even if born in the country or the issue of multiple generations. The result has been a historical trajectory of exploitation and exclusion as well as a contemporary demand for exoticness. As model minority, moreover, they are regarded as an ideal group, most assimilated to the dominant model, on the basis of their traditional values. The result has been disparaging treatment as exemplary though "colored" and inferior as well as tactical deployment against other minority groups. In both regards, Yee argues, Ruth, undeniably a foreigner, qualifies in eminent fashion. As convert and immigrant, she becomes not just an exemplary Jew but a model of behavior for all Jews, yet she disappears altogether from the narrative after the birth of her son—a model minority. Though immigrant and convert, she remains marked throughout as foreign, and a Moabite to boot, subjected to exploitation and exclusion as well as eroticization—a perpetual foreigner.

Such reading turns sharply ideological at both levels. Ultimately, Yee proposes, Ruth and Asian Americans alike are used—as racialized constructs—as rhetorical and ideological tools on behalf of their respective dominant societies and cultures. They become weapons of propaganda pointing in dialectical fashion: in the case of Asian Americans, to the justice and fairness of the United States—and away from the structural system of discrimination in American society and culture; in the case of Ruth, to the greatness of Israel, plus either the soundness of David's line or a policy of intermarriage (depending on time of composition)—and away from economic and sexual oppression in Judean society and culture. Hers is, therefore, an Asian American reading committed to the exposé and denunciation of racial minoritization and its consequences—one that involves problematization of biblical authority, appeal to intersectionality, and transposition onto a geopolitical stage as an indictment of the "First World" in the face of its treatment of labor from the "developing countries."

Expanding the Field of Studies

Expanding Antiquity—Gay Byron. Byron sets up minority criticism—the work of scholars "from various underrepresented racial and ethnic minority groups"—as focal point of reference, addressing not only character and ramifications but also scope in the process. Its breadth she portrays as ever-growing: certainly in terms of volume and range of production, but no less so in terms of the "social and cultural locations" of the critics involved. Its nature and consequences she summarizes by way of comparison with dominant criticism. Minority critics pursue matters of race and ethnicity in the texts of antiquity, in modern and postmodern frameworks of interpretation, and in their "locations" and "subjectivities" as interpreters. This last focus on inquiry differentiates their criticism from the work of "white" scholars—critics "with Anglo-European racial and ethnic origins"—on race and ethnicity, whose beginnings she traces to the mid 1990s. Moreover, minority critics carry out their task "in the midst of struggle"—for life in the world at large and for voice in the biblical guild. Consequently, Byron calls on "white" interpreters not only to vent their own "struggles" in critical fashion but also to identify with minority critics in theirs. Byron situates herself and her work entirely within this critical matrix. In so doing, she has recourse to puncturing objectivity and universality, while adopting expanding the field as primary strategy.

Her reading strategy proceeds in crescendo fashion: setting the reader in context; analyzing the text in context, arguing for a much broader vision of such context; challenging all readers regarding context. Regarding her own stance in reading, Byron contextualizes herself, within the minority matrix, as African American—more concretely, as a gendered and Christian subject, although neither religion nor gender plays a pivotal role in this study. Regarding her approach to the text, she has in mind a recontextualization of early Christian literary production through a distinctly African lens, that of Ethiopia.

As an African American critic, Byron casts—in an exercise of contextual enlightenment at both a personal and social-cultural level—a critical glance at the whole of her work. Looking back, she set out to examine the symbolic-political representations of Egyptians, Ethiopians, and black—with a particular focus on women—in the writings of the Greco-Roman and early Christian world. Looking ahead, she seeks to expand such work radically: extending beyond the established parameters of the discipline by moving beyond the confines of the Roman Empire and bringing the Axumite Empire of Ethiopia to bear, materially and discursively, on the configuration and construction of early Christianity. Throughout, a driving ideological commitment, grounded in her own sense of struggle, is evident: invoking "African origins and influences" in pointed and unapologetic fashion.

As text, Byron proposes—drawing upon scholarly denuding/investing and heightening the discourse as resources—a rereading of early Christian literature, with the encounter between Philip and the Ethiopian eunuch in Luke-Acts (Acts 8:26–40) as test case. To begin with, the discipline must revise its geographical obsession with the Greco-Roman world as central point of reference for early Christianity. Such exclusion needs correction in various directions, among them through a consideration of "sources and insights" from "African (specifically Ethiopian) civilizations," for which she proposes the Axumite Empire, whose reach and influence she proceeds to outline. Further, such correction demands attention to racial-ethnic "subtexts" in texts and interpretation alike. Consequently, a critical exposé of traditional criticism is in order, given its silence on this problematic and its critical stance of nonracial and nonethnic identification. Lastly, she argues, such correction should draw on postcolonial and critical race studies for theoretical assistance, with intersectionality in mind. While the postcolonial optic lifts up the marginal, leading to a retrieval of ancient Ethiopia from oblivion and installation as "a *necessary* frame of reference" for Christian origins, the racial-ethnic optic moves racialized subtexts to the center, at all levels of inquiry.

In the light of such a recentered rereading, the Ethiopian eunuch emerges as a point of contention in need of intersectional attention: not only in terms of his representation as a "*black* man" in highly ascetic and submissive terms, but also in light of the untold consequences of such a representation for African American males today and the construction of "black masculinities." In the end, Byron reissues her universal challenge. Only through unsparing attention to racialized subtexts—from texts, through readings, to interpreters—will the discipline be able to undergo the much-needed shift from a "politics of omission" to a "politics of recognition," including the role of Ethiopia and Africa as a central point of reference for early Christianity.

Problematizing Criticism

Pursuing Self-Identity—Fernando F. Segovia. Given his focus on joint projects undertaken by African American, Asian American, and Latino/a American critics, Segovia places the issue of minority criticism directly on the table. At the same time, given his overriding emphasis on what Latino/a criticism implies and entails, critical analysis of minority criticism as a common endeavor remains on the whole rather limited, yet sufficiently ample as to provide a clear sense of meaning and consequences. In both respects Segovia espouses interruptive stock-taking as primary critical strategy, with recourse to a heightening of the discourse throughout.

The concern with minority criticism surfaces in various ways: indirectly, in the remarks on minority projects as well as in the account of the path of racial-ethnic theory; pointedly, in the exposition of the various postulates that inform and guide all such endeavors. Reflection on joint projects yields a distinct view of such cooperation as: strictly tactical, opting for exclusion of the dominant "gaze" only for the sake of opening a space for mutual "assessment, interchange, and planning"; defyingly convoluted, given the countless "variations and tensions" that mark each group; and enormously challenging, calling for engagement with the problematic of race-ethnicity through racial ethnic studies—in itself a discourse described as not only "highly complex and constantly shifting" but also bearing within itself a broad set of closely related discourses. Reflection on racial-ethnic theory yields the following assessment: both categories should be seen as constructs, variously invoked by observers and agents alike; these constructs are dialectical, defining the self as superior through a definition of the Other as inferior; this process takes place as a result of migration, producing "dominant" and "minority" formations; the latter should be viewed as "minoritized," so emplaced through a process of racialization-ethnicization. What applies to minority projects and groups applies to discourses as well.

Minority criticism thus involves the following set of "driving" postulates: "overt and active" connection between critic and community; such a connection has a bearing on reading and teaching the Bible at all levels; the communities in question are "historically marginalized"; as such, minority production is confined to the periphery in both the academy and the profession. Consequently, for Segovia minority criticism constitutes a tactical way of struggling against marginalization through a type of criticism, both highly demanding and highly challenging, that foregrounds the problematic of race-ethnicity throughout. Various objectives are identified as central in this regard: examining how the various ethnic-racial groups do criticism, without obviating differences; developing skills for survival in dominant contexts; reimagining the discipline in the light of such different ways of knowledge production and transmission.

Within this overall framework, Segovia addresses what it means to be a Latino/a critic and to do Latino/a criticism. Toward this end, a threefold rhetorical strategy is adopted: a beginning unfolding of Latin(o/a)ness as optic; subsequent problematization of this optic from various perspectives; and a concluding personal vision for Latino/a criticism. The optic itself is advanced in terms of the modern concept of "ethnie" as a community of descent and culture: a Latino/a critic must be both "born" and "reborn" as such—must have membership in the community and must exhibit conscientization from within it. However, as soon as such a circumscription of Latin(o/a)ness is advanced, it is deconstructed: on the one hand, by emphasizing the highly constructive and conflicted nature of both racial-ethnic theory in general and Latino/a theory in particular; on the other hand, by bringing out the enormously varied character of contemporary Latino/a reality and experience in the United States. In the end, therefore, Segovia describes Latino/a criticism as involving a multitude of "births" as well as a multitude of "rebirths," of which his emerges as but a particular variation—a "limited and limiting … activation of the Latino imaginary." From this perspective a vision emerges: broad parameters of range, character, and specifics; the sense of a collective task; a demand for engagement at all times; attunement to local as well as global material and cultural realities; and in pursuit of human and social rights.

Taking an Interdisciplinary Turn

Ethnicity Genderized and Sexualized—Randall Bailey. Bailey does not entertain minority criticism as such, its mode or consequences. His focus is on African American life in general and ecclesial life in particular, and his concern is for the ramifications of such experience and reality for criticism. These reflections constitute, therefore, an exercise in contextual enlightenment, formulated through a heightening of discourse by way of critical race theory. Yet they are of such a nature that they can be readily expanded into a working project for minority criticism of all stripes. To begin with, the oppression suffered by the group, described as akin to "living under genocidal conditions," is foregrounded. At the same time, the national discourse of oppression is marked as multidimensional, with reference to gender and especially sexuality (impingement on "lesbian, gay, bisexual, and transgendered people"), and brought to bear on the African American community itself, insofar as it engages in the reproduction of such "othering" within its own ranks. This internal reproduction of dominant oppression is then explained as a racialized response to a racialized construct: black men as hyper-heterosexual, versus their "white" portrayal as weak; black women as exploitable—versus their "white" portrayal as strong. Lastly, Bailey calls for a race criticism that is keenly aware of and in opposition to any system of "interlocking" oppressions. Such a call can be readily transferred onto a broader minority key: a mission out of racial-ethnic oppression to combat other oppressions through unfailing attention to gender and sexuality in matters racial-ethnic. While Bailey clearly uses puncturing objectivity and universality as a critical point of entry, the main strategy at work involves, to my mind, taking an interdisciplinary turn.

The reading strategy, as evidenced in this study on the book of Esther, begins with extensive analysis of the text in context (the Greco-Roman period) and concludes with brief analysis of the reader in context; the latter, however, ultimately grounds and informs the interpretive process. The explication of the text proceeds sequentially: attention to racial-ethnic construction followed by complexification by way of gender and sexuality. The explication of the reader, as already outlined, foregrounds such complexification within the African American community.

Bailey begins, therefore, by examining the rendition of the Jewish *ethnos* advanced by the text, which is accepted by the scholarly tradition and embraced in African American circles: a Jewish "struggle to survive" in the face of genocide. This he does by way of discourse heightening, now through close attention to narrative rhetorics. The result is a fundamental problematization—a privileging of the Jews as an ethnic group over against all others. The evidence marshaled is broad: an underlying anti-Greek polemic; a view of the empire as requiring not total cultural assimilation but full accord with oppressive policies; a conflicted representation of Jewish identity in terms of descent and culture; a sanctioning of violence by the Jewish *ethnos* against other ethnic groups. Bailey then turns to analyze the characterization of Esther in established interpretation: desexualization as a "good Jewish prince." This he does by examining all major figures of the narrative through the lens of sexuality and gender ("cruising"). The conclusion is a similarly radical problematization: a deployment of sexuality for ethnic critique and of gender for androcentric and mysogynistic aims. The evidence adduced is wide: homoeroticizing as a negative signifier in the depiction of outsiders (Ahasuerus and Haman); female portrayal in terms of child exploitation and sexual seduction (Esther); homoeroticizing as a negative signifier in the depiction of assimilated insiders (Mordecai).

Such reading leads, in the end, to ideological critique: of the biblical text—textual desacralizing; of dominant interpretation—scholarly denuding/investing; and of the reader—contextual enlightenment. Esther emerges, in its portrayal of interethnic conflict, as a narrative that is not only deeply ethnocentric but also profoundly heterocentric. The scholarly tradition emerges, in its interpretation of the text, as utterly blind to, if not complicit with, both ethnocentrism, given ready identification with its racial-ethnic project, and heterocentrism, given absolute repression of its gender and sexual agenda. The African American community emerges, in its appropriation of the text and its own attitudes toward gender and sexuality, as thoroughly myopic in terms of its own ethnocentrism, its disregard for the gender "other," and its rejection of the sexual "other." For Bailey, there is but one response: a reading of resistance at all levels to oppression of all sorts.

Oppositional Agent—Tat-siong Benny Liew. One finds in Liew no direct reflection on minority criticism as such, nor on Asian American criticism per se. One does find throughout, however, manifold references to Asian American and other minority contexts as well as repeated invocations of Asian American and other minority scholars, in biblical criticism and in the academic world at large—alongside similar references to and invocations of dominant frameworks and scholars. Such reticence is the result of the particular subject-position adopted by Liew as critic. In response to observations from a variety of minority critics regarding a perceived downplaying of his own "commitments and stance," he reveals a "stubbornly" conscious choice on his part: to play the role of "elusive" writer and to produce a "trickster piece." Light, however, is shed immediately on this strategy, given its explicit grounding—"partly"—on a racial-ethnic dialectic at play in "coming out": unlike "whites," who, as unmarked norm, remain "(racially-ethnically) transparent" and demand or claim "visibility" when under threat, "people of color" know full well that "(racial-ethnic) readability" can be easily rendered into "(social) invisibility." Consequently, elusiveness emerges thereby as a racial-ethnic tactic designed to preserve "(social) visibility" in order to engage in "tricking." Such a tactic can be readily applied to minority critics across the spectrum. Liew's principal strategy in this regard is taking the interdisciplinary turn, with emphasis on heightening the discourse.

The reading strategy, given the suspension of self-analysis as a reader in context, remains intent on the text: the Gospel of John, a "trickster piece," and the figure of Jesus, a character marked by "elusiveness." Its overall discursive framework brings together race, gender, and sexuality as "entwined and imbricated" identity factors—positing intersectional deployment as indispensable. Its development is sequential: a reading of the text as text from the perspective of sexual constructions and relations, followed by a reading of the text in context from the angle of racial-ethnic and imperial-colonial constructions and relations, yielding in the end a complex intersectional interpretation. Throughout, moreover, numerous discursive frameworks and theoretical positions are invoked and applied—engaging in sustained though shifting theoretical heightening. Its objective, "trickery," is destabilization: exposing how "hegemonic systems" of race-gender-sexuality mark some bodies as mainstream (signifying containment, security, social order) and others as "deviant" (signifying excess, threats, social chaos). Lastly, while his own context as reader remains unpacked, in order to remain "elusive," that of racial-ethnic minorities is broached in sustained though intermittent fashion, in both discursive and social-cultural terms.

From the point of view of sexual constructions and relations, first of all, Liew uncovers in the Gospel a Jesus who, as Sophia or Wisdom, functions as a "cross-dresser"—a "transvestite" or "*drag* king." This "transgendering" identity of Jesus, highlighted through use of clothing and mode of speech, upsets the determinacy of gender (gender as "a truly porous and polysemous site/sight," in which there is no "essential core identity" but an "effect of bodily acts"), leading, in turn, to crisis in various other identity categories as well (the image of the deity; the representation of sexuality; the play of absence and presence; the structure of the family). Then, from the point of view of racial-ethnic and imperial-colonial relations, Liew expands on this "cross-dresser" Jesus as a "cross-bearer"—a "*Ioudaios*" or "racial-ethnic drag" and a "double agent." This "masquerading" identity of Jesus, traced through his relations to the *Ioudaioi* and Pilate in light of historical reality and experience, is said to trouble racial-ethnic and nationalist ideology ("masculinist" and "heteronormative" as well as "complicit" with Roman colonialism), yielding, in turn, displacement and pollution (a "transnational or even transworld alliance"). This transgendering and masquerading Jesus of the Gospel emerges for Liew, therefore, as a consummate elusive trickster—the "oppositional agent" who destabilizes all hegemonic systems and categories, dismantling all "traditions" and bringing about "all forms of transformations."

It is this role of Jesus and the Gospel, then, that Liew takes upon himself as critic: a similarly "elusive trickster" who wishes to trouble and upset "the multiple and intersecting forms of hegemonic" systems and categories in criticism and beyond. It is a call issued to minority and dominant critics alike: to take up intersectional criticism by reading "across more worlds," a call, it would seem, to become "elusive tricksters."

Universalism and Intersectionality—Demetrius K. Williams. Williams does not reflect on minority criticism, yet his comments as an African American on the task of criticism provide a glimpse of what such criticism would signify and entail in his eyes. Generally, Williams situates himself within ideological criticism, in twofold fashion: attentive to the rhetorical and ideological strategies of the text; forthcoming regarding the location and agenda of the reader in interpretation. These are mandates that can be readily applied across the minority spectrum. Specifically, he locates himself—socioculturally and ecclesially—within the African American tradition: personally, in descriptive terms; communally, in analytical terms. Such positioning is twofold. On the one hand, he argues, African Americans have embraced, in the face of racial oppression, a universalist-egalitarian model of human relations, invoking Scripture as a charter in this regard—but uncritically so, given a much too innocent reading of conflicted texts. On the other hand, he adds, this model has failed in its driving vision of inclusivity, insofar as its emphasis on race has bypassed the interstructural nature of oppression, especially with regard to gender and class, and has thus reproduced oppression within African American communities—following, ironically, the conflicted pattern of Scripture in this regard. Consequently, Williams calls for intersectional analysis with regard to texts and readers alike. This too is a mandate that can be readily extended across the minority spectrum. Williams's primary strategy represents, therefore, a taking of the interdisciplinary turn, involving a puncturing of objectivity and universality as well.

Its reading strategy emerges, on the surface, as sequential: detailed analysis of the text in context followed by succinct examination of the reader in context. In point of fact, however, the second stage provides the theoretical grounding for the initial reading of the text, insofar as it outlines the specific angle of vision employed in interpretation. The result is a thoroughgoing ideological reading focused on intersectionality, derived from contextual enlightenment and involving denuding/investing, but not of the scholarly tradition, as well as textual desacralizing. The text in question is Acts 2; the reader, the African American religious tradition.

Acts 2 unfolds what Williams describes as the "Pentecost paradigm" of universalism, brought about through reception of the Spirit—an updating of the prophecy of Joel concerning the "last days." On the surface, as widely noted, this Lukan vision foresees the inclusion of "all flesh" and the elimination of all social-cultural divisions—not only race-ethnicity but also gender (male-female), age (young-old), and class (male-female). Yet a pointed intersectional reading of Luke-Acts, focused on the unfolding narrative representations of these categories, proves highly deconstructive, in two respects: (1) gender and status distinctions are preserved, to the benefit of male disciples and the status quo; (2) racial-ethnic distinctions, while addressed through extension of the Jewish covenant promises to the Gentiles, remain subject to ethnocentrism and gradation. As a result, Luke-Acts emerges for Williams as a "deficient implementation" of such a model of inclusivity. The reception of Acts 2 among African American Christians Williams describes as quite positive. On the surface, this vision of universalism has been warmly appropriated—even to the point of serving as the basis for the first denomination of African American origins, the Church of God in Christ, arising out of the Pentecostal movement—in its drive for "inclusive and just practices" in both the social and the ecclesial fabric of the country. Yet a pointed intersectional analysis of the tradition proves highly deconstructive as well: the foregrounding of race has occluded other dimensions of oppression, such as gender and class. Consequently, in drawing upon Luke-Acts for scriptural sanction, the African American religious tradition has reproduced the exclusions of Scripture itself, yielding a "deficient implementation" of universalism as well.

In the end, the key to this intersectional optic comes from within the African American tradition itself, as Williams turns to a variety of dissenting discourses: the contrarian historical reception of Acts 2 by African American women, with its call for gender inclusion; contemporary feminist and womanist discourse on intersectionality; and African American studies on identity construction. The result is thoroughgoing ideological analysis of the contextualized text and the contextualized reader, deemed by Williams as essential for African Americans as they "explore the Bible in search of healing models and paradigms of liberation."

Concluding Remarks

The results of this analysis can be readily summarized in terms of the two steps identified at the beginning. From the point of view of any notion of minority criticism, the studies have to be characterized as inchoative. For the most part, the category is not formally addressed as such; when mentioned, it is either by way of allusion or insufficiently elaborated. From the point of view of activation and interlacing of critical moves, the studies reveal the following tendencies: in terms of major strategy, decided preference for interpretative contextualization, with discursive cross-fertilization as a strong second and both border transgressionism and interruptive stock-taking as individual options; in terms of supporting tactics, extensive intermingling within each major category and across all such categories. The richness of the venture in terms of mechanics is thus undeniable.

Yet while its accomplishments in this regard are praiseworthy, certain limitations are no less clear.

A first key lacuna can be immediately discerned from the preceding summary of the analysis: an under-theorization of criticism, at the level of each group as well as at the level of the ensemble. While one finds references to African American, Asian American, and Latino/a American traditions of criticism, not enough attention is bestowed on what is it that makes or distinguishes criticism as African American, Asian American, and Latino/a American. Is it a claim to descent-and-culture on the part of the critic? Is it a standpoint adopted by the critic and evident in interpretation? Is it a combination of both? Likewise, while one comes across references to minority criticism, not enough consideration is given to what constitutes or differentiates criticism as minority, beyond yet bringing together in some distinct fashion African American, Asian American, and Latino/a American criticism. Is it a sense of position in the face of dominant criticism? Is it a specific awareness driving the critic and clear in interpretation? Is it a combination of both? Much remains to be done here.

A second key lacuna, not unrelated to the first, insofar as it involves a different type of under-theorization, has to do with critical interchange. The studies tend to stand on their own in activating and interlacing rhetorical strategies as they do. There is not enough awareness of and reference to similar moves among critics from either the same group or other groups. This does not mean among the contributors to the volume themselves, for such engagement would demand a different type of publication altogether, namely, one that would integrate and reflect this dialectical procedure—one in which the finished essays were circulated, commented upon, responded to, and published with such comments and responses appended in some fashion. Such a comparative perspective would yield enormous benefits. It would lend a much sharper foundation for the critical move in question, allowing the critic to see what others have done and how they have done it. It would lead as well to much greater insight regarding the move as such among minority critics: its rationale, its character, its ramifications. It would also serve as a keen tool for expanding our base of knowledge about the realities and experiences of the critics behind such moves and of the groups to which they belong. The critical interchange would become thereby deeply relational and multicultural. Much remains to be done in this respect as well.

INTERDISCIPLINARY FRAMEWORK OF DISCUSSION

A third salient marker of achievement has to do with the prominent interdisciplinary dimension surrounding the undertaking as a whole. The design of the venture in this regard was to involve a group of interlocutors from various other fields of study, both within (religious education; constructive theology) and outside (ethnic studies) the traditional set of theological disciplines that together make up Christian studies. These scholars served as both internal participants and external observers throughout. On the one hand, they functioned as active partners in the conversations and as constructive contributors to the volume, no different from anyone else. On the other hand, they brought to bear on both discussions and publication an invaluable comparative dimension from their own respective disciplines in the academy. As a result, the problematic of race-ethnicity in biblical criticism was set, at all times, within a variety of discursive frameworks and analytical modes of inquiry.

In addition, it should be noted, the intent of inclusion and parity in group representation was very much at work here as well. The interlocutors were drawn from all three minority groups, with due attention given as well to gender and national origins or descent, so that this comparative setting of the problematic would be highly diffracted as well. From the perspective of interdisciplinarity, therefore, minority criticism is situated as resolutely and profoundly embedded in the academy. The quest for the location and role of minority critics in discipline and profession alike casts them as discursively imbricated and dialogical.

In what follows, I shall pursue a detailed analysis of the various assessments of the venture from outside the field. I shall do so with three concerns in mind: to establish the theoretical and ideological foundations of each piece; to unpack their critical visions of the project and volume; and to note the implications of such visions. I shall proceed in order of disciplinary distance, from the closest to the furthest—from the theological, through the pedagogical, to the ethnic-racial. This analysis will prepare the way for identifying key lacunae in need of critical consideration.

Exercise in Postmodernist Hermeneutics and Relational Theology— Mayra Rivera

From the discipline of theological studies in general and the angle of constructive theology in particular, Rivera approaches the venture from a cosmo-logical-interpretive perspective. This assessment is set against a multilevel binary framework—more functional than essentialist in character—involving a threefold set of oppositions. The various levels are arranged in vertical order, from most concrete to most general, with the corresponding sides of the oppositions flow-ing from and supporting one another. These levels may be identified as follows, from surface to foundation: disciplinary; hermeneutical; theological. As with any binary framework, this one also presents a positive and a negative side. Rivera places the venture decidedly on the positive side—an exercise in postmodernist hermeneutics and relational theology.

Two oppositions set up an overall interpretive-cosmological framework. At the middle level, the hermeneutical binary involves diametrically different interpretations of language and subjectivity. At the grounding level, the theo-logical binary involves diametrically different conceptions of God and creation. This framework is concretized as follows. On one side, there stands modernist hermeneutics: textual meaning as stable and univocal; the reader as independent and universal; interpretation as controlled. Underlying this interpretive model, there is a cosmological vision: God as transcendent and creation as mechanistic. On the other side, there is postmodernist hermeneutics: textual meaning as embodied and particular; reader as embedded and embodied; interpretation as uncontrollable. Beneath it there stands a corresponding cosmological vision: God as immanent and creation as relational. At the surface level, then, the disciplinary opposition involves diametrically different approaches to texts. On the modernist, transcendentalist side, there stands traditional historical criticism, as well as a number of other approaches; on the postmodernist, relational side, minority criticism, of the sort represented by the venture, as well as a number of other approaches. It is this variety of approaches on both sides of the divide that makes the binary framework a functional one.

Both the postmodernist hermeneutics and the relational theology at work in minority criticism are, Rivera argues, the result of foregrounding material realities and relations in texts, contexts, and readers, specifically by way of race and ethnicity in marginalized communities. Interpretively, any notion of independence of and between texts and readers is rejected. Against a concept of language as transparent, meaning is viewed as produced through language; there is no meaning outside particular words in relation to one another. Further, words are polysemic in nature, hence open to multiple and conflicted interpretations. Against an idea of "man" as universal, subjectivity is regarded as complex and immersed in power relations; there is no subject outside particular contexts. Further, contexts are legion in nature, thus open to multiple and conflicted standpoints of interpretation. Consequently, its mode of interpretation is not univocal or objective but open-ended and multiperspectival. Cosmologically, any notion of independence between God and creation is rejected. Against a concept of God as transcendent from creation, divinity is presupposed as immanent; there is no "absolutely external" and "self-enclosed" God. Against any idea of creation as mechanistic, the world is taken as opaque; there is no "self-enclosed" and "manipulable" creation. As a result, its vision of cosmology is not external and disembodied, but relational.

Rivera draws out the consequences of minority criticism as a postmodernist and relational undertaking. From the point of view of hermeneutics, it shatters any illusion of coherence and unity on the part of a dominant society and culture, whether in biblical texts and contexts or among contemporary readers and contexts. As such, it opens the way for attention to and engagement with the excluded throughout. What emerges thereby is a free-flow vision of interpretation in which endless encounters among texts, contexts, and readers produce revelation amidst "the messy realities of life"—a revelation that breaks beyond the universal, given its perspective as Other. From the point of view of theology, it shatters any illusion of race and ethnicity as essentialist categories of the sort produced by dominant society and culture, again whether in texts and their contexts or among readers and their contexts. As such, it seeks to transform, while affirming, the material "inscriptions" of race and ethnicity. What emerges thereby is an "apophatic" vision of theology in which creation is seen as mysterious, overflowing all categories, and in which God is viewed as working through all creation, a relational transcendence that is, at once, "incarnate" and "dynamic."

In conclusion, minority criticism points at once to and beyond these, and all, categories of oppression and exclusion. It posits excess in all categories and in all relations. Such transcendence is present in particular persons. When individuals come together, transcendence touches and is touched, leading to the possibility of transformation in self and in the Other. The same applies to interpretation as a contact with texts and contexts, leading to the possibility of transformation in self and in the text. For Rivera, such an ongoing process constitutes revelation in creation, the imprint of a God who unfolds in creation. Minority criticism is, in the end, a "hermeneutics of hope."

EXERCISE IN TEACHING FOR COLOR CONSCIOUSNESS—EVELYN L. PARKER

Grounded in the field of education in general and the theological discipline of religious education in particular, Parker comes to the venture from a pedagogical-political perspective. The assessment is cast within a double binary framework, in which two sets of oppositions entail and undergird one another. The first set involves teaching philosophies with diametrically opposed methods and objectives. The second set, the result of a systemic ideological critique of U.S. society and culture, concerns attitudes toward national policies and goals, involving diametrically opposed reactions to the social-cultural fabric of the country. On one side, one philosophy, teaching for (white) assimilation, is identified as supporting and promoting the country's social-cultural formations and relations. On the other side, the other philosophy, teaching for color consciousness, is depicted as questioning and resisting the fabric of national formations and relations in place. In light of this pedagogical-political framework, Parker situates the venture squarely within the realm of problematizing and resisting, pedagogically as well as ideologically—an exercise in teaching for color consciousness.

Parker identifies white supremacy as the "foundational ideology" of the country, thus informing and guiding all others. For her, this is a system based on the concept of a superior race ("whiteness"). Its character is overarching, encompassing the set of ideas and beliefs, values and attitudes, as well as driving the constellation of practices of white men and women. Its objective lies in the social-political dominance of whites, whether liberals or conservatives, over ethnic-racial minority groups, "people of color." Its effects are exploitation and dehumanization. Drawing on the work of Louis Althusser, Parker posits the preservation of capitalist relations of oppression as the goal of such ideology and its exploitative and dehumanizing identities and relations. Toward this end, all ideological apparatuses are geared, engendering rituals of all sorts in the service of power, out of which emerge the comprehensive practices of white supremacy. This has been so, she argues, from the beginning of the country, as evidenced by the imperial policies adopted toward Native Americans, through the present, as continued in the imperial policies exercised toward racial-ethnic minorities. Further, both the Christian churches and religious-theological education have been deeply involved, as apparatuses, in the support and furtherance of this ideology. Indeed, Parker sees the Bible as having played, and still playing, no small part in such a task, serving as grounds for the set of unjust policies—social, economic, political—that stand behind white supremacy. As a result, she argues, the Bible's own hegemonic identities and relations have been invoked, through the reading and impartation of texts, over the marginalized.

This type of biblical pedagogy constitutes, for Parker, a variation on teaching by assimilation in the realm of religion. The goal of education in general becomes thereby the uncritical appropriation—through the method of banking—of hegemonic identities and relations in society and culture, with assimilation of the marginalized to the foundational ideology: "honorary whiteness." Within this optic, the goal of biblical pedagogy, as practiced in religious-theological education, becomes a parallel appropriation of hegemonic identities and relations in the biblical texts. Even the goal of teaching for color blindness, espoused by white liberals and adopted by some minorities, proves insufficient, since the problem is only addressed at the individual level (overcoming racial prejudice), while the material matrix of white supremacy (pervasive presence) remains untouched. In opposition, drawing on the work of Paulo Freire and bell hooks, Parker proposes an alternative biblical pedagogy, a variation on teaching for color consciousness in the realm of religion. Here the goal of education in general becomes the dismantling and transformation—through the method of conscientization—of white supremacy, its rituals and practices, with critical thinking and engagement in mind. Within this optic, the goal of biblical pedagogy becomes a parallel surfacing of power dynamics in the biblical texts through a foregrounding of the lens of race and ethnicity and its intersections with class and culture, gender and sexuality.

Such teaching for color consciousness—an admittedly difficult process, she observes, given the socialization of students in the banking approach with respect to the Bible—involves a variety of strategies: (1) the creation of a pedagogical context in which a sense of hospitality prevails for the process of learning to question—a questioning not only of the realities of U.S. society and culture but also of the Scriptures; (2) the use of the Scriptures as a mirror for the hard realities of U.S. society and culture in order to move toward a call for justice—a questioning that leads to social action; (3) particular attention to the issue of colorism, defined as the emphasis on gradations in skin color and somatic features as a basis for discrimination, in both country and texts alike—a questioning that takes into consideration interracial and interethnic identities and relations. While the venture is praised for its sharp deployment of the first two strategies, openness to questioning and use of mirroring, it is found largely wanting with regard to the third. The participants, Parker observes, found it "difficult" to deal with colorism, leaving such a necessary discussion, given its prominence in racial-ethnic groups, "uneven and voiceless."

In sum, from a pedagogical perspective, this joint exercise in minority biblical criticism is viewed as a crucial step forward in teaching for color consciousness, both in the religious-theological realm and in the social-cultural realm at large. Insofar as the Bible has been read and taught with assimilation in mind, serving thereby as a foundation for white supremacy, a contrarian way of reading and teaching with transformation in mind, through recourse to the lens of race-ethnicity, is imperative for religious-theological education. Minority biblical criticism emerges thereby as a key social-cultural tool, essential to the dismantlement and transformation of the country's foundational ideology. What remains to be incorporated, however, is the problematic of colorism, which affects all groups materially and discursively.

EXERCISE IN COMPLICIT RESISTANCE—JAMES KYUNG-JIN LEE

From the field of ethnic studies in general and the discipline of Asian American literary studies in particular, Lee scrutinizes the venture from the perspective of minority formations and relations. This assessment is rendered in the light of a spectrum of positions open to minority individuals and groups in coming to terms with dominant society and culture. At one end, there lies the path of assimilation, which yields to the project of "uniform universalism" on the part of the dominant; at the other end, there stands the path of affirmation, which leads to a project of "horizontal assimilation" on the part of one's "own kind." In the middle, one finds a way of engaged disconnection, which does result in a project of one's own kind, but one that is both fully aware of inevitable complicity in the dominant project and consciously at work in offering resistance to it nonetheless. Lee identifies the venture as very much at the center of the spectrum—an exercise in complicit resistance.

This theoretical range of responses to dominant society and culture Lee concretizes within the context of the U.S. This he does by way of a systemic ideological critique of the country, primarily conveyed through the eyes of Asian American writers and critics but ultimately applicable to other minority critics and writers as well. He identifies the fundamental ideology, and underlying political economy, of the nation as one of warfare, in which the boundaries of what is acceptable and what is not are dictated by the state, in shifting fashion. All is geared toward warfare, including the deployment of race as a consequence of racism, and hence the resulting formations and relations of dominant and minority groups; race is seen thereby as a particular channel of such warfare, white supremacy. For minorities, the outcome is profound alienation, out of which may come a move toward assimilation, taken in terror, or toward affirmation, taken in opposition. The latter, a position represented by traditional ethnic studies, constitutes a quest for solace and identity, for voice and justice, on the part of those victimized by white supremacy.

For Lee, however, at the heart of such a quest, and of ethnic studies as initially conceived, lies a contradiction: affirmation entails ultimate obeisance to the warfare imperative. The appropriate strategy lies, rather, in acknowledging such complicity and in moving beyond it, not by surpassing it, for that proves impossible, but by refusing to serve its ends. Consequently, the way for minority groups and individuals is to envision a situation of multilateralism, a different way of relating to one another, and to work toward it. That is precisely what he sees the venture as doing, as minority critics come together to read the stories of the Bible, stories so beloved yet stories responsible for so much damage, with a different story in mind.

The different story in question is one that foregrounds and theorizes the concepts of race and ethnicity in texts and interpretations alike. It is also a story that has not victimization in mind but transformation, moving beyond racism. As such, it is a story of "wild readers": readers who are often looked upon as crazy by the dominant, who violate the accepted protocols of reading, who read with those in shadows, and who look upon reading as a political act—all in the service of a different kind of cultural logic. In such critical activity, born of crisis, the possibility of revelation becomes open, as we listen to and respond to the suffering of the Other. Rather than an ethic of universalism, one contemplates polyculturalism. Rather than a view of hybridity as defilement, one approaches it as holiness. Rather than a sense of exile as what has been lost, one draws upon it as strength for a new life. It is precisely such a cultural logic, the imperative of "unavailability for servitude," that the venture represents, as it stares the warfare imperative in the face and refuses to collaborate with it. In so doing, it looks not only at what is "killing us" but at what is "killing someone else." In the end, however, it is a story that has no certain outcomes, only possibilities, which Lee characterizes as "the gift of responding" to the "shadow of justice" that is "nothing more and nothing less than the face of God."

CONCLUDING REMARKS

The assessments of the venture offered by the interlocutors from outside the discipline are most incisive. From a theological standpoint, it comes across as a timely conveyor, within the matrix of postmodernism, of a vision of God and creation as embodied and relational, making room for transcendence and hope, built on a view of criticism as irretrievably embodied and relational. From a pedagogical perspective, it is welcomed as a keen tool, within the context of the United States, on behalf of color consciousness, allowing for transformation and justice, resting on a foregrounding of race and ethnicity in the face of a social-cultural fabric of white supremacy. From a minority standpoint, it is embraced as a savvy commitment, within the context of the United States, to a contrarian ethic of polyculturalism, allowing for the possibility of revelation and transformation, based on a nuanced projection of race-ethnicity in the face of a national warfare imperative. From each perspective, therefore, minority criticism is praised as a highly positive development, not only for biblical interpretation but also for theology, for education, and for ethnic studies—and, ultimately, for the nation, materially as well as culturally. At the same time, these assessments do bring out lacunae in such work that are very much in need of critical attention.

A first lacuna has to do with the theological presuppositions of minority criticism, which, as Rivera points out, invariably remain in the background. In approaching the Bible by prioritizing race and ethnicity in texts and interpretations alike, minority critics should address their cosmological convictions in so doing as well as the consequences of such convictions. It is not sufficient to speak about questions of literary method and theory. It is also not sufficient to consider questions of intersectionality with gender and economics or sexuality and geopolitics. It is imperative to deal with questions of God and creation and how interpretation impacts upon such questions.

A second lacuna involves the pedagogical dimension of minority criticism. On the one hand, a point implicit in Parker, is the need for close attention to national contexts, pedagogical methods, and political objectives in teaching biblical interpretation. In projecting race-ethnicity as crucial categories in texts and interpretations, minority critics should examine carefully how to impart such an approach, where such impartation is carried on, and to what ends it is geared. It is not sufficient to interpret; it is imperative to deal with questions of how to deliver and pass on such a way of interpreting. On the other hand, an explicit critique in Parker is the need to attend to colorism. This is certainly true at a base level: how to deal with interracial and interethnic formations and relations beyond the usual categories (e.g., African, Asian, and Latino/a American). This is a pressing matter as well, given the increasing number of such formations on the contemporary scene. It is also true, I would add, at a metaphorical level: how to do so with respect to teaching interpretation with a full spectrum of minority groups in mind. This too is a pressing matter, given the expanding complex variations of minority ranks in the classroom.

A final lacuna has to do with the "minority" characteristics of minority criticism as such. In highlighting race and ethnicity in texts and interpretations, Lee utters an implicit call for careful consideration of dominant-majority relations: their definition within a state as part of the cultural logic of that state; the choice of reaction to the dominant society and culture; the option of assimilation as highly nuanced; the option of affirmation as highly complicit; the elaboration of a contrarian cultural logic. It is not sufficient to erect oneself in affirmation and opposition. It is imperative to analyze the driving logic of the state, to articulate a different cultural logic, and to situate the various options available in terms of such imperatives.

RETURNING TO THE BEGINNING

This critical reflection has, as it set out to do, established salient markers of achievement as well as key lacunae for development, across various fundamental dimensions of such work, in this first joint venture in minority biblical criticism. In the process its two main aims stand fulfilled: the location and role of such criticism and its practitioners have been mapped within the discipline and profession of biblical studies; and the stage for future work has been clarified by a thorough account of what has already transpired. At this point, therefore, the task conveyed by the subtitle, *Toward Minority Biblical Criticism*, may be summarized as follows: much good work has been done, but much work remains to be done. To borrow a term that comes up in each external assessment of the venture: much transformation has taken place, but much transformation still needs to take place in coalitions of racial-ethnic minority critics.

CONTRIBUTORS

Cheryl B. Anderson is an Associate Professor of Old Testament at Garrett-Evangelical Theological Seminary in Evanston, Illinois. She is the author of *Interpreting the Bible: Confronting the Legacy of Ancient Biblical Laws in Contemporary Controversies*, which will be published in the fall of 2009. Her current research interests involve contextual and liberationist readings of Scripture in the age of HIV and AIDS. She serves as a member of the Council of the Society of Biblical Literature, and she is the chair of the society's Committee on Underrepresented Racial and Ethnic Minorities in the Profession.

Randall C. Bailey is Andrew W. Mellon Professor of Hebrew Bible at Interdenominational Theological Center in Atlanta, Georgia. He is an ideological critic concentrating on the intersections of race/ethnicity, class, gender, sexuality, and power in the biblical text. He is co-editor with Jacquelyn Grant of *The Recovery of Black Presence: An Interdisciplinary Exploration* (Abingdon, 1995), co-editor with Tina Pippin of *Race, Class, and the Politics of Bible Translation* (*Semeia* 76, 1996), editor of *Yet with a Steady Beat: Contemporary U.S. Afrocentric Biblical Interpretation* (Society of Biblical Literature, 2003), and author of *David in Love and War: The Pursuit of Power in 2 Samuel 10–12* (Sheffield: 1990) and *Open with Caution: The Bible and Sexuality* (Westminster John Knox, forthcoming).

Gay L. Byron is Baptist Missionary Training School Professor of New Testament and Christian Origins at Colgate Rochester Crozer Divinity School in Rochester, New York. She is the author of *Symbolic Blackness and Ethnic Difference in Early Christian Literature* (Routledge, 2002). Her research analyzes ancient Ethiopic (Geʿez) sources and theorizes how these sources facilitate our understanding of the New Testament and other early Christian writings.

Francisco O. García-Treto, JFR King Professor of Religion, Emeritus, at Trinity University in San Antonio Texas, was born in Cuba, the son of a Presbyterian minister, and grew up in Havana, where his father was pastor of the First Presbyterian Church. He came to the U.S. to pursue his higher education and here received the A.B., B.D., and Ph.D. degrees, the latter in Biblical Studies (Old Testament). Before his retirement in 2006, he taught for forty years in the

Department of Religion at Trinity University. His most recent publications are contributions to the *New Interpreter's Dictionary of the Bible* (Abingdon) and to *The Peoples' Bible* (Fortress), as well as a commentary in Spanish, *Salmos*, in the series Conozca su Biblia (Augsburg Fortress).

Jae Won Lee grew up in Seoul, Korea, and studied at Union Theological Seminary in New York. She teaches at McCormick Theological Seminary in Chicago as Assistant Professor of New Testament. Her teaching and research focus on critical, contextual, and emancipatory interpretations of Paul, in engagement with theoretical and hermeneutical issues regarding empire, race/ethnicity, gender, class, and culture. She approaches Asian American biblical studies from a global perspective. Among her recent articles are "Justification of Difference in Galatians" and "Reading the Bible from a Postcolonial Perspective."

James Kyung-Jin Lee is an associate professor of Asian American Studies and English at the University of California, Santa Barbara. He is the author of *Urban Triage: Race and the Fictions of Multiculturalism* (University of Minnesota Press, 2004), serves as an associate editor for *American Quarterly*, and sits on the editorial board of the *Heath Anthology of American Literature*.

Tat-siong Benny Liew is Professor of New Testament at the Pacific School or Religion in Berkeley, California. He is the author of *What Is Asian American Biblical Hermeneutics? Reading the New Testament* (University of Hawai'i Press, 2008) and *Politics of Parousia: Reading Mark Iner(con)textually* (Brill, 1999), as well as guest editor of the *Semeia* volume on *The Bible in Asian America* (Society of Biblical Literature, 2002).

Evelyn L. Parker is Associate Professor of Christian Education at Perkins School of Theology, Southern Methodist University, in Dallas, Texas. Her research interests include religious identity and spiritual formation in African American adolescents and adolescent spirituality as influenced by sociocultural context and social policy. She is the author of *Trouble Don't Last Always: Emancipatory Hope among African American Adolescents* (Pilgrim, 2003), *The Sacred Selves of Adolescent Girls: Hard Stories of Race, Class and Gender* (Pilgrim, 2006), and co-editor with Anne S. Wimberly of *In Search of Wisdom: Faith Formation in the Black Church* (Abingdon, 2002).

Mayra Rivera Rivera is Assistant Professor of Theology at Pacific School of Religion in Berkeley, California. Her research is in the field of constructive theology informed by postcolonial, feminist, and Latina/o studies. She is author of *The Touch of Transcendence: A Postcolonial Theology of God* (2007) and co-editor of *Postcolonial Theologies: Divinity and Empire* (2004) and *Planetary Loves: Gayatri Spivak, Postcoloniality and Theology* (forthcoming).

Jean-Pierre Ruiz is Associate Professor of Biblical Studies at St. John's University in New York, where he is also director of the Master of Arts in Liberal Studies and a senior research fellow of the Vincentian Center for Church and Society. Ruiz earned his doctorate from the Pontifical Gregorian University, and his research interests include prophetic and apocalyptic literature. He is editor of the electronic *Journal of Hispanic/Latino Theology*.

Fernando F. Segovia is the Oberlin Graduate Professor of New Testament and Early Christianity at the Divinity School and the Graduate Department of Religion at Vanderbilt University, where he is also a member of the faculty in the Center for Latin American Studies. Among a variety of academic and professional interests, he has long been active in Latino/a American critical and theological circles and presently functions as co-chair of the Society of Biblical Literature program unit and project on "Latin and Latino/a American Biblical Criticism."

Demetrius K. Williams completed his graduate and doctoral studies at Harvard Divinity School in New Testament and Christian Origins. He taught at Tulane University, New Orleans, from 1996 to 2006. Relocating to Milwaukee, Wisconsin, after the Katrina hurricane, he has taught at Marquette University and Central Baptist Theological School (Shawnee, Kansas) at its Milwaukee Center. In September of 2007 he joined the faculty of the University of Wisconsin-Milwaukee as an Associate Professor in the Department of French, Italian and Comparative Literature and the Religious Studies Program. He also serves as pastor of the Community Baptist Church of Greater Milwaukee.

Frank M. Yamada is Associate Professor of Hebrew Bible and Director of the Center for Asian American Ministries at McCormick Theological Seminary. His scholarly emphasis is in the areas of hermeneutics and culturally contextual interpretation, especially Asian American biblical interpretation. He is the author of *Configurations of Rape in the Hebrew Bible* (Peter Lang, 2008) and an editor and contributor for *The Peoples' Bible* (Fortress, 2008).

Gale A. Yee is currently Nancy W. King Professor of Biblical Studies at Episcopal Divinity School, Cambridge, Massachusetts. She is the author of *Poor Banished Children of Eve* (Fortress, 2003); *Jewish Feasts and the Gospel of John* (Michael Glazier, 1989); "The Book of Hosea" commentary in *The New Interpreter's Bible* (Abingdon), as well as many articles and essays. She is the editor of *Judges and Method: New Approaches in Biblical Studies*, which is now in its second edition (Fortress, 2007), and General Editor of Semeia Studies.

Printed in the United States
210680BV00001B/2/P